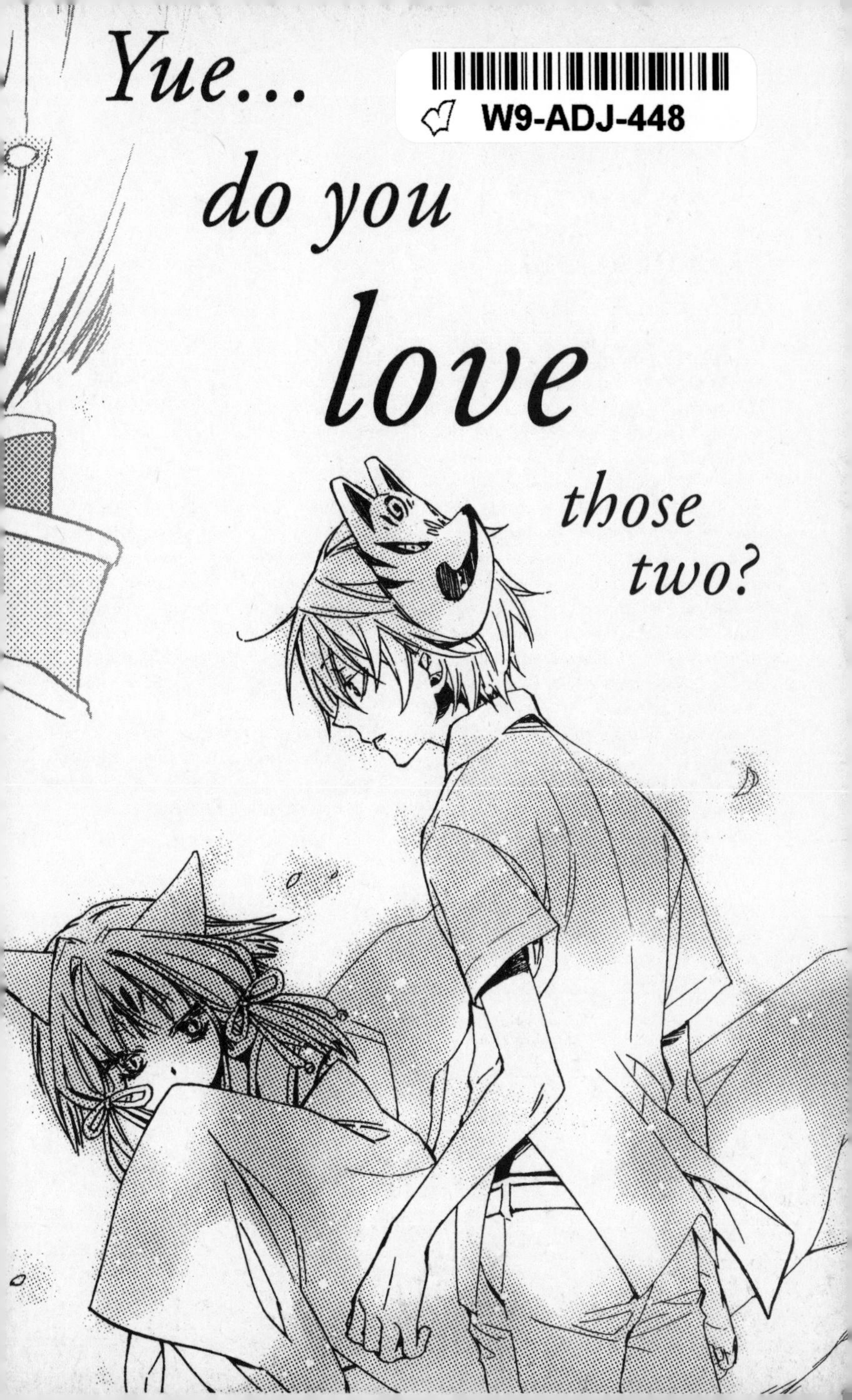
Yue...
do you
love
those
two?

TRANSLATION NOTES

COMMON HONORIFICS

no honorific: Indicates familiarity or closeness; if used without permission or reason, addressing someone in this manner would be an insult.

-san: The Japanese equivalent of Mr./Mrs./Miss. If a situation calls for politeness, this is the fail-safe honorific.

-sama: Conveys great respect; may also indicate that the social status of the speaker is lower than that of the addressee.

-kun: Used most often when referring to boys, this indicates affection or familiarity. Occasionally used by older men among their peers, but it may also be used by anyone referring to a person of lower standing.

-chan, -tan: An affectionate honorific indicating familiarity used mostly in reference to girls; also used in reference to cute persons or animals.

Ayakashi is a general term for ghosts, monsters, haunted objects, mythical animals, and all sorts of uncanny things from Japanese folklore.

PAGE 3

Kurogitsune literally means "black fox." In Japanese folklore, black foxes can be either good or bad omens.

PAGE 5

¥5 coins are considered the best denomination to use in shrine offering boxes because "five yen" in Japanese (*go en*) is homophonous with "relationship" (with a respectful prefix). The implication is that the supplicant would like to have a good relationship with the god of the shrine.

PAGE 15

Tsubaki is the Japanese word for "camellia." This flower is sometimes called the Japanese rose and has associations of love and longing in Japanese culture.

PAGE 75

Akujiki is a Japanese word that means "eating disgusting things."

Of the Red, the Light, and the Ayakashi

ART BY Nanao
STORY BY HaccaWorks*

Translation: Jocelyne Allen + Lettering: Alexis Eckerman

AKAYA AKASHIYA AYAKASHINO
© Nanao 2013
© Hacca Works* 2013
Edited by MEDIA FACTORY
First published in Japan in 2013 by KADOKAWA CORPORATION. English translation rights reserved by HACHETTE BOOK GROUP, INC. under the license from KADOKAWA COPORATION, Tokyo through TUTTLE-MORI AGENCY, Inc., Tokyo.

Translation © 2015 by Hachette Book Group, Inc.

Yen Press
Hachette Book Group
1290 Avenue of the Americas,
New York, NY 10104

www.HachetteBookGroup.com + www.YenPress.com

Yen Press is an imprint of Hachette Book Group, Inc.
The Yen Press name and logo are trademarks of Hachette Book Group, Inc.

The publisher is not responsible for websites (or their content) not owned by the publisher.

First Yen Press Edition: December 2015

ISBN: 978-0-316-35196-6

10 9 8 7 6 5 4 3 2 1

BVG

Printed in the United States of America

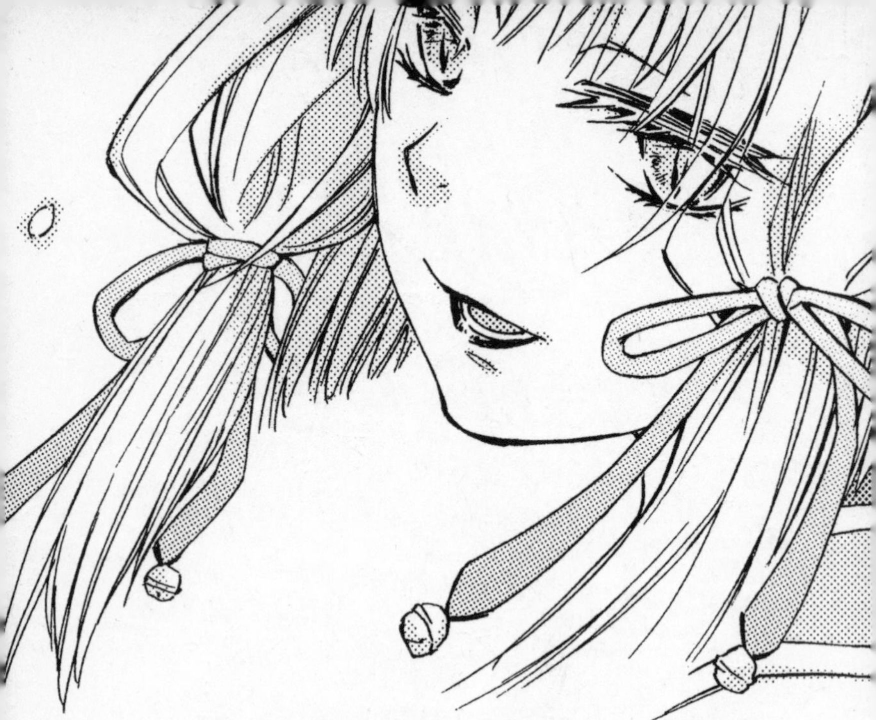

Yue must choose one of the people for

whom he has grown to care as his Meal—

Tsubasa or Akiyoshi.

What will he do...?

Of the Red, the Light, and the Ayakashi ②

COMING IN MARCH 2016

AFTERWORD

HELLO THERE! I'M Nanao, THE PERSON RESPONSIBLE FOR ADAPTING OF THE RED INTO COMICS FORM!

I MADE EVERY EFFORT TO MAKE IT SO THAT THOSE OF YOU NEW TO OF THE RED AND THOSE OF YOU WHO ARE ALREADY PLAYING THE GAME WOULD BE ABLE TO ENJOY IT AT LEAST A LITTLE.

I'M SO HAPPY YOU GOT TO WANDER AROUND THE TOWN OF UTSUWA WITH YUE-KUN. I HOPE YOU'LL STICK AROUND!

Special ThanX! HaccaWorks*
Y-san (my editor)
K-san (my first editor)
Aie-san
Fumki-san
Pesun
All my readers

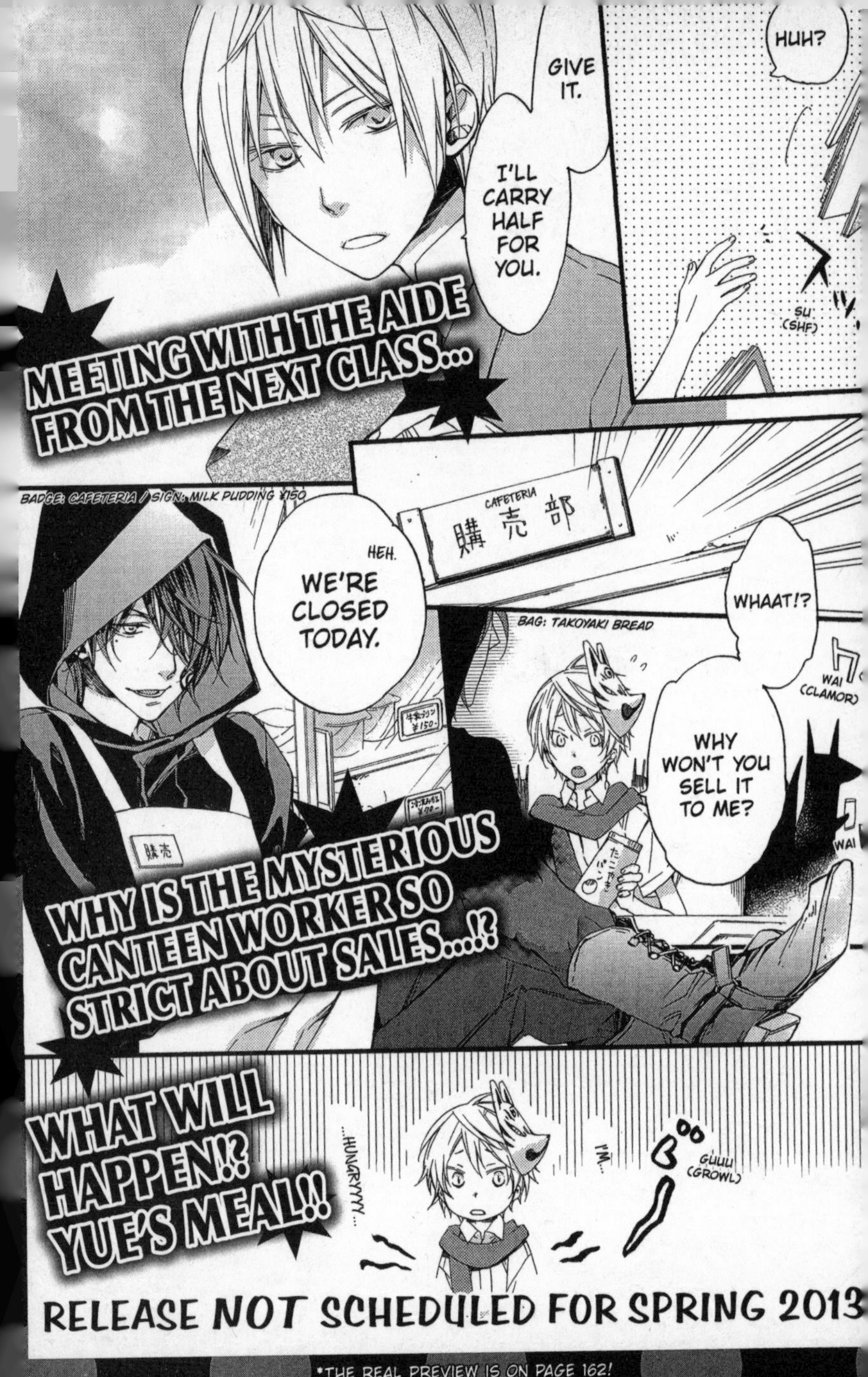
HUH?
SU (SHF)
GIVE IT.
I'LL CARRY HALF FOR YOU.
MEETING WITH THE AIDE FROM THE NEXT CLASS...
CAFETERIA
購売部
WHAAT!?
BAG: TAKOYAKI BREAD
WHY WON'T YOU SELL IT TO ME?
WAI (CLAMOR)
WAI
BADGE: CAFETERIA / SIGN: MILK PUDDING ¥150
HEH.
WE'RE CLOSED TODAY.
WHY IS THE MYSTERIOUS CANTEEN WORKER SO STRICT ABOUT SALES...!?
GUUU (GROWL)
I'M...
...HUNGRYYYY...
WHAT WILL HAPPEN!? YUE'S MEAL!!
RELEASE NOT SCHEDULED FOR SPRING 2013

*THE REAL PREVIEW IS ON PAGE 162!

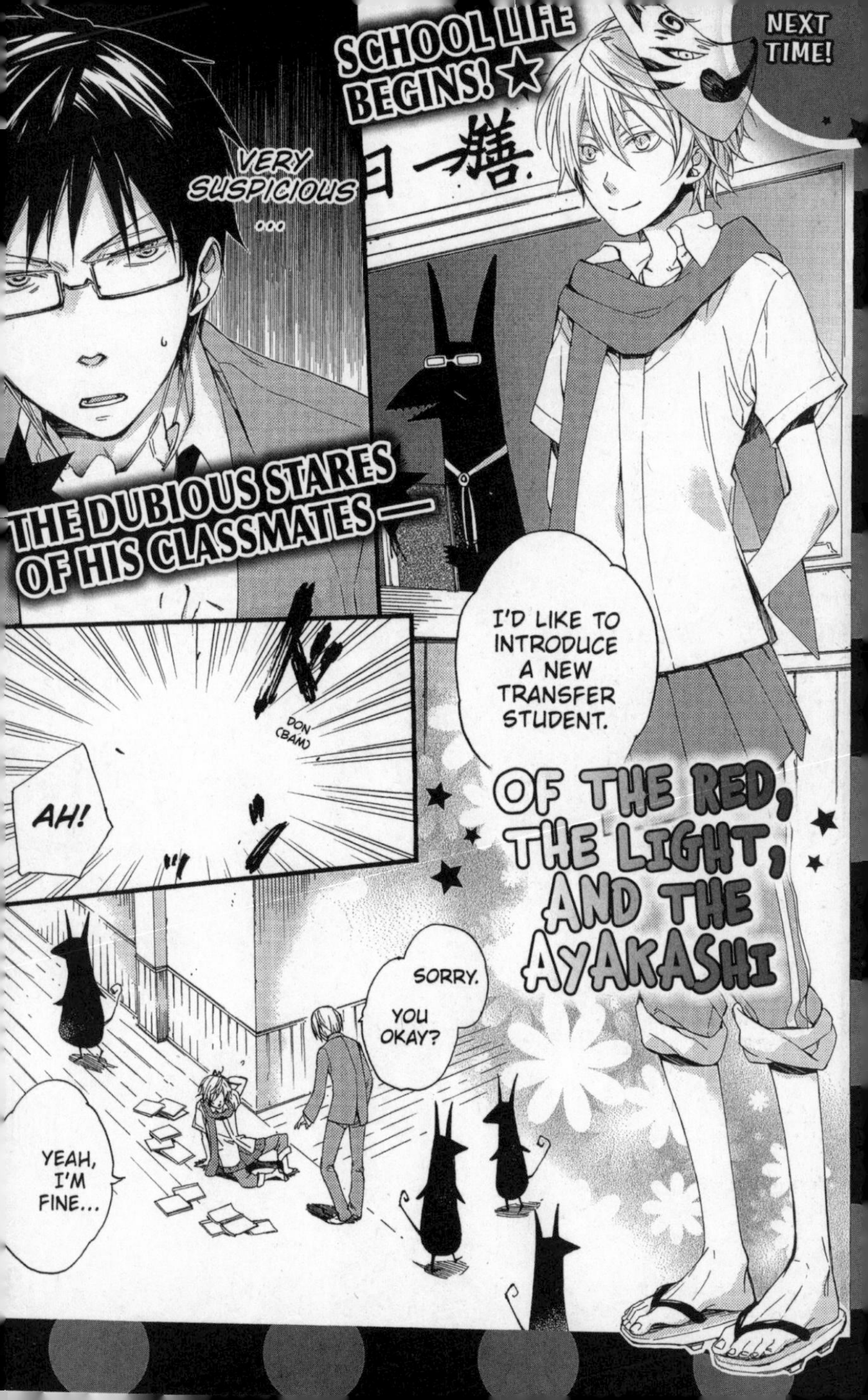
NEXT TIME!
SCHOOL LIFE BEGINS! ★
I'D LIKE TO INTRODUCE A NEW TRANSFER STUDENT.
OF THE RED, THE LIGHT, AND THE AYAKASHI
VERY SUSPICIOUS ...
THE DUBIOUS STARES OF HIS CLASSMATES —
DON (BAM)
AH!
SORRY.
YOU OKAY?
YEAH, I'M FINE...

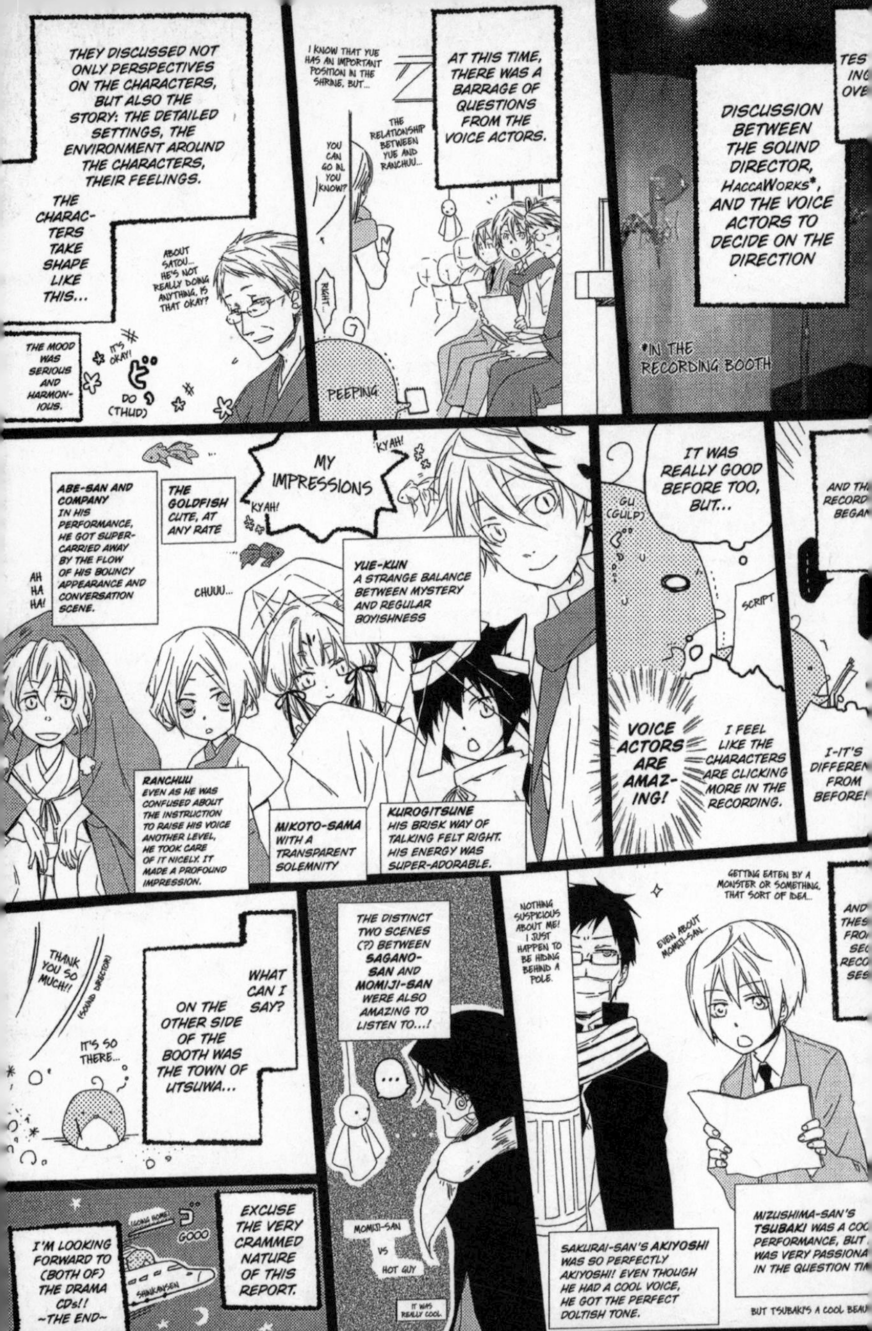

TES
ING
OVE
DISCUSSION BETWEEN THE SOUND DIRECTOR, HaccaWorks*, AND THE VOICE ACTORS TO DECIDE ON THE DIRECTION
*IN THE RECORDING BOOTH
AT THIS TIME, THERE WAS A BARRAGE OF QUESTIONS FROM THE VOICE ACTORS.
I KNOW THAT YUE HAS AN IMPORTANT POSITION IN THE SHRINE, BUT...
THE RELATIONSHIP BETWEEN YUE AND RANCHUU...
YOU CAN GO IN, YOU KNOW?
RIGHT...
PEEPING
THEY DISCUSSED NOT ONLY PERSPECTIVES ON THE CHARACTERS, BUT ALSO THE STORY: THE DETAILED SETTINGS, THE ENVIRONMENT AROUND THE CHARACTERS, THEIR FEELINGS.
THE CHARACTERS TAKE SHAPE LIKE THIS...
ABOUT SATOU... HE'S NOT REALLY DOING ANYTHING, IS THAT OKAY?
IT'S OKAY!
DO (THUD)
THE MOOD WAS SERIOUS AND HARMONIOUS.
AND TH
RECORD
BEGAN
I-IT'S DIFFEREN FROM BEFORE!
IT WAS REALLY GOOD BEFORE TOO, BUT...
GU (GULP)
SCRIPT
VOICE ACTORS ARE AMAZING!
I FEEL LIKE THE CHARACTERS ARE CLICKING MORE IN THE RECORDING.
MY IMPRESSIONS
KYAH!
KYAH!
YUE-KUN A STRANGE BALANCE BETWEEN MYSTERY AND REGULAR BOYISHNESS
THE GOLDFISH CUTE, AT ANY RATE
ABE-SAN AND COMPANY IN HIS PERFORMANCE, HE GOT SUPER-CARRIED AWAY BY THE FLOW OF HIS BOUNCY APPEARANCE AND CONVERSATION SCENE.
AH HA HA!
CHUUU...
KUROGITSUNE HIS BRISK WAY OF TALKING FELT RIGHT. HIS ENERGY WAS SUPER-ADORABLE.
MIKOTO-SAMA WITH A TRANSPARENT SOLEMNITY
RANCHUU EVEN AS HE WAS CONFUSED ABOUT THE INSTRUCTION TO RAISE HIS VOICE ANOTHER LEVEL, HE TOOK CARE OF IT NICELY. IT MADE A PROFOUND IMPRESSION.
AND
THES
FRO
SEC
RECO
SES
GETTING EATEN BY A MONSTER OR SOMETHING, THAT SORT OF IDEA...
EVEN ABOUT MOMIJI-SAN
MIZUSHIMA-SAN'S TSUBAKI WAS A COO PERFORMANCE, BUT WAS VERY PASSIONA IN THE QUESTION TIM
BUT TSUBAKI'S A COOL BEAU
NOTHING SUSPICIOUS ABOUT ME! I JUST HAPPEN TO BE HIDING BEHIND A POLE.
SAKURAI-SAN'S AKIYOSHI WAS SO PERFECTLY AKIYOSHI! EVEN THOUGH HE HAD A COOL VOICE, HE GOT THE PERFECT DOLTISH TONE.
THE DISTINCT TWO SCENES (?) BETWEEN SAGANO-SAN AND MOMIJI-SAN WERE ALSO AMAZING TO LISTEN TO...!
...
MOMIJI-SAN VS HOT GUY
IT WAS REALLY COOL.
WHAT CAN I SAY?
ON THE OTHER SIDE OF THE BOOTH WAS THE TOWN OF UTSUWA...
THANK YOU SO MUCH!! (SOUND DIRECTOR)
IT'S SO THERE...
EXCUSE THE VERY CRAMMED NATURE OF THIS REPORT.
(GOING HOME)
GOOO
SHINKANSEN
I'M LOOKING FORWARD TO (BOTH OF) THE DRAMA CDs!! ~THE END~

*THIS REPORT IS FROM THE RECORDING OF ANTHOLOGY DRAMA CD 1.

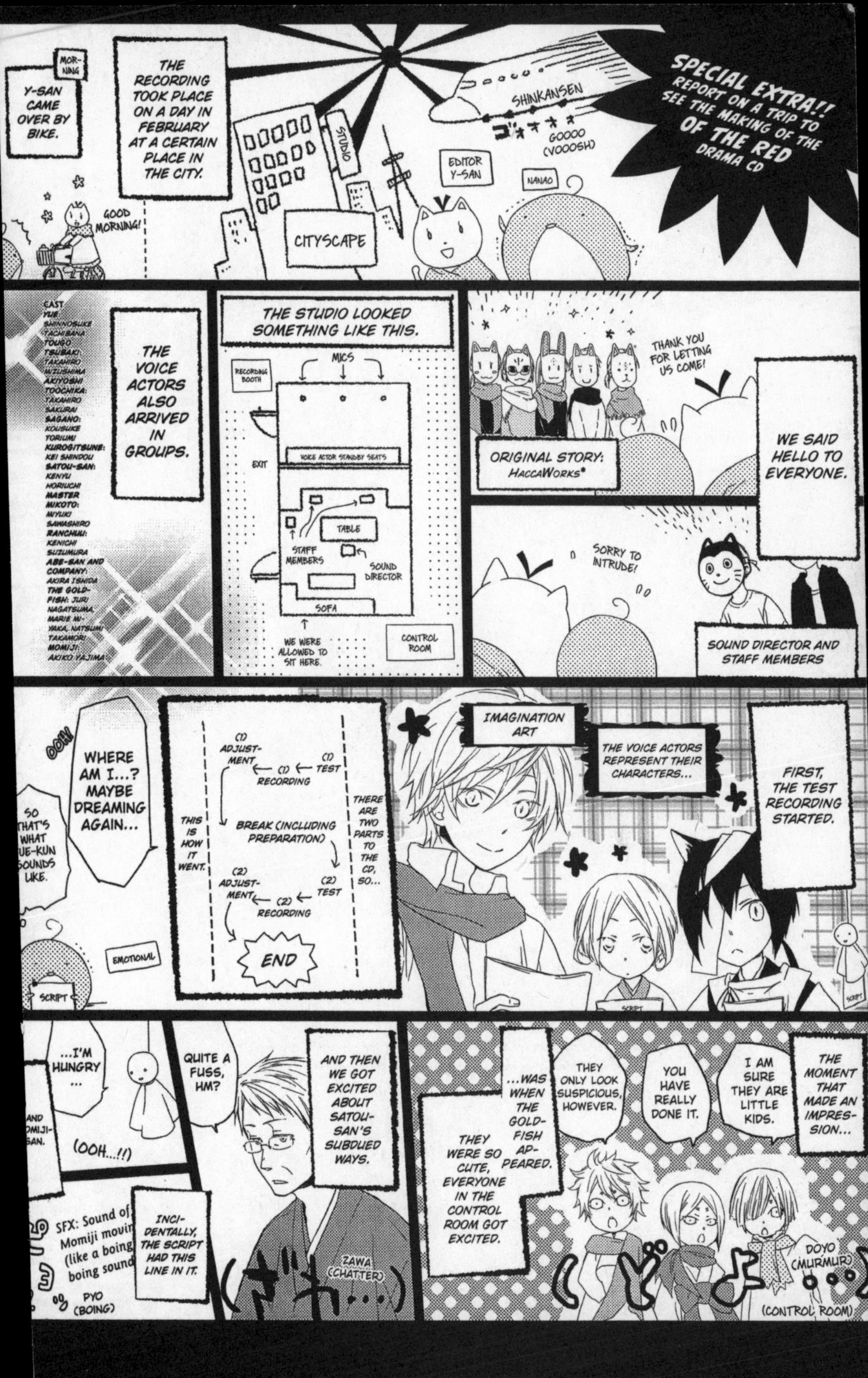
SPECIAL EXTRA!! REPORT ON A TRIP TO SEE THE MAKING OF THE RED DRAMA CD
SHINKANSEN
GOOOO (VOOOSH)
EDITOR Y-SAN
NANAO
STUDIO
CITYSCAPE
THE RECORDING TOOK PLACE ON A DAY IN FEBRUARY AT A CERTAIN PLACE IN THE CITY.
MOR-NING
Y-SAN CAME OVER BY BIKE.
GOOD MORNING!
THANK YOU FOR LETTING US COME!
WE SAID HELLO TO EVERYONE.
ORIGINAL STORY: HaccaWorks*
SORRY TO INTRUDE!
SOUND DIRECTOR AND STAFF MEMBERS
THE STUDIO LOOKED SOMETHING LIKE THIS.
MICS
RECORDING BOOTH
VOICE ACTOR STANDBY SEATS
EXIT
TABLE
STAFF MEMBERS
SOUND DIRECTOR
SOFA
WE WERE ALLOWED TO SIT HERE.
CONTROL ROOM
THE VOICE ACTORS ALSO ARRIVED IN GROUPS.
CAST
YUE: SHINNOSUKE TACHIBANA
TOUGO TSUBAKI: TAKAHIRO MIZUSHIMA
AKIYOSHI TOOCHIKA: TAKAHIRO SAKURAI
SAGANO: KOUSUKE TORIUMI
KUROGITSUNE: KEI SHINDOU
SATOU-SAN: KENYU HORIUCHI
MASTER MIKOTO: MYUKI SAWASHIRO
RANCHUU: KENICHI SUZUMURA
ABE-SAN AND COMPANY: AKIRA ISHIDA
THE GOLDFISH: JURI NAGATSUMA, MARIE MIYAKE, NATSUMI TAKAMORI
MOMIJI: AKIKO YAJIMA
FIRST, THE TEST RECORDING STARTED.
IMAGINATION ART
THE VOICE ACTORS REPRESENT THEIR CHARACTERS...
SCRIPT
THERE ARE TWO PARTS TO THE CD, SO...
(1) TEST
(1) RECORDING
(1) ADJUSTMENT
BREAK (INCLUDING PREPARATION)
(2) TEST
(2) RECORDING
(2) ADJUSTMENT
END
THIS IS HOW IT WENT.
WHERE AM I...? MAYBE DREAMING AGAIN...
OOH!
SO THAT'S WHAT YUE-KUN SOUNDS LIKE.
EMOTIONAL
SCRIPT
THE MOMENT THAT MADE AN IMPRESSION...
I AM SURE THEY ARE LITTLE KIDS.
YOU HAVE REALLY DONE IT.
THEY ONLY LOOK SUSPICIOUS, HOWEVER.
...WAS WHEN THE GOLDFISH APPEARED.
THEY WERE SO CUTE, EVERYONE IN THE CONTROL ROOM GOT EXCITED.
DOYO (MURMUR)
(CONTROL ROOM)
AND THEN WE GOT EXCITED ABOUT SATOU-SAN'S SUBDUED WAYS.
QUITE A FUSS, HM?
INCIDENTALLY, THE SCRIPT HAD THIS LINE IN IT.
ZAWA (CHATTER)
...I'M HUNGRY...
AND MOMIJI-SAN.
(OOH...!!)
SFX: Sound of Momiji movin (like a boing boing sound
PYO (BOING)

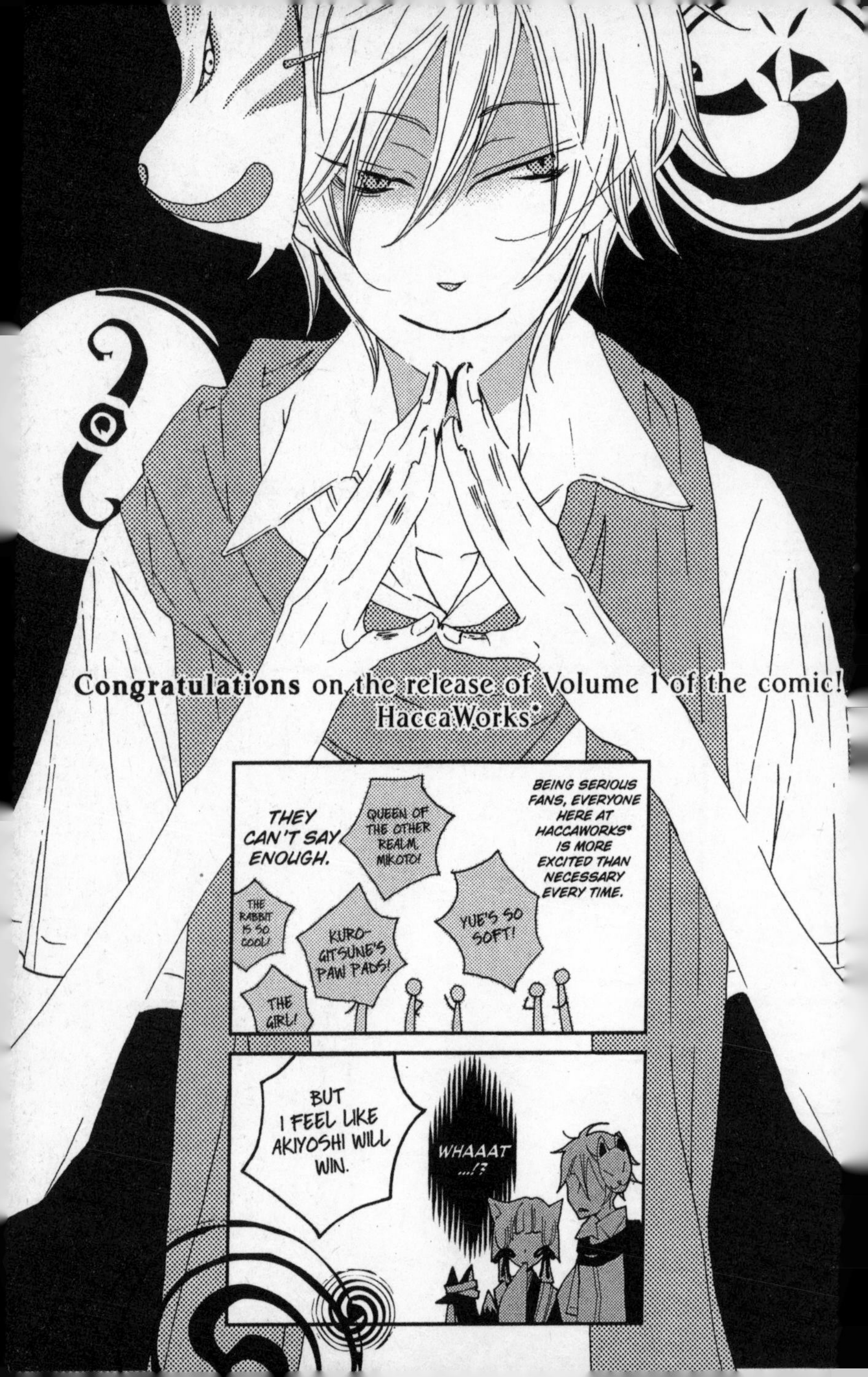
Congratulations on the release of Volume 1 of the comic!
HaccaWorks*
BEING SERIOUS FANS, EVERYONE HERE AT HACCAWORKS* IS MORE EXCITED THAN NECESSARY EVERY TIME.
QUEEN OF THE OTHER REALM, MIKOTO!
THEY CAN'T SAY ENOUGH.
YUE'S SO SOFT!
KURO-GITSUNE'S PAW PADS!
THE RABBIT IS SO COOL!
THE GIRL!
BUT I FEEL LIKE AKIYOSHI WILL WIN.
WHAAAT ...!?

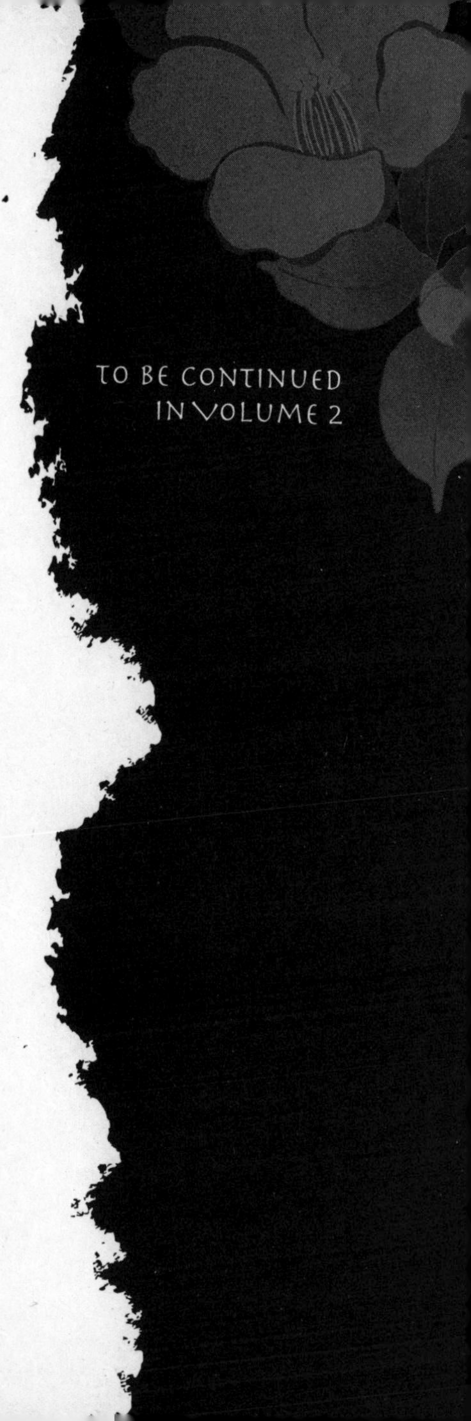
TO BE CONTINUED
IN VOLUME 2

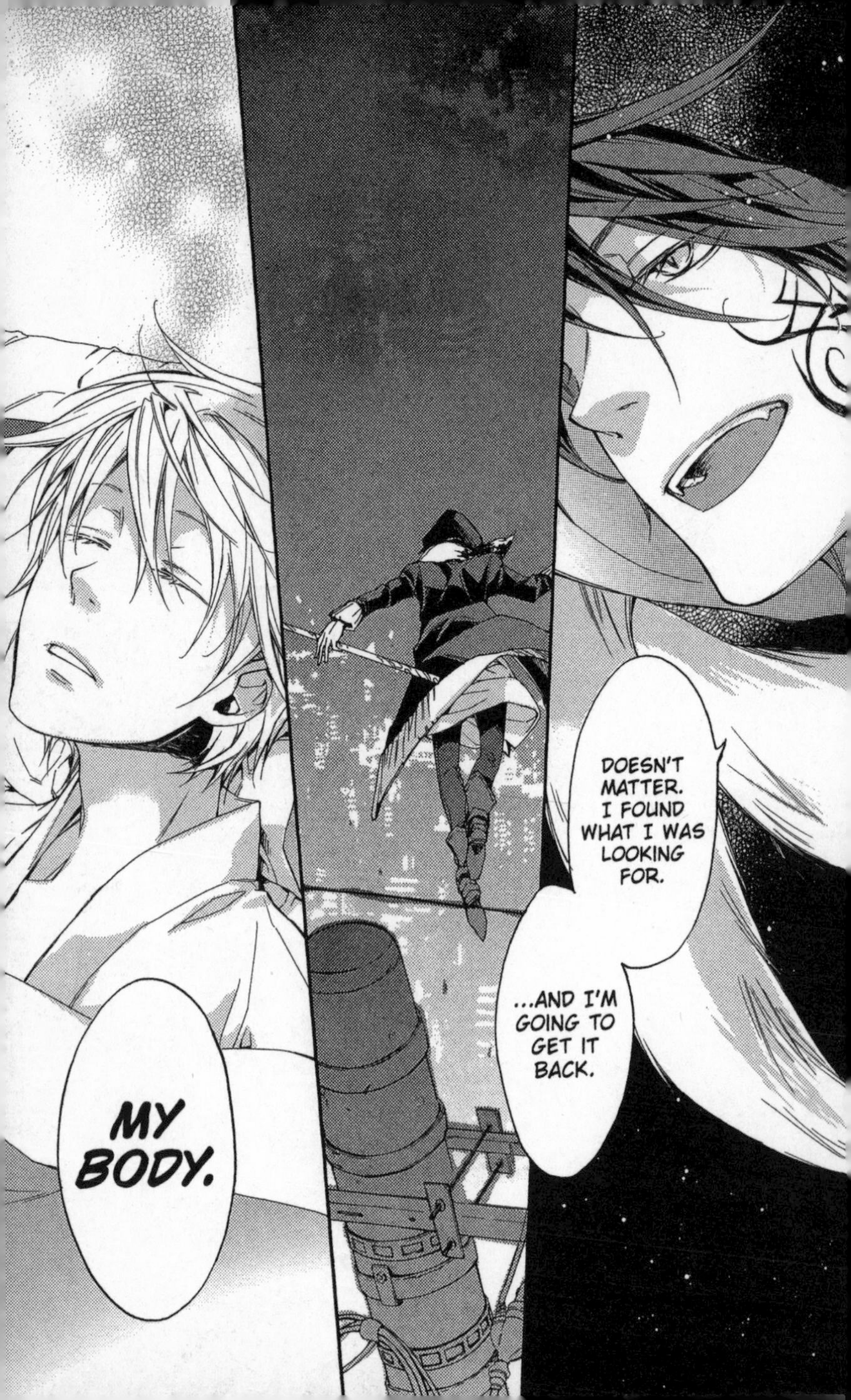
DOESN'T MATTER. I FOUND WHAT I WAS LOOKING FOR.
...AND I'M GOING TO GET IT BACK.
MY BODY.

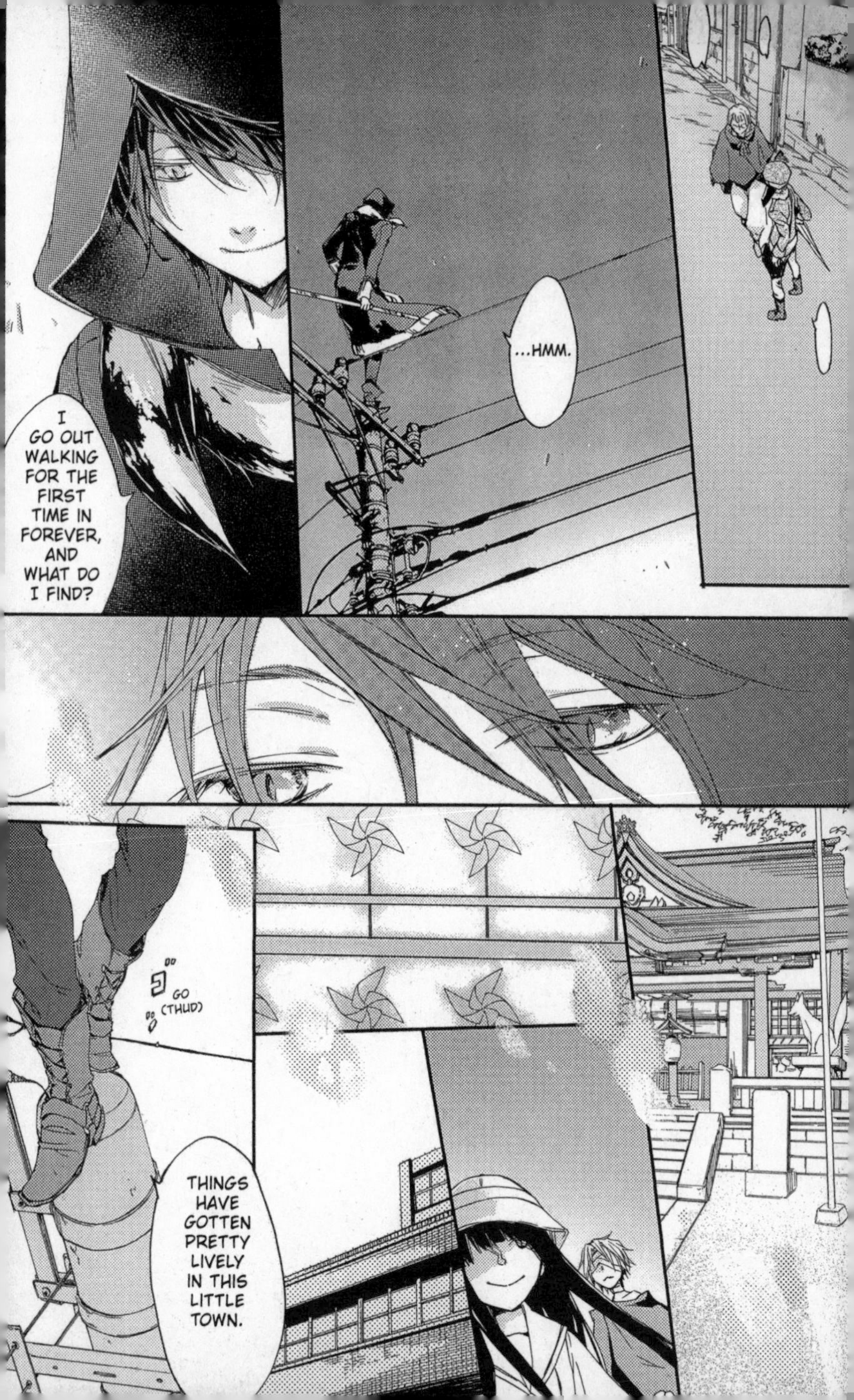
...HMM.
I GO OUT WALKING FOR THE FIRST TIME IN FOREVER, AND WHAT DO I FIND?
GO (THUD)
THINGS HAVE GOTTEN PRETTY LIVELY IN THIS LITTLE TOWN.

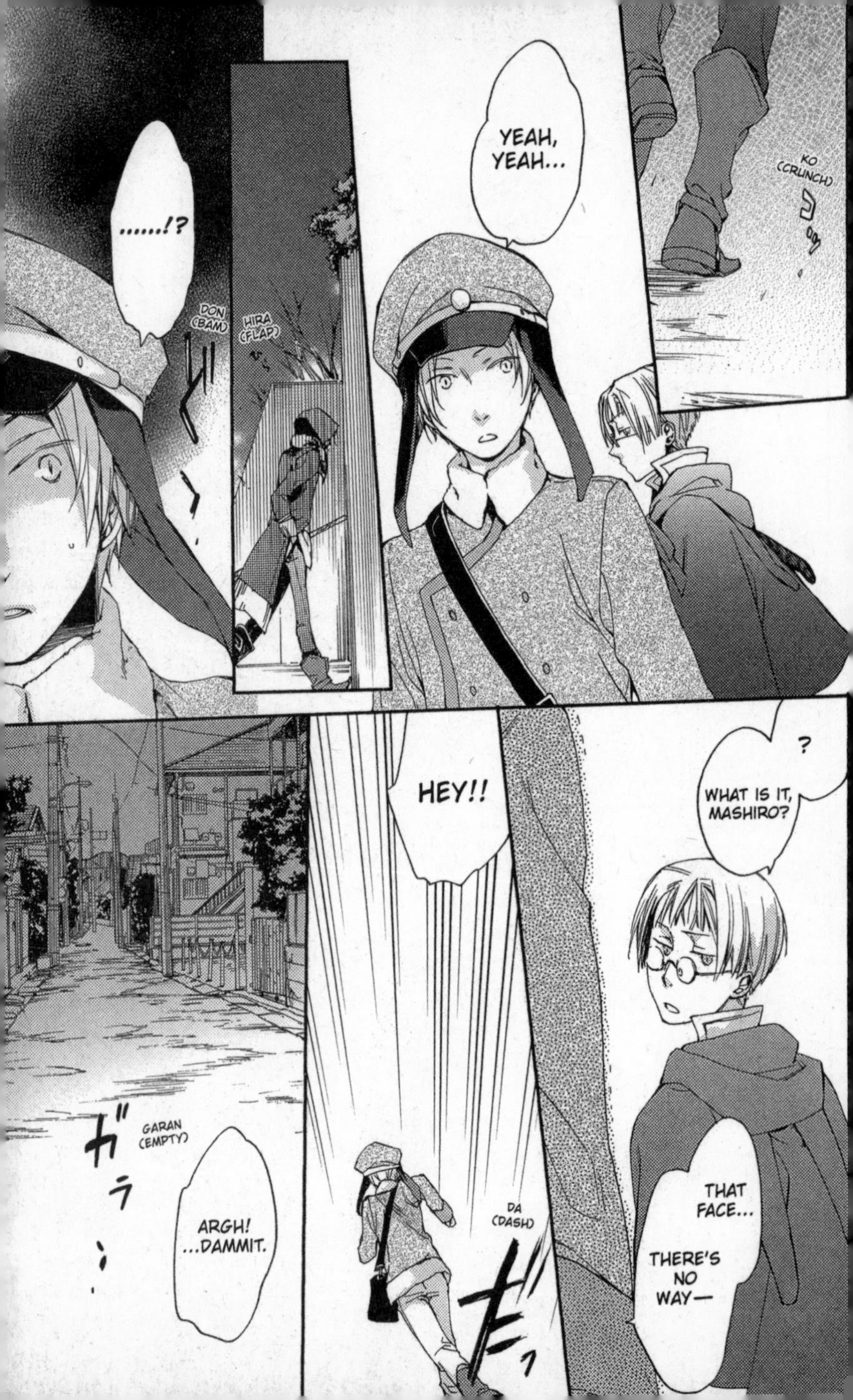
KO (CRUNCH)
YEAH, YEAH...
HIRA (FLAP)
......!?
DON (BAM)
?
WHAT IS IT, MASHIRO?
THAT FACE...
THERE'S NO WAY—
HEY!!
DA (DASH)
GARAN (EMPTY)
ARGH! ...DAMMIT.

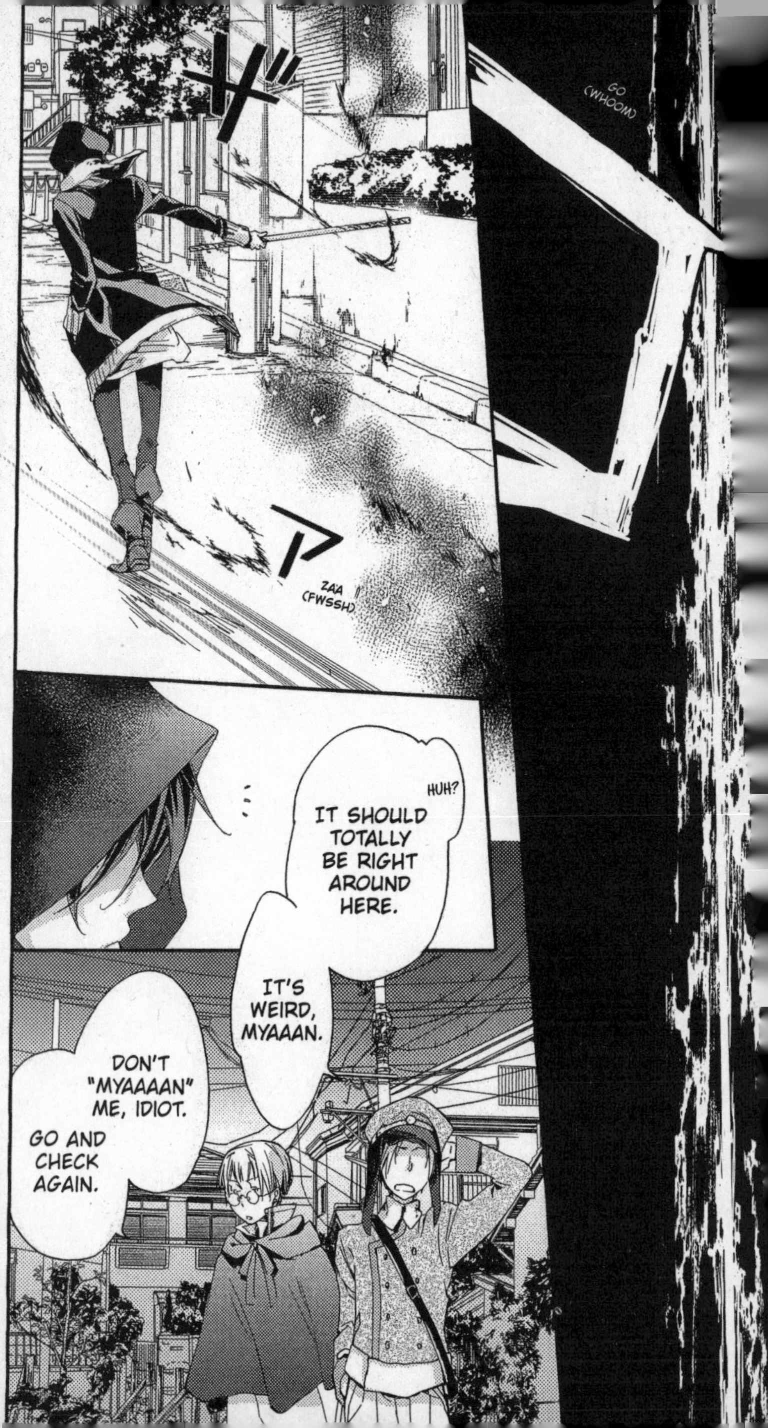
GO (WHOOM)
ZAA (FWSSH)
HUH?
IT SHOULD TOTALLY BE RIGHT AROUND HERE.
IT'S WEIRD, MYAAAN.
DON'T "MYAAAAN" ME, IDIOT.
GO AND CHECK AGAIN.

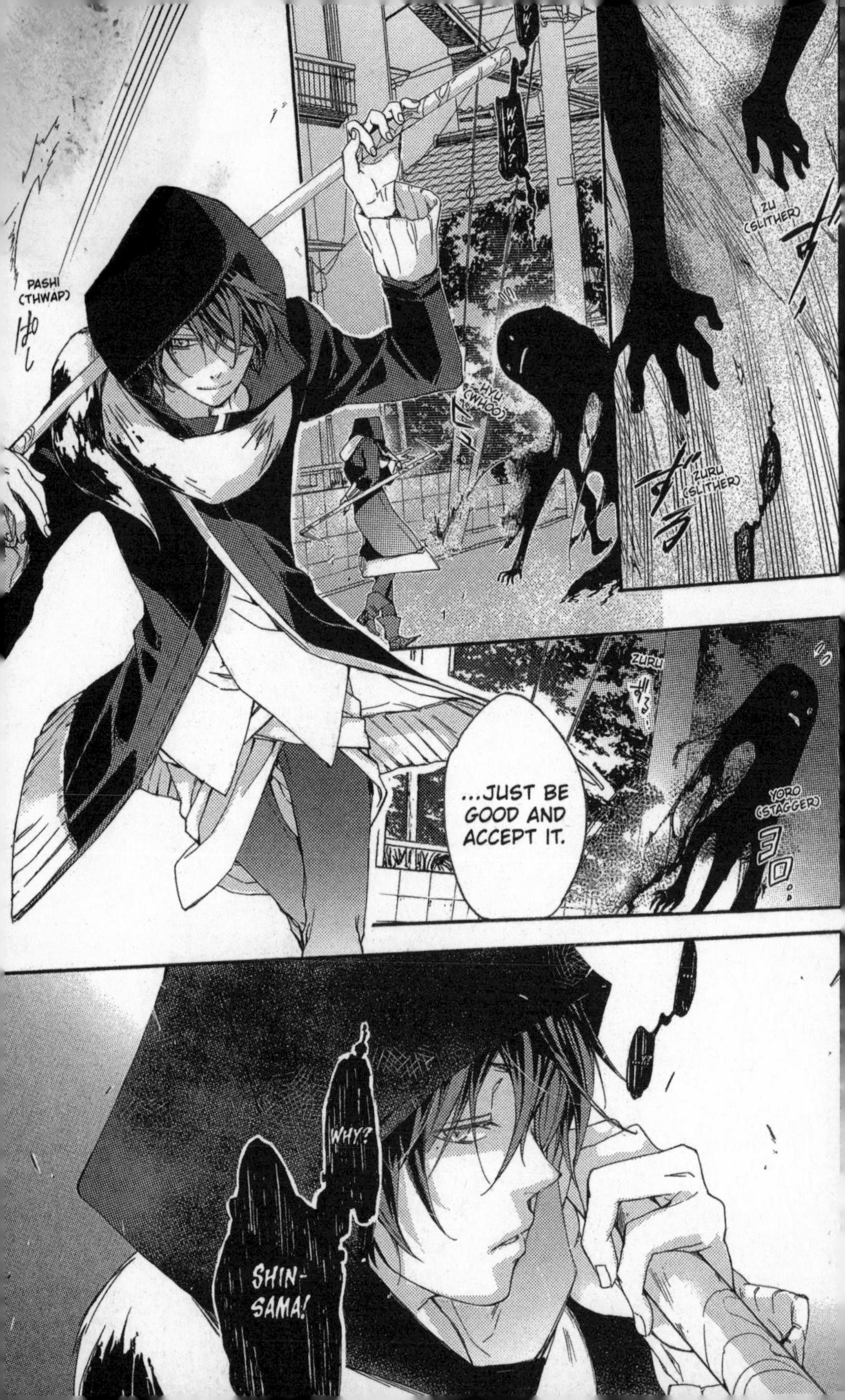
ZU (SLITHER)
ZURU (SLITHER)
WHY?
WHY?
HYU (WHOO)
ZURU
YORO (STAGGER)
...JUST BE GOOD AND ACCEPT IT.
PASHI (THWAP)
WHY?
SHIN-SAMA!

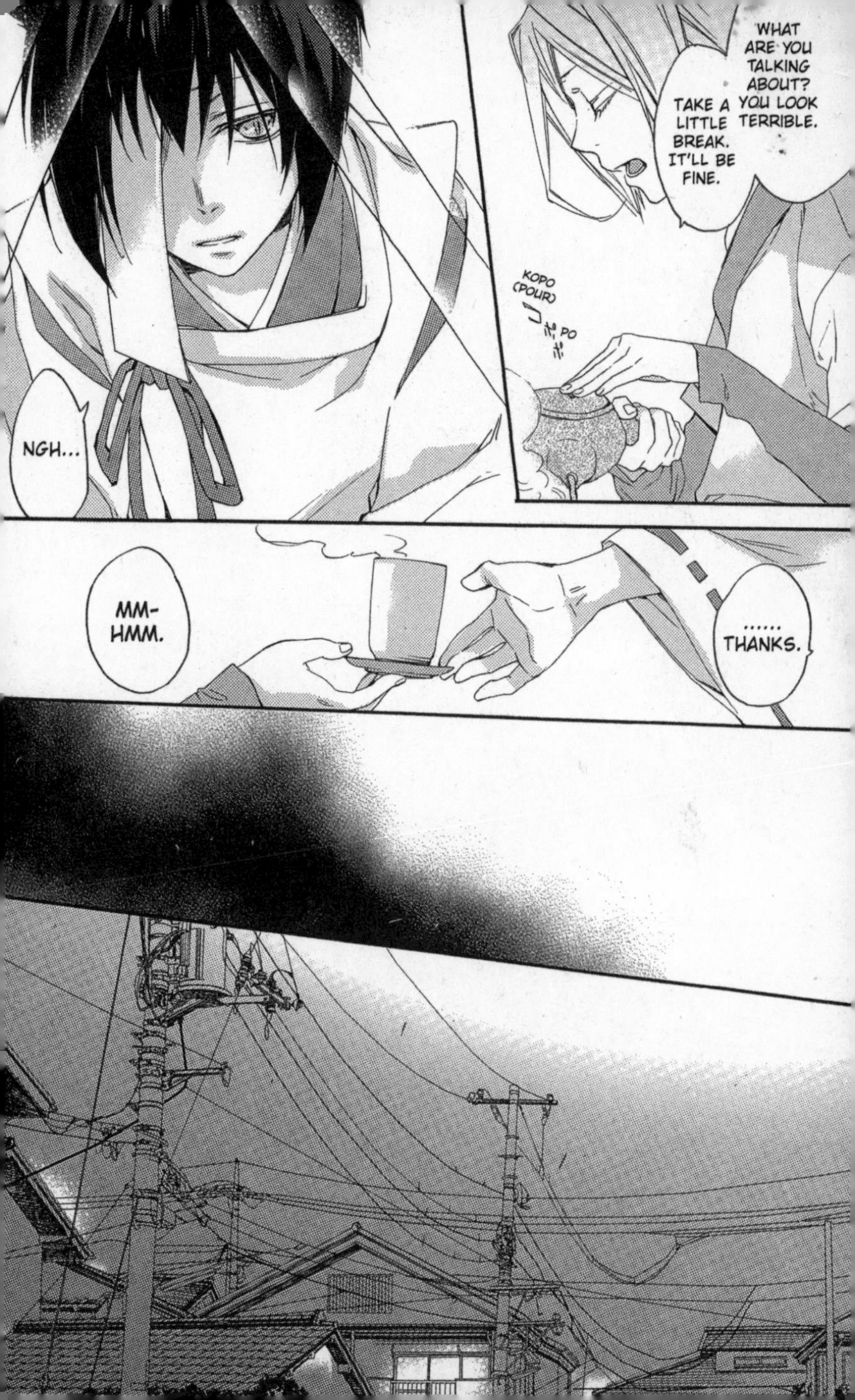
WHAT ARE YOU TALKING ABOUT? YOU LOOK TERRIBLE.
TAKE A LITTLE BREAK. IT'LL BE FINE.
KOPO (POUR)
PO
NGH...
......THANKS.
MM-HMM.

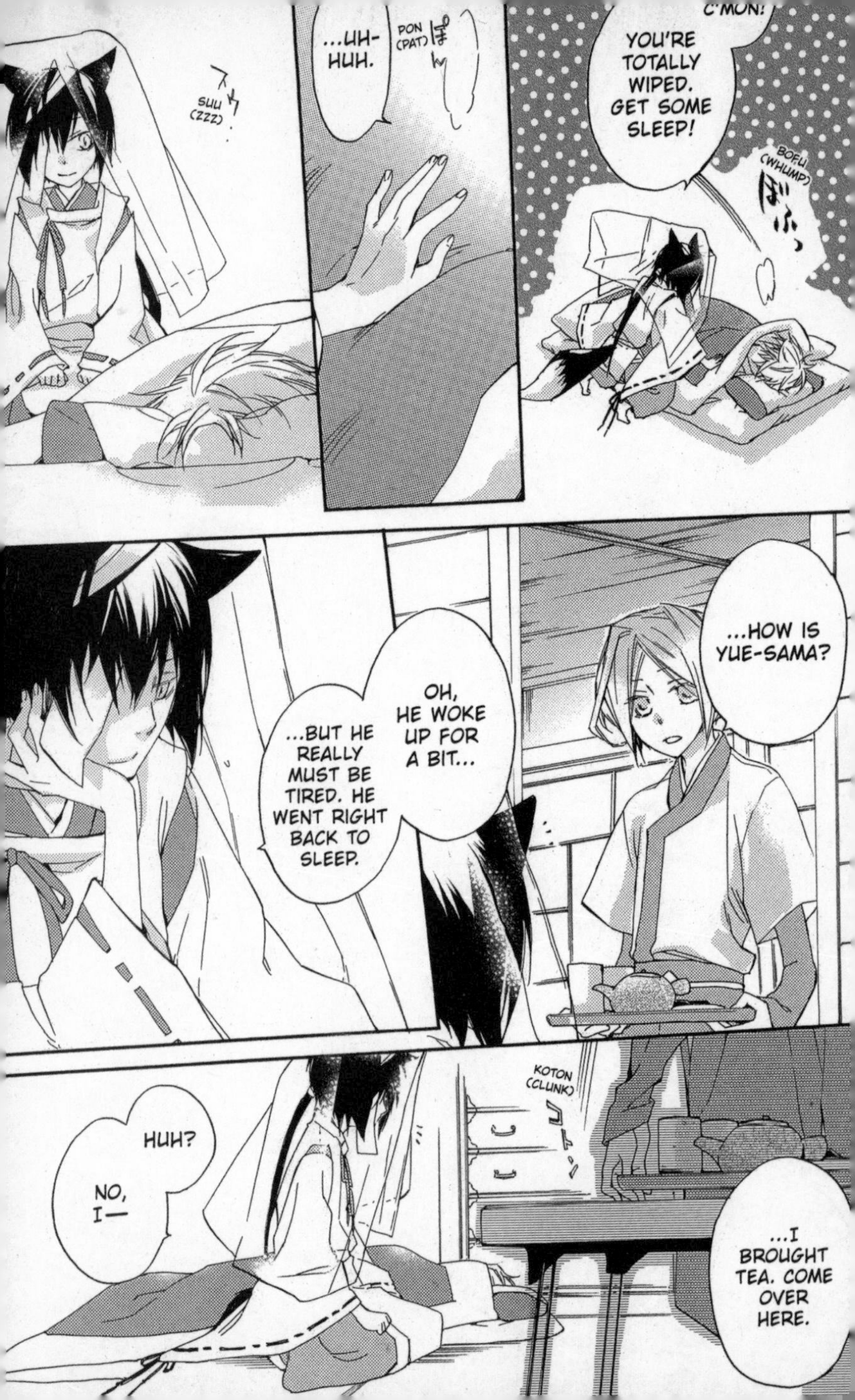
C'MON!
YOU'RE TOTALLY WIPED. GET SOME SLEEP!
BOFU (WHUMP)
...UH-HUH.
PON (PAT)
SUU (ZZZ)
...HOW IS YUE-SAMA?
OH, HE WOKE UP FOR A BIT...
...BUT HE REALLY MUST BE TIRED. HE WENT RIGHT BACK TO SLEEP.
KOTON (CLUNK)
...I BROUGHT TEA. COME OVER HERE.
HUH?
NO, I—

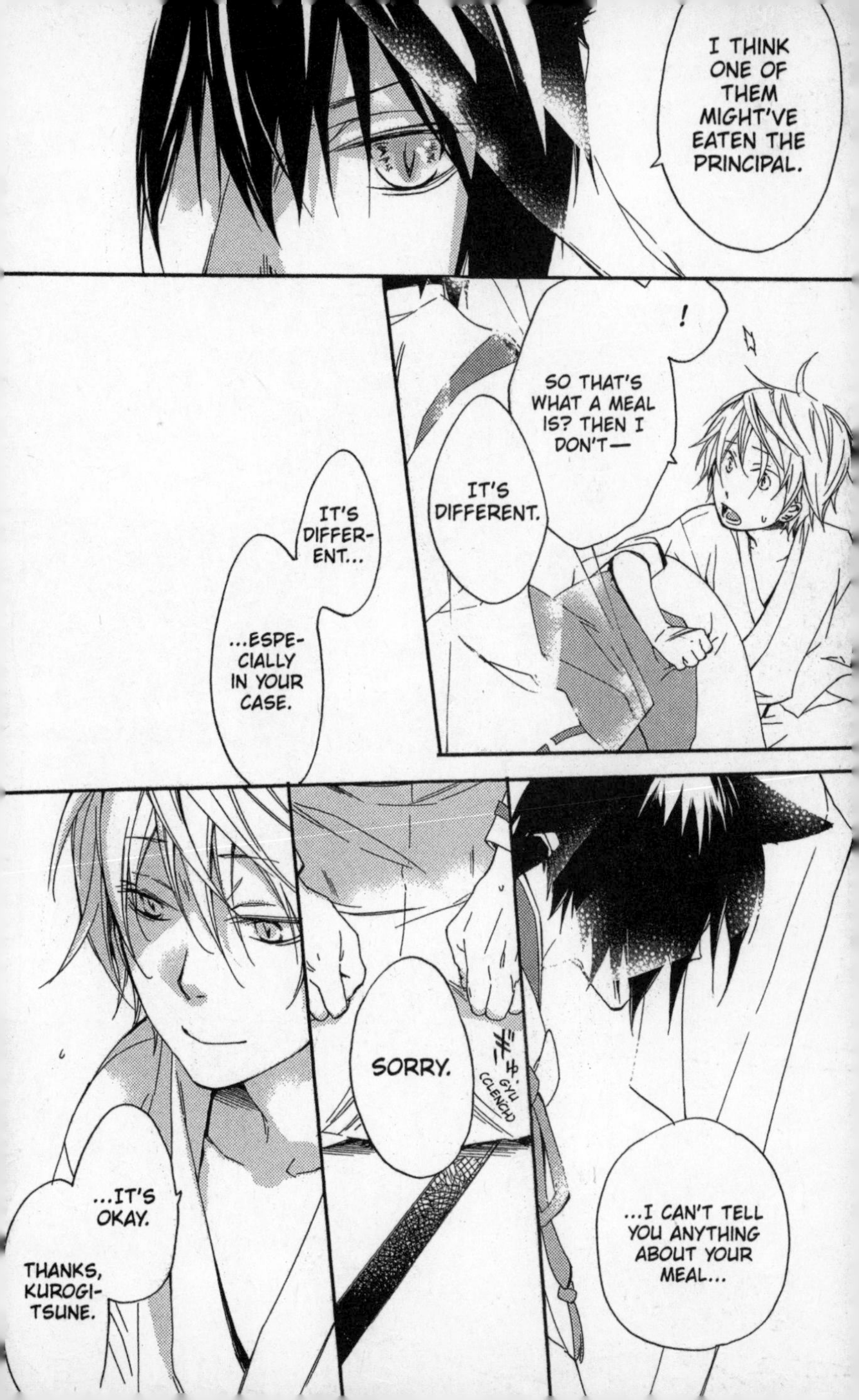
I THINK ONE OF THEM MIGHT'VE EATEN THE PRINCIPAL.
!
SO THAT'S WHAT A MEAL IS? THEN I DON'T—
IT'S DIFFERENT.
IT'S DIFFER-ENT...
...ESPE-CIALLY IN YOUR CASE.
...I CAN'T TELL YOU ANYTHING ABOUT YOUR MEAL...
GYU (CLENCH)
SORRY.
...IT'S OKAY.
THANKS, KUROGI-TSUNE.

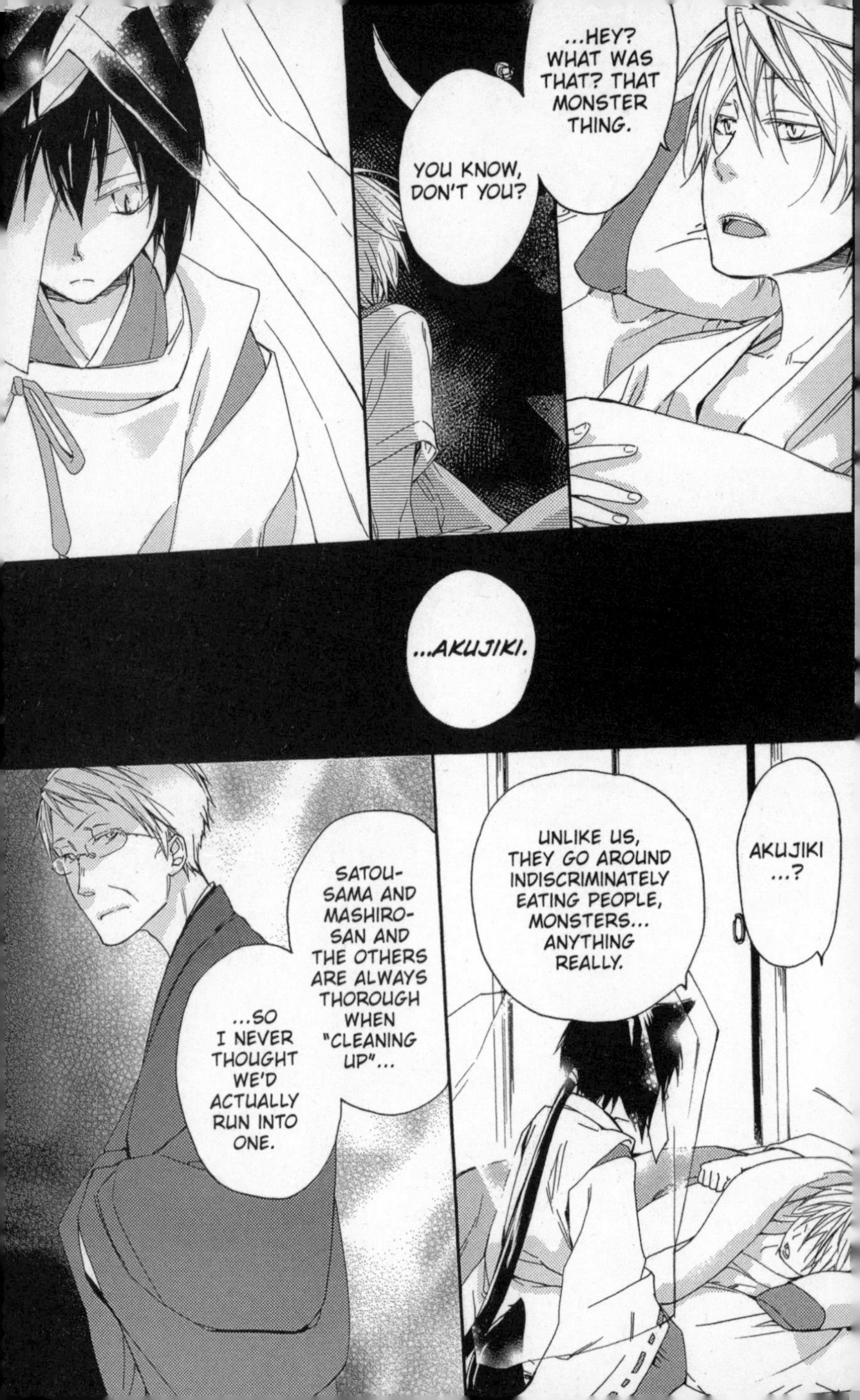
...HEY? WHAT WAS THAT? THAT MONSTER THING.
YOU KNOW, DON'T YOU?
...AKUJIKI.
AKUJIKI ...?
UNLIKE US, THEY GO AROUND INDISCRIMINATELY EATING PEOPLE, MONSTERS... ANYTHING REALLY.
SATOU-SAMA AND MASHIRO-SAN AND THE OTHERS ARE ALWAYS THOROUGH WHEN "CLEANING UP"...
...SO I NEVER THOUGHT WE'D ACTUALLY RUN INTO ONE.

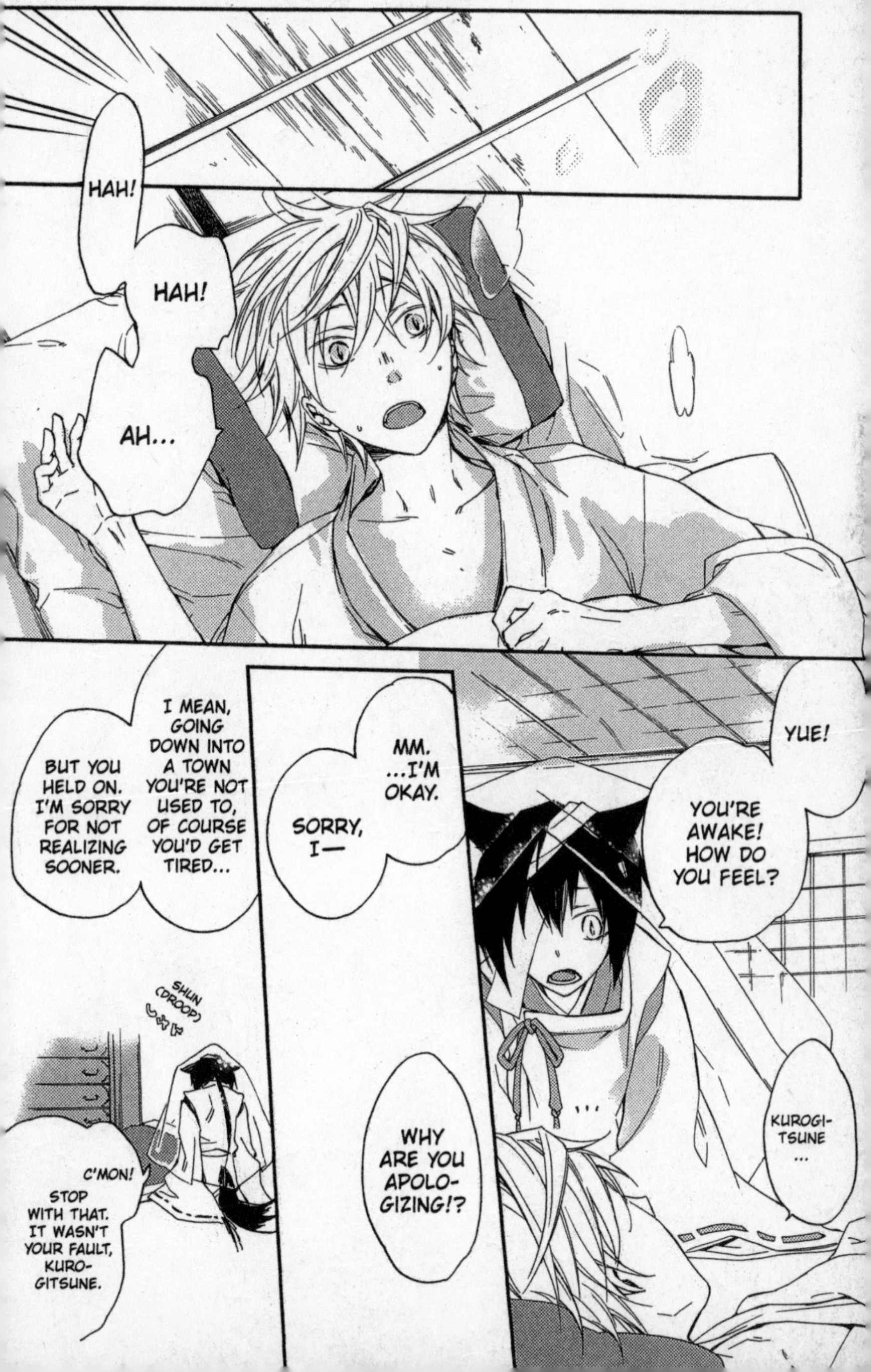
HAH!
HAH!
AH...
YUE!
YOU'RE AWAKE! HOW DO YOU FEEL?
...
KUROGI-TSUNE ...
MM. ...I'M OKAY.
SORRY, I—
WHY ARE YOU APOLO-GIZING!?
I MEAN, GOING DOWN INTO A TOWN YOU'RE NOT USED TO, OF COURSE YOU'D GET TIRED...
BUT YOU HELD ON. I'M SORRY FOR NOT REALIZING SOONER.
しゅん
SHUN (DROOP)
C'MON!
STOP WITH THAT. IT WASN'T YOUR FAULT, KURO-GITSUNE.

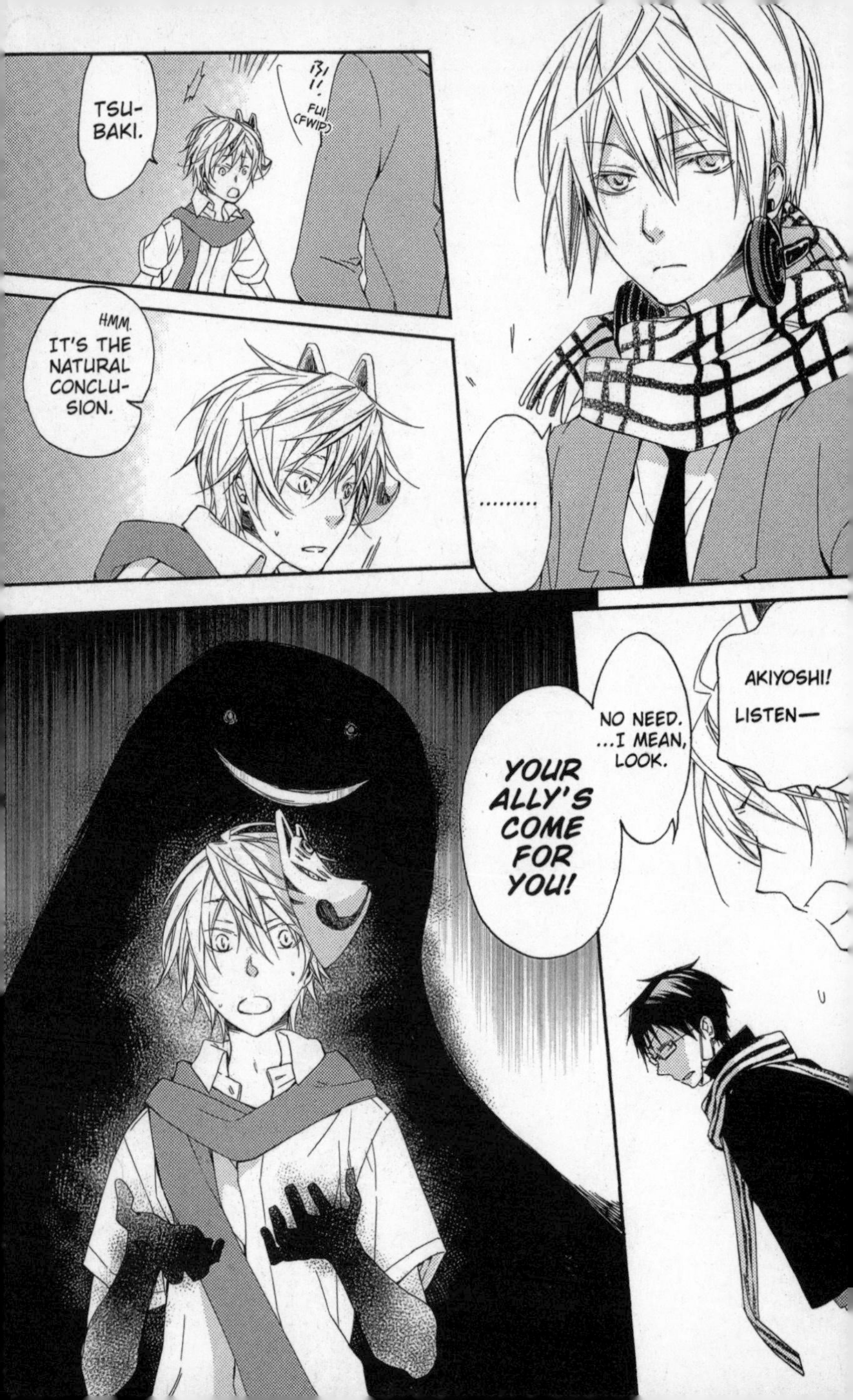

....
FUI (FWIP)
TSU-BAKI.
HMM. IT'S THE NATURAL CONCLU-SION.
AKIYOSHI! LISTEN—
NO NEED. ...I MEAN, LOOK.
YOUR ALLY'S COME FOR YOU!

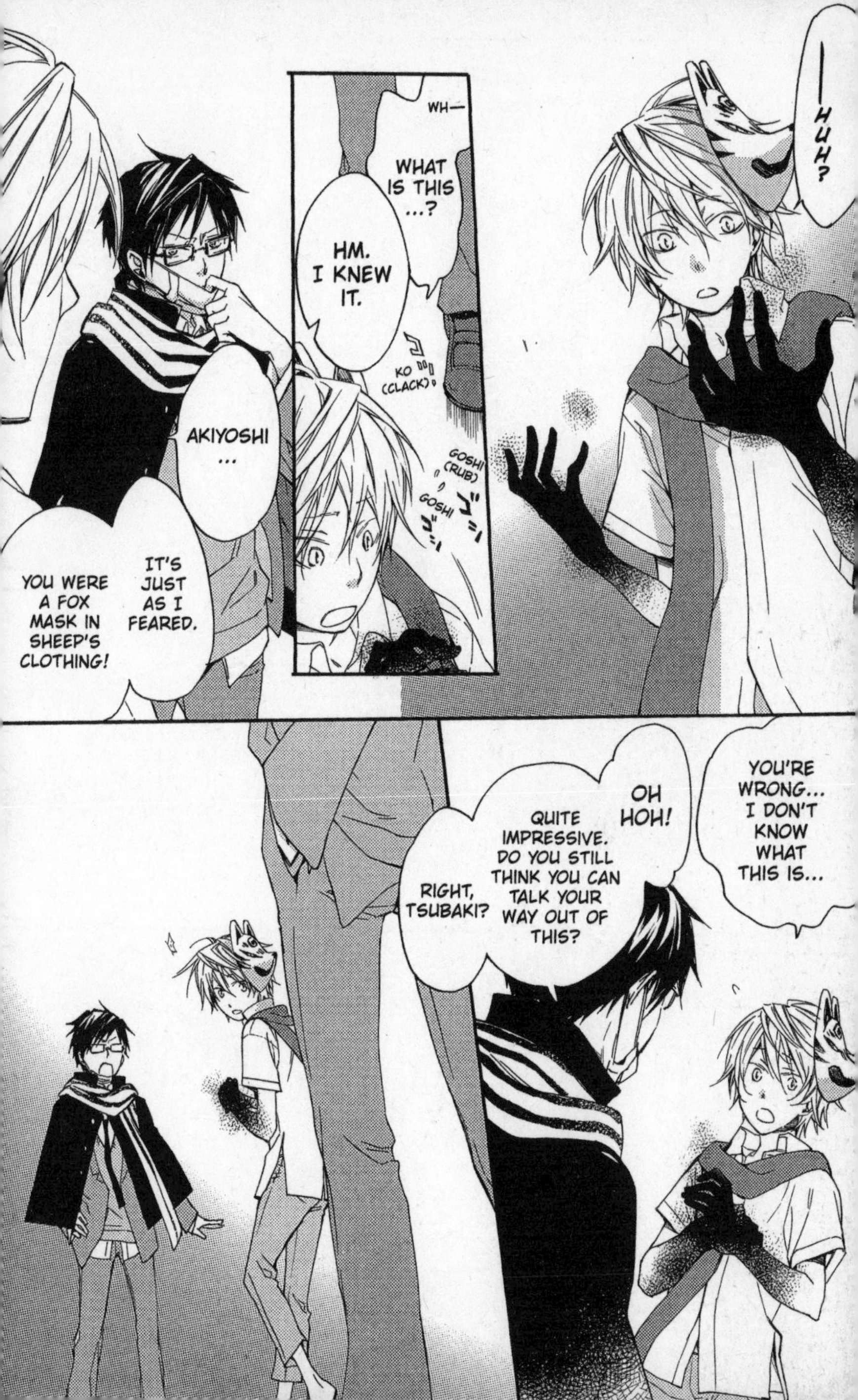
—HUH?
WH—
WHAT IS THIS ...?
HM. I KNEW IT.
KO (CLACK)
GOSHI (RUB) GOSHI
AKIYOSHI ...
IT'S JUST AS I FEARED.
YOU WERE A FOX MASK IN SHEEP'S CLOTHING!
YOU'RE WRONG... I DON'T KNOW WHAT THIS IS...
OH HOH!
QUITE IMPRESSIVE. DO YOU STILL THINK YOU CAN TALK YOUR WAY OUT OF THIS?
RIGHT, TSUBAKI?

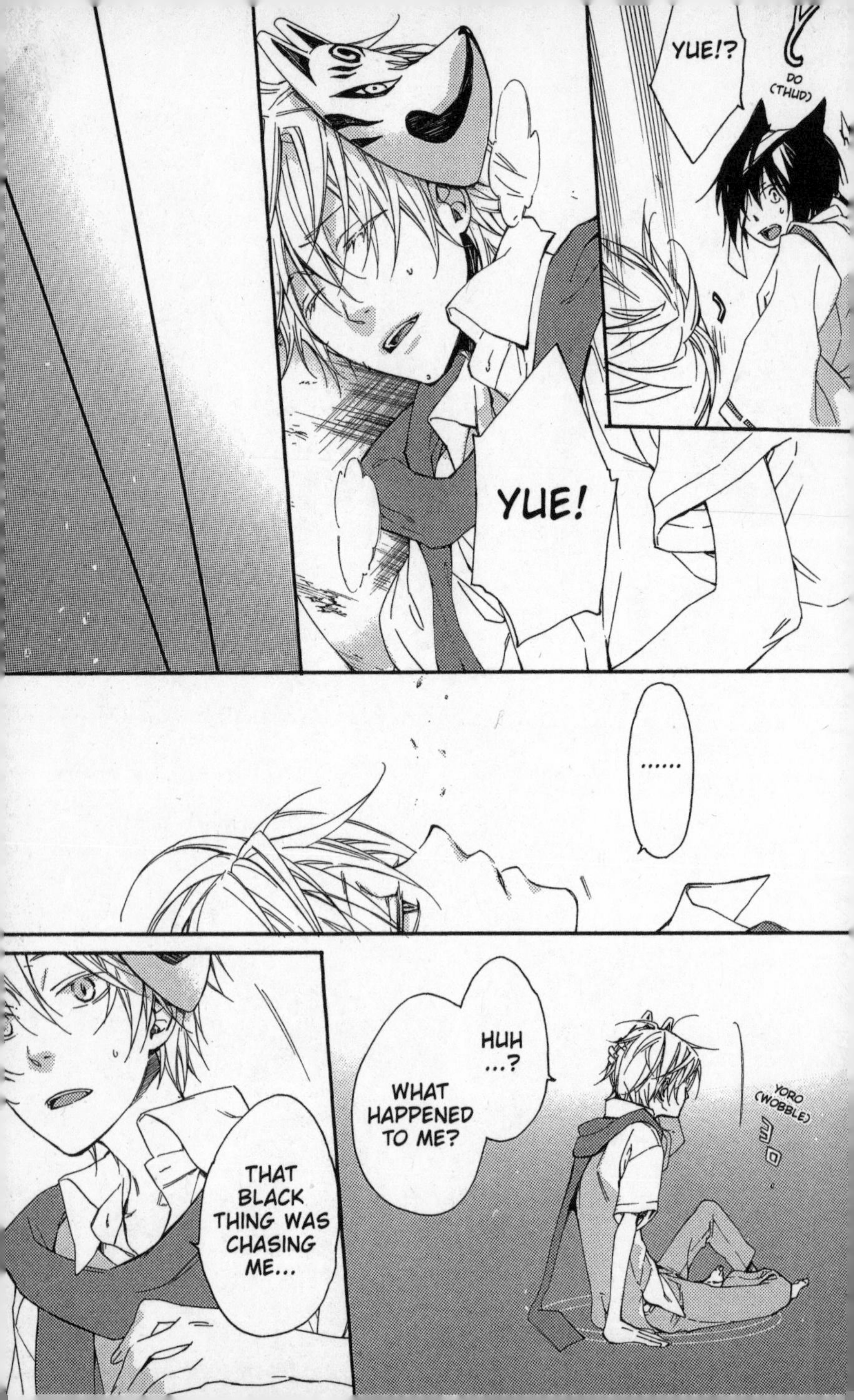
YUE!?
DO (THUD)
YUE!
......
HUH ...?
WHAT HAPPENED TO ME?
YORO (WOBBLE)
THAT BLACK THING WAS CHASING ME...

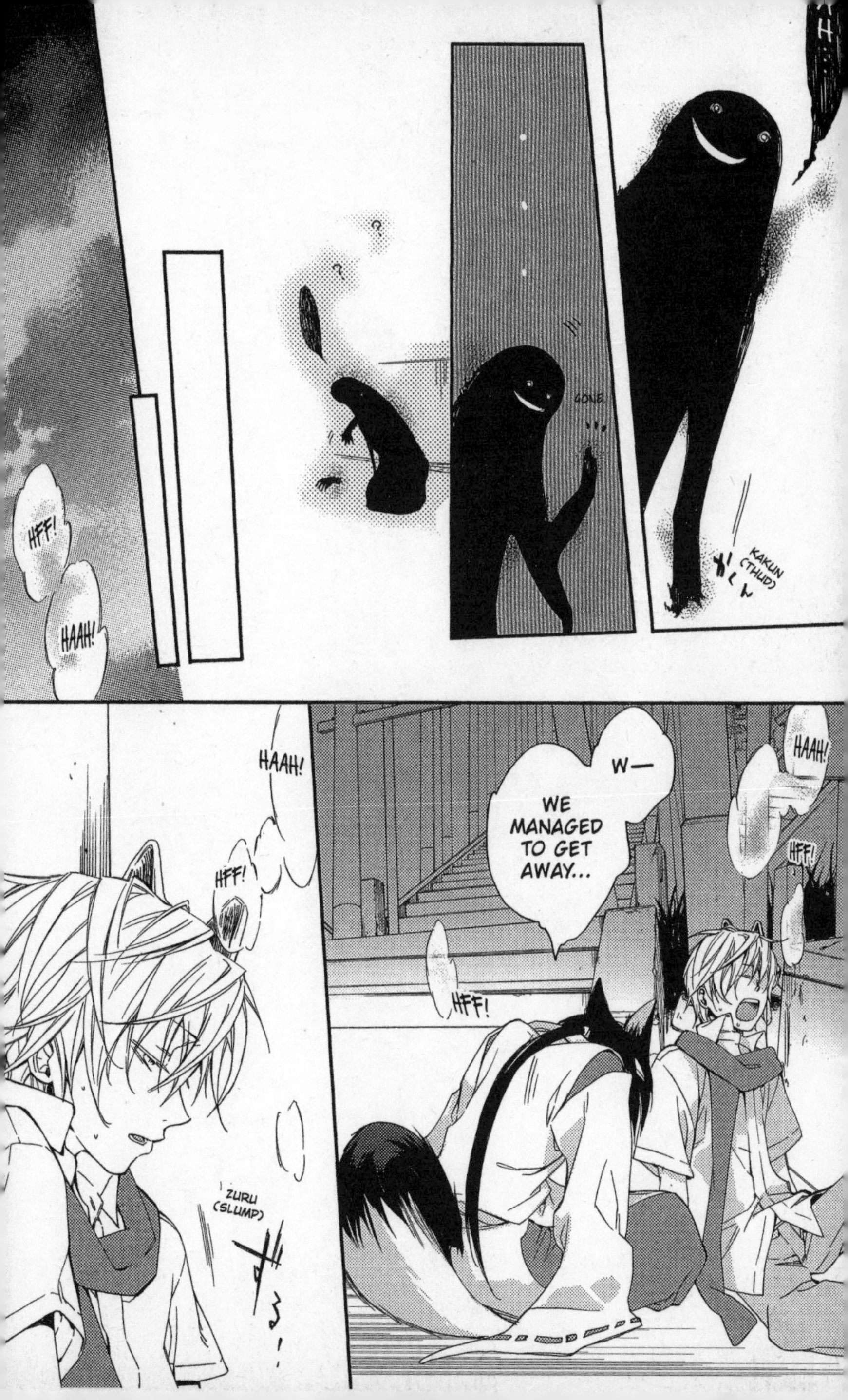
KAKUN (THUD)
GONE
?
?
HFF!
HAAH!
W—
WE MANAGED TO GET AWAY...
HAAH!
HFF!
HFF!
HAAH!
HFF!
ZURU (SLUMP)

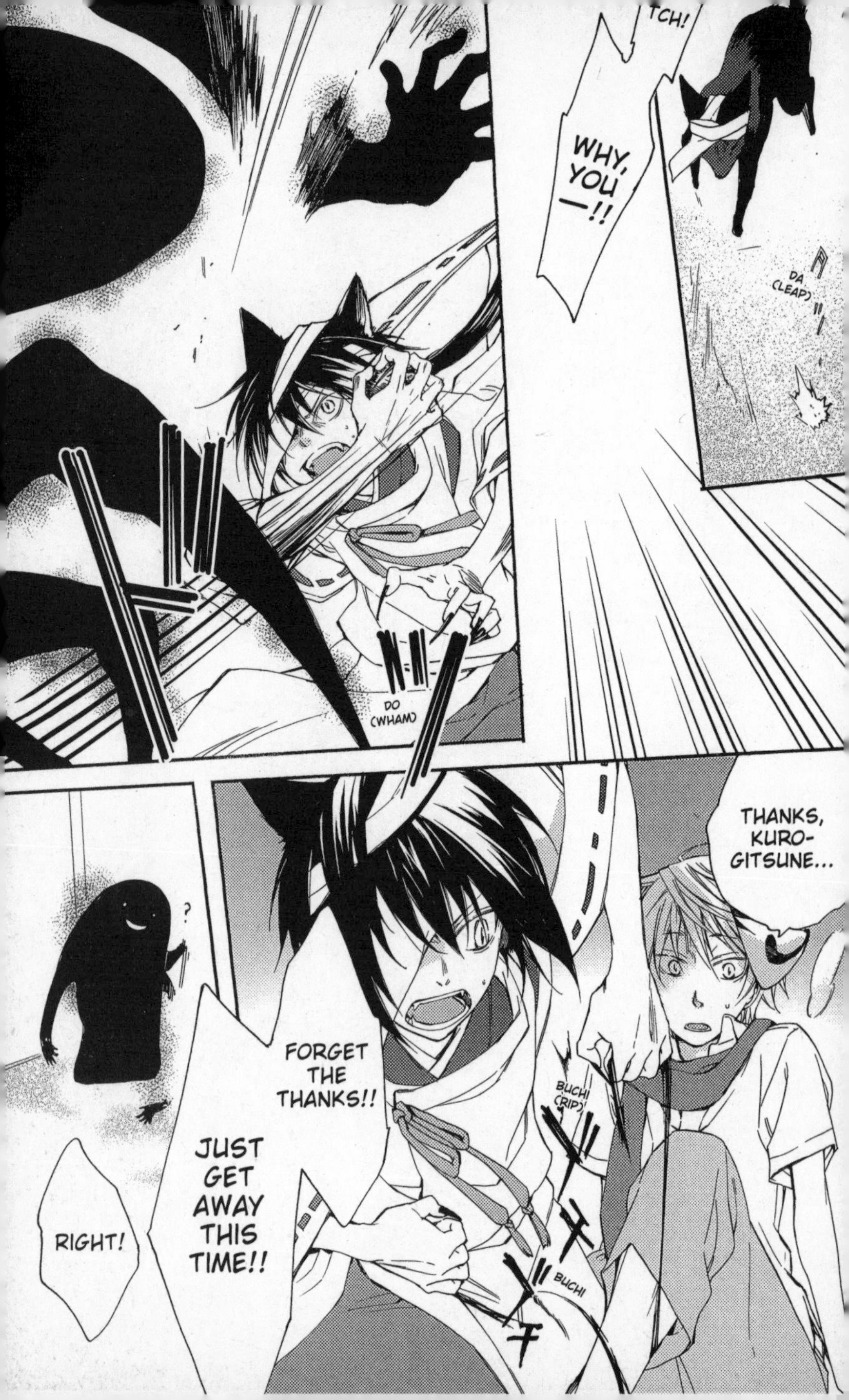
TCH!
DA (LEAP)
WHY, YOU—!!
DO (WHAM)
THANKS, KURO-GITSUNE...
BUCHI (RIP)
BUCHI
FORGET THE THANKS!!
JUST GET AWAY THIS TIME!!
?
RIGHT!

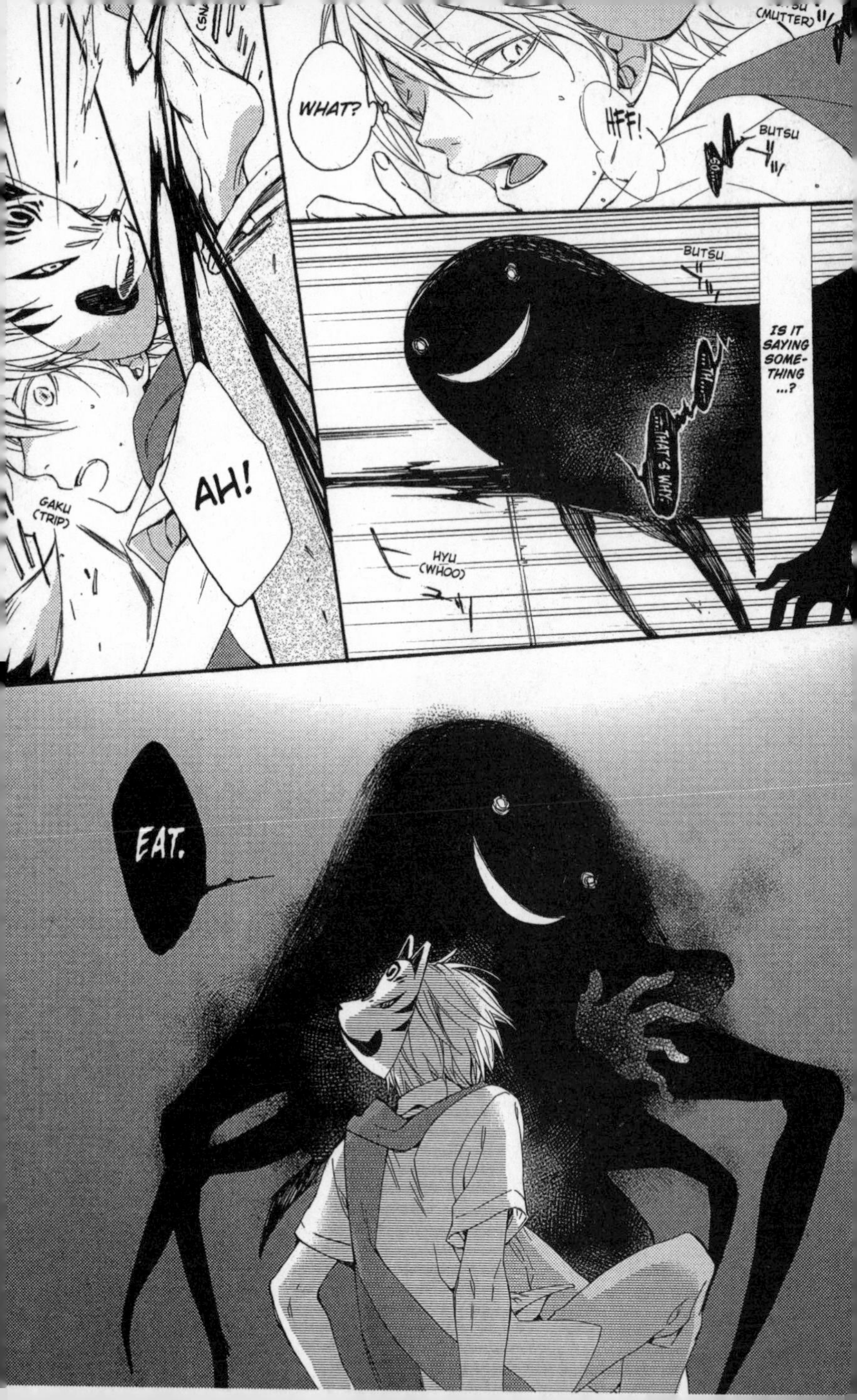
(MUTTER)
HFF!
WHAT?
BUTSU
SO...
BUTSU
IS IT SAYING SOMETHING ...?
...TH...
...THAT'S WHY.
HYU (WHOO)
AH!
GAKU (TRIP)
EAT.

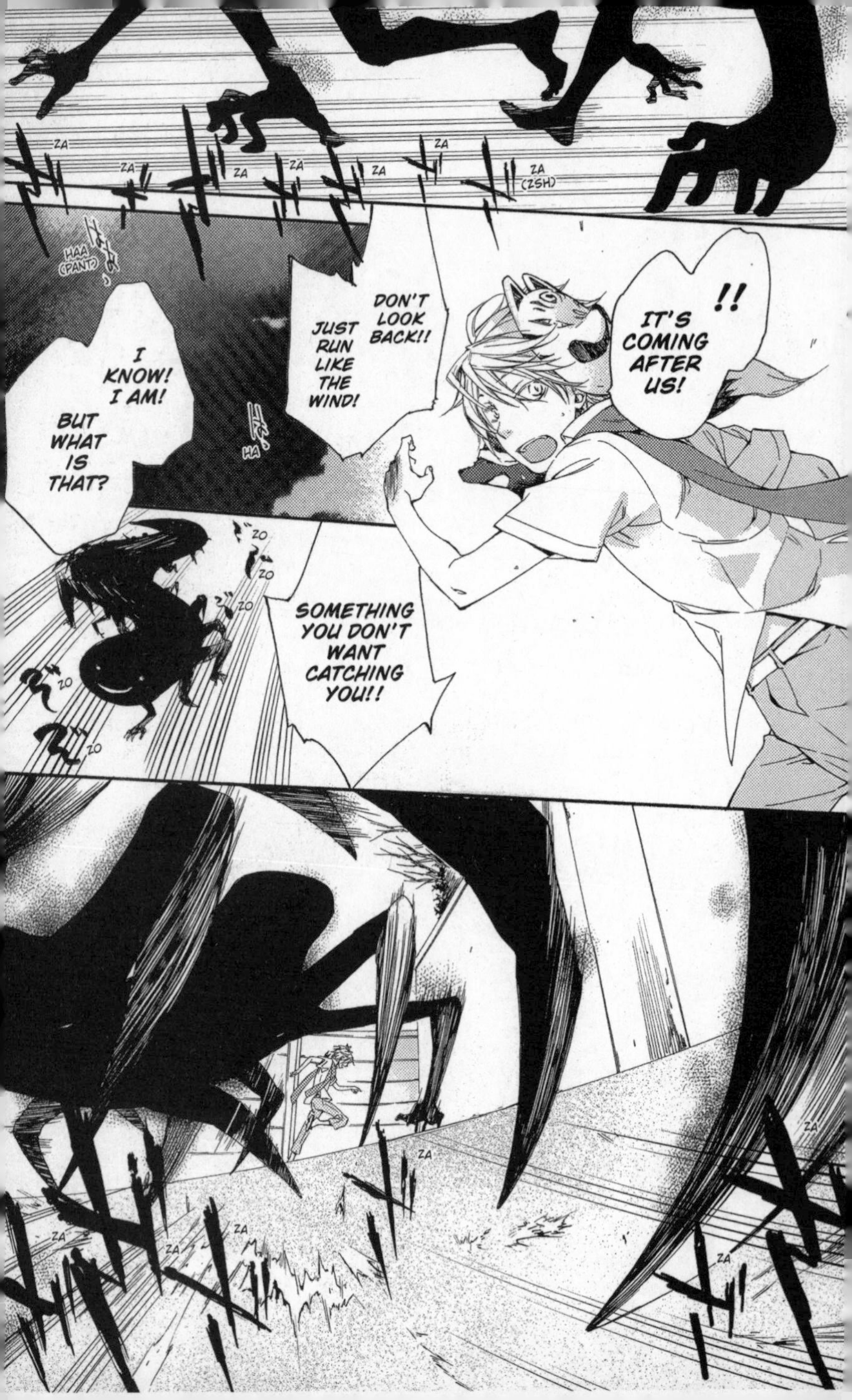
ZA (ZSH)
ZA
ZA
ZA
ZA
ZA
ZA
!!
IT'S COMING AFTER US!
DON'T LOOK BACK!!
JUST RUN LIKE THE WIND!
HAA (PANT)
I KNOW! I AM!
BUT WHAT IS THAT?
HA
SOMETHING YOU DON'T WANT CATCHING YOU!!
ZO
ZO
ZO
ZO
ZO
ZA
ZA
ZA
ZA
ZA
ZA

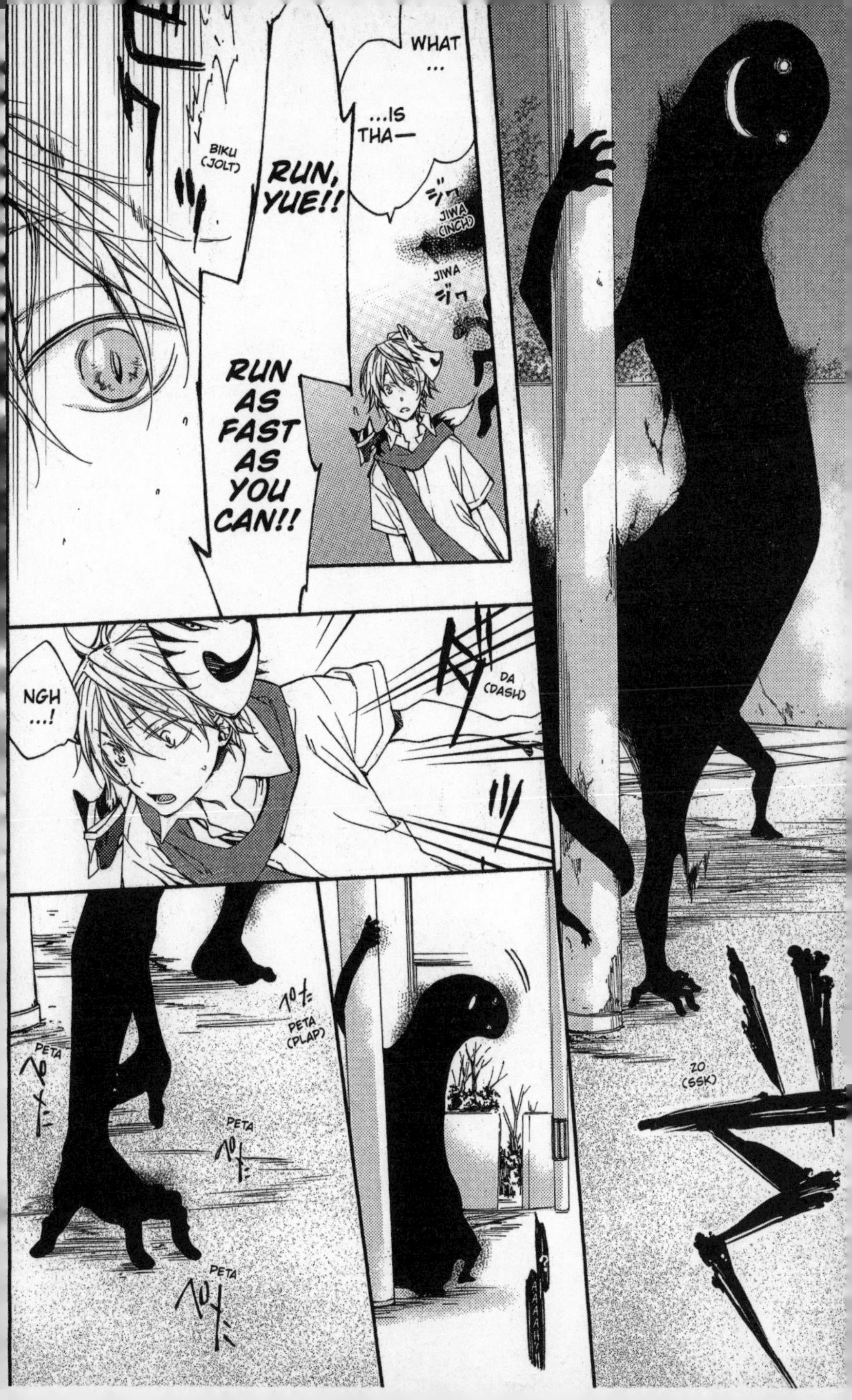
ZO
(SSK)
WHAT
...
...IS
THA—
JIWA
(INCH)
JIWA
RUN,
YUE!!
RUN
AS
FAST
AS
YOU
CAN!!
BIKU
(JOLT)
DA
(DASH)
NGH
...!
?
AAAAH!
PETA
(PLAP)
PETA
PETA
PETA

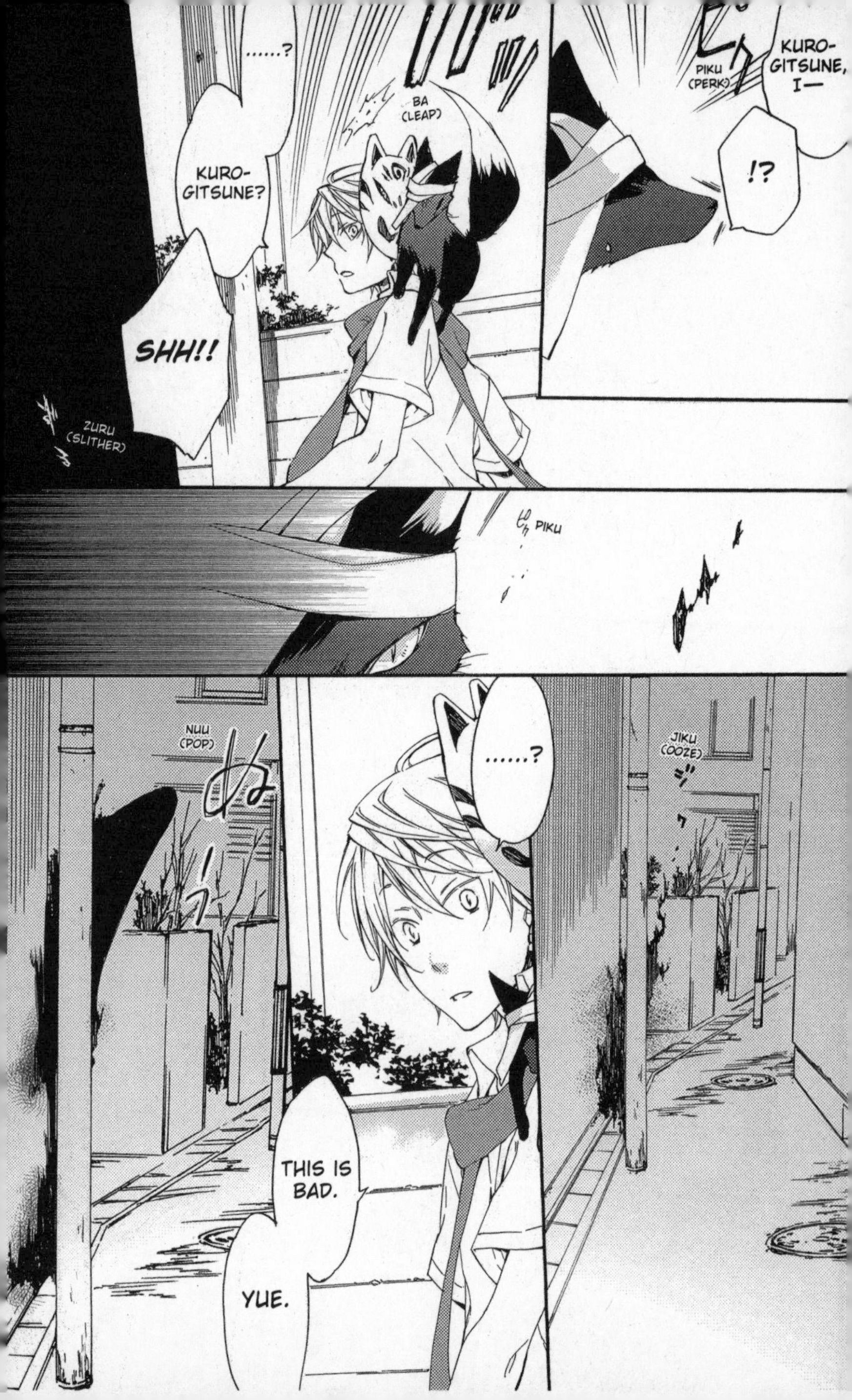
KURO-GITSUNE, I—
PIKU (PERK)
!?
......?
BA (LEAP)
KURO-GITSUNE?
SHH!!
ZURU (SLITHER)
PIKU
JIKU (OOZE)
......?
NUU (POP)
THIS IS BAD.
YUE.

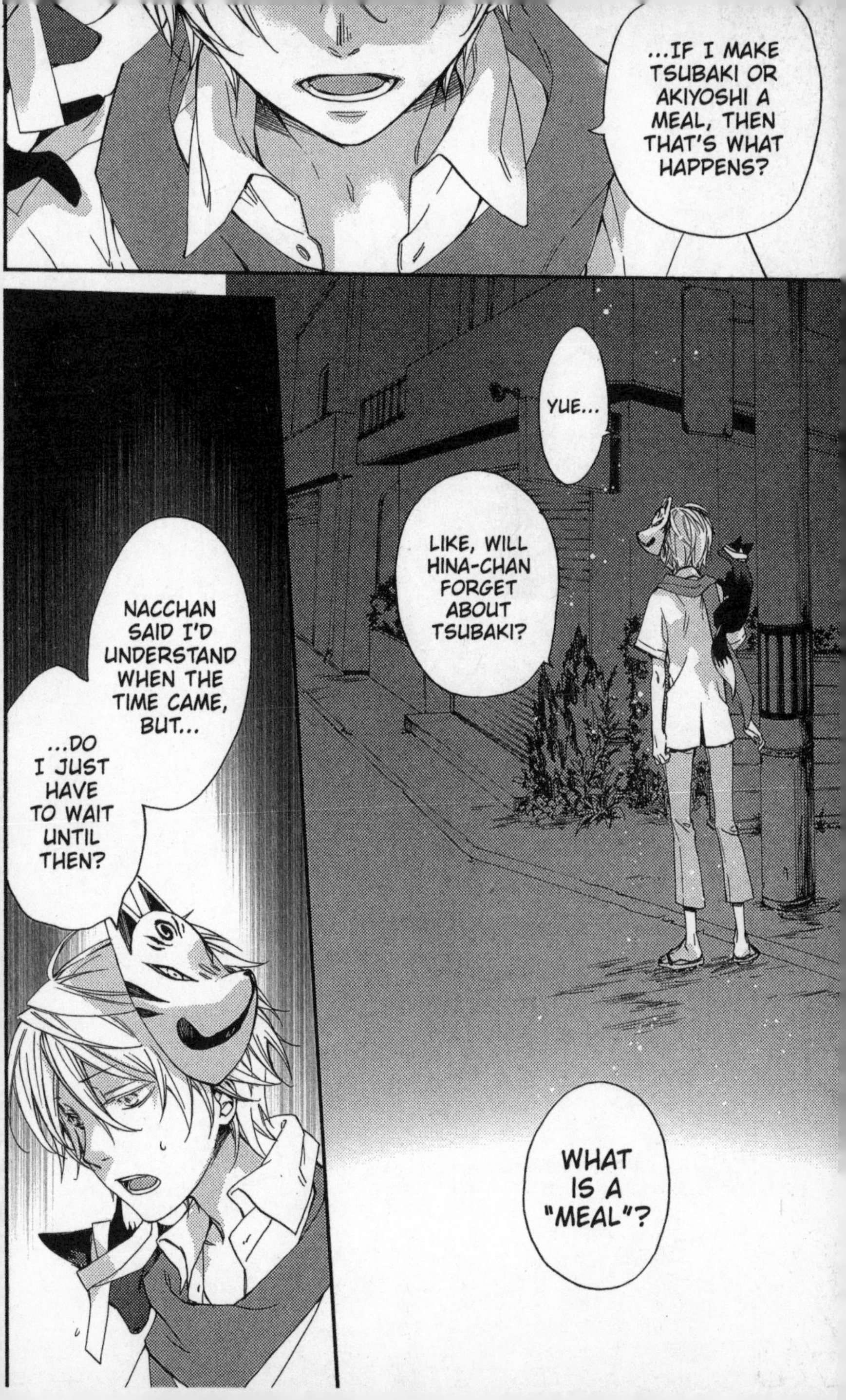
...IF I MAKE TSUBAKI OR AKIYOSHI A MEAL, THEN THAT'S WHAT HAPPENS?
YUE...
LIKE, WILL HINA-CHAN FORGET ABOUT TSUBAKI?
WHAT IS A "MEAL"?
NACCHAN SAID I'D UNDERSTAND WHEN THE TIME CAME, BUT...
...DO I JUST HAVE TO WAIT UNTIL THEN?

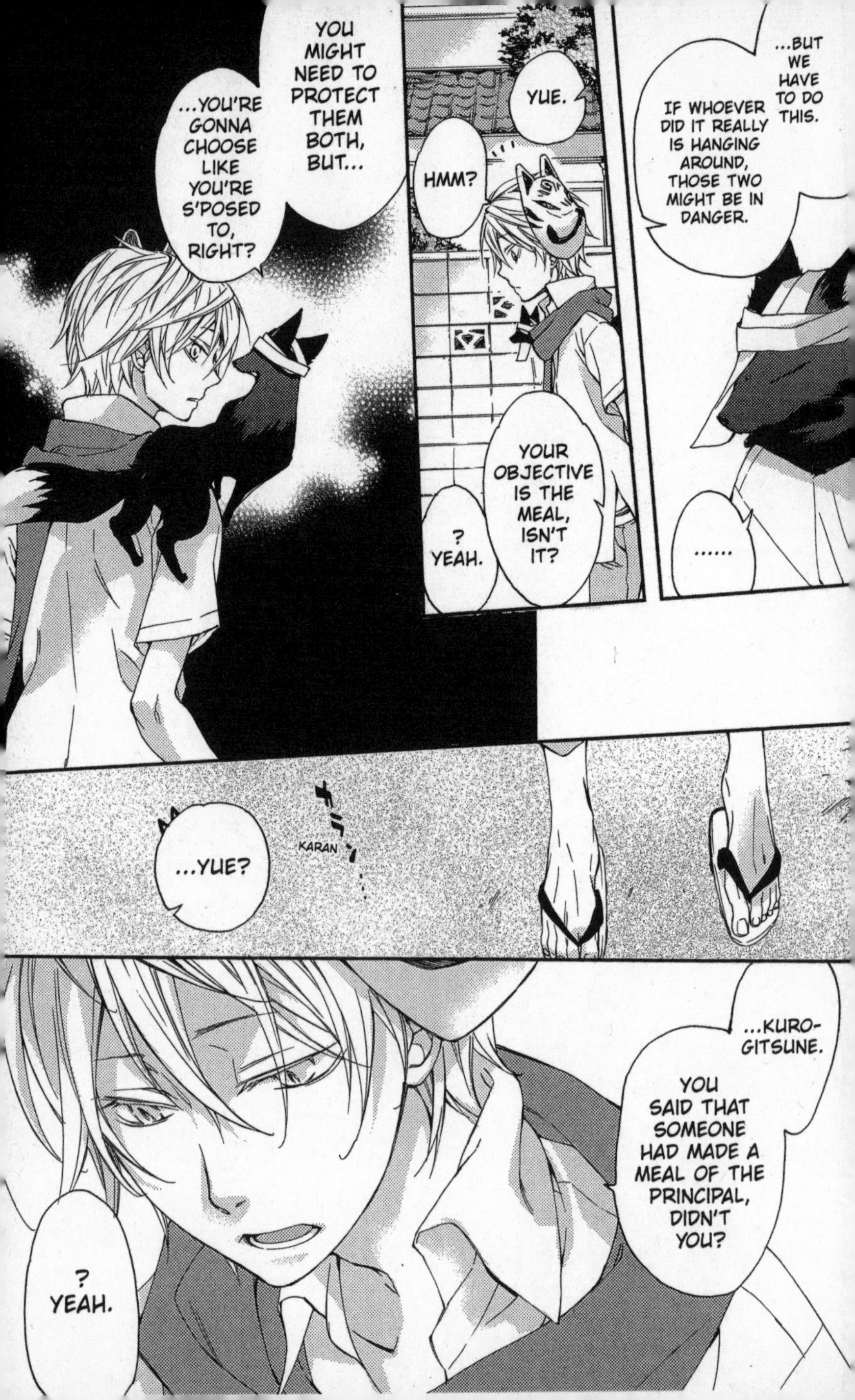
...BUT WE HAVE TO DO THIS.
IF WHOEVER DID IT REALLY IS HANGING AROUND, THOSE TWO MIGHT BE IN DANGER.
......
YUE.
HMM?
YOUR OBJECTIVE IS THE MEAL, ISN'T IT?
? YEAH.
YOU MIGHT NEED TO PROTECT THEM BOTH, BUT...
...YOU'RE GONNA CHOOSE LIKE YOU'RE S'POSED TO, RIGHT?
KARAN
...YUE?
...KURO-GITSUNE.
YOU SAID THAT SOMEONE HAD MADE A MEAL OF THE PRINCIPAL, DIDN'T YOU?
? YEAH.

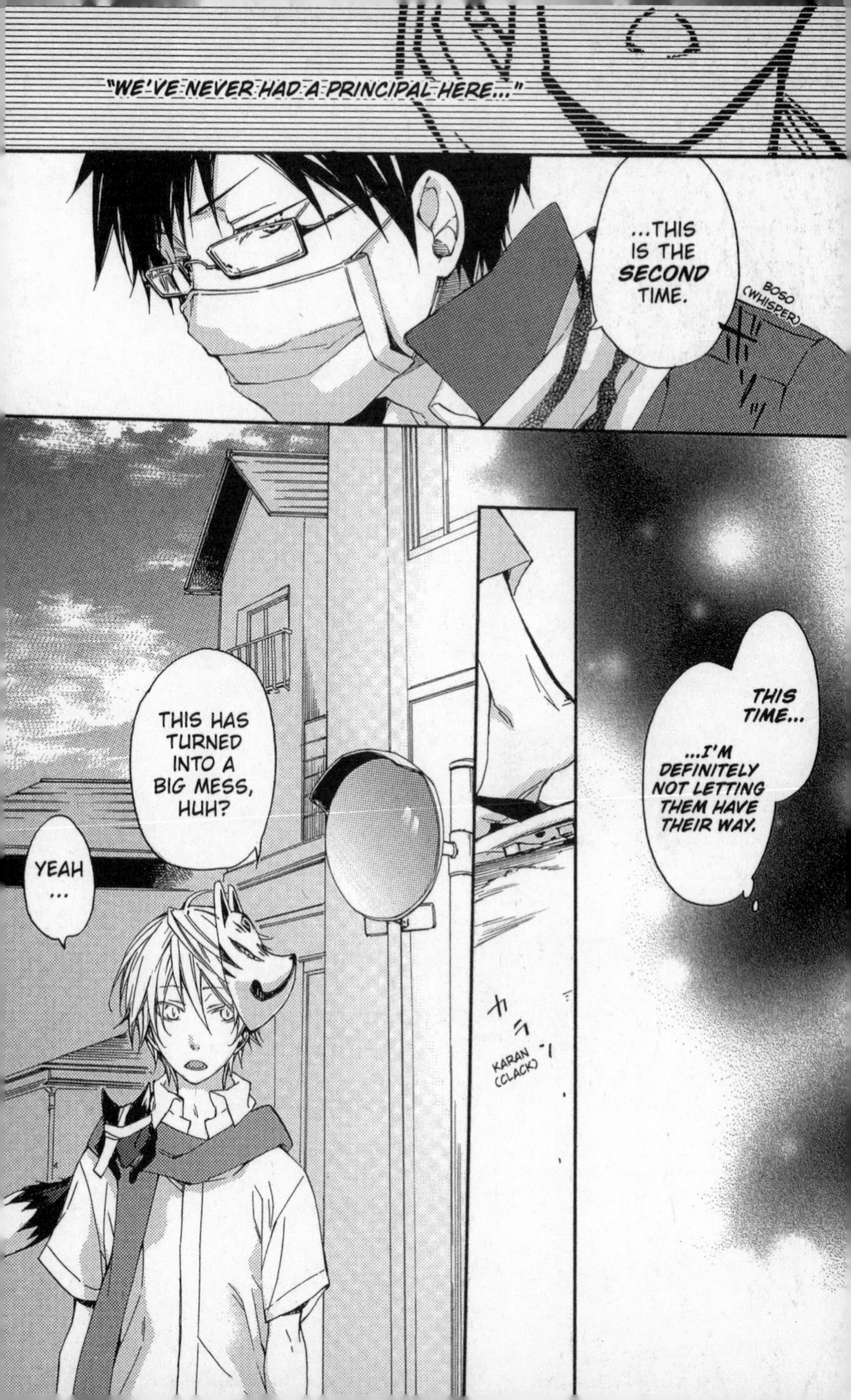
"WE'VE NEVER HAD A PRINCIPAL HERE..."
...THIS IS THE SECOND TIME.
BOSO (WHISPER)
THIS TIME...
...I'M DEFINITELY NOT LETTING THEM HAVE THEIR WAY.
KARAN (CLACK)
THIS HAS TURNED INTO A BIG MESS, HUH?
YEAH...

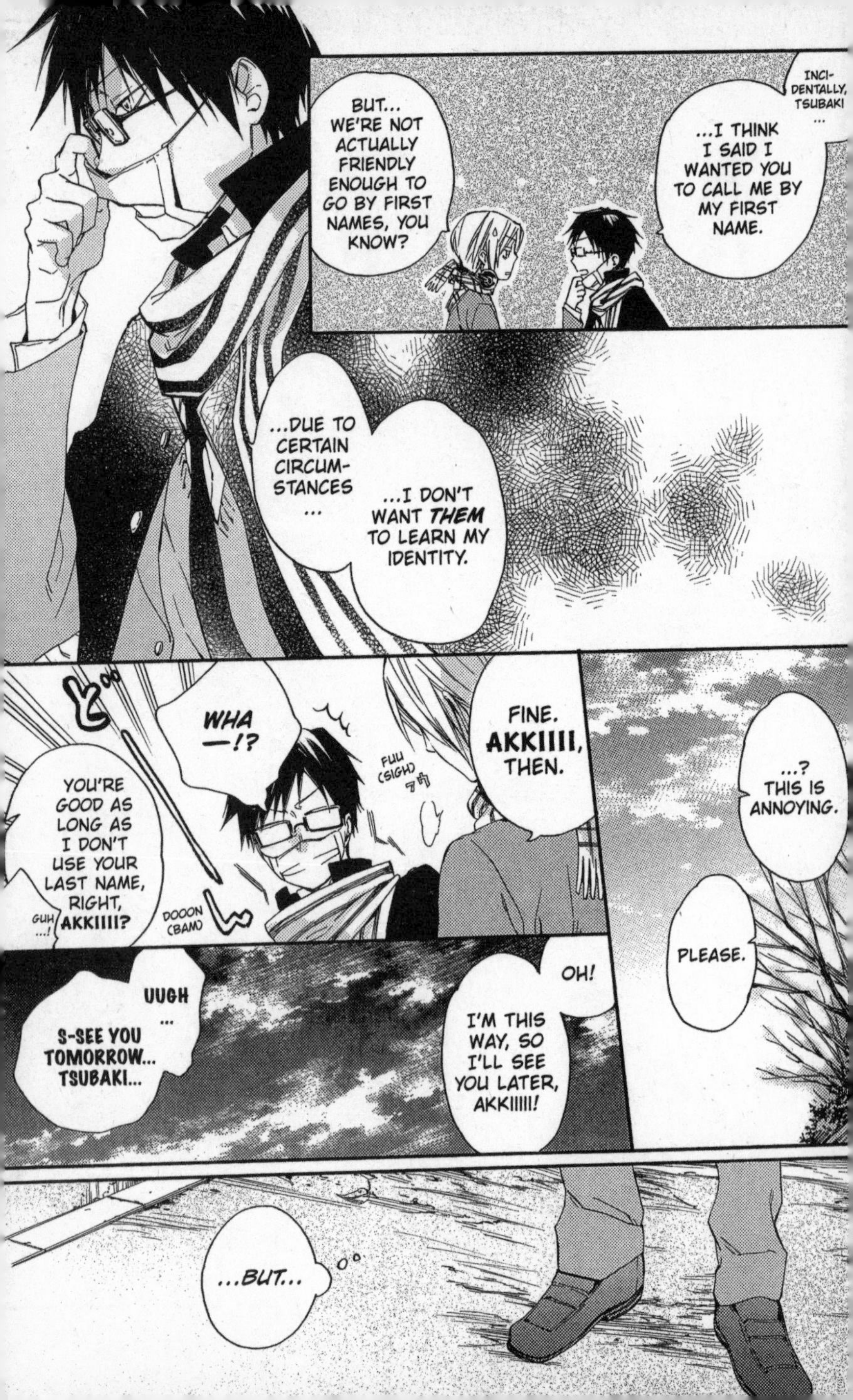
INCI-DENTALLY, TSUBAKI ...
...I THINK I SAID I WANTED YOU TO CALL ME BY MY FIRST NAME.
BUT... WE'RE NOT ACTUALLY FRIENDLY ENOUGH TO GO BY FIRST NAMES, YOU KNOW?
...DUE TO CERTAIN CIRCUM-STANCES ...
...I DON'T WANT *THEM* TO LEARN MY IDENTITY.
...? THIS IS ANNOYING.
PLEASE.
FINE. **AKKIIII**, THEN.
FUU (SIGH)
WHA —!?
YOU'RE GOOD AS LONG AS I DON'T USE YOUR LAST NAME, RIGHT, **AKKIIII?**
GUH ...!
DOOON (BAM)
OH!
I'M THIS WAY, SO I'LL SEE YOU LATER, AKKIIII!
UUGH ...
S-SEE YOU TOMORROW... TSUBAKI...
...BUT...

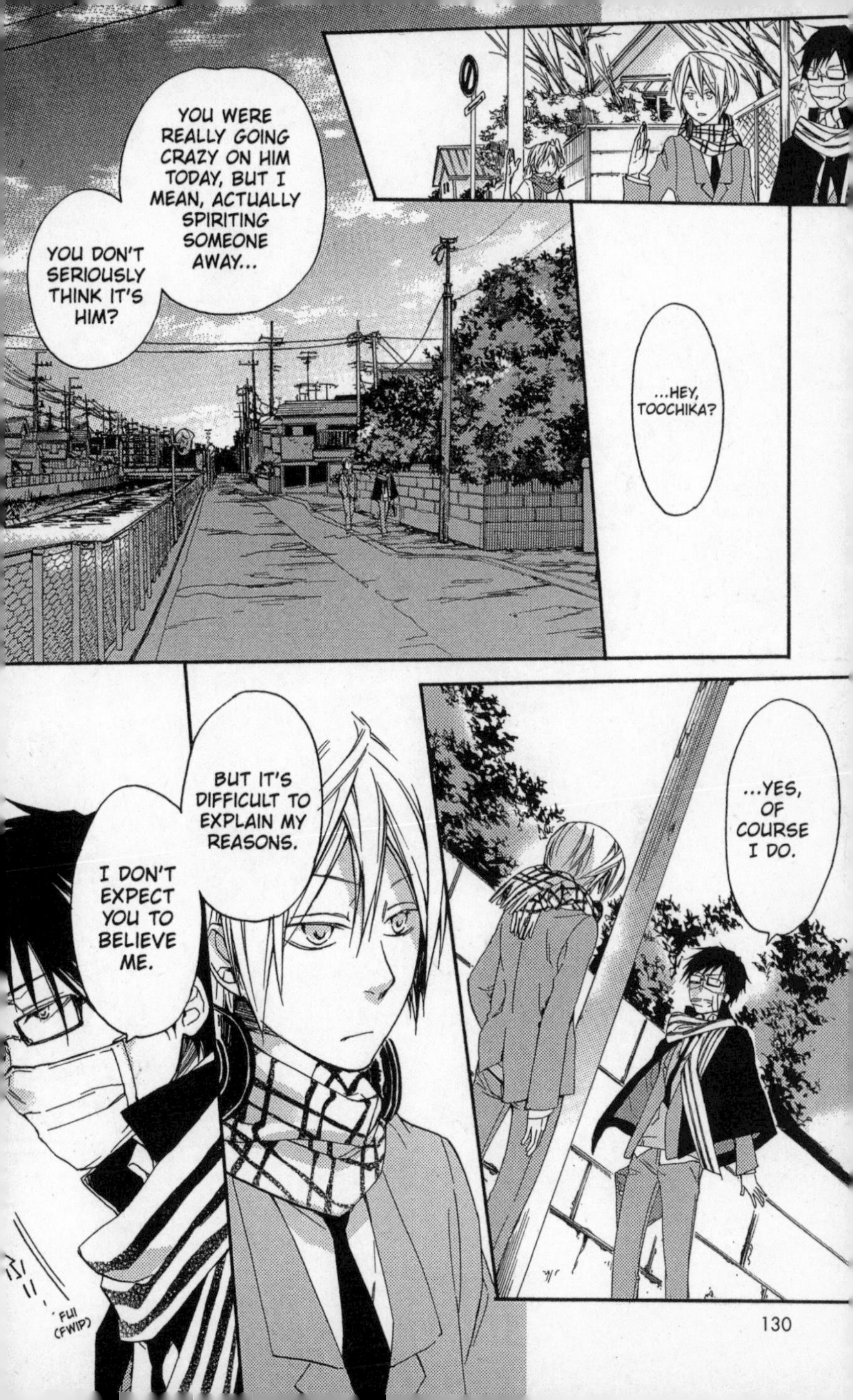
...HEY, TOOCHIKA?
YOU WERE REALLY GOING CRAZY ON HIM TODAY, BUT I MEAN, ACTUALLY SPIRITING SOMEONE AWAY...
YOU DON'T SERIOUSLY THINK IT'S HIM?
...YES, OF COURSE I DO.
BUT IT'S DIFFICULT TO EXPLAIN MY REASONS.
I DON'T EXPECT YOU TO BELIEVE ME.
FUI (FWIP)

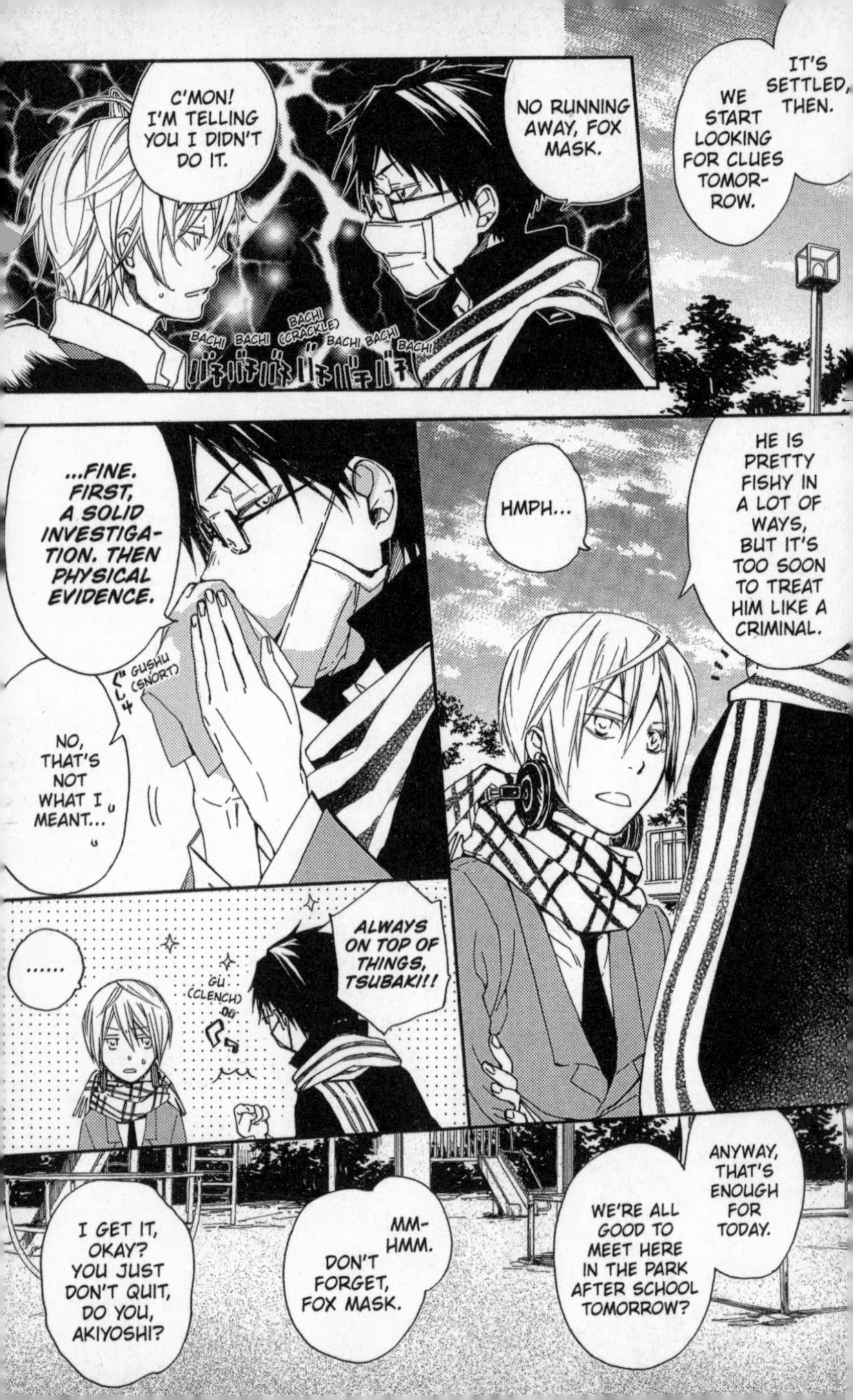
IT'S SETTLED, THEN.
WE START LOOKING FOR CLUES TOMORROW.
NO RUNNING AWAY, FOX MASK.
C'MON! I'M TELLING YOU I DIDN'T DO IT.
BACHI BACHI BACHI (CRACKLE) BACHI BACHI BACHI
HE IS PRETTY FISHY IN A LOT OF WAYS, BUT IT'S TOO SOON TO TREAT HIM LIKE A CRIMINAL.
HMPH...
...FINE. FIRST, A SOLID INVESTIGATION. THEN PHYSICAL EVIDENCE.
GUSHU (SNORT)
NO, THAT'S NOT WHAT I MEANT...
ALWAYS ON TOP OF THINGS, TSUBAKI!!
GU (CLENCH)
......
ANYWAY, THAT'S ENOUGH FOR TODAY.
WE'RE ALL GOOD TO MEET HERE IN THE PARK AFTER SCHOOL TOMORROW?
MM-HMM.
DON'T FORGET, FOX MASK.
I GET IT, OKAY? YOU JUST DON'T QUIT, DO YOU, AKIYOSHI?

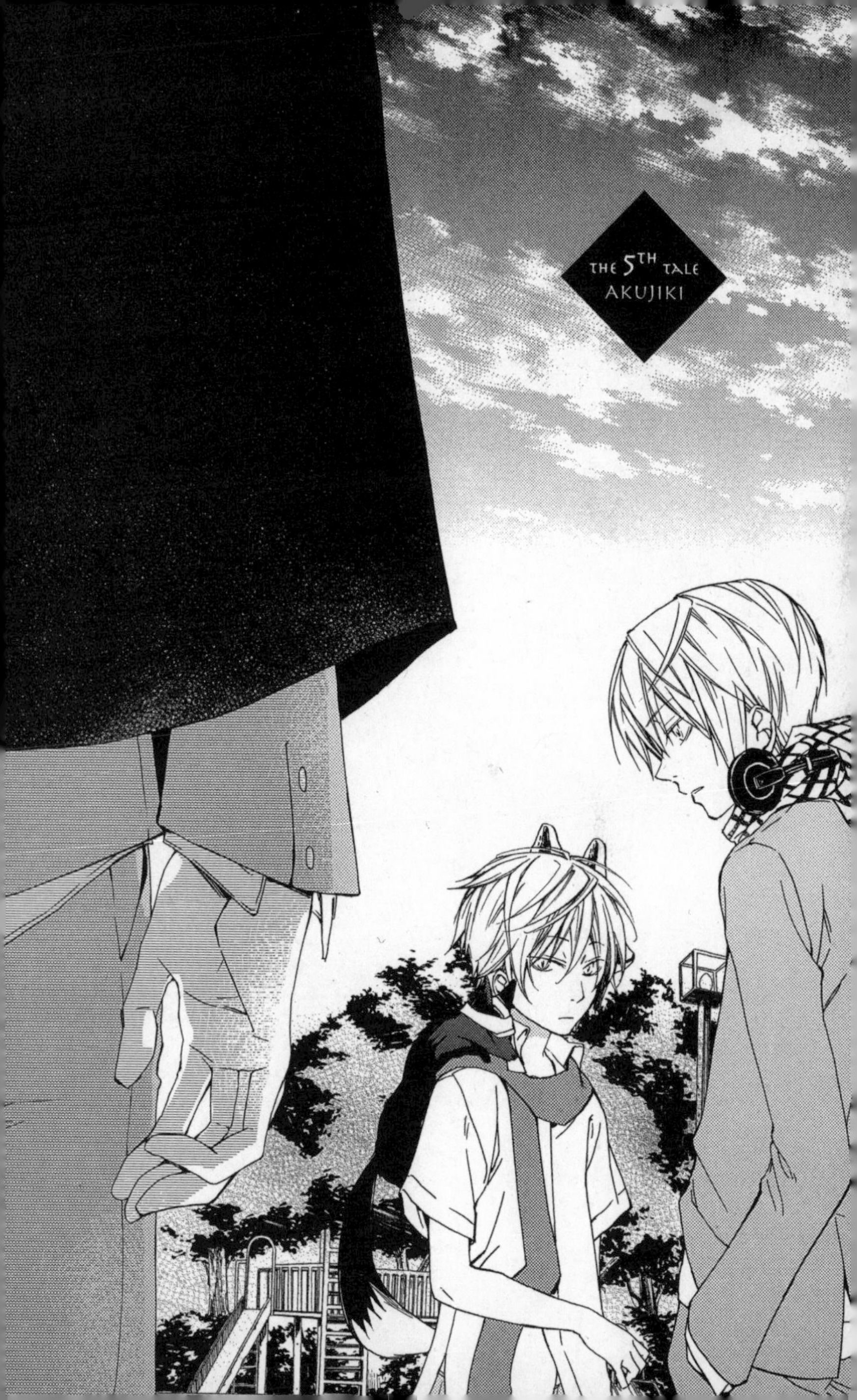
THE 5TH TALE
AKUJIKI

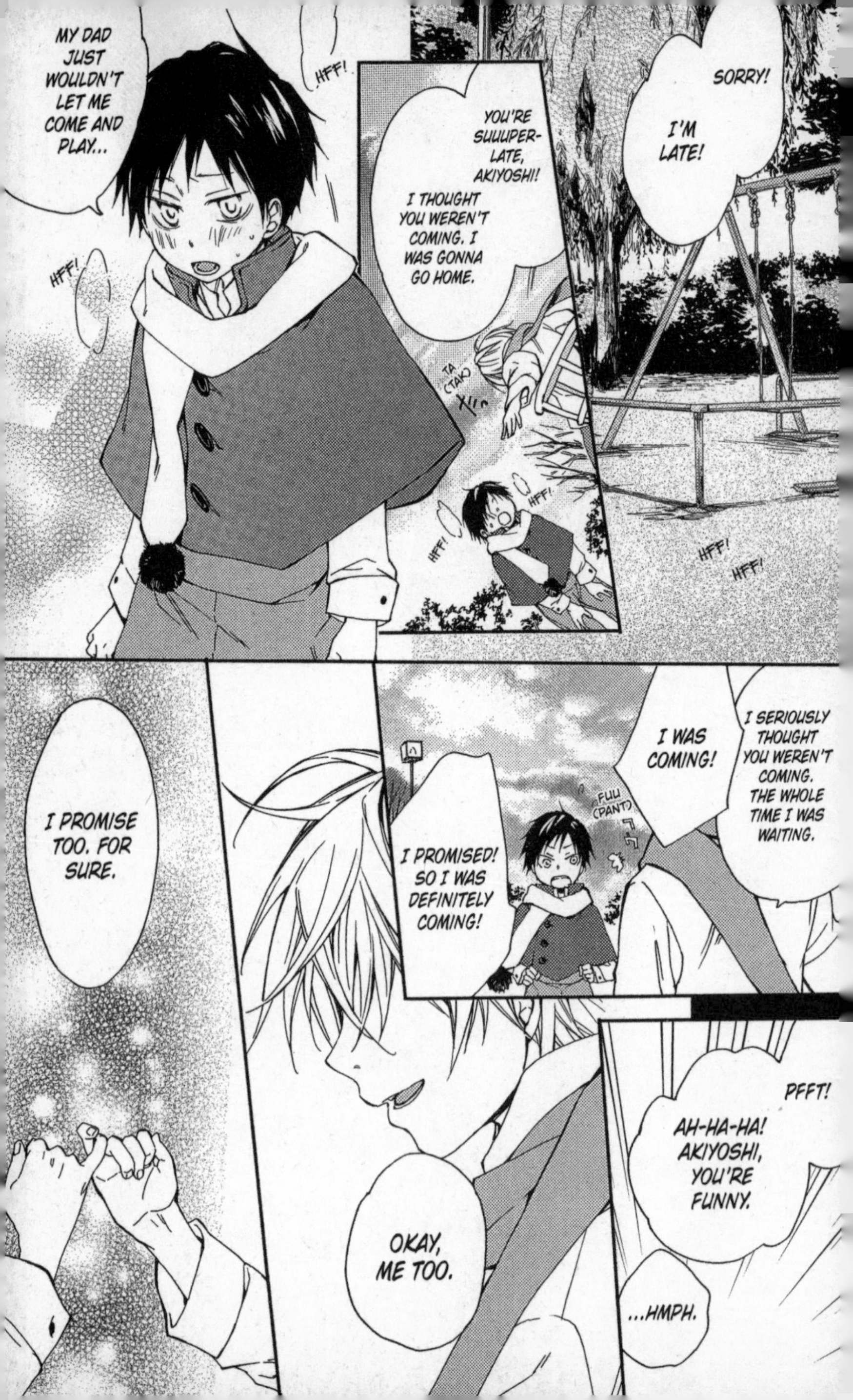
SORRY!
I'M LATE!
HFF!
HFF!
YOU'RE SUUUPER-LATE, AKIYOSHI!
I THOUGHT YOU WEREN'T COMING. I WAS GONNA GO HOME.
TA (TAK)
HFF!
HFF!
HFF!
MY DAD JUST WOULDN'T LET ME COME AND PLAY...
HFF!
I SERIOUSLY THOUGHT YOU WEREN'T COMING. THE WHOLE TIME I WAS WAITING.
I WAS COMING!
FUU (PANT)
I PROMISED! SO I WAS DEFINITELY COMING!
PFFT!
AH-HA-HA! AKIYOSHI, YOU'RE FUNNY.
...HMPH.
OKAY, ME TOO.
I PROMISE TOO. FOR SURE.

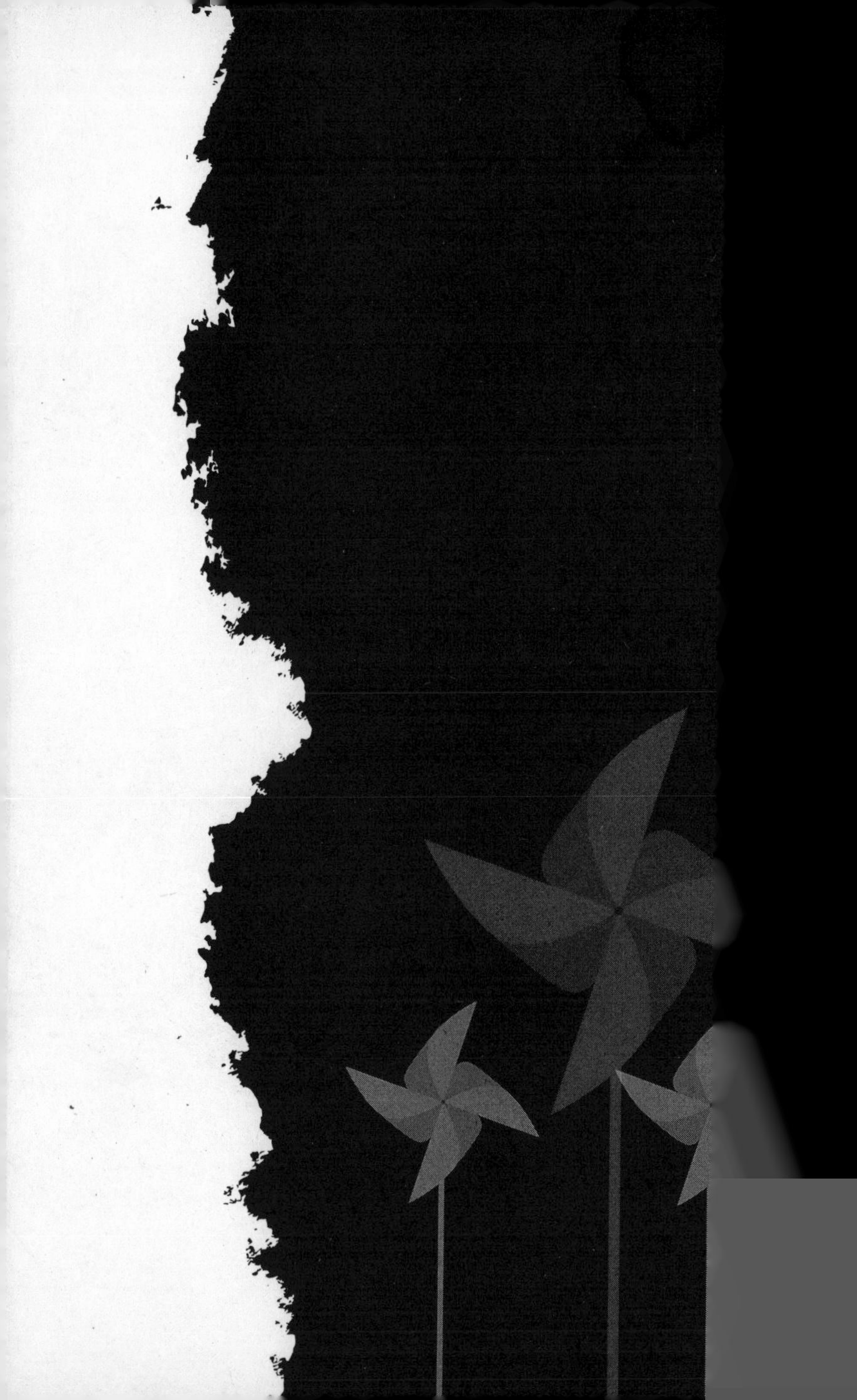

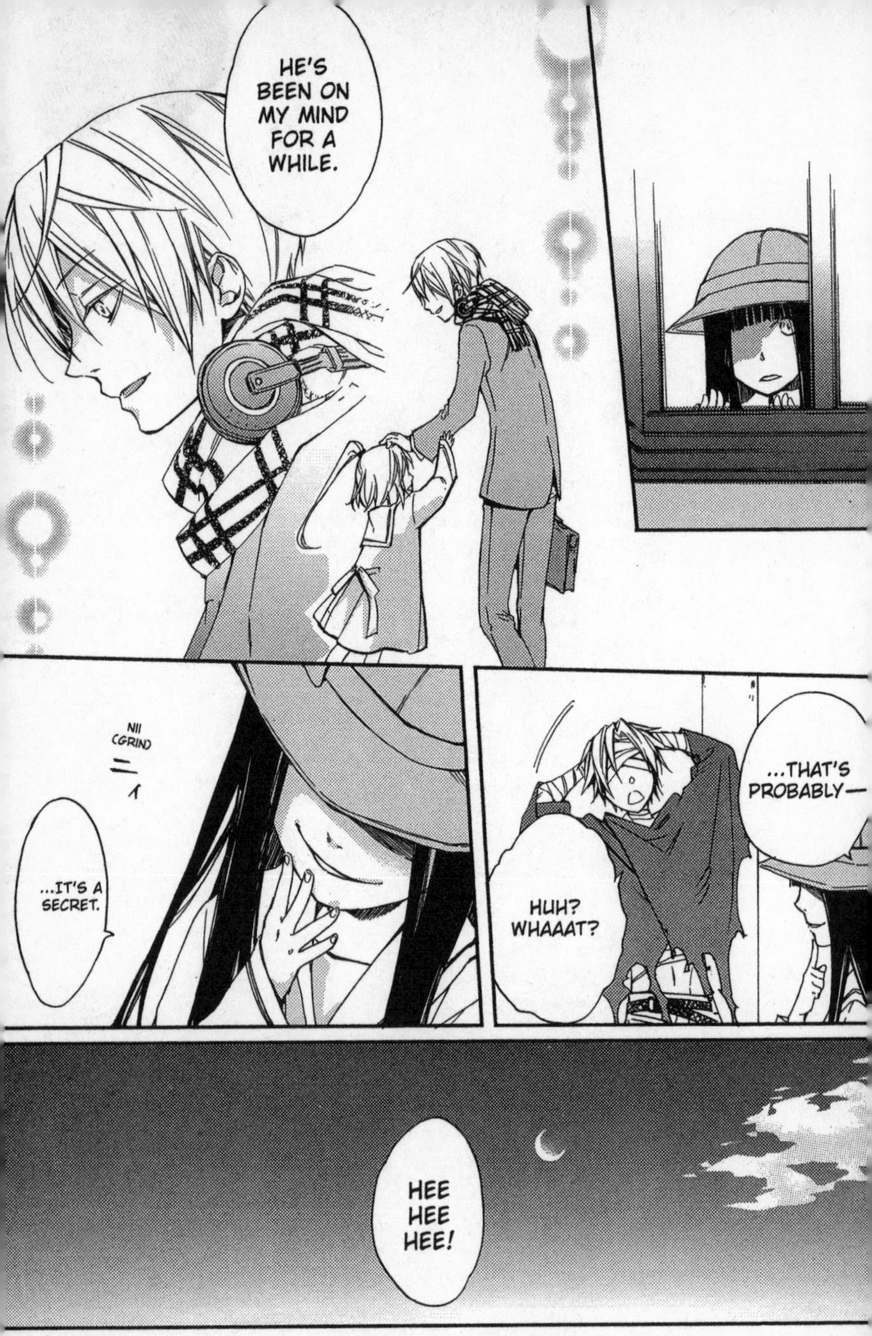
HE'S BEEN ON MY MIND FOR A WHILE.
...THAT'S PROBABLY—
HUH? WHAAAT?
NII (GRIND)
...IT'S A SECRET.
HEE HEE HEE!

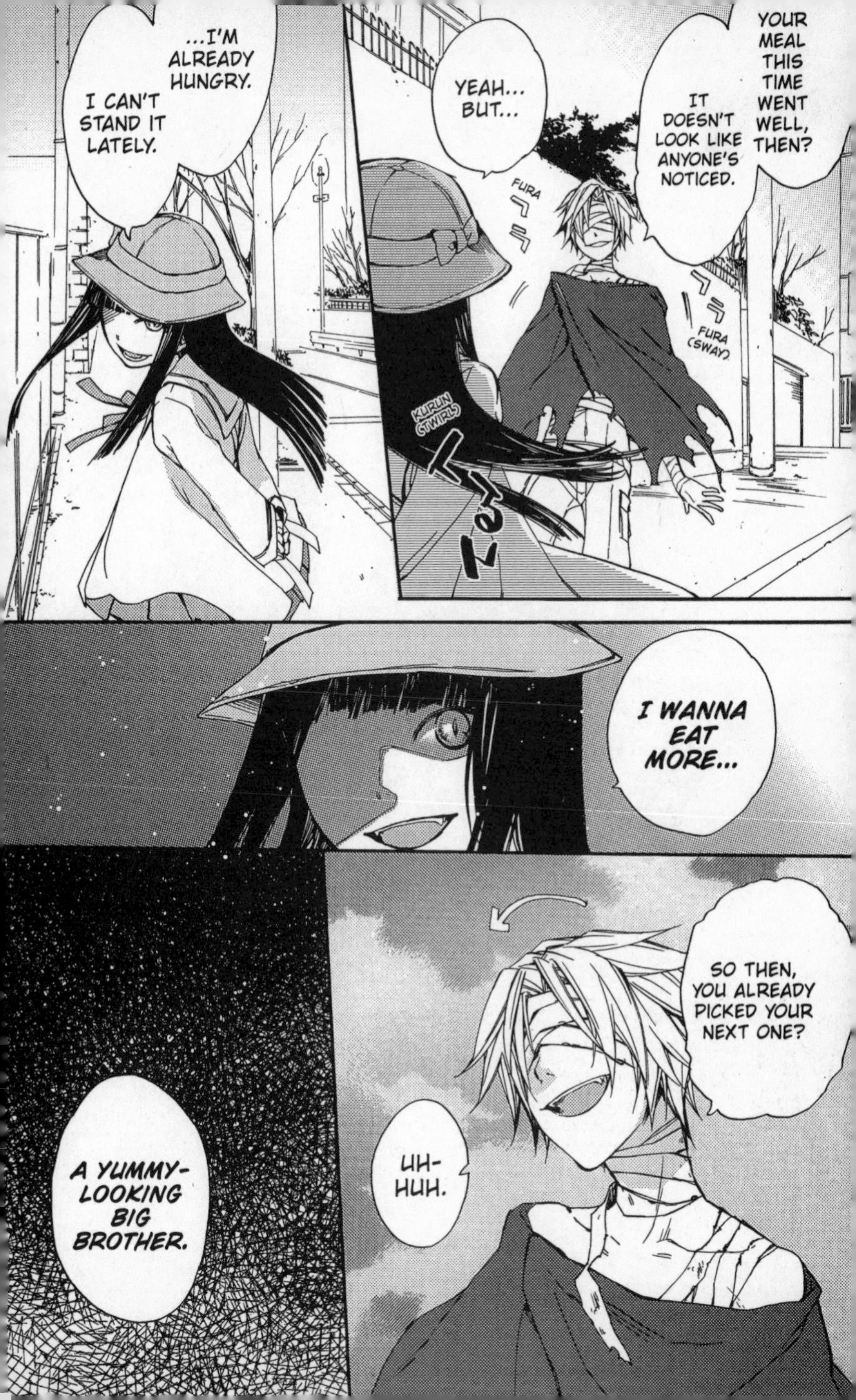
YOUR MEAL THIS TIME WENT WELL, THEN?
IT DOESN'T LOOK LIKE ANYONE'S NOTICED.
FURA
FURA (SWAY)
YEAH... BUT...
KURUN (TWIRL)
...I'M ALREADY HUNGRY.
I CAN'T STAND IT LATELY.
I WANNA EAT MORE...
SO THEN, YOU ALREADY PICKED YOUR NEXT ONE?
UH-HUH.
A YUMMY-LOOKING BIG BROTHER.

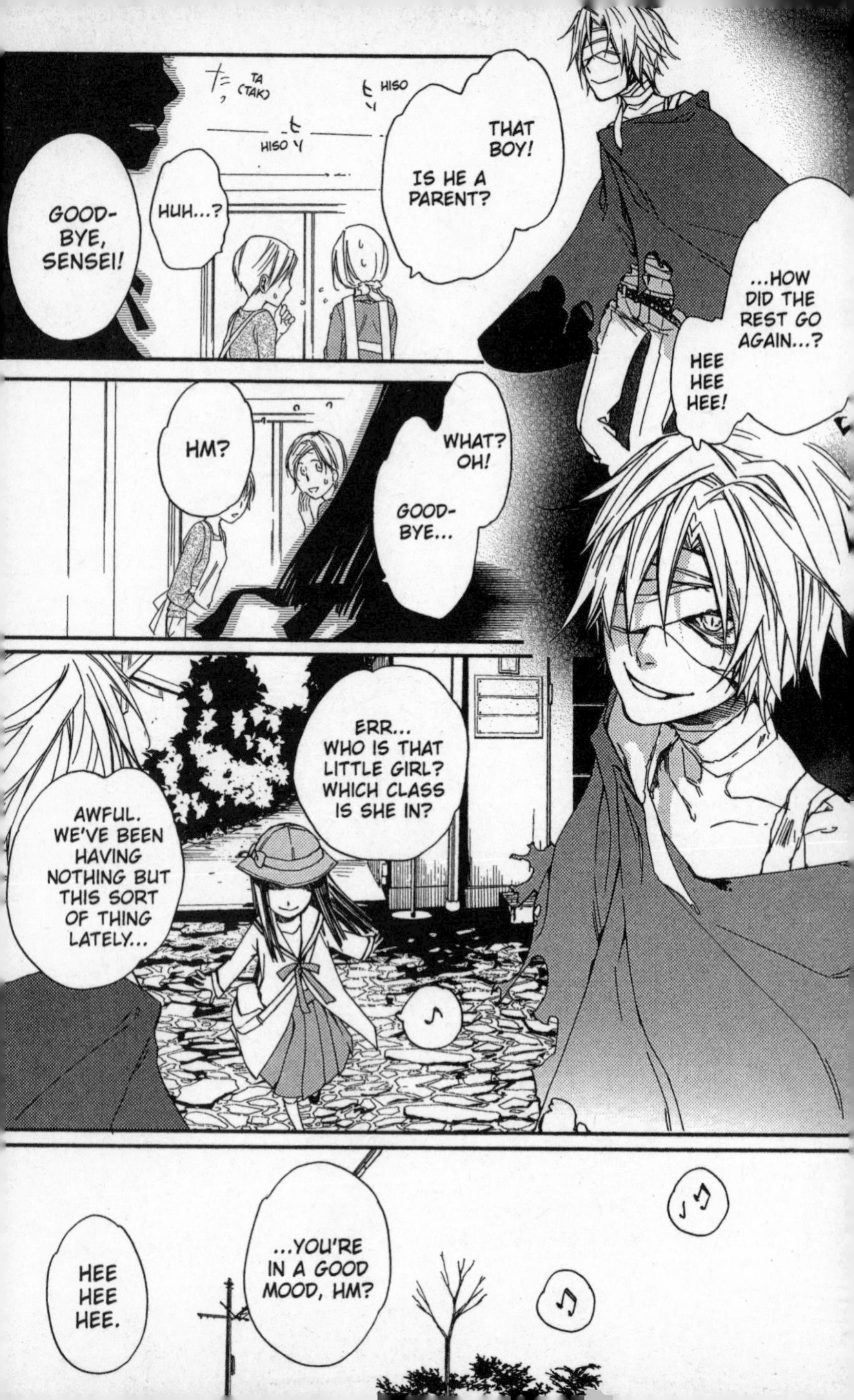
...HOW DID THE REST GO AGAIN...?
HEE HEE HEE!
THAT BOY! IS HE A PARENT?
HISO
HISO
TA (TAK)
HUH...?
GOOD-BYE, SENSEI!
WHAT? OH! GOOD-BYE...
HM?
ERR... WHO IS THAT LITTLE GIRL? WHICH CLASS IS SHE IN?
AWFUL. WE'VE BEEN HAVING NOTHING BUT THIS SORT OF THING LATELY...
...YOU'RE IN A GOOD MOOD, HM?
HEE HEE HEE.

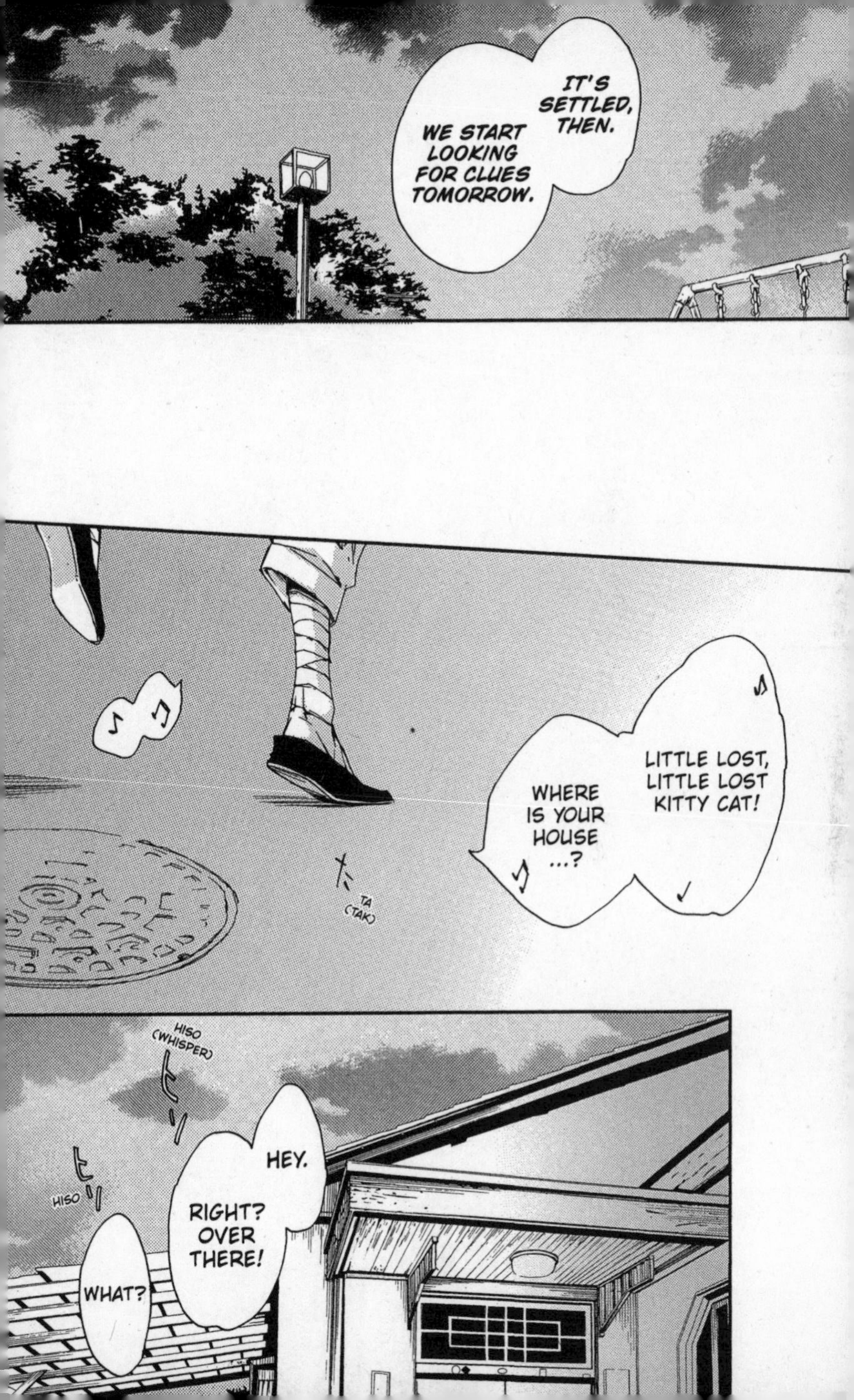
IT'S SETTLED, THEN.
WE START LOOKING FOR CLUES TOMORROW.
LITTLE LOST, LITTLE LOST KITTY CAT!
WHERE IS YOUR HOUSE ...?
TA (TAK)
HISO (WHISPER)
HEY.
RIGHT? OVER THERE!
HISO
WHAT?

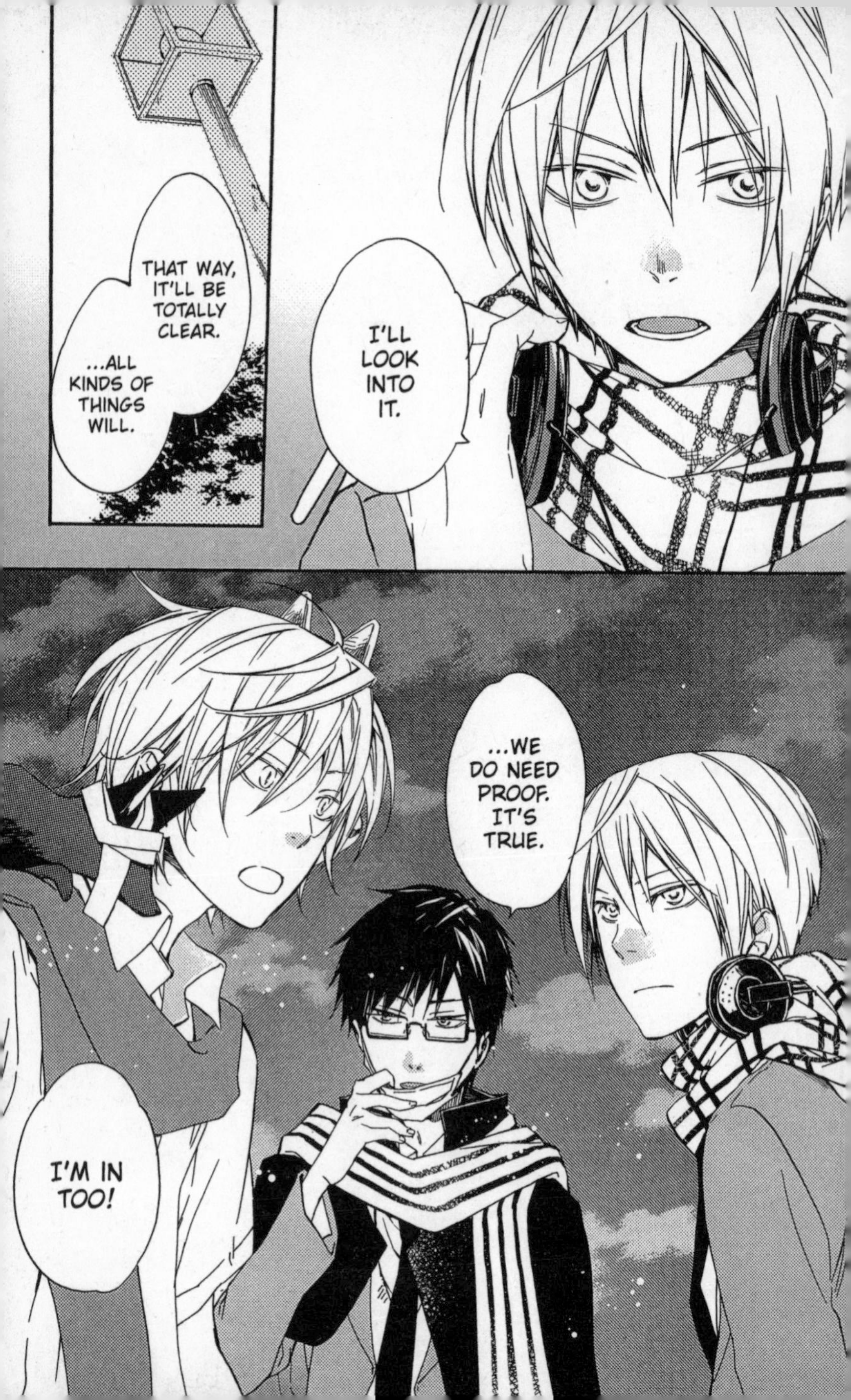
I'LL LOOK INTO IT.
THAT WAY, IT'LL BE TOTALLY CLEAR.
...ALL KINDS OF THINGS WILL.
...WE DO NEED PROOF. IT'S TRUE.
I'M IN TOO!

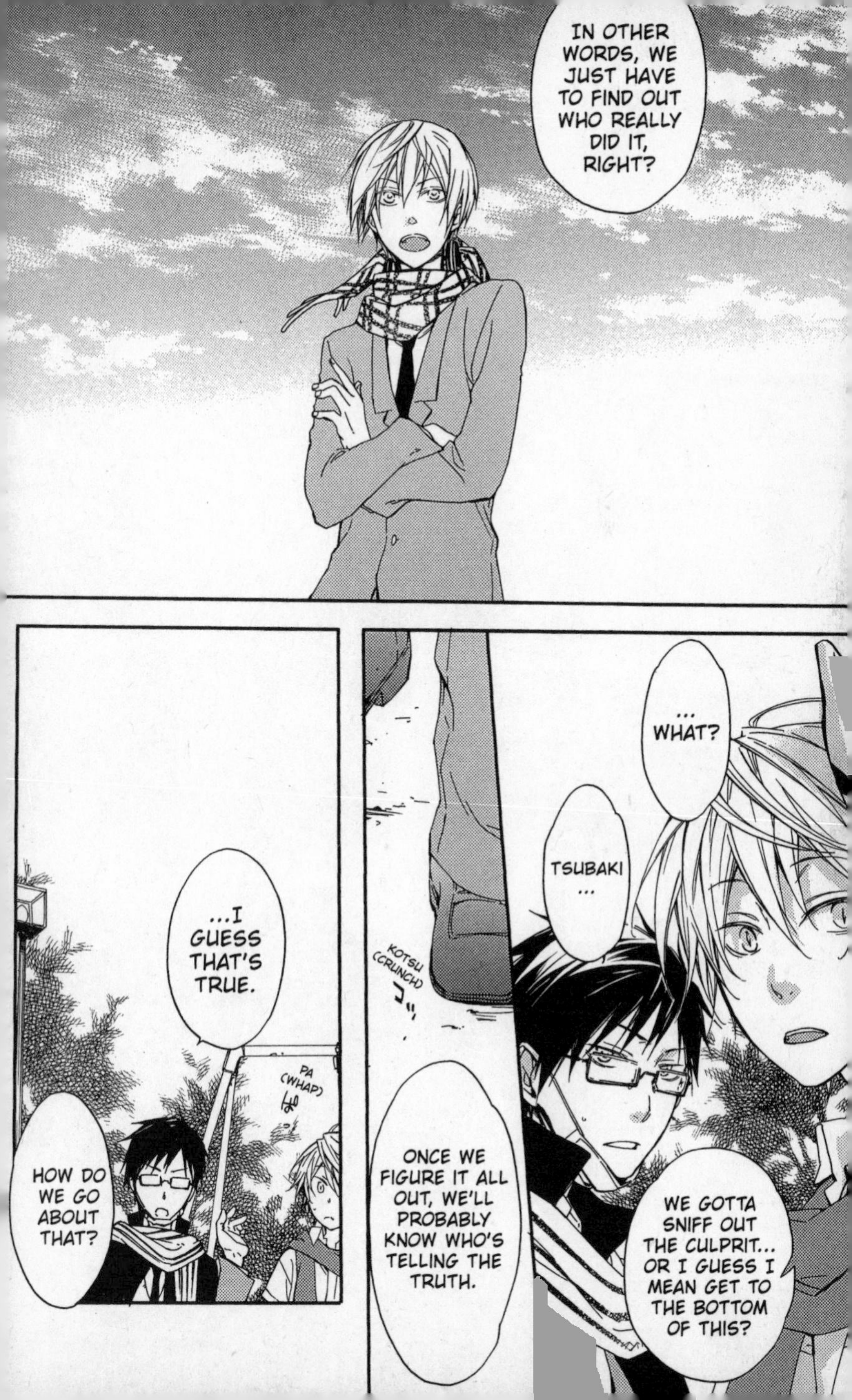
IN OTHER WORDS, WE JUST HAVE TO FIND OUT WHO REALLY DID IT, RIGHT?
...WHAT?
TSUBAKI...
WE GOTTA SNIFF OUT THE CULPRIT... OR I GUESS I MEAN GET TO THE BOTTOM OF THIS?
KOTSU (CRUNCH)
ONCE WE FIGURE IT ALL OUT, WE'LL PROBABLY KNOW WHO'S TELLING THE TRUTH.
...I GUESS THAT'S TRUE.
PA (WHAP)
HOW DO WE GO ABOUT THAT?

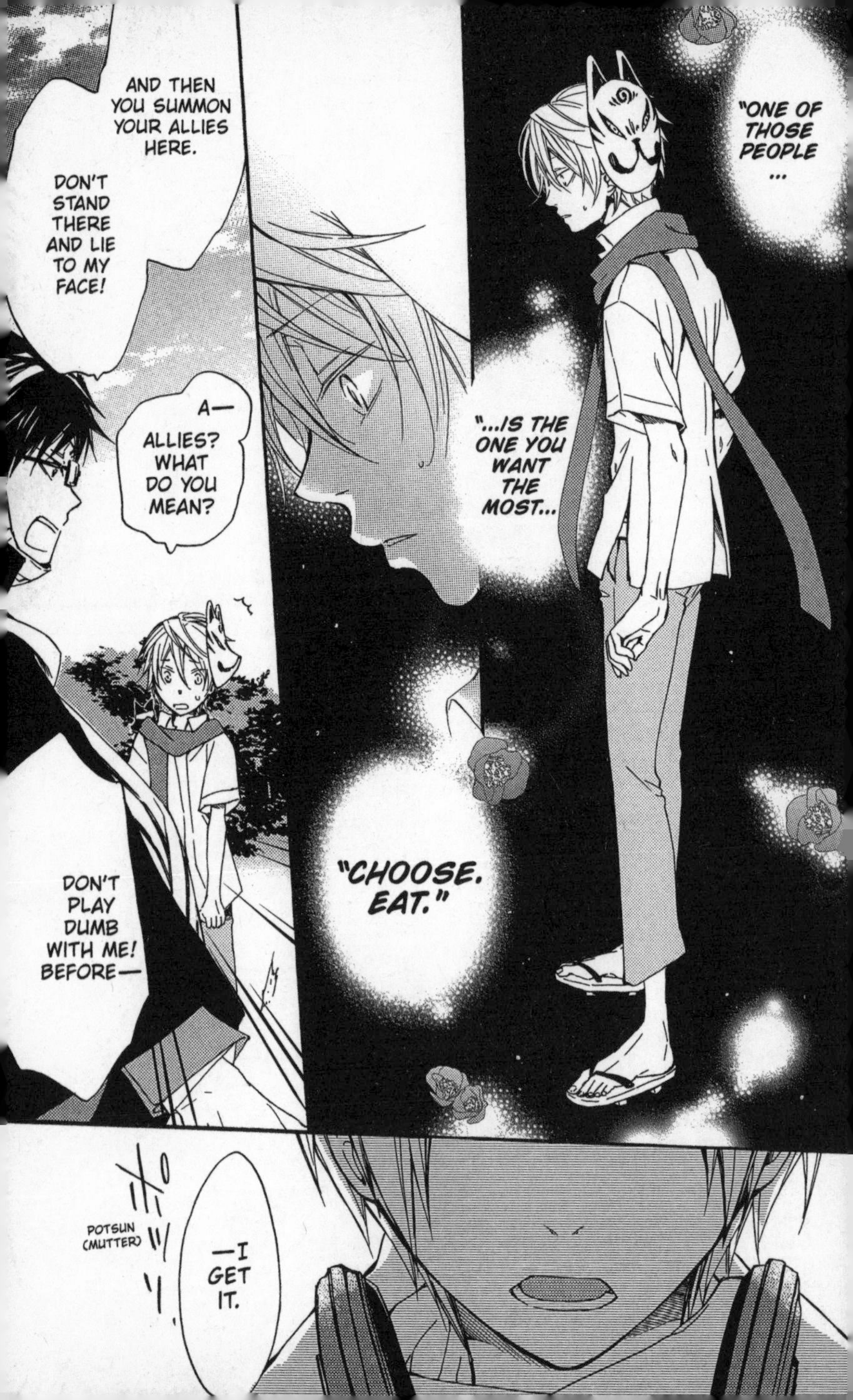

"ONE OF THOSE PEOPLE ...
"...IS THE ONE YOU WANT THE MOST...
"CHOOSE. EAT."
AND THEN YOU SUMMON YOUR ALLIES HERE.
DON'T STAND THERE AND LIE TO MY FACE!
A— ALLIES? WHAT DO YOU MEAN?
DON'T PLAY DUMB WITH ME! BEFORE—
—I GET IT.
POTSUN (MUTTER)

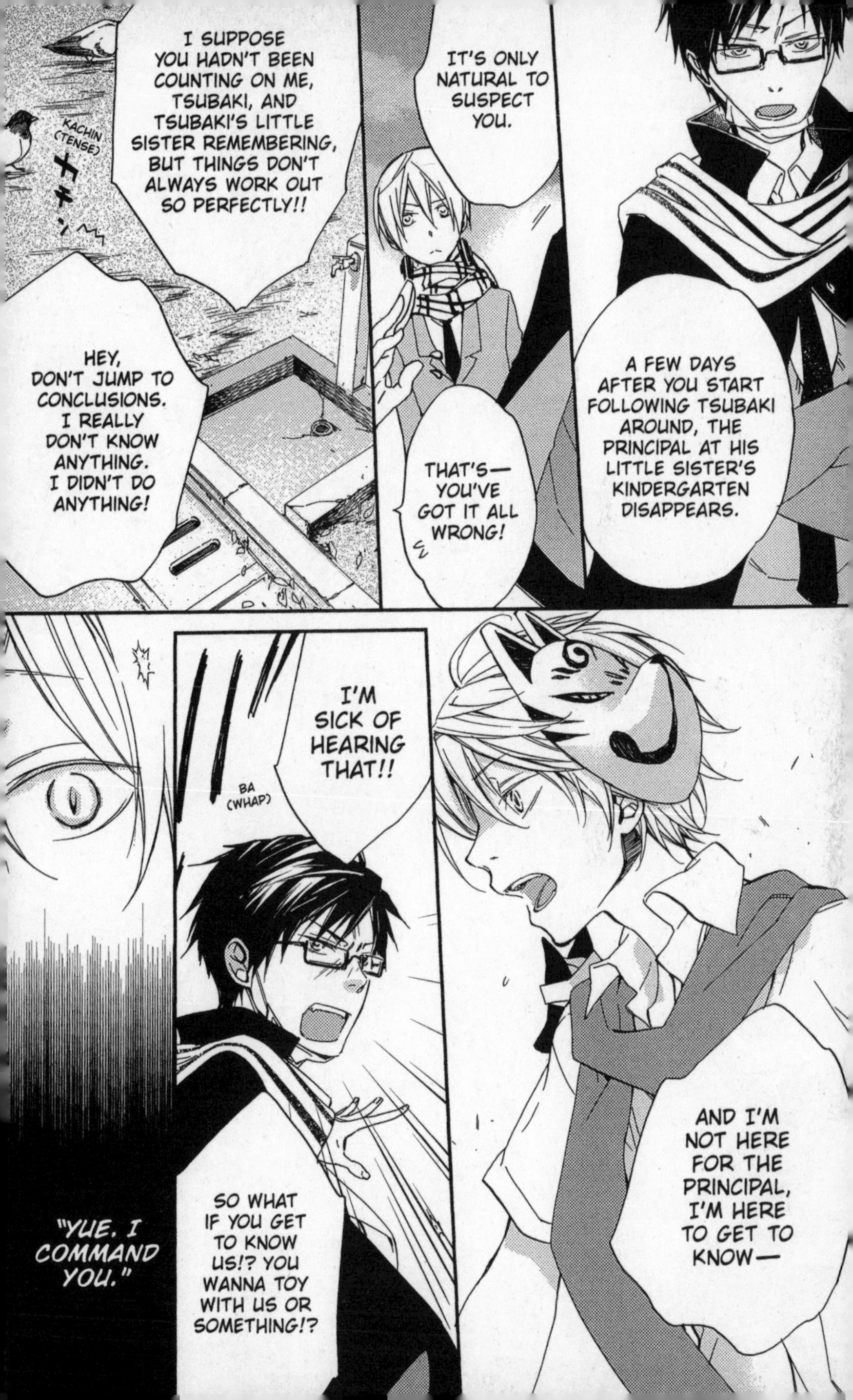
IT'S ONLY NATURAL TO SUSPECT YOU.
A FEW DAYS AFTER YOU START FOLLOWING TSUBAKI AROUND, THE PRINCIPAL AT HIS LITTLE SISTER'S KINDERGARTEN DISAPPEARS.
THAT'S— YOU'VE GOT IT ALL WRONG!
I SUPPOSE YOU HADN'T BEEN COUNTING ON ME, TSUBAKI, AND TSUBAKI'S LITTLE SISTER REMEMBERING, BUT THINGS DON'T ALWAYS WORK OUT SO PERFECTLY!!
KACHIN (TENSE)
HEY, DON'T JUMP TO CONCLUSIONS. I REALLY DON'T KNOW ANYTHING. I DIDN'T DO ANYTHING!
AND I'M NOT HERE FOR THE PRINCIPAL, I'M HERE TO GET TO KNOW—
I'M SICK OF HEARING THAT!!
BA (WHAP)
SO WHAT IF YOU GET TO KNOW US!? YOU WANNA TOY WITH US OR SOMETHING!?
"YUE. I COMMAND YOU."

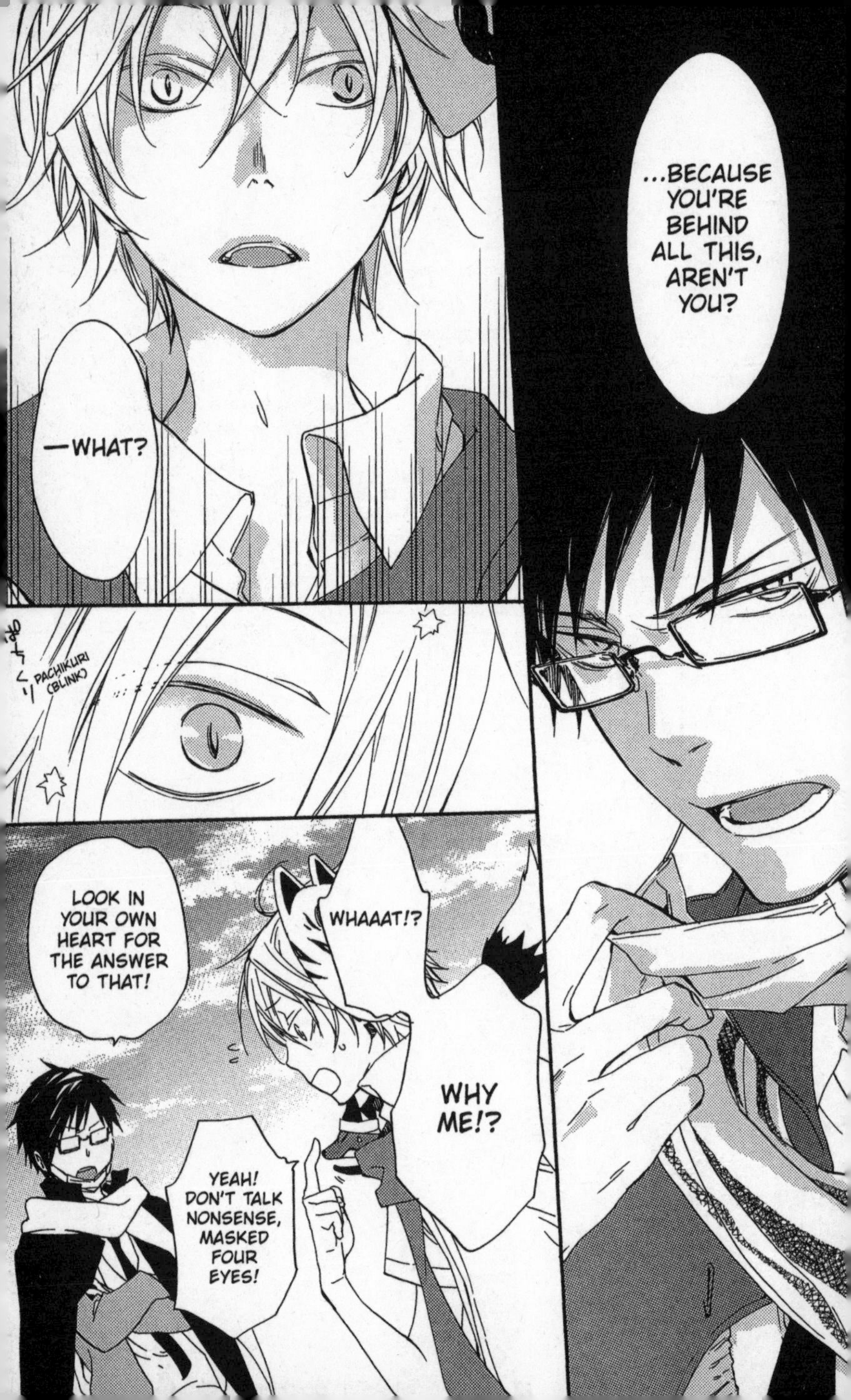
...BECAUSE YOU'RE BEHIND ALL THIS, AREN'T YOU?
—WHAT?
PACHIKURI (BLINK)
WHAAAT!?
WHY ME!?
LOOK IN YOUR OWN HEART FOR THE ANSWER TO THAT!
YEAH! DON'T TALK NONSENSE, MASKED FOUR EYES!

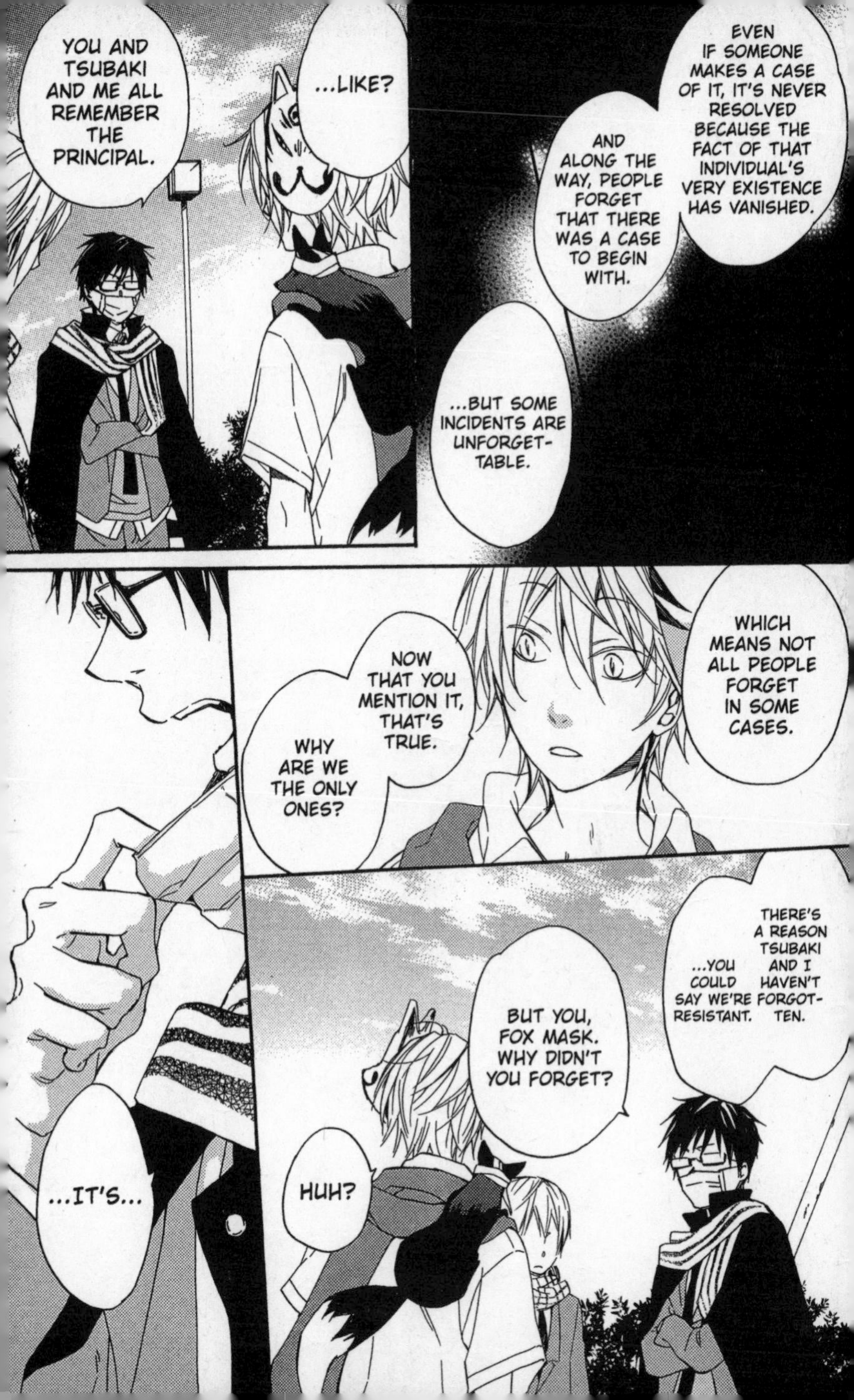
EVEN IF SOMEONE MAKES A CASE OF IT, IT'S NEVER RESOLVED BECAUSE THE FACT OF THAT INDIVIDUAL'S VERY EXISTENCE HAS VANISHED.
AND ALONG THE WAY, PEOPLE FORGET THAT THERE WAS A CASE TO BEGIN WITH.
...BUT SOME INCIDENTS ARE UNFORGET-TABLE.
...LIKE?
YOU AND TSUBAKI AND ME ALL REMEMBER THE PRINCIPAL.
WHICH MEANS NOT ALL PEOPLE FORGET IN SOME CASES.
NOW THAT YOU MENTION IT, THAT'S TRUE.
WHY ARE WE THE ONLY ONES?
THERE'S A REASON TSUBAKI AND I HAVEN'T FORGOT-TEN.
...YOU COULD SAY WE'RE RESISTANT.
BUT YOU, FOX MASK. WHY DIDN'T YOU FORGET?
HUH?
...IT'S...

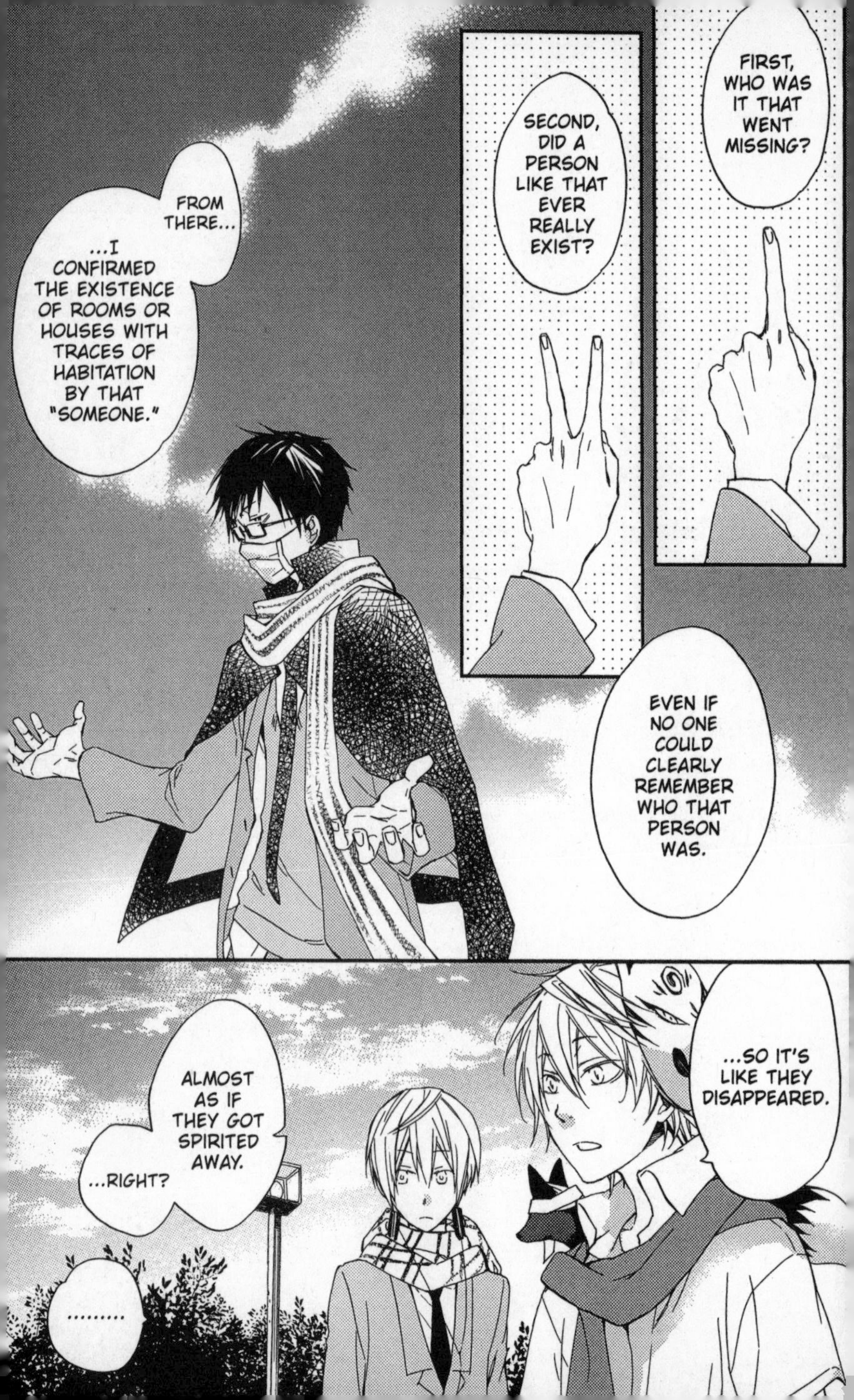

FIRST, WHO WAS IT THAT WENT MISSING?
SECOND, DID A PERSON LIKE THAT EVER REALLY EXIST?
FROM THERE...
...I CONFIRMED THE EXISTENCE OF ROOMS OR HOUSES WITH TRACES OF HABITATION BY THAT "SOMEONE."
EVEN IF NO ONE COULD CLEARLY REMEMBER WHO THAT PERSON WAS.
...SO IT'S LIKE THEY DISAPPEARED.
ALMOST AS IF THEY GOT SPIRITED AWAY.
...RIGHT?
....

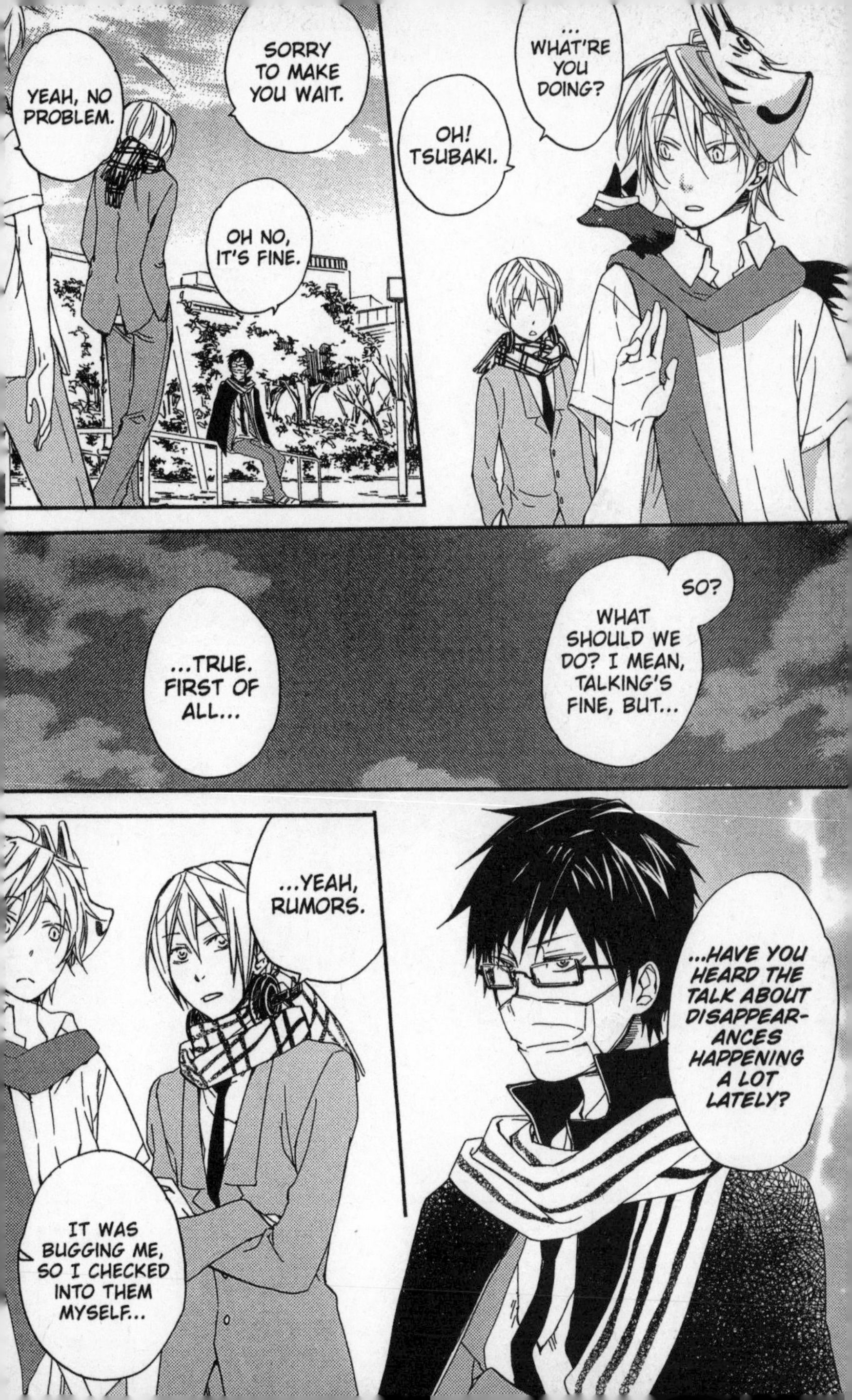
...WHAT'RE YOU DOING?
OH! TSUBAKI.
SORRY TO MAKE YOU WAIT.
YEAH, NO PROBLEM.
OH NO, IT'S FINE.
SO?
WHAT SHOULD WE DO? I MEAN, TALKING'S FINE, BUT...
...TRUE. FIRST OF ALL...
...HAVE YOU HEARD THE TALK ABOUT DISAPPEAR-ANCES HAPPENING A LOT LATELY?
...YEAH, RUMORS.
IT WAS BUGGING ME, SO I CHECKED INTO THEM MYSELF...

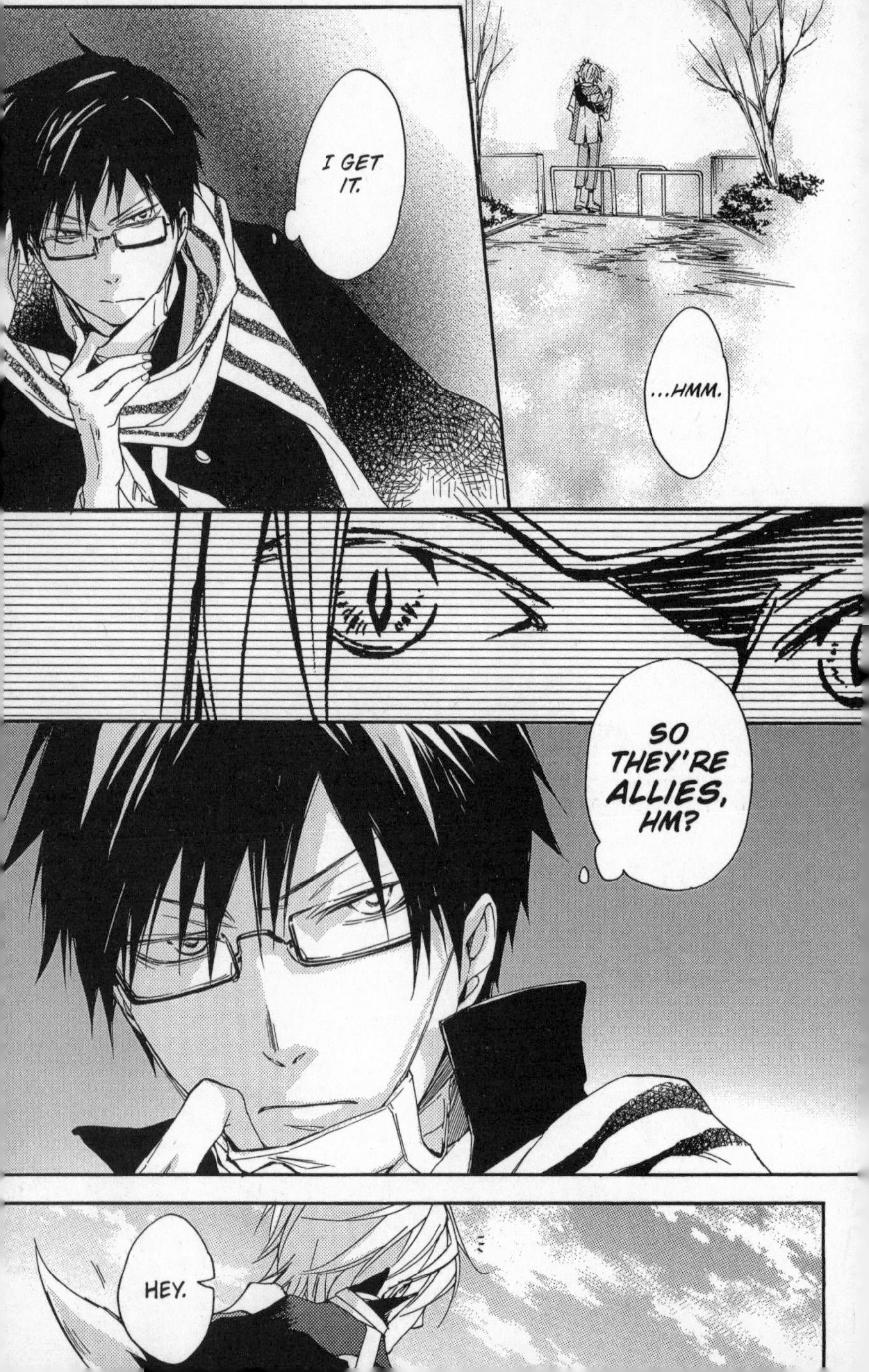
...HMM.
I GET IT.
SO THEY'RE ALLIES, HM?
HEY.

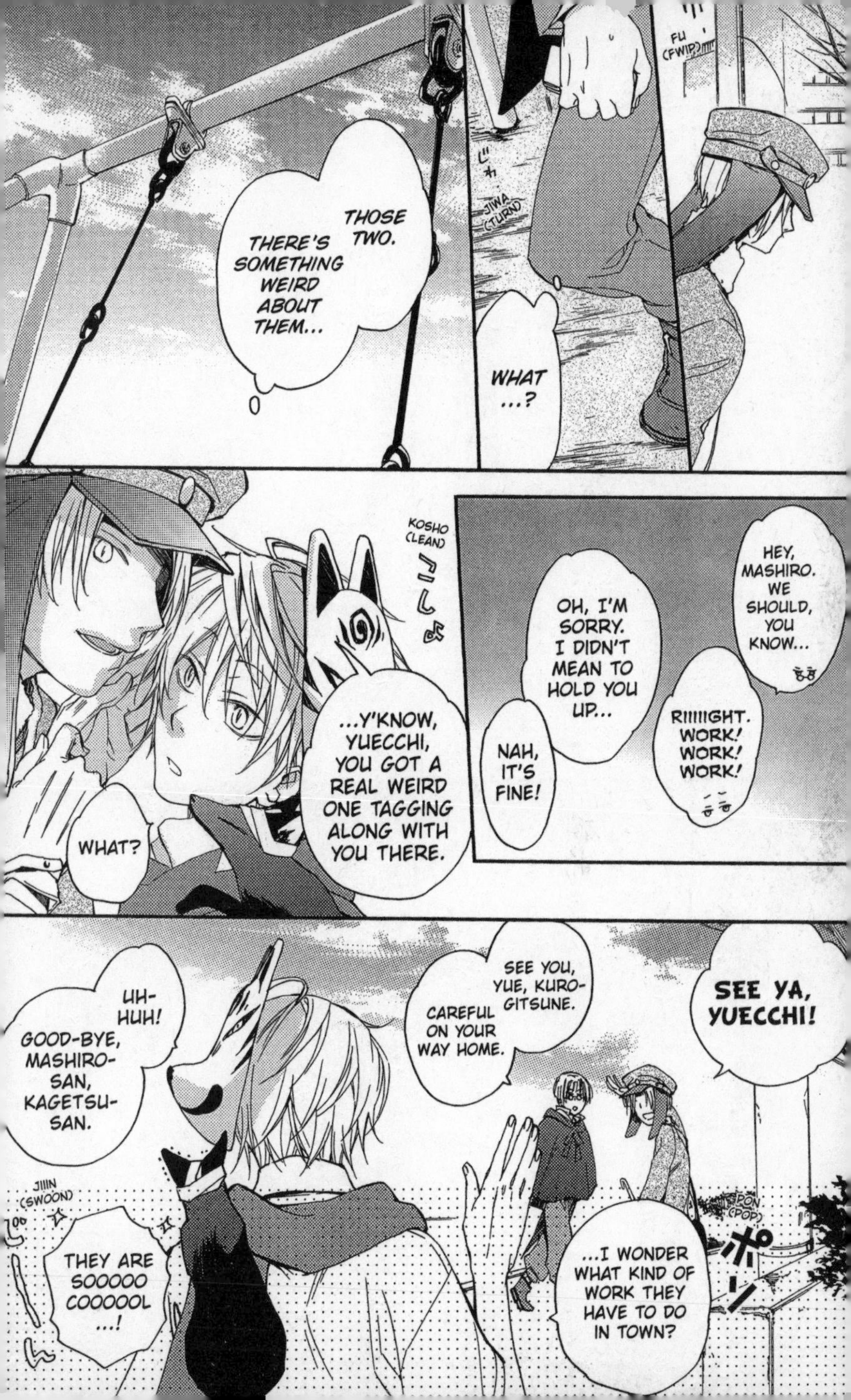
FU
(FWIP)
JIWA
(TURN)
WHAT ...?
THOSE TWO. THERE'S SOMETHING WEIRD ABOUT THEM...
HEY, MASHIRO. WE SHOULD, YOU KNOW...
RIIIIGHT. WORK! WORK! WORK!
OH, I'M SORRY. I DIDN'T MEAN TO HOLD YOU UP...
NAH, IT'S FINE!
KOSHO
(LEAN)
...Y'KNOW, YUECCHI, YOU GOT A REAL WEIRD ONE TAGGING ALONG WITH YOU THERE.
WHAT?
SEE YA, YUECCHI!
SEE YOU, YUE, KURO-GITSUNE.
CAREFUL ON YOUR WAY HOME.
UH-HUH! GOOD-BYE, MASHIRO-SAN, KAGETSU-SAN.
SPON
(POP)
...I WONDER WHAT KIND OF WORK THEY HAVE TO DO IN TOWN?
JIIIN
(SWOON)
THEY ARE SOOOOO COOOOOL ...!

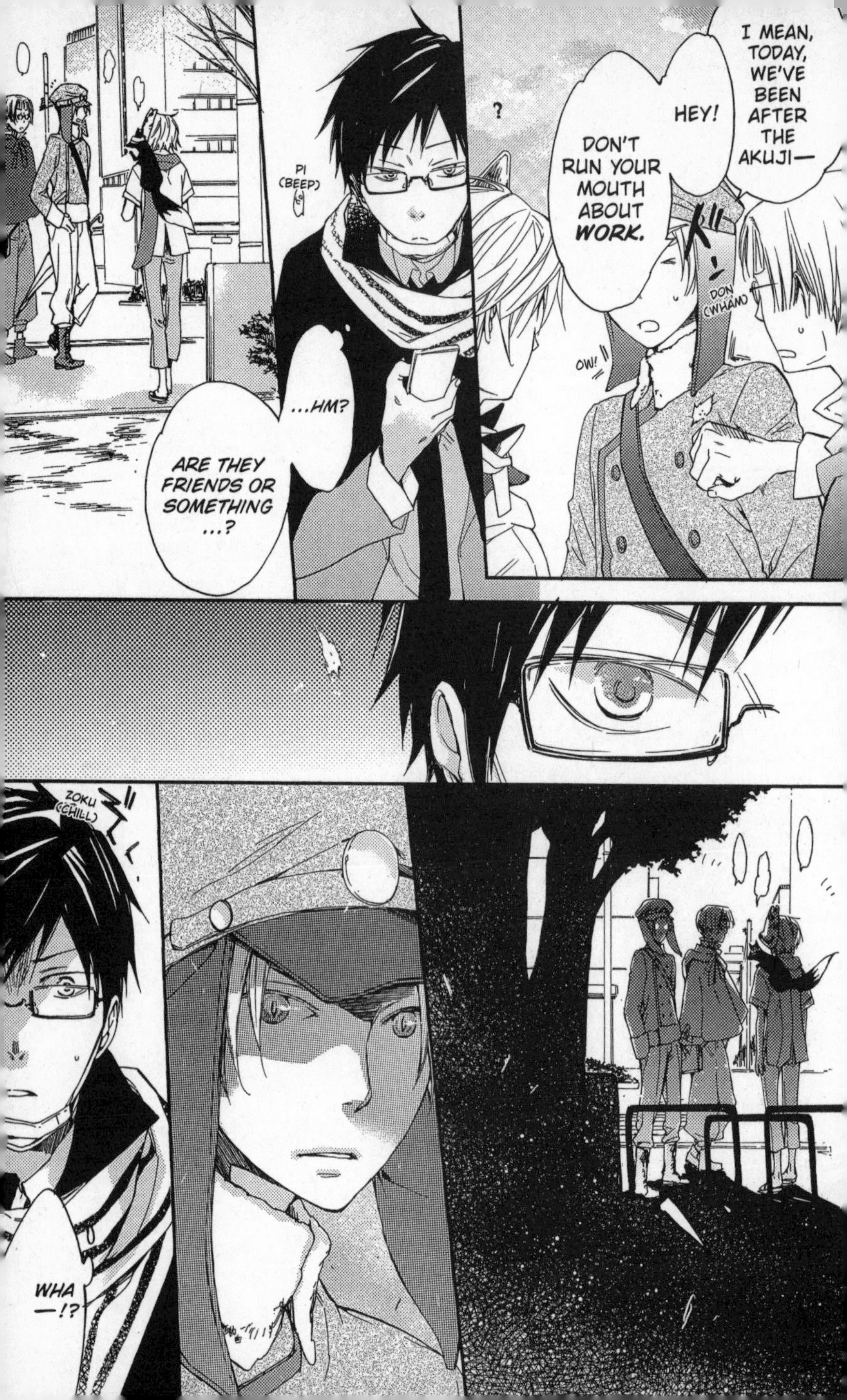
I MEAN, TODAY, WE'VE BEEN AFTER THE AKUJI—
HEY!
DON (WHAM)
DON'T RUN YOUR MOUTH ABOUT WORK.
OW!
?
PI (BEEP)
...HM?
ARE THEY FRIENDS OR SOMETHING ...?
ZOKU (CHILL)
WHA—!?

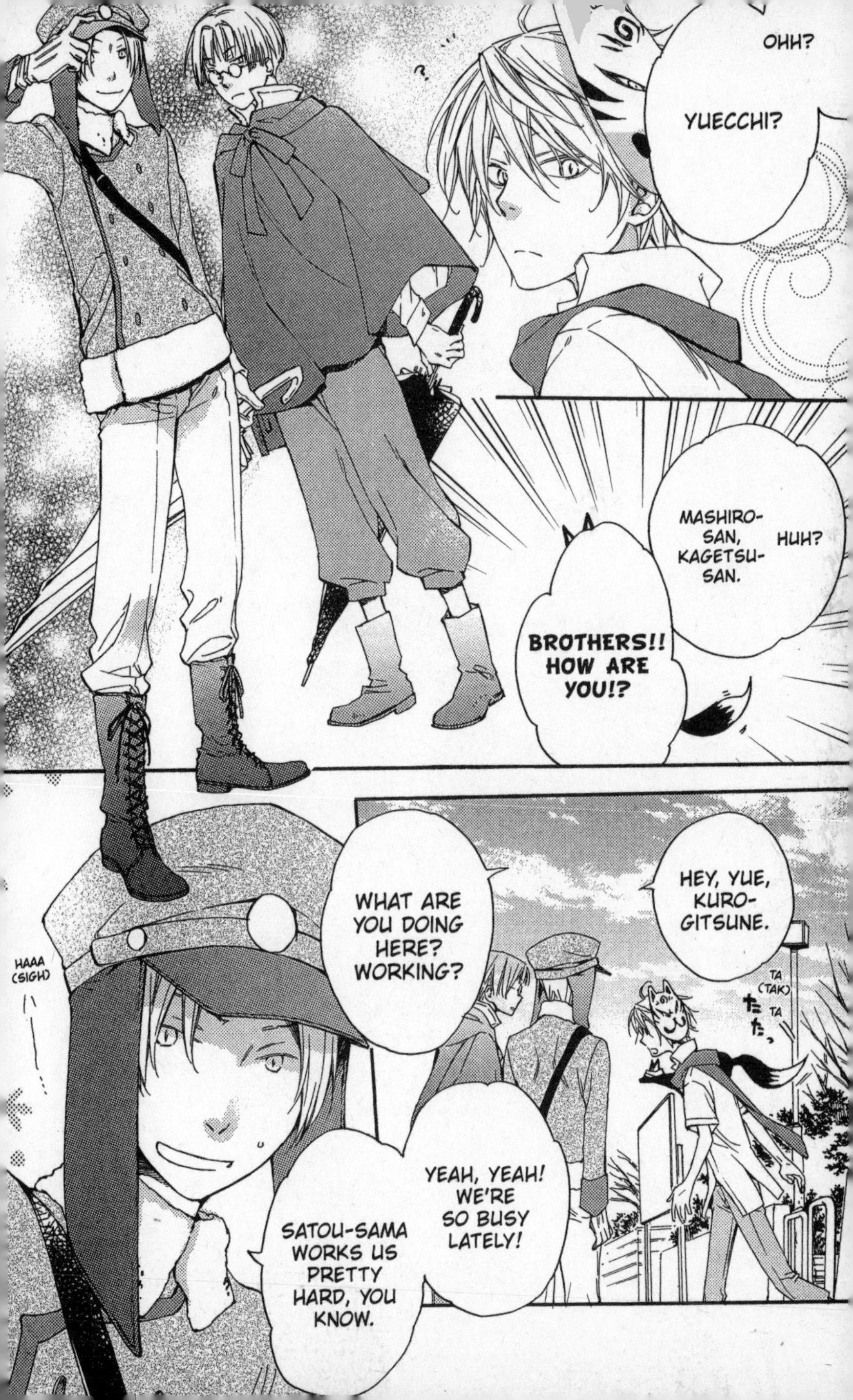
OHH?
YUECCHI?
HUH?
MASHIRO-SAN, KAGETSU-SAN.
BROTHERS!! HOW ARE YOU!?
HEY, YUE, KURO-GITSUNE.
TA (TAK) TA
WHAT ARE YOU DOING HERE? WORKING?
HAAA (SIGH)
YEAH, YEAH! WE'RE SO BUSY LATELY!
SATOU-SAMA WORKS US PRETTY HARD, YOU KNOW.

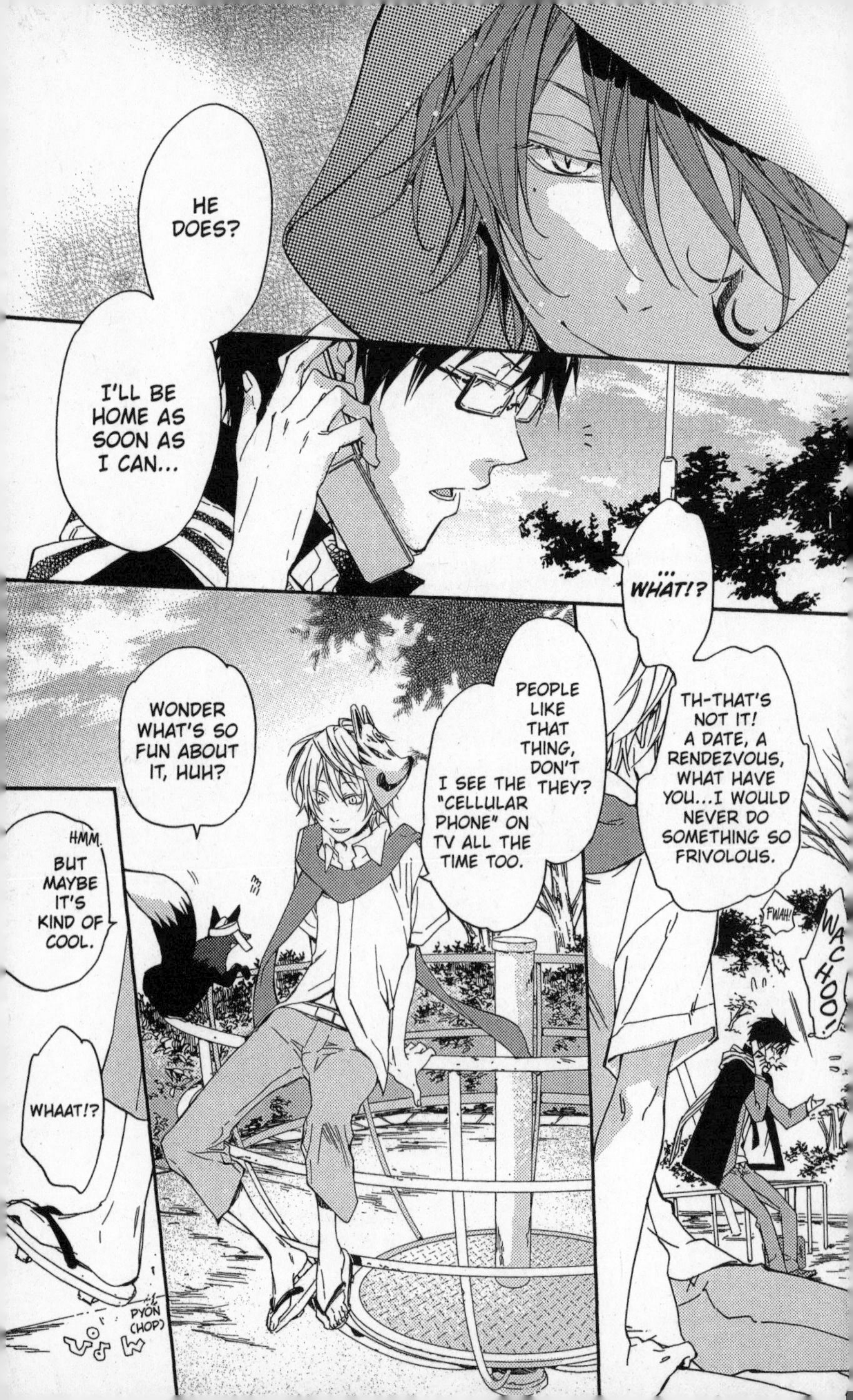

HE DOES?
I'LL BE HOME AS SOON AS I CAN...
...WHAT!?
TH-THAT'S NOT IT! A DATE, A RENDEZVOUS, WHAT HAVE YOU...I WOULD NEVER DO SOMETHING SO FRIVOLOUS.
FWAH!
WACHOO!
PEOPLE LIKE THAT THING, DON'T THEY?
I SEE THE "CELLULAR PHONE" ON TV ALL THE TIME TOO.
WONDER WHAT'S SO FUN ABOUT IT, HUH?
HMM.
BUT MAYBE IT'S KIND OF COOL.
WHAAT!?
PYON (HOP)

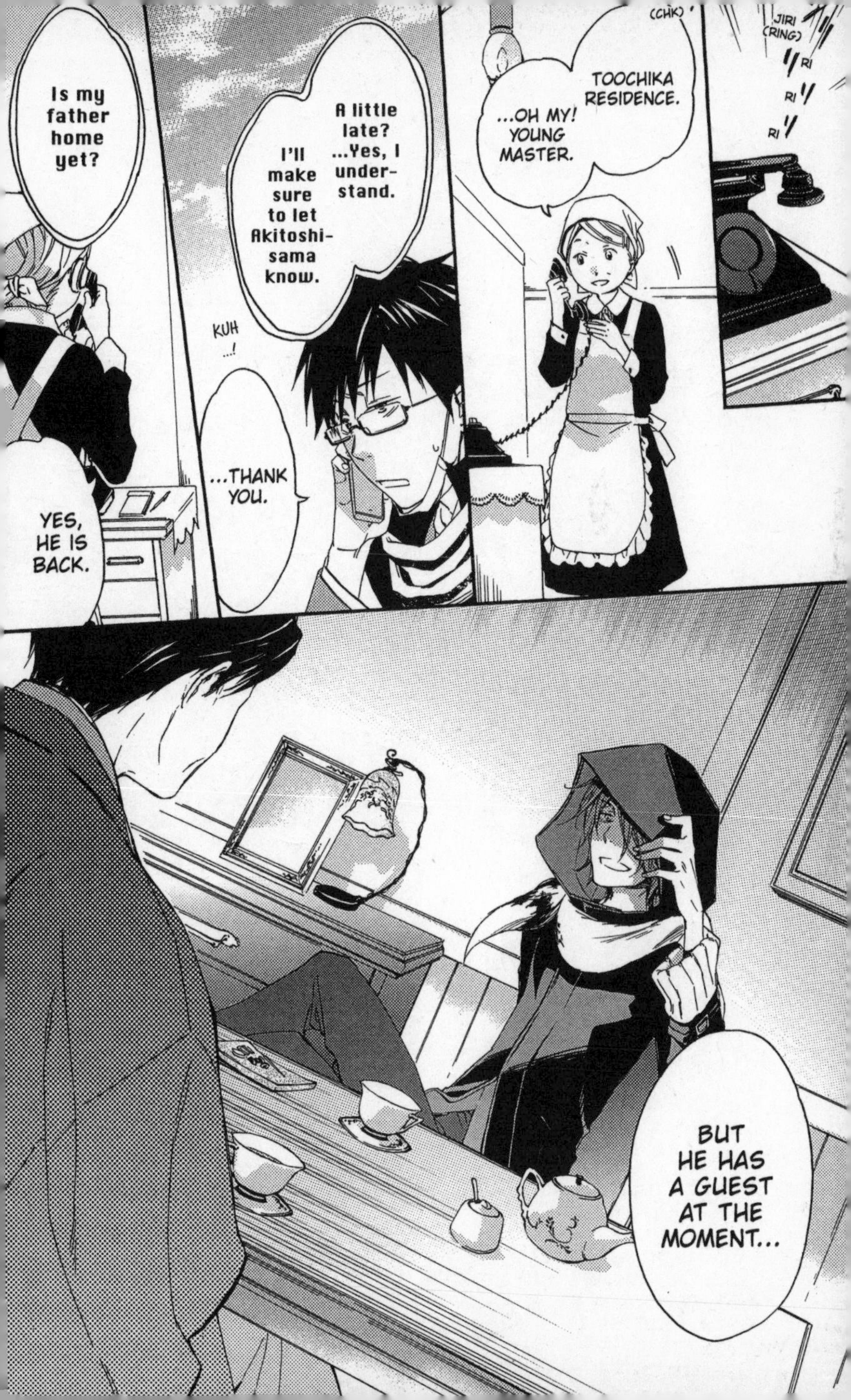
JIRI (RING)
RI
RI
RI
(CHK)
TOOCHIKA RESIDENCE.
...OH MY! YOUNG MASTER.
A little late? ...Yes, I understand.
I'll make sure to let Akitoshi-sama know.
KUH ...!
...THANK YOU.
Is my father home yet?
YES, HE IS BACK.
BUT HE HAS A GUEST AT THE MOMENT...

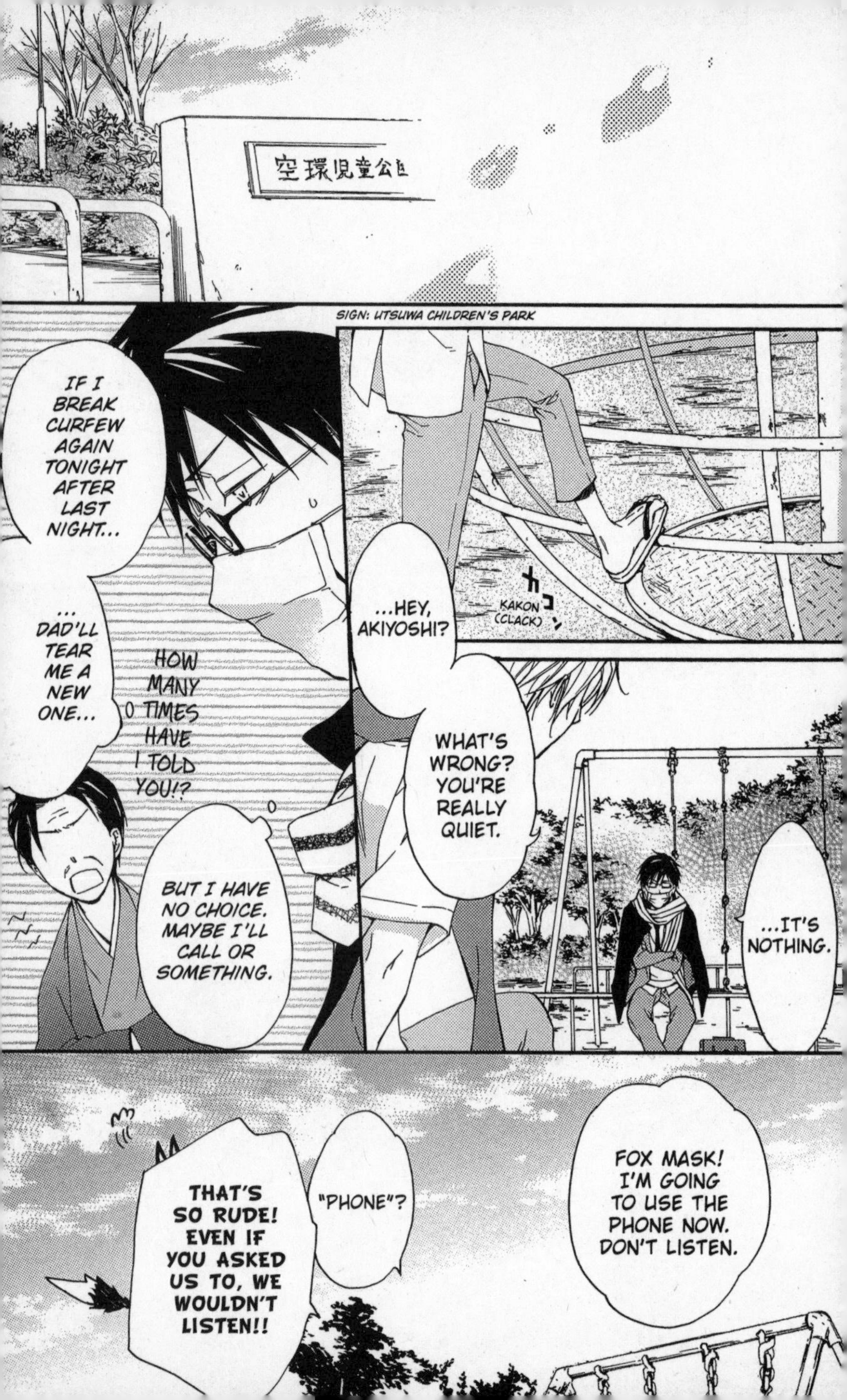
空環児童公
SIGN: UTSUWA CHILDREN'S PARK
...HEY, AKIYOSHI?
KAKON (CLACK)
WHAT'S WRONG? YOU'RE REALLY QUIET.
...IT'S NOTHING.
IF I BREAK CURFEW AGAIN TONIGHT AFTER LAST NIGHT...
...DAD'LL TEAR ME A NEW ONE...
HOW MANY TIMES HAVE I TOLD YOU!?
BUT I HAVE NO CHOICE. MAYBE I'LL CALL OR SOMETHING.
FOX MASK! I'M GOING TO USE THE PHONE NOW. DON'T LISTEN.
"PHONE"?
THAT'S SO RUDE! EVEN IF YOU ASKED US TO, WE WOULDN'T LISTEN!!

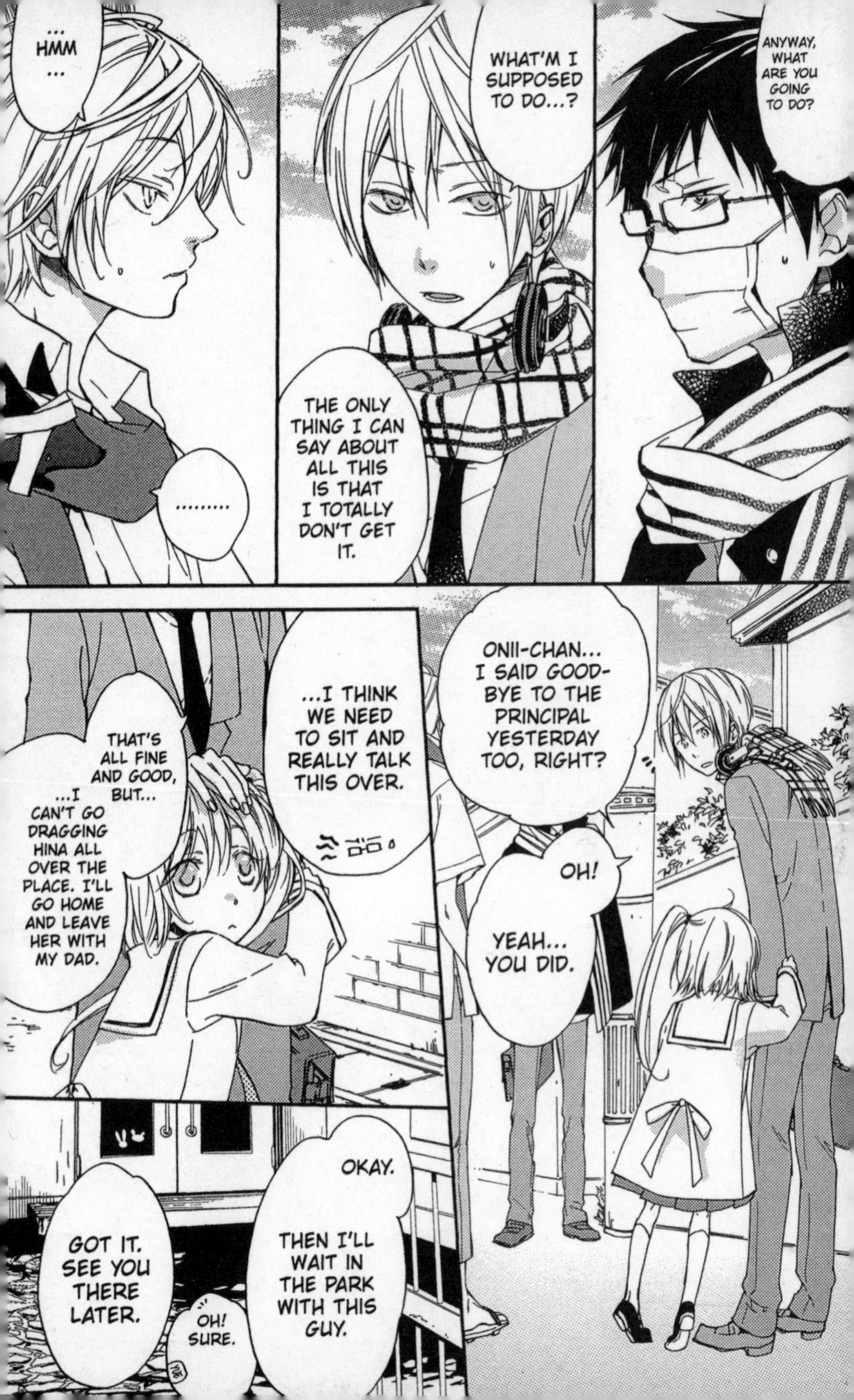
ANYWAY, WHAT ARE YOU GOING TO DO?
WHAT'M I SUPPOSED TO DO...?
THE ONLY THING I CAN SAY ABOUT ALL THIS IS THAT I TOTALLY DON'T GET IT.
... HMM ...
....
ONII-CHAN... I SAID GOOD-BYE TO THE PRINCIPAL YESTERDAY TOO, RIGHT?
OH!
YEAH... YOU DID.
...I THINK WE NEED TO SIT AND REALLY TALK THIS OVER.
THAT'S ALL FINE AND GOOD, BUT...
...I CAN'T GO DRAGGING HINA ALL OVER THE PLACE. I'LL GO HOME AND LEAVE HER WITH MY DAD.
OKAY.
THEN I'LL WAIT IN THE PARK WITH THIS GUY.
GOT IT. SEE YOU THERE LATER.
OH! SURE.

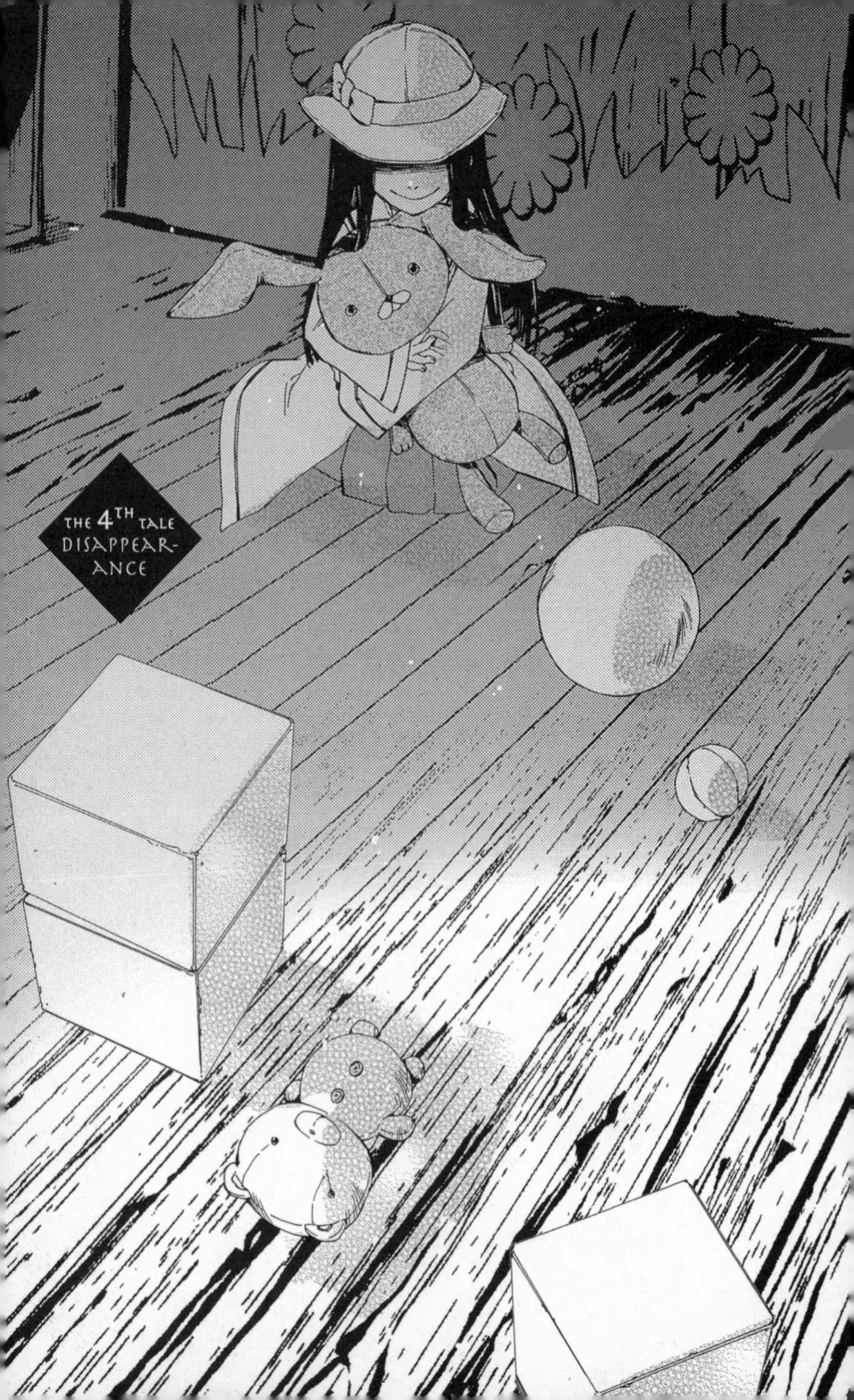
THE 4TH TALE
DISAPPEAR-
ANCE

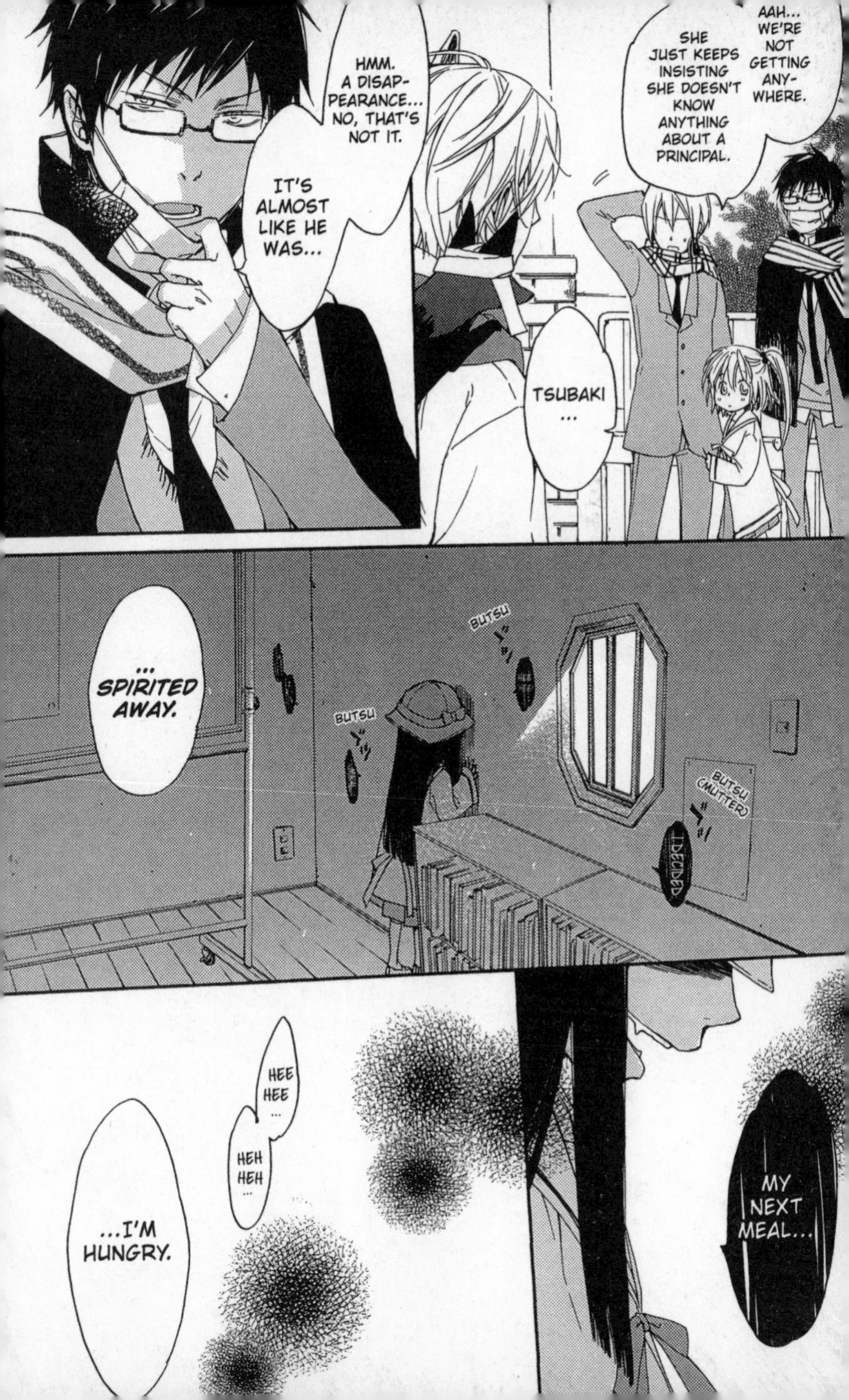
AAH... WE'RE NOT GETTING ANY-WHERE.
SHE JUST KEEPS INSISTING SHE DOESN'T KNOW ANYTHING ABOUT A PRINCIPAL.
TSUBAKI ...
HMM. A DISAP-PEARANCE... NO, THAT'S NOT IT.
IT'S ALMOST LIKE HE WAS...
BUTSU (MUTTER)
I DECIDED
BUTSU
BUTSU
... SPIRITED AWAY.
MY NEXT MEAL...
HEE HEE ...
HEH HEH ...
...I'M HUNGRY.

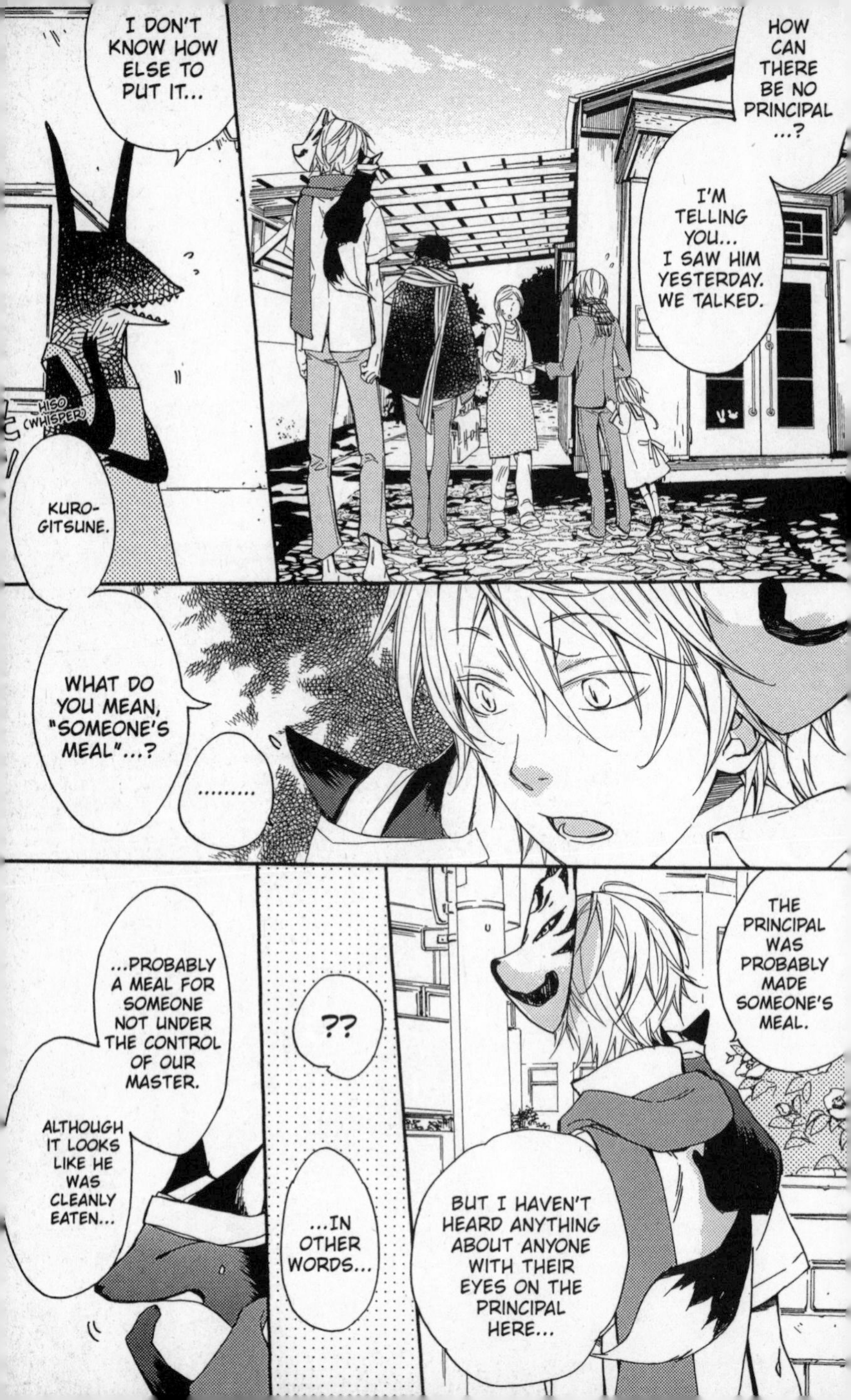
HOW CAN THERE BE NO PRINCIPAL ...?
I'M TELLING YOU... I SAW HIM YESTERDAY. WE TALKED.
I DON'T KNOW HOW ELSE TO PUT IT...
HISO (WHISPER)
KURO-GITSUNE.
WHAT DO YOU MEAN, "SOMEONE'S MEAL"...?
....
THE PRINCIPAL WAS PROBABLY MADE SOMEONE'S MEAL.
BUT I HAVEN'T HEARD ANYTHING ABOUT ANYONE WITH THEIR EYES ON THE PRINCIPAL HERE...
??
...IN OTHER WORDS...
...PROBABLY A MEAL FOR SOMEONE NOT UNDER THE CONTROL OF OUR MASTER.
ALTHOUGH IT LOOKS LIKE HE WAS CLEANLY EATEN...

*Of the Red,
the Light,
and the
Ayakashi*

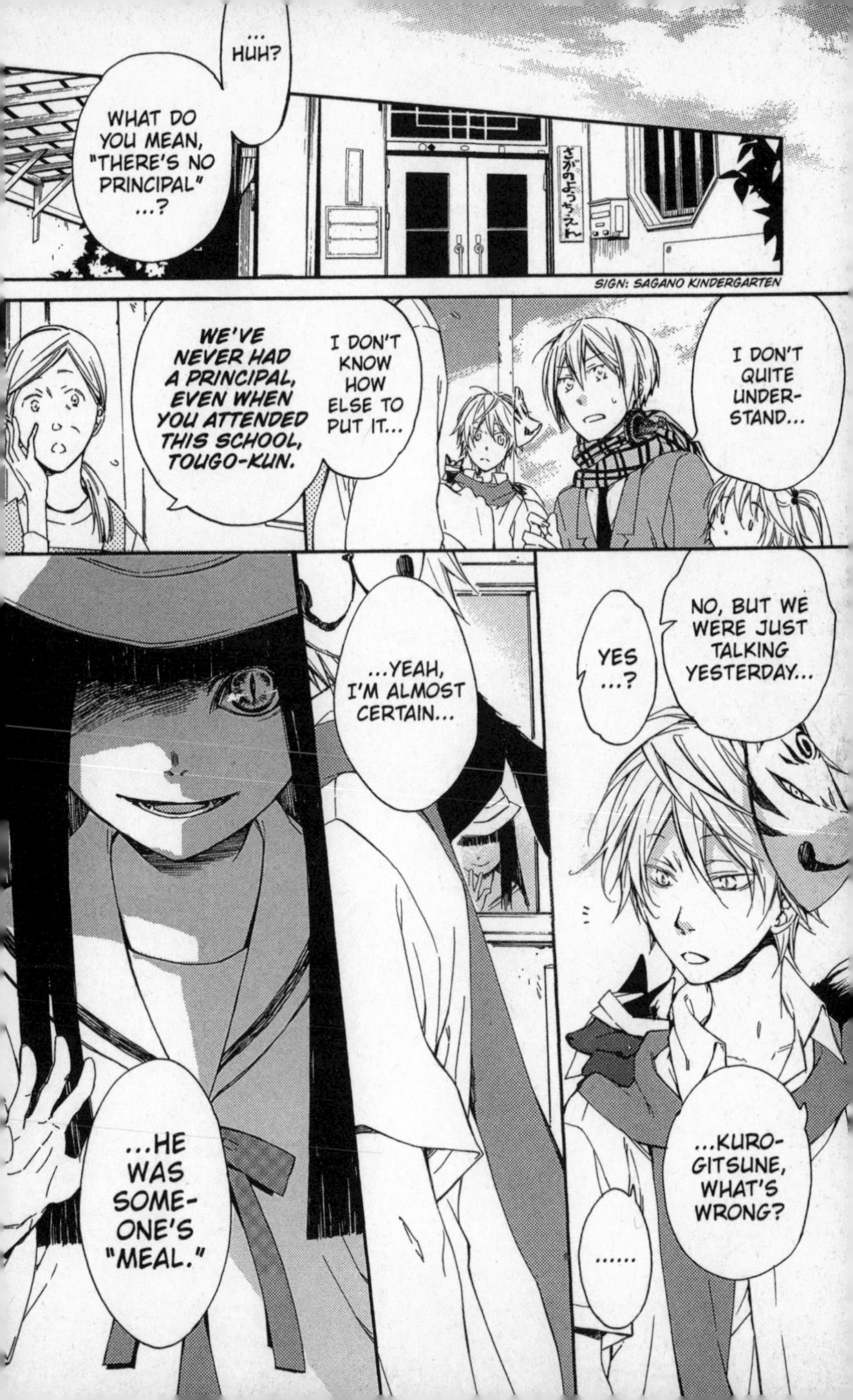
... HUH?
WHAT DO YOU MEAN, "THERE'S NO PRINCIPAL" ...?
さがのようちえん
SIGN: SAGANO KINDERGARTEN
I DON'T QUITE UNDER-STAND...
I DON'T KNOW HOW ELSE TO PUT IT...
WE'VE NEVER HAD A PRINCIPAL, EVEN WHEN YOU ATTENDED THIS SCHOOL, TOUGO-KUN.
NO, BUT WE WERE JUST TALKING YESTERDAY...
YES ...?
...KURO-GITSUNE, WHAT'S WRONG?
......
...YEAH, I'M ALMOST CERTAIN...
...HE WAS SOME-ONE'S "MEAL."

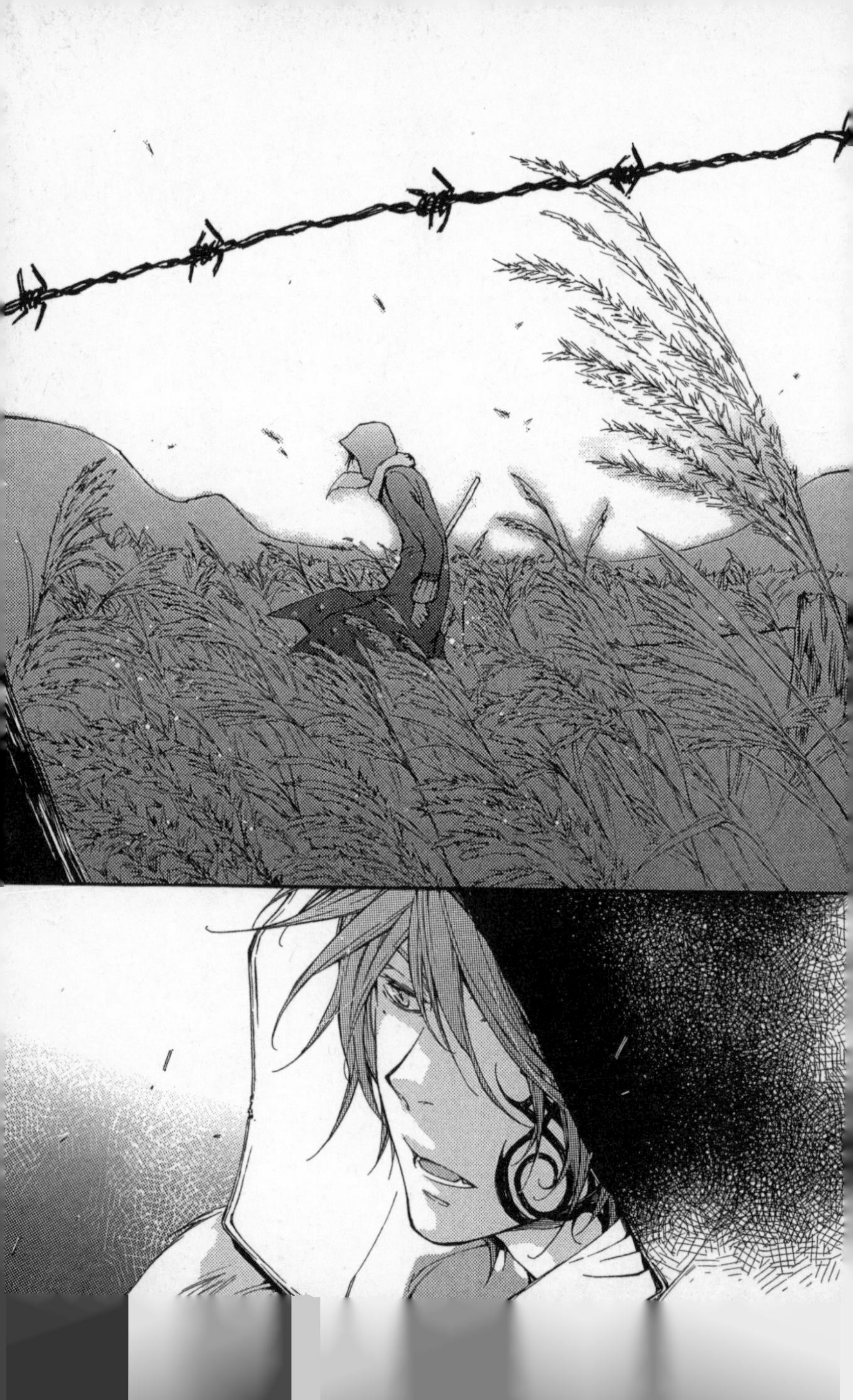

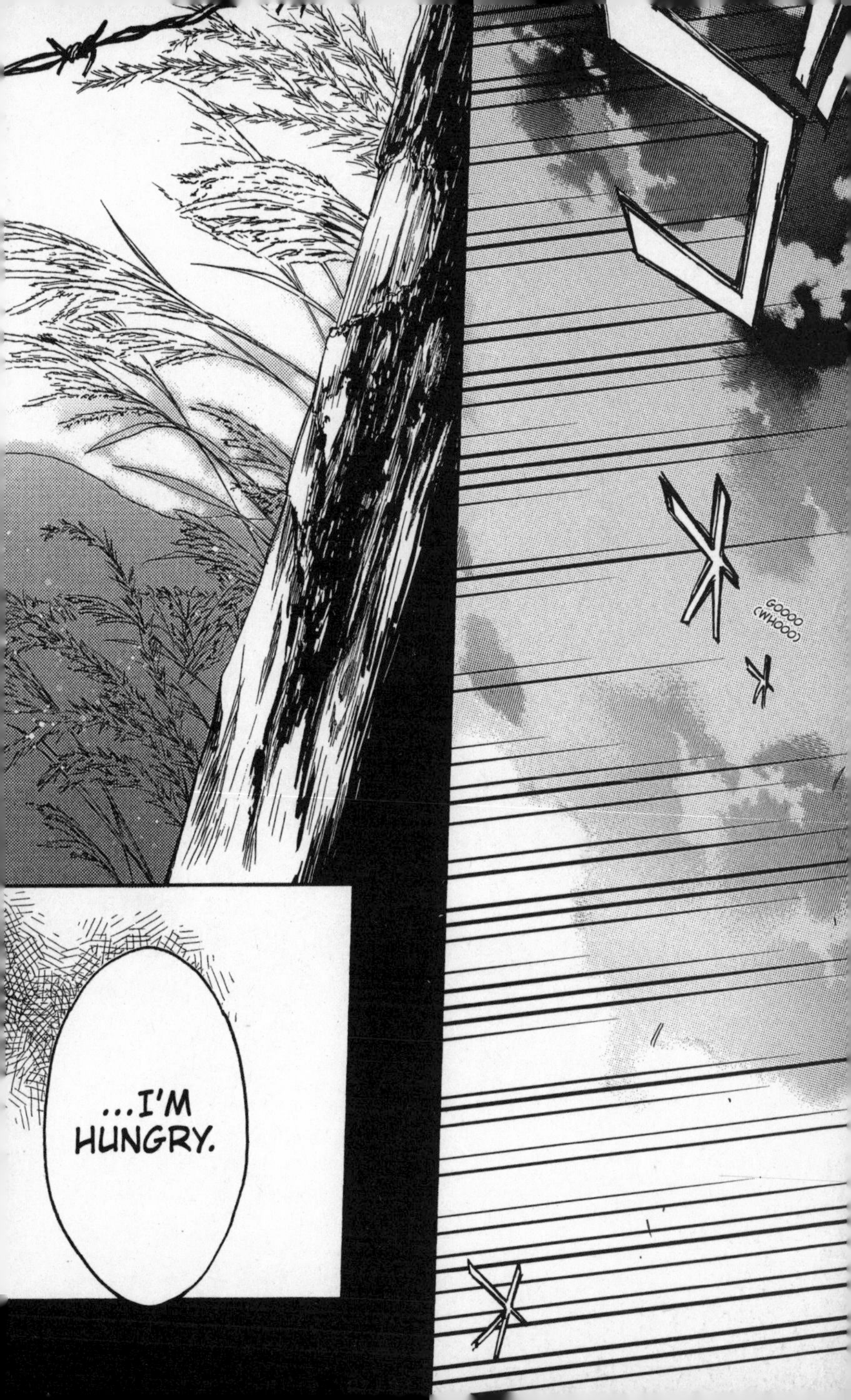
GOOOO
(WHOOO)
...I'M HUNGRY.

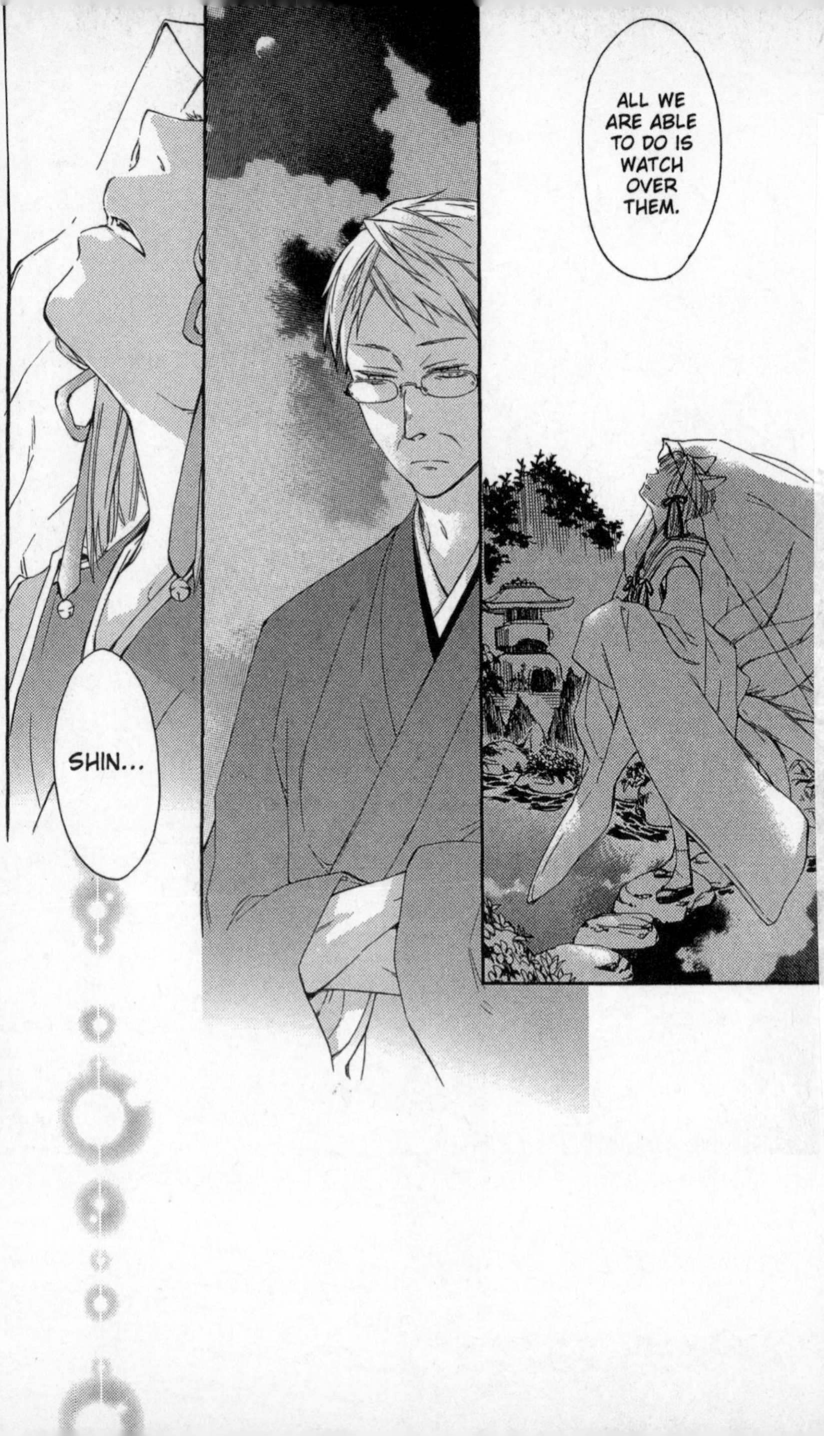
ALL WE ARE ABLE TO DO IS WATCH OVER THEM.
SHIN...

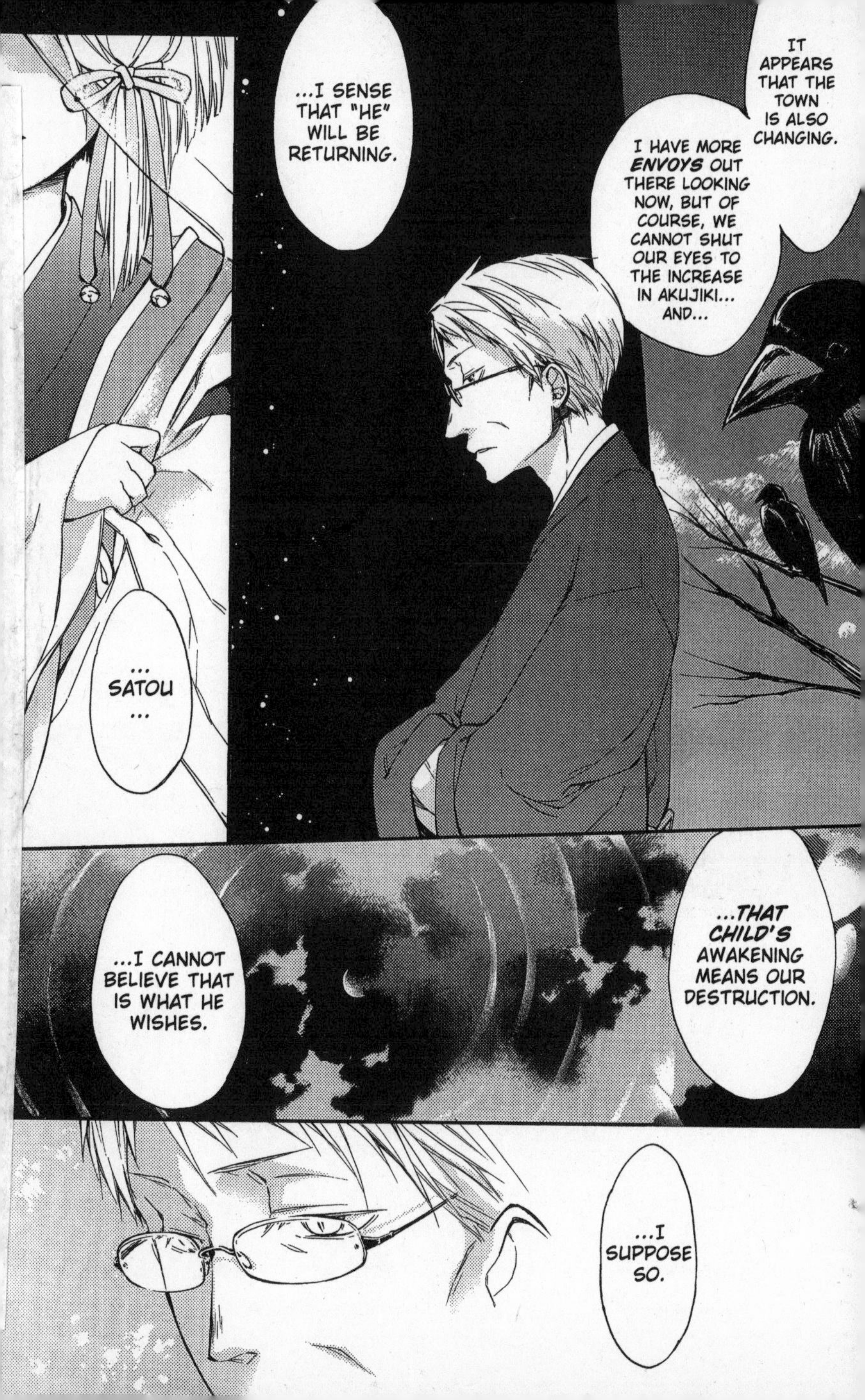
IT APPEARS THAT THE TOWN IS ALSO CHANGING.
I HAVE MORE *ENVOYS* OUT THERE LOOKING NOW, BUT OF COURSE, WE CANNOT SHUT OUR EYES TO THE INCREASE IN AKUJIKI... AND...
...I SENSE THAT "HE" WILL BE RETURNING.
...SATOU...
...*THAT CHILD'S* AWAKENING MEANS OUR DESTRUCTION.
...I CANNOT BELIEVE THAT IS WHAT HE WISHES.
...I SUPPOSE SO.

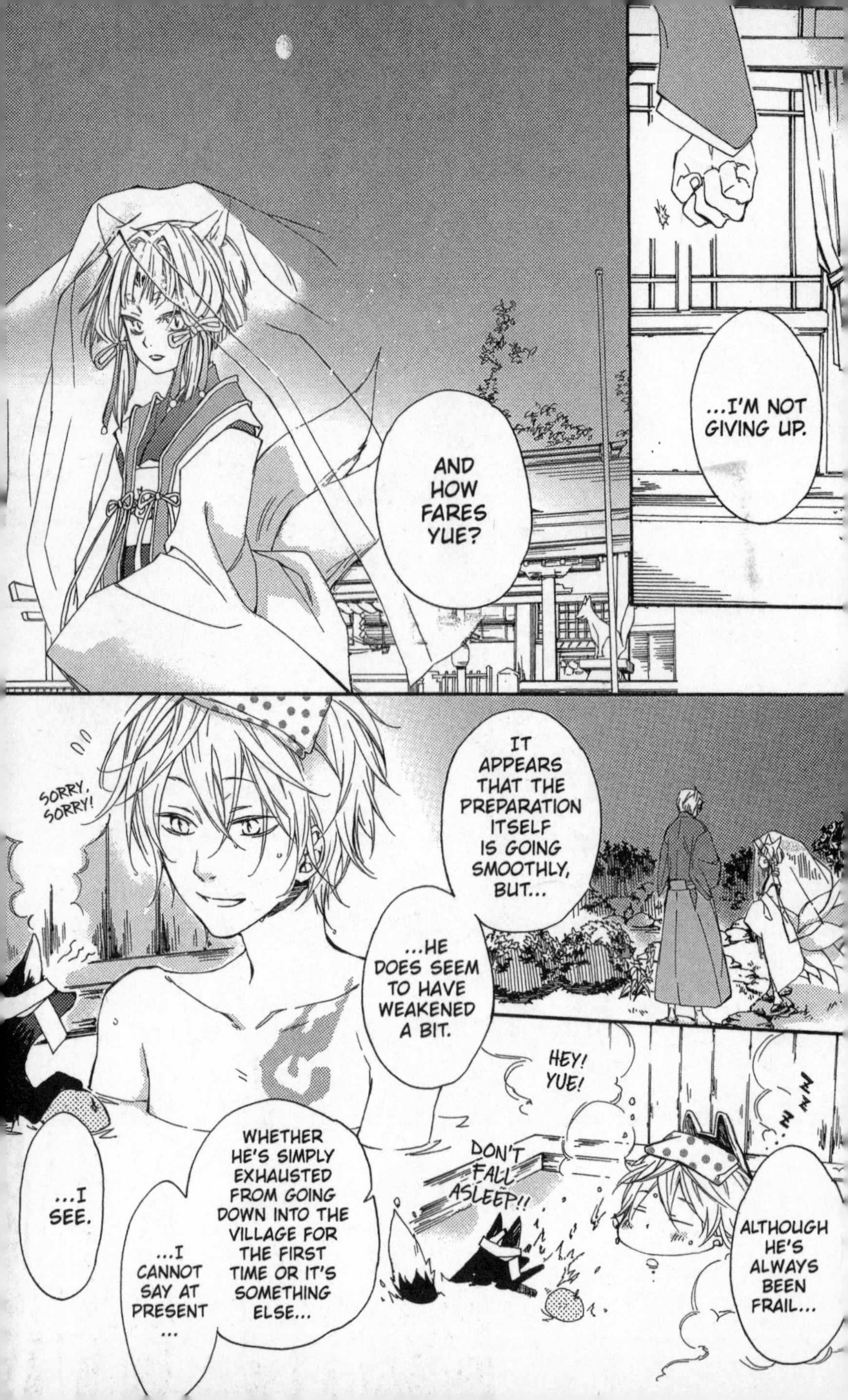
...I'M NOT GIVING UP.
AND HOW FARES YUE?
IT APPEARS THAT THE PREPARATION ITSELF IS GOING SMOOTHLY, BUT...
...HE DOES SEEM TO HAVE WEAKENED A BIT.
HEY! YUE!
ALTHOUGH HE'S ALWAYS BEEN FRAIL...
DON'T FALL ASLEEP!!
WHETHER HE'S SIMPLY EXHAUSTED FROM GOING DOWN INTO THE VILLAGE FOR THE FIRST TIME OR IT'S SOMETHING ELSE...
...I CANNOT SAY AT PRESENT...
SORRY, SORRY!
...I SEE.

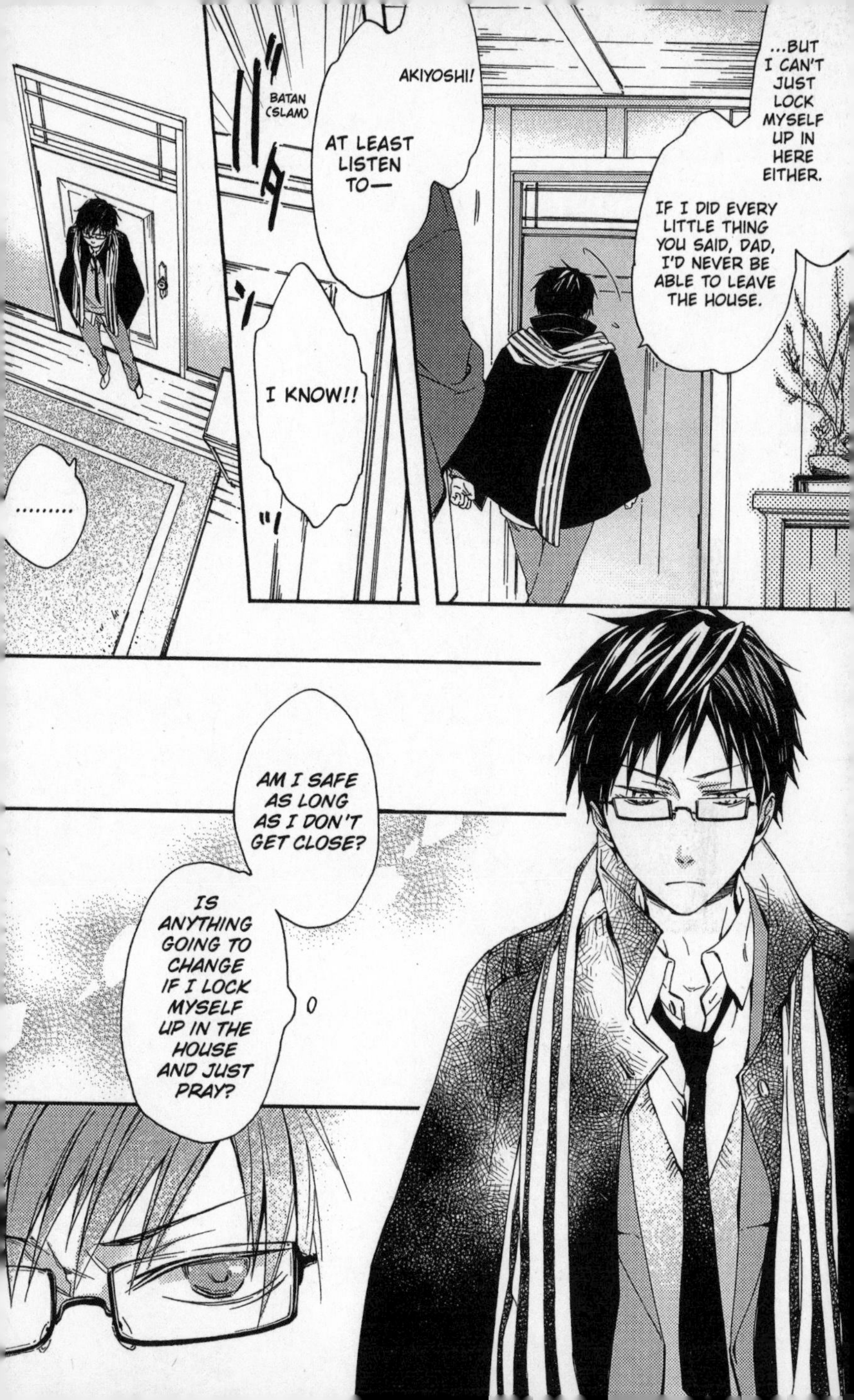
...BUT I CAN'T JUST LOCK MYSELF UP IN HERE EITHER.
IF I DID EVERY LITTLE THING YOU SAID, DAD, I'D NEVER BE ABLE TO LEAVE THE HOUSE.
AKIYOSHI!
AT LEAST LISTEN TO—
I KNOW!!
BATAN (SLAM)
....
AM I SAFE AS LONG AS I DON'T GET CLOSE?
IS ANYTHING GOING TO CHANGE IF I LOCK MYSELF UP IN THE HOUSE AND JUST PRAY?

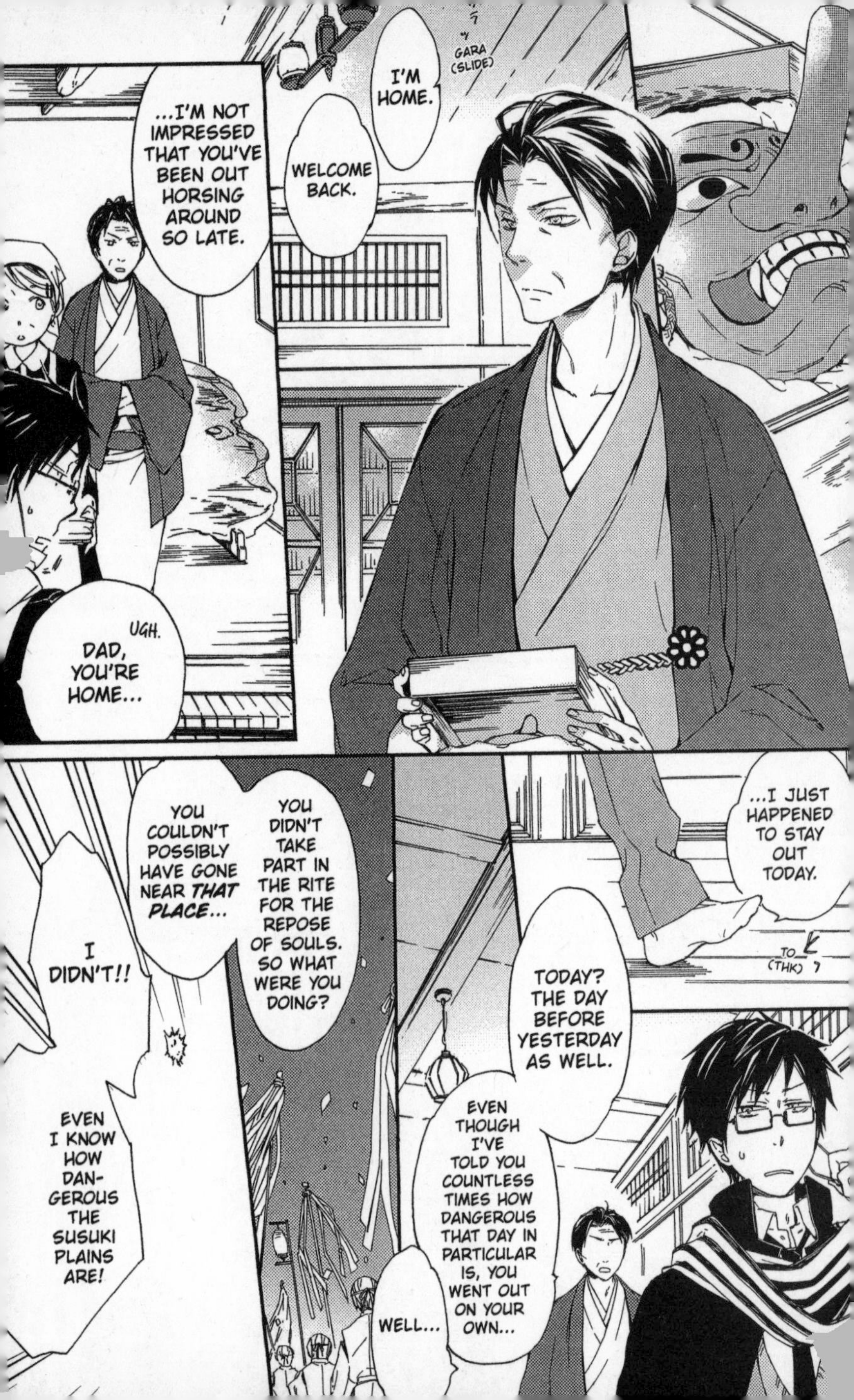

GARA (SLIDE)
I'M HOME.
WELCOME BACK.
...I'M NOT IMPRESSED THAT YOU'VE BEEN OUT HORSING AROUND SO LATE.
UGH.
DAD, YOU'RE HOME...
...I JUST HAPPENED TO STAY OUT TODAY.
TO (THK)
TODAY? THE DAY BEFORE YESTERDAY AS WELL.
EVEN THOUGH I'VE TOLD YOU COUNTLESS TIMES HOW DANGEROUS THAT DAY IN PARTICULAR IS, YOU WENT OUT ON YOUR OWN...
WELL...
YOU DIDN'T TAKE PART IN THE RITE FOR THE REPOSE OF SOULS. SO WHAT WERE YOU DOING?
YOU COULDN'T POSSIBLY HAVE GONE NEAR *THAT PLACE*...
I DIDN'T!!
EVEN I KNOW HOW DAN-GEROUS THE SUSUKI PLAINS ARE!

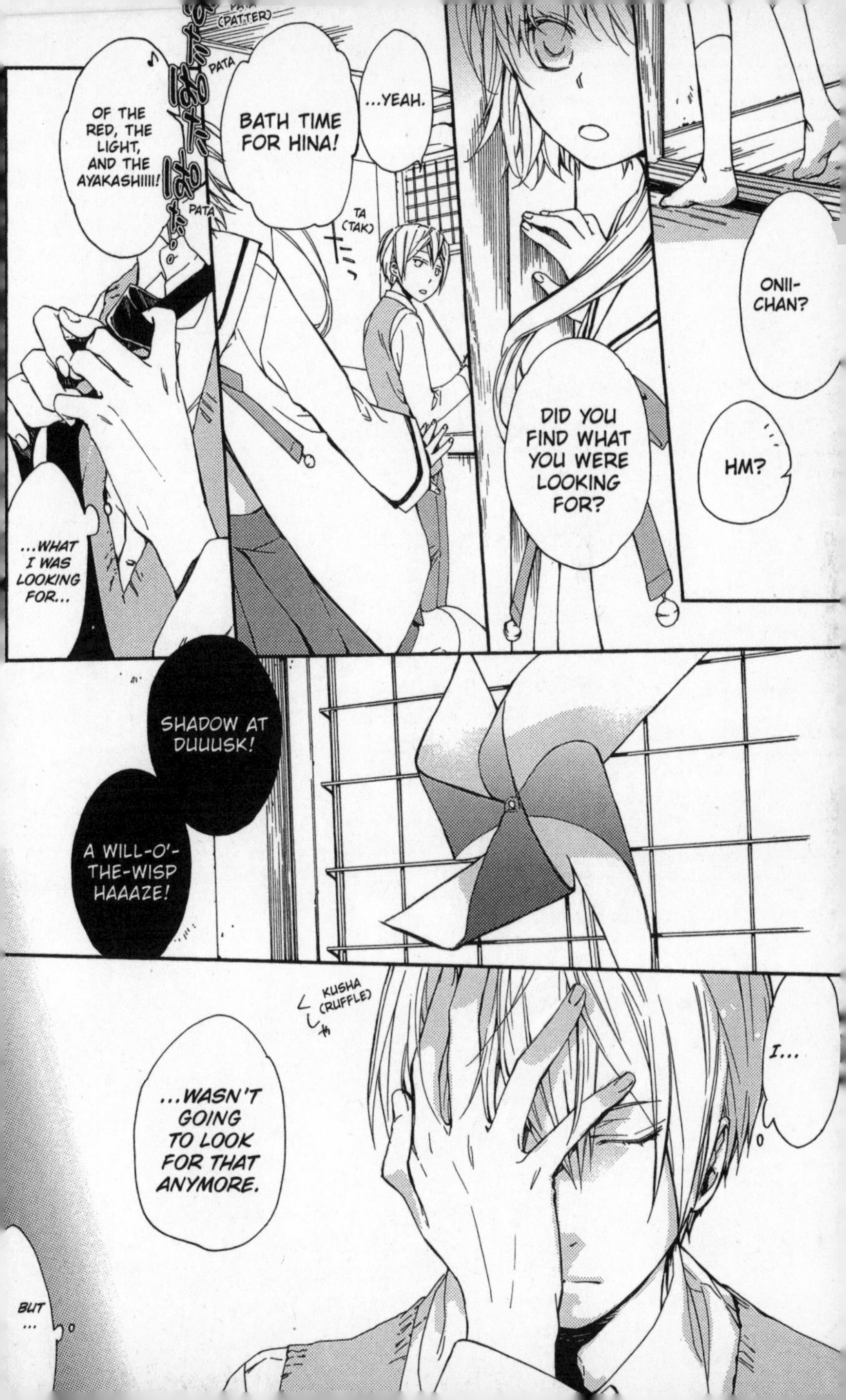
ONII-CHAN?
HM?
DID YOU FIND WHAT YOU WERE LOOKING FOR?
...YEAH.
TA (TAK)
BATH TIME FOR HINA!
PATA (PATTER)
PATA
PATA
OF THE RED, THE LIGHT, AND THE AYAKASHIIII!
...WHAT I WAS LOOKING FOR...
SHADOW AT DUUUSK!
A WILL-O'-THE-WISP HAAAZE!
I...
KUSHA (RUFFLE)
...WASN'T GOING TO LOOK FOR THAT ANYMORE.
BUT...

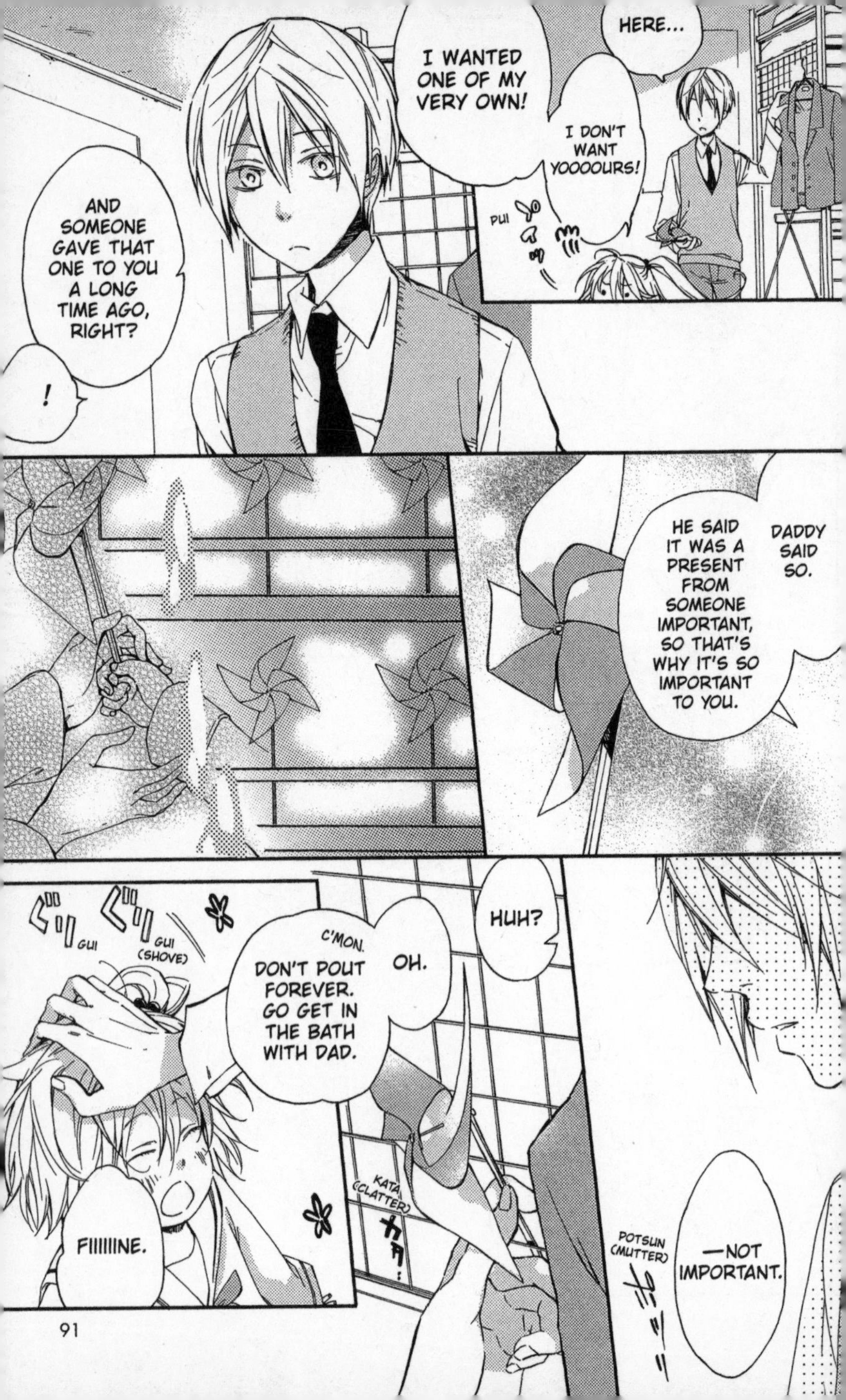
HERE...
I DON'T WANT YOOOOURS!
PUI
I WANTED ONE OF MY VERY OWN!
AND SOMEONE GAVE THAT ONE TO YOU A LONG TIME AGO, RIGHT?
!
DADDY SAID SO.
HE SAID IT WAS A PRESENT FROM SOMEONE IMPORTANT, SO THAT'S WHY IT'S SO IMPORTANT TO YOU.
—NOT IMPORTANT.
POTSUN (MUTTER)
HUH?
OH.
C'MON.
DON'T POUT FOREVER. GO GET IN THE BATH WITH DAD.
KATA (CLATTER)
GUI GUI (SHOVE)
FIIIIINE.

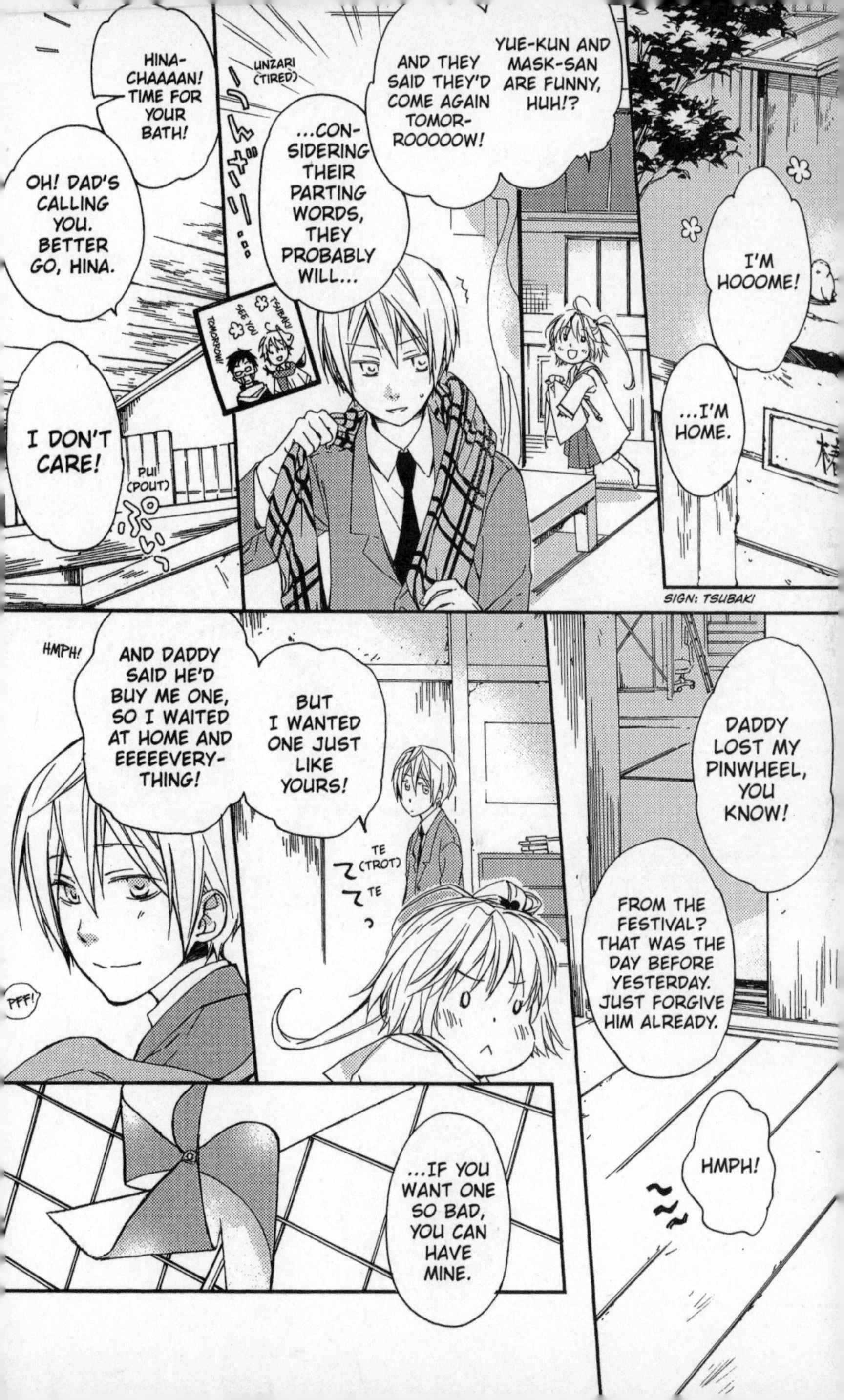
I'M HOOOME!
...I'M HOME.
SIGN: TSUBAKI
YUE-KUN AND MASK-SAN ARE FUNNY, HUH!?
AND THEY SAID THEY'D COME AGAIN TOMOR-ROOOOOW!
UNZARI (TIRED)
...CON-SIDERING THEIR PARTING WORDS, THEY PROBABLY WILL...
TSUBAKI! SEE YOU TOMORROW!
HINA-CHAAAAN! TIME FOR YOUR BATH!
OH! DAD'S CALLING YOU. BETTER GO, HINA.
I DON'T CARE!
PUI (POUT)
DADDY LOST MY PINWHEEL, YOU KNOW!
FROM THE FESTIVAL? THAT WAS THE DAY BEFORE YESTERDAY. JUST FORGIVE HIM ALREADY.
BUT I WANTED ONE JUST LIKE YOURS!
TE (TROT) TE
AND DADDY SAID HE'D BUY ME ONE, SO I WAITED AT HOME AND EEEEVERY-THING!
HMPH!
PFF!
HMPH!
...IF YOU WANT ONE SO BAD, YOU CAN HAVE MINE.

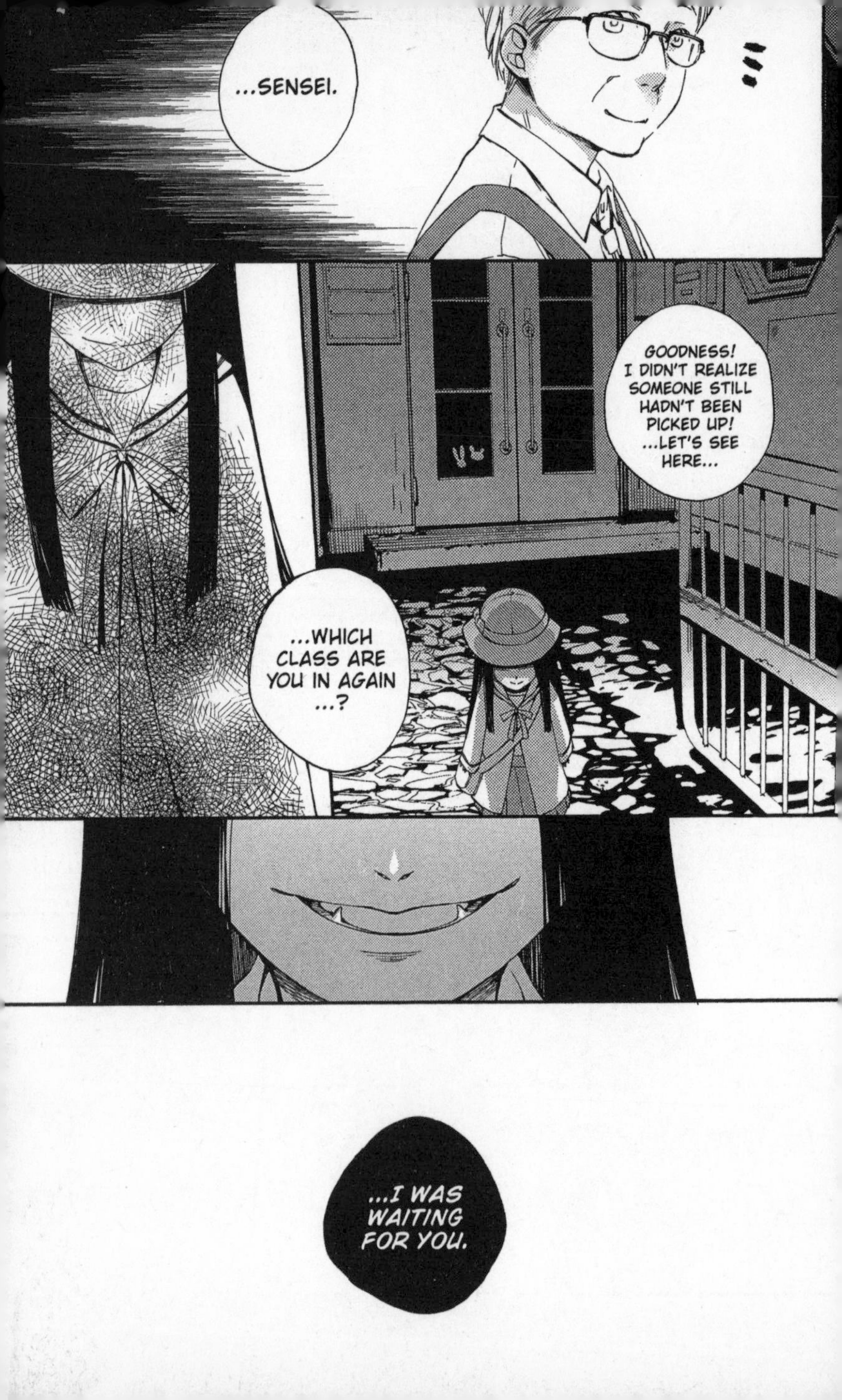
...SENSEI.
GOODNESS! I DIDN'T REALIZE SOMEONE STILL HADN'T BEEN PICKED UP! ...LET'S SEE HERE...
...WHICH CLASS ARE YOU IN AGAIN ...?
...I WAS WAITING FOR YOU.

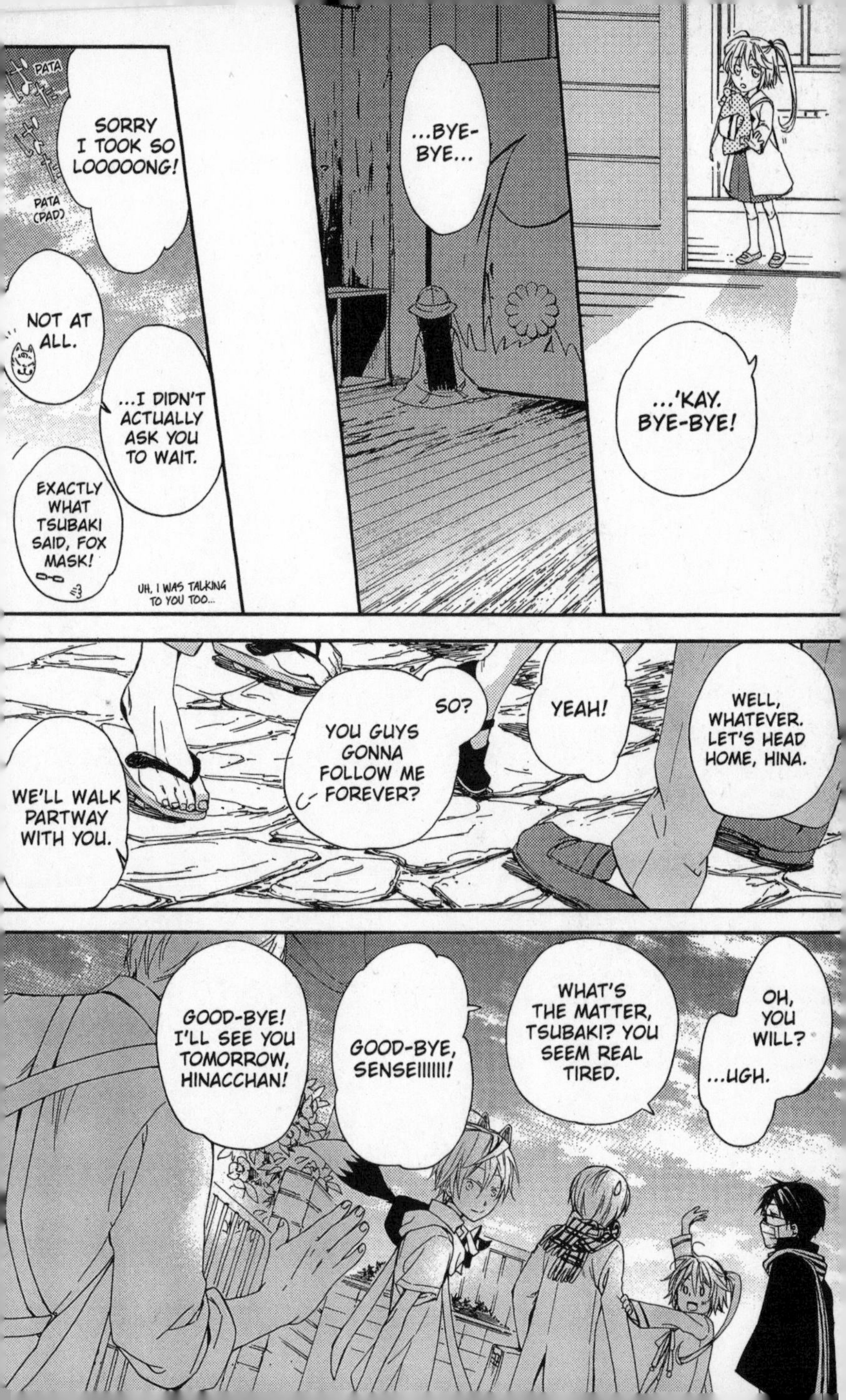
...BYE-BYE...
...'KAY. BYE-BYE!
PATA
SORRY I TOOK SO LOOOOONG!
PATA (PAD)
NOT AT ALL.
...I DIDN'T ACTUALLY ASK YOU TO WAIT.
EXACTLY WHAT TSUBAKI SAID, FOX MASK!
UH, I WAS TALKING TO YOU TOO...
WELL, WHATEVER. LET'S HEAD HOME, HINA.
YEAH!
SO?
YOU GUYS GONNA FOLLOW ME FOREVER?
WE'LL WALK PARTWAY WITH YOU.
OH, YOU WILL?
...UGH.
WHAT'S THE MATTER, TSUBAKI? YOU SEEM REAL TIRED.
GOOD-BYE, SENSEIIIIIII!
GOOD-BYE! I'LL SEE YOU TOMORROW, HINACCHAN!

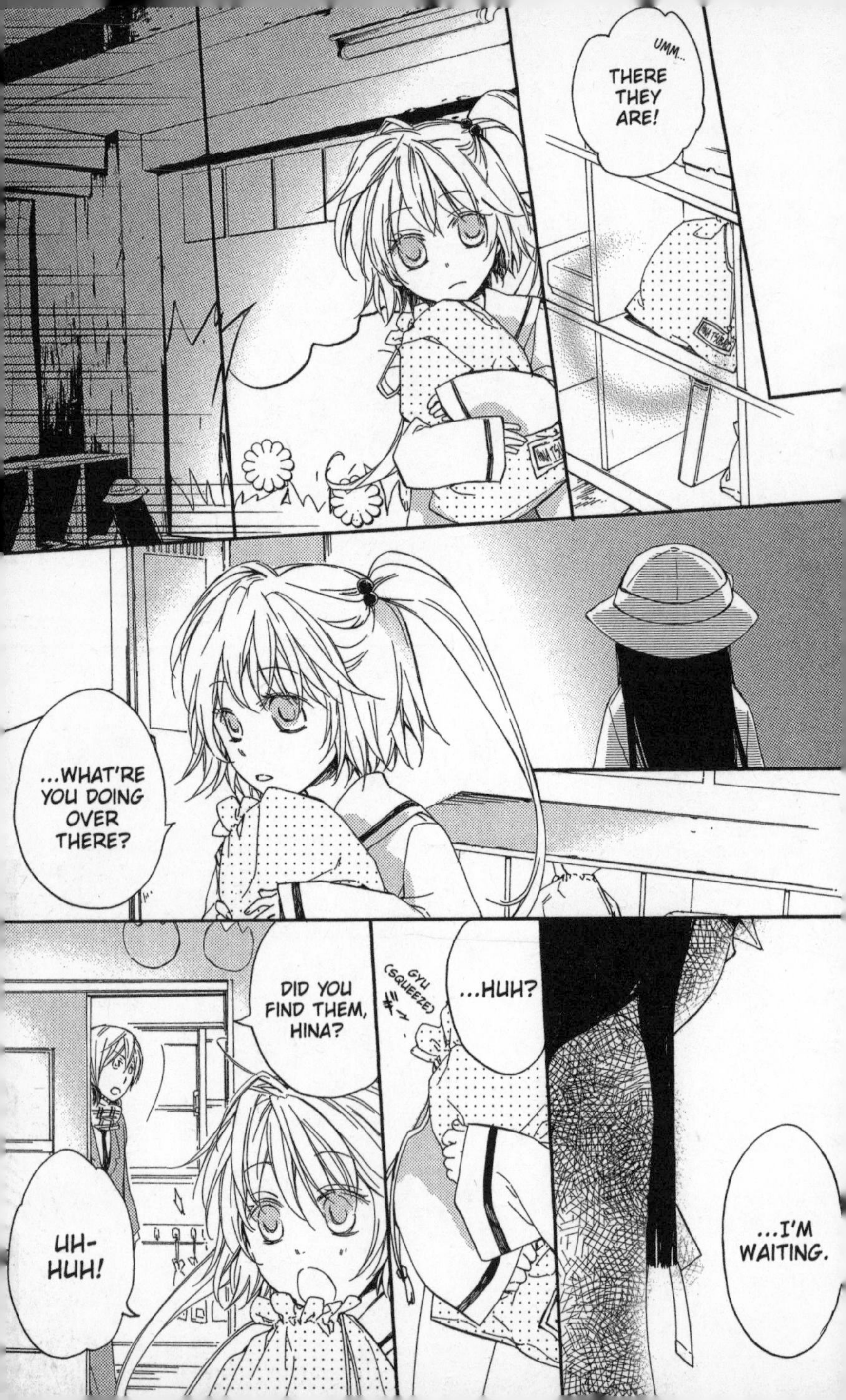
UMM...
THERE THEY ARE!
HINA TSUBAKI
...WHAT'RE YOU DOING OVER THERE?
...I'M WAITING.
...HUH?
GYU (SQUEEZE)
DID YOU FIND THEM, HINA?
UH-HUH!

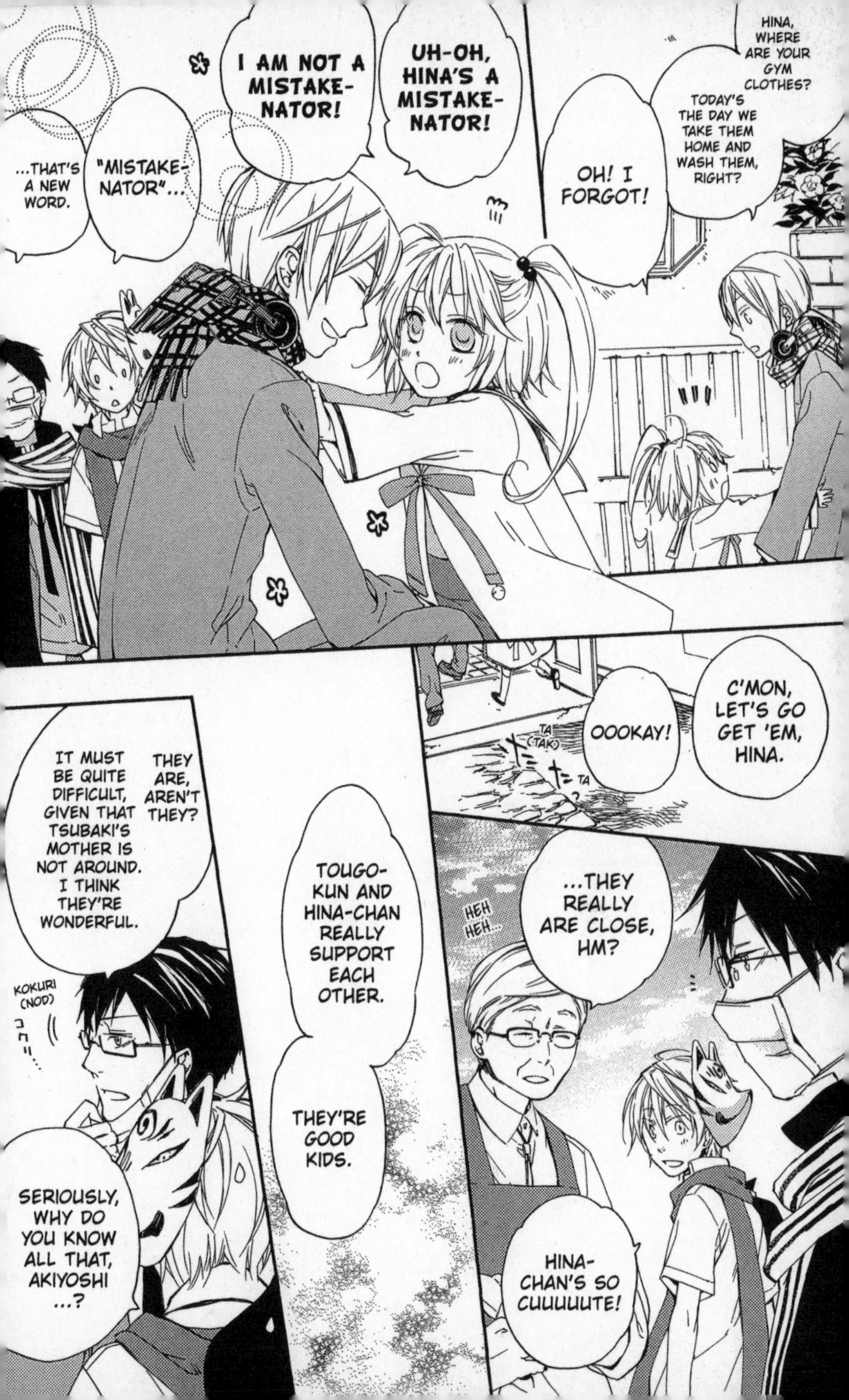

HINA, WHERE ARE YOUR GYM CLOTHES?
TODAY'S THE DAY WE TAKE THEM HOME AND WASH THEM, RIGHT?
OH! I FORGOT!
UH-OH, HINA'S A MISTAKE-NATOR!
I AM NOT A MISTAKE-NATOR!
"MISTAKE-NATOR"...
...THAT'S A NEW WORD.
C'MON, LET'S GO GET 'EM, HINA.
OOOKAY!
TA (TAK)
TA
...THEY REALLY ARE CLOSE, HM?
HEH HEH...
HINA-CHAN'S SO CUUUUUTE!
TOUGO-KUN AND HINA-CHAN REALLY SUPPORT EACH OTHER.
THEY'RE GOOD KIDS.
THEY ARE, AREN'T THEY?
IT MUST BE QUITE DIFFICULT, GIVEN THAT TSUBAKI'S MOTHER IS NOT AROUND. I THINK THEY'RE WONDERFUL.
KOKURI (NOD)
SERIOUSLY, WHY DO YOU KNOW ALL THAT, AKIYOSHI ...?

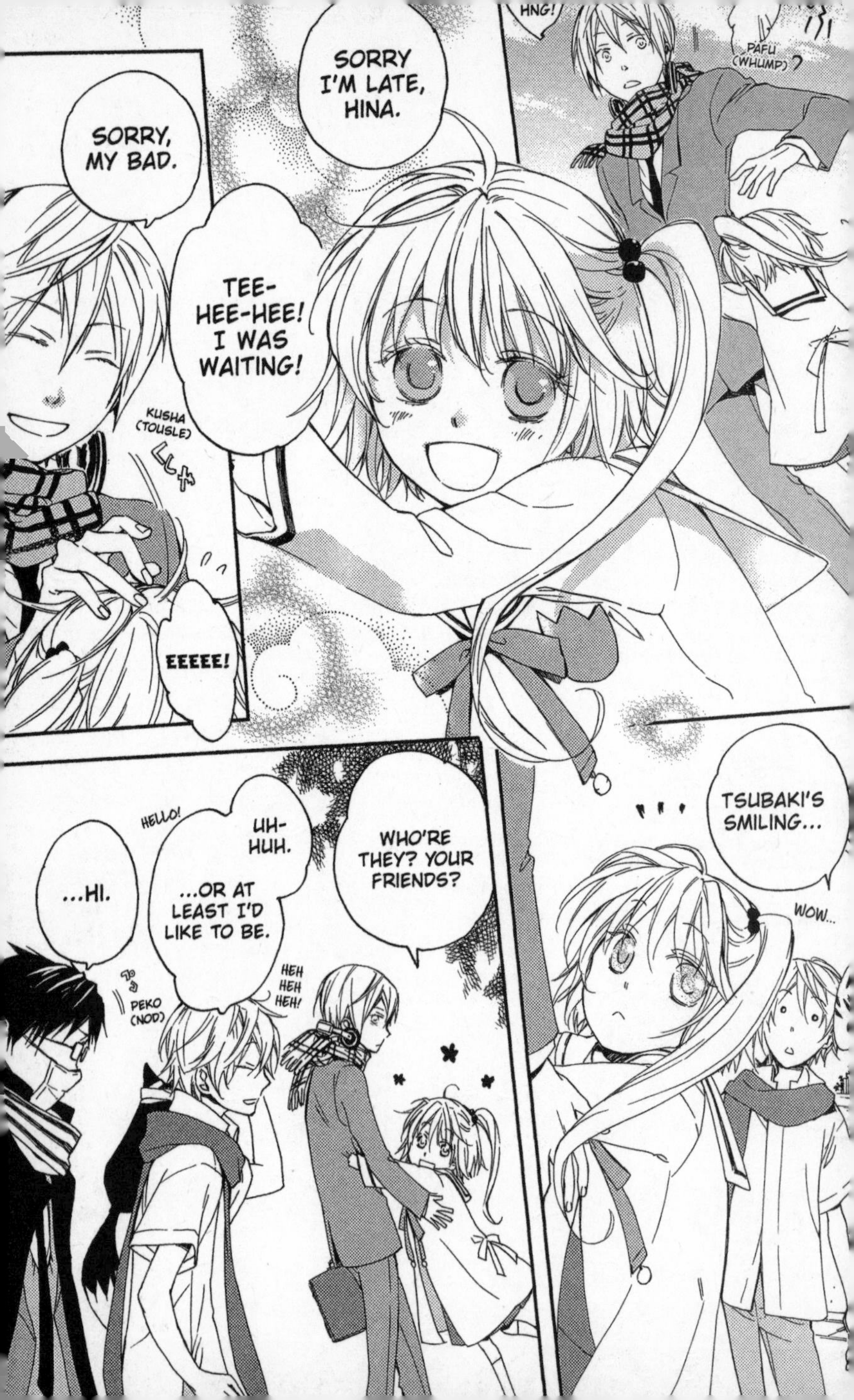
HNG!
PAFU (WHUMP)
SORRY I'M LATE, HINA.
TEE-HEE-HEE! I WAS WAITING!
SORRY, MY BAD.
KUSHA (TOUSLE)
EEEEE!
TSUBAKI'S SMILING...
WOW...
WHO'RE THEY? YOUR FRIENDS?
UH-HUH.
...OR AT LEAST I'D LIKE TO BE.
HEH HEH HEH!
HELLO!
...HI.
PEKO (NOD)

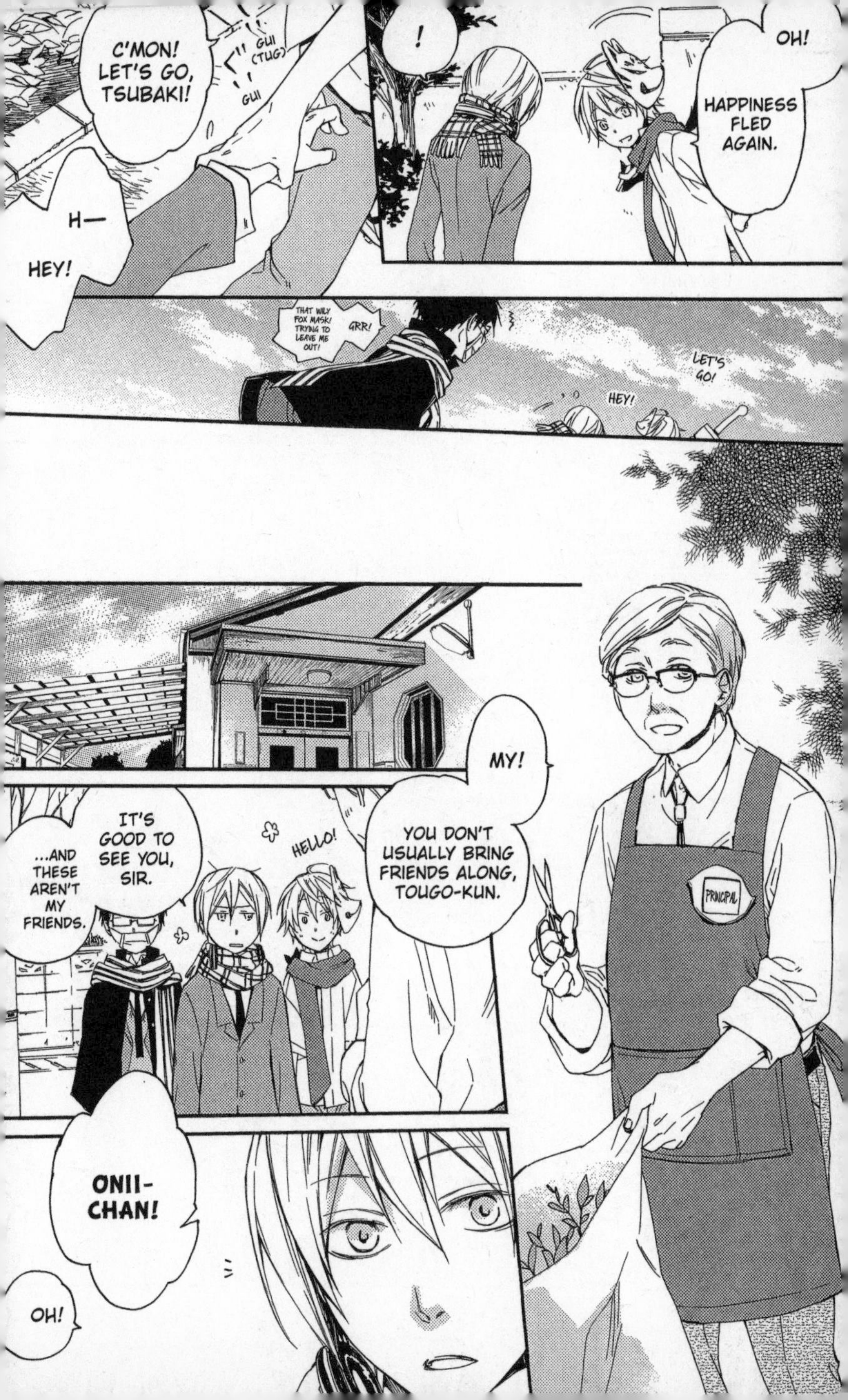
OH!
HAPPINESS FLED AGAIN.
!
C'MON! LET'S GO, TSUBAKI!
GUI (TUG)
GUI
H—
HEY!
LET'S GO!
HEY!
GRR!
THAT WILY FOX MASK! TRYING TO LEAVE ME OUT!
MY!
YOU DON'T USUALLY BRING FRIENDS ALONG, TOUGO-KUN.
PRINCIPAL
HELLO!
IT'S GOOD TO SEE YOU, SIR.
...AND THESE AREN'T MY FRIENDS.
ONII-CHAN!
OH!

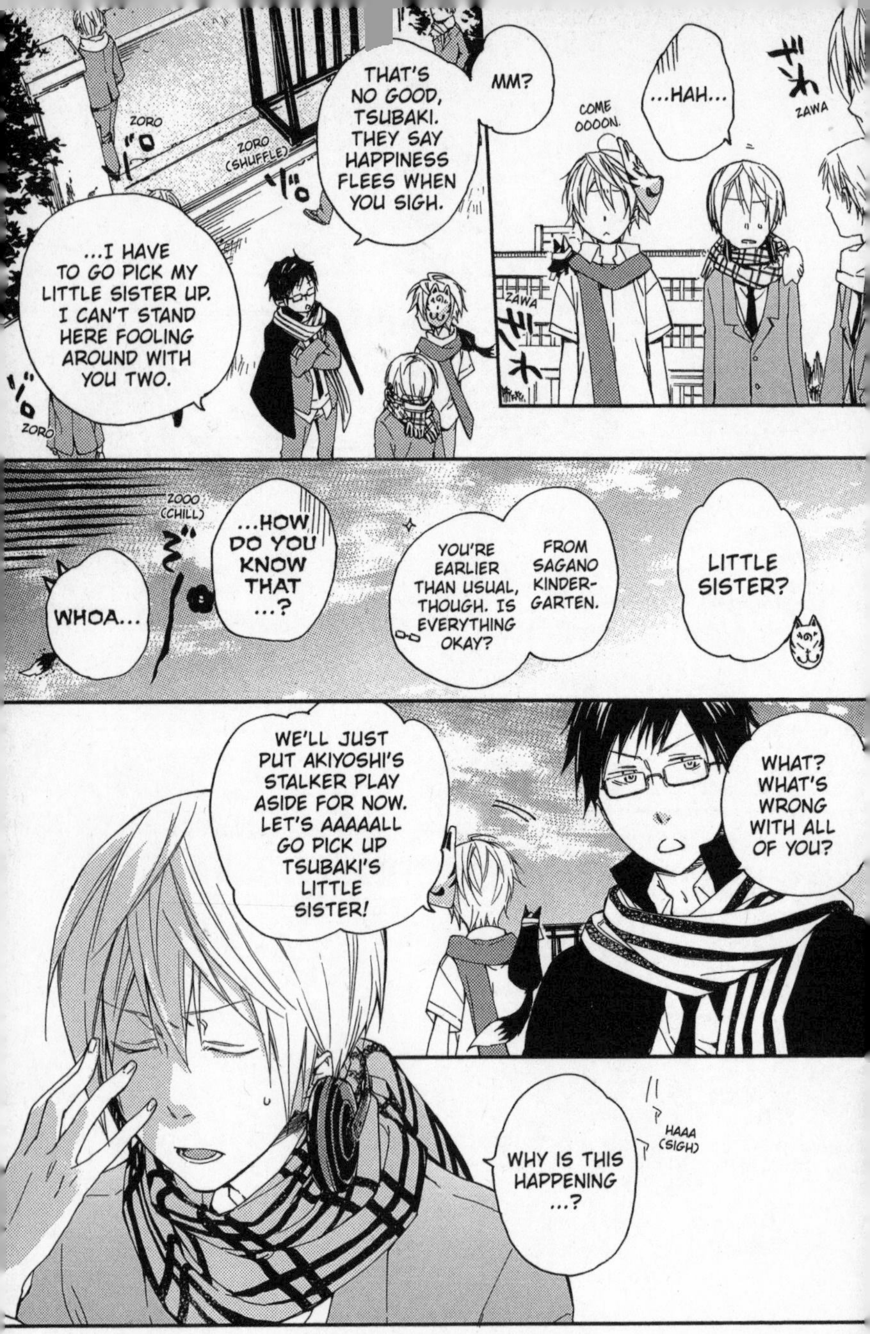
ZAWA
...HAH...
COME OOOON.
ZAWA
MM?
THAT'S NO GOOD, TSUBAKI. THEY SAY HAPPINESS FLEES WHEN YOU SIGH.
ZORO (SHUFFLE)
ZORO
...I HAVE TO GO PICK MY LITTLE SISTER UP. I CAN'T STAND HERE FOOLING AROUND WITH YOU TWO.
ZORO
LITTLE SISTER?
FROM SAGANO KINDERGARTEN.
YOU'RE EARLIER THAN USUAL, THOUGH. IS EVERYTHING OKAY?
...HOW DO YOU KNOW THAT ...?
ZOOO (CHILL)
WHOA...
WHAT? WHAT'S WRONG WITH ALL OF YOU?
WE'LL JUST PUT AKIYOSHI'S STALKER PLAY ASIDE FOR NOW. LET'S AAAAALL GO PICK UP TSUBAKI'S LITTLE SISTER!
HAAA (SIGH)
WHY IS THIS HAPPENING ...?

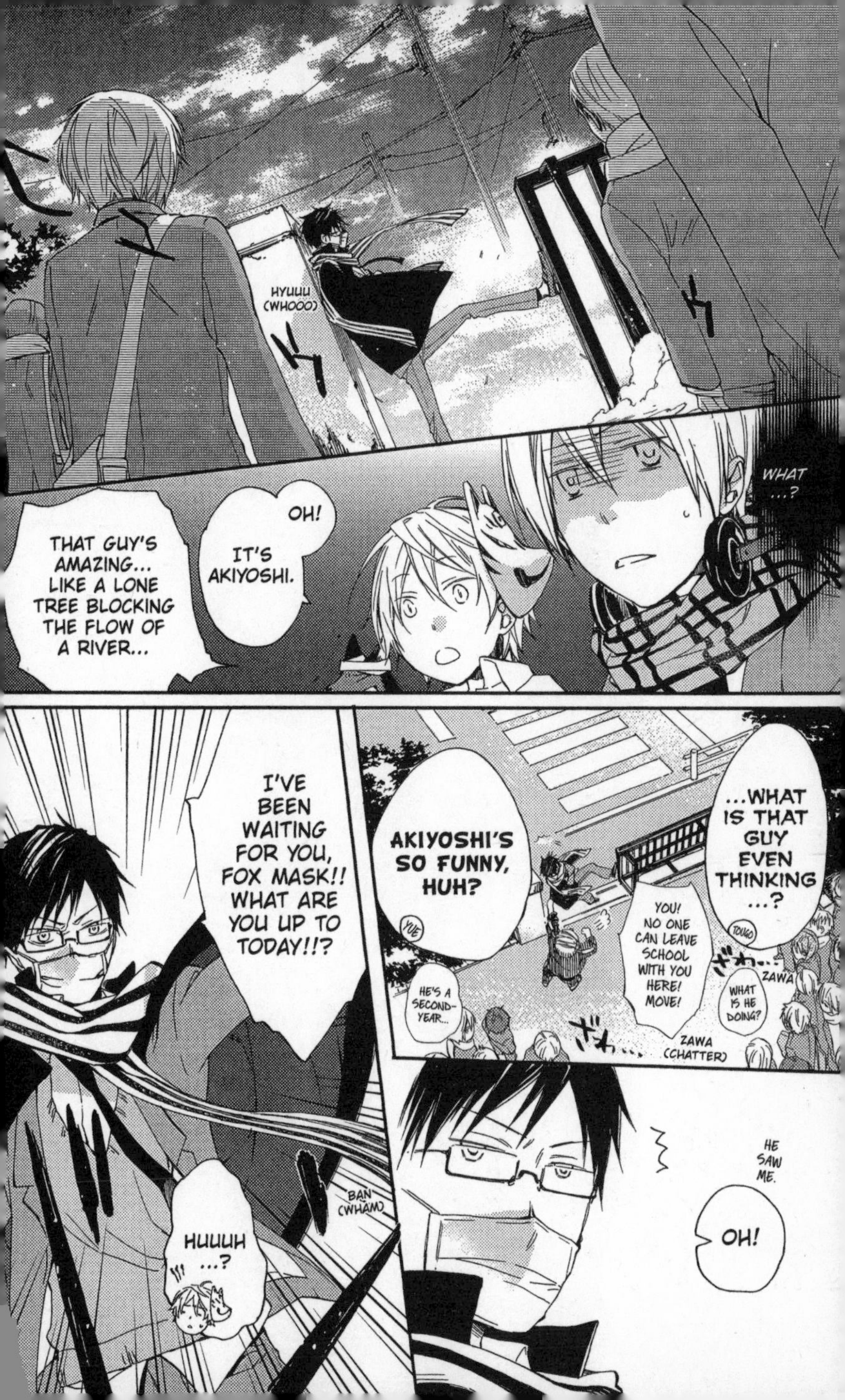
HYUUU (WHOOO)
WHAT ...?
OH!
IT'S AKIYOSHI.
THAT GUY'S AMAZING... LIKE A LONE TREE BLOCKING THE FLOW OF A RIVER...
...WHAT IS THAT GUY EVEN THINKING ...?
TOUGO
AKIYOSHI'S SO FUNNY, HUH?
YUE
ZAWA
WHAT IS HE DOING?
YOU! NO ONE CAN LEAVE SCHOOL WITH YOU HERE! MOVE!
ZAWA (CHATTER)
HE'S A SECOND-YEAR...
HE SAW ME.
OH!
I'VE BEEN WAITING FOR YOU, FOX MASK!! WHAT ARE YOU UP TO TODAY!!?
BAN (WHAM)
HUUUH ...?

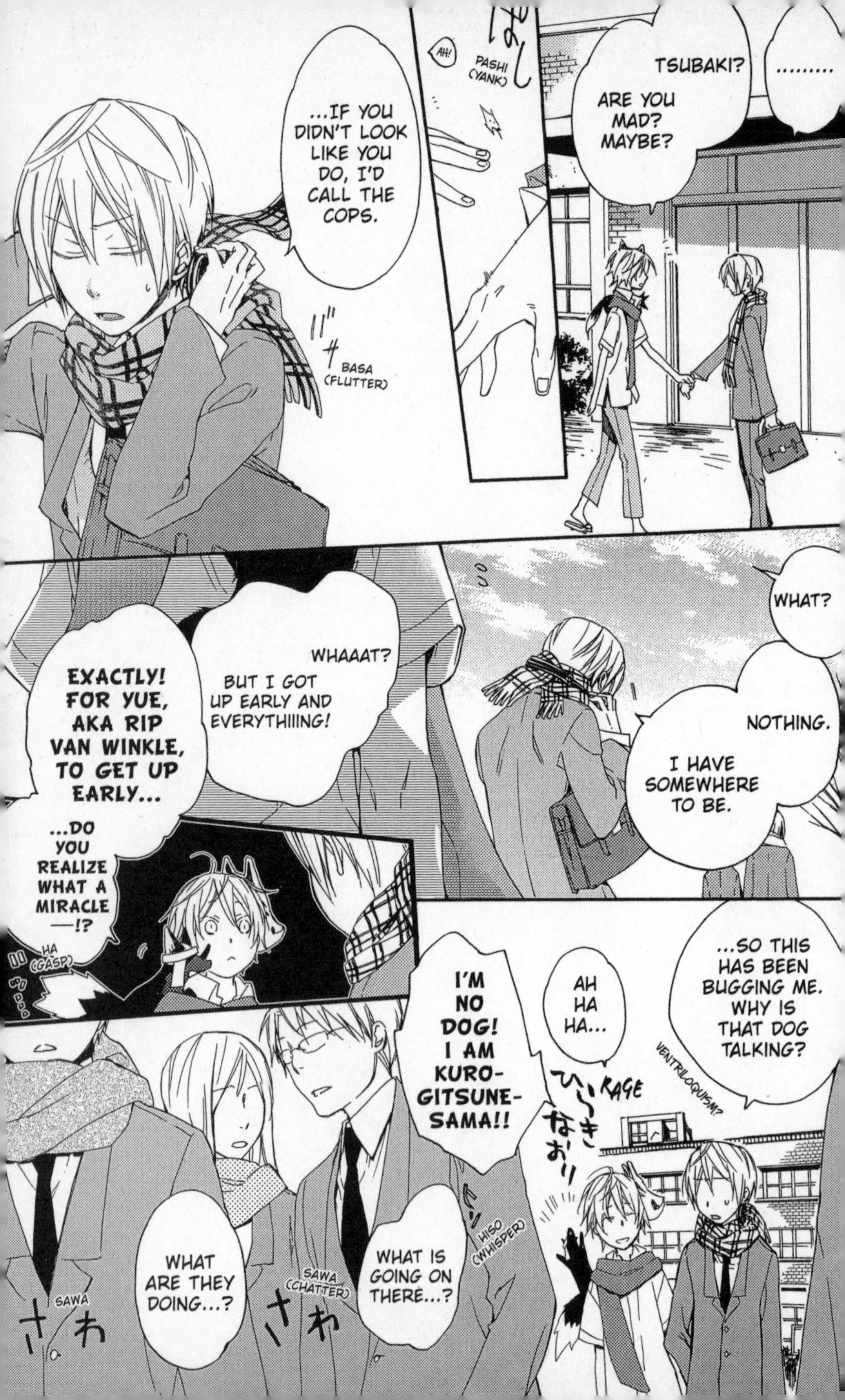
....
TSUBAKI? ARE YOU MAD? MAYBE?
AH!
PASHI (YANK)
...IF YOU DIDN'T LOOK LIKE YOU DO, I'D CALL THE COPS.
BASA (FLUTTER)
WHAT?
NOTHING. I HAVE SOMEWHERE TO BE.
WHAAAT? BUT I GOT UP EARLY AND EVERYTHIIIING!
EXACTLY! FOR YUE, AKA RIP VAN WINKLE, TO GET UP EARLY...
...DO YOU REALIZE WHAT A MIRACLE—!?
HA (GASP)
...SO THIS HAS BEEN BUGGING ME. WHY IS THAT DOG TALKING?
VENTRILOQUISM?
AH HA HA...
I'M NO DOG! I AM KURO-GITSUNE-SAMA!!
RAGE
HISO (WHISPER)
WHAT IS GOING ON THERE...?
SAWA (CHATTER)
WHAT ARE THEY DOING...?
SAWA

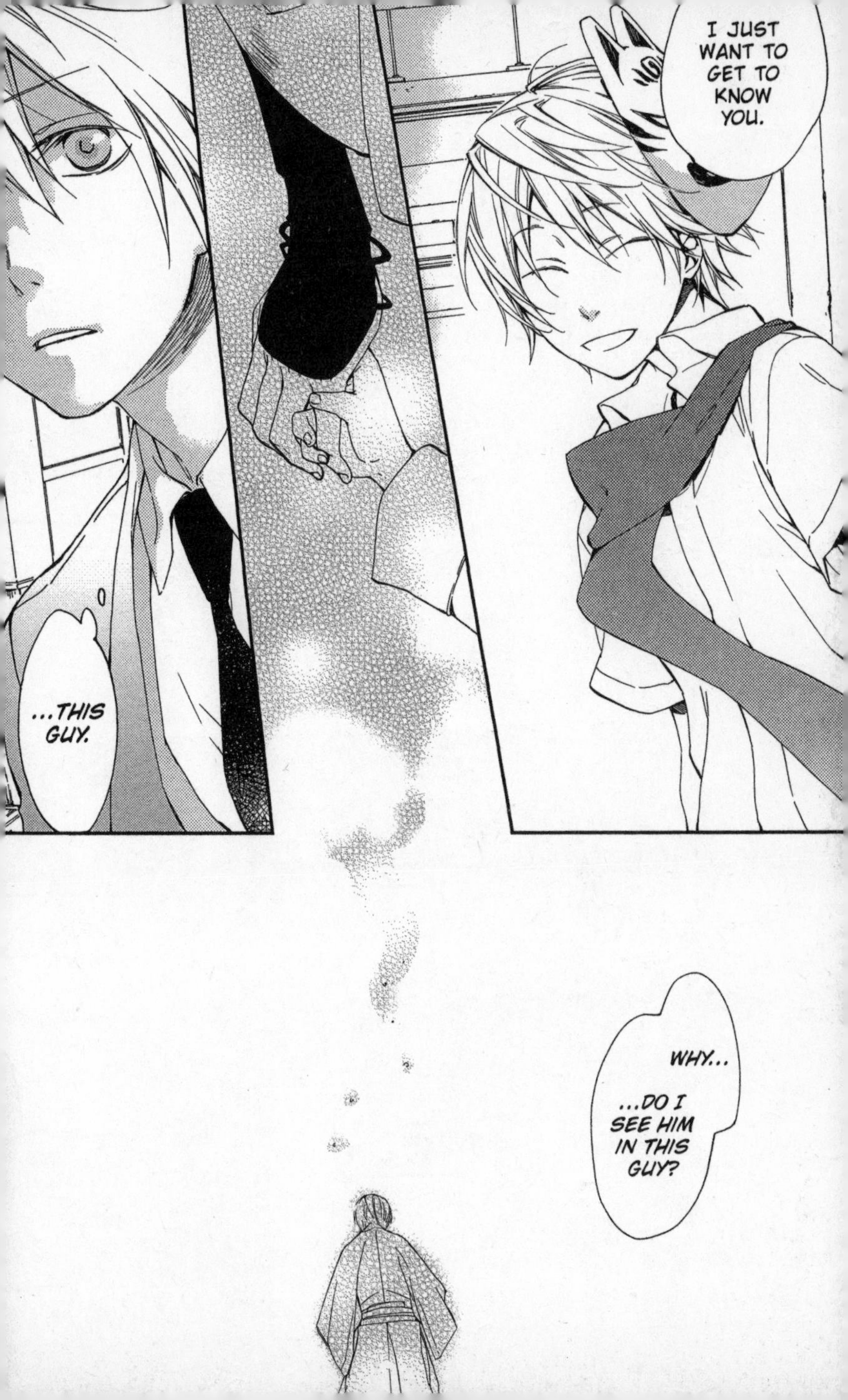
I JUST WANT TO GET TO KNOW YOU.
...THIS GUY.
WHY...
...DO I SEE HIM IN THIS GUY?

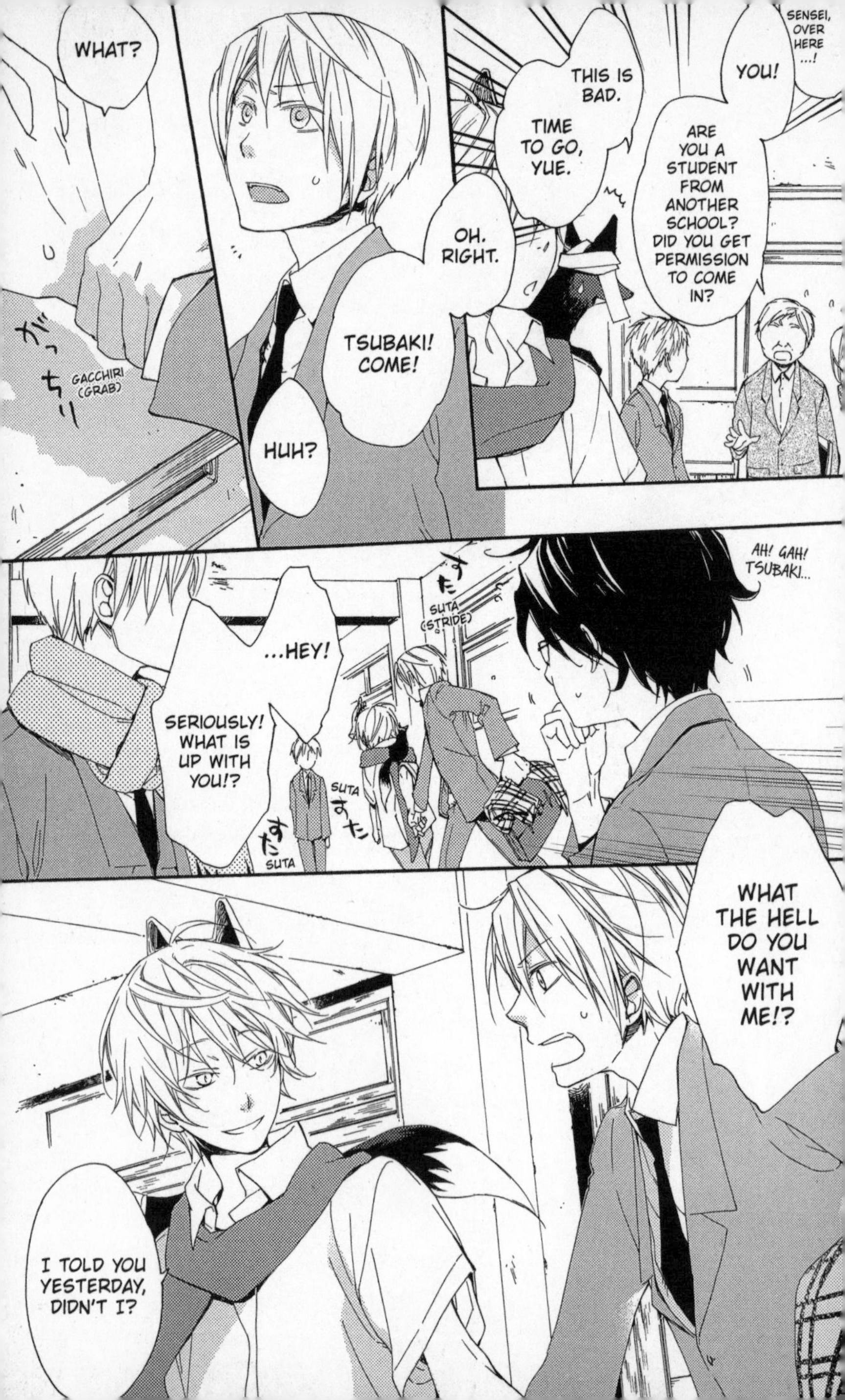
SENSEI, OVER HERE ...!
YOU!
ARE YOU A STUDENT FROM ANOTHER SCHOOL? DID YOU GET PERMISSION TO COME IN?
THIS IS BAD.
TIME TO GO, YUE.
OH. RIGHT.
TSUBAKI! COME!
HUH?
WHAT?
GACCHIRI (GRAB)
AH! GAH! TSUBAKI...
SUTA (STRIDE)
...HEY!
SERIOUSLY! WHAT IS UP WITH YOU!?
SUTA
SUTA
WHAT THE HELL DO YOU WANT WITH ME!?
I TOLD YOU YESTERDAY, DIDN'T I?

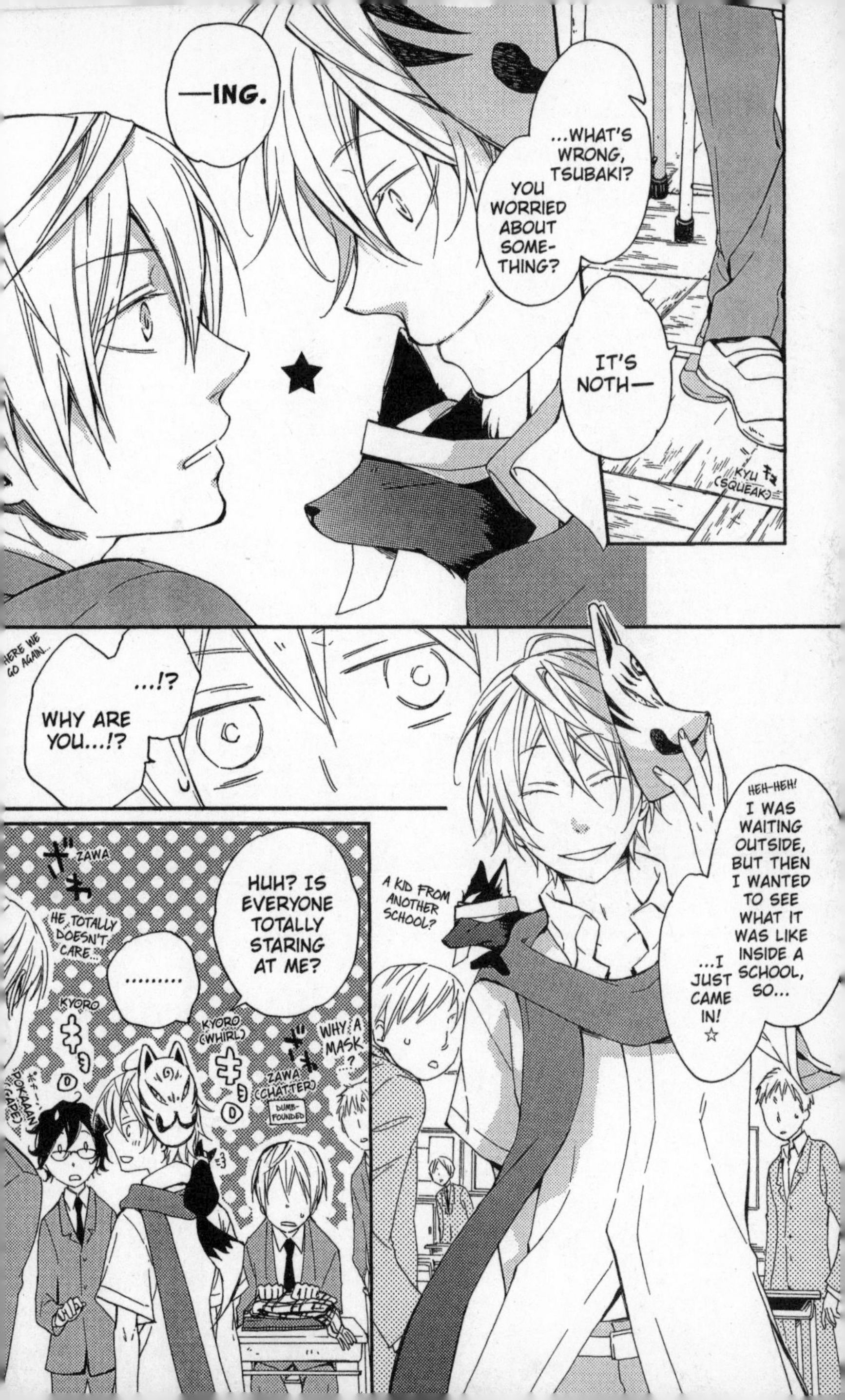

...WHAT'S WRONG, TSUBAKI? YOU WORRIED ABOUT SOMETHING?
IT'S NOTH—
KYU (SQUEAK)
—ING.
HEH-HEH! I WAS WAITING OUTSIDE, BUT THEN I WANTED TO SEE WHAT IT WAS LIKE INSIDE A SCHOOL, SO...
...I JUST CAME IN! ☆
A KID FROM ANOTHER SCHOOL?
HERE WE GO AGAIN...
...!?
WHY ARE YOU...!?
HUH? IS EVERYONE TOTALLY STARING AT ME?
ZAWA
....
HE TOTALLY DOESN'T CARE...
KYORO
KYORO (WHIRL)
WHY A MASK?
ZAWA (CHATTER)
DUMB-FOUNDED
POKAAAN (GAPE)

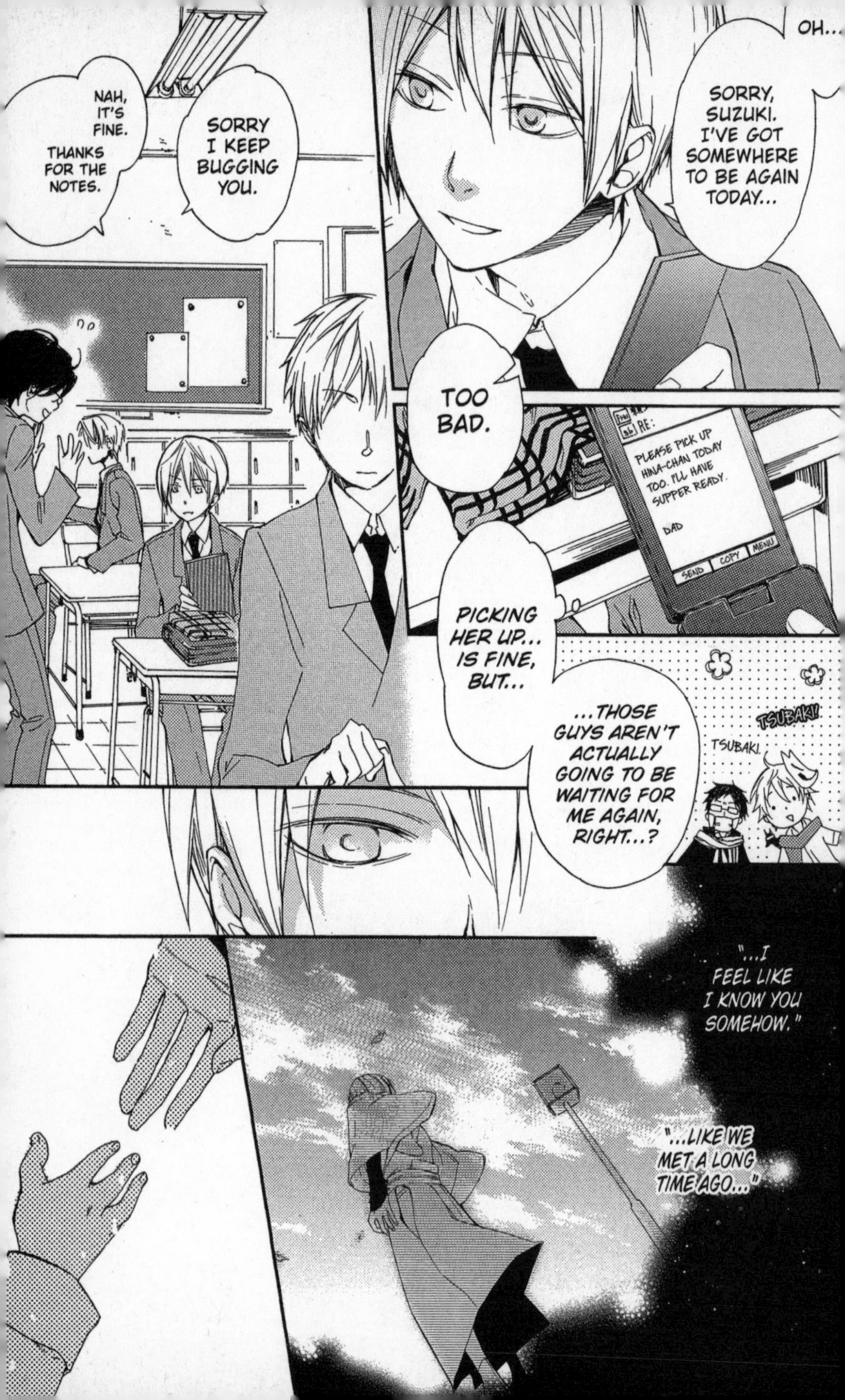
OH...
SORRY, SUZUKI. I'VE GOT SOMEWHERE TO BE AGAIN TODAY...
TOO BAD.
SORRY I KEEP BUGGING YOU.
NAH, IT'S FINE. THANKS FOR THE NOTES.
RE:
PLEASE PICK UP HINA-CHAN TODAY TOO. I'LL HAVE SUPPER READY.
DAD
SEND
COPY
MENU
PICKING HER UP... IS FINE, BUT...
TSUBAKI!
TSUBAKI.
...THOSE GUYS AREN'T ACTUALLY GOING TO BE WAITING FOR ME AGAIN, RIGHT...?
"...I FEEL LIKE I KNOW YOU SOMEHOW."
"...LIKE WE MET A LONG TIME AGO..."

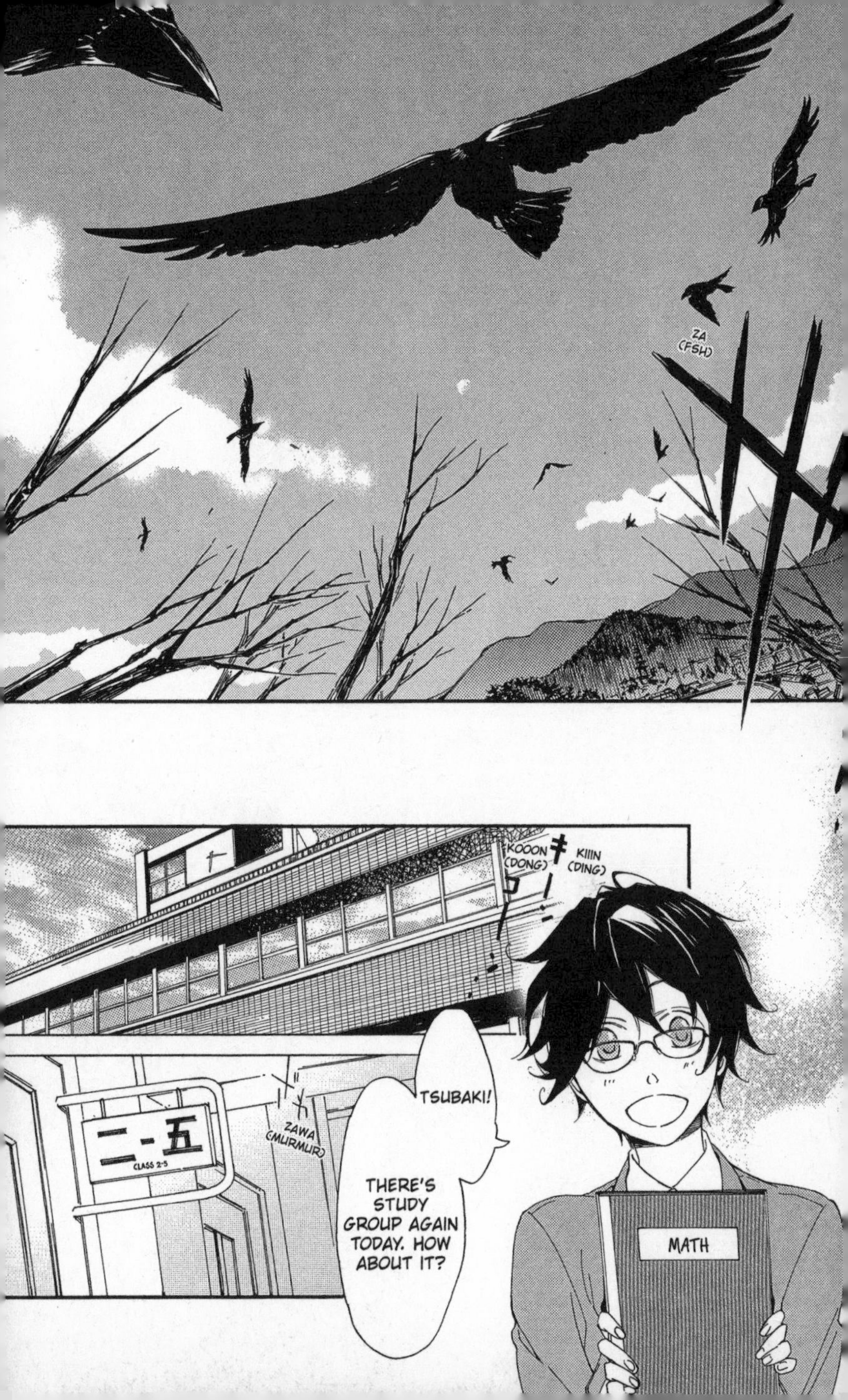
ZA
(FSH)
KIIN
(DING)
KOOON
(DONG)
TSUBAKI!
THERE'S STUDY GROUP AGAIN TODAY. HOW ABOUT IT?
MATH
ZAWA
(MURMUR)
二-五
CLASS 2-5

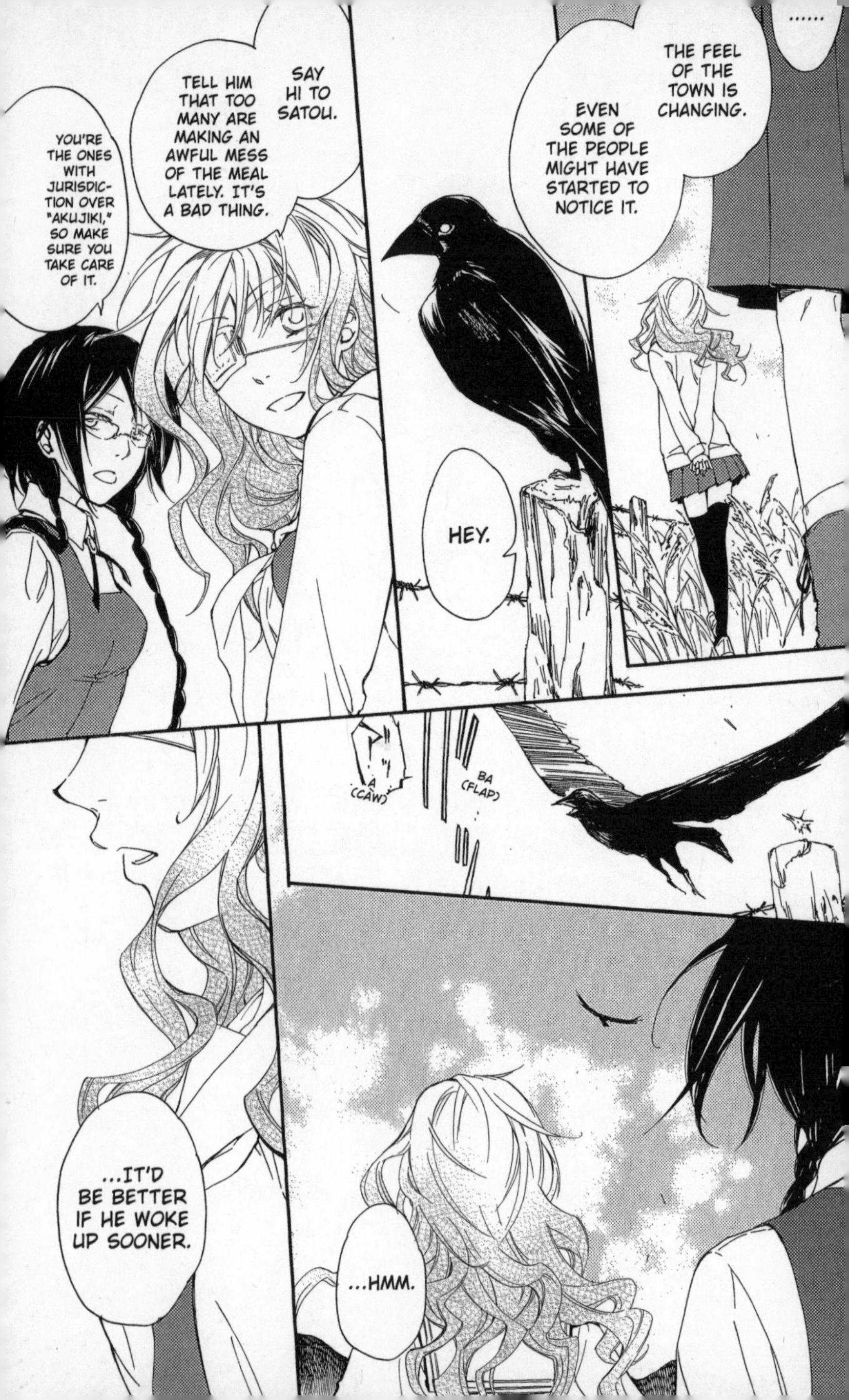
......
THE FEEL OF THE TOWN IS CHANGING.
EVEN SOME OF THE PEOPLE MIGHT HAVE STARTED TO NOTICE IT.
HEY.
SAY HI TO SATOU.
TELL HIM THAT TOO MANY ARE MAKING AN AWFUL MESS OF THE MEAL LATELY. IT'S A BAD THING.
YOU'RE THE ONES WITH JURISDICTION OVER "AKUJIKI," SO MAKE SURE YOU TAKE CARE OF IT.
BA (FLAP)
A (CAW)
...HMM.
...IT'D BE BETTER IF HE WOKE UP SOONER.

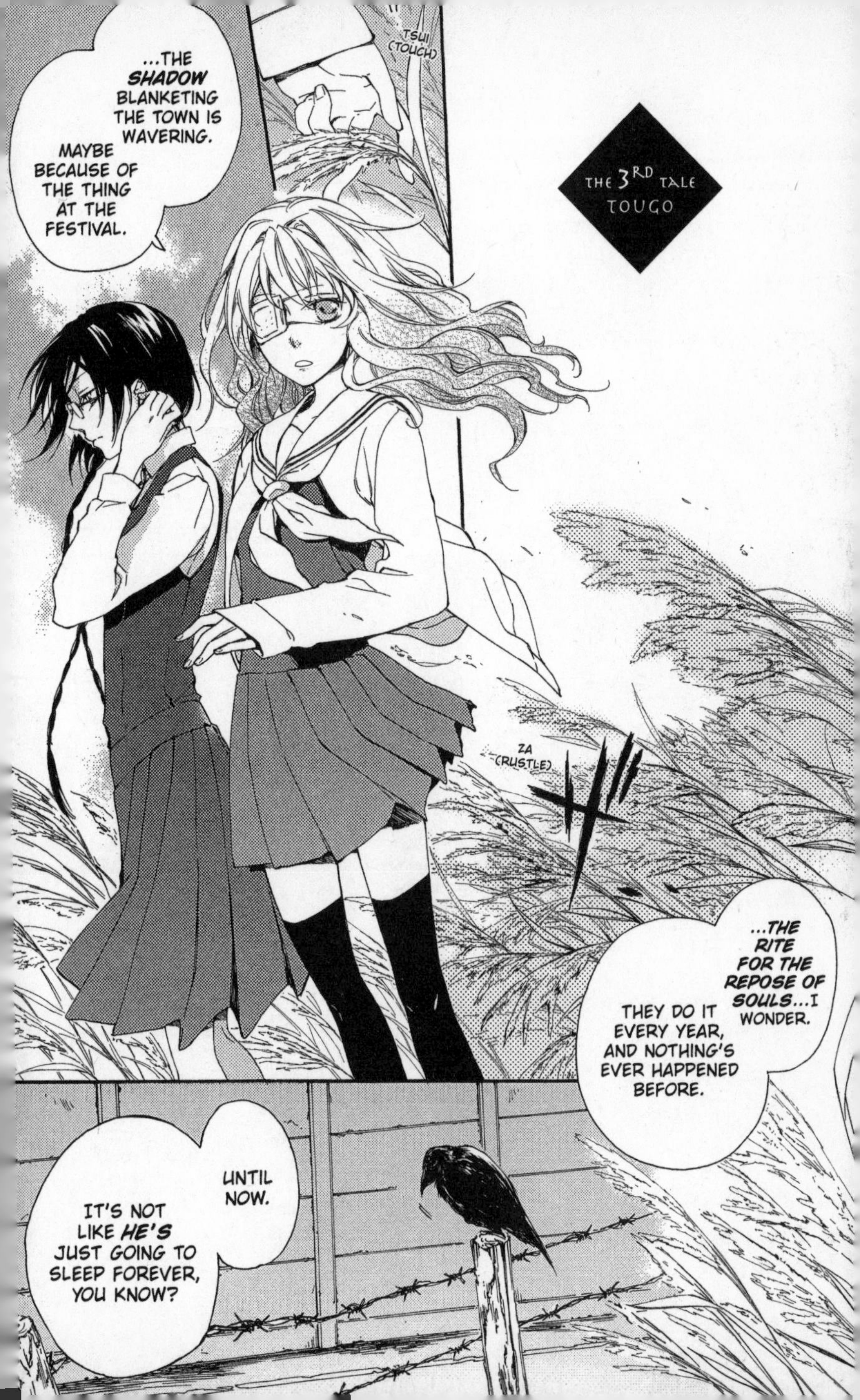
THE 3RD TALE
TOUGO
TSUI (TOUCH)
...THE SHADOW BLANKETING THE TOWN IS WAVERING.
MAYBE BECAUSE OF THE THING AT THE FESTIVAL.
ZA (RUSTLE)
...THE RITE FOR THE REPOSE OF SOULS...I WONDER.
THEY DO IT EVERY YEAR, AND NOTHING'S EVER HAPPENED BEFORE.
UNTIL NOW.
IT'S NOT LIKE HE'S JUST GOING TO SLEEP FOREVER, YOU KNOW?

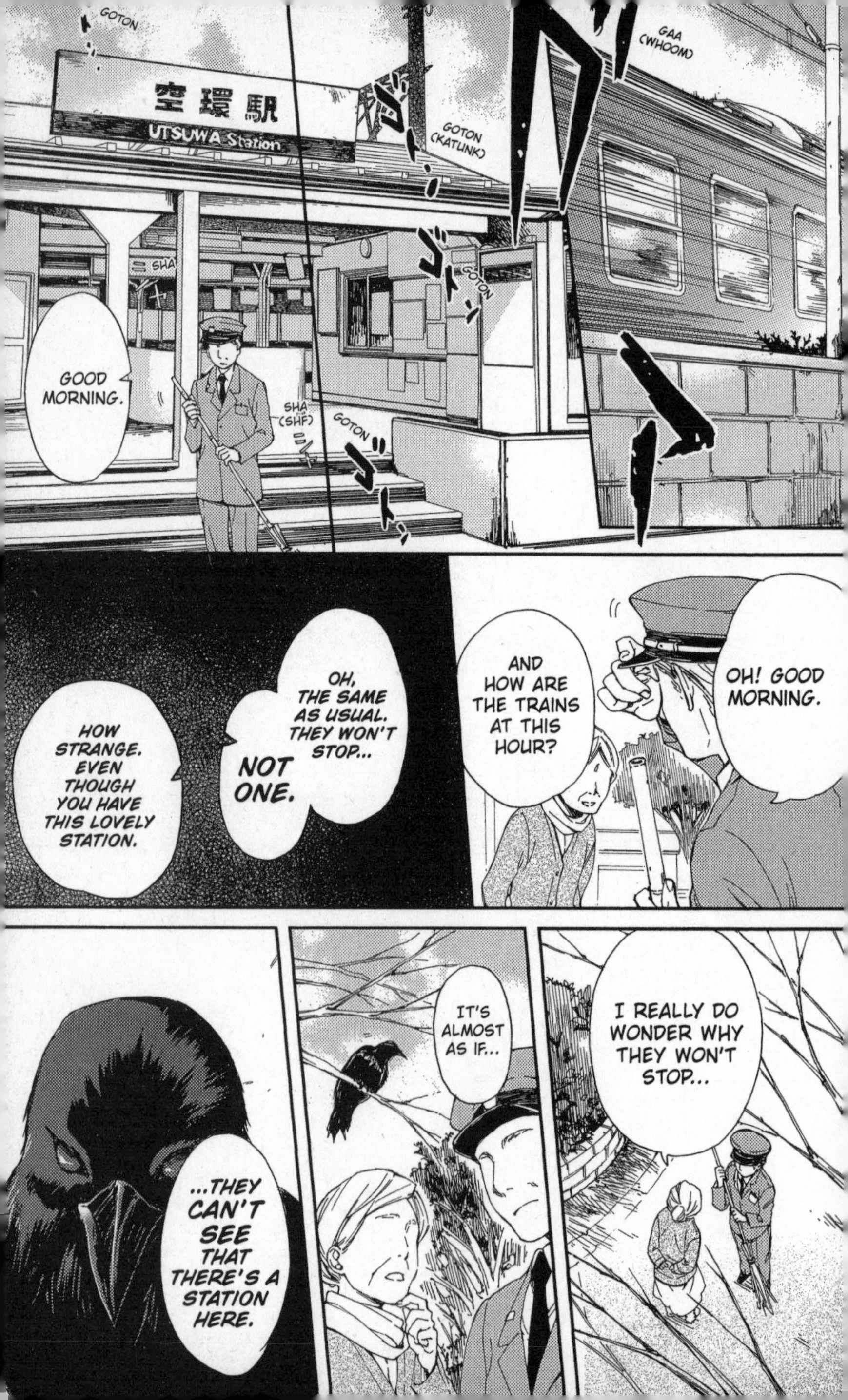
GAA (WHOOM)
GOTON (KATUNK)
GOTON
GOTON
空環駅
UTSUWA Station
SHA
SHA (SHF)
GOTON
GOOD MORNING.
OH! GOOD MORNING.
AND HOW ARE THE TRAINS AT THIS HOUR?
OH, THE SAME AS USUAL. THEY WON'T STOP...
NOT ONE.
HOW STRANGE. EVEN THOUGH YOU HAVE THIS LOVELY STATION.
I REALLY DO WONDER WHY THEY WON'T STOP...
IT'S ALMOST AS IF...
...THEY CAN'T SEE THAT THERE'S A STATION HERE.

Of the Red,
the Light,
and the
Ayakashi

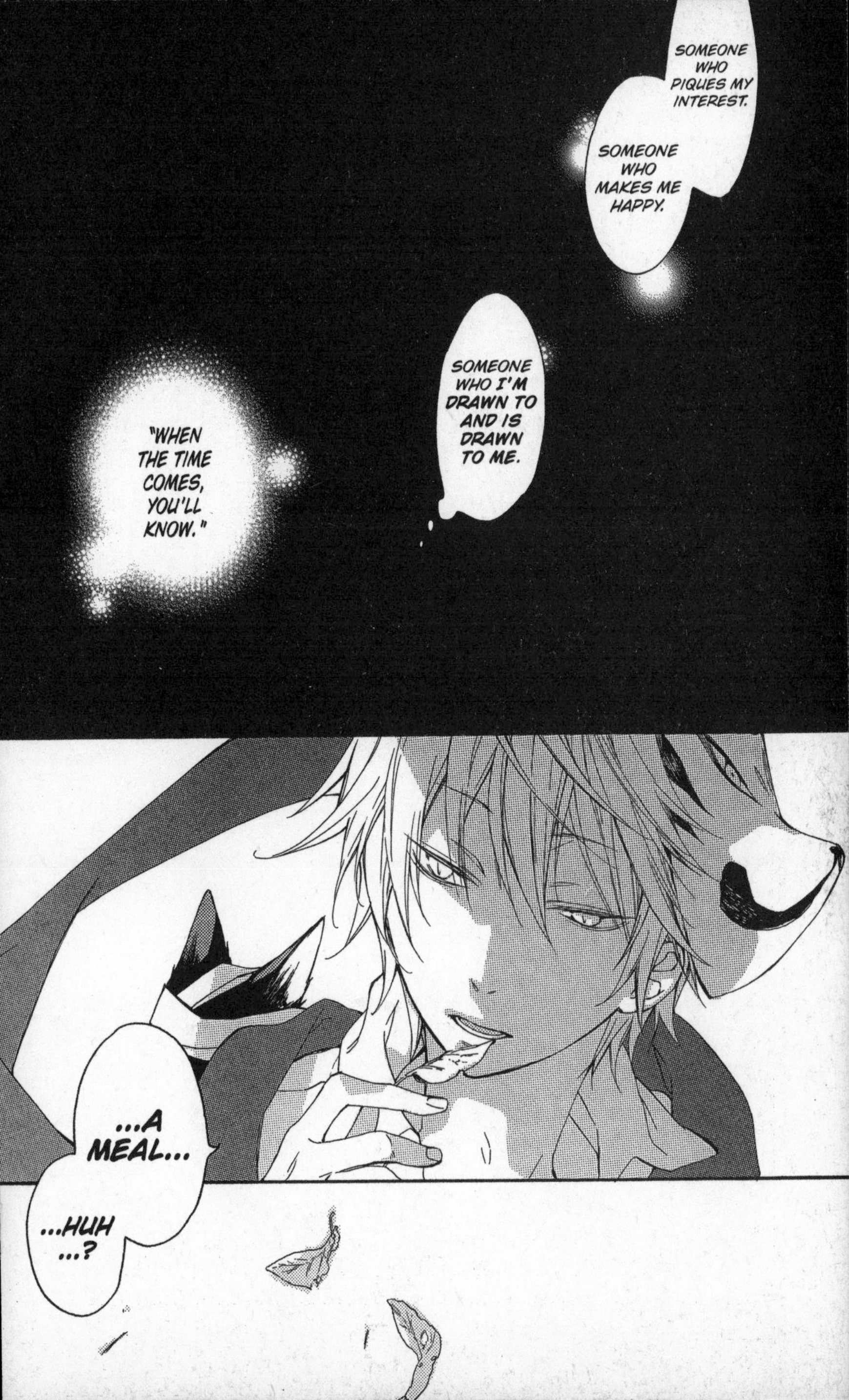
SOMEONE WHO PIQUES MY INTEREST.
SOMEONE WHO MAKES ME HAPPY.
SOMEONE WHO I'M DRAWN TO AND IS DRAWN TO ME.
"WHEN THE TIME COMES, YOU'LL KNOW."
...A MEAL...
...HUH ...?

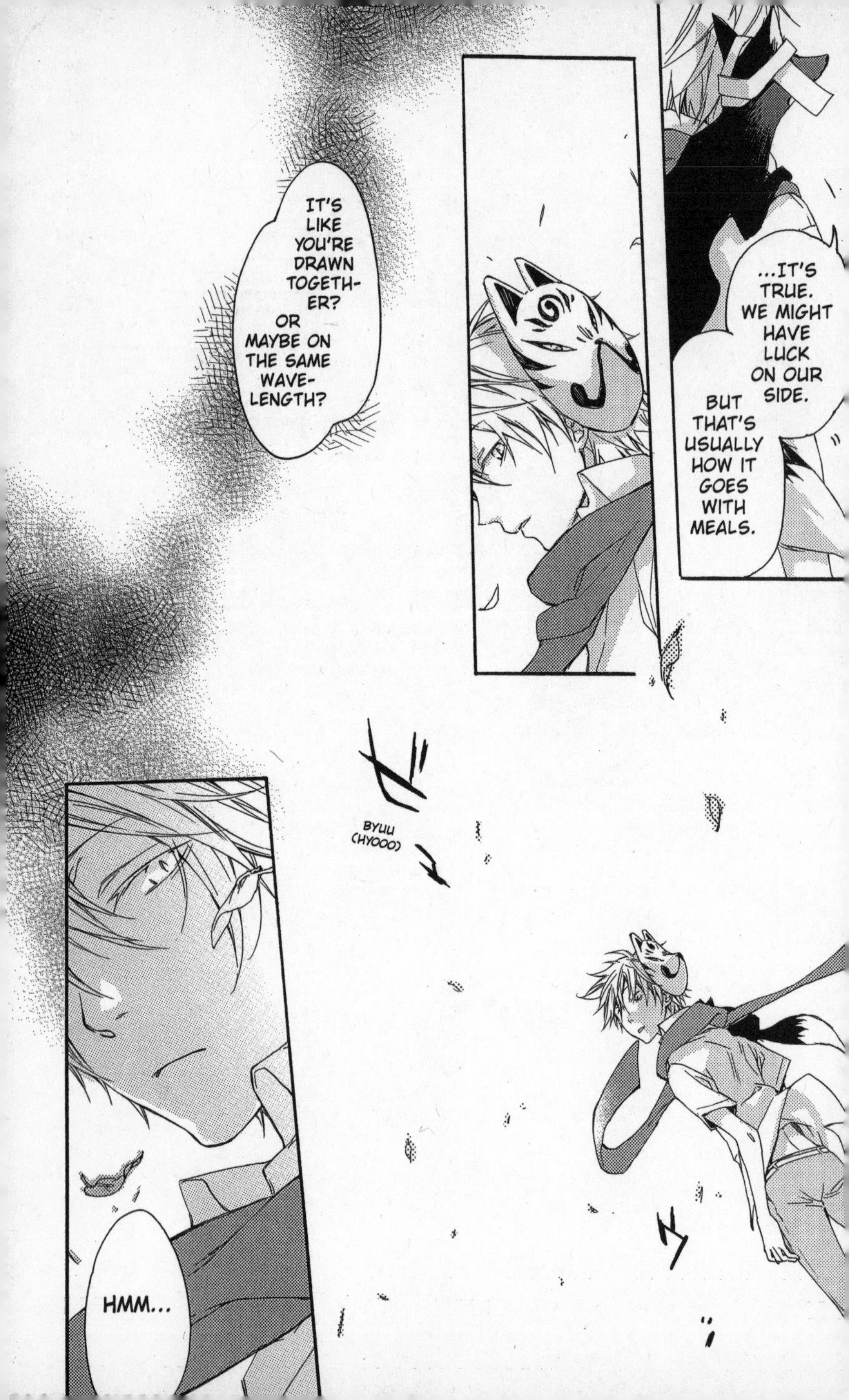
...IT'S TRUE. WE MIGHT HAVE LUCK ON OUR SIDE.
BUT THAT'S USUALLY HOW IT GOES WITH MEALS.
IT'S LIKE YOU'RE DRAWN TOGETHER? OR MAYBE ON THE SAME WAVE-LENGTH?
BYUU (HYOOO)
HMM...

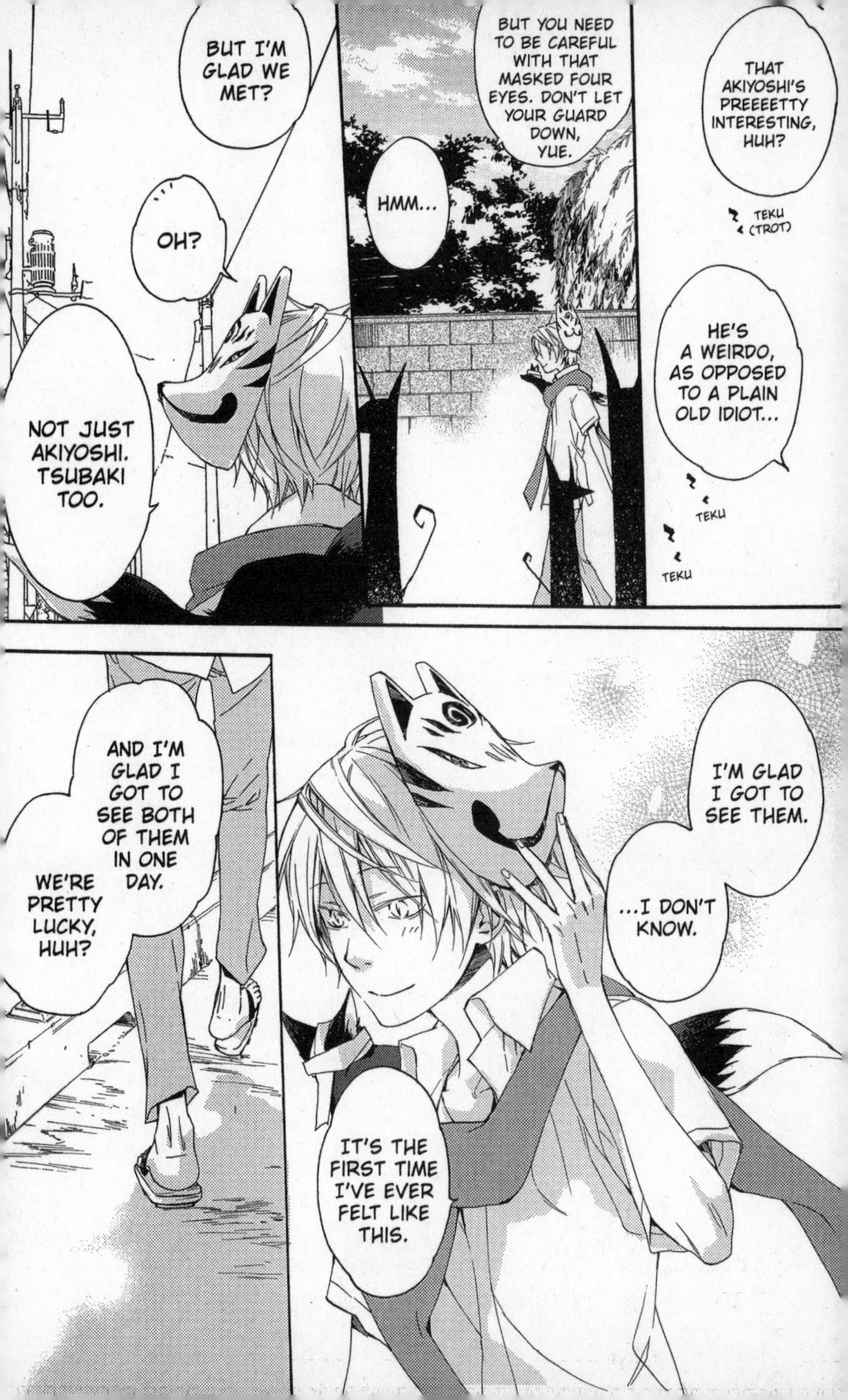
THAT AKIYOSHI'S PREEEETTY INTERESTING, HUH?
TEKU (TROT)
HE'S A WEIRDO, AS OPPOSED TO A PLAIN OLD IDIOT...
TEKU
TEKU
BUT YOU NEED TO BE CAREFUL WITH THAT MASKED FOUR EYES. DON'T LET YOUR GUARD DOWN, YUE.
HMM...
BUT I'M GLAD WE MET?
OH?
NOT JUST AKIYOSHI. TSUBAKI TOO.
I'M GLAD I GOT TO SEE THEM.
...I DON'T KNOW.
IT'S THE FIRST TIME I'VE EVER FELT LIKE THIS.
AND I'M GLAD I GOT TO SEE BOTH OF THEM IN ONE DAY.
WE'RE PRETTY LUCKY, HUH?

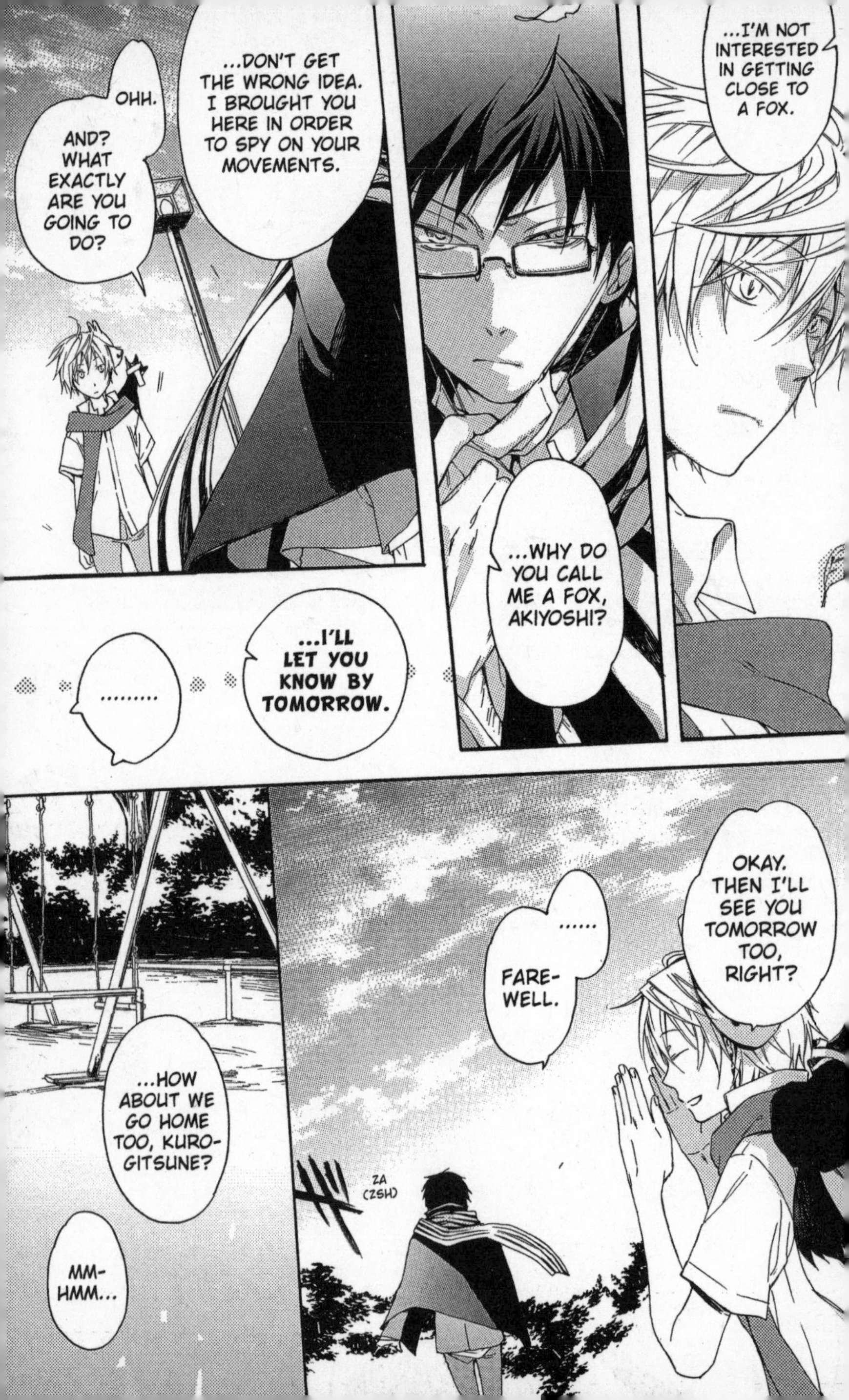
...I'M NOT INTERESTED IN GETTING CLOSE TO A FOX.
...WHY DO YOU CALL ME A FOX, AKIYOSHI?
...DON'T GET THE WRONG IDEA. I BROUGHT YOU HERE IN ORDER TO SPY ON YOUR MOVEMENTS.
OHH.
AND? WHAT EXACTLY ARE YOU GOING TO DO?
...I'LL LET YOU KNOW BY TOMORROW.
....
OKAY. THEN I'LL SEE YOU TOMORROW TOO, RIGHT?
......
FARE-WELL.
ZA (ZSH)
...HOW ABOUT WE GO HOME TOO, KURO-GITSUNE?
MM-HMM...

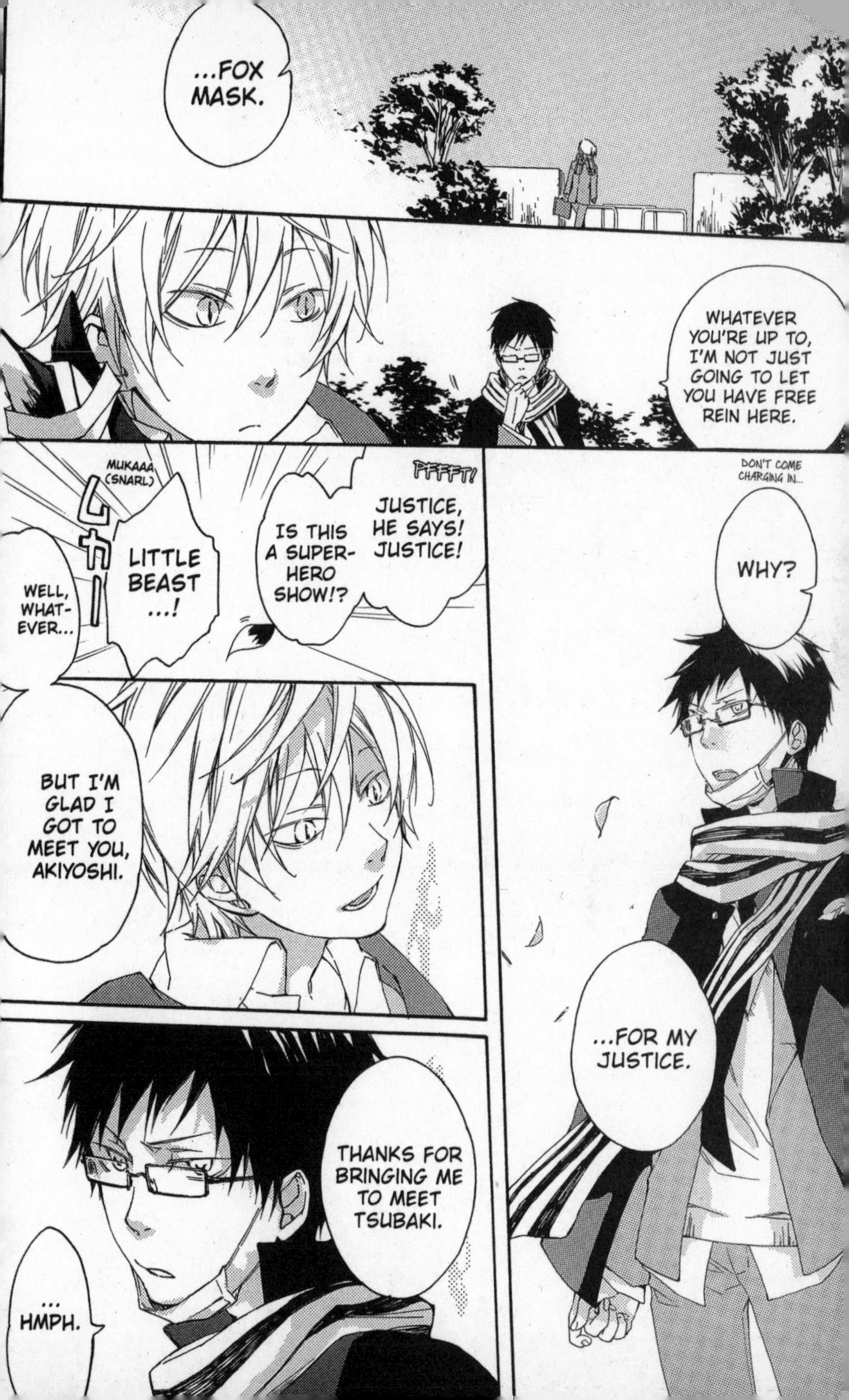
...FOX MASK.
WHATEVER YOU'RE UP TO, I'M NOT JUST GOING TO LET YOU HAVE FREE REIN HERE.
DON'T COME CHARGING IN...
WHY?
...FOR MY JUSTICE.
PFFFT!
JUSTICE, HE SAYS! JUSTICE!
IS THIS A SUPER-HERO SHOW!?
ムカー
MUKAAA (SNARL)
LITTLE BEAST ...!
WELL, WHAT-EVER...
BUT I'M GLAD I GOT TO MEET YOU, AKIYOSHI.
THANKS FOR BRINGING ME TO MEET TSUBAKI.
... HMPH.

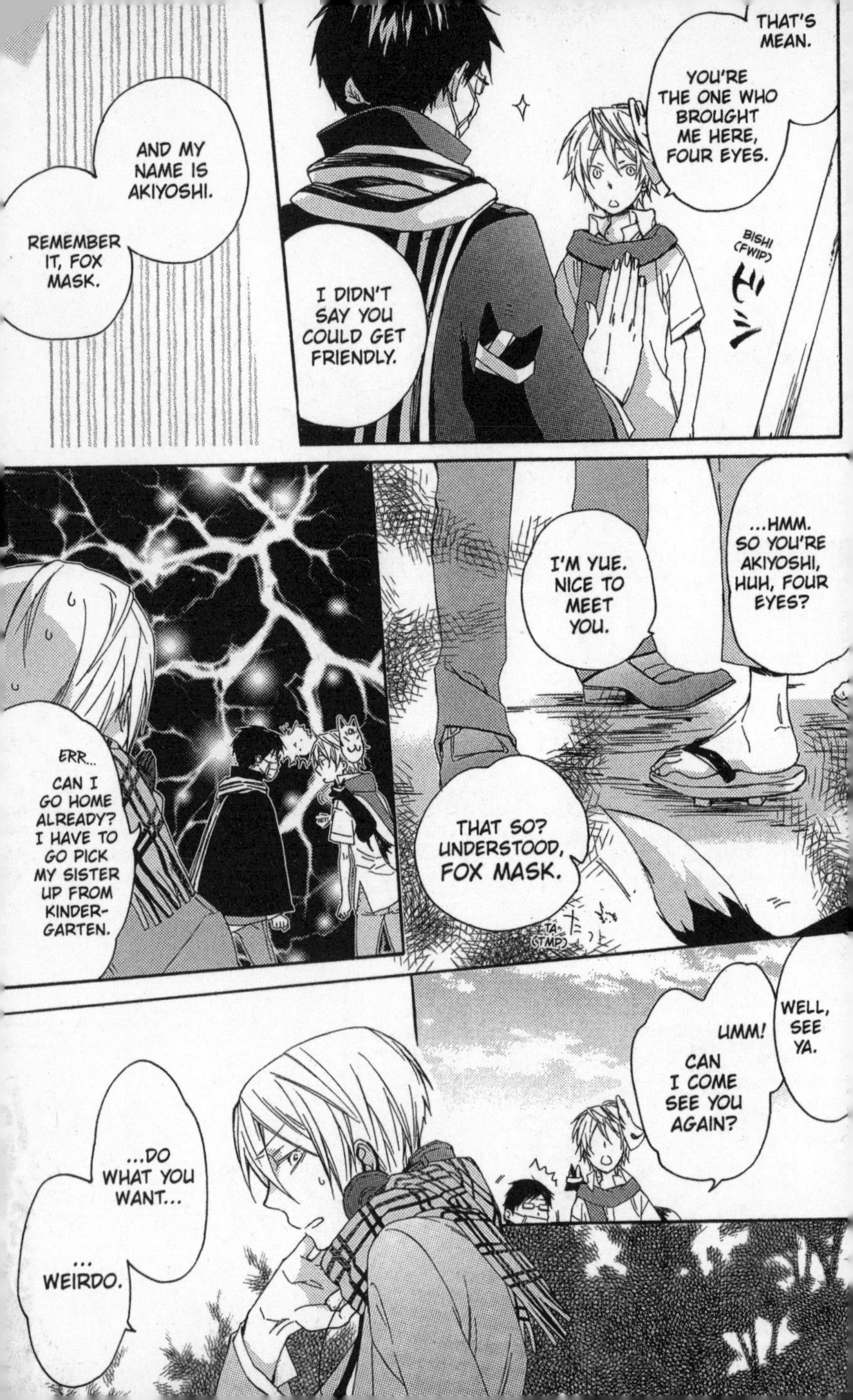
THAT'S MEAN.
YOU'RE THE ONE WHO BROUGHT ME HERE, FOUR EYES.
BISHI (FWIP)
I DIDN'T SAY YOU COULD GET FRIENDLY.
AND MY NAME IS AKIYOSHI.
REMEMBER IT, FOX MASK.
...HMM. SO YOU'RE AKIYOSHI, HUH, FOUR EYES?
I'M YUE. NICE TO MEET YOU.
THAT SO? UNDERSTOOD, FOX MASK.
TA (STMP)
ERR... CAN I GO HOME ALREADY? I HAVE TO GO PICK MY SISTER UP FROM KINDER-GARTEN.
WELL, SEE YA.
UMM! CAN I COME SEE YOU AGAIN?
...DO WHAT YOU WANT...
... WEIRDO.

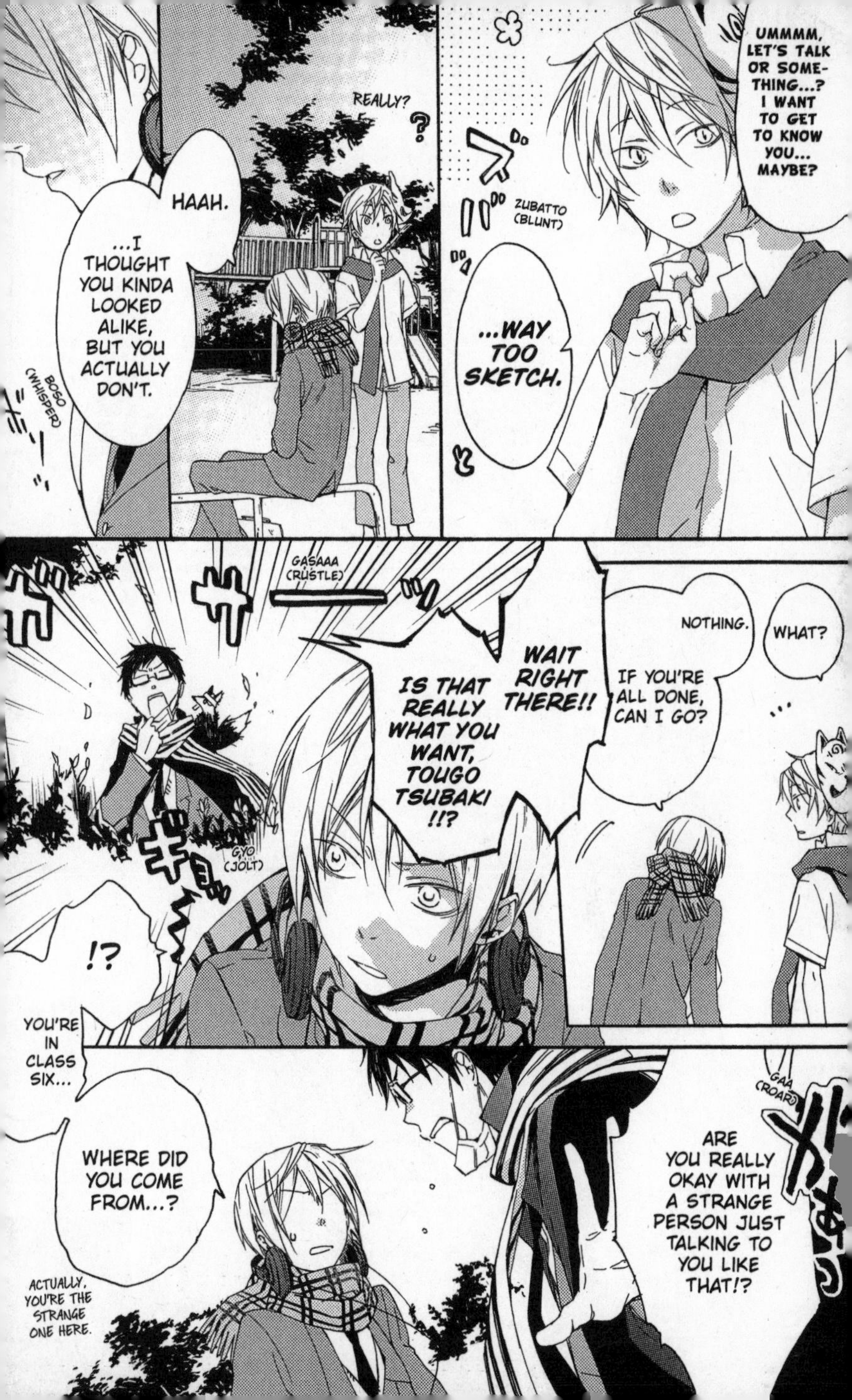
UMMMM, LET'S TALK OR SOME-THING...? I WANT TO GET TO KNOW YOU... MAYBE?
ZUBATTO (BLUNT)
...WAY TOO SKETCH.
REALLY?
HAAH.
...I THOUGHT YOU KINDA LOOKED ALIKE, BUT YOU ACTUALLY DON'T.
BOSO (WHISPER)
WHAT?
NOTHING.
IF YOU'RE ALL DONE, CAN I GO?
...
GASAAA (RUSTLE)
WAIT RIGHT THERE!!
IS THAT REALLY WHAT YOU WANT, TOUGO TSUBAKI!!?
GYO (JOLT)
!?
GAA (ROAR)
ARE YOU REALLY OKAY WITH A STRANGE PERSON JUST TALKING TO YOU LIKE THAT!?
YOU'RE IN CLASS SIX...
WHERE DID YOU COME FROM...?
ACTUALLY, YOU'RE THE STRANGE ONE HERE.

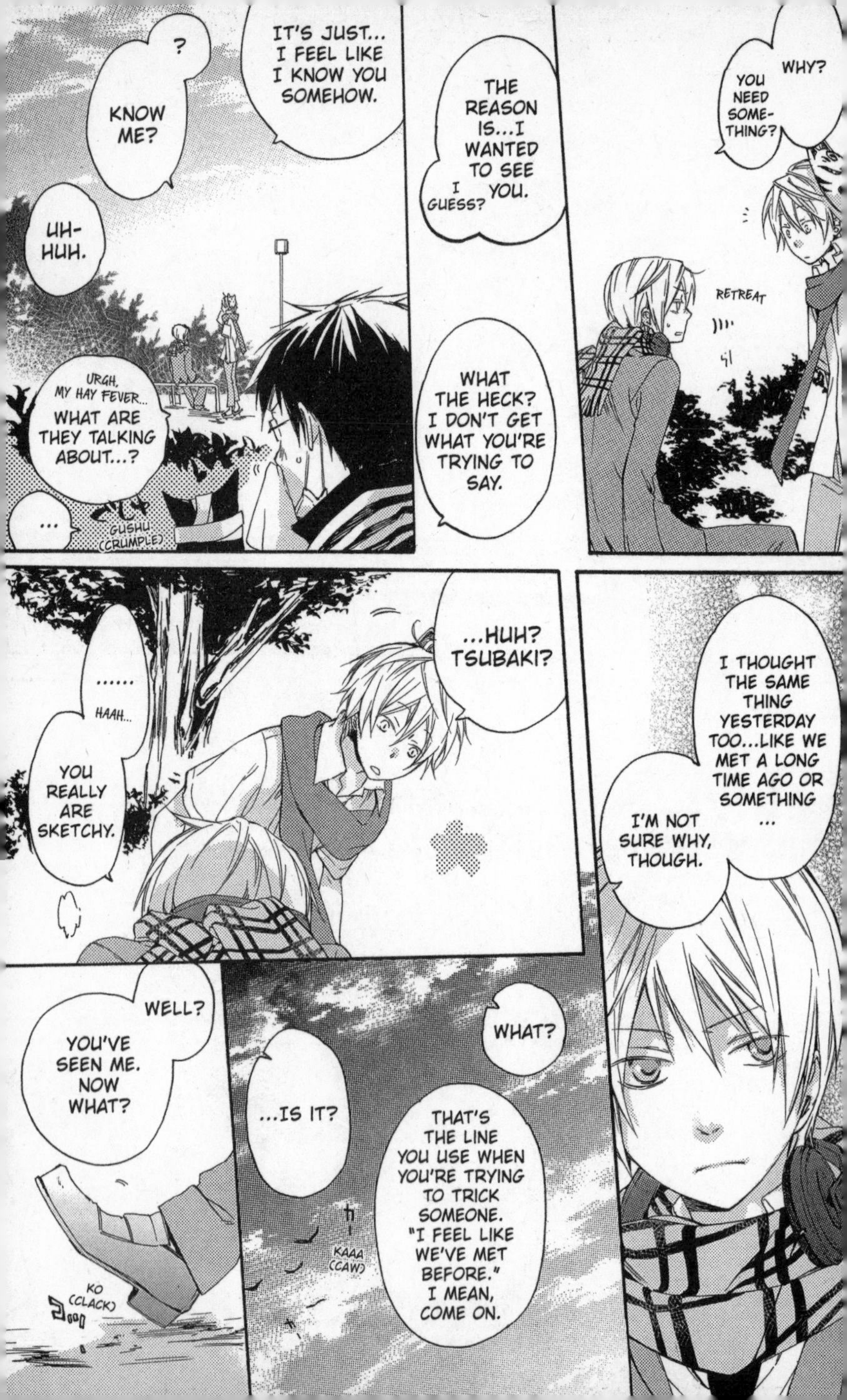
WHY?
YOU NEED SOME-THING?
RETREAT
THE REASON IS...I WANTED TO SEE YOU.
I GUESS?
WHAT THE HECK? I DON'T GET WHAT YOU'RE TRYING TO SAY.
IT'S JUST... I FEEL LIKE I KNOW YOU SOMEHOW.
?
KNOW ME?
UH-HUH.
URGH, MY HAY FEVER...
WHAT ARE THEY TALKING ABOUT...?
...
GUSHU (CRUMPLE)
I THOUGHT THE SAME THING YESTERDAY TOO...LIKE WE MET A LONG TIME AGO OR SOMETHING...
I'M NOT SURE WHY, THOUGH.
...HUH? TSUBAKI?
......
HAAH...
YOU REALLY ARE SKETCHY.
WHAT?
...IS IT?
THAT'S THE LINE YOU USE WHEN YOU'RE TRYING TO TRICK SOMEONE. "I FEEL LIKE WE'VE MET BEFORE." I MEAN, COME ON.
KAAA (CAW)
WELL?
YOU'VE SEEN ME. NOW WHAT?
KO (CLACK)

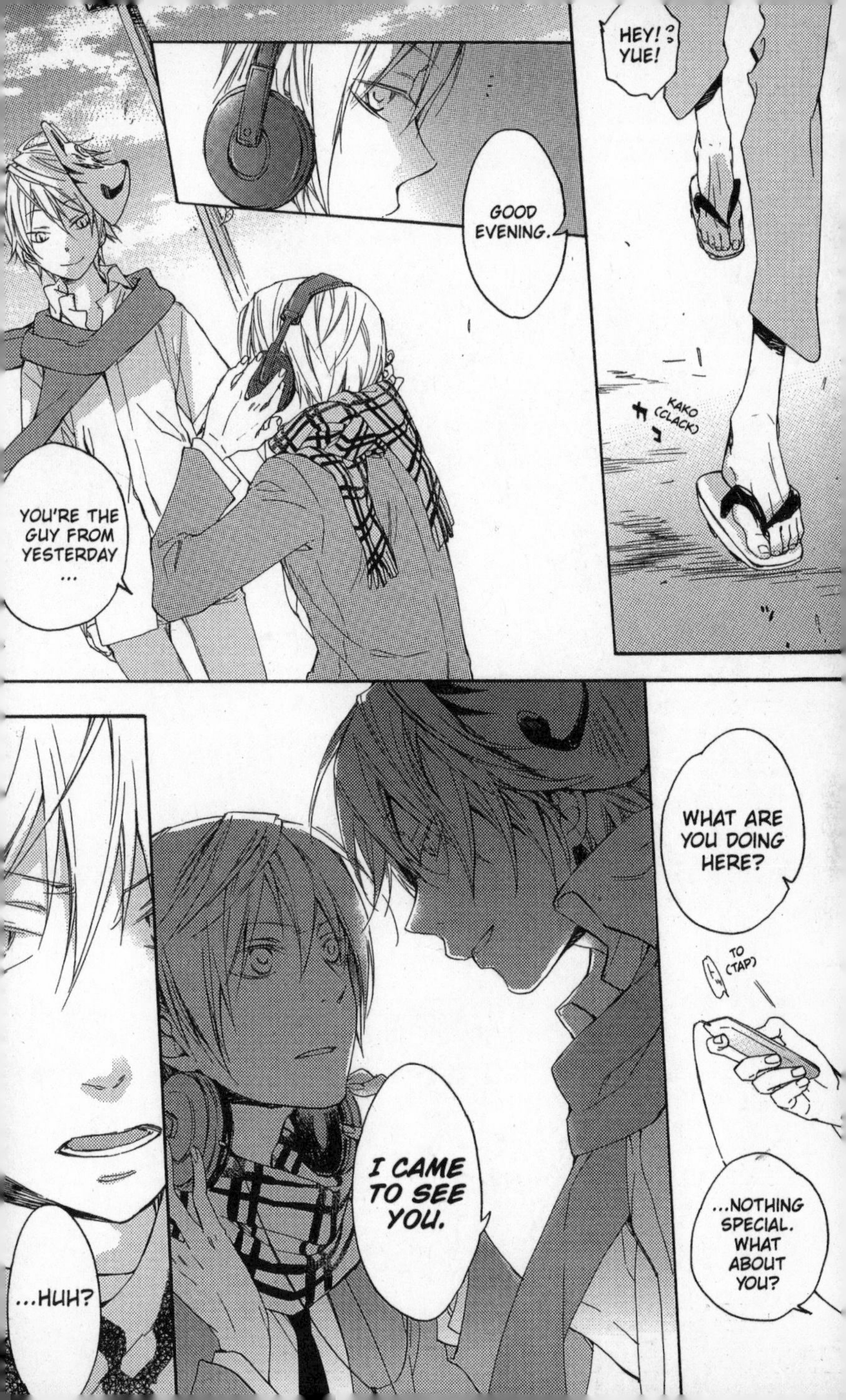
HEY! YUE!
KAKO (CLACK)
GOOD EVENING.
YOU'RE THE GUY FROM YESTERDAY ...
WHAT ARE YOU DOING HERE?
TO (TAP)
...NOTHING SPECIAL. WHAT ABOUT YOU?
I CAME TO SEE YOU.
...HUH?

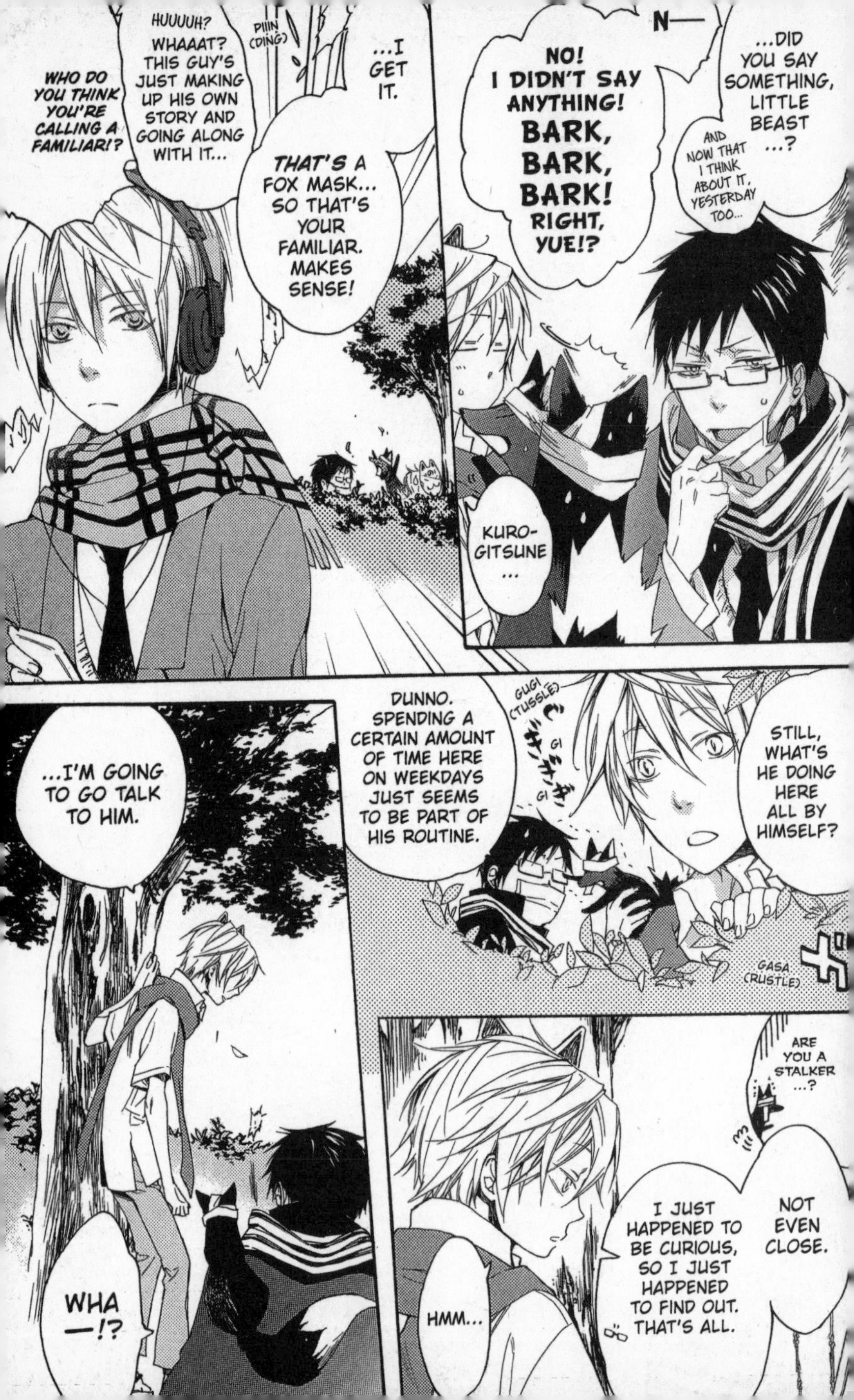
N—
...DID YOU SAY SOMETHING, LITTLE BEAST ...?
AND NOW THAT I THINK ABOUT IT, YESTERDAY TOO...
NO! I DIDN'T SAY ANYTHING! BARK, BARK, BARK! RIGHT, YUE!?
KURO-GITSUNE ...
...I GET IT.
PIIIN (DING)
THAT'S A FOX MASK... SO THAT'S YOUR FAMILIAR. MAKES SENSE!
HUUUUH? WHAAAT? THIS GUY'S JUST MAKING UP HIS OWN STORY AND GOING ALONG WITH IT...
WHO DO YOU THINK YOU'RE CALLING A FAMILIAR!?
STILL, WHAT'S HE DOING HERE ALL BY HIMSELF?
GUGI (TUSSLE)
GI
GI
DUNNO. SPENDING A CERTAIN AMOUNT OF TIME HERE ON WEEKDAYS JUST SEEMS TO BE PART OF HIS ROUTINE.
GASA (RUSTLE)
ARE YOU A STALKER ...?
NOT EVEN CLOSE.
I JUST HAPPENED TO BE CURIOUS, SO I JUST HAPPENED TO FIND OUT. THAT'S ALL.
HMM...
...I'M GOING TO GO TALK TO HIM.
WHA—!?

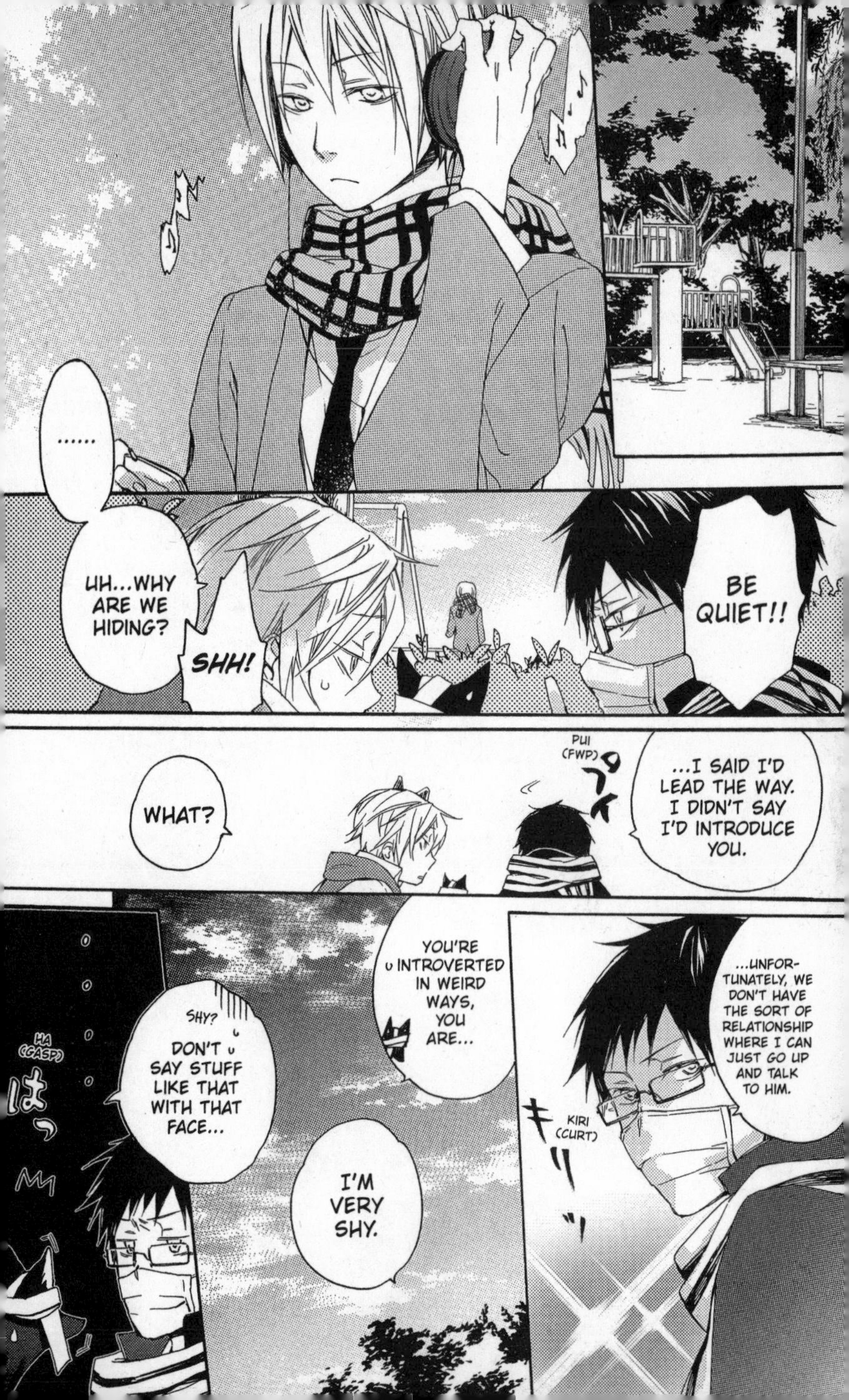
......
BE QUIET!!
UH...WHY ARE WE HIDING?
SHH!
...I SAID I'D LEAD THE WAY. I DIDN'T SAY I'D INTRODUCE YOU.
PUI (FWP)
WHAT?
...UNFOR-TUNATELY, WE DON'T HAVE THE SORT OF RELATIONSHIP WHERE I CAN JUST GO UP AND TALK TO HIM.
KIRI (CURT)
YOU'RE INTROVERTED IN WEIRD WAYS, YOU ARE...
SHY? DON'T SAY STUFF LIKE THAT WITH THAT FACE...
I'M VERY SHY.
HA (GASP)

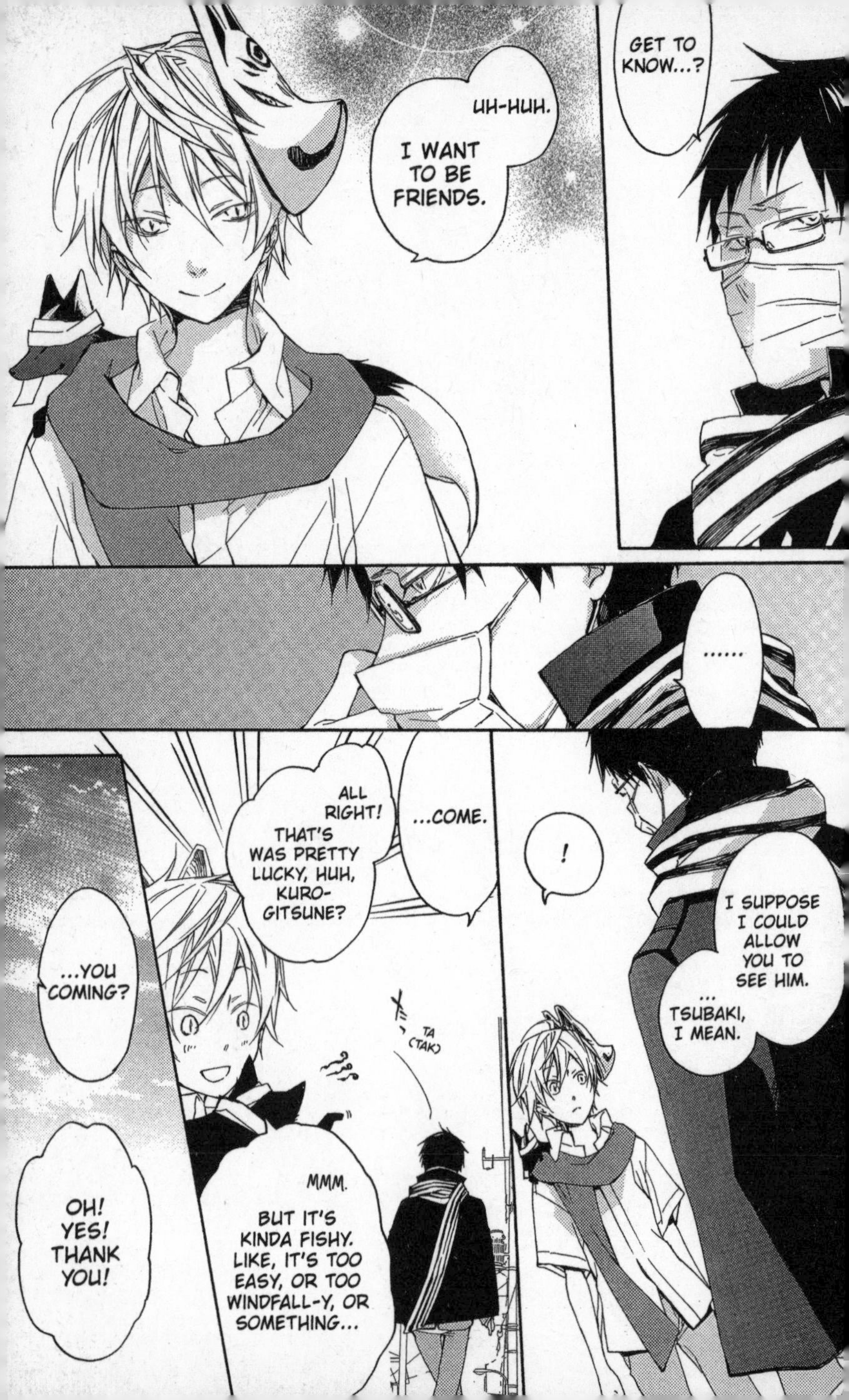

GET TO KNOW...?
UH-HUH.
I WANT TO BE FRIENDS.
......
I SUPPOSE I COULD ALLOW YOU TO SEE HIM.
... TSUBAKI, I MEAN.
!
...COME.
TA (TAK)
ALL RIGHT! THAT'S WAS PRETTY LUCKY, HUH, KURO-GITSUNE?
MMM.
BUT IT'S KINDA FISHY. LIKE, IT'S TOO EASY, OR TOO WINDFALL-Y, OR SOMETHING...
...YOU COMING?
OH! YES! THANK YOU!

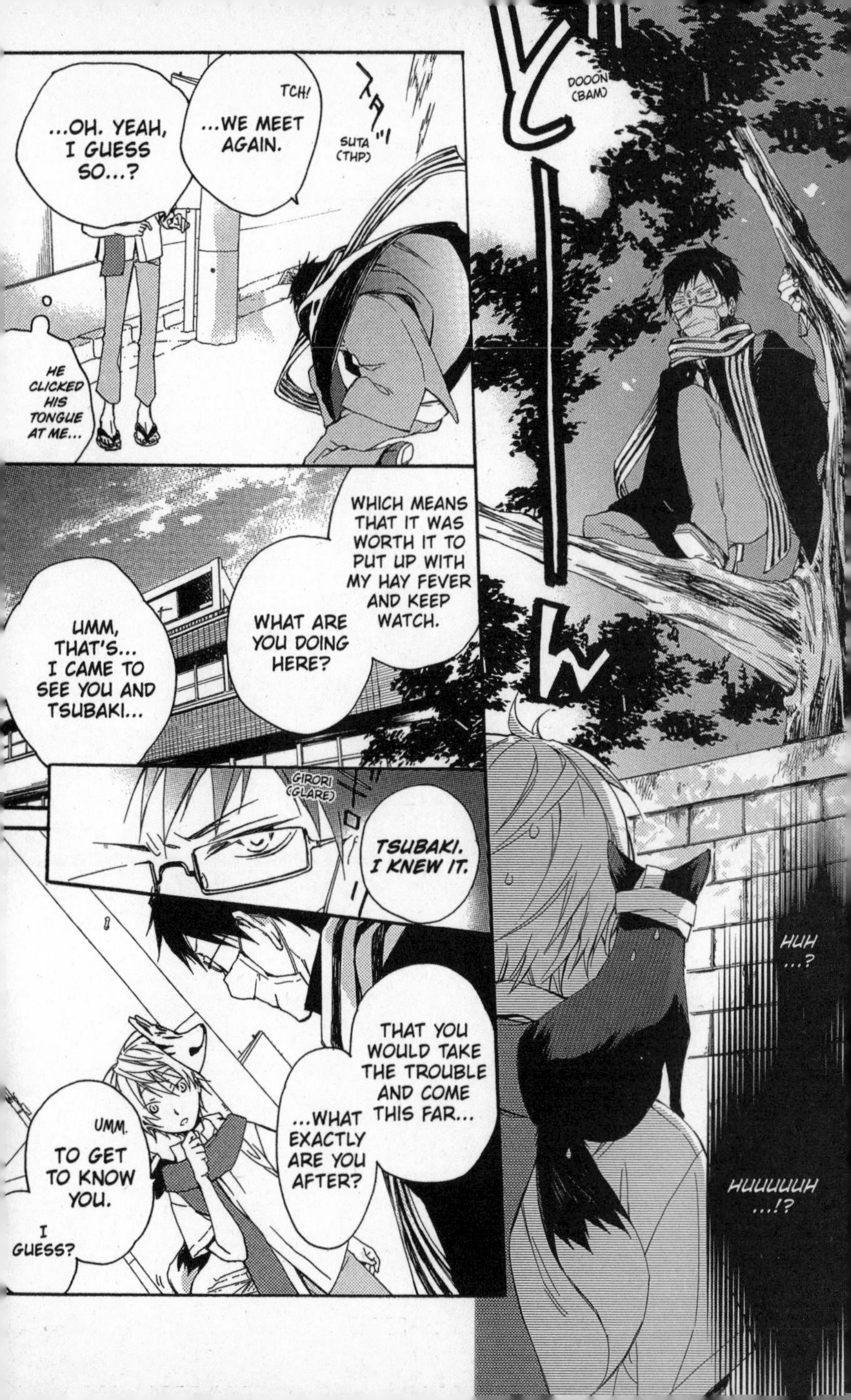
DOOON (BAM)
HUH ...?
HUUUUUH ...!?
TCH!
SUTA (THP)
...WE MEET AGAIN.
...OH. YEAH, I GUESS SO...?
HE CLICKED HIS TONGUE AT ME...
WHICH MEANS THAT IT WAS WORTH IT TO PUT UP WITH MY HAY FEVER AND KEEP WATCH.
WHAT ARE YOU DOING HERE?
UMM, THAT'S... I CAME TO SEE YOU AND TSUBAKI...
GIRORI (GLARE)
TSUBAKI. I KNEW IT.
THAT YOU WOULD TAKE THE TROUBLE AND COME THIS FAR...
...WHAT EXACTLY ARE YOU AFTER?
UMM. TO GET TO KNOW YOU.
I GUESS?

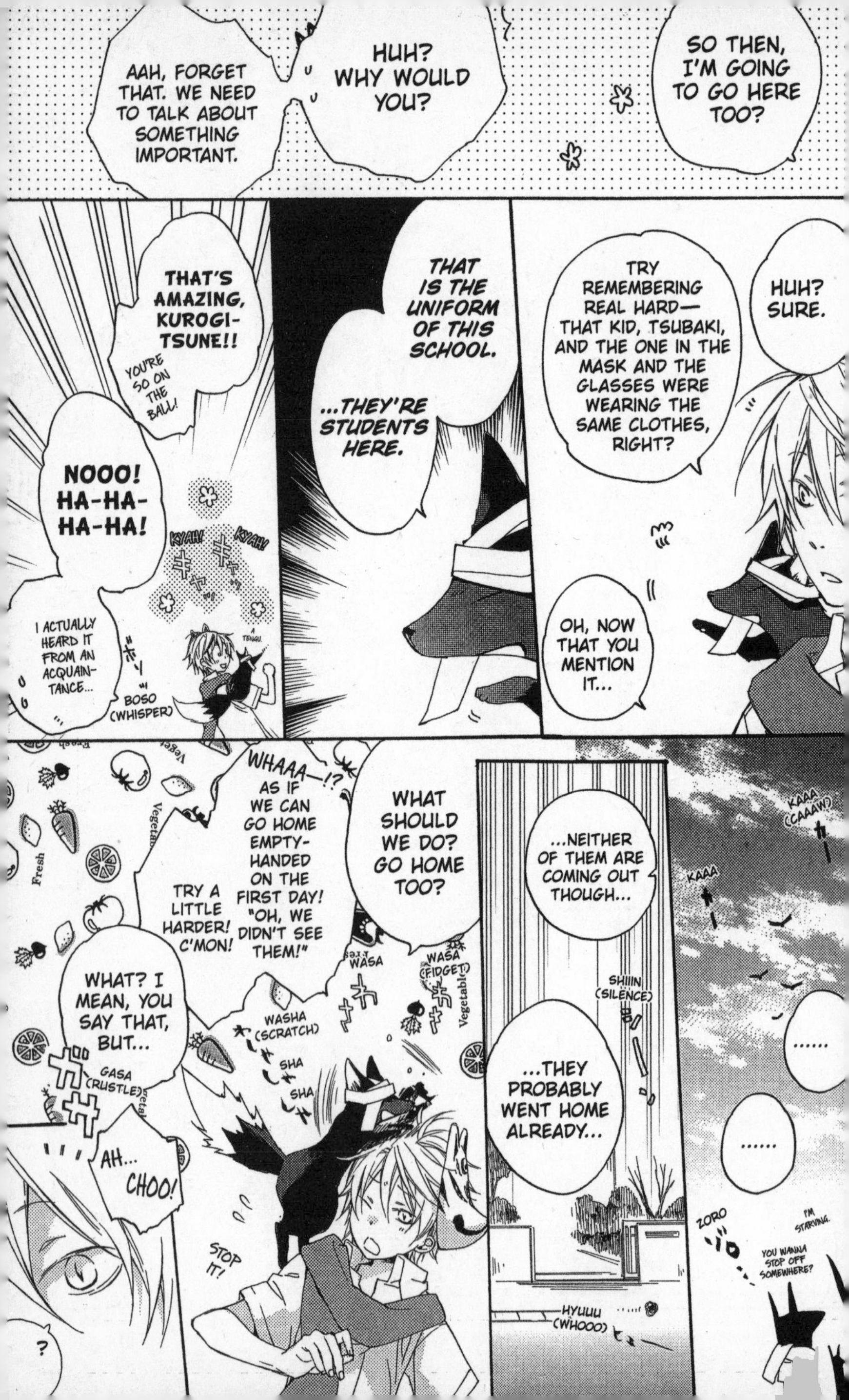
SO THEN, I'M GOING TO GO HERE TOO?
HUH? WHY WOULD YOU?
AAH, FORGET THAT. WE NEED TO TALK ABOUT SOMETHING IMPORTANT.
HUH? SURE.
TRY REMEMBERING REAL HARD—THAT KID, TSUBAKI, AND THE ONE IN THE MASK AND THE GLASSES WERE WEARING THE SAME CLOTHES, RIGHT?
OH, NOW THAT YOU MENTION IT...
THAT IS THE UNIFORM OF THIS SCHOOL.
...THEY'RE STUDENTS HERE.
THAT'S AMAZING, KUROGI-TSUNE!!
YOU'RE SO ON THE BALL!
NOOO! HA-HA-HA-HA!
KYAH!
KYAH!
A TENGU.
I ACTUALLY HEARD IT FROM AN ACQUAINTANCE...
BOSO (WHISPER)
KAAA (CAAAW)
KAAA
......
......
I'M STARVING.
YOU WANNA STOP OFF SOMEWHERE?
ZORO
...NEITHER OF THEM ARE COMING OUT THOUGH...
SHIIIN (SILENCE)
...THEY PROBABLY WENT HOME ALREADY...
HYUUU (WHOOO)
WHAT SHOULD WE DO? GO HOME TOO?
WHAAA—!? AS IF WE CAN GO HOME EMPTY-HANDED ON THE FIRST DAY! "OH, WE DIDN'T SEE THEM!"
TRY A LITTLE HARDER! C'MON!
WASA (FIDGET)
WASA
WHAT? I MEAN, YOU SAY THAT, BUT...
WASHA (SCRATCH)
SHA
SHA
GASA (RUSTLE)
AH... CHOO!
STOP IT!
?

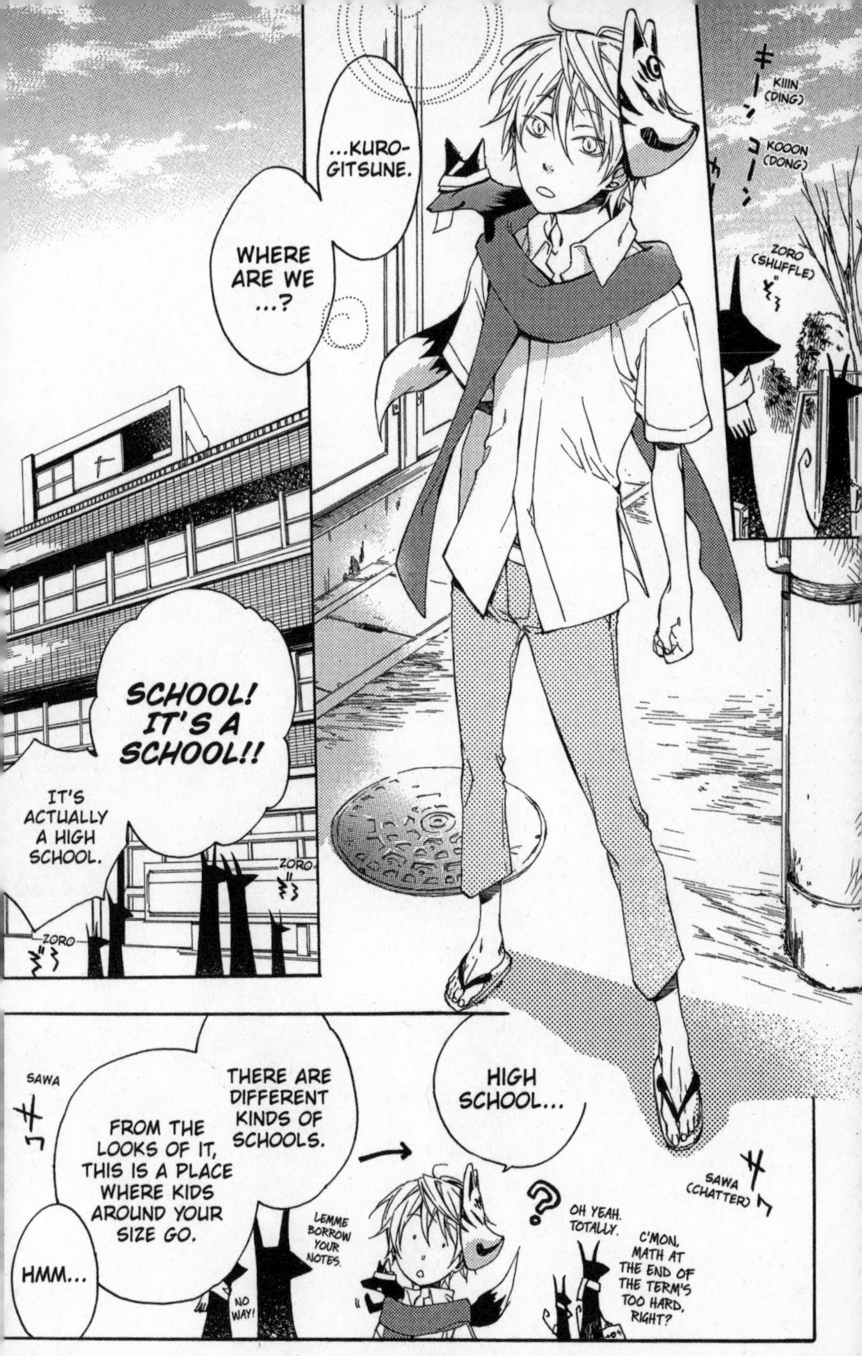
KIIN (DING)
KOOON (DONG)
ZORO (SHUFFLE)
...KURO-GITSUNE.
WHERE ARE WE ...?
SCHOOL! IT'S A SCHOOL!!
IT'S ACTUALLY A HIGH SCHOOL.
ZORO
ZORO
SAWA (CHATTER)
C'MON, MATH AT THE END OF THE TERM'S TOO HARD, RIGHT?
OH YEAH. TOTALLY.
HIGH SCHOOL...
LEMME BORROW YOUR NOTES.
NO WAY!
THERE ARE DIFFERENT KINDS OF SCHOOLS.
FROM THE LOOKS OF IT, THIS IS A PLACE WHERE KIDS AROUND YOUR SIZE GO.
HMM...
SAWA

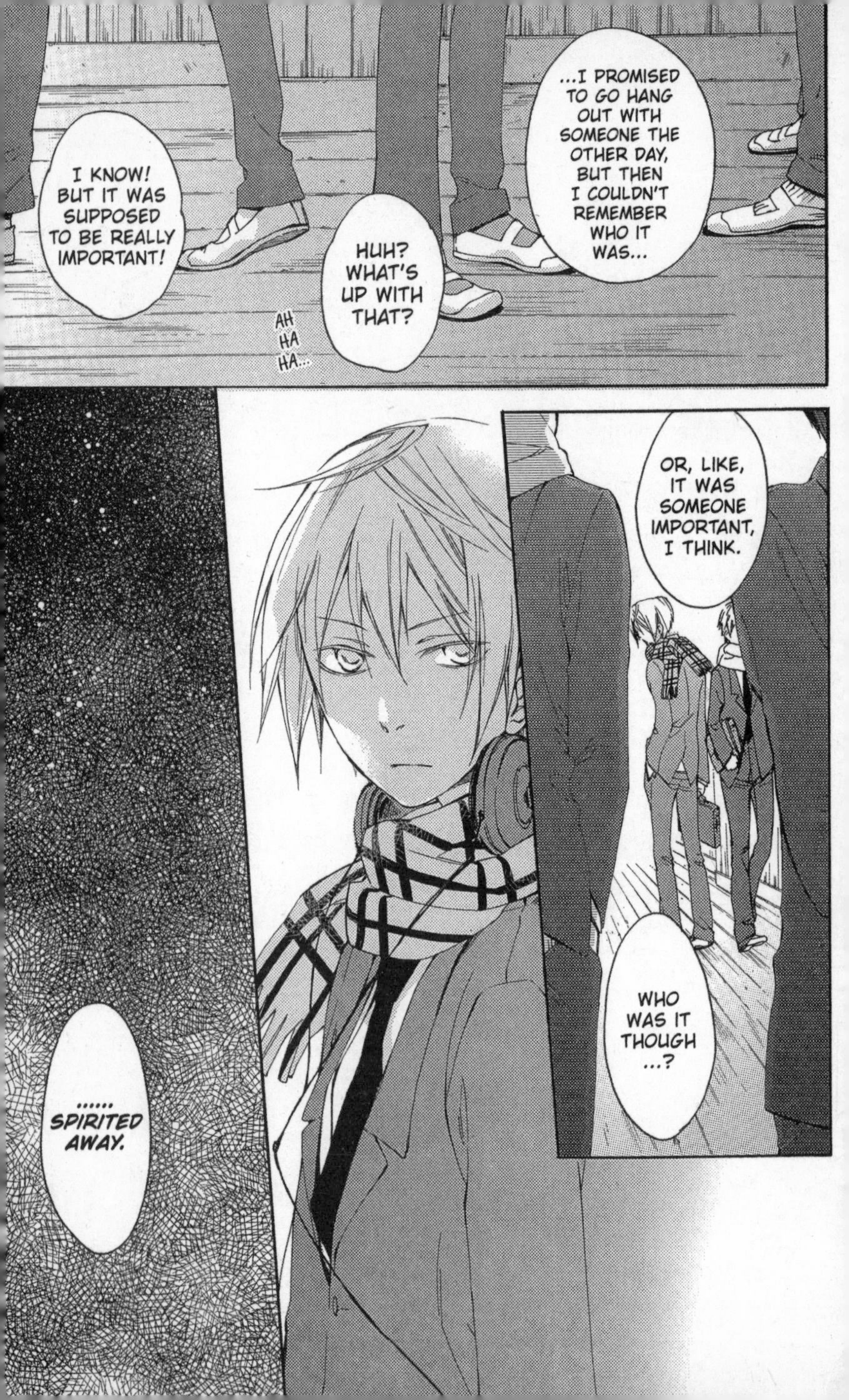
...I PROMISED TO GO HANG OUT WITH SOMEONE THE OTHER DAY, BUT THEN I COULDN'T REMEMBER WHO IT WAS...
HUH? WHAT'S UP WITH THAT?
I KNOW! BUT IT WAS SUPPOSED TO BE REALLY IMPORTANT!
AH HA HA...
OR, LIKE, IT WAS SOMEONE IMPORTANT, I THINK.
WHO WAS IT THOUGH ...?
...... SPIRITED AWAY.

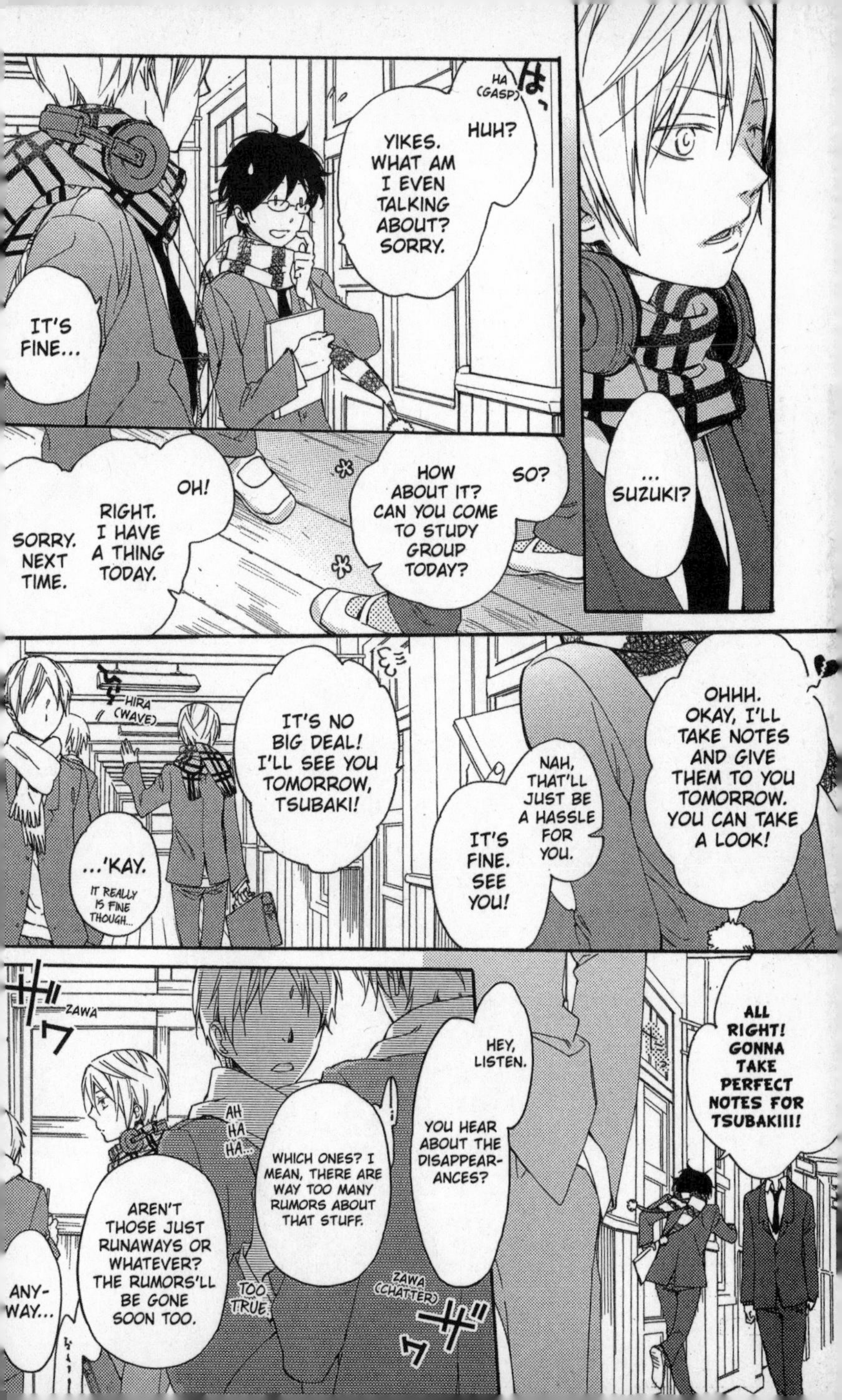

... SUZUKI?
HA (GASP)
HUH?
YIKES. WHAT AM I EVEN TALKING ABOUT? SORRY.
IT'S FINE...
SO?
HOW ABOUT IT? CAN YOU COME TO STUDY GROUP TODAY?
OH!
RIGHT. I HAVE A THING TODAY.
SORRY. NEXT TIME.
OHHH. OKAY, I'LL TAKE NOTES AND GIVE THEM TO YOU TOMORROW. YOU CAN TAKE A LOOK!
NAH, THAT'LL JUST BE A HASSLE FOR YOU.
IT'S FINE. SEE YOU!
IT'S NO BIG DEAL! I'LL SEE YOU TOMORROW, TSUBAKI!
HIRA (WAVE)
...'KAY.
IT REALLY IS FINE THOUGH...
ALL RIGHT! GONNA TAKE PERFECT NOTES FOR TSUBAKIII!
HEY, LISTEN.
YOU HEAR ABOUT THE DISAPPEARANCES?
ZAWA (CHATTER)
WHICH ONES? I MEAN, THERE ARE WAY TOO MANY RUMORS ABOUT THAT STUFF.
AH HA HA...
TOO TRUE
AREN'T THOSE JUST RUNAWAYS OR WHATEVER? THE RUMORS'LL BE GONE SOON TOO.
ZAWA
ANY-WAY...

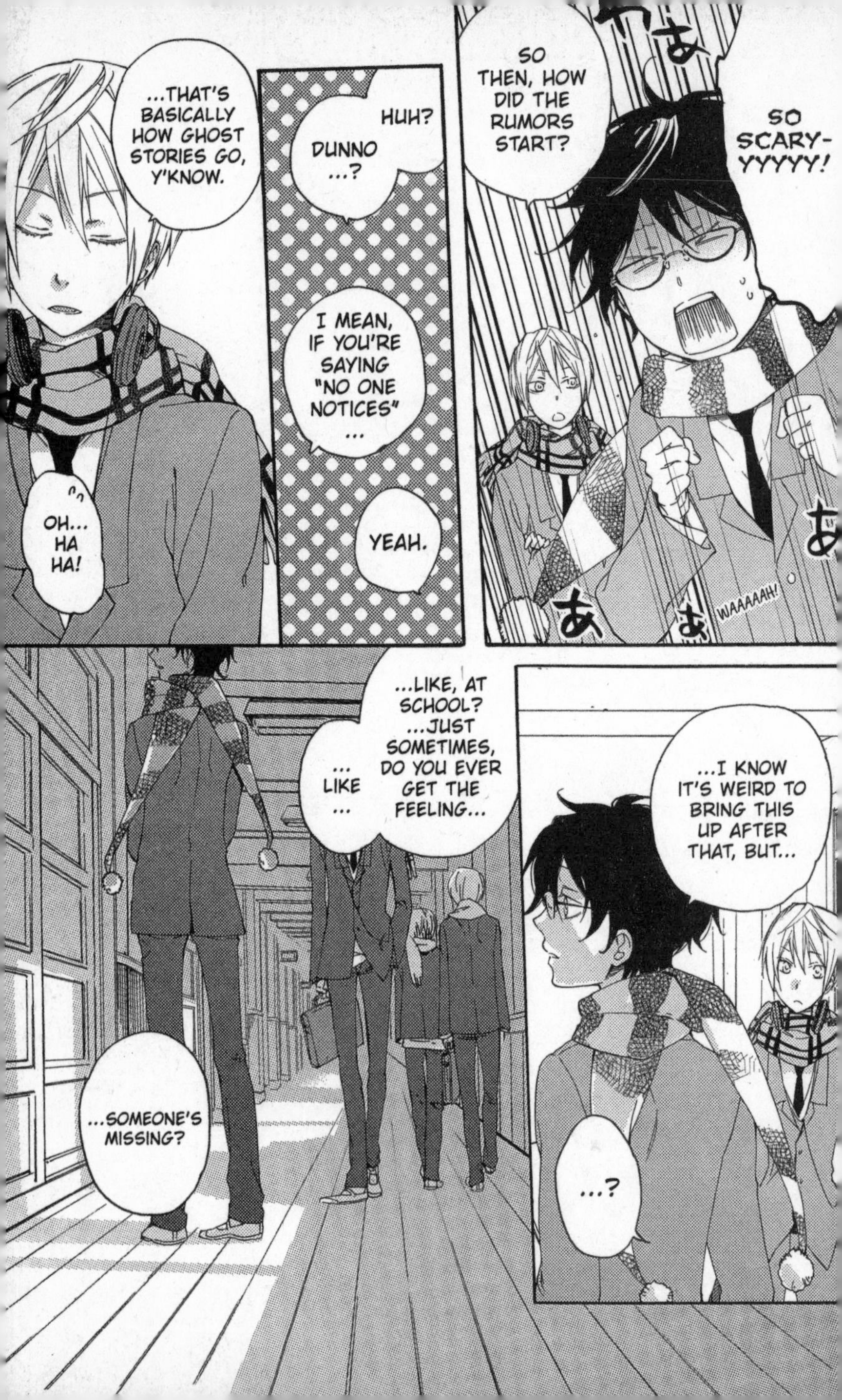
SO THEN, HOW DID THE RUMORS START?
SO SCARY-YYYYY!
WAAAAAH!
HUH?
DUNNO ...?
I MEAN, IF YOU'RE SAYING "NO ONE NOTICES" ...
YEAH.
...THAT'S BASICALLY HOW GHOST STORIES GO, Y'KNOW.
OH... HA HA!
...I KNOW IT'S WEIRD TO BRING THIS UP AFTER THAT, BUT...
...?
...LIKE, AT SCHOOL? ...JUST SOMETIMES, DO YOU EVER GET THE FEELING...
... LIKE ...
...SOMEONE'S MISSING?

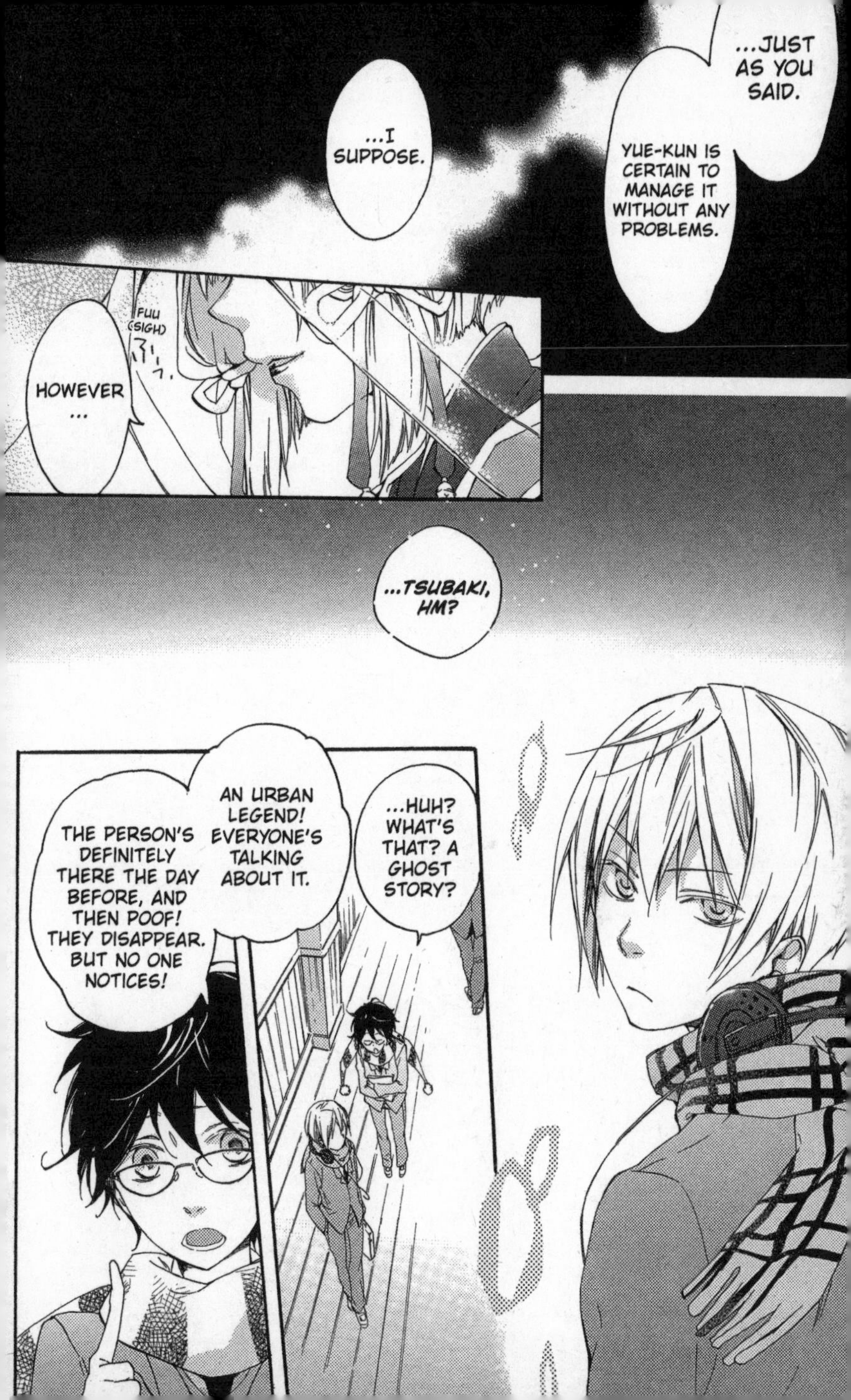
...JUST AS YOU SAID.
YUE-KUN IS CERTAIN TO MANAGE IT WITHOUT ANY PROBLEMS.
...I SUPPOSE.
FUU (SIGH)
HOWEVER ...
...TSUBAKI, HM?
...HUH? WHAT'S THAT? A GHOST STORY?
AN URBAN LEGEND! EVERYONE'S TALKING ABOUT IT.
THE PERSON'S DEFINITELY THERE THE DAY BEFORE, AND THEN POOF! THEY DISAPPEAR. BUT NO ONE NOTICES!

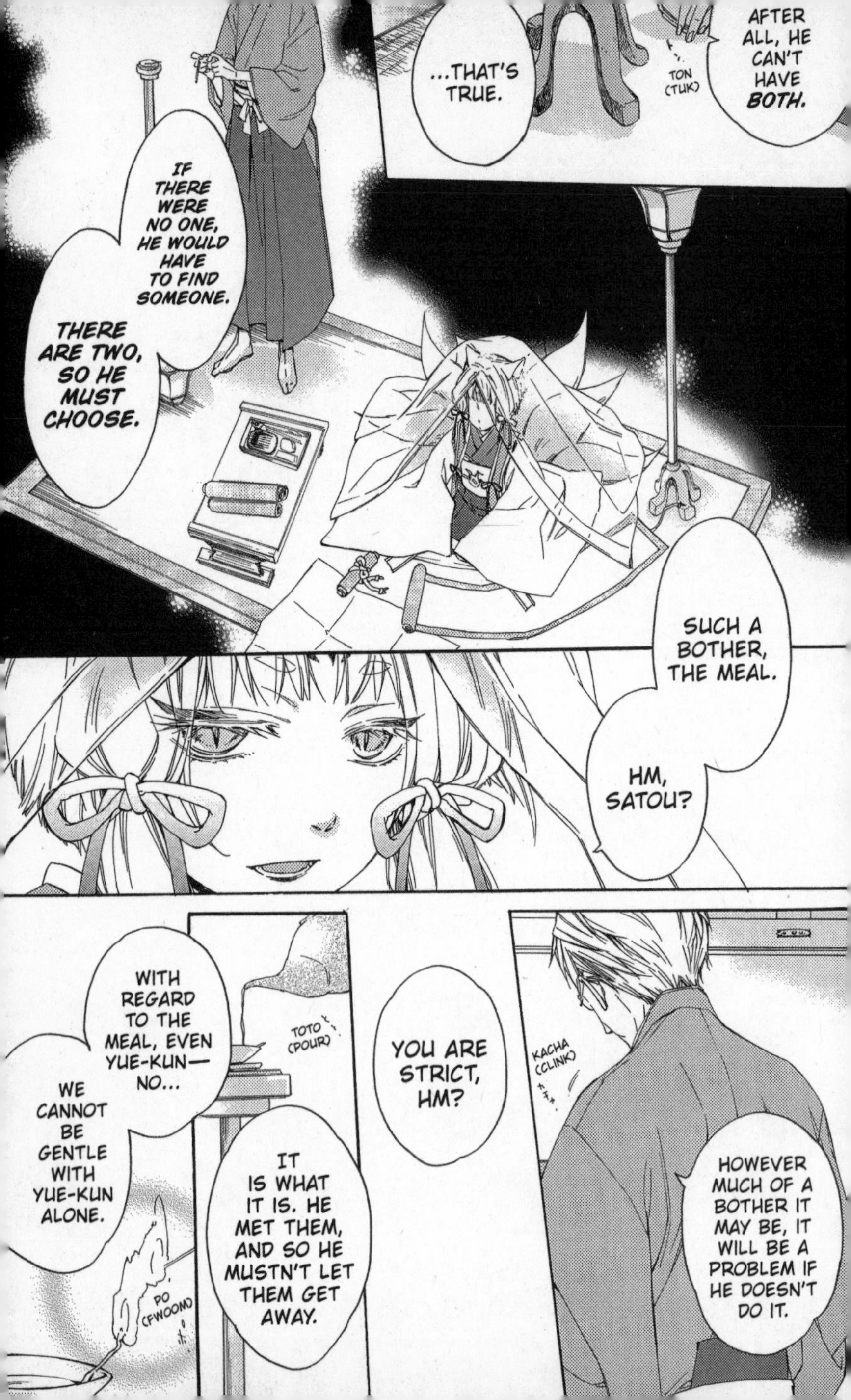
AFTER ALL, HE CAN'T HAVE BOTH.
TON (TUK)
...THAT'S TRUE.
IF THERE WERE NO ONE, HE WOULD HAVE TO FIND SOMEONE.
THERE ARE TWO, SO HE MUST CHOOSE.
SUCH A BOTHER, THE MEAL.
HM, SATOU?
KACHA (CLINK)
HOWEVER MUCH OF A BOTHER IT MAY BE, IT WILL BE A PROBLEM IF HE DOESN'T DO IT.
YOU ARE STRICT, HM?
IT IS WHAT IT IS. HE MET THEM, AND SO HE MUSTN'T LET THEM GET AWAY.
TOTO (POUR)
WITH REGARD TO THE MEAL, EVEN YUE-KUN— NO...
WE CANNOT BE GENTLE WITH YUE-KUN ALONE.
PO (FWOOM)

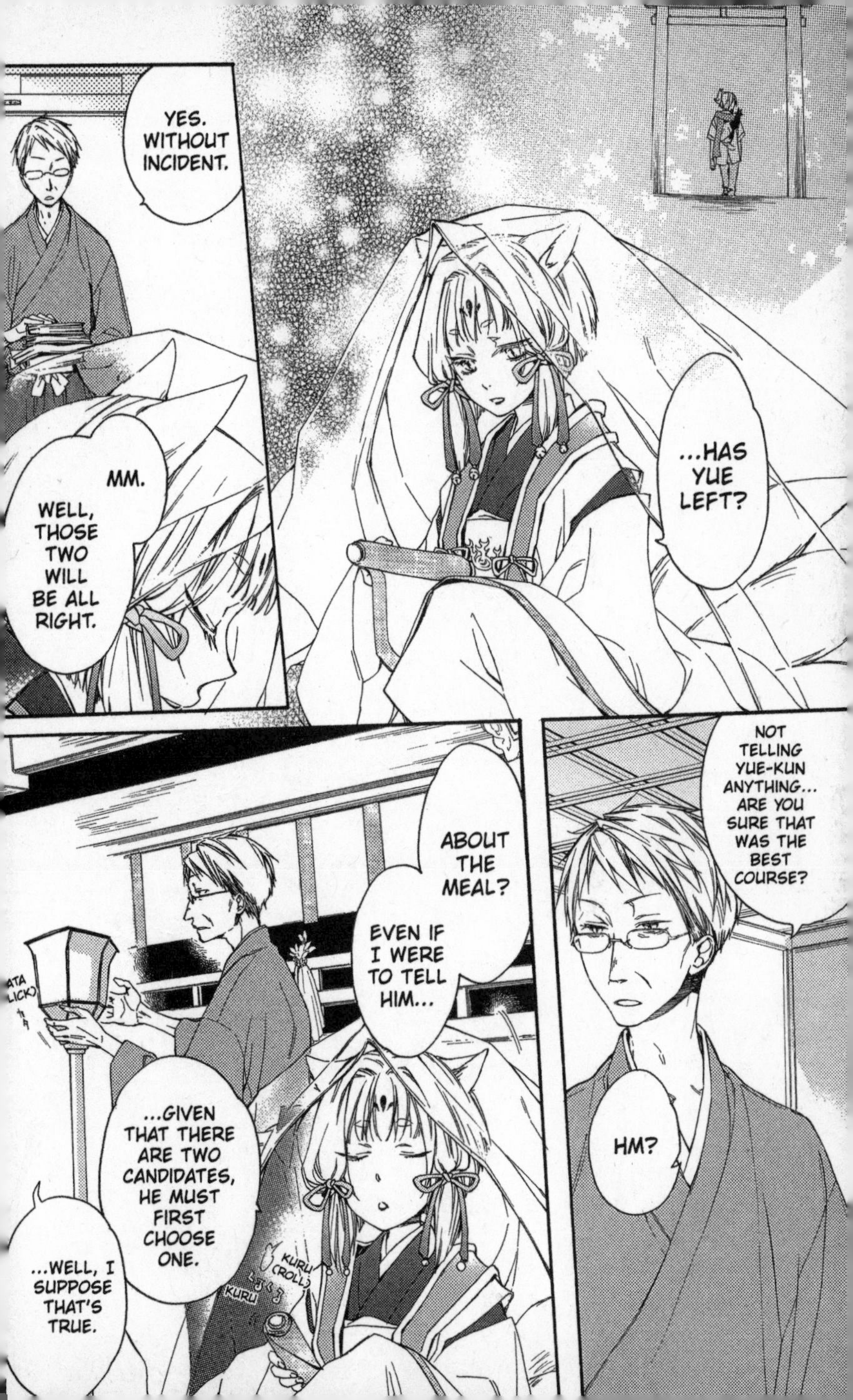
...HAS YUE LEFT?
YES. WITHOUT INCIDENT.
MM.
WELL, THOSE TWO WILL BE ALL RIGHT.
NOT TELLING YUE-KUN ANYTHING... ARE YOU SURE THAT WAS THE BEST COURSE?
HM?
ABOUT THE MEAL?
EVEN IF I WERE TO TELL HIM...
...GIVEN THAT THERE ARE TWO CANDIDATES, HE MUST FIRST CHOOSE ONE.
KURU (ROLL)
KURU
...WELL, I SUPPOSE THAT'S TRUE.

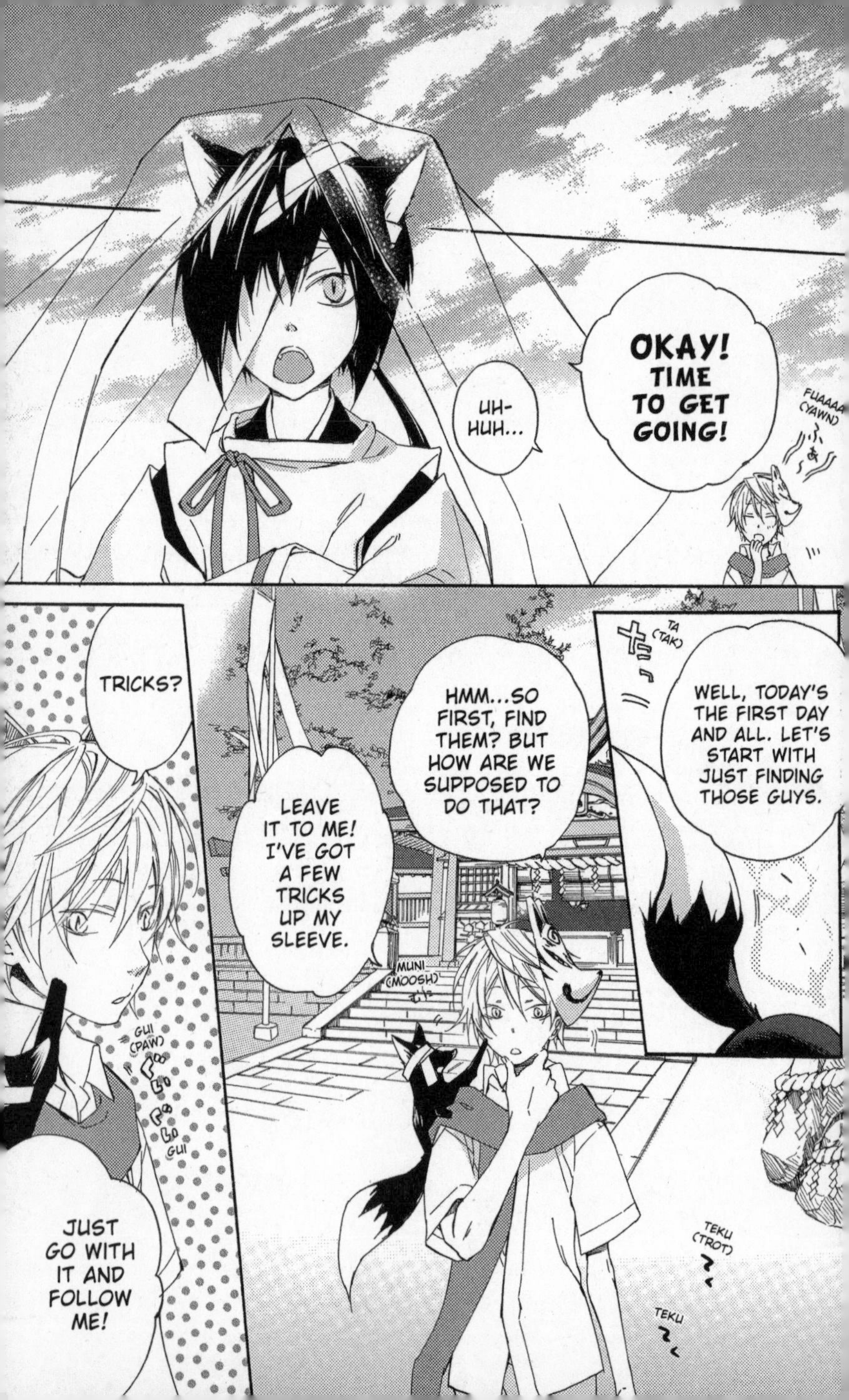
FUAAAA (YAWN)
OKAY! TIME TO GET GOING!
UH-HUH...
TA (TAK)
WELL, TODAY'S THE FIRST DAY AND ALL. LET'S START WITH JUST FINDING THOSE GUYS.
HMM...SO FIRST, FIND THEM? BUT HOW ARE WE SUPPOSED TO DO THAT?
LEAVE IT TO ME! I'VE GOT A FEW TRICKS UP MY SLEEVE.
MUNI (MOOSH)
TEKU (TROT)
TEKU
TRICKS?
GUI (PAW)
GUI
JUST GO WITH IT AND FOLLOW ME!

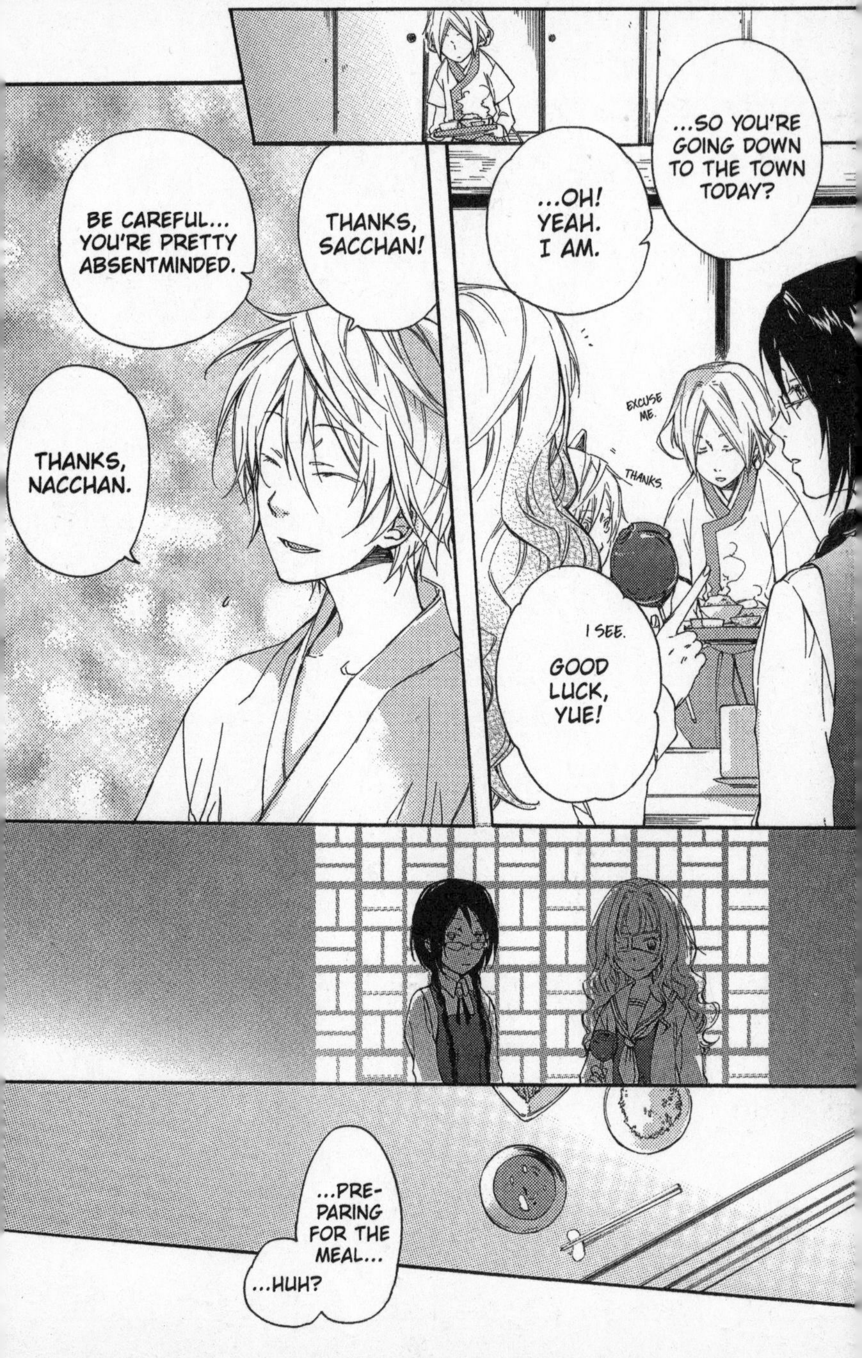
...SO YOU'RE GOING DOWN TO THE TOWN TODAY?
...OH! YEAH. I AM.
EXCUSE ME.
THANKS.
I SEE.
GOOD LUCK, YUE!
THANKS, SACCHAN!
BE CAREFUL... YOU'RE PRETTY ABSENTMINDED.
THANKS, NACCHAN.
...PRE-PARING FOR THE MEAL...
...HUH?

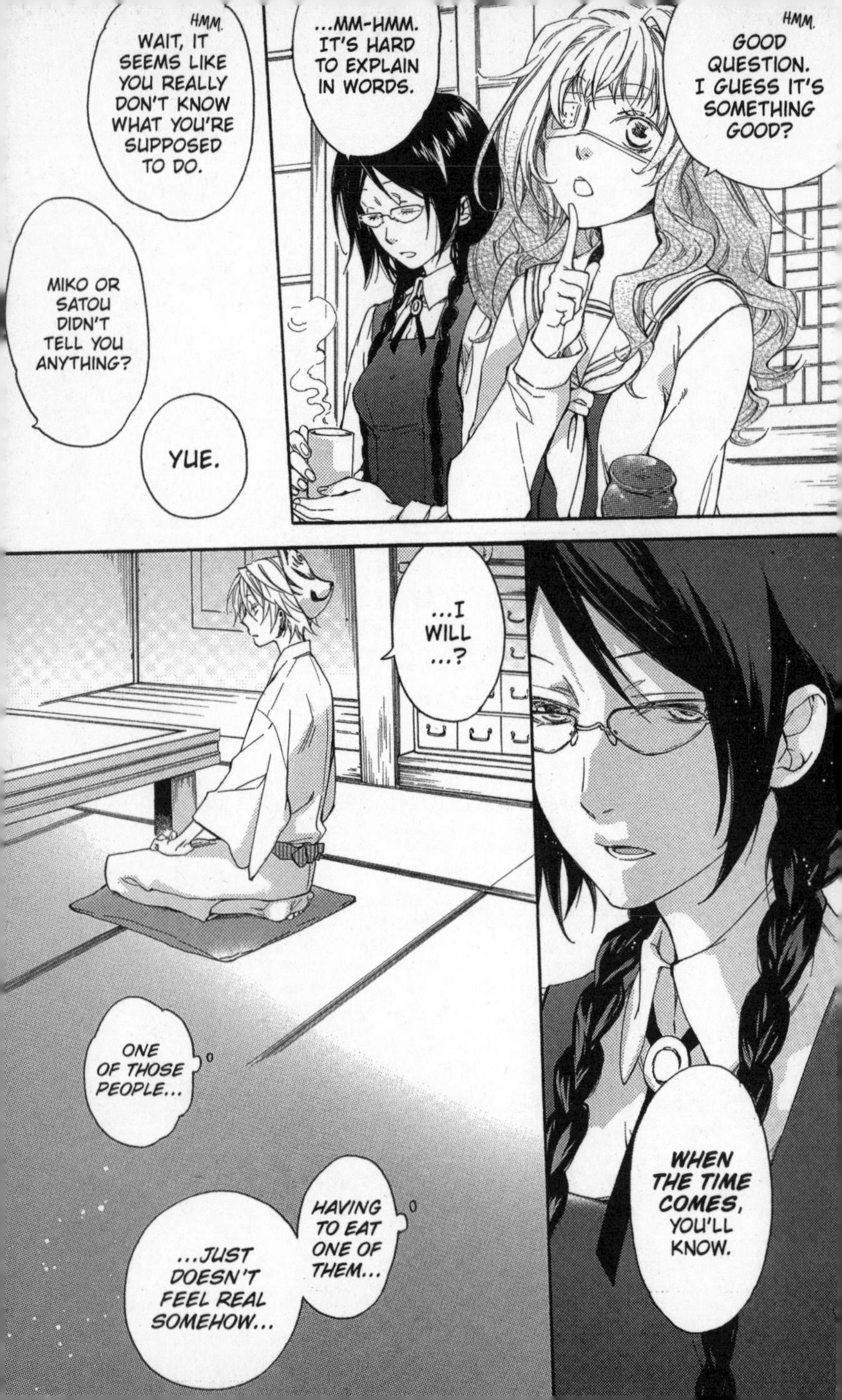
HMM. GOOD QUESTION. I GUESS IT'S SOMETHING GOOD?
...MM-HMM. IT'S HARD TO EXPLAIN IN WORDS.
HMM. WAIT, IT SEEMS LIKE YOU REALLY DON'T KNOW WHAT YOU'RE SUPPOSED TO DO.
MIKO OR SATOU DIDN'T TELL YOU ANYTHING?
YUE.
WHEN THE TIME COMES, YOU'LL KNOW.
...I WILL ...?
ONE OF THOSE PEOPLE...
HAVING TO EAT ONE OF THEM...
...JUST DOESN'T FEEL REAL SOMEHOW...

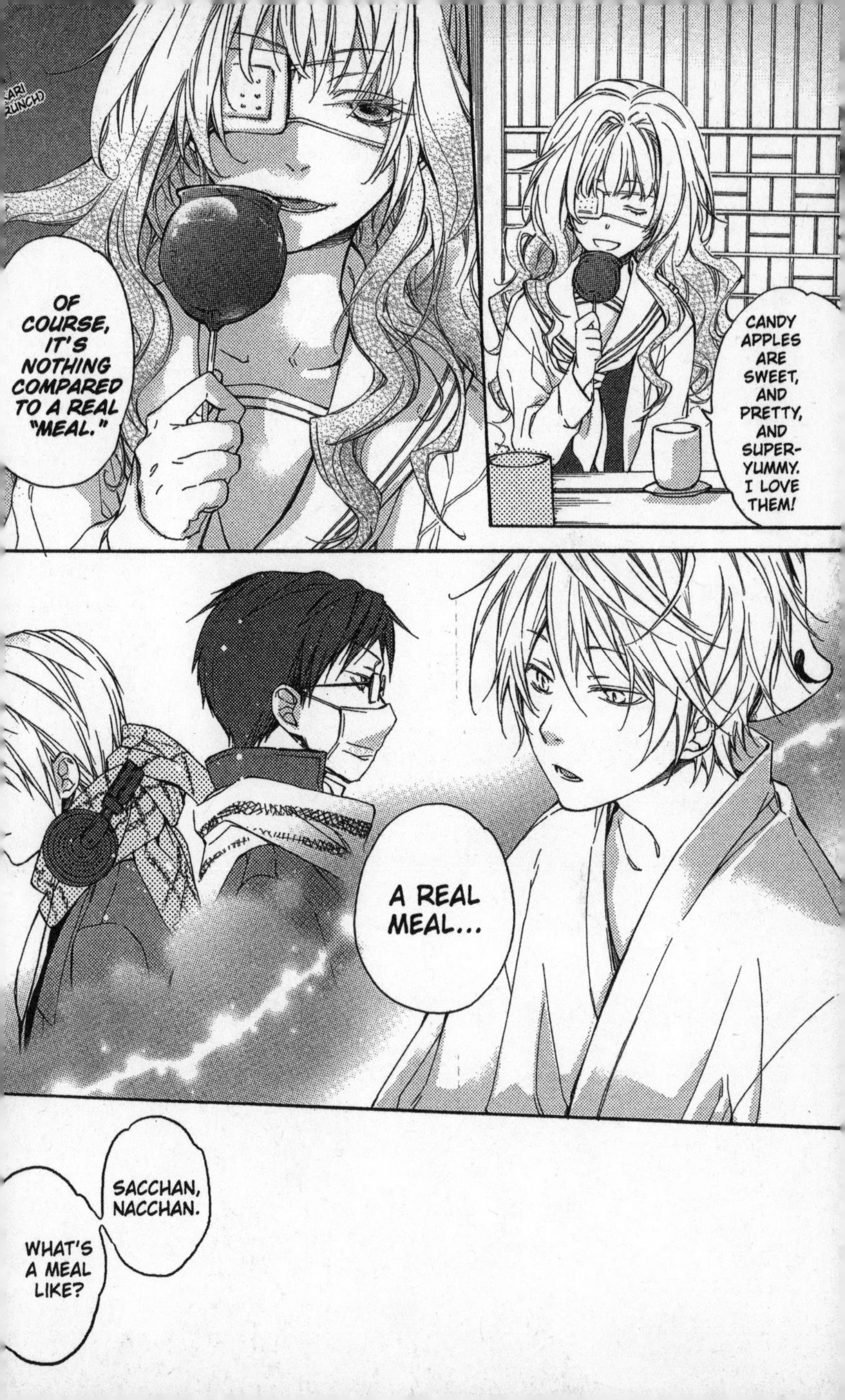
CANDY APPLES ARE SWEET, AND PRETTY, AND SUPER-YUMMY. I LOVE THEM!
OF COURSE, IT'S NOTHING COMPARED TO A REAL "MEAL."
A REAL MEAL...
SACCHAN, NACCHAN.
WHAT'S A MEAL LIKE?

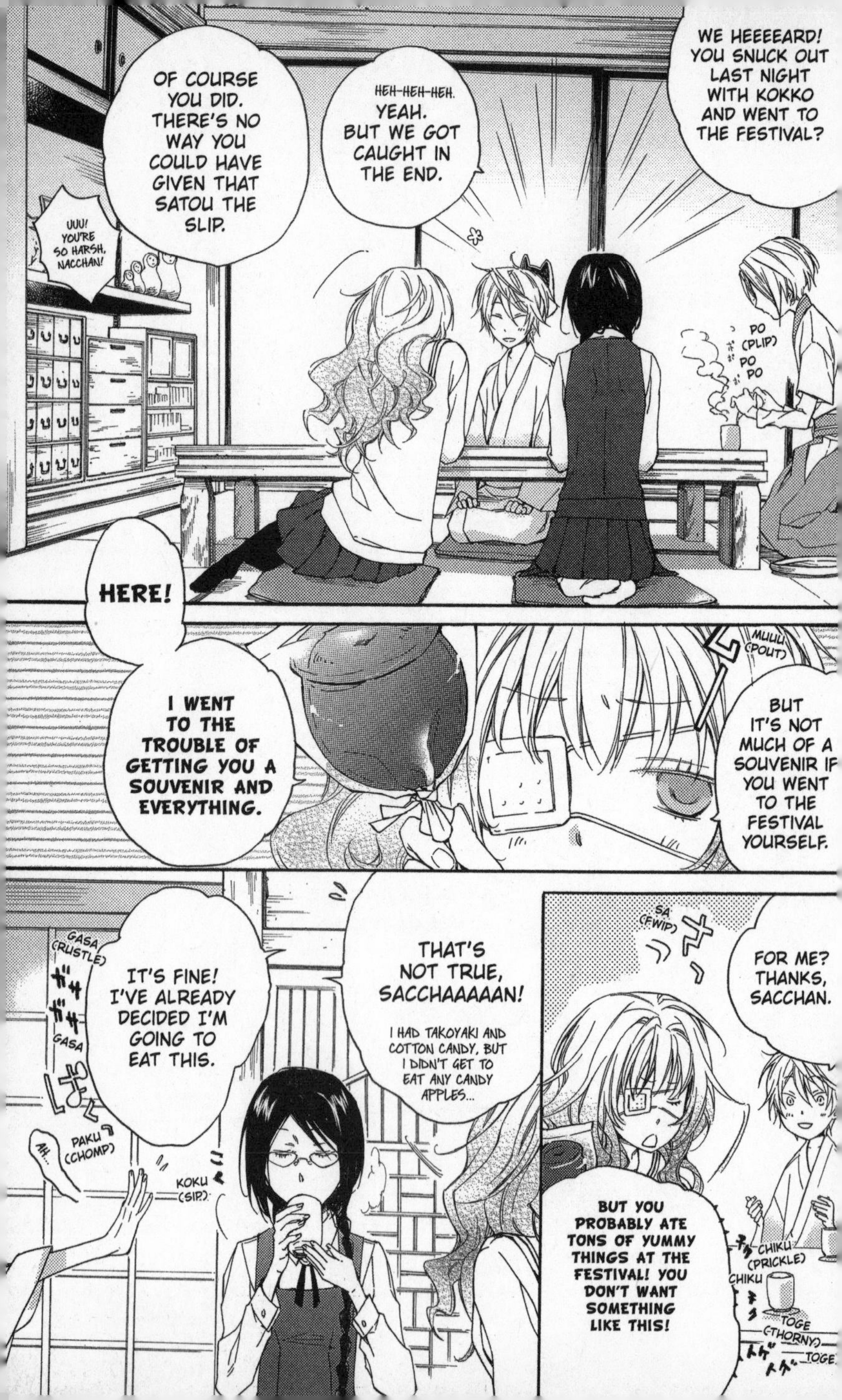
WE HEEEEARD! YOU SNUCK OUT LAST NIGHT WITH KOKKO AND WENT TO THE FESTIVAL?
HEH-HEH-HEH.
YEAH. BUT WE GOT CAUGHT IN THE END.
OF COURSE YOU DID. THERE'S NO WAY YOU COULD HAVE GIVEN THAT SATOU THE SLIP.
UUU! YOU'RE SO HARSH, NACCHAN!
PO (PLIP) PO PO
HERE!
MUUU (POUT)
BUT IT'S NOT MUCH OF A SOUVENIR IF YOU WENT TO THE FESTIVAL YOURSELF.
I WENT TO THE TROUBLE OF GETTING YOU A SOUVENIR AND EVERYTHING.
SA (FWIP)
FOR ME? THANKS, SACCHAN.
BUT YOU PROBABLY ATE TONS OF YUMMY THINGS AT THE FESTIVAL! YOU DON'T WANT SOMETHING LIKE THIS!
CHIKU (PRICKLE) CHIKU
TOGE (THORNY) TOGE
THAT'S NOT TRUE, SACCHAAAAAN!
I HAD TAKOYAKI AND COTTON CANDY, BUT I DIDN'T GET TO EAT ANY CANDY APPLES...
GASA (RUSTLE) GASA
IT'S FINE! I'VE ALREADY DECIDED I'M GOING TO EAT THIS.
PAKU (CHOMP)
AH...
KOKU (SIP)

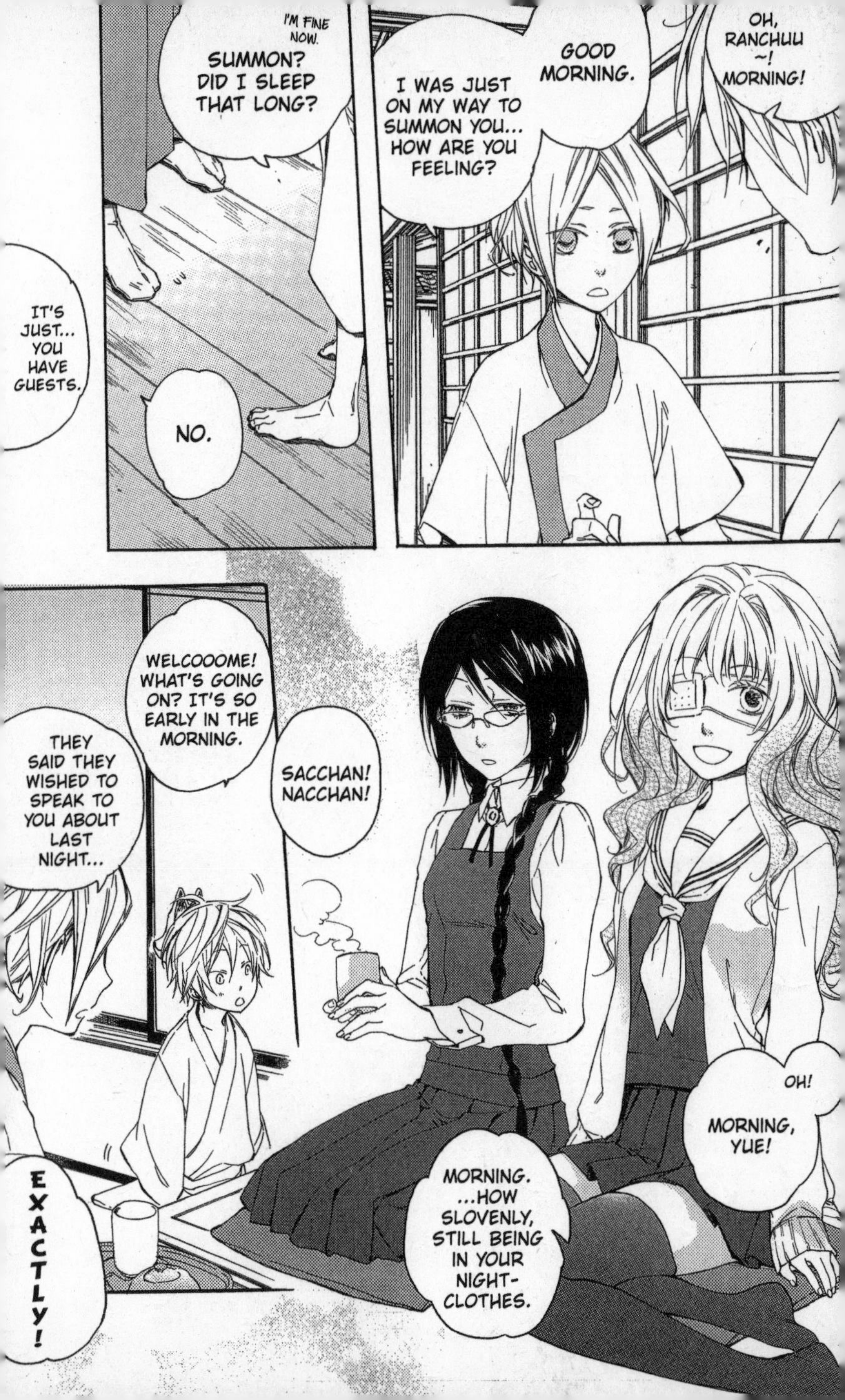
OH, RANCHUU~! MORNING!
GOOD MORNING.
I WAS JUST ON MY WAY TO SUMMON YOU... HOW ARE YOU FEELING?
SUMMON? DID I SLEEP THAT LONG?
I'M FINE NOW.
NO.
IT'S JUST... YOU HAVE GUESTS.
SACCHAN! NACCHAN!
WELCOOOME! WHAT'S GOING ON? IT'S SO EARLY IN THE MORNING.
THEY SAID THEY WISHED TO SPEAK TO YOU ABOUT LAST NIGHT...
EXACTLY!
OH!
MORNING, YUE!
MORNING. ...HOW SLOVENLY, STILL BEING IN YOUR NIGHT-CLOTHES.

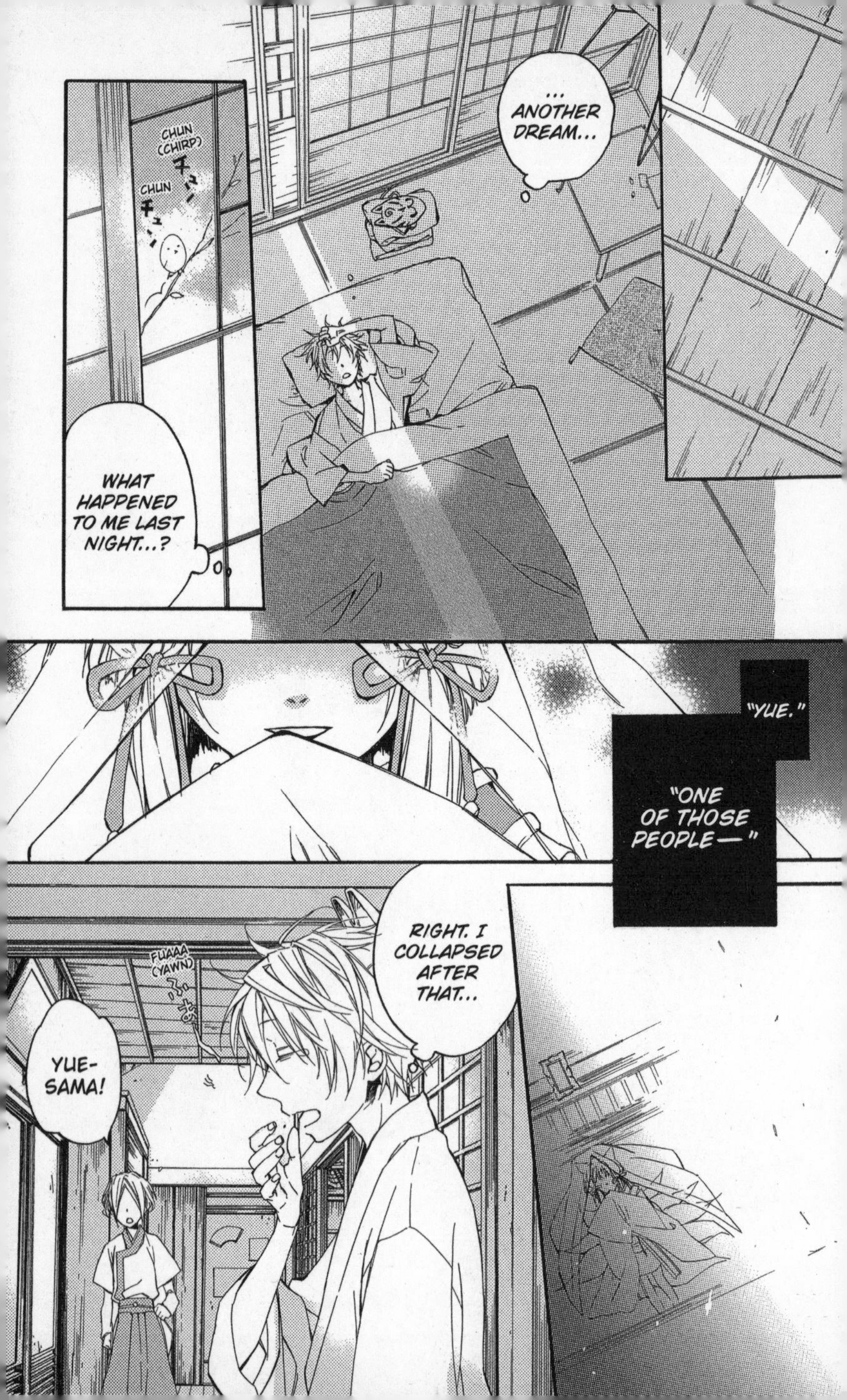
...ANOTHER DREAM...
CHUN (CHIRP)
CHUN
WHAT HAPPENED TO ME LAST NIGHT...?
"YUE."
"ONE OF THOSE PEOPLE—"
RIGHT. I COLLAPSED AFTER THAT...
FUAAA (YAWN)
YUE-SAMA!

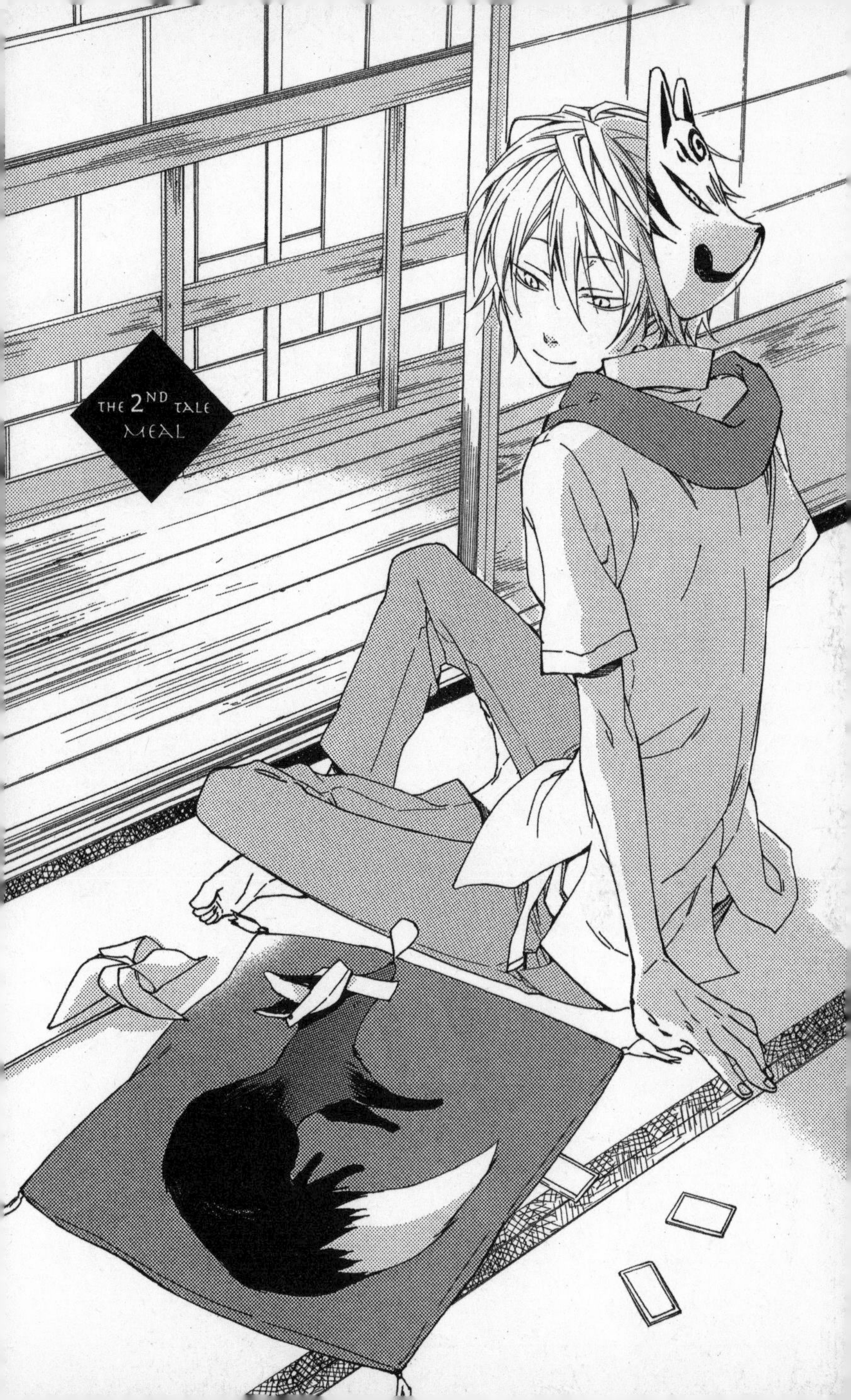
THE 2ND TALE
MEAL

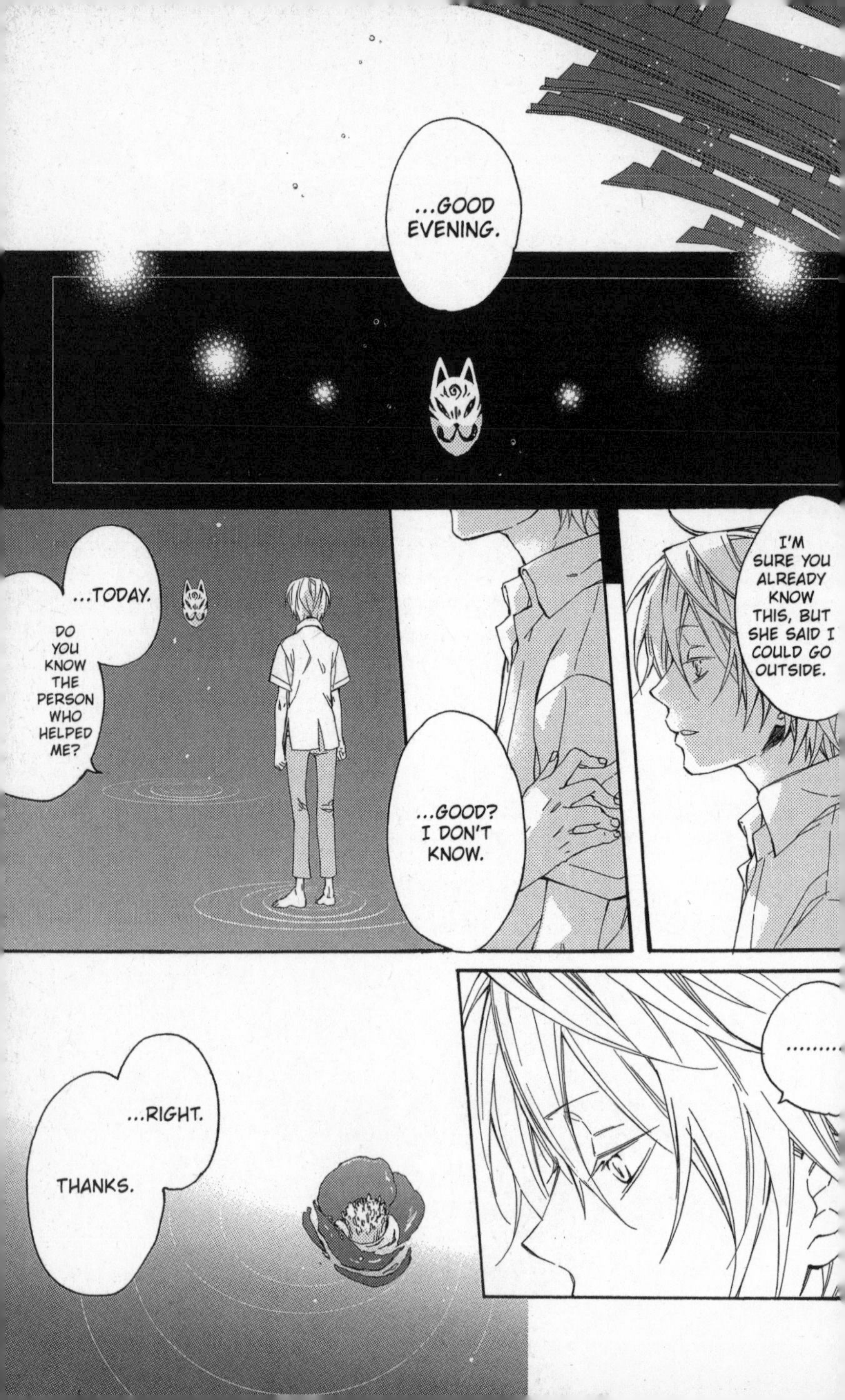
...GOOD EVENING.
I'M SURE YOU ALREADY KNOW THIS, BUT SHE SAID I COULD GO OUTSIDE.
...GOOD? I DON'T KNOW.
...TODAY.
DO YOU KNOW THE PERSON WHO HELPED ME?
....
...RIGHT.
THANKS.

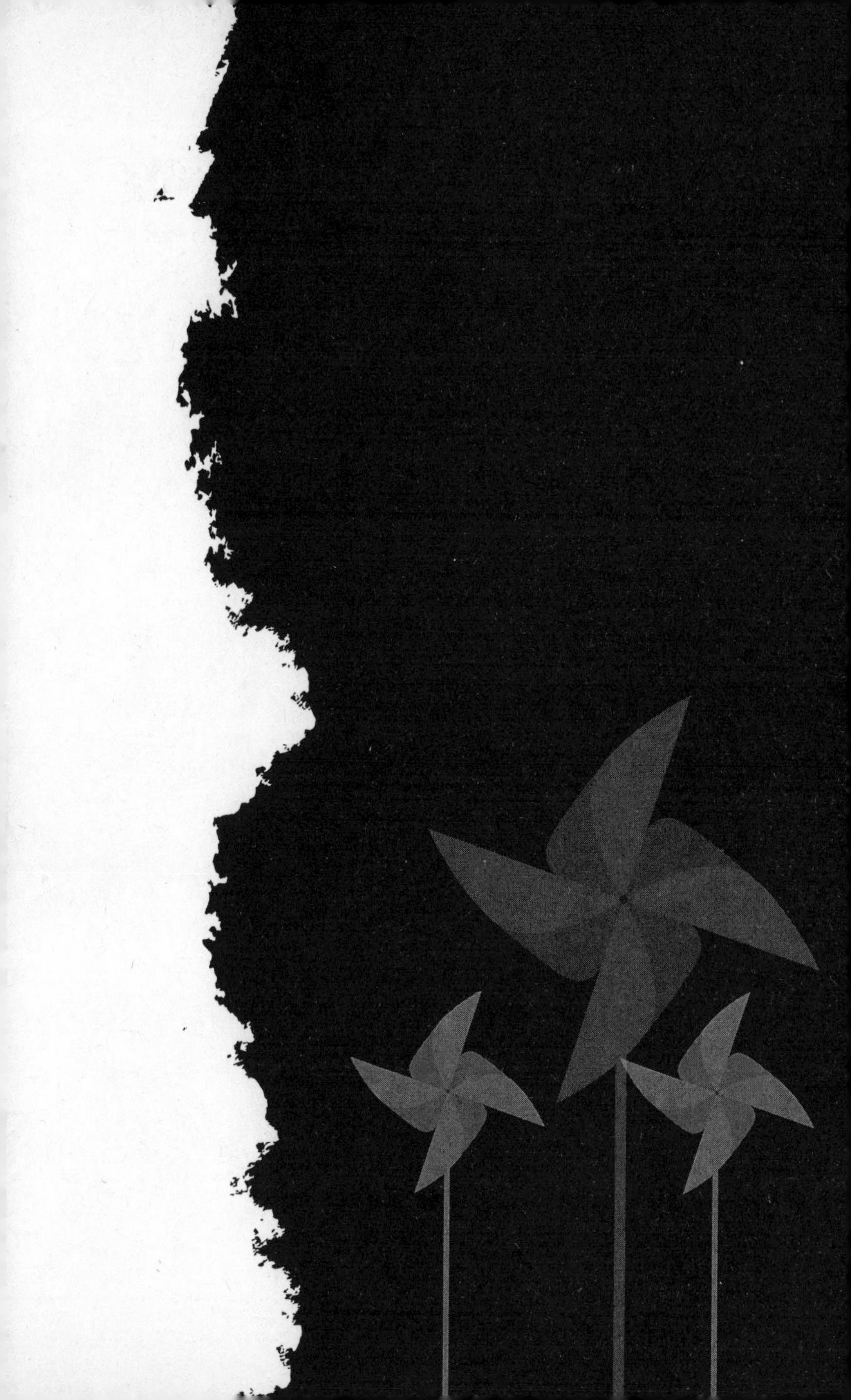

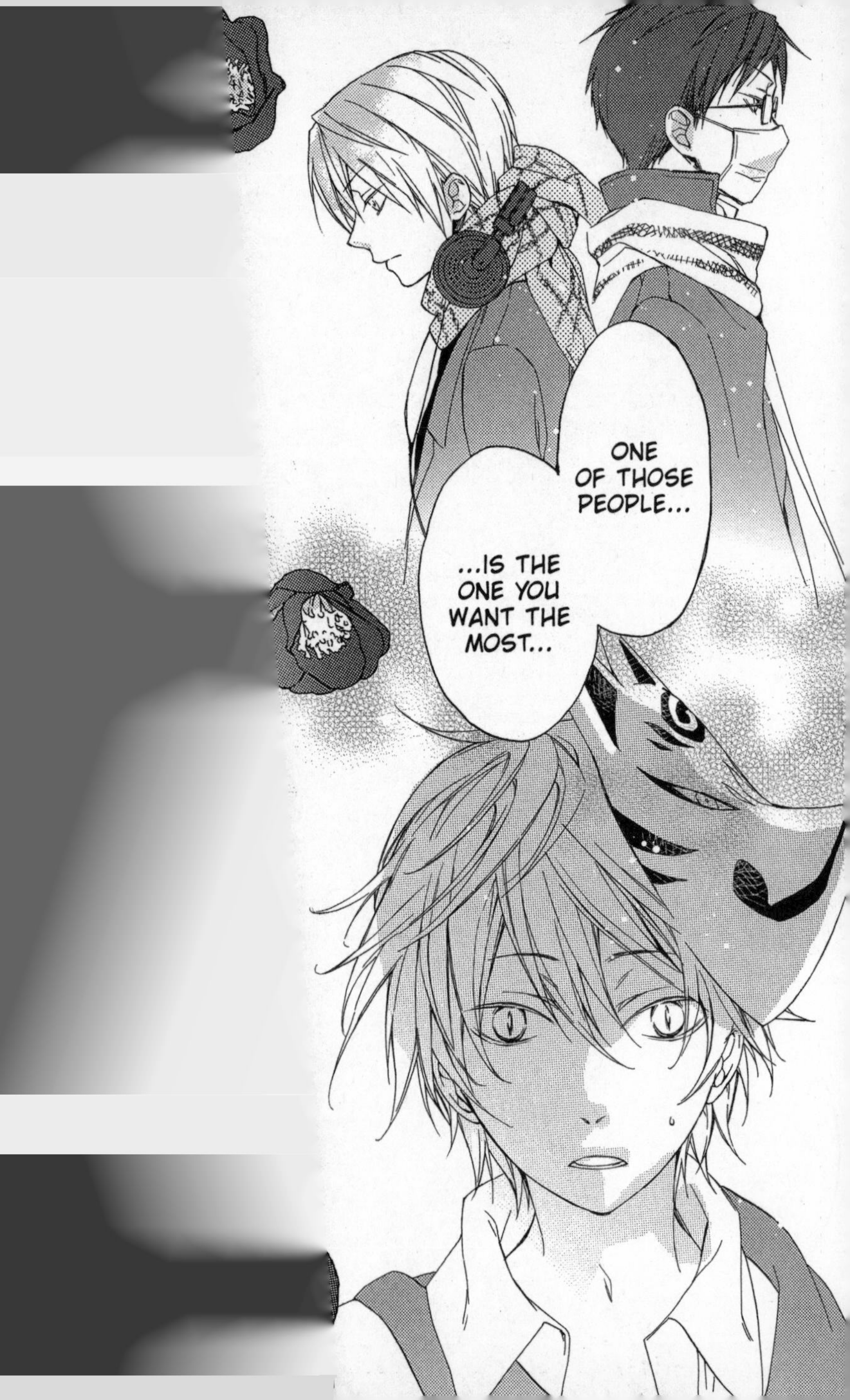
ONE OF THOSE PEOPLE...
...IS THE ONE YOU WANT THE MOST...

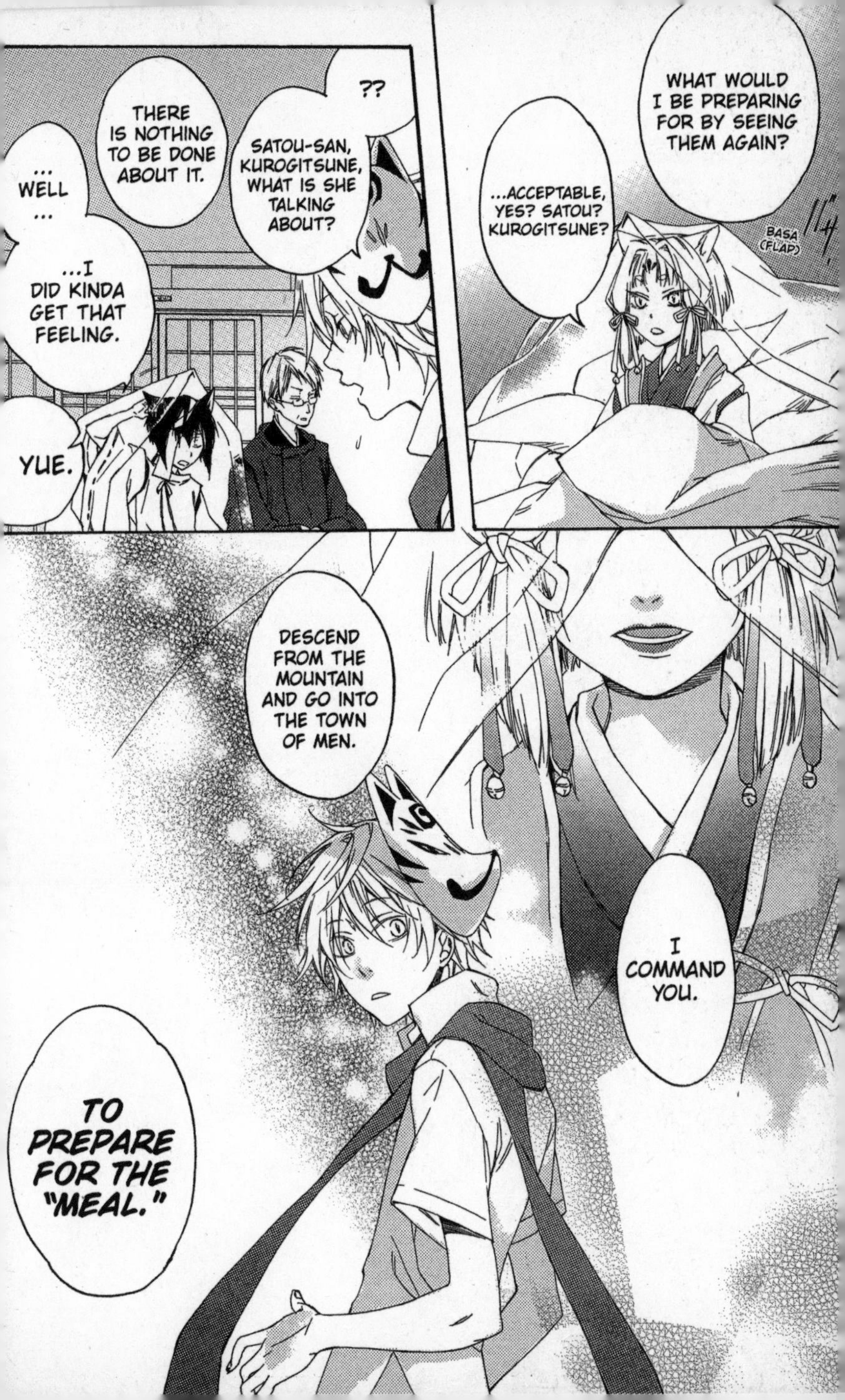

WHAT WOULD I BE PREPARING FOR BY SEEING THEM AGAIN?
BASA (FLAP)
...ACCEPTABLE, YES? SATOU? KUROGITSUNE?
??
SATOU-SAN, KUROGITSUNE, WHAT IS SHE TALKING ABOUT?
THERE IS NOTHING TO BE DONE ABOUT IT.
... WELL ...
...I DID KINDA GET THAT FEELING.
YUE.
DESCEND FROM THE MOUNTAIN AND GO INTO THE TOWN OF MEN.
I COMMAND YOU.
TO PREPARE FOR THE "MEAL."

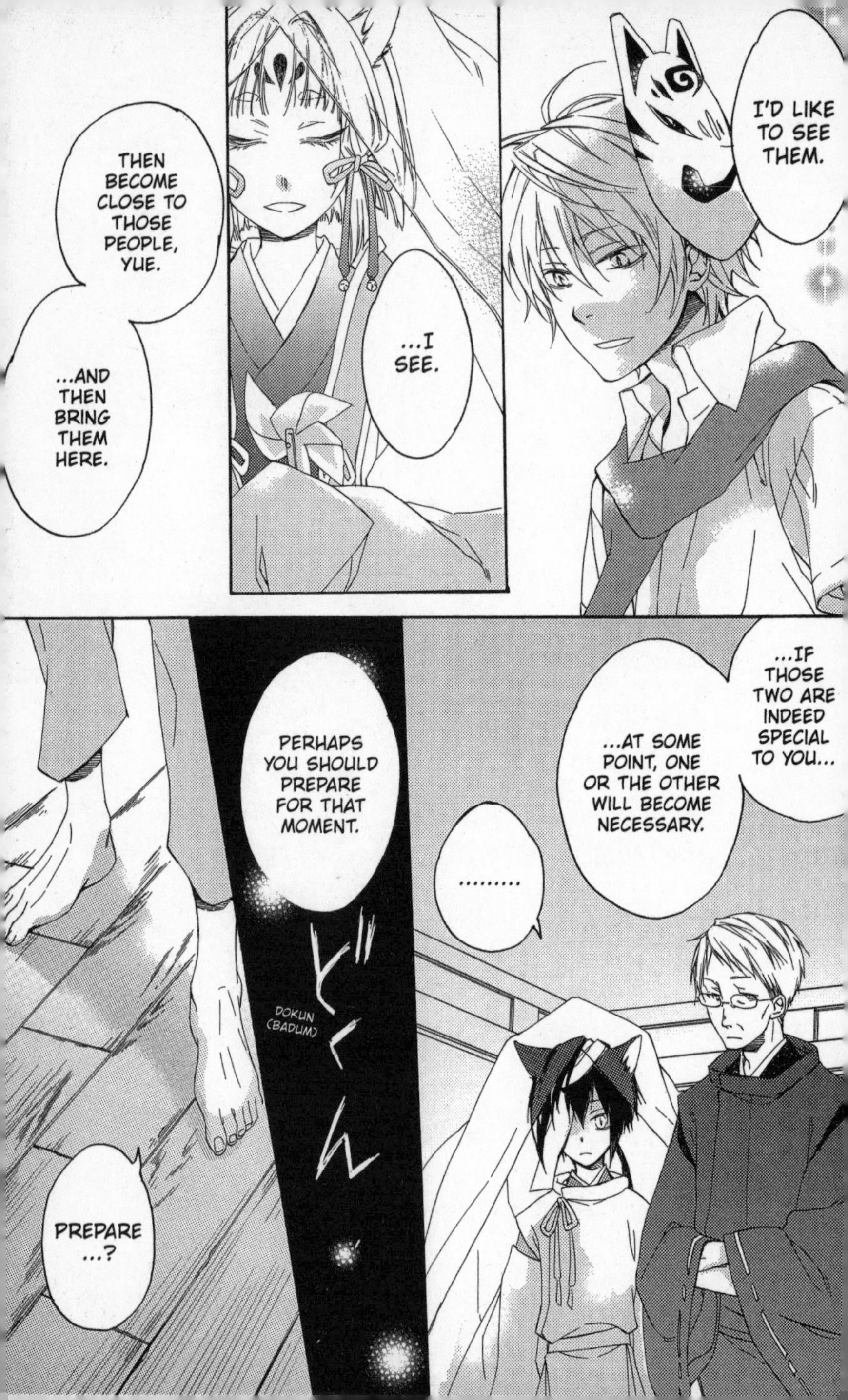
I'D LIKE TO SEE THEM.
...I SEE.
THEN BECOME CLOSE TO THOSE PEOPLE, YUE.
...AND THEN BRING THEM HERE.
...IF THOSE TWO ARE INDEED SPECIAL TO YOU...
...AT SOME POINT, ONE OR THE OTHER WILL BECOME NECESSARY.
....
PERHAPS YOU SHOULD PREPARE FOR THAT MOMENT.
DOKUN (BADUM)
PREPARE ...?

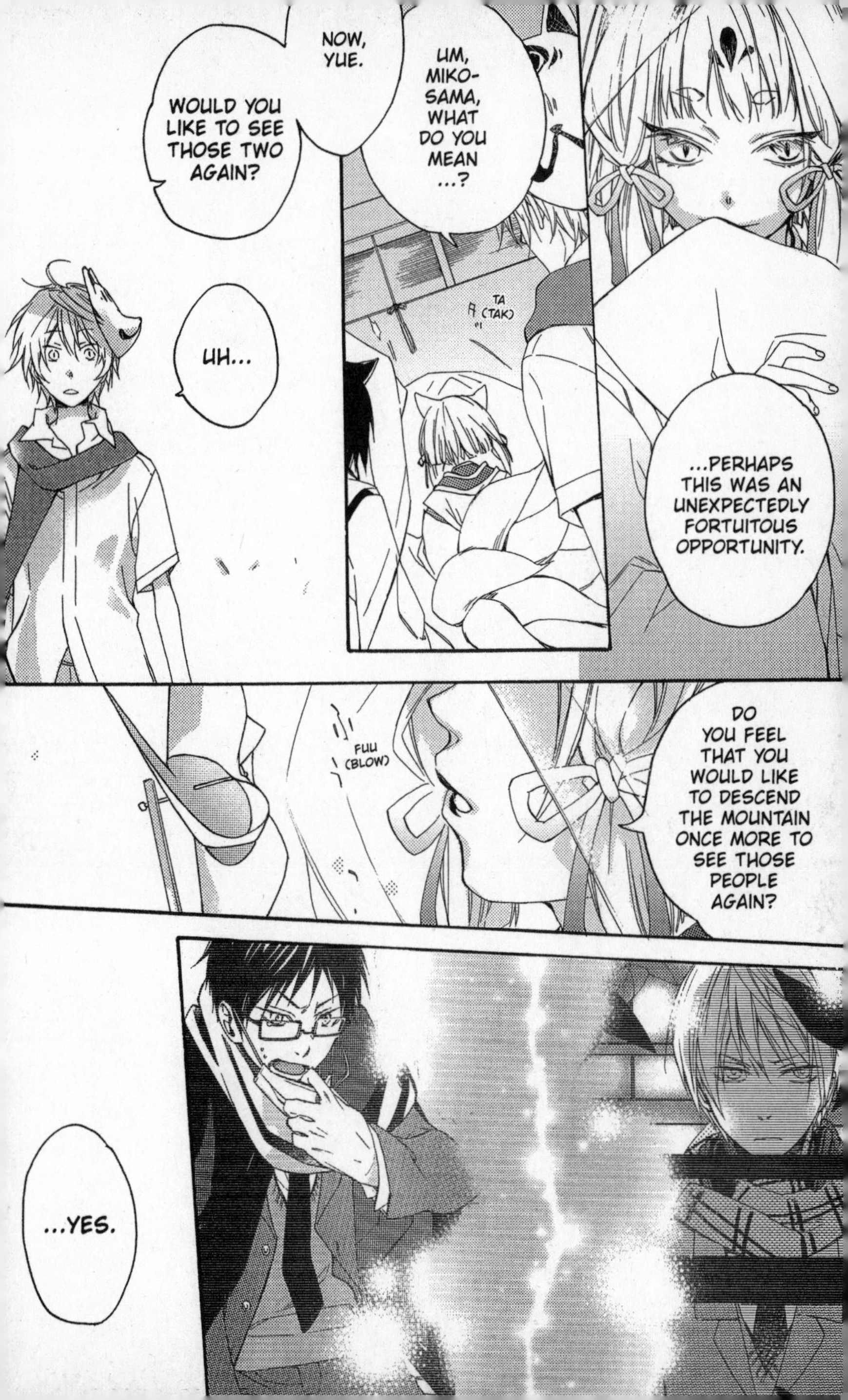
...PERHAPS THIS WAS AN UNEXPECTEDLY FORTUITOUS OPPORTUNITY.
UM, MIKO-SAMA, WHAT DO YOU MEAN ...?
TA (TAK)
NOW, YUE.
WOULD YOU LIKE TO SEE THOSE TWO AGAIN?
UH...
DO YOU FEEL THAT YOU WOULD LIKE TO DESCEND THE MOUNTAIN ONCE MORE TO SEE THOSE PEOPLE AGAIN?
FUU (BLOW)
...YES.

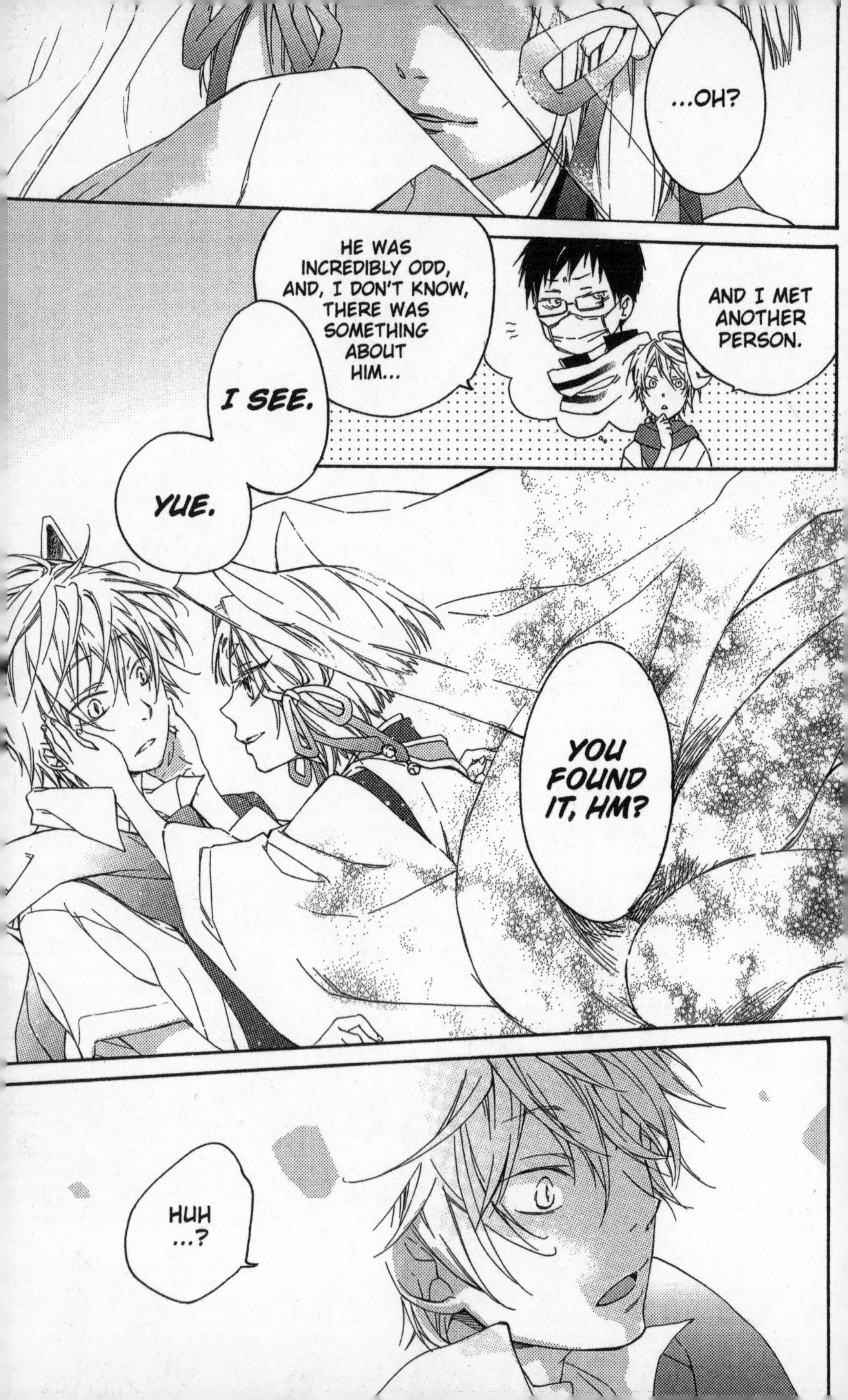
...OH?
AND I MET ANOTHER PERSON.
HE WAS INCREDIBLY ODD, AND, I DON'T KNOW, THERE WAS SOMETHING ABOUT HIM...
I SEE.
YUE.
YOU FOUND IT, HM?
HUH ...?

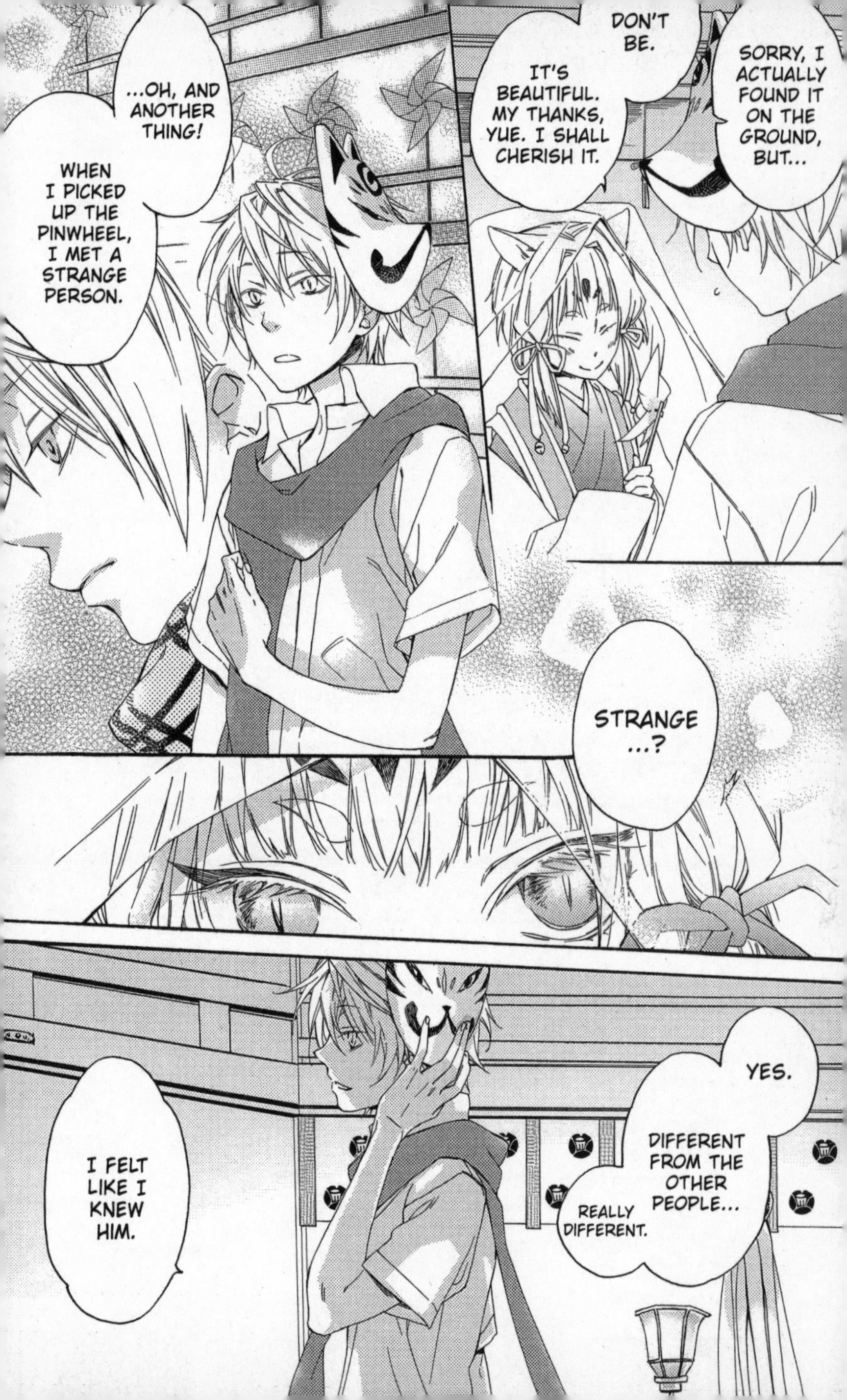
SORRY, I ACTUALLY FOUND IT ON THE GROUND, BUT...
DON'T BE.
IT'S BEAUTIFUL. MY THANKS, YUE. I SHALL CHERISH IT.
...OH, AND ANOTHER THING!
WHEN I PICKED UP THE PINWHEEL, I MET A STRANGE PERSON.
STRANGE ...?
YES.
DIFFERENT FROM THE OTHER PEOPLE...
REALLY DIFFERENT.
I FELT LIKE I KNEW HIM.

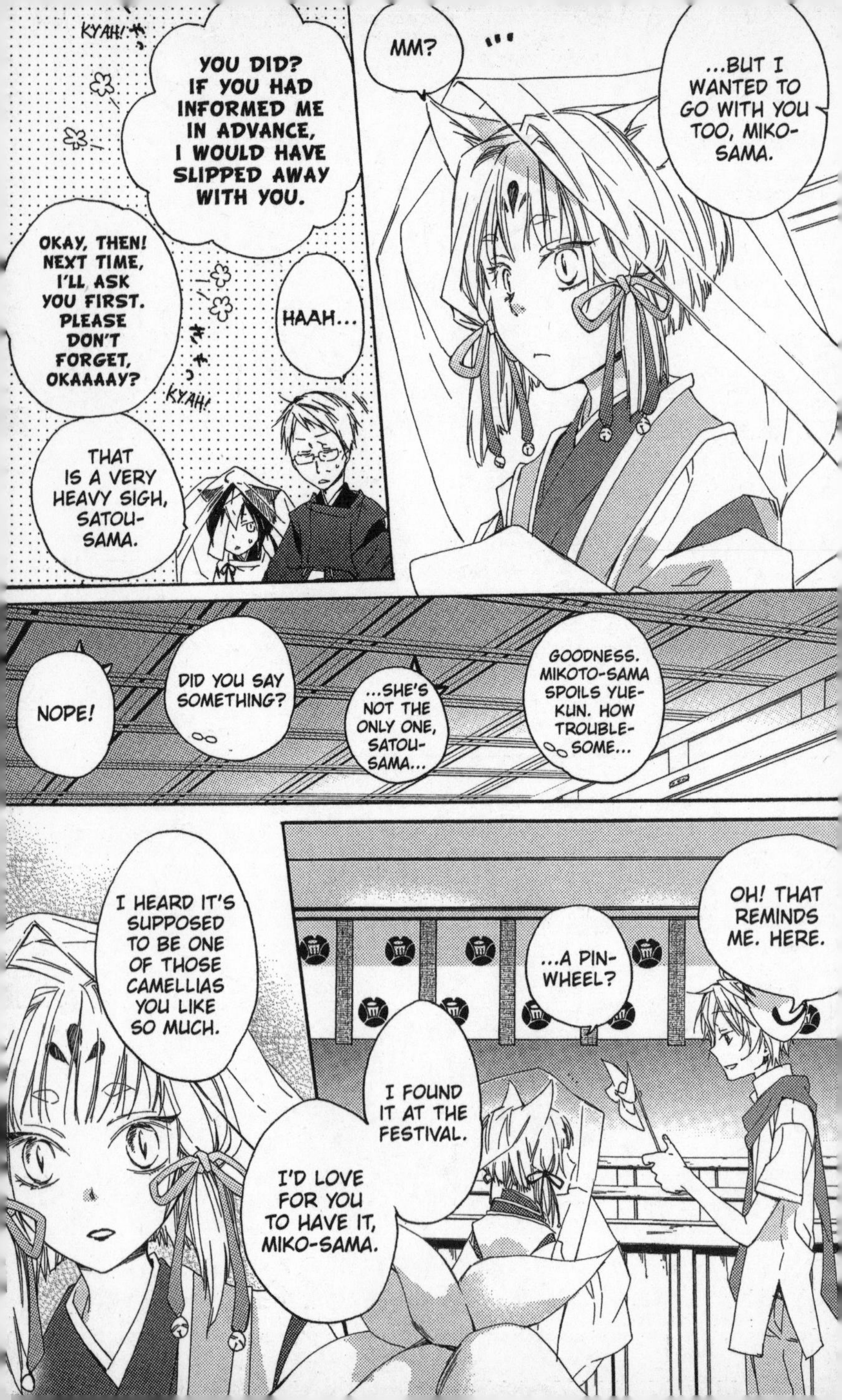
...BUT I WANTED TO GO WITH YOU TOO, MIKO-SAMA.
MM?
...
YOU DID? IF YOU HAD INFORMED ME IN ADVANCE, I WOULD HAVE SLIPPED AWAY WITH YOU.
KYAH!
OKAY, THEN! NEXT TIME, I'LL ASK YOU FIRST. PLEASE DON'T FORGET, OKAAAAY?
HAAH...
KYAH!
THAT IS A VERY HEAVY SIGH, SATOU-SAMA.
GOODNESS. MIKOTO-SAMA SPOILS YUE-KUN. HOW TROUBLE-SOME...
...SHE'S NOT THE ONLY ONE, SATOU-SAMA...
DID YOU SAY SOMETHING?
NOPE!
OH! THAT REMINDS ME. HERE.
...A PIN-WHEEL?
I FOUND IT AT THE FESTIVAL.
I'D LOVE FOR YOU TO HAVE IT, MIKO-SAMA.
I HEARD IT'S SUPPOSED TO BE ONE OF THOSE CAMELLIAS YOU LIKE SO MUCH.

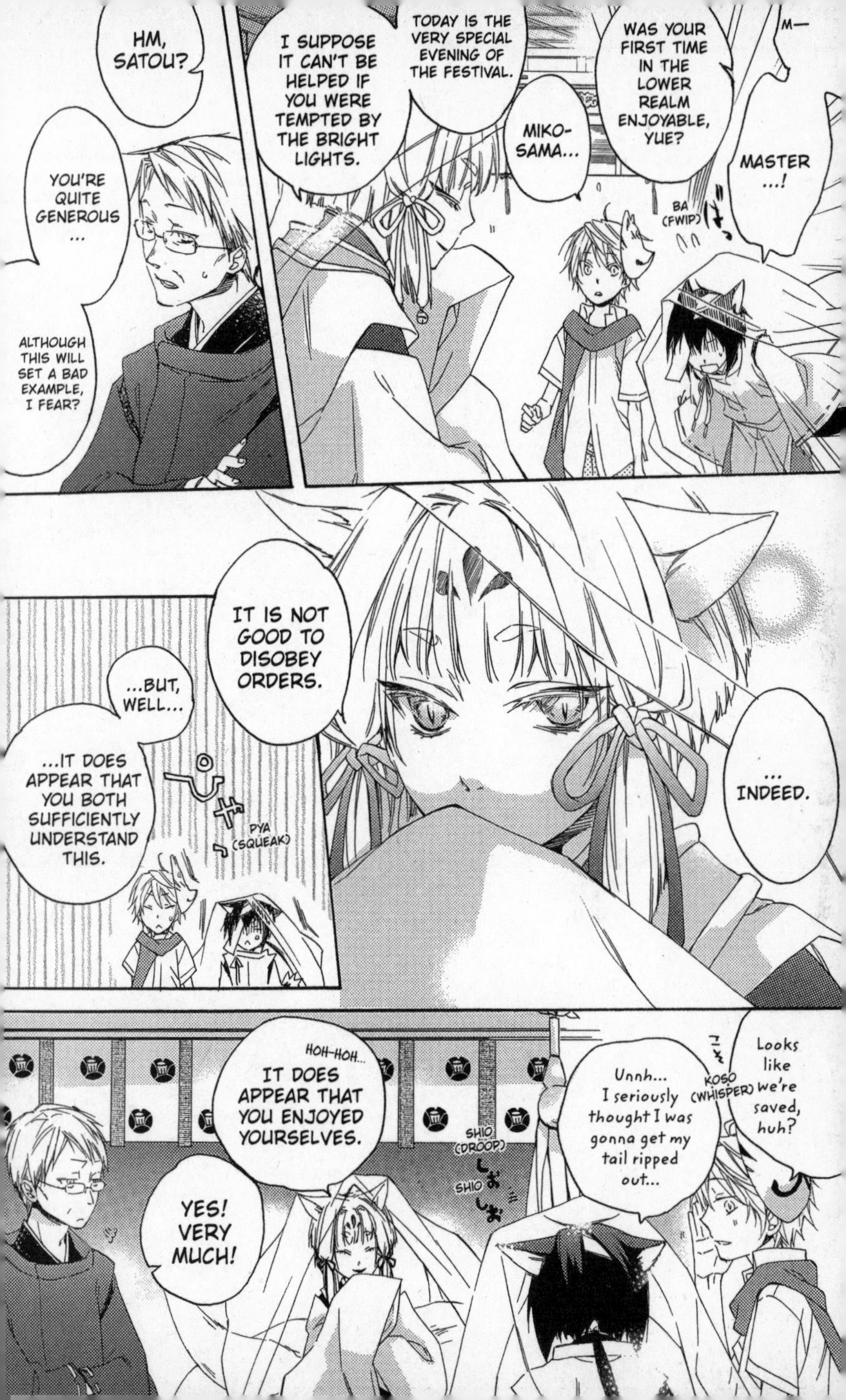
M—
MASTER ...!
WAS YOUR FIRST TIME IN THE LOWER REALM ENJOYABLE, YUE?
TODAY IS THE VERY SPECIAL EVENING OF THE FESTIVAL.
MIKO-SAMA...
I SUPPOSE IT CAN'T BE HELPED IF YOU WERE TEMPTED BY THE BRIGHT LIGHTS.
BA (FWIP)
HM, SATOU?
YOU'RE QUITE GENEROUS ...
ALTHOUGH THIS WILL SET A BAD EXAMPLE, I FEAR?
IT IS NOT GOOD TO DISOBEY ORDERS.
... INDEED.
...BUT, WELL...
...IT DOES APPEAR THAT YOU BOTH SUFFICIENTLY UNDERSTAND THIS.
PYA (SQUEAK)
Looks like we're saved, huh?
KOSO (WHISPER)
Unnh... I seriously thought I was gonna get my tail ripped out...
HOH-HOH...
IT DOES APPEAR THAT YOU ENJOYED YOURSELVES.
SHIO SHIO (DROOP)
YES! VERY MUCH!

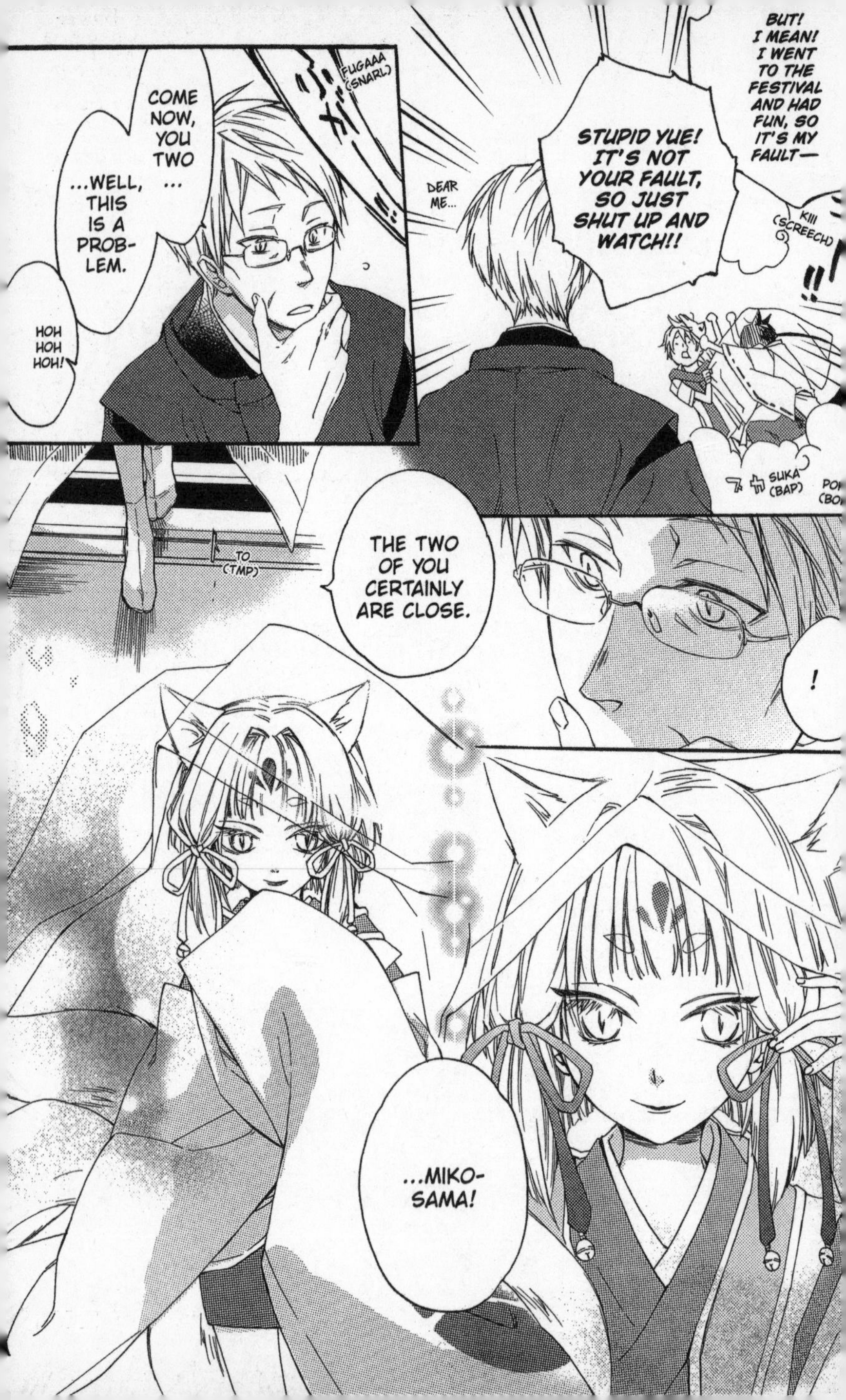
BUT! I MEAN! I WENT TO THE FESTIVAL AND HAD FUN, SO IT'S MY FAULT—
STUPID YUE! IT'S NOT YOUR FAULT, SO JUST SHUT UP AND WATCH!!
KIII (SCREECH)
DEAR ME...
SUKA (BAP)
FUGAAA (SNARL)
COME NOW, YOU TWO ...
...WELL, THIS IS A PROB-LEM.
HOH HOH HOH!
!
THE TWO OF YOU CERTAINLY ARE CLOSE.
TO (TMP)
...MIKO-SAMA!

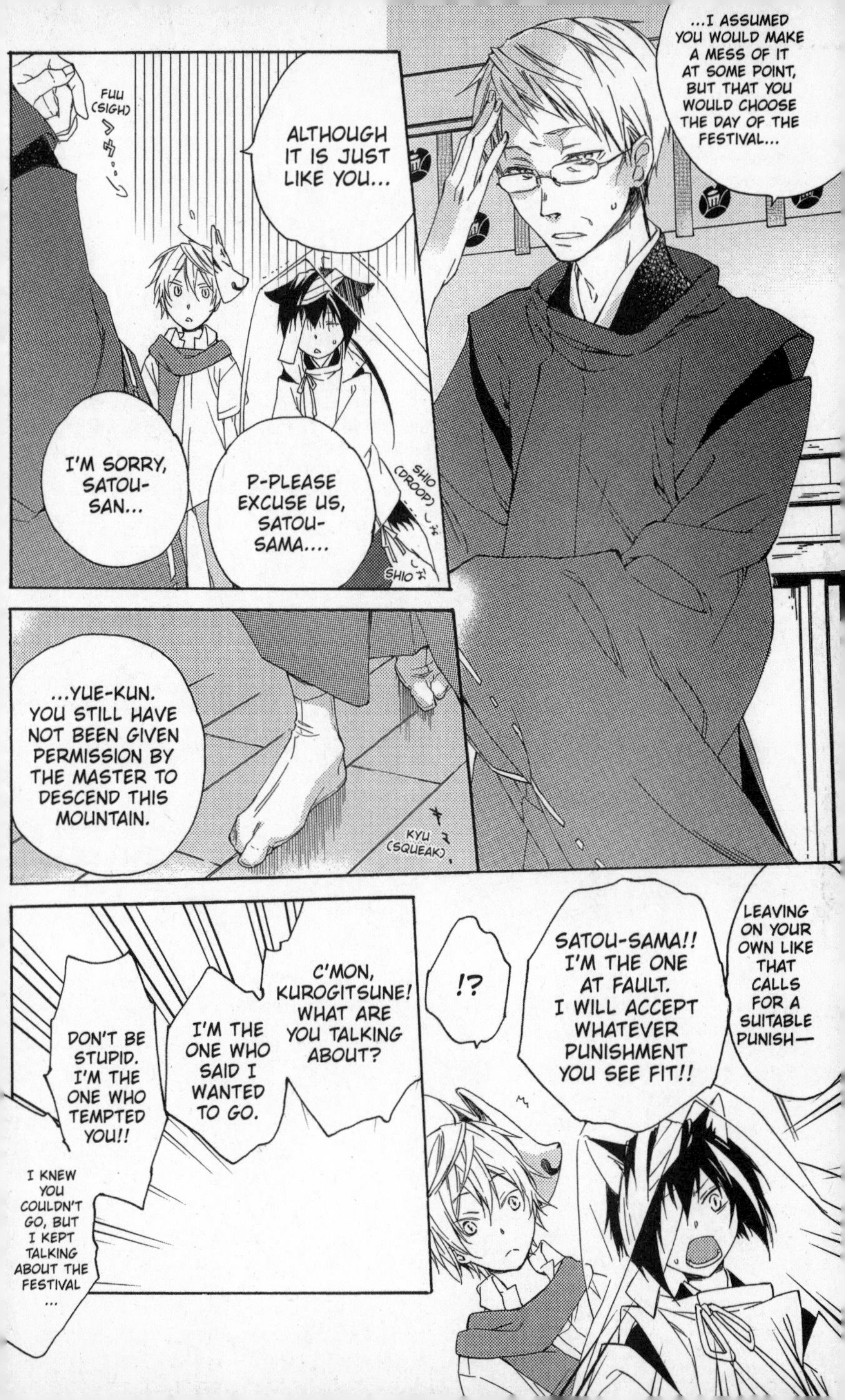
...I ASSUMED YOU WOULD MAKE A MESS OF IT AT SOME POINT, BUT THAT YOU WOULD CHOOSE THE DAY OF THE FESTIVAL...
FUU (SIGH)
ALTHOUGH IT IS JUST LIKE YOU...
SHIO (DROOP)
SHIO
P-PLEASE EXCUSE US, SATOU-SAMA....
I'M SORRY, SATOU-SAN...
KYU (SQUEAK)
...YUE-KUN. YOU STILL HAVE NOT BEEN GIVEN PERMISSION BY THE MASTER TO DESCEND THIS MOUNTAIN.
LEAVING ON YOUR OWN LIKE THAT CALLS FOR A SUITABLE PUNISH—
SATOU-SAMA!! I'M THE ONE AT FAULT. I WILL ACCEPT WHATEVER PUNISHMENT YOU SEE FIT!!
!?
C'MON, KUROGITSUNE! WHAT ARE YOU TALKING ABOUT?
I'M THE ONE WHO SAID I WANTED TO GO.
DON'T BE STUPID. I'M THE ONE WHO TEMPTED YOU!!
I KNEW YOU COULDN'T GO, BUT I KEPT TALKING ABOUT THE FESTIVAL ...

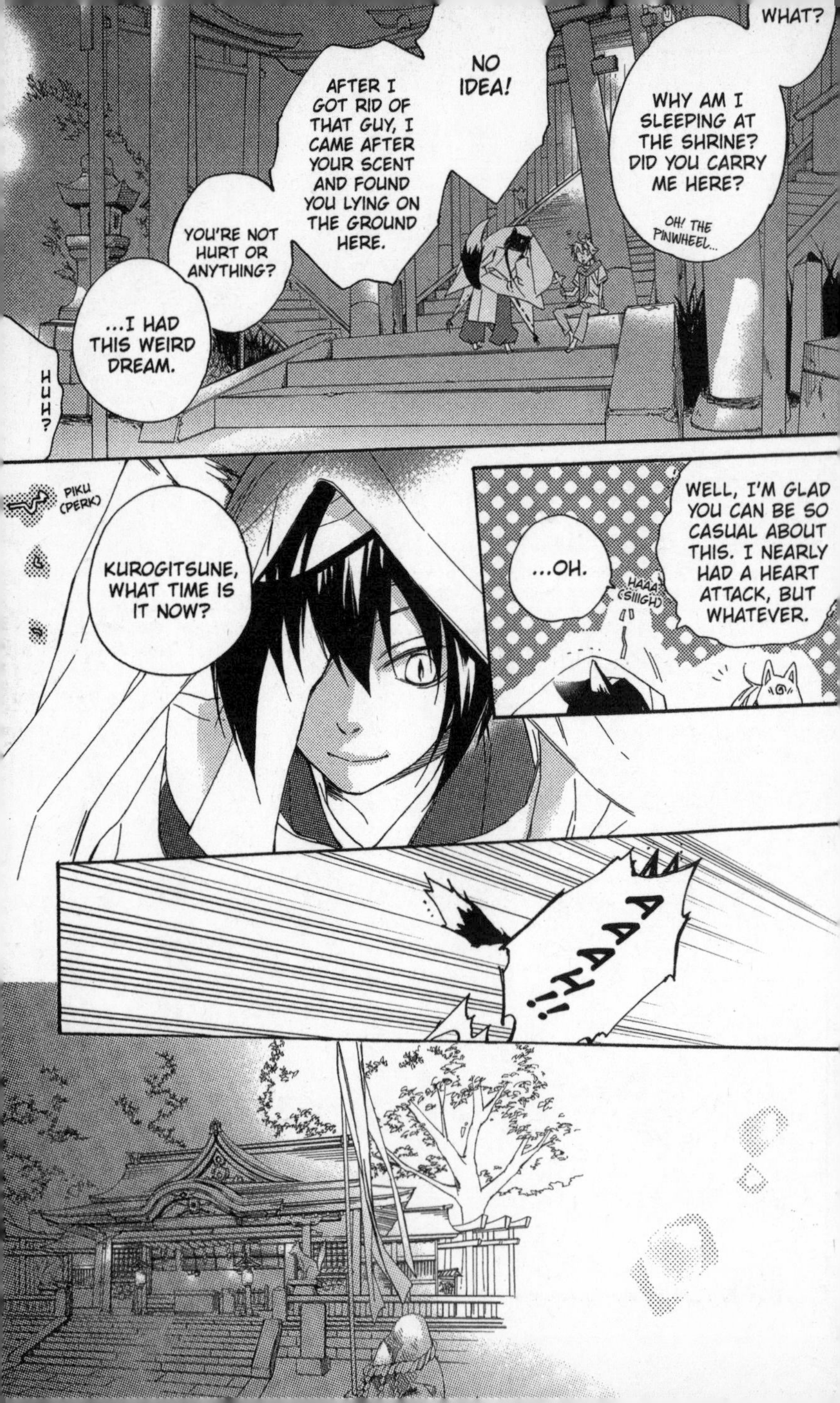
WHAT?
WHY AM I SLEEPING AT THE SHRINE? DID YOU CARRY ME HERE?
OH! THE PINWHEEL...
NO IDEA!
AFTER I GOT RID OF THAT GUY, I CAME AFTER YOUR SCENT AND FOUND YOU LYING ON THE GROUND HERE.
YOU'RE NOT HURT OR ANYTHING?
...I HAD THIS WEIRD DREAM.
HUH?
WELL, I'M GLAD YOU CAN BE SO CASUAL ABOUT THIS. I NEARLY HAD A HEART ATTACK, BUT WHATEVER.
HAAA (SIIIGH)
...OH.
PIKU (PERK)
KUROGITSUNE, WHAT TIME IS IT NOW?
AAAAH!!

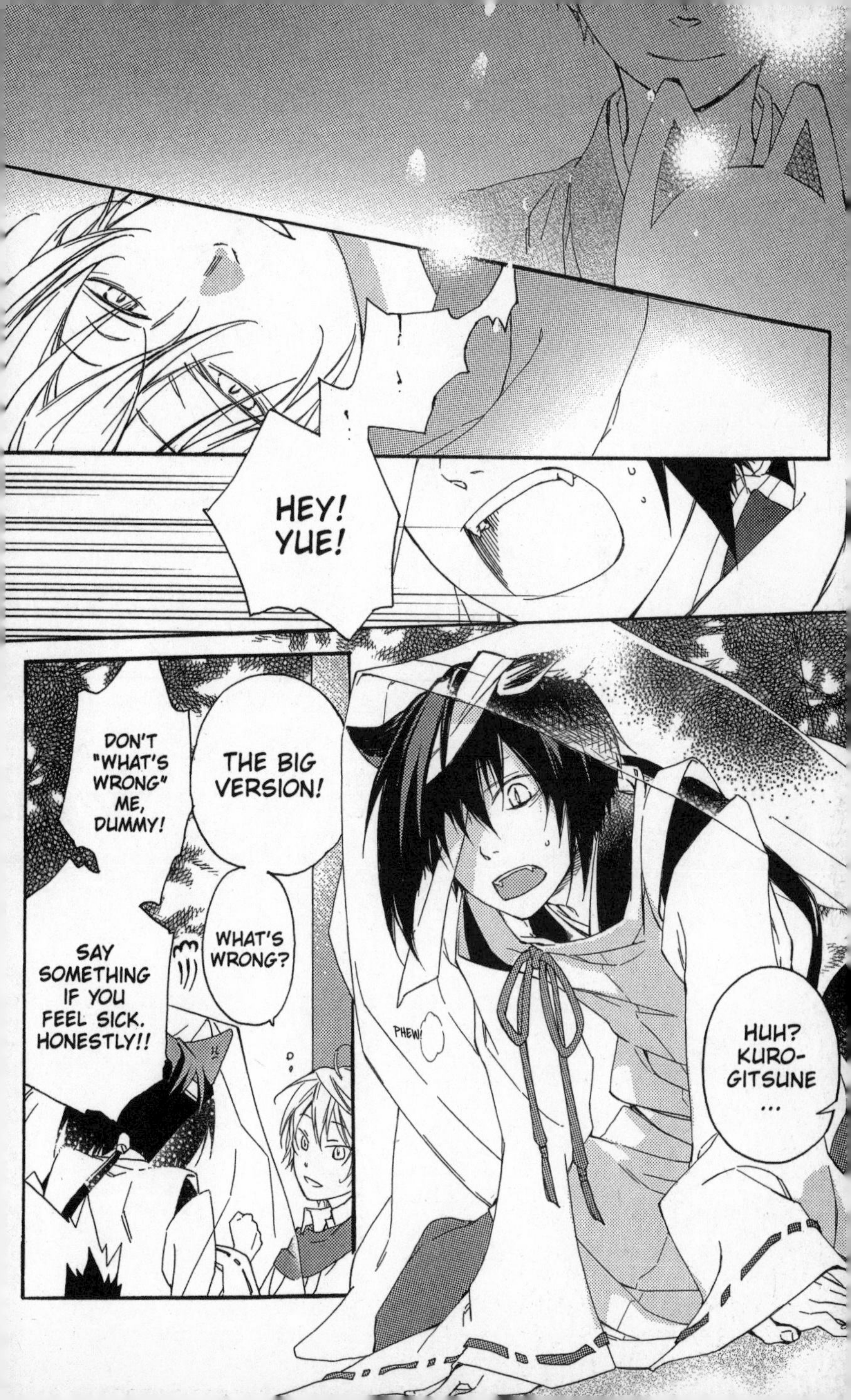
HEY! YUE!
HUH? KURO-GITSUNE ...
PHEW!
THE BIG VERSION!
WHAT'S WRONG?
DON'T "WHAT'S WRONG" ME, DUMMY!
SAY SOMETHING IF YOU FEEL SICK. HONESTLY!!

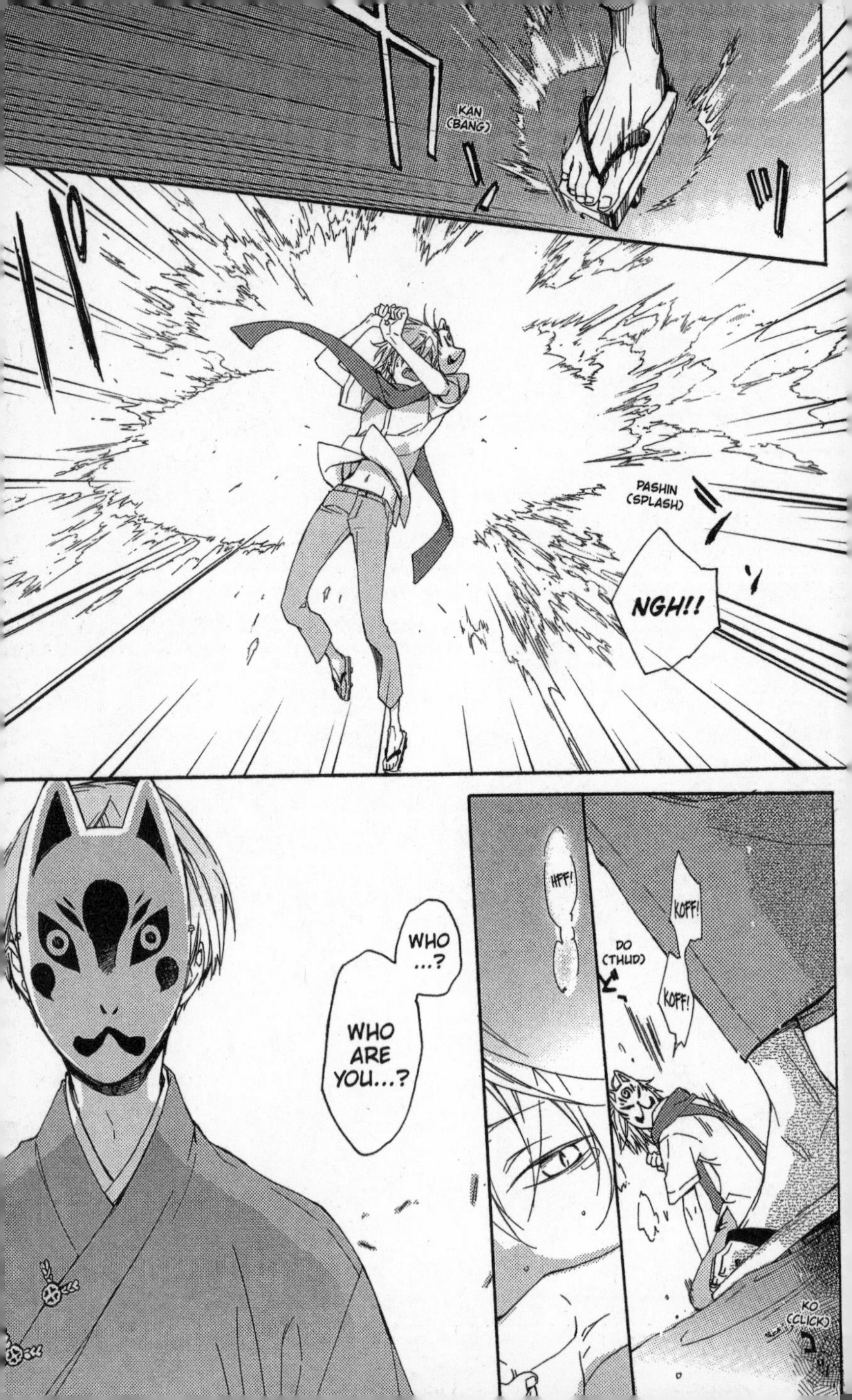
KAN (BANG)
PASHIN (SPLASH)
NGH!!
KOFF!
HFF!
DO (THUD)
KOFF!
KO (CLICK)
WHO ...?
WHO ARE YOU...?

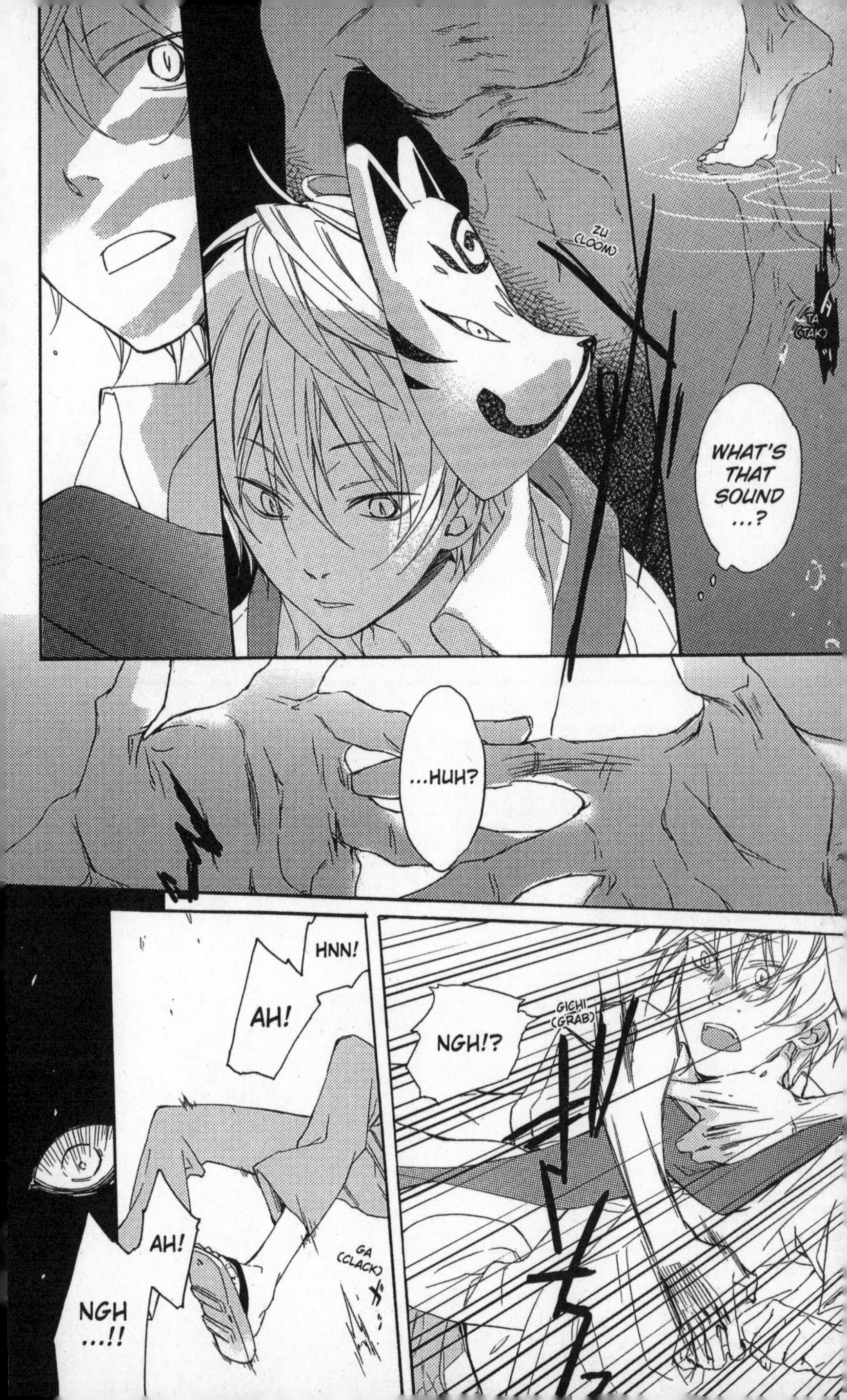

TA (TAK)
WHAT'S THAT SOUND ...?
ZU (LOOM)
...HUH?
GICHI (GRAB)
NGH!?
HNN!
AH!
AH!
GA (CLACK)
NGH ...!!

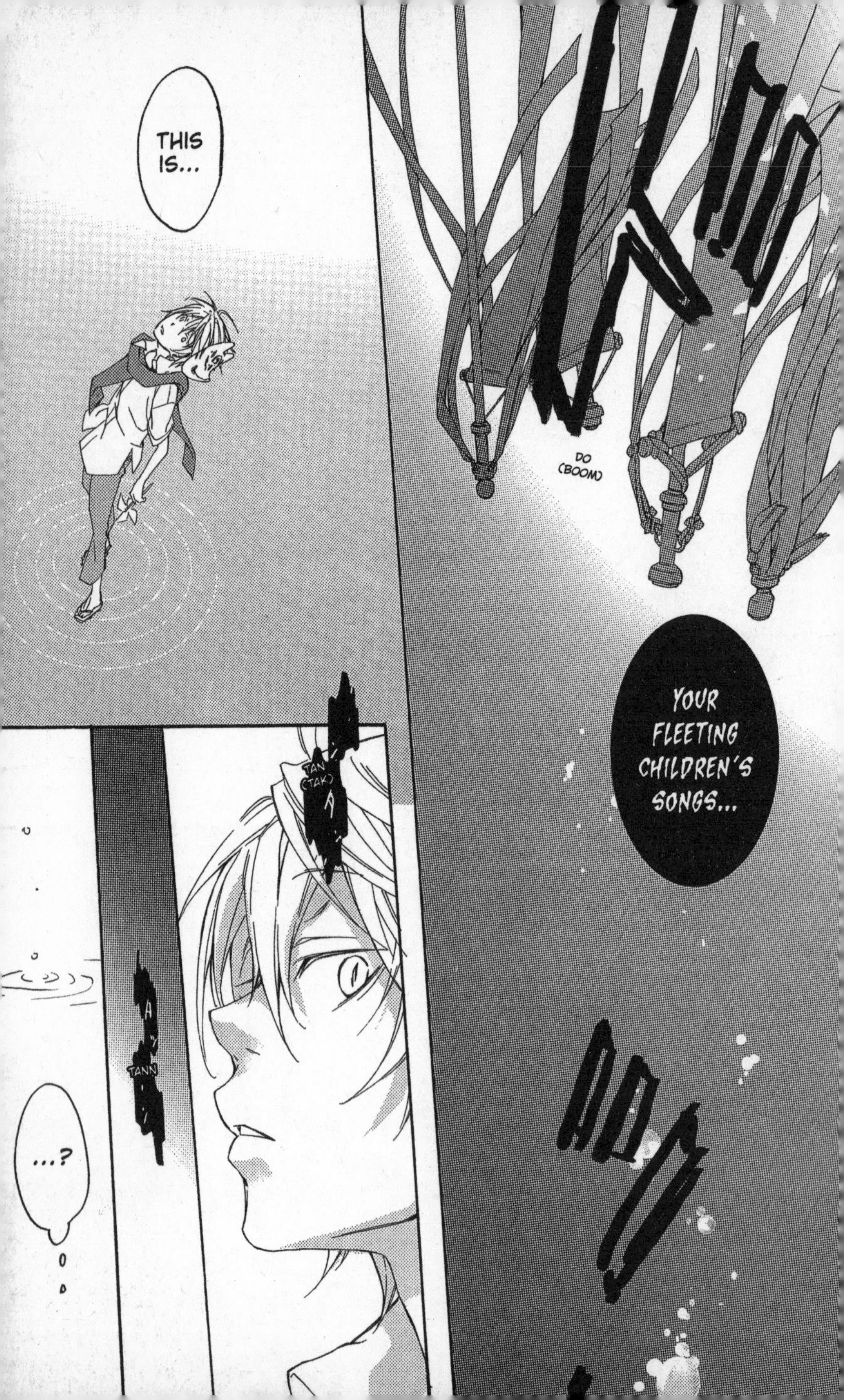
DO (BOOM)
YOUR FLEETING CHILDREN'S SONGS...
THIS IS...
TAN (TAK)
TANN
...?

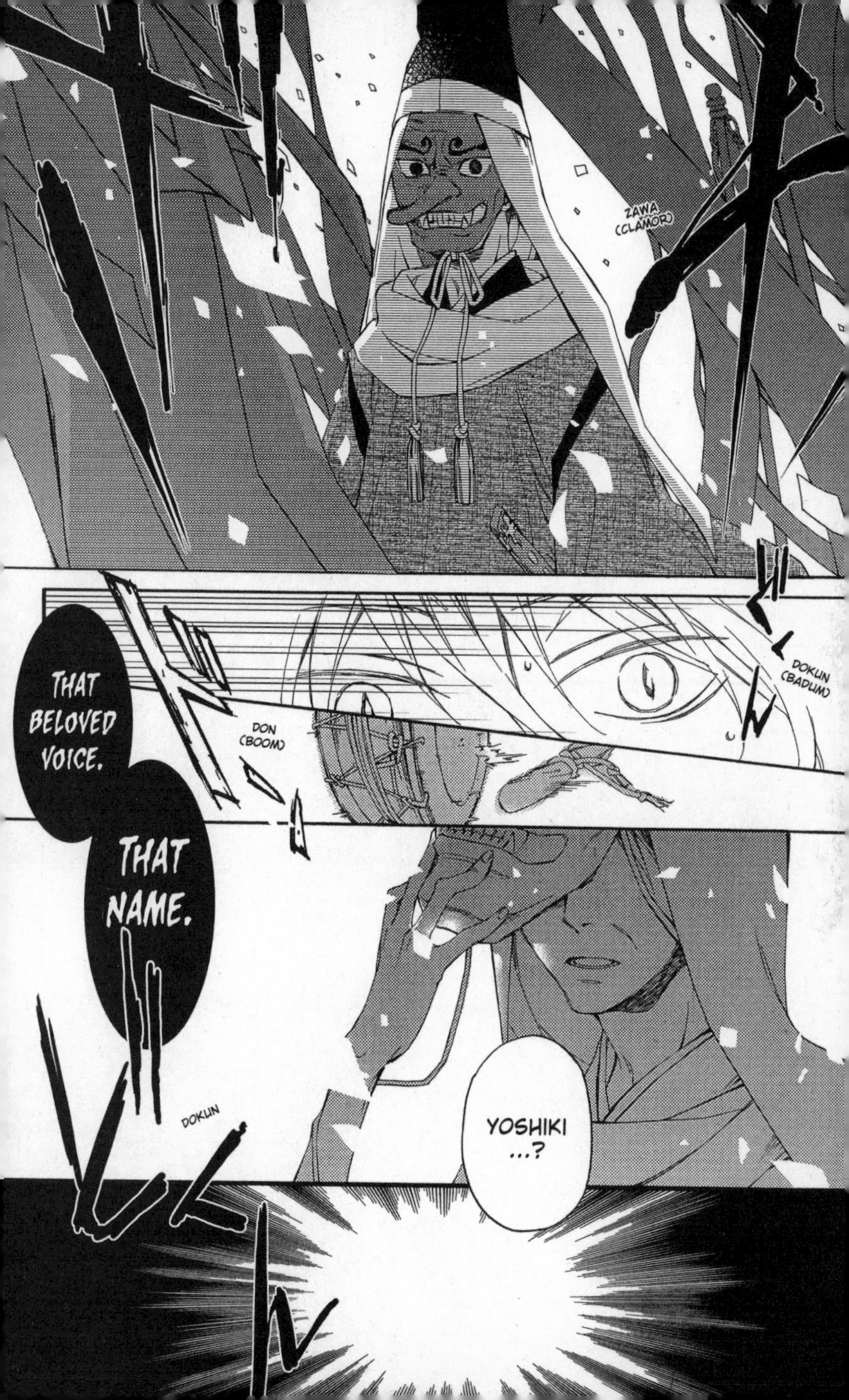
ZAWA (CLAMOR)
DOKUN (BADUM)
DON (BOOM)
THAT BELOVED VOICE.
THAT NAME.
YOSHIKI ...?
DOKUN

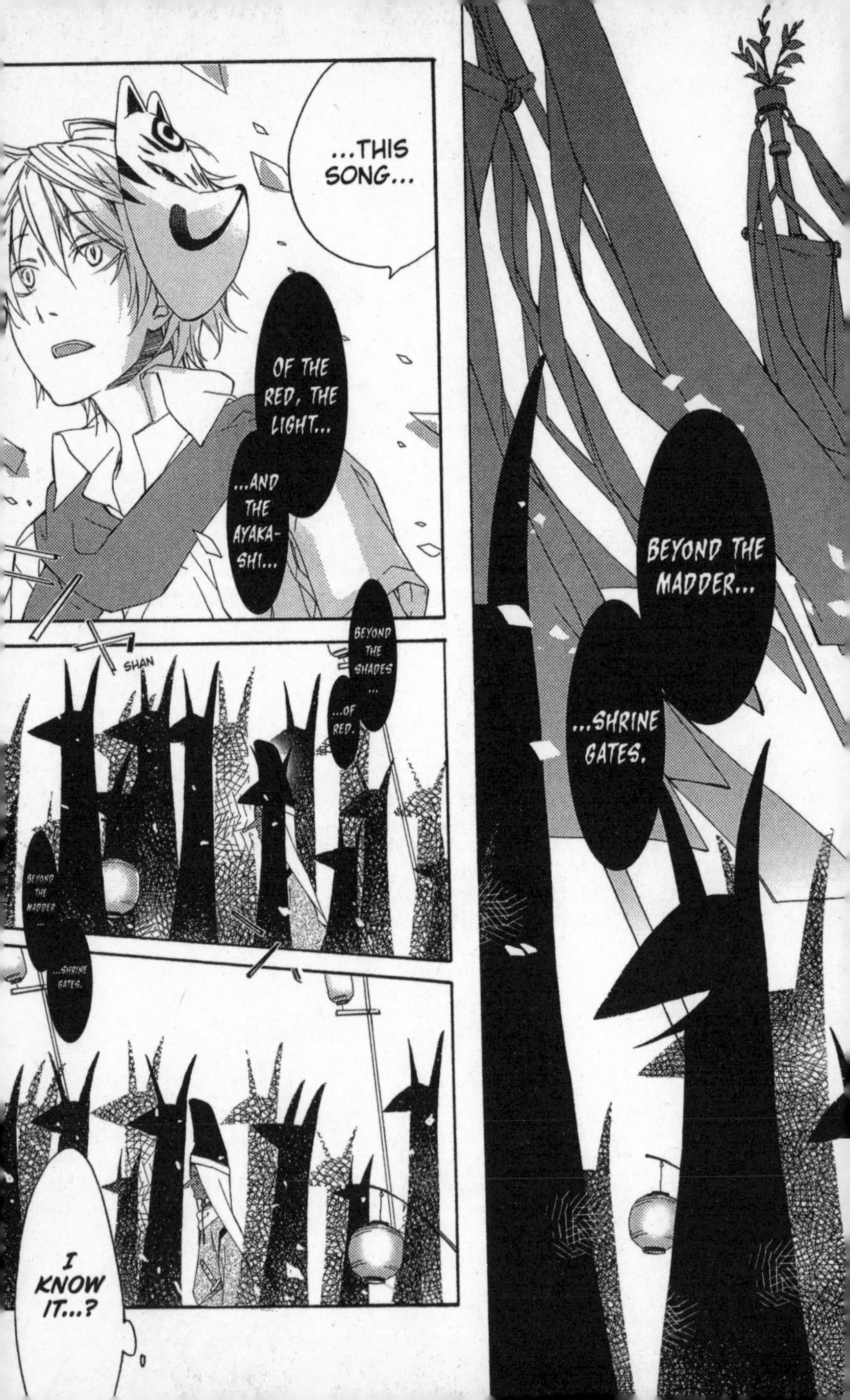
BEYOND THE MADDER...
...SHRINE GATES.
...THIS SONG...
OF THE RED, THE LIGHT...
...AND THE AYAKA-SHI...
SHAN
BEYOND THE SHADES...
...OF RED.
BEYOND THE MADDER...
...SHRINE GATES.
I KNOW IT...?

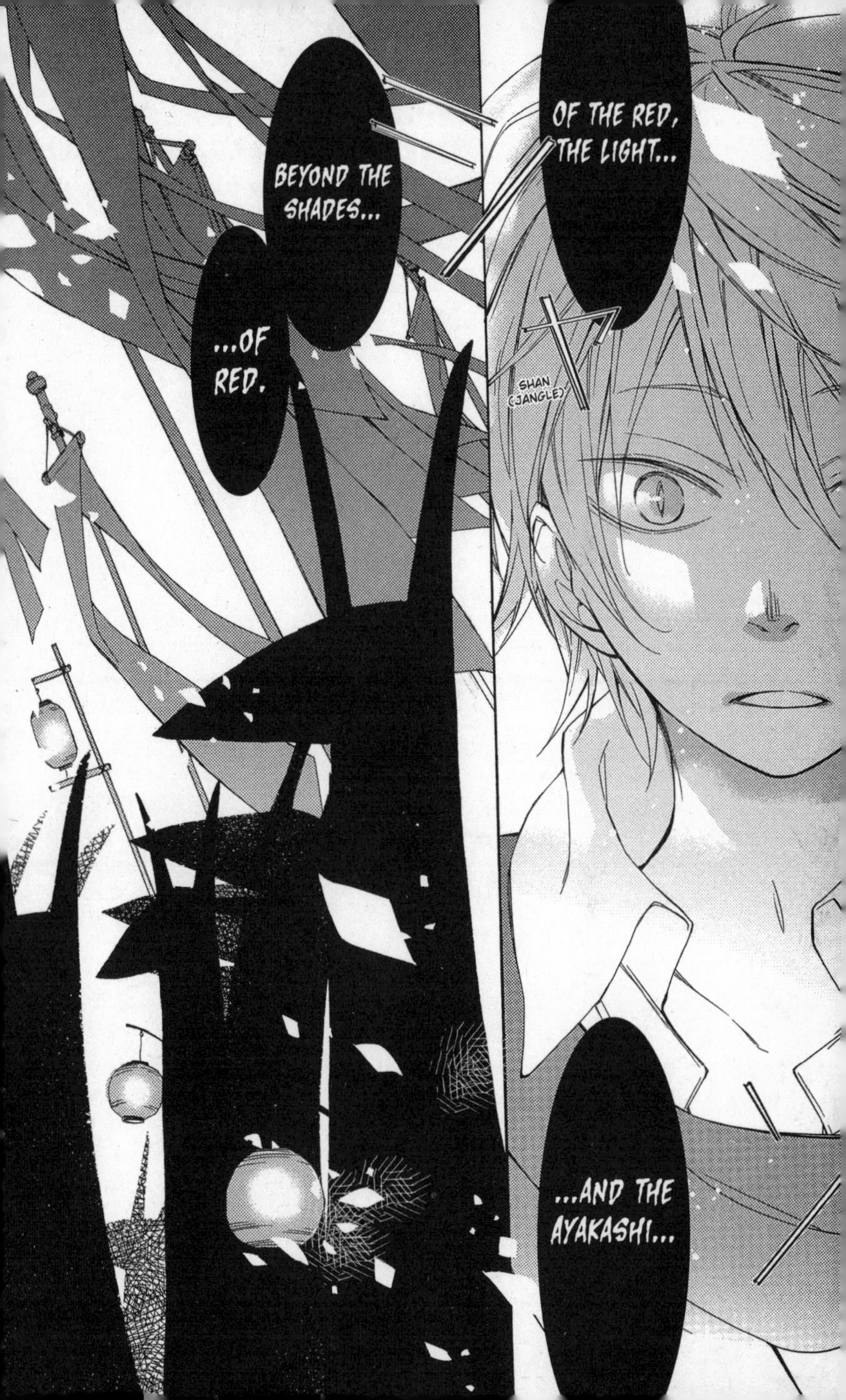
OF THE RED, THE LIGHT...
SHAN (JANGLE)
...AND THE AYAKASHI...
BEYOND THE SHADES...
...OF RED.

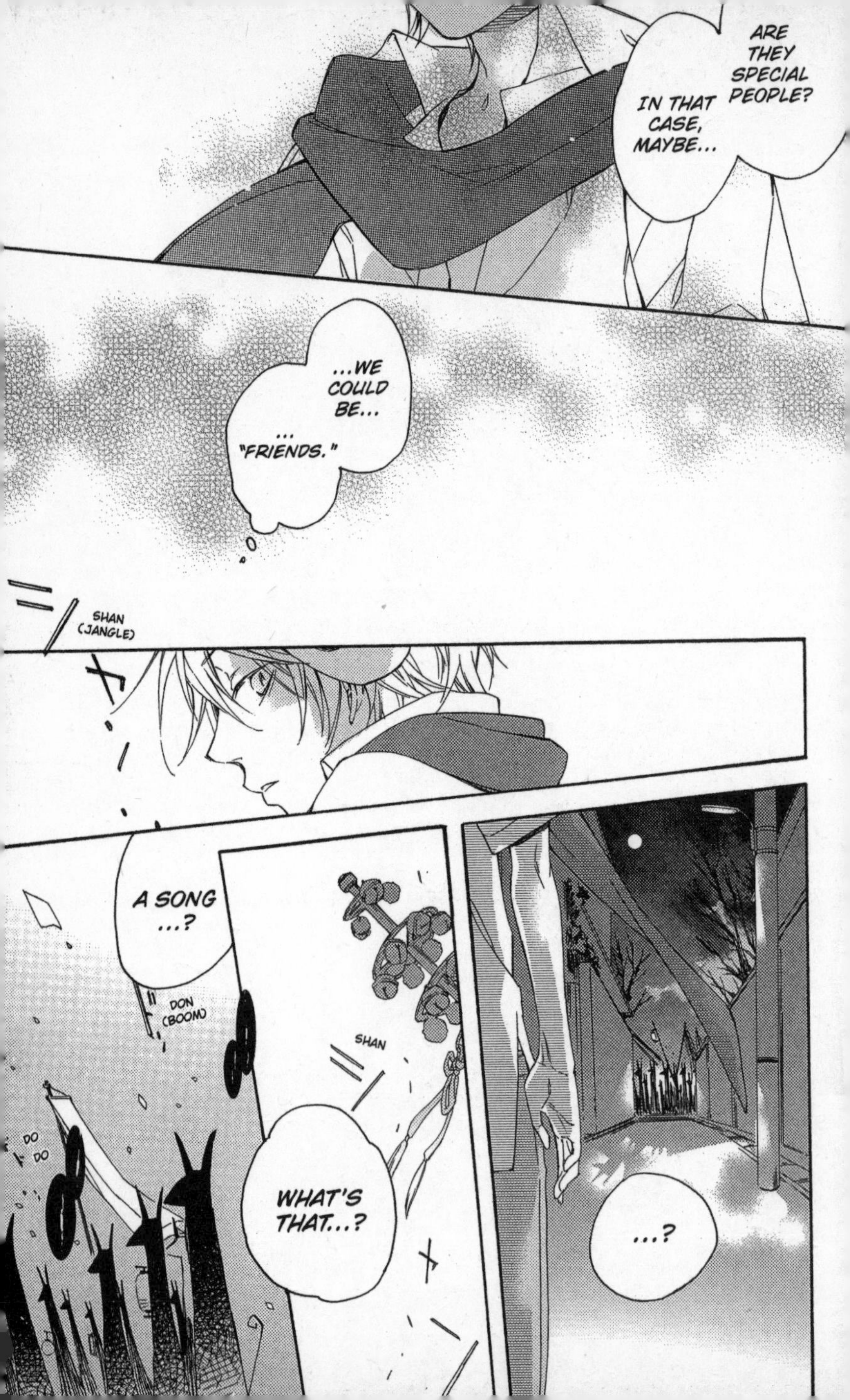
ARE THEY SPECIAL PEOPLE?
IN THAT CASE, MAYBE...
...WE COULD BE... ... "FRIENDS."
SHAN (JANGLE)
...?
SHAN
WHAT'S THAT...?
A SONG ...?
DON (BOOM)
DO DO

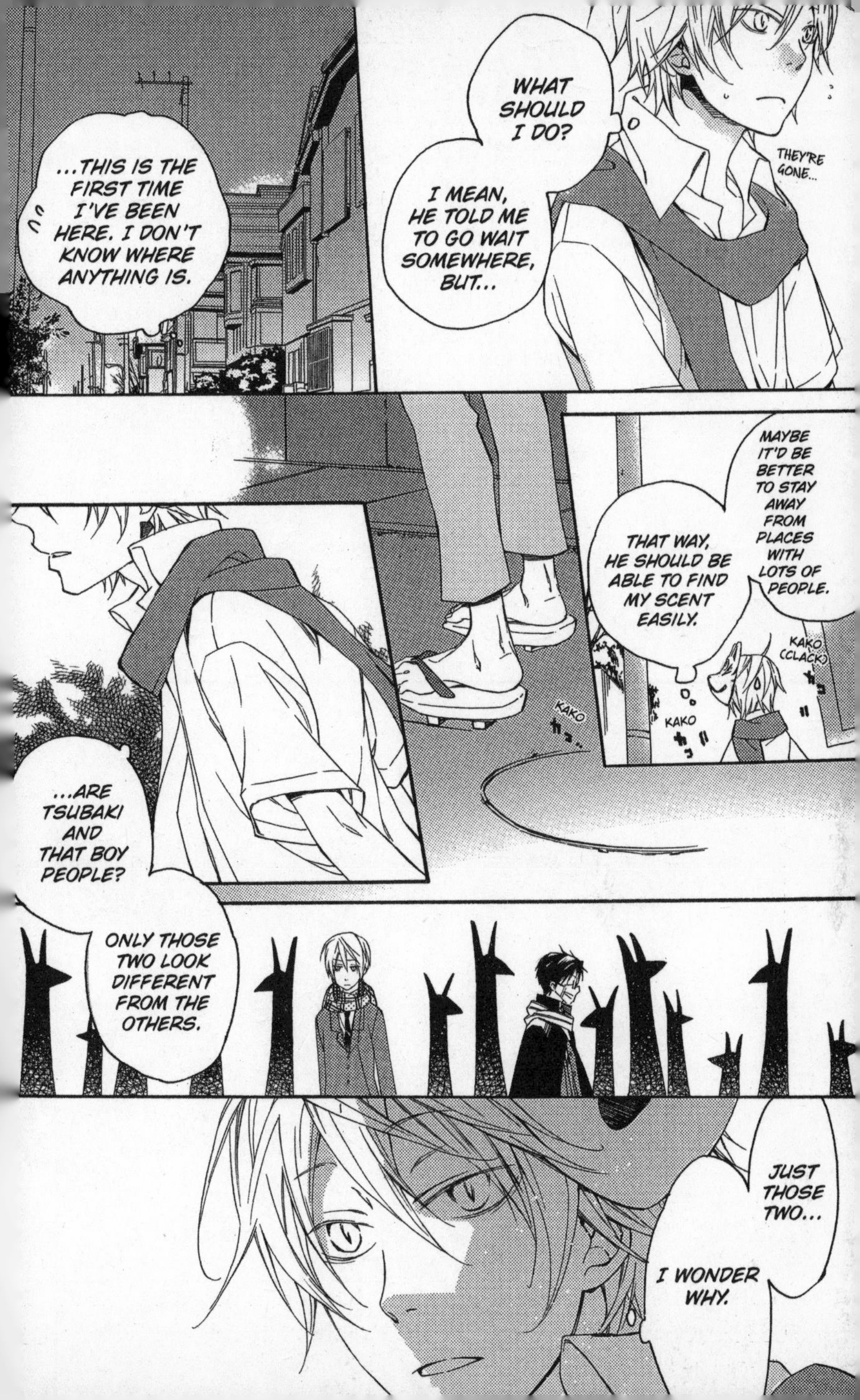
WHAT SHOULD I DO?
I MEAN, HE TOLD ME TO GO WAIT SOMEWHERE, BUT...
THEY'RE GONE...
...THIS IS THE FIRST TIME I'VE BEEN HERE. I DON'T KNOW WHERE ANYTHING IS.
MAYBE IT'D BE BETTER TO STAY AWAY FROM PLACES WITH LOTS OF PEOPLE.
THAT WAY, HE SHOULD BE ABLE TO FIND MY SCENT EASILY.
KAKO (CLACK)
KAKO
KAKO
...ARE TSUBAKI AND THAT BOY PEOPLE?
ONLY THOSE TWO LOOK DIFFERENT FROM THE OTHERS.
JUST THOSE TWO...
I WONDER WHY.

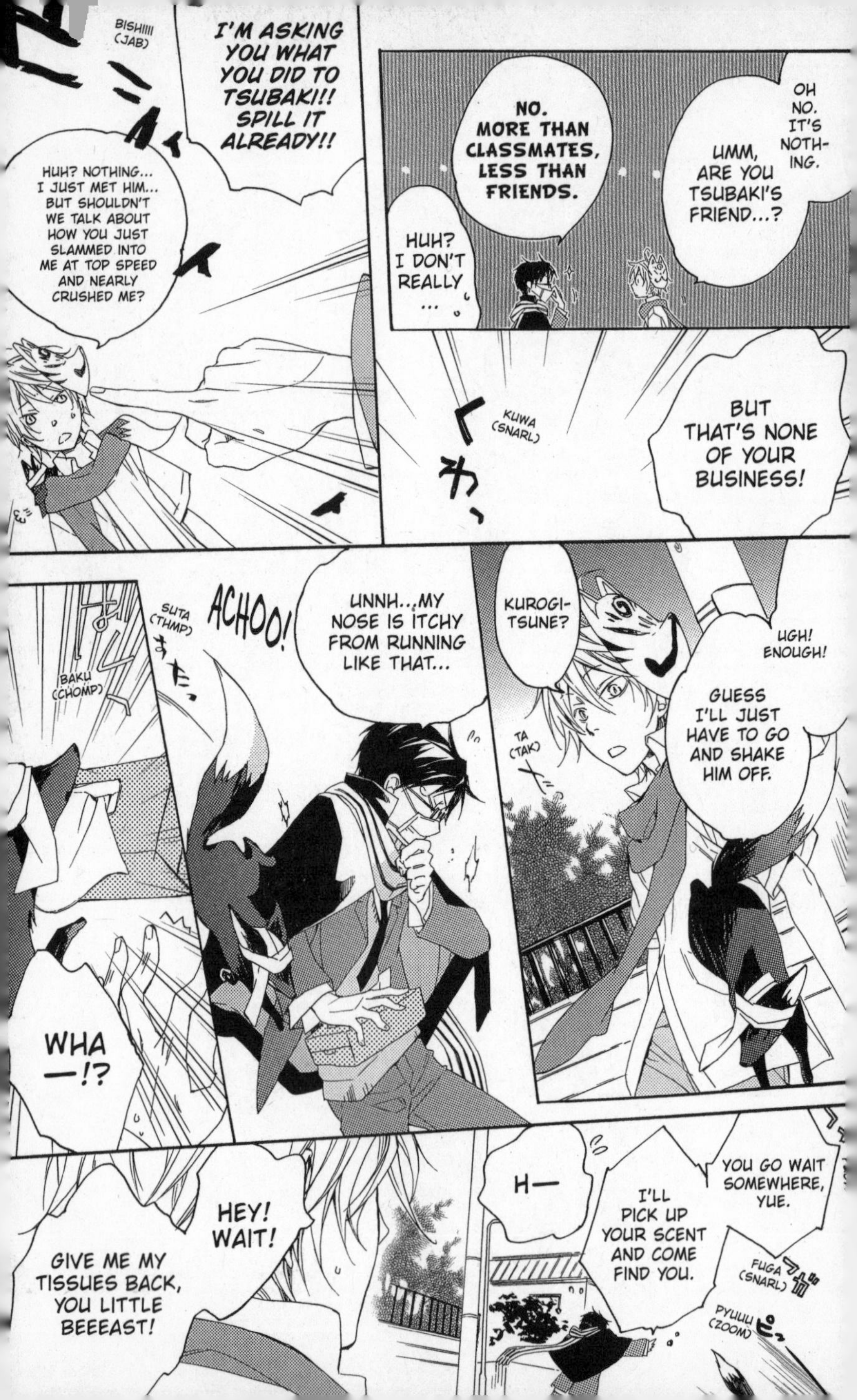
OH NO. IT'S NOTHING.
UMM, ARE YOU TSUBAKI'S FRIEND...?
NO. MORE THAN CLASSMATES, LESS THAN FRIENDS.
HUH? I DON'T REALLY...
KUWA (SNARL)
BUT THAT'S NONE OF YOUR BUSINESS!
BISHIIII (JAB)
I'M ASKING YOU WHAT YOU DID TO TSUBAKI!! SPILL IT ALREADY!!
HUH? NOTHING... I JUST MET HIM... BUT SHOULDN'T WE TALK ABOUT HOW YOU JUST SLAMMED INTO ME AT TOP SPEED AND NEARLY CRUSHED ME?
KUROGI-TSUNE?
UGH! ENOUGH!
GUESS I'LL JUST HAVE TO GO AND SHAKE HIM OFF.
TA (TAK)
ACHOO!
UNNH...MY NOSE IS ITCHY FROM RUNNING LIKE THAT...
SUTA (THMP)
BAKU (CHOMP)
WHA—!?
YOU GO WAIT SOMEWHERE, YUE.
I'LL PICK UP YOUR SCENT AND COME FIND YOU.
H—
FUGA (SNARL)
PYUUU (ZOOM)
HEY! WAIT!
GIVE ME MY TISSUES BACK, YOU LITTLE BEEEAST!

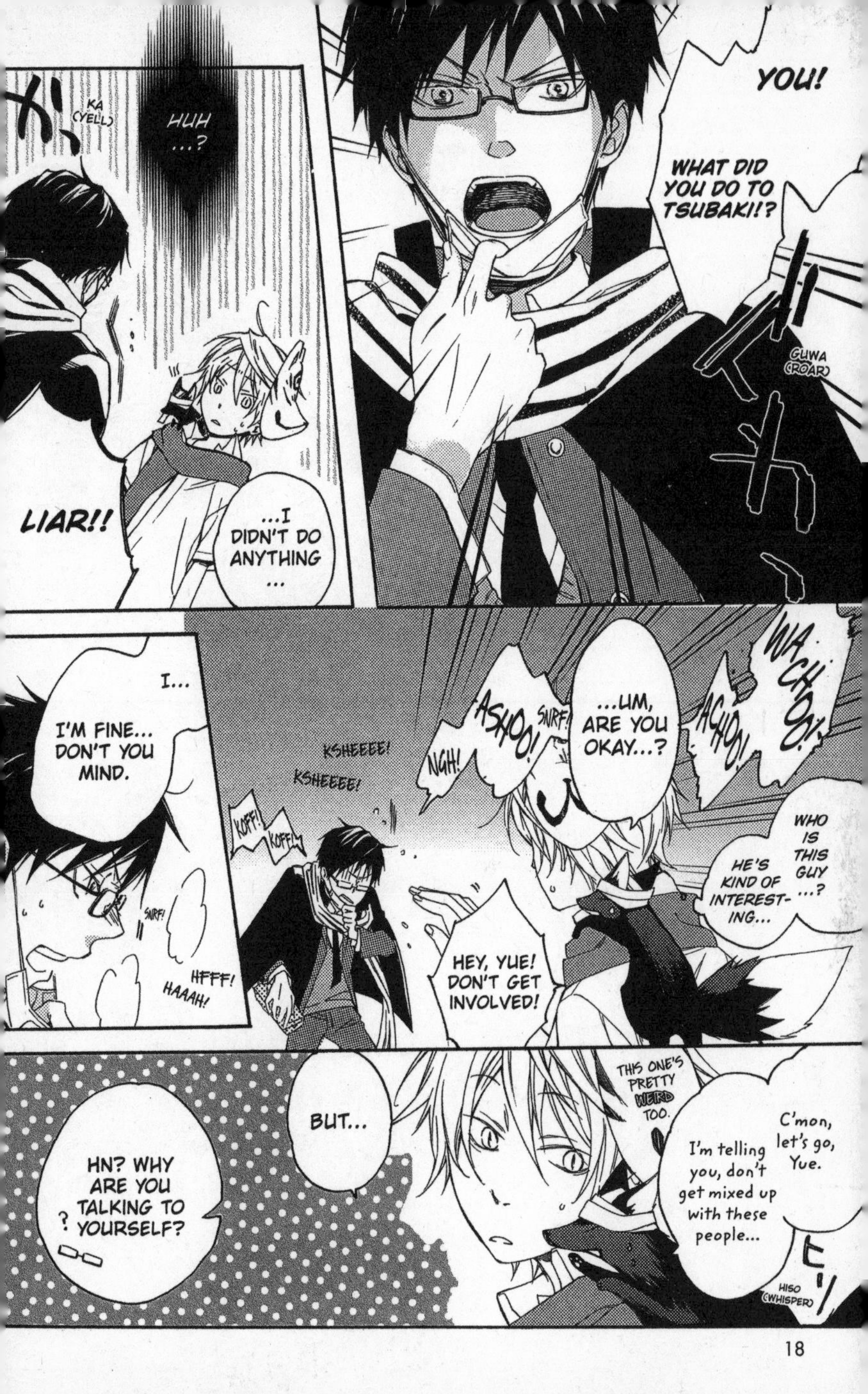
YOU!
WHAT DID YOU DO TO TSUBAKI!?
GUWA (ROAR)
HUH ...?
KA (YELL)
...I DIDN'T DO ANYTHING ...
LIAR!!
WACHOO!
ACHOO!
WHO IS THIS GUY ...?
HE'S KIND OF INTEREST-ING...
...UM, ARE YOU OKAY...?
SNIRF!
ASHOO!
NGH!
KSHEEEE!
KSHEEEE!
KOFF!
KOFF!
HEY, YUE! DON'T GET INVOLVED!
I...
I'M FINE... DON'T YOU MIND.
SNIRF!
HFFF! HAAAH!
HISO (WHISPER)
C'mon, let's go, Yue.
I'm telling you, don't get mixed up with these people...
THIS ONE'S PRETTY WEIRD TOO.
BUT...
HN? WHY ARE YOU TALKING TO YOURSELF?

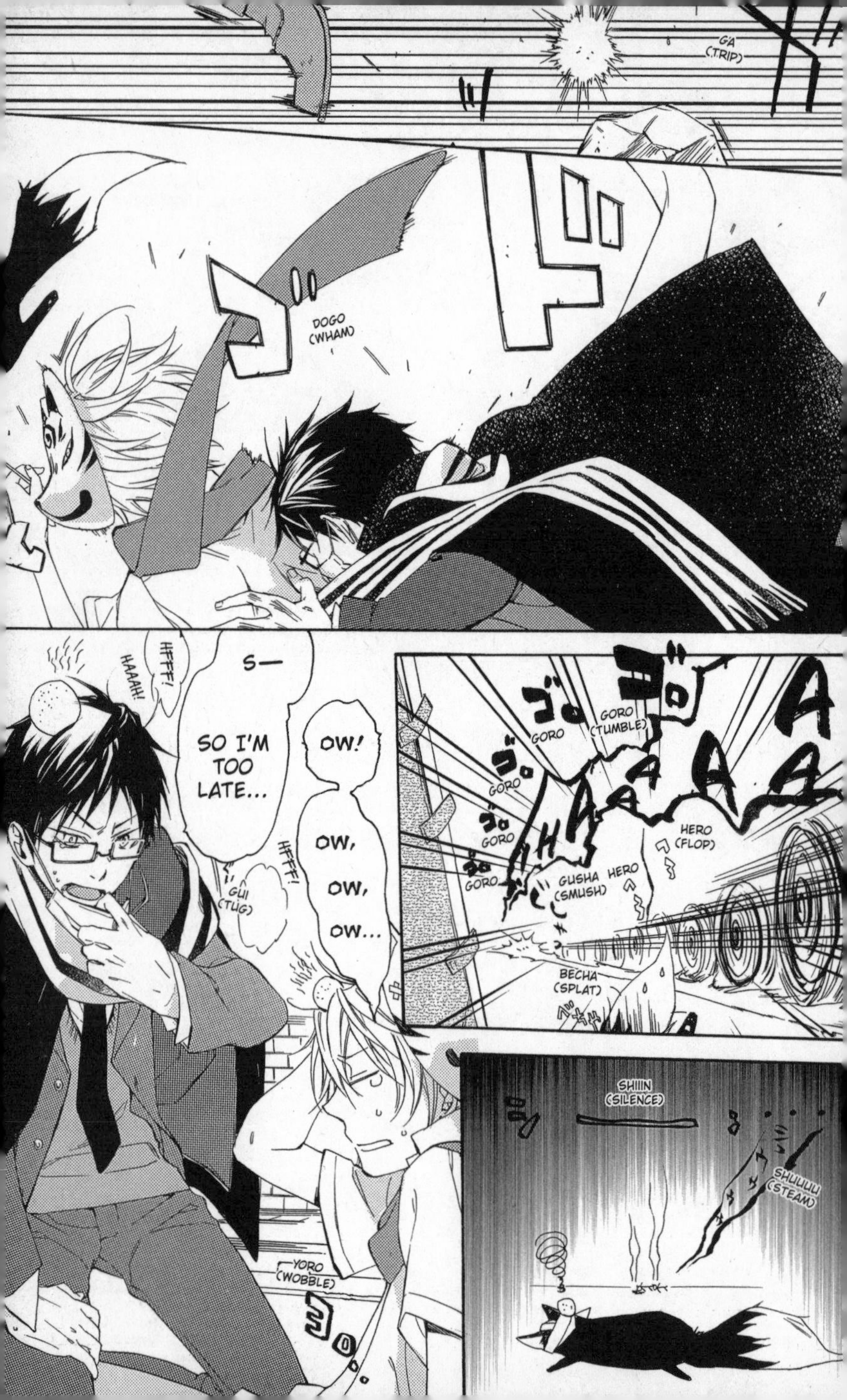
GA (TRIP)
DOGO (WHAM)
GORO (TUMBLE)
GORO
GORO
GORO
GORO
AAAAAAAH
HERO (FLOP)
HERO
GUSHA (SMUSH)
BECHA (SPLAT)
SHIIIN (SILENCE)
SHUUUU (STEAM)
OW!
OW, OW, OW...
S—
SO I'M TOO LATE...
HFFF! HAAAH!
HFFF!
GUI (TUG)
YORO (WOBBLE)

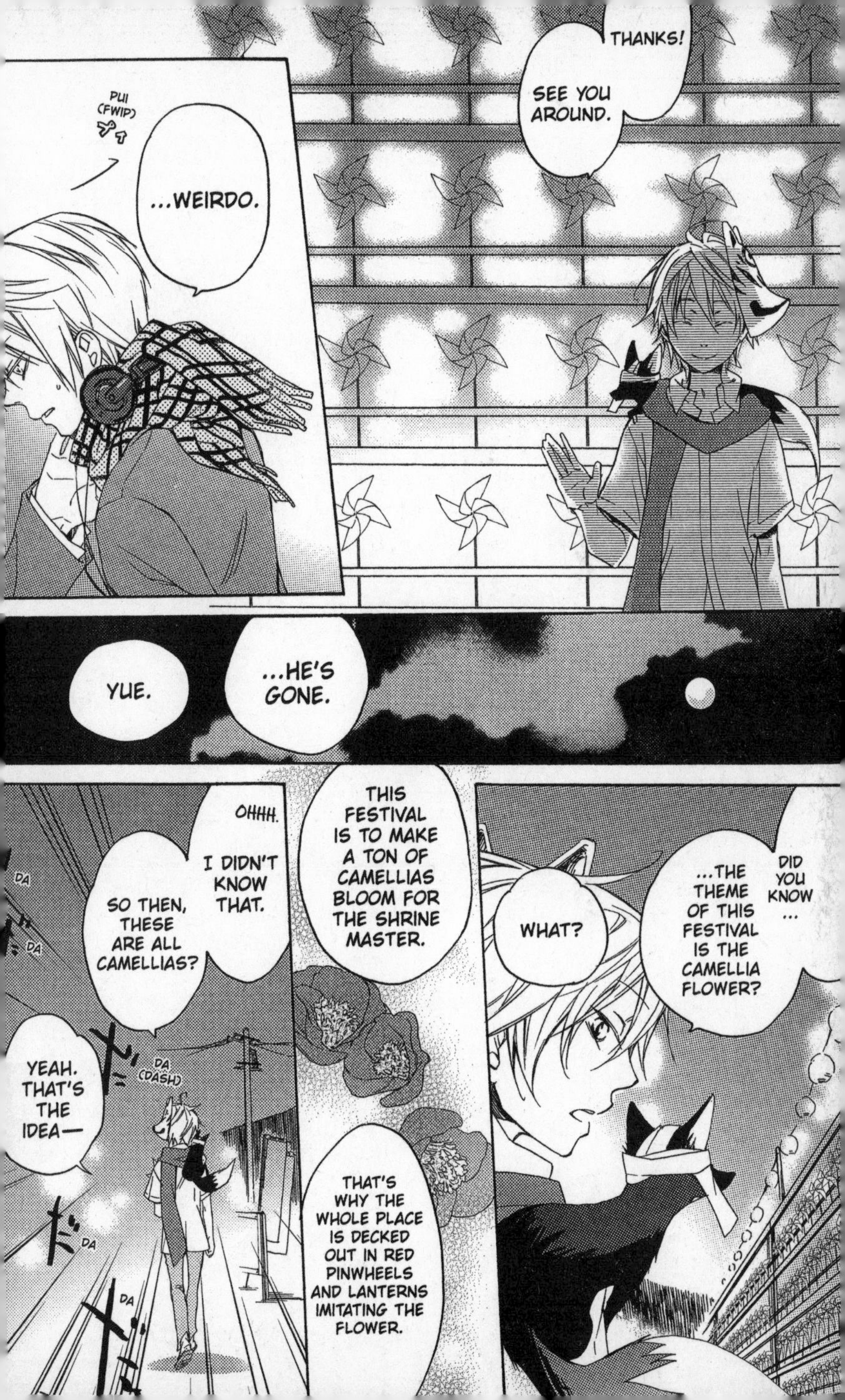
THANKS!
SEE YOU AROUND.
PUI (FWIP)
...WEIRDO.
...HE'S GONE.
YUE.
DID YOU KNOW ...
...THE THEME OF THIS FESTIVAL IS THE CAMELLIA FLOWER?
WHAT?
THIS FESTIVAL IS TO MAKE A TON OF CAMELLIAS BLOOM FOR THE SHRINE MASTER.
THAT'S WHY THE WHOLE PLACE IS DECKED OUT IN RED PINWHEELS AND LANTERNS IMITATING THE FLOWER.
OHHH.
I DIDN'T KNOW THAT.
SO THEN, THESE ARE ALL CAMELLIAS?
YEAH. THAT'S THE IDEA—
DA
DA
DA (DASH)
DA
DA

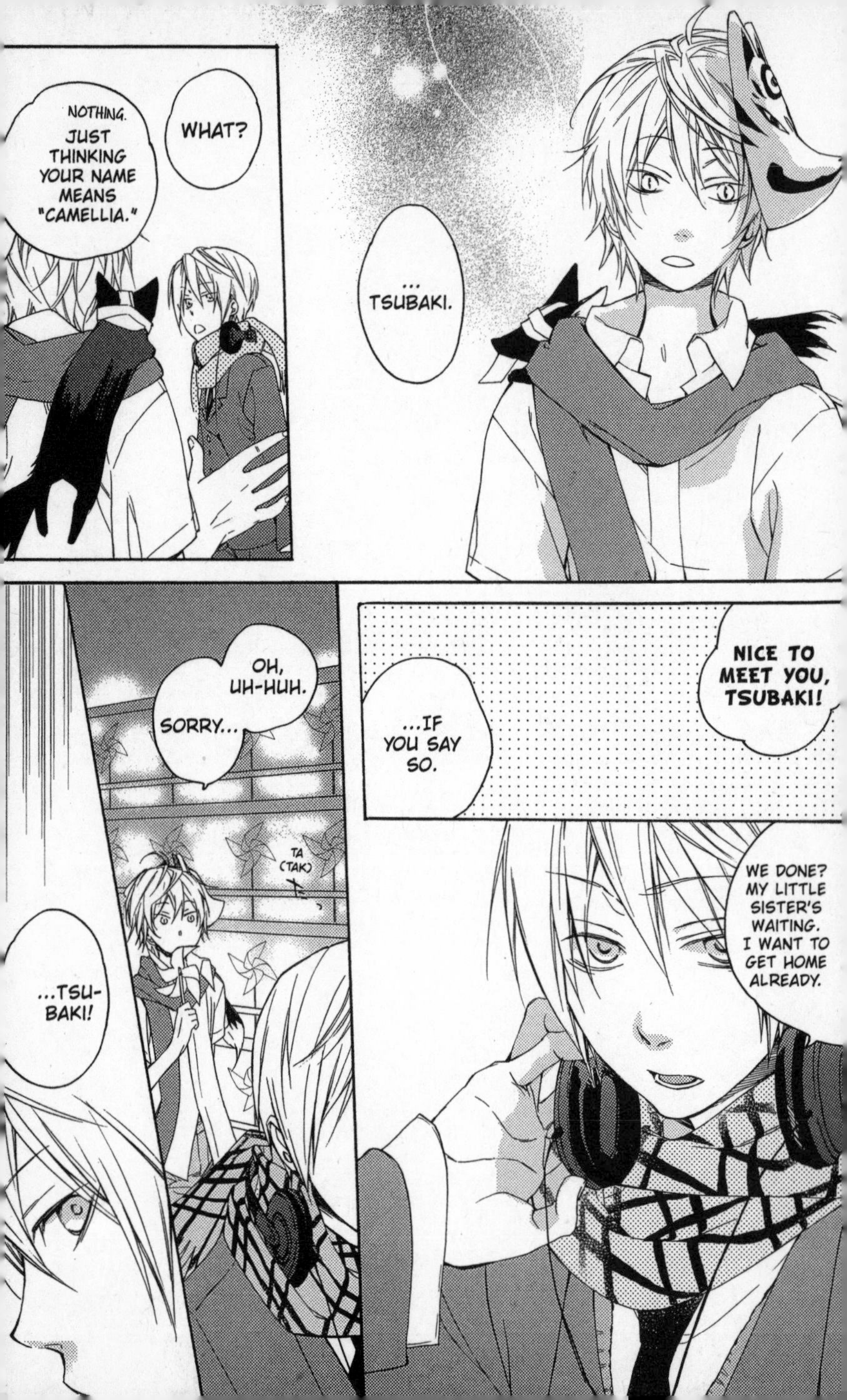
... TSUBAKI.
WHAT?
NOTHING. JUST THINKING YOUR NAME MEANS "CAMELLIA."
NICE TO MEET YOU, TSUBAKI!
...IF YOU SAY SO.
WE DONE? MY LITTLE SISTER'S WAITING. I WANT TO GET HOME ALREADY.
OH, UH-HUH.
SORRY...
TA (TAK)
...TSU-BAKI!

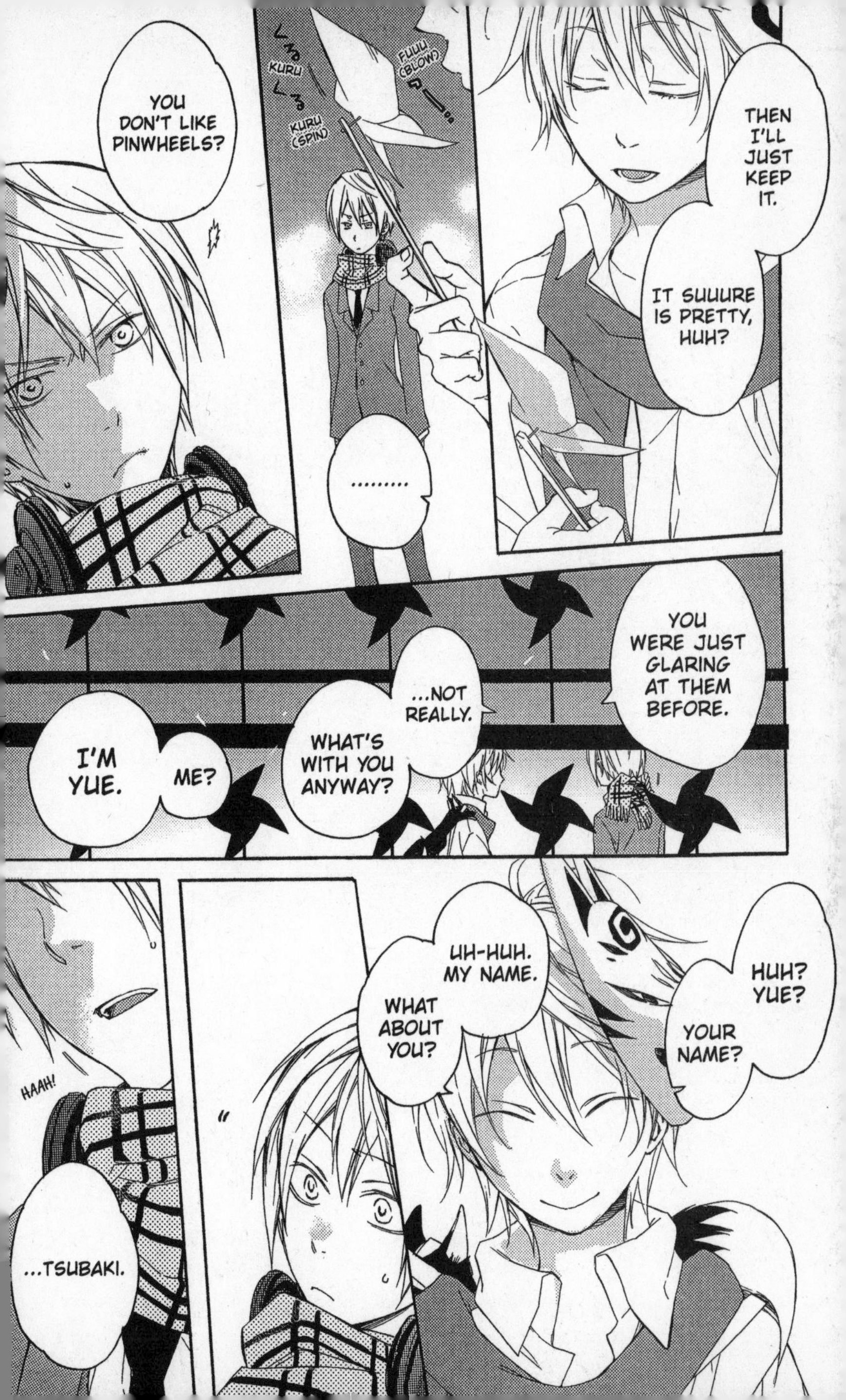
THEN I'LL JUST KEEP IT.
IT SUUURE IS PRETTY, HUH?
FUUU (BLOW)
KURU
KURU (SPIN)
....
YOU DON'T LIKE PINWHEELS?
YOU WERE JUST GLARING AT THEM BEFORE.
...NOT REALLY.
WHAT'S WITH YOU ANYWAY?
ME?
I'M YUE.
HUH? YUE?
YOUR NAME?
UH-HUH. MY NAME.
WHAT ABOUT YOU?
HAAH!
...TSUBAKI.

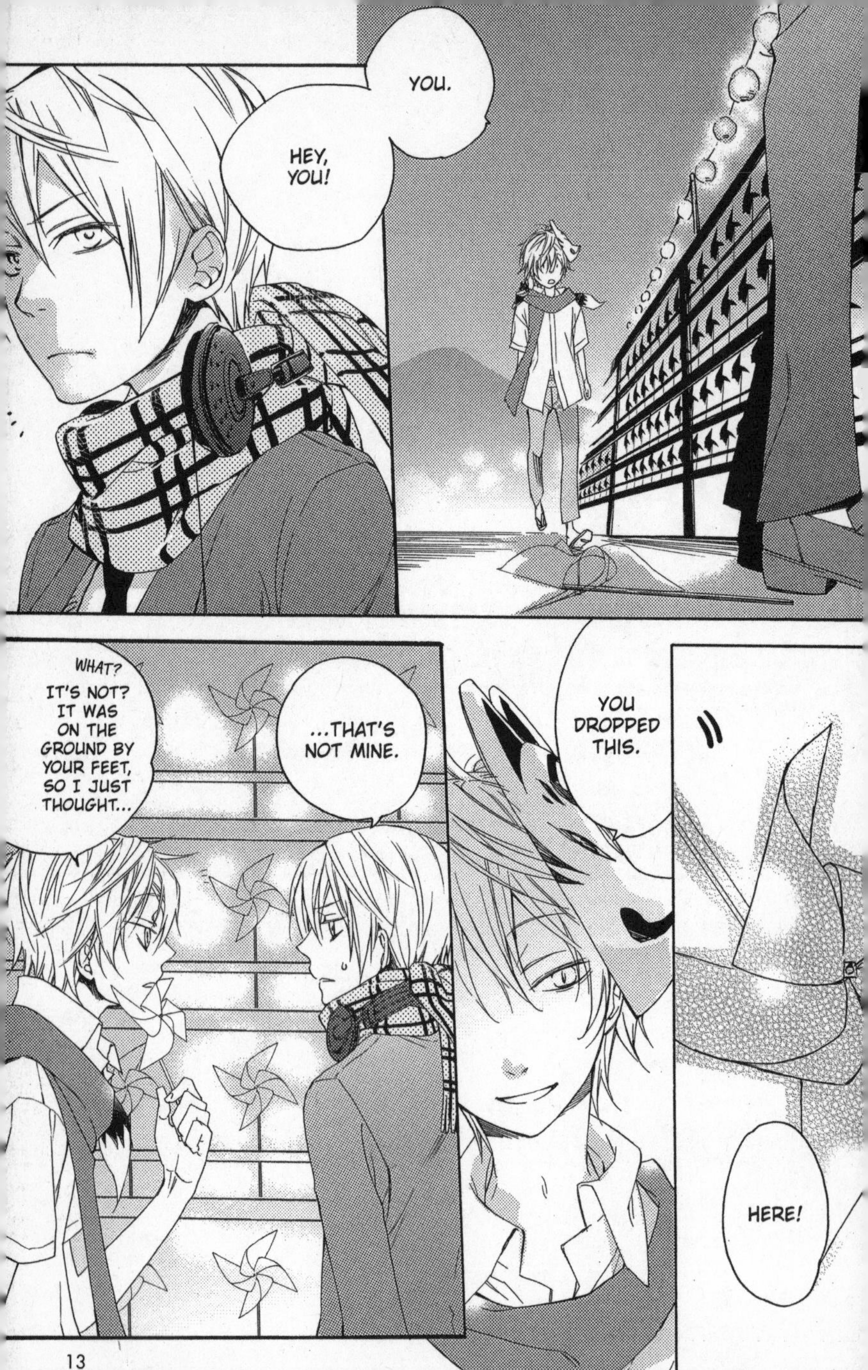
YOU.
HEY, YOU!
HERE!
YOU DROPPED THIS.
...THAT'S NOT MINE.
WHAT? IT'S NOT? IT WAS ON THE GROUND BY YOUR FEET, SO I JUST THOUGHT...

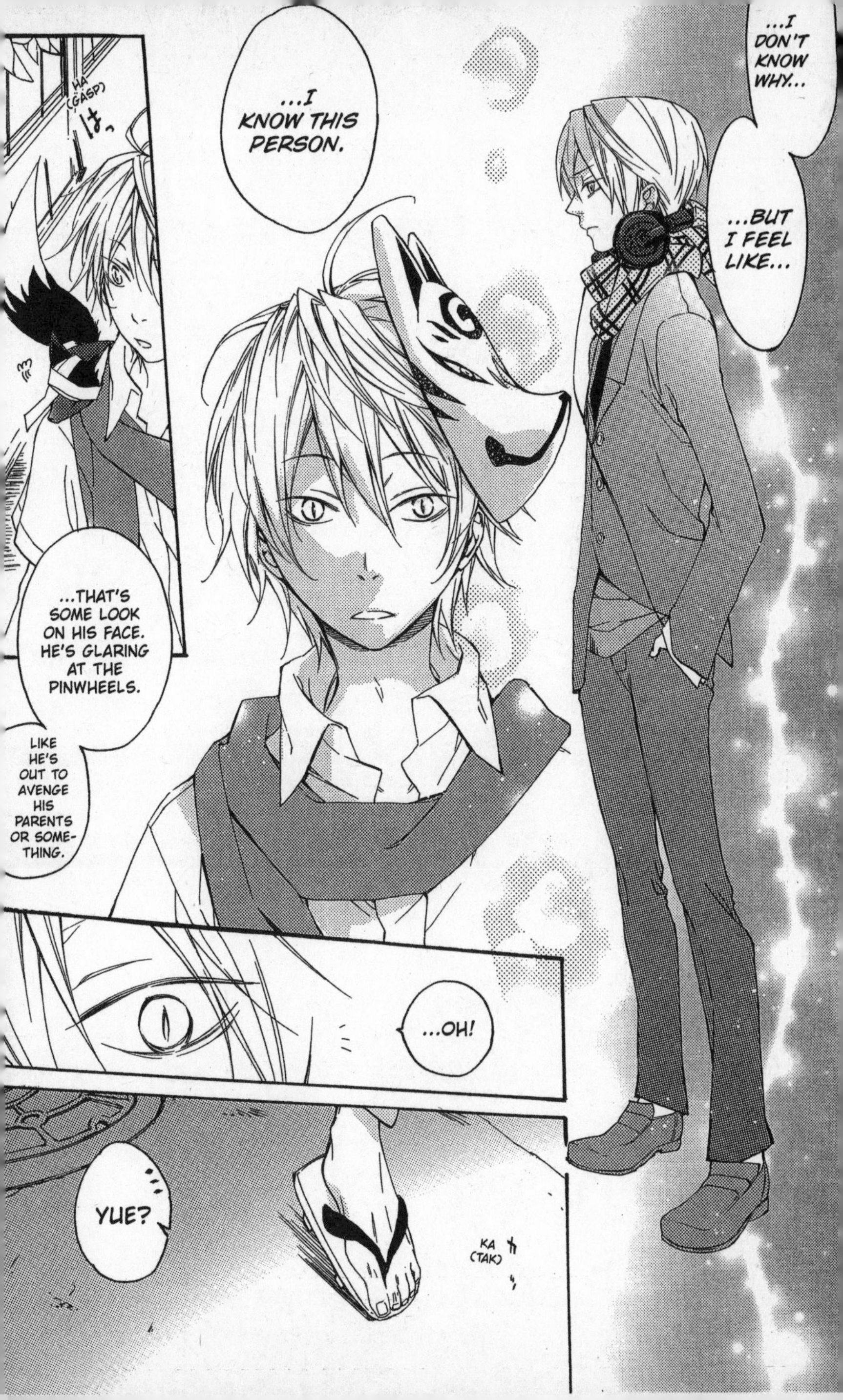
...I DON'T KNOW WHY...
...BUT I FEEL LIKE...
...I KNOW THIS PERSON.
HA (GASP) は、
...THAT'S SOME LOOK ON HIS FACE. HE'S GLARING AT THE PINWHEELS.
LIKE HE'S OUT TO AVENGE HIS PARENTS OR SOME-THING.
...OH!
KA (TAK) カッ
... YUE?

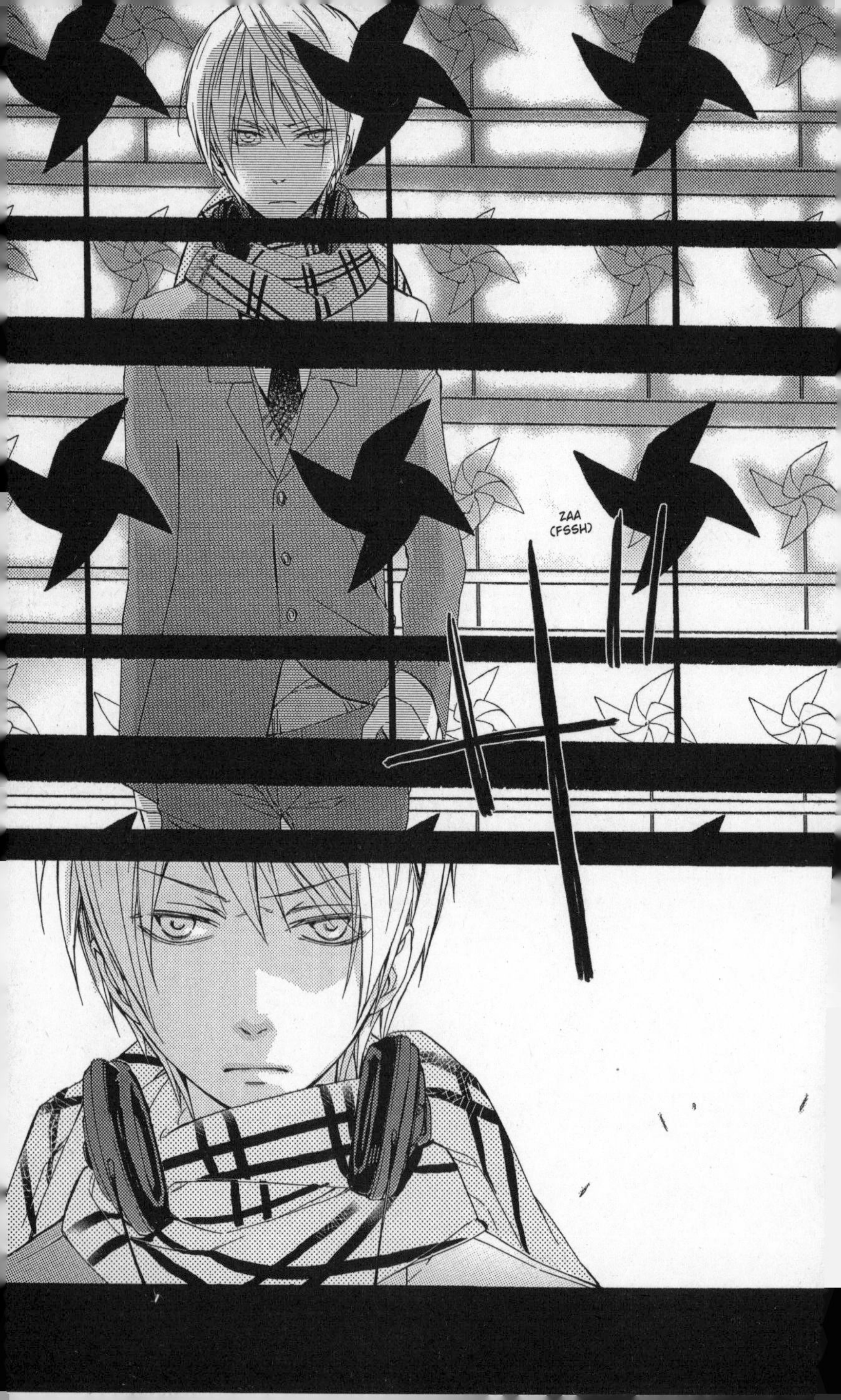
ZAA
(FSSH)

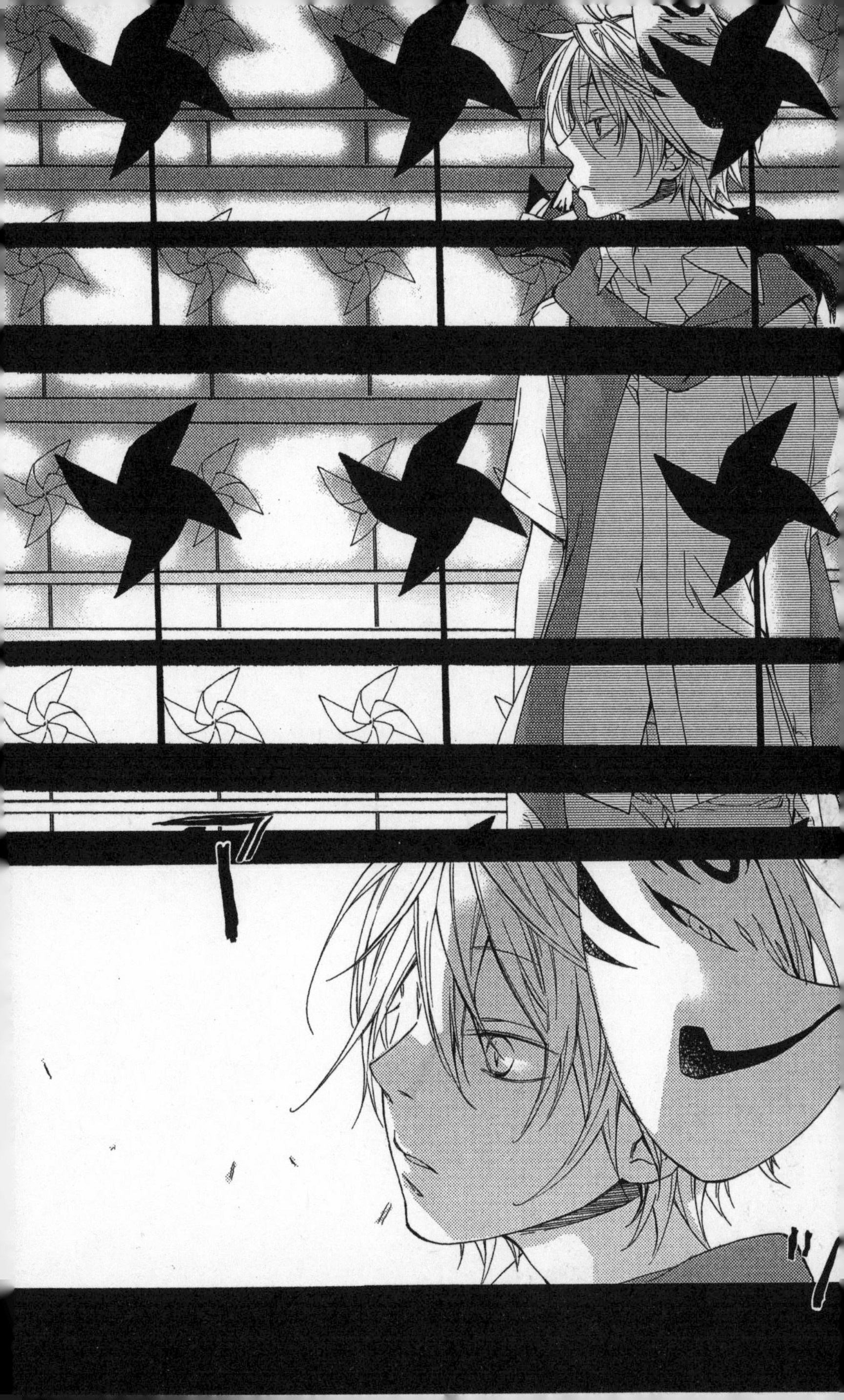

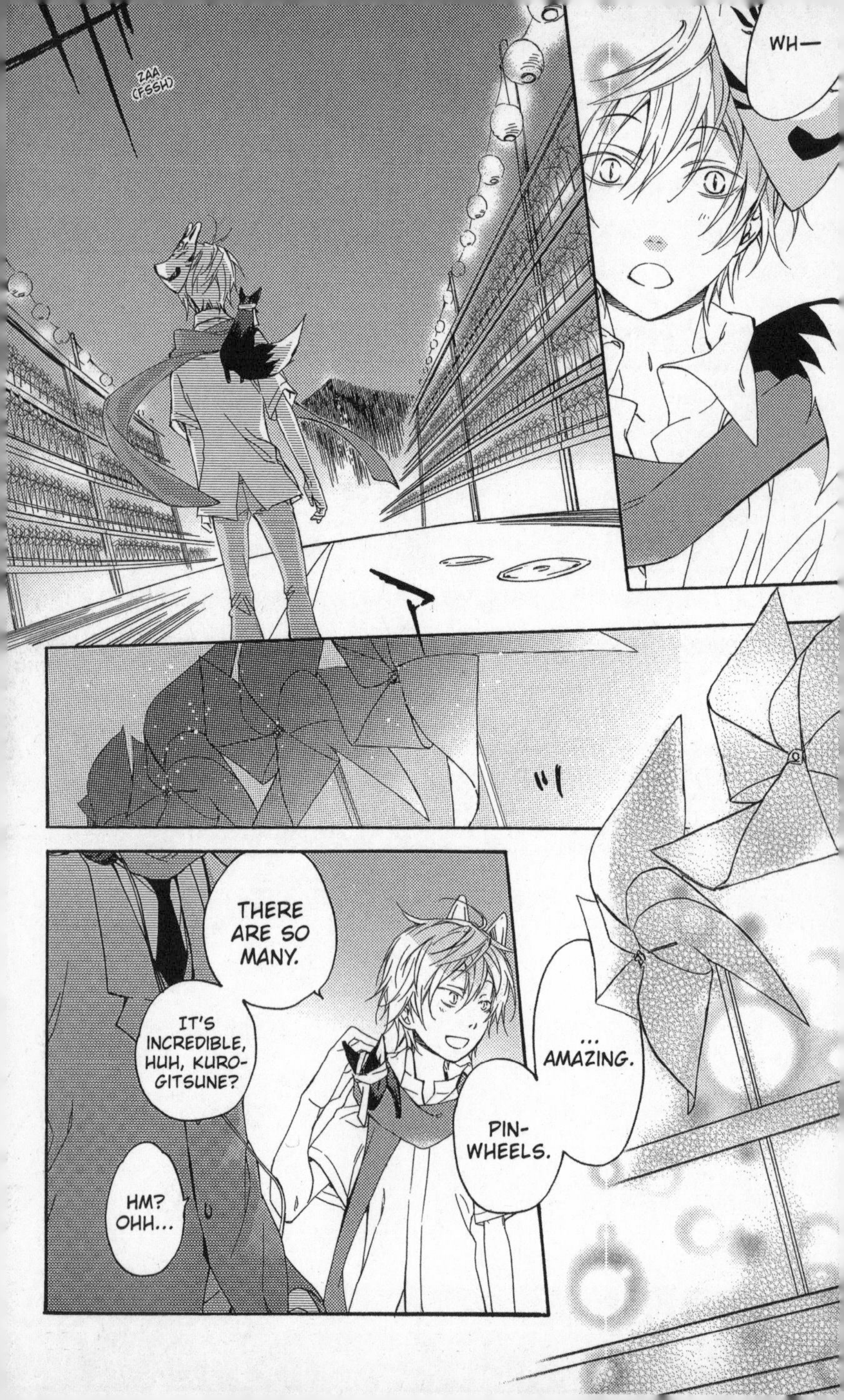
WH—
ZAA (FSSH)
... AMAZING.
PIN-WHEELS.
THERE ARE SO MANY.
IT'S INCREDIBLE, HUH, KURO-GITSUNE?
HM? OHH...

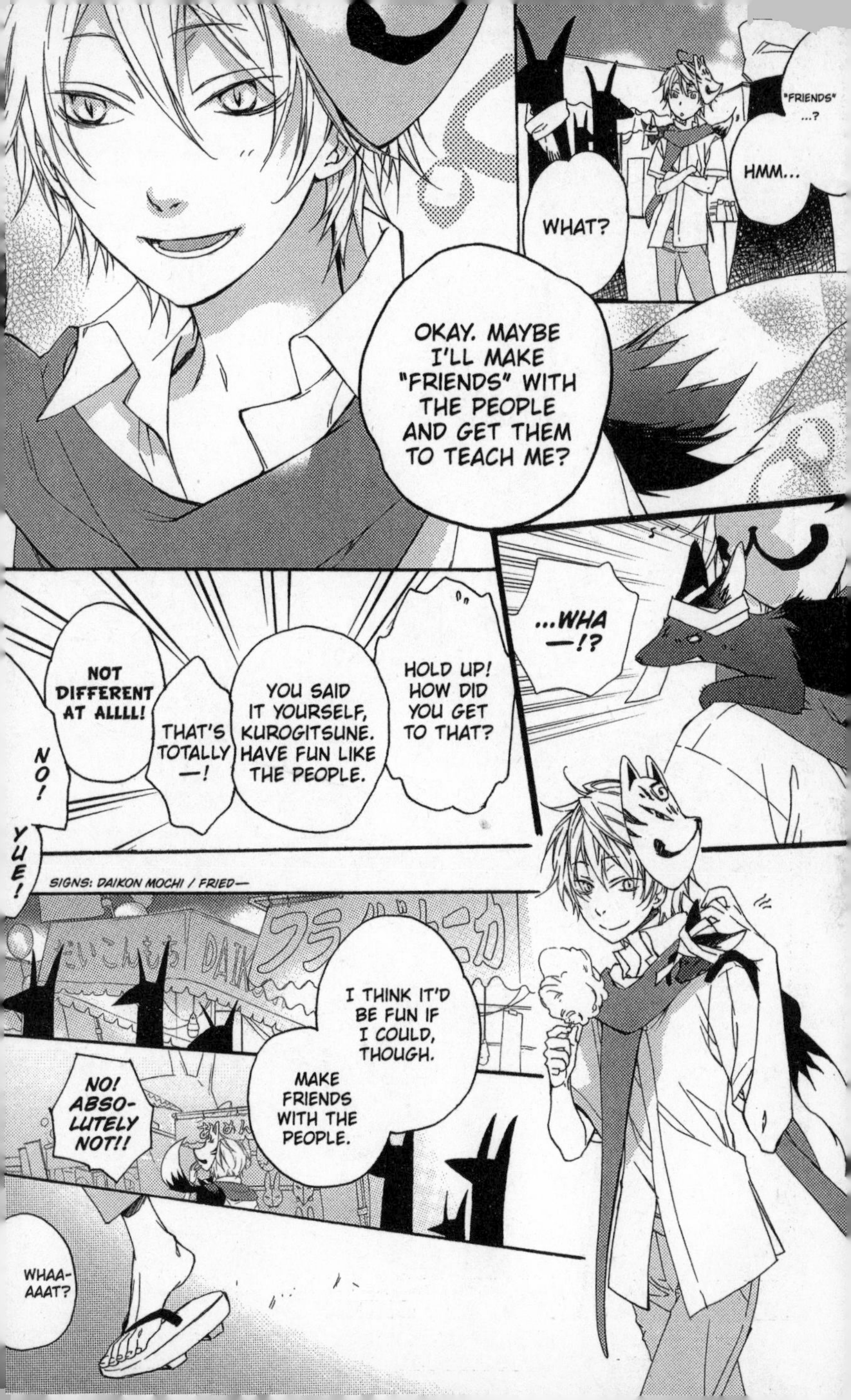
"FRIENDS" ...?
HMM...
WHAT?
OKAY. MAYBE I'LL MAKE "FRIENDS" WITH THE PEOPLE AND GET THEM TO TEACH ME?
...WHA—!?
HOLD UP! HOW DID YOU GET TO THAT?
YOU SAID IT YOURSELF, KUROGITSUNE. HAVE FUN LIKE THE PEOPLE.
THAT'S TOTALLY—!
NOT DIFFERENT AT ALLLL!
NO! YUE!
SIGNS: DAIKON MOCHI / FRIED—
I THINK IT'D BE FUN IF I COULD, THOUGH.
MAKE FRIENDS WITH THE PEOPLE.
NO! ABSOLUTELY NOT!!
WHAA-AAAT?

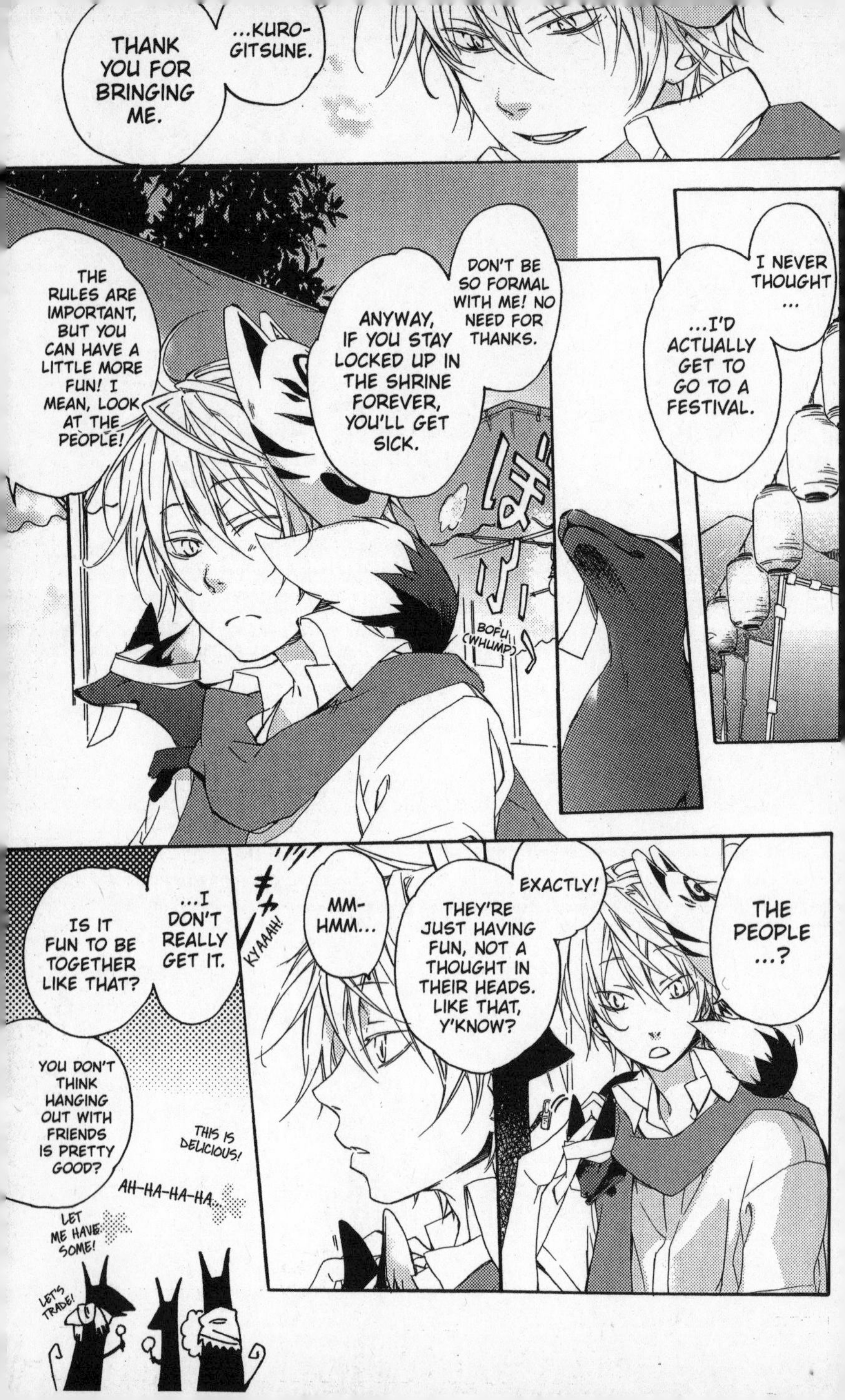
...KURO-GITSUNE.
THANK YOU FOR BRINGING ME.
I NEVER THOUGHT...
...I'D ACTUALLY GET TO GO TO A FESTIVAL.
DON'T BE SO FORMAL WITH ME! NO NEED FOR THANKS.
ANYWAY, IF YOU STAY LOCKED UP IN THE SHRINE FOREVER, YOU'LL GET SICK.
BOFU (WHUMP)
THE RULES ARE IMPORTANT, BUT YOU CAN HAVE A LITTLE MORE FUN! I MEAN, LOOK AT THE PEOPLE!
THE PEOPLE...?
EXACTLY!
THEY'RE JUST HAVING FUN, NOT A THOUGHT IN THEIR HEADS. LIKE THAT, Y'KNOW?
MM-HMM...
KYAAAH!
...I DON'T REALLY GET IT.
IS IT FUN TO BE TOGETHER LIKE THAT?
YOU DON'T THINK HANGING OUT WITH FRIENDS IS PRETTY GOOD?
THIS IS DELICIOUS!
AH-HA-HA-HA
LET ME HAVE SOME!
LET'S TRADE!

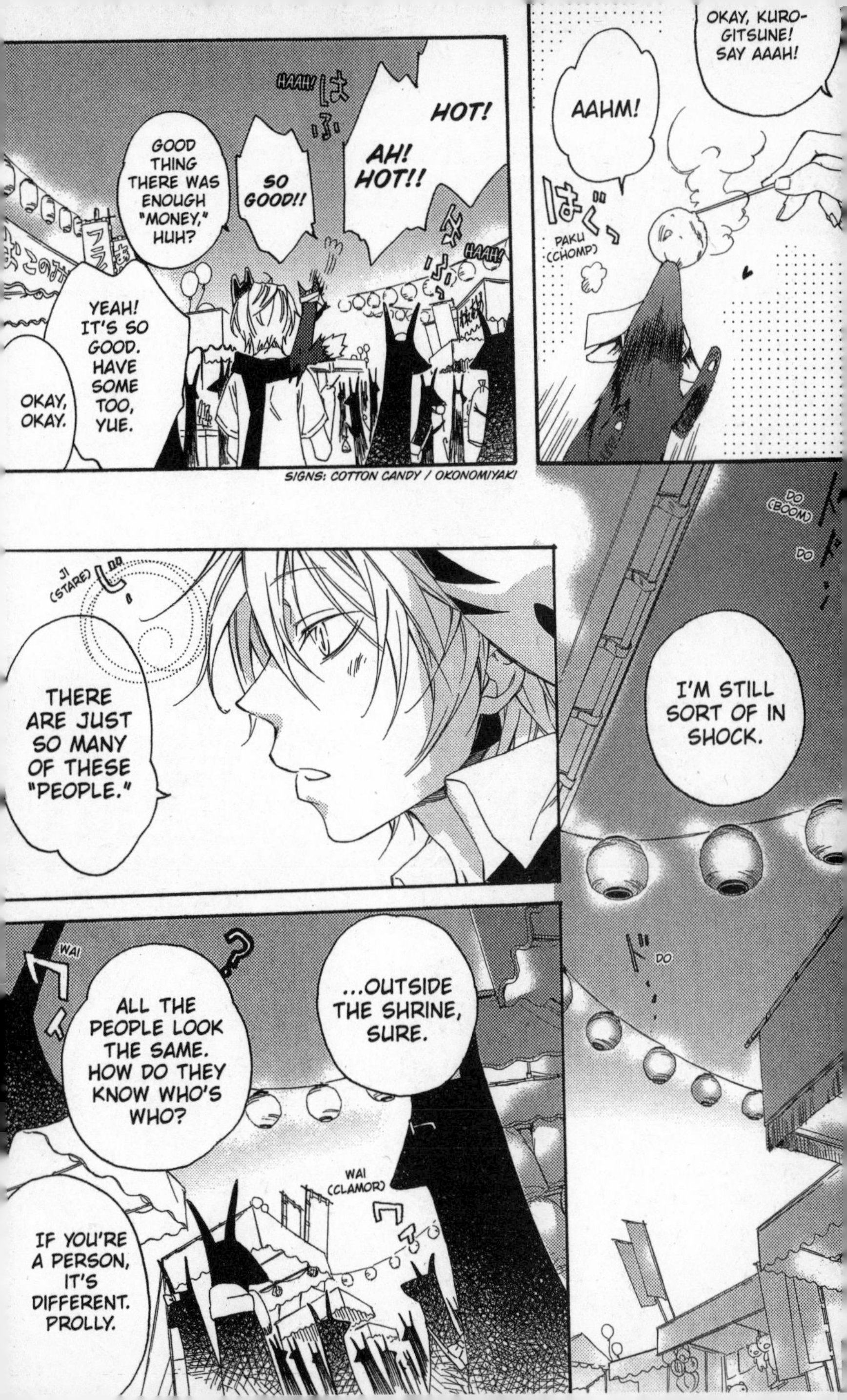
OKAY, KURO-GITSUNE! SAY AAAH!
AAHM!
PAKU (CHOMP)
HAAH!
HOT!
AH! HOT!!
HAAH!
SO GOOD!!
GOOD THING THERE WAS ENOUGH "MONEY," HUH?
YEAH! IT'S SO GOOD. HAVE SOME TOO, YUE.
OKAY, OKAY.
SIGNS: COTTON CANDY / OKONOMIYAKI
DO (BOOM)
DO
I'M STILL SORT OF IN SHOCK.
DO
JI (STARE)
THERE ARE JUST SO MANY OF THESE "PEOPLE."
WAI
...OUTSIDE THE SHRINE, SURE.
ALL THE PEOPLE LOOK THE SAME. HOW DO THEY KNOW WHO'S WHO?
WAI (CLAMOR)
IF YOU'RE A PERSON, IT'S DIFFERENT. PROLLY.

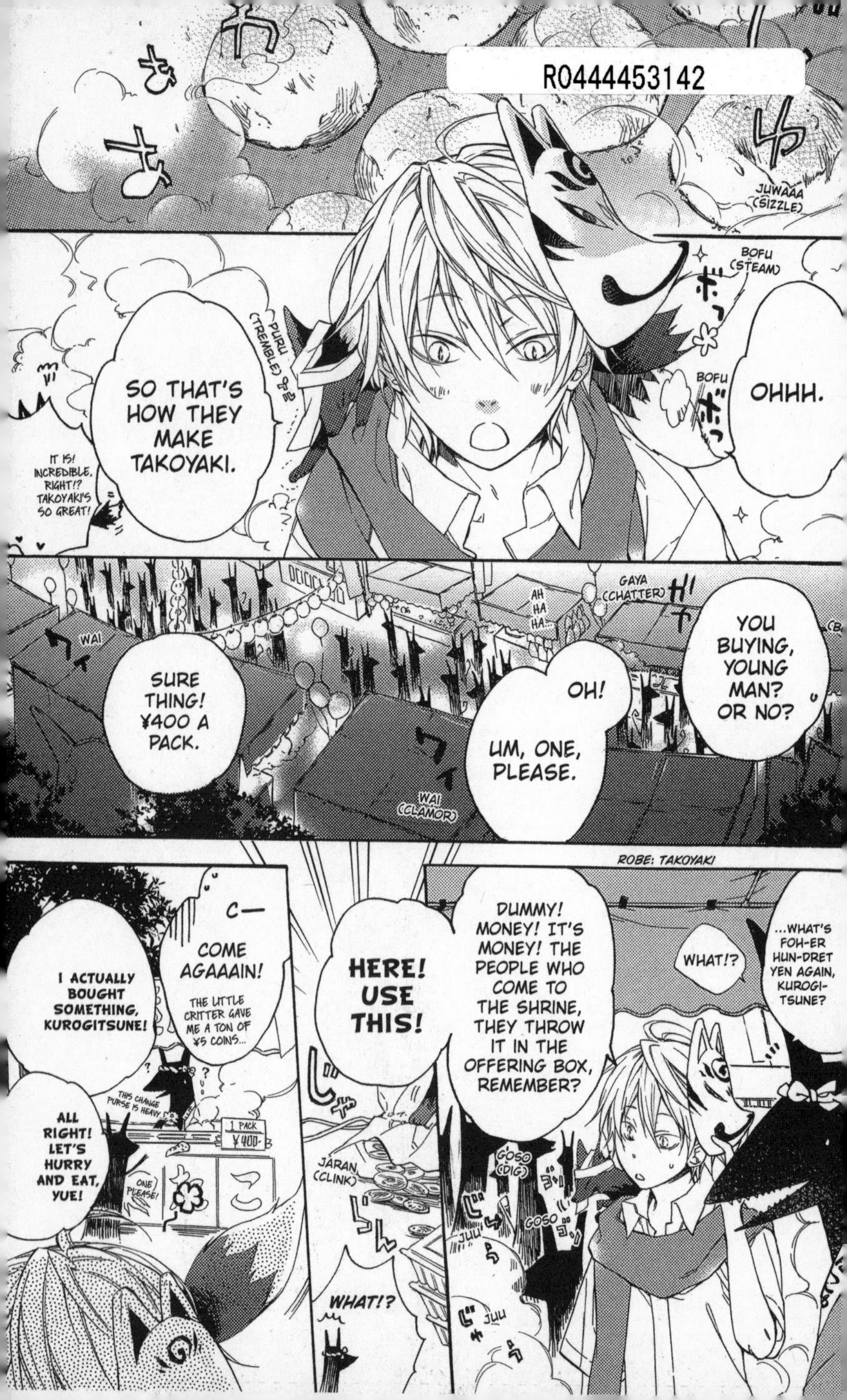
JUWAAA (SIZZLE)
BOFU (STEAM)
OHHH.
BOFU
SO THAT'S HOW THEY MAKE TAKOYAKI.
PURU (TREMBLE)
IT IS! INCREDIBLE, RIGHT!? TAKOYAKI'S SO GREAT!
YOU BUYING, YOUNG MAN? OR NO?
GAYA (CHATTER)
AH HA HA...
OH!
UM, ONE, PLEASE.
WAI (CLAMOR)
SURE THING! ¥400 A PACK.
WAI
ROBE: TAKOYAKI
...WHAT'S FOH-ER HUN-DRET YEN AGAIN, KUROGI-TSUNE?
WHAT!?
DUMMY! MONEY! IT'S MONEY! THE PEOPLE WHO COME TO THE SHRINE, THEY THROW IT IN THE OFFERING BOX, REMEMBER?
GOSO (DIG)
GOSO
JUU
JUU
HERE! USE THIS!
JARAN (CLINK)
WHAT!?
C—
COME AGAAAIN!
THE LITTLE CRITTER GAVE ME A TON OF ¥5 COINS...
I ACTUALLY BOUGHT SOMETHING, KUROGITSUNE!
THIS CHANGE PURSE IS HEAVY
1 PACK ¥400
ONE PLEASE!
ALL RIGHT! LET'S HURRY AND EAT, YUE!

CONTENTS

THE 1ST TALE: FESTIVAL   001

THE 2ND TALE: MEAL   041

THE 3RD TALE: TOUGO   073

THE 4TH TALE: DISAPPEARANCE   103

THE 5TH TALE: AKUJIKI   127

SPECIAL BONUS
OF THE RED DRAMA CD REPORT MANGA   156

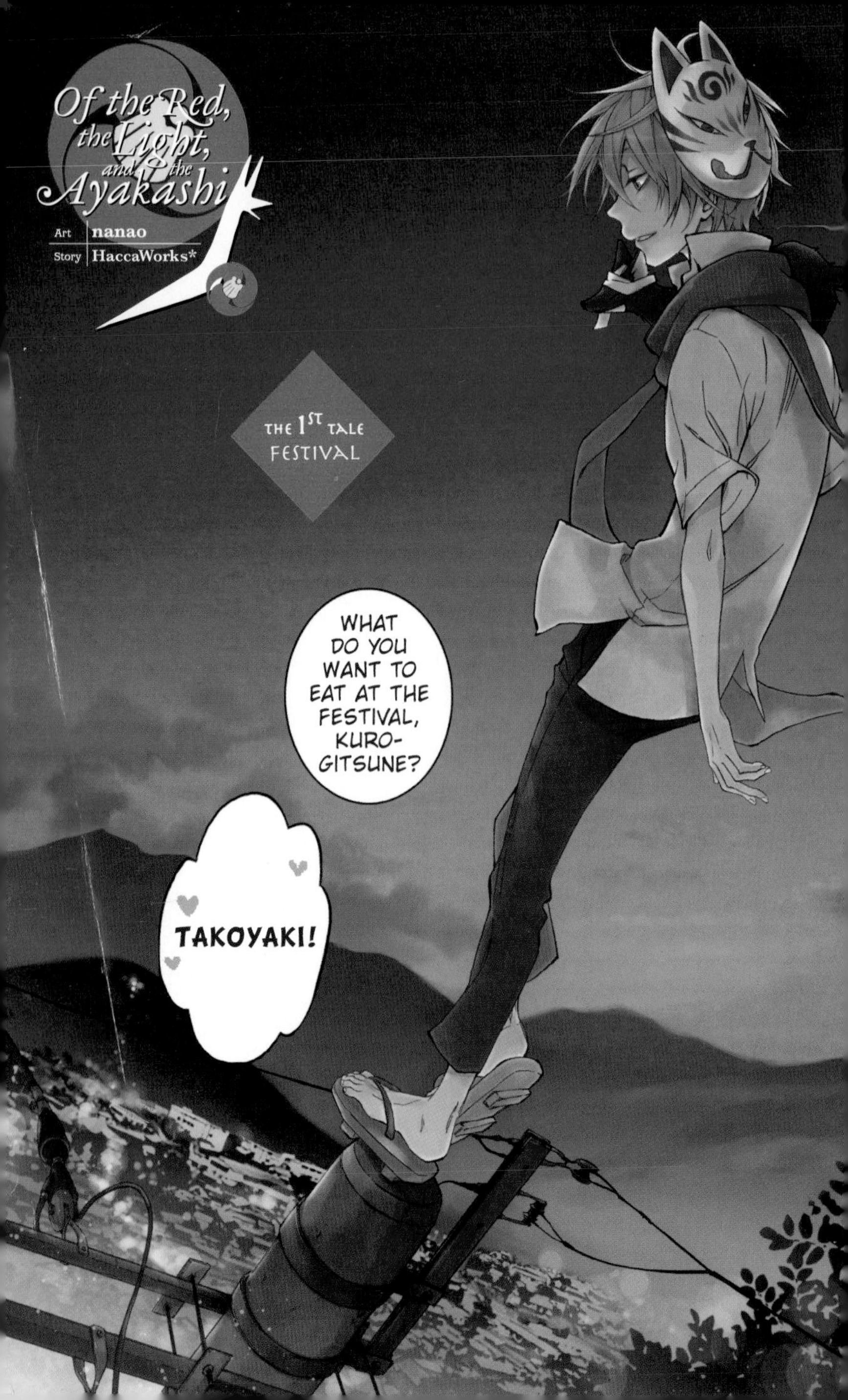
Of the Red, the Light, and the Ayakashi
Art nanao
Story HaccaWorks*
THE 1ST TALE FESTIVAL
WHAT DO YOU WANT TO EAT AT THE FESTIVAL, KURO-GITSUNE?
TAKOYAKI!

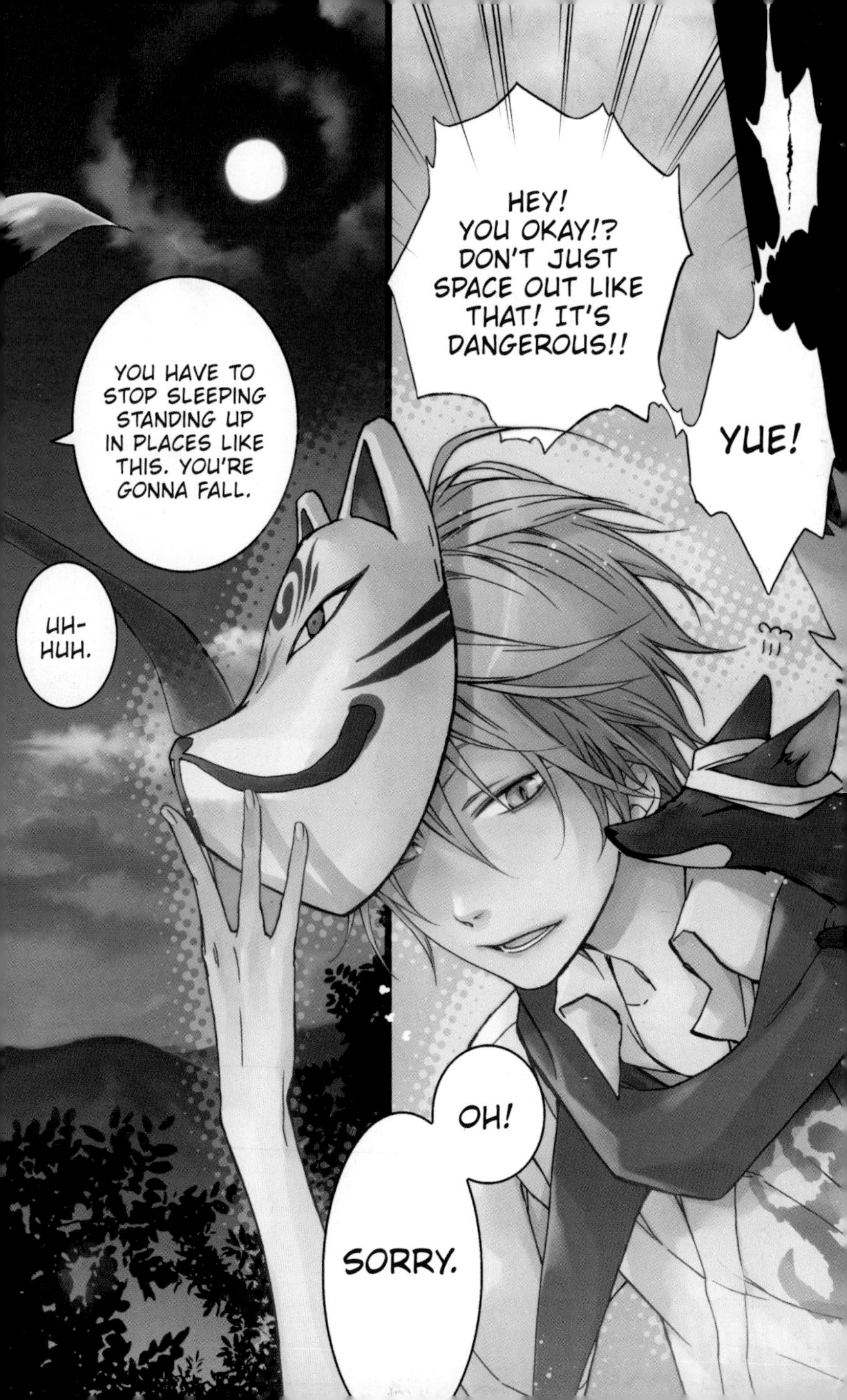
YUE!
HEY! YOU OKAY!? DON'T JUST SPACE OUT LIKE THAT! IT'S DANGEROUS!!
OH!
SORRY.
YOU HAVE TO STOP SLEEPING STANDING UP IN PLACES LIKE THIS. YOU'RE GONNA FALL.
UH-HUH.

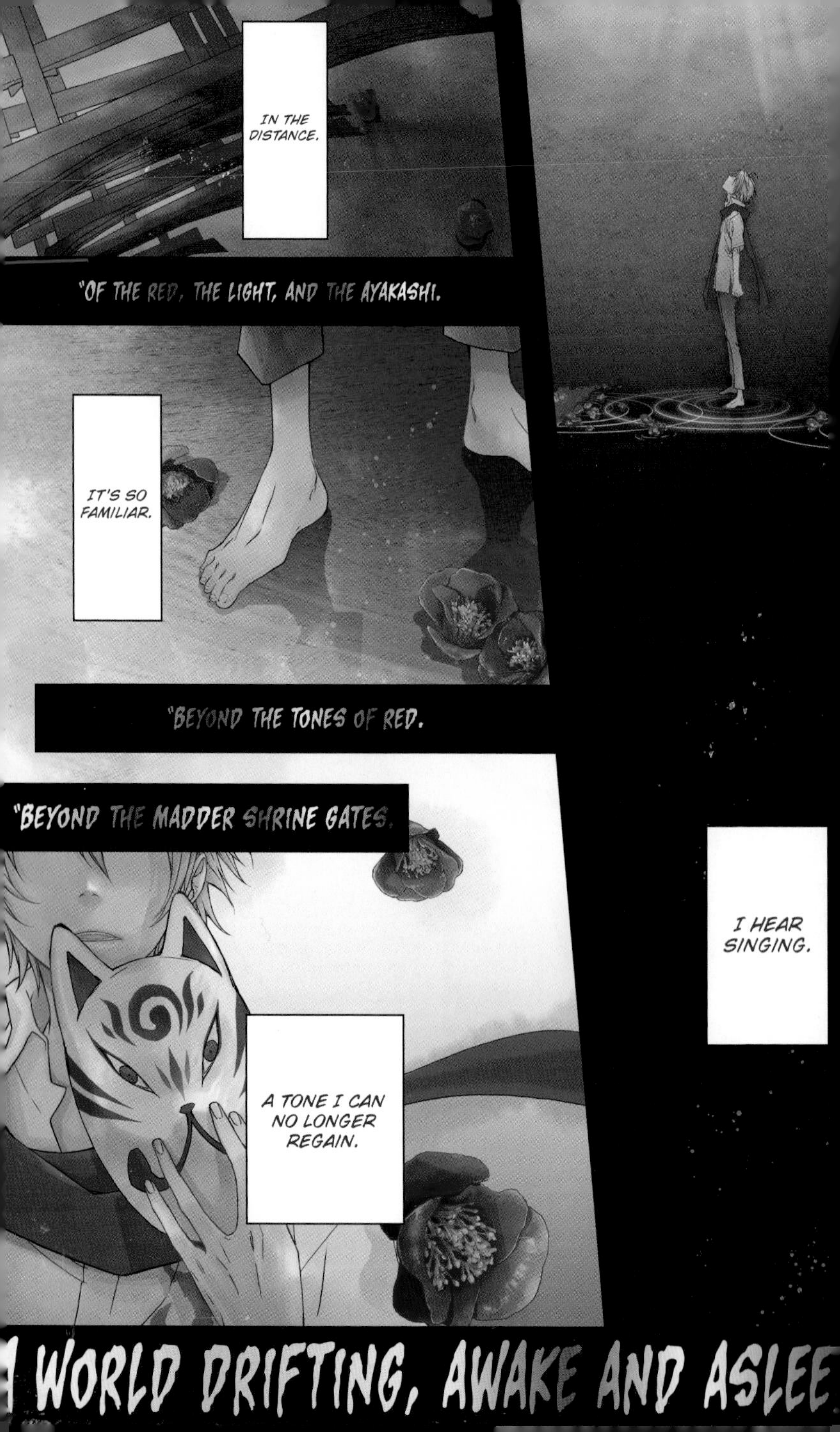
I HEAR SINGING.
IN THE DISTANCE.
"OF THE RED, THE LIGHT, AND THE AYAKASHI.
IT'S SO FAMILIAR.
"BEYOND THE TONES OF RED.
"BEYOND THE MADDER SHRINE GATES.
A TONE I CAN NO LONGER REGAIN.
WORLD DRIFTING, AWAKE AND ASLEE

The Cat of Bubastes
A Tale of Ancient Egypt

by

G. A. Henty

PrestonSpeed
Publications
Exciting Books of History & Historical Fiction

A note about the name PrestonSpeed Publications:
Living in an age when it has become fashionable to denigrate fathers, we decided to honor ours. Thus the name PrestonSpeed Publications was chosen in loving memory of Preston Louis Schmitt and Lester Herbert Maynard (nicknamed "Speed" for prowess in baseball).

Originally published by Blackie & Son, Limited, on September 3, 1888 (t.p. date 1889)

The Cat of Bubastes A Tale of Ancient Egypt, by G. A. Henty
© 1997 by PrestonSpeed Publications
Published by PrestonSpeed Publications, 51 Ridge Road, Mill Hall, Pennsylvania 17751.

Printed in the United States of America

ISBN 1-887159-16-9 (cloth)
ISBN 1-887159-23-1 (pbk)
ISBN 1-887159-68-1 (mass pbk)

My Dear Lads,

Thanks to the care with which the Egyptians depicted upon the walls of their sepulchres the minutest doings of their daily life, to the dryness of the climate which has preserved these records uninjured for so many thousand years, and to the indefatigable labour of modern investigators, we know far more of the manners and customs of the Egyptians, of their methods of work, their sports and amusements, their public festivals, and domestic life, than we do of those of peoples comparatively modern. My object in the present story has been to give you as lively a picture as possible of that life, drawn from the bulky pages of Sir J. Gardner Wilkinson and other writers on the same subject. I have laid the scene in the time of Thotmes III., one of the greatest of the Egyptian monarchs, being surpassed only in glory and the extent of his conquests by Ramses the Great. It is certain that Thotmes carried the arms of Egypt to the shores of the Caspian, and a people named the Rebu, with fair hair and blue eyes, were among those depicted in the Egyptian sculptures as being conquered and made tributary. It is open to discussion whether the Exodus of the Jews from Egypt took place in the reign of Thotmes or many years subsequently, some authors assigning it to the time of Ramses. Without attempting to enter this much discussed question, I have assumed that the Israelites were still in Egypt at the time of Thotmes, and by introducing Moses just at the time he began to take up the cause of the people to whom he belonged, I leave it to be inferred that the Exodus took place some forty years later. I wish you to understand, however, that you are not to accept this date as being absolutely correct. Opinions differ widely upon it; and as no allusion whatever has been discovered either to the Exodus, or to any of the events which preceded it, among the records of Egypt, there is nothing to fix the date as occurring during the reign of any one among the long line of Egyptian kings. The term Pharaoh used in the Bible throws no light on the subject, as Pharaoh simply means king, and the name of no monarch bearing that appellation is to be found on the Egyptian monuments. I have in no way exaggerated the consequences arising from the slaying of the sacred cat, as the accidental killing of any cat whatever was an offence punished by death throughout the history of Egypt down to the time of the Roman connection with that country.

Yours sincerely,

G. A. Henty

Chapter 1

THE sun was blazing down upon a city on the western shore of the Caspian. It was a primitive city, and yet its size and population rendered it worthy of the term. It consisted of a vast aggregation of buildings, which were for the most part mere huts. Among them rose, however, a few of more solid build and of higher pretensions. These were the abodes of the chiefs and great men, the temples, and places of assembly. But although larger and more solidly built, these buildings could lay no claim to architectural beauty of any kind, but were little more than magnified huts, and even the king's palace was but a collection of such buildings closely adjoining each other.

The town was surrounded by a lofty wall with battlements and loopholes, and a similar but higher wall girt in the dwellings of the king and of his principal captains. The streets were alive with the busy multitude; and it was evident that although in the arts of peace the nation had made but little progress, they had in everything appertaining to war made great advances. Most of the men wore helmets closely fitting to the head and surmounted by a spike. These were for the most part composed of hammered brass, although some of the head-pieces were made of tough hide, studded with knobs of metal. All carried round shields—those of the soldiers, of leather stiffened with metal; those of the captains, of brass, worked with considerable elaboration.

In their belts all wore daggers, while at their backs were slung quivers of iron; painted bows hung over one shoulder, and some had at their waist a pouch of smooth flat stones and leather slings. Their chief garment was a sort of kilt falling to the knee. Above the waist some wore only a thin vest of white linen, others a garment not unlike the nightgown of modern times, but with short sleeves. The kilt was worn over this. Some had breast-pieces of thick leather confined by straps behind; while in the case of the officers the leather was covered with small pieces of metal, forming a cuirass.

All carried two or three javelins in the left hand, and a spear some ten feet long in the right. Horsemen galloped about at full speed to and from the royal palace, while occasionally chariots, drawn sometimes by one, sometimes by two horses, dashed along. These chariots were small, the wheels not exceeding three feet in height. Between them was placed the body of the vehicle, which was but just large enough for two men to stand on. It consisted only of a small platform, with a semicircular rail running round the front some eighteen inches above it. A close observer would have perceived at once that not only were the males of the city upon the point of marching out on a military expedition, but that it was no mere foray against a neighbouring people, but a war on which the safety of the city depended.

Women were standing in tearful groups as they watched the soldiers making towards the gates. The men themselves had a resolute and determined look, but there was none of the light-hearted gaiety among them which betokened the expectation of success and triumph. Inside the palace the bustle of preparation was as marked as without. The king and his principal councillors and leaders were assembled in the great circular hut which formed the audience-room and council-chamber. Messengers arrived in close succession with news of the progress and strength of the enemy, or with messages from the neighbouring towns and tribes as to the contingents they had furnished, and the time at which these had set out to join the army.

The king himself was a tall and warlike figure, in the prime of life. He had led his warriors on many successful expeditions far to the west, and had repulsed with great loss the attempts of the Persians to encroach upon his territory. Standing behind him was his son, Amuba, a lad of some fifteen years of age. The king and his councillors, as well as all the wealthier inhabitants of the city, wore, in addition to the kilt and linen jacket, a long robe highly coloured and ornamented with fanciful devices, and having a broad rich border. It was fastened at the neck with a large brooch, fell loosely from the shoulders to the ankles, and was open in front. The girdles which retained the kilts and in which the daggers were worn were highly ornamented, and the ends fell down in front and terminated in large tassels.

All wore a profusion of necklaces, bracelets, and other ornaments of gold; many of the chiefs wore feathers in their helmets, and the greater portion of all ranks had figures tattooed on their arms and legs. They were fair in complexion, with blue eyes; their hair was for the most part golden or red, and they wore their beards short and pointed. The young Prince Amuba was attired for the field; his helmet was of gold, and his cuirass covered with plates of the same metal. He listened with suppressed impatience to the arguments of his elders, for he was eager to be off, this being the first time that he had been permitted to take part in the military expeditions of his country.

After listening for some time and perceiving that there was no prospect of the council breaking up, he retired to the large hut adjoining the council-chamber. This served as the dwelling-place of the ladies and their family. It was divided into several apartments by screens formed of hide sewn together and hidden from sight by coloured hangings. In one of these a lady was seated on a low couch covered with panthers' skins.

"They have not done talking yet, mother. It has been a question as to where we shall assemble to give battle. It does not seem to me to make much difference where we fight, but they seem to think that it is most important; and of course they know more about it than I do. They have fixed upon a place at last—it is about fifteen miles from here. They say that the ground in front is marshy and can hardly be traversed by the enemy's chariots; but if they cannot get at us, it seems to me that we cannot get at them. Messengers have been sent off to order all the contingents to assemble at that spot. Six thousand men are to remain behind to guard the city; but as we mean to beat them I do not think there can be much occasion for that; for you think we shall beat them—don't you mother?"

"I hope so, Amuba; but I am very fearful."

"But we have several times repulsed them when they have invaded our country, mother; why should we not do so this time?"

"They are much stronger than they have ever been before when they have come against us, my boy; and their king is a great

4 G.A. Henty

warrior, who has been successful in almost every enterprise he has undertaken."

"I cannot think why he wants to conquer us, mother. They say the riches of Egypt are immense and the splendour of their temples and buildings such as we have no idea of. We have no quarrel with them if they will but let us alone."

"No country is so rich that it does not desire more, my son. We have gold and are skilled in the working of it, and no doubt they anticipate that they will capture much treasure in the land; besides, as you say, their expeditions against the Rebu have been several times repulsed, and therefore their monarch will reap all the greater honour if he should defeat us. As to their having no quarrel with us, have we not made many expeditions to the west, returning with captives and much booty? And yet the people had no quarrel with us—many of them, indeed, could scarcely have known us by name when our army appeared among them. Some day, my son, things may be managed differently; but at present kings who have power make war upon people that are weaker than themselves, spoil them of their goods, and make slaves of them.

"I hope, Amuba, you will not expose yourself too much in the conflict. You have not come to man's strength yet; and remember you are my only child. See that your charioteer covers you with his shield when you have entered the battle, for the Egyptians are terrible as archers. Their bows carry much further than do ours, and the arrows will pierce even the strongest armour. Our spearman have always shown themselves as good as theirs—nay, better, for they are stronger in body and full of courage. It is in the goodness of her archers and the multitude of her chariots that the strength of Egypt lies. Remember that although your father, as king, must needs go into the thick of the battle to encourage his soldiers, there is no occasion why you, who are yet a boy, should so expose yourself.

"It will doubtless be a terrible battle. The Egyptians have the memory of past defeats to wipe out, and they will be fighting under the eye of their king. I am terrified, Amuba. Hitherto when your father has gone out to battle I have never doubted as to the result. The Persians were not foes whom brave men need dread; nor was it difficult to force the hordes passing us from the eastward towards the setting sun to respect our country, for we had the advantage in arms and discipline. But the Egyptians are terrible foes, and the arms of their king have been everywhere victorious. My heart is filled with dread at the thought of the approaching conflict, though I try to keep up a brave face when your father is with me, for I would not that he should deem me cowardly."

"I trust, mother, that your fears are groundless, and I cannot think that our men will give way when fighting for their homes and country upon ground chosen by themselves."

"I hope not, Amuba. But there is the trumpet sounding; it is the signal that the council have broken up and that your father is about to start. Bless you, my dear boy, and may you return safe and sound from the conflict!"

The queen fondly embraced her son, who left the apartment hastily as his father entered in order that the latter might not see the traces of tears on his cheeks. A few minutes later the king, with his captains, started from the palace. Most of them rode in chariots, the rest on horseback. The town was quiet now and the streets almost deserted. With the exception of the garrison, all the men capable of bearing arms had gone forth; the women with anxious faces stood in groups at their doors and watched the royal party as it drove out.

The charioteer of Amuba was a tall and powerful man; he carried a shield far larger than was ordinarily used, and had been specially selected by the king for the service. His orders were that he was not to allow Amuba to rush into the front line of fighters, and that he was even to disobey the orders of the prince if he wished to charge into the ranks of the enemy.

"My son must not shirk danger," his father said, "and he must needs go well into the fight; but he is still but a boy, not fit to enter upon a hand-to-hand contest with the picked warriors of Egypt. In time I hope he will fight abreast of me, but at present you must restrain his ardour. I need not bid you shield him as well as you can from the arrows of the Egyptians. He is my eldest son, and if aught happens to me he will be the King of the Rebu; and his life is therefore a precious one."

Half an hour later they came upon the tail of the stragglers making their way to the front. The king stopped his chariot and sharply reproved some of them for their delay in setting out, and urged them to hasten on to the appointed place. In two hours the king arrived at this spot, where already some forty thousand men were assembled. The scouts who had been sent out reported that although the advance-guard of the Egyptians might arrive in an hour's time the main body were some distance behind, and would not be up in time to attack before dark.

This was welcome news, for before night the rest of the forces of the Rebu, fully thirty thousand more, would have joined. The king at once set out to examine the ground chosen by his general for the conflict. It sloped gently down in front to a small stream which ran through soft and marshy ground, and would oppose a formidable obstacle to the passage of chariots. The right rested upon a dense wood, while a village a mile and a half distant from the wood was held by the left wing.

A causeway which led from this across the marsh had been broken up, and heavy blocks of stone were scattered thickly upon it to impede the passage of chariots. The archers were placed in front to harass the enemy attempting to cross. Behind them were the spearmen in readiness to advance and aid them if pressed. The chariots were on the higher ground in the rear ready to dash in and join in the conflict should the enemy succeed in forcing their way through the marsh.

The visit of inspection was scarcely finished when a cloud of dust was seen rising over the plain. It approached rapidly. The flash of arms could be seen in the sun, and presently a vast number of horses were seen approaching in even line.

"Are they horsemen, father?" Amuba asked.

"No, they are chariots, Amuba. The Egyptians do not, like us, fight on horseback, although there may be a few small bodies of horsemen with the army; their strength lies in their chariots. See, they have halted; they have perceived our ranks drawn up in order of battle."

The chariots drew up in perfect line, and as the clouds of dust blew away four lines of chariots could be made out ranged at a distance of a hundred yards apart.

"There are about a thousand in each line," the king said, "and this is but their advance guard; we have learned from fugitives that there are fully fifteen thousand chariots with their army."

"Is there no other place where they can pass this swamp, father?"

"Not so well as here, Amuba; the valley deepens further on, and the passage would be far more difficult than here. Above, beyond the wood, there is a lake of considerable extent, and beyond that the ground is broken and unsuited for the action of chariots as far as the sea. Besides, they have come to fight us, and the pride of their king would not permit of their making a detour. See, there is some great personage, probably the king himself, advancing beyond their ranks to reconnoiter the ground."

A chariot was indeed approaching the opposite brow of the depression; there were two figures in it; by the side walked numerous figures, who, although too far off to be distinguished, were judged to be the attendants and courtiers of the king. The sun flashed from the side of the chariot, which appeared at this distance to be composed of burnished gold. Great fans carried on wands shaded the king from the heat of the sun.

He drove slowly along the edge of the brow until he reached a point opposite the wood, and then, turning, went the other way till he reached the causeway which passed on through the village. After this he rode back to the line of chariots and evidently gave a word of command, for instantly the long line of figures seen above the horses disappeared as the men stepped off the chariots to the ground. No movement took place for an hour; then there was a sudden stir, and the long lines broke up and wheeled round to the right and left, where they took up their position in two solid masses.

"The main army are at hand," the king said. "Do you see that great cloud, ruddy in the setting sun? That is the dust raised by their advance; in another hour they will be here, but by that time the sun will have set, and assuredly they will not attack until morning."

The front line were ordered to remain under arms for a time; the others were told to fall out and prepare their food for the night. The Egyptian army halted about a mile distant, and as soon as it was evident that no further movement was intended, the whole of the soldiers were ordered to fall out. A line of archers were placed along the edge of the swamp, and ere long a party of Egyptian bowmen took up their post along the opposite crest. Great fires were lighted, and a number of oxen, which had been driven forward in readiness, were slaughtered for food.

"If the Egyptians can see what is going on," the king said to his son, "they must be filled with fury, for they worship the oxen as among their chief gods."

"Is it possible, father, that they can believe that cattle are gods?" Amuba asked in surprise.

"They do not exactly look upon them as gods, my son, but as sacred to their gods. Similarly they reverence the cat, the ibis, and many other creatures."

"How strange!" Amuba said. "Do they not worship, as we and the Persians do, the sun, which, as all must see, is the giver of light and heat, which ripens our crops and gives fertility in abundance?"

"Not, so far as I know, Amuba; but I know that they have many gods who they believe give them victory over their enemies."

"They don't always give them victory," Amuba said, "since four times they have been repulsed in their endeavours to invade our land; perhaps our gods are more powerful than theirs."

"It may be that, my son; but so far as I can see the gods give victory to the bravest and most numerous armies."

"That is to say, they do not interfere at all, father."

"I do not say that, my son; we know little of the ways of the gods. Each nation has its own, and as some nations overthrow others, it must be that either some gods are more powerful than others, or that they do not interfere to save those who worship them from destruction. But these things are all beyond our knowledge. We have but to do our part bravely, and we need assuredly not fear the bulls and the cats and other creatures which the Egyptians trust."

Some hours were spent by the king, his leaders, and his captains in going about among the troops seeing that all the contingents had arrived well-armed and in good order, notifying to the leaders of each the position they should take up in the morning, and doing all in their power to animate and encourage the soldiers. When all was done the king sat down on a pile of skins which had been prepared for him, and talked long and earnestly with his son, giving him advice as to his conduct in future, if aught should befall him in the coming fight.

"You are my heir," he said, "and as is customary to the country the throne goes down from father to son. Were I to survive for another eight or ten years you would, of course, succeed me, but should I fall to-morrow and should the Egyptians overrun the land, things may happen otherwise. In that case the great need of the people would be a military leader who would rouse them to prolonged resistance and lead them again and again against the Egyptians until these, worn out by the perpetual fighting, abandon the idea of subjecting us and turn their attention to less stubborn minded people.

"For such work you are far too young, and the people would look to Amusis or one of my other captains as their leader. Should success crown his efforts they may choose him as their king. In that case I would say, Amuba, it will be far better for you to acquiesce in the public choice than to struggle against it. A lad like you would have no prospect of success against a victorious general, the choice of the people, and you would only bring ruin and death upon yourself and your mother by opposing him.

"I can assure you that there is nothing so very greatly to be envied in the lot of a king, and as one of the nobles of the land your position would be far more pleasant here than as king. A cheerful acquiescence on your part to their wishes will earn you the good-will of the people, and at the death of him whom they may choose for their king their next choice may fall upon you. Do all in your power to win the good-will of whoever may take the place of leader at my death by setting an example of prompt and willing obedience to his orders. It is easy for an ambitious man to remove a lad from his path, and your safety absolutely demands that you shall give him no reason whatever to regard you as a rival.

"I trust that all this advice may not be needed, and that we may conquer in to-morrow's fight, but if we are beaten the probability that I shall escape is very small, and it is therefore as well that you should be prepared for whatever may happen. If you find that in spite of following my advice the leader of the people, whoever he may be, is ill-disposed towards you, withdraw to the borders of the country, collect as large a band as you can—there are always plenty of restless spirits ready to take part in any adventure—and journey with them to the far west, as so many of our people have done before, and establish yourself there and found a kingdom.

"None of those who have ever gone in that direction have returned, and they must therefore have found space to establish themselves, for had they met with people skilled in war and been defeated, some at least would have found their way back, but so long as traditions have been handed down to us tribes from the east have poured steadily westward to the unknown land, and no band has ever returned."

His father spoke so seriously that Amuba lay down that night on his couch of skins in a very different mood to that in which he had ridden out; he had thought little of his mother's forebodings, and had looked upon it as certain that the Rebu would beat the Egyptians as they had done before, but his father's tone showed him that he too felt by no means confident of the issue of the day.

As soon as daylight broke the Rebu stood to their arms, and an hour later dense masses of the Egyptians were seen advancing. As soon as these reached the edge of the slope and began to descend towards the stream, the king ordered his people to advance to the edge of the swamp and to open fire with their arrows.

A shower of missiles flew through the air and fell among the ranks of the Egyptian footmen who had just arrived at the edge of the swamp. So terrible was the discharge that the Egyptians recoiled and, retreating half-way up the slope where they would be beyond the reach of the Rebu, in turn discharged their arrows. The superiority of the Egyptian bowmen was at once manifest; they carried very powerful bows, and standing sideways drew them to the ear, just as the English archers did at Crecy, and therefore shot their arrows a vastly greater distance than did their opponents, who were accustomed to draw their bows only to the breast.

Scores of the Rebu fell at the first discharge, and as the storm of arrows continued, they, finding themselves powerless to damage the Egyptians at that distance, retired half-way up the side of the slope. Now from behind the lines of the Egyptian archers a column of men advanced a hundred abreast, each carrying a great faggot; their object was evident, they were about to prepare a wide causeway across the marsh by which the chariots could pass. Again the Rebu advanced to the edge of the swamp and poured in their shower of arrows; but the Egyptians, covering themselves with the bundles of faggots they carried, suffered but little harm, while the Rebu were mown down by the arrows of the Egyptians archers shooting calmly and steadily beyond the range of their missiles.

As soon as the front rank of the Egyptian column reached the edge of the swampy ground the men of the front line laid down their faggots in a close row, and then retired in the intervals between their comrades behind them. Each rank as it arrived at the edge did the same. Many fell beneath the arrows of the Rebu, but the operation went on steadily, the faggots being laid down two deep as the ground became more marshy, and the Rebu saw, with a feeling approaching dismay, the gradual but steady advance of the causeway two hundred yards wide across the swamp.

The king himself and his bravest captains, alighting from their chariots, went down among the footmen and urged them to stand firm, pointing out that every yard the causeway advanced their arrows inflicted more fatal damage among the men who were forming it. Their entreaties, however, were in vain; the ground facing the causeway was already thickly encumbered with dead, and the hail of the Egyptian arrows was so fast and deadly that even the bravest shrank from withstanding it. At last even their leaders ceased to urge them, and the king gave the order for all to fall back beyond the range of the Egyptian arrows.

Some changes were made in the formation of the troops, and the best and most disciplined bands were placed facing the causeway so as to receive the charge of the Egyptian chariots. The two front lines were of spearmen, while on the higher ground behind them were placed archers whose orders were to shoot at the horses, and pay no heed to those in the chariots; then came the chariots, four hundred in number. Behind these again was a deep line of spearmen; on the right and left extending to the wood and village were the main body of the army, who were to oppose the Egyptian footmen advancing across the swamp.

The completion of the last portion of the causeway cost the Egyptians heavily, for while they were exposed to the arrows of the Rebu archers these were now beyond the range of the Egyptians on the opposite crest. But at last the work was completed. Just as it was finished and the workmen had retired, the king leaped from his chariot, and, leading a body of a hundred men carrying blazing brands, dashed down the slope. As soon as they were seen the Egyptian archers ran forward and a storm of arrows was poured into the little band. Two-thirds of them fell ere they reached the causeway; the others applied their torches to the faggots.

The Egyptian footmen rushed across to extinguish the flames, while the Rebu poured down to repel them. A desperate fight ensued, but the bravery of the Rebu prevailed, and the Egyptians were driven back. Their attack, however, had answered its purpose, for in the struggle the faggots had been trodden deeper into the mire, and the fire was extinguished. The Rebu now went back to their first position and waited the attack which they were powerless to avert. It was upwards of an hour before it began, then the long line of Egyptian footmen opened, and their chariots were seen fifty abreast, then with a mighty shout the whole army advanced down the slope. The Rebu replied with their war-cry.

At full speed the Egyptian chariots dashed down the declivity to the causeway. This was the signal for the Rebu archers to draw their bows, and in an instant confusion was spread among the first line of chariots. The horses wounded by the missiles plunged madly. Many, stepping between the faggots, fell. For a moment the advance was checked, but the Egyptian footmen, entering the swamp waist-deep, opened such a terrible fire with their arrows that the front line of the Rebu were forced to fall back, and the aim of their archers became wild and uncertain.

In vain the king endeavoured to steady them. While he was doing so, the first of the Egyptian chariots had already made their way across the causeway, and behind them the others poured on in an unbroken column. Then through the broken lines of spearmen the Rebu chariots dashed down upon them, followed by the host of spearmen. The king's object was to arrest the first onslaught of the Egyptians, to overwhelm the leaders, and prevent the mass behind from emerging from the crowded causeway.

The shock was terrible. Horses and chariots rolled over in wild confusion, javelins were hurled, bows twanged, and the shouts of the combatants and the cries of the wounded as they fell beneath the feet of the struggling horses created a terrible din. Light and active, the Rebu footmen mingled in the fray, diving under the bellies of the Egyptian horses, and inflicting vital stabs with their long knives or engaging in hand-to-hand conflicts with the dismounted Egyptians. Amuba had charged down with the rest of the chariots. He was stationed in the second line, immediately behind his father; and his charioteer, mindful of the orders he had received, strove, in spite of the angry orders of the lad, to keep the chariot stationary; but the horses, accustomed to manoeuver in line, were not to be restrained, and in spite of their driver's efforts charged down the slope with the rest.

Amuba, who had hunted the lion and leopard, retained his coolness, and discharged his arrows among the Egyptians with steady aim. For a time the contest was doubtful. The Egyptian chariots crowded on the causeway were unable to move forward, and in many places their weight forced the faggots so deep in the mire that the vehicles were immovable. Meanwhile, along the swamp on both sides a terrible contest was going on. The Egyptians, covered by the fire of their arrows, succeeded in making their way across the swamp, but here they were met by the Rebu spearmen, and the fight raged along the whole line.

Then two thousand chosen men, the body-guard of the Egyptian king, made their way across the swamp close to the causeway, while at the same time there was a movement among the densely packed vehicles. A tremendous impulse was given to them from behind: some were pressed off into the swamp, some were overthrown or trampled under foot, some were swept forward on to the firm ground beyond, and thus a mass of the heaviest chariots drawn by the most powerful horses forced their way across the causeway over all obstacles.

In their midst was the King of Egypt himself, the great Thotmes.

The weight and impetus of the mass of horses and chariots pressed all before it up the hill. This gave to the chariots which came on behind room to open to the right and left. The king's body-guard shook the solid formation of the Rebu spearmen with their thick flights of arrows, and the chariots then dashed in among them. The Rebu fought with the valour of their race. The Egyptians who first charged among them fell pierced with their arrows, while their horses were stabbed in innumerable places. But as the stream of chariots poured over without a check, and charged in sections upon them, bursting their way through the mass of footmen by the force and fury with which they charged, the infantry became broken up into groups, each fighting doggedly and desperately.

At this moment the officer in command of the Rebu horse, a thousand strong, charged down upon the Egyptian chariots, drove them back towards the swamp, and for a time restored the conflict; but the breaks which had occurred between the Rebu centre and its two flanks had enabled the Egyptian body-guard to thrust themselves through and fall upon the Rebu chariots and spearmen, who were still maintaining the desperate conflict. The Rebu king had throughout fought in the front line of his men, inspiriting them with his voice and valour. Many times, when his chariot was so jammed in the mass that all movement was impossible, he leapt to the ground, and, making his way through the throng, slew many of the occupants of the Egyptian chariots.

But his efforts and those of his captains were unavailing. The weight of the attack was irresistible. The solid phalanx of Egyptian chariots pressed onward, and the Rebu were forced steadily back. Their chariots, enormously outnumbered, were destroyed rather than defeated. The horses fell pierced by the terrible rain of arrows, and the wave of Egyptians passed over them. The king, looking round in his chariot, saw that all was lost here, and that the only hope was to gain one or other of the masses of his infantry on the flank, and to lead them off the field in solid order. But as he turned to give orders, a shaft sent by a bowman in a chariot a few yards away struck him in the eye and he fell back dead in his chariot.

Chapter 2

AMUBA saw his father fall, and leaping from his chariot, strove to make his way through the mingled mass of footmen and chariots to the spot. Jethro followed close behind him. He, too, had caught sight of the falling figure, and knew what Amuba did not—that the Rebu had lost their king. He was not forgetful of the charge which had been laid on him, but the lad was for a moment beyond his control, and he, too, was filled with fury at the fall of the king, and determined if possible to save his body. He reached Amuba's side just in time to interpose his shield between the boy and an Egyptian archer in a chariot he was passing. The arrow pierced the shield and the arm that held it. Jethro paused an instant, broke off the shaft at the shield, and seizing the point, which was projecting two inches beyond the flesh, pulled the arrow through the wound.

It was but a moment's work, but short as it was it almost cost Amuba his life, for the archer, leaning forward, dropped the end of his bow over the lad's head—a trick common among the Egyptian archers—and in a moment dragged him to the ground, while his comrade in the chariot raised his spear to despatch him. Jethro sprang forward with a shout of rage, and with a blow of his sword struck off the head of the spear as it was descending. Then shortening his sword, he sprang into the chariot, ran the man holding the bow through the body, and grappled with the spearman.

The struggle was a short one. Leaving his sword in the body of the archer, Jethro drew his dagger and speedily despatched his foe. Then he jumped down, and lifting Amuba, who was insensible from the sharp jerk of the bowstring upon his throat and the violence of his fall, carried him back to his chariot. This with the greatest difficulty he managed to draw out of the heat of the conflict, which was for the moment raging more fiercely than before. The Rebu who had seen the fall of their king had dashed forward to rescue the body and to avenge his death. They cleared a space round him, and as it was impossible to extricate his chariot, they carried his body through the chaos of plunging horses, broken chariots, and fiercely struggling men to the rear.

Then it was placed in another chariot, and the driver started with it at full speed for the city. Jethro, on emerging from the crowd, paused for a moment to look round. He saw at once that the battle was lost. The centre was utterly broken, and the masses of the Egyptians who had crossed the swamp were pressing heavily on the flanks of the Rebu footmen, who were still opposing a firm stand to those attacking them in front. For the moment the passage of the Egyptian chariots was arrested; so choked was the causeway with chariots and horses which were imbedded in the mire, or had sunk between the faggots, that further passage was impossible, and a large body of footmen were now forming a fresh causeway by the side of the other.

This would soon be completed, for they were now working undisturbed by opposition, and Jethro saw that as soon as it was done the Egyptian host would sweep across and fall upon the rear of the Rebu. Jethro ran up to two mounted men, badly wounded, who had like himself made their way out of the fight. "See," he said, "in a quarter of an hour a new causeway will be completed, and the Egyptians will pour over. In that case resistance will be impossible, and all will be lost. Do one of you ride to each flank and tell the captains that the king is dead, that there are none to give orders here, and that their only chance to save their troops is to retreat at full speed but keeping good order to the city."

The horsemen rode off immediately, for Jethro, as the king's own charioteer, was a man of some importance. After despatching the messengers he returned to his chariot and at once drove off. Amuba was now recovering, and the rough motion of the vehicle as it dashed along at full speed aroused him.

"What is it, Jethro? What has happened?"

"The battle is lost, prince, and I am conveying you back to the city. You have had a rough fall and a narrow escape of your life, and can do no more fighting even if fighting were of any good, which it is not."

"And the king, my father?" Amuba said, struggling to his feet. "What of him? Did I not see him fall?"

"I know nought of him for certain," Jethro replied. "There was a terrible fight raging, and as I had you to carry out I could take no share in it. Besides, I had an arrow through my left arm— if I had been a moment later it would have gone through your body instead. And now, if you do not mind taking the reins, I will bandage it up. I have not had time to think about it yet, but it is bleeding fast, and I begin to feel faint."

This was indeed true; but Jethro had called Amuba's attention to his wound principally for the sake of diverting his thoughts for a moment from his fear for his father. As Amuba drove, he looked back. The plain behind him was covered with a mass of fugitives.

"I see that all is lost," he said mournfully. "But how is it that we are not pursued?"

"We shall be pursued before long," Jethro answered. "But I fancy that few of the Egyptians chariots which first passed are in a condition to follow. Most of them have lost horses or drivers. Numbers were broken to pieces in the melée. But they are making a fresh causeway, and when that is completed those who cross will take up the pursuit. As for their footmen, they have small chance of catching the Rebu."

"Surely our men ought to retreat in good order, Jethro. Scattered as they are, they will be slaughtered in thousands by the Egyptian chariots."

"They could not oppose much resistance to them anyhow," Jethro replied. "On a plain footmen cannot withstand a chariot charge. As it is, many will doubtless fall; but they will scatter to the right and left, numbers will reach the hills in safety, some will take refuge in the woods and jungles, while many will outrun the chariots. The new causeway is narrow, and a few only can cross abreast, and thus, though many of our men will be overtaken and killed, I trust that the greater part will escape."

"Let us draw up here for a short time, Jethro. I see there are several chariots and some horsemen behind, and as they are with the main body of the fugitives, they are doubtless friends. Let us join them and proceed in a body to the town. I should not like to be the first to enter with the news of our defeat."

"You are right, prince. As our horses are good, we need not fear being overtaken. We can therefore wait a few minutes."

A score of chariots presently came up, and all halted on seeing Amuba. One of them contained Amusis, the chief captain of the army. He leaped from his chariot when he saw Amuba, and advanced to him.

"Prince," he said, "why do you delay? I rejoice at seeing that you have escaped in the battle, for I marked you bravely fighting in the midst; but let me beg you to hasten on. A few minutes and the host of Egyptian chariots will be upon us."

"I am ready to proceed, Amusis, since you have come. Have you any news of my father?"

"The king has been sorely wounded," the general said, "and was carried off out of the battle; but come, prince, we must hasten on. Our presence will be sorely needed in the city, and we must get all in readiness for defence before the Egyptians arrive."

The chariots again started, and reached the city without seeing anything of the Egyptians, who did not indeed arrive before the walls until an hour later, having been delayed by the slaughter of the fugitives. As the party entered the town they found confusion and terror prevailing. The arrival of the body of the king was the first intimation of disaster, and this had been followed by several horsemen and chariots, who had spread the news of the defeat of the army. The cries of women filled the air; some in their grief and terror ran wildly here and there; some sat at their doors with their faces hidden by their hands, wailing loudly; others tore their garments and behaved as if demented.

On their way to the palace they met the troops who had been left behind to guard the city, moving down stern and silent to take their places on the wall. During the drive Amusis, who had driven in Amuba's chariot had broken to the boy the news that his father was dead, and Amuba was prepared for the loud lamentation of women which met him as he entered the royal inclosure.

"I will see my mother," he said to Amusis, "and then I will come down with you to the walls and will take whatever part you may assign me in the defence. It is to your experience and valour we must now trust."

"I will do all that I can, prince. The walls are strong, and if, as I hope, the greater part of our army find their way back, I trust we may be able to defend ourselves successfully against the Egyptian host. Assure your royal mother of my deep sympathy for her in her sorrow, and of my devotion to her personally."

The general now drove off, and Amuba entered the royal dwellings. In the principal apartment the body of the king was laid upon a couch in the middle of the room. The queen stood beside it in silent grief, while the attendants raised loud cries, wrung their hands, and filled the air with their lamentation, mingled with praises of the character and bravery of the king. Amuba advanced to his mother's side. She turned and threw her arms round him.

"Thank the gods, my son, that you are restored to me; but what a loss, what a terrible loss is ours!"

"It is indeed, mother. No better father ever lived than mine. But I pray you, mother, lay aside your grief for a while; we shall have time to weep and mourn for him afterward. We have need of all our courage. In a few hours the Egyptian hosts will be before our walls, and every arm will be needed for their defence. I am going down to take my place among the men, to do what I can to encourage them; but the confusion in the city is terrible. None know whether they have lost husbands or fathers, and the cries and lamentations of the women cannot but dispirit and dishearten the men. I think, mother, that you might do much if you would; and I am sure that my father in his resting place with the gods would far rather see you devoting yourself to the safety of his people than to lamentations here."

"What would you have me do?"

"I should say, mother, mount a chariot and drive through the streets of the town; bid the women follow the example of their queen and defer their lamentation for the fallen until the foe has been repelled. Bid each do her part in the defence of the city; there is work for all—stones to be carried to the walls, food to be cooked for the fighting men, hides to be prepared in readiness to be carried to the ramparts where the attack is hottest, to shield our soldiers from arrows. In these and other tasks all can find employment, and in thus working for the defence of the town, the women would find distraction from their sorrows and anxieties."

"Your advice is wise, Amuba, and I will follow it. Order a chariot to be brought down. My maidens shall come with me; and see that two trumpeters are in readiness to precede us. This will insure attention and silence, and my words will be heard as we pass along. How did you escape from the conflict?"

"The faithful Jethro bore me off, mother, or I, too, should have fallen; and now, with your permission, I will go to the wall."

"Do so, Amuba, and may the gods preserve you. You must partake of some food before you go, for you will need all your strength, my son."

Amuba hastily ate the food that was placed before him in another apartment, and drank a goblet of wine, and then hurried down to the wall.

The scene was a heart-rending one. All over the plain were scattered groups of men hurrying towards the city, while among them dashed the Egyptian chariots, overthrowing and slaying them; but not without resistance. The Rebu were well disciplined, and, as the chariots thundered up, little groups gathered together, shield overlapping shield, and spears projecting, while those within the circle shot their arrows or whirled stones from their slings. The horses wounded by the arrows often refused to obey their drivers, but rushed headlong across the plain; others charged up only to fall pierced with the spears, while the chariots were often empty of their occupants before they broke into the phalanx.

Thus, although many fell, many succeeded in gaining the gates of the town, and the number of men available for the defence had already largely increased when Amuba reached the walls. Although the Egyptian chariots came up in great numbers, night fell without the appearance of the main body of the Egyptian army. After darkness set in great numbers of the Rebu troops who had escaped to the hills made their way into the town. The men of the contingents furnished by the other Rebu cities naturally made their way direct to their homes, but before morning the six thousand men left behind to guard the city when the army set out had been swelled to four times their numbers.

Although this was little more than half the force which had marched out to battle, the return of so large a number of the fugitives caused a great abatement of the panic and misery that had prevailed. The women whose husbands or sons had returned rejoiced over those whom they had regarded as lost, while those whose friends had not yet returned gained hopes from the narratives of the fresh comers that their loved ones might also have survived, and would ere long make their way back. The example of the queen had already done much to restore confidence. All knew the affection that existed between the king and her, and the women all felt that if she could lay aside her deep sorrow, and set such an example of calmness and courage at such a time, it behoved all others to set aside their anxieties and do their best for the defence of the town.

Amusis gave orders that all those who had returned from the battle should rest for the night in their homes, the troops who had remained in the city keeping guard upon the walls. In the morning, however, all collected at the trumpet-call, and were formed up according to the companies and battalions to which they belonged. Of some of these which had borne the brunt of the combat there were but a handful of survivors, while of others the greater portion were present; weak battalions were joined to the strong, fresh officers were appointed to take the place of those who were missing; the arms were examined, and all deficiencies made good from the public stores.

Ten thousand men were set aside as reserve to be brought up to the points most threatened, while to the rest were allotted those portions of the wall which they were to occupy. As soon as morning broke the women recommenced the work that had been interrupted by night, making their way to the walls in long trains, carrying baskets of stones on their heads. Disused houses were pulled down for the sake of their stones and timber, parties of women with ropes dragging the latter to the walls in readiness to be hurled down upon the heads of the enemy. Even the children joined in the work, carrying small baskets of earth to those portions of the wall which Amusis had ordered to be strengthened.

The position of the city had been chosen with a view to defence. It stood on a plateau of rock raised some fifty feet above the plain. The Caspian washed its eastern face; on the other three sides a high wall, composed of earth roughly faced with stones, ran along at the edge of the plateau; above it, at distances of fifty yards apart, rose towers. The entire circuit of the walls was about three miles. Since its foundation by the grandfather of the late king the town had never been taken, although several times besieged, and the Rebu had strong hopes that here, when the chariots of the Egyptians were no longer to be feared, they could oppose a successful resistance to all the efforts of the enemy.

At noon the Egyptian army was seen advancing, and, confident as the defenders of the city felt, they could not resist a feeling of apprehension at the enormous force which was seen upon the plain. The Egyptian army was over three hundred thousand strong. It moved in regular order according to the arms or nationality of the men. Here were Nubians, Sardinians, Etruscans, Oscans, Dauni, Maxyes, Kahaka, a race from Iberia, and bodies of other mercenaries from every tribe and people with whom the Egyptians had any dealings.

The Sardinians bore round shields, three or four spears or javelins, a long straight dagger, and a helmet surmounted by a spike, with a ball at the top. The Etruscans carried no shields, and instead of the straight dagger were armed with a heavy curved chopping-knife; their head-dress resembled somewhat in shape that now worn by the Armenians. The Dauni were Greek in the character of their arms, carrying a round shield, a single spear, a short straight sword, and a helmet of the shape of a cone.

The Egyptians were divided according to their arms. There were regiments of archers, who carried, for close combat, a slightly-curved stick of heavy wood; other regiments of archers carried hatchets. The heavy infantry all bore the Egyptian shield, which was about three feet long. It was widest at the upper part, where it was semicircular, while the bottom was cut off straight. The shields had a boss near the upper part. Some regiments carried, in addition to the spears, heavy maces, others axes. Their helmets all fitted closely to the head; most of them wore metal tassels hanging from the top. The helmets were for the most part made of thick material, quilted and padded; these were preferred to metal, being a protection from the heat of the sun.

Each company carried its own standard; these were all of religious character, and represented animals sacred to the gods, sacred boats, emblematic devices, or the names of the king or queen. These were in metal, and were raised at the ends of spears or staves. The standard-bearers were all officers of approved valour. Behind the army followed an enormous baggage-train; and as soon as this had arrived on the ground the tents of the king and the principal officers were pitched.

"What a host!" Jethro said to Amuba, who, after having his arm dressed on his arrival at the palace, had accompanied the young prince to the walls. "It seems a nation rather than an army. I do not wonder now that we were defeated yesterday, but that we so long held our ground, and that so many escaped from the battle."

"It is wonderful, truly, Jethro. Look at the long line of chariots moving in as regular order as the footmen. It is well for us that they will now be forced to be inactive. As to the others, although they are countless in numbers, they cannot do much against our walls. No towers that they can erect upon the plains will place them on a level with us here, and the rock is so steep that it is only here and there that it can be climbed."

"It would seem impossible for them to take it, prince; but we must not be too confident. We know that many towns which believed themselves impregnable have been captured by the Egyptians, and must be prepared for the most daring enterprises. The gates have been already fastened, and so great a thickness of rocks piled against them, that they are now the strongest part of the wall; those parts of the roads leading up to them that were formed of timber have been burned, and they cannot now reach the gates except by climbing, as at other points. We have provisions enough to last for well-nigh a year, for all the harvest has been brought in from the whole district round, together with many thousands of cattle; of wells there are abundance."

"Yes, I heard the preparations that were being made, Jethro, and doubt not that if we can resist the first onslaught of the Egyptians we can hold out far longer than they can, for the difficulty of victualling so huge an army will be immense. In what way do you think they will attack? For my part I do not see any method which offers a hope of success."

"That I cannot tell you. We know that to us and to the peoples around our cities seem impregnable. But the Egyptians are skilled in all the devices of war. They have laid siege to and captured great numbers of cities, and are doubtless full of plans and expedients of which we know nothing. However, to-morrow morning will show us something. Nothing will be attempted to-day. The generals have first to inspect our walls and see where the assault is to be delivered, and the army will be given a day's rest at least before being called upon to assault such a position."

In the afternoon a cortege of chariots made the circuit of the walls from the shore of the sea round the great plateau to the sea again, keeping just beyond the range of arrows.

"If we had but a few of their archers here," Jethro said, "the Egyptian king would not be so overbold in venturing so near. It is wonderful how strongly they shoot. Their arrows have fully double the range of ours, and their power is sufficient to carry them through the strongest shields, even when strengthened with metal. Had I not seen it I should have thought it impossible that living men, and those no bigger or stronger than we, could have sent their arrows with such power. They stand in a different attitude to that of our archers, and though their shafts are fully a foot longer than ours they draw them to the head. I regarded myself as a good bowman till I met the Egyptians, and now I feel as a child might do when watching a man performing feats of strength of which he had not even imagined a possibility."

In the evening the great council met. It included all the principal officers of the army, the priests, the royal councillors, and the leading men in the state. After a discussion it was determined that in the present crisis it were best to postpone taking any steps to appoint a successor to the late king, but that so long as the siege lasted Amusis should be endowed with absolute powers. In order that there should be no loss of time for the necessity of consulting anyone Amuba was present with his mother at the council, though neither of them took any active part in it. But at its commencement an announcement was made in their name that they were willing to abide by whatever the council should decide, and that indeed both mother and son desired that while this terrible danger hung over the state the supreme power should be placed in the hands of whomsoever the general voice might select as the person best fitted to take the command in such an extremity.

That night the body of the king was consumed on a great funeral pile. Under ordinary occasions the ceremony would have taken place on a narrow promontory jutting out into the sea, about five miles from the city. Here the previous monarchs had been consumed in sight of a multitude of their people, and had been buried beneath great mounds of earth. The priests had long ago pronounced this place the most sacred in the kingdom, and had declared that the anger of the gods would fall upon any who ventured to set foot upon the holy ground. But it was impossible for the present to lay the ashes of the king by the side of those of his forefathers, and the ceremony was therefore conducted within the royal inclosure, only the officiating priests and the wife and son of the deceased being present. When all was over the ashes were collected and were placed in a casket, which was destined, when better times returned, to be laid, in the sight of the whole people, in the sacred inclosure on the promontory.

Early next morning the trumpets of the guards on the walls called all the troops to arms. As soon as Amuba reached his post, he saw the Egyptian army marching against the city. When they arrived within bow-shot the archers, who formed the front lines, opened fire upon the defenders on the walls. Their arrows, however, for the most part fell short, while those of the besieged rained down upon them with effect. They were therefore withdrawn a short distance, and contracting their ranks a vast number of footmen poured through, and in irregular order ran forward to the foot of the rock, where they were sheltered from the arrows of those on the wall.

"What can they be going to do now?" Amuba exclaimed, laying aside his bow.

Jethro shook his head.

"They are working with a plan," he said. "We shall see before long. Listen."

Even above the din caused by so vast a multitude a sharp metallic sound was presently heard like that of innumerable hammers striking on steel.

"Surely," Amuba exclaimed, "they can never be thinking of quarrying the rock away! That is too great a task even were the whole people of Egypt here."

"It certainly is not that," Jethro agreed; "and yet I cannot think what else can be their intentions."

It was nigh an hour before the mystery was solved. Then, at the blast of a trumpet sounded at the post where the Egyptian king had placed himself, and taken up along the whole of the line, a great number of heads appeared along the edge of rock at the foot of the walls. The Egyptians had been employed in driving spikes in the crevices of the rock. Standing on the first so driven, they then inserted others three feet higher, and so had proceeded until a number of men had climbed up the face of the rock. These let down ropes, and ladders had been hauled up the steepest places. Great numbers of ropes were hung down to assist those who followed in the ascent, and the men who first showed themselves over the brow were followed by a stream of others, until the ledge, which was in most cases but a few feet wide, was crowded with soldiers.

The ladders were now hauled up and placed against the wall, and the Egyptians swarmed up in great numbers; but the Rebu were prepared for the assault, and a storm of stones, beams of wood, arrows, javelins, and other missiles rained down on the Egyptians. Many of the ladders, in spite of the number of men upon them, were thrown back by the defenders, and fell with a crash over the edge of the rock to the plain below. Here and there the Egyptians gained a footing on the wall before the Rebu had recovered from their first surprise at their daring manner of attack; but so soon as they rallied they attacked the Egyptians with such fury that in every case the latter were slain fighting or were thrown over the embattlements.

For several hours the Egyptians continued their efforts, but after losing vast numbers of men without obtaining any success they were recalled by the sound of the trumpet.

"That has not been very serious, Jethro," Amuba said, wiping the perspiration from his forehead; for he had been encouraging the men by assisting in the lifting and casting over the massive stones and beams of wood.

"It was not difficult to repulse them under such conditions," Jethro said; "but the manner of their attack was a surprise indeed to us, and they have fought with the greatest bravery. You will see that the next time they will have benefited by the lesson, and that we shall have some new device to cope with. Now that they have once found a way to scale the rock we may expect but little rest."

The fight was not renewed until evening, when, just as darkness fell, a large number of the Egyptians again ascended the rock. As before, the Rebu poured missiles down upon them; but this time only a sufficient number had climbed up to be able to stand along close to the foot of the wall, where they were to a great extent sheltered from the missiles from above. The night was a dark one, and all night long the Rebu continued to shower down missiles upon their invisible foe, of whose continued presence they were assured by the sounds which from time to time were heard.

When daylight enabled the defenders to see what was going on at the foot of their walls they raised a shout of surprise and dismay. During the night the Egyptians had hoisted up by ropes a quantity of the timber brought with them for the construction of shelters for those who were engaged on siege operations. The timbers were all cut and prepared for fitting together, and were easily jointed even in the dark. Thus then, when the besiegers looked over, they saw forty or fifty of these shelters erected against the foot of their walls. They were so formed that they sloped down like a pent-house and were thickly covered with hides.

The besieged soon found that so solid were these constructions that the beams and great stones which they dropped upon them simply bounded off and leapt down into the plain. Ladders fastened together had been fixed by the Egyptians from each of these shelters to the plain below, so that the men at work could be relieved or reinforced as the occasion required.

In vain the besieged showered down missiles, in vain poured over the caldrons of boiling oil they had prepared in readiness. The strength of the beams defied the first; the hides lapped over each other prevented the second from penetrating to those below.

"Truly these are terrible foes, prince," Jethro said. "I told you that we might expect new plans and devices, but I did not think that the very day after the siege began we should find that they had overcome all the difficulties of our natural defences, and should have established themselves in safety at the foot of our walls."

"But what is to be done, Jethro? The men working in these shelters will speedily dislodge these stones facing the walls, and will then without difficulty dig through the earthwork behind."

"The matter is serious," Jethro agreed; "but as yet there is no reason to alarm ourselves. The greater portion of our troops will be assembled behind the wall, and should the Egyptians gain a way through we should pour in at the openings, and as they can be only reinforced slowly, would speedily hurl them all over the edge of the cliff. It is not that I fear."

"What is it that you do fear, Jethro?"

"I fear, prince, because I do not know what it is I have to fear. We are as children in the struggle of this kind as opposed to the Egyptians. Already they have wholly over-thrown all our calculations, and it is just because I do not know what they will do next that I am afraid. It must be as plain to them as it is to us that if they dig through the walls we shall rush in and overpower them."

"Perhaps they intend to work right and left and to undermine the walls, until large portions of them tumble over and breaches are made."

Jethro shook his head.

"That would destroy the Egyptian shelters and bury their workmen; or, even did they manage to retire before the walls fell, they would gain nothing by it. In fact, I wish that we ourselves could tumble the walls over, for in that case the heap of earth and stones would rise from the very edge of the rock, and as the Egyptians could only climb up in small numbers at a time, we could destroy them without difficulty. I see now that our builders made a mistake in surrounding the city with a high wall; it would have been best to have built a bare breastwork at the very edge of the cliff all around. Here comes Amusis; we shall hear what his opinion of the matter is."

Amusis looked flushed and anxious, although when he saw the prince he assumed an expression of carelessness.

"The Egyptians are going to burrow through our walls," he said; "but when they do we will drive them like rats out of the holes. Do you not think so, Jethro?"

"I do not know," Jethro said gravely. "If they dig through our walls we shall certainly, as you say, drive them out of their holes; but I cannot believe that that is what they are going to do."

"What do you think they are going to do?" Amusis asked roughly.

"I have no idea, Amusis. I wish that I had; but I am quite sure that they haven't taken all this trouble for nothing."

Chapter 3

SO confident were the Rebu that if the Egyptians dug through their walls, or even threw them down by undermining them, they could repel their assault, that they took but little heed to the huts established at the foot of the wall, except that a strong body of men were stationed behind the walls, half of whom were always to be under arms in readiness to repel the Egyptians should they burrow through. This confidence proved their ruin. The Egyptians were thoroughly accustomed to mining operations, and were fully aware that were they to pierce the wall the Rebu could at once overwhelm the small working parties; they therefore, after penetrating a considerable distance into the embankment, drove right and left, making an excavation of considerable size, the roof being supported by beams and planks hauled up at night.

The number of those employed in the work was increased as fast as there was room for them; and, while the Rebu thought that there were at most a dozen men in each of the sheltered places, there were, at the end of twenty-four hours, fully two hundred men at work in the heart of the embankment at each point. The Egyptian king had ordered the chief of his engineers to have everything in readiness for the capture of the city by the end of the third day.

Each night the numbers of workmen increased, while the excavations were carried in further and further. No picks were used in the work, the earth being cut away with wide daggers. Absolute silence was enjoined among the workers, and they were thus enabled to extend their excavations close to the surface without the defenders having an idea of their proximity. The distance that they were from the inner face was ascertained by boring through at night-time with spears. By the end of the third day the excavations had been carried so far that there was but a foot or so of earth remaining, this being kept from moving, on pressure from the outside, by a lining of boards supported by beams. Thus at twenty points the Egyptians were in readiness to burst through among the unsuspecting defenders.

As soon as it was dark the preparations for the assault began. Great numbers of stagings of vast length had been prepared, together with an immense number of broad and lofty ladders. These last were brought forward noiselessly to the foot of the cliff, and great numbers of the Egyptians mounted before the alarm was given by those on the walls. But by this time the excavations were all crowded with men. The Egyptian army now advanced with shouts to the assault. The great stages were brought forward by the labour of thousands of men and placed against the cliff.

The besieged had now rushed to defend the walls, and volleys of missiles of all sorts were poured down upon the Egyptians as they strove to mount the ladders and stages. No one thought of any possible danger from the little shelters lying at the foot of the wall, and the din was so great that the work of digging through the remaining wall of earth was unheard. The troops who had been specially told off to watch these points had joinded their comrades on the walls, and none marked the stream of dark figures which presently began to pour out from the embankment at twenty different points.

At last the besieged, whose hopes were rising as the Egyptians appeared to falter under the showers of missiles poured down, were startled by the sound of a trumpet in their rear—a sound which was answered instantly from a score of points. Rushing with cries of dismay to the back of the rampart, they saw dark bodies of footmen drawn up in regular order, and a rain of arrows was opened upon them. The Rebu, without a moment's hesitation, rushed down to attack the foes who had gained a footing, they scarce knew how, in their fortress. But each of the Egyptian companies was four hundred strong, composed of picked troops, and these for a time easily beat off the irregular attacks of the Rebu.

Amusis and the other leaders of the Rebu strove to get their men into solid order, for so alone could they hope to break the phalanxes of the Egyptians; but the confusion was too great. In the meantime the Egyptians outside had taken advantage of the diversion created by the attack within, and poured up their ladders and stagings in vast numbers. Some dragging up ladders after them planted them against the walls, others poured through by the passages which had been dug, and these, as soon as they were numerous enough, ascended the embankments from behind and fell upon the Rebu still defending the wall.

Never did the tribesmen fight with greater bravery; but the completeness of the surprise, the number of the Egyptians who had established themselves in their rear, the constant pushing in of reinforcements both through and over the wall, rendered it impossible for them to retrieve their fortress; and in the confusion and darkness they were unable to distinguish friend from foe. The various battalions and companies were hopelessly mixed together; the orders of their leaders and officers were unheard in the din.

Upon the Egyptian side everything had been carefully planned. One of the companies which first entered had made their way quietly along the foot of the wall, and were not noticed until they suddenly threw themselves upon the defenders of one of the gates. As soon as they had obtained possession of this great fires were lighted, and a large body of Egyptian troops, headed by engineers carrying beams and planks, advanced. The gaps across the roadway were bridged over, and the Egyptians poured in at the gate before the Rebu could dislodge the party which had taken possession of it. Every moment added to the confusion of the scene. To the Rebu it seemed as if their foes were springing from the very earth upon them, and, despairing of regaining the ground that had been lost, they began to break away and make some for their homes, some for the water face of the city—the only one which was open to them, for the Egyptians were now pressing forward from the three other faces of the town. The boats lying along the sand were quickly crowded with fugitives and pushed off from the shore, and those who arrived later found all means of escape gone. Some threw down their arms and made their way to their homes, others ran back to meet the Egyptians and die fighting.

It was some hours before the conflict ceased, for the Egyptians too were confused with the darkness, and many desperate fights took place between different battalions before they discovered they were friends. Light was gained by firing numbers of the houses lying nearest to the walls; but as soon as the Egyptians advanced beyond the arc of light they were fiercely attacked by the Rebu, and at last the trumpet sounded the order for the troops to remain in the positions they occupied until daylight.

As soon as morning broke a vast crowd of women were seen advancing from the centre of the town. As they neared the Egyptians they threw themselves on the ground with loud cries for mercy. There was a pause; and then some Egyptian officers advanced and bade a score of the women follow them to the presence of the king. Thotmes had entered with the troops who made their way into the city by the gate, but yielding to the entreaties of the officers that he would not expose himself to be killed in the confusion, perhaps by an arrow shot by his own soldiers, he had retired to the plain, and had just returned to take part in the occupation of the city.

The Rebu women were led to him over ground thickly covered with dead. Fully half the defenders of the city had fallen, while the loss of the Egyptians had been almost as large. The women threw themselves on their faces before the great monarch and implored mercy for themselves, their children, and the remnant of the men of the city.

Thotmes was well satisfied. He had captured a city which was regarded as impregnable; he had crushed the people who had inflicted defeats upon his predecessors; he had added to his own glory and to the renown of the Egyptian arms. The disposition of the Egyptians was lenient. Human sacrifices were unknown to their religion, and they do not appear at any time to have slain in cold blood captives taken in war. Human life was held at a far higher value in Egypt than among any other nation of antiquity, and the whole teaching of their laws tended to create a disposition towards mercy.

An interpreter translated to the king the words of the women.

"Has all resistance ceased?" the king asked. "Have all the men laid down their arms?"

The women exclaimed that there was not now an armed man in the city, all the weapons having been collected during the night and placed in piles in the open space in front of the entrance to the palace.

"Then I give to all their lives," the king said graciously. "When I fight with cowards I have little mercy upon them, for men who are not brave are unfit to live; but when I fight with men I treat them as men. The Rebu are a valiant people, but as well might the jackal fight with the lion as the Rebu oppose themselves to the might of Egypt. They fought bravely in the field, and they have bravely defended their walls; therefore I grant life to all in the city—men, women, and children. Where is your king?"

"He died in the battle four days since," the women replied.

"Where is your queen?"

"She drank poison last night, preferring to join her husband than to survive the capture of her city."

Thotmes had now ordered the whole of the inhabitants to be taken out to the plain and kept there under a guard. The town was then methodically searched and everything of value brought together. The king set aside a certain portion of the golden vessels for the services of the temple, some he chose for himself, and after presenting others to his generals, ordered the rest to be divided among the troops. He then ordered a hundred captives—fifty young men and fifty maidens of the highest rank—to be selected to be taken to Egypt as slaves, and then fixed the tribute which the Rebu were in future to pay. The army then evacuated the city and the inhabitants were permitted to return.

The next day messengers arrived from the other Rebu towns. The fall of the capital, which had been believed to be impregnable, after so short a siege had struck terror into the minds of all, and the messengers brought offers of submission to the king, with promises to pay any tribute that he might lay upon them.

The king, well satisfied with his success and anxious to return to Egypt, from which he had been absent nearly two years, replied graciously to the various deputations, informing them that he had already fixed the tribute that the nation was to pay annually, and ordered a contribution to be sent in at once by each city in proportion to its size. In a few days the required sums, partly in money, partly in vessels of gold, embroidered robes, and other articles of value, were brought in. When the full amount had been received the camp was struck and the army started on their long march back to Egypt, an officer of high rank being left as governor of the newly-captured province, with ten thousand men as a garrison.

Amuba was one of the fifty selected as slaves. Amusis had escaped in the confusion, as had many others. Jethro was also one of the selected band. Amuba was for a time careless of what befell him. The news of the death of his mother, which had met him as, after fighting to the last, he returned to the palace, had been a terrible blow, following as it did so closely upon the loss of his father and the overthrow of the nation. His mother had left the message for him that, although as life had no longer a charm for her, she preferred death to the humiliation of being carried a prisoner to Egypt, she trusted that he would bear the misfortunes which had fallen on him and his people with submission and patience; he was young, and there was no saying what the future had in store for him.

"You will doubtless, my son," were the words of her message, "be carried away captive into Egypt, but you may yet escape some day and rejoin your people, or may meet with some lot in which you may find contentment or even happiness there. At any rate, my last words to you are, bear patiently whatever may befall you, remember always that your father was king of the Rebu, and whatever your station in life may be, try to be worthy of the rank to which you were born. There is no greater happiness on a throne than in a cottage. Men make their own happiness, and a man may be respected even though only a slave. May the gods of your country preside over and protect you always."

The message was delivered by an old woman who had been with the queen since her birth, and, struck down with grief as Amuba was at his mother's death, he yet acknowledged to himself that even this loss was less hard to bear than the knowledge that she who had been so loved and honoured by the people should undergo the humiliation of being dragged a slave in the train of the conquering Egyptians. He was, however, so prostrate with grief that he obeyed with indifference the order to leave the city, and was scarcely moved when the Egyptian officer appointed to make the selection chose him as one of the party that were to be taken as slaves to Egypt.

Prostrate as he was, however, he felt it to be a satisfaction and comfort when he found that Jethro was also of the party set aside.

"It is selfish, Jethro," he said, "for me to feel glad that you too are to be dragged away as a slave, but it will be a great comfort to have you with me. I know almost all the others of the party, but to none shall I be able to talk of my father and mother and my home here as I should to you whom I have known so long."

"I am not sorry that I have been chosen," Jethro said, "for I have no family ties, and now that the Rebu are a conquered people I should have little satisfaction in my life here. When we get to Egypt we shall probably be separated, but there is a march of months' duration before us, and during that time we may at least be together; since, then, my being with you is as you say, prince, a comfort to you, I am well content that I have been chosen. I thought it a hard thing when my wife died but a few weeks after our marriage. Now I rejoice that it was so, and that I can leave without anyone's heart being wrung at my departure. You and I, prince, perhaps of all those chosen will feel the least misery at the fate that has befallen us. Most of those here are leaving wives and children behind; some of the youngest are still unmarried, but they have fathers and mothers from whom they will be separated. Therefore, let us not bemoan our lot, for it might have been worse, and our life in Egypt may not be wholly unbearable."

"That is just what my dear mother said, Jethro," Amuba replied, repeating the message the queen had sent him.

"My dear mistress was right," Jethro said. "We may find happiness in Egypt as elsewhere; and now let us try to cheer up our companions, for in cheering them we shall forget our own misfortunes."

Jethro and Amuba went among the rest of the captives, most of whom were prostrated with grief, and did their best to rouse them from their stupor.

"The Egyptians have seen that the Rebu are men in the field," Amuba said to some of them. "Let them see that we can also bear misfortune like men. Grieving will not mitigate our lot, nay, it will add to its burden. If the Egyptians see that we bear our fate manfully they will have far more compassion upon us than if they see that we bemoan ourselves. Remember we have a long and toilsome journey before us, and shall need all our strength. After all the hardship of our lot is as nothing to that of the women yonder. We are accustomed to exercise and toil, but the journey, which we can support as well as the Egyptians, will be terrible to them, delicate in nature as they are. Let us therefore set them an example of courage and patience, let us bear ourselves as men whose suffering is unmerited, who have been conquered but not disgraced, who are prepared to defy fate and not to succumb to it."

Amuba's words had a great effect upon the captives. They regarded him with respect as the son of their late king, and as one who would have been king himself had not this misfortune befallen them; and his calmness and manly speech encouraged them to strive against their grief and to look their fate more hopefully in the face. As long as the army remained in camp the hands of the captives were tied behind them, but when the march was begun they were relieved of their bonds and were placed in the centre of an Egyptian regiment.

It was a long and tedious journey. On the way the train of captives was very largely increased by those who had been taken in the earlier conquests of the army, and who had been left in charge of the troops told off to the various provinces brought into subjection by the Egyptians until the army passed through on its homeward march. Provisions had been everywhere collected to supply it on its progress, and as the distance traversed each day was small the captives suffered but little until they entered upon the passage of the desert tract between the southern point of Syria and the mouth of the Nile.

Here, although vast quantities of water were carried in the train of the army, the supply given to the captives was extremely small, and as the sun blazed down with tremendous heat, and they were half suffocated by the dust which rose in clouds under the feet of the vast body of men, their sufferings were very severe. The Rebu captives had gained the respect of the troops who escorted them by their manly bearing and the absence of the manifestations of grief which were betrayed by most of the other captives.   The regiment was composed of Libyan mercenaries, hardy, active men, inured alike to heat and fatigue.

During the three months which the march had occupied Amuba and Jethro, and indeed most of the captives, had acquired some knowledge of the Egyptian language. Jethro had from the first impressed upon the young prince the great advantage this would be to them.   In the first place, it would divert their thoughts from dwelling upon the past, and in the second, it would make their lot more bearable in Egypt.

"You must remember," he said, "that we shall be slaves, and masters are not patient with their slaves. They give them orders, and if the order is not understood so much the worse for the slaves.

It will add to our value, and therefore obtain for us better treatment, if we are able to converse in their tongue."

Amuba was thankful indeed when the gray monotony of the desert was succeeded by the bright verdure of the plains of Egypt. As they entered the land the order in which they had marched was changed, and the long line of captives followed immediately after the chariot of the king. Each of them was laden with a portion of the spoils taken from their native country. Amuba bore on his head a large golden vase which had been used in the ceremonies of the temple. Jethro carried a rich helmet and armour which had belonged to the king.

The first city they entered Amuba was astonished at the massive splendour of the buildings and at the signs of comfort and wealth which everywhere met his eye. The streets were thronged with people who, bending to the ground, shouted their acclamations as the king passed along, and who gazed with interest and surprise at the long procession of captives representing the various nations who had been subjected to his arms. Most of all he was surprised at the temples with their long avenues of sphinxes, the gigantic figures representing the gods, the rows of massive pillars, the majesty and grandeur of the edifices themselves.

"How were they built, Jethro?" he exclaimed over and again. "How were these massive stones placed in order? How did they drag these huge figures across the plains? What tools could they have used to carve them out of the solid granite?"

"I am afraid, Amuba," Jethro said grimly, for the lad had positively forbidden him to address him any longer as prince, saying that such title addressed to a slave was no better than mockery, "we are likely to learn to our cost before long how they manage these marvels, for marvels they assuredly are. It must have taken the strength of thousands of men to have transported even one of these strange figures, and although the people themselves may have aided in the work, you may be sure the slaves bore the brunt of it."

"But what is the meaning of these figures, Jethro? Surely neither in this country nor in any other are there creatures with the faces of women and the bodies of lions and great wings such as these have. Some, too, have the faces of men and the bodies of bulls, while others have heads like birds and bodies like those of men."

"Assuredly there can be no such creatures, Amuba; and I wonder that a people so enlightened and wise as the Egyptians should choose such strange figures for their gods. I can only suppose that these figures represent their attributes rather than the gods themselves. Do you see, the human head may represent their intelligence, the bodies of the lions or bulls their strength and power, the wings of the bird their swiftness. I do not know that it is so, but it seems to me that it is possible that it may be something of this sort. We cannot but allow that their gods are powerful since they give them victory over all other people; but no doubt we shall learn more of them and of many other things in time."

The journey was continued for another three weeks, and was the cause of constant surprises to the captives. The extraordinary fertility of the land especially struck them. Cultivation among the Rebu was of a very primitive description, and the abundance and variety of the crops that everywhere met their eye seemed to them absolutely marvellous. Irrigation was not wholly unknown to the Rebu, and was carried on to a considerable extent in Persia; but the enormous works for the purpose in Egypt, the massive embankments of the river, the network of canals and ditches, the order and method everywhere apparent, filled them with surprise and admiration.

Many of the cities and temples greatly surpassed in magnificence and splendour those they had first met with, and Amuba's wonder reached its climax when they arrived at Memphis, till lately the capital of Egypt. The wealth and contents of the city astonished the captives, but most of all were they surprised when they saw the enormous bulk of the pyramids rising a few miles distant from the town, and learned that these were some of the tombs of the kings.

The country had now altered in character. On the left a range of steep hills approached the river, and as the march proceeded similar though not so lofty hills were seen on the right.

At last after another fortnight's travelling, a shout of joy from the army proclaimed that Thebes, the capital of Egypt, the goal of the long and weary march, was in view.

Thebes stood on both sides of the Nile. On the eastern bank the largest portion of the population was gathered, but this part of the city was inhabited principally by the poorer class. There was, too, a large population on the Libyan side of the Nile, the houses being densely packed near the bank of the river. Behind these were numbers of temples and palaces, while the tombs of the kings and queens were excavated in a valley further back, whose precipitous sides were indeed honeycombed with the rock sepulchres of the wealthy. As the dwelling-houses were all low, the vast piles of the temples, palaces, and public buildings rose above them, and presented a most striking appearance to those approaching the city, which lay in a great natural amphitheatre, the hills on both sides narrowing towards the river both above and below it. The march of the royal army from Memphis had been on the western bank of the river, and it was the great Libyan suburb with its palaces and temples that they were approaching. As they neared the city an enormous multitude poured out to welcome the king and the returning army. Shouts of enthusiasm were raised, the sound of trumpets and other musical instruments filled the air, religious processions from the great temples moved with steady course through the dense crowd, which separated at once to allow of the passage of the figures of the gods, and of the priests and attendants bearing their emblems.

"Indeed, Jethro," Amuba exclaimed with enthusiasm, "it is almost worth while being made a slave if it is only to witness this glorious scene. What a wonderful people are these; what knowledge, and power, and magnificence. Why, my father's palace would be regarded as a mere hut in Thebes, and our temples, of which we thought so much, are pigmies by the side of these immense edifices."

"All that is true enough, Amuba, and I do not say that I, too, am not filled with admiration, and yet you know the Rebu several times drove back their forces, and man for man are more than a match for their soldiers. Our people are taller than they by half a head. We have not so much luxury, nor did we want it. All this must make people effeminate."

"Perhaps so," Amuba assented; "but you must remember it is not so very long ago that we were a people living in tents, and wandering at will in search of pasture, and we have not, I think, become effeminate because we have settled down and built towns. No one can say that the Egyptians are not brave, certainly it is not for us to say so, though I agree with you that physically they are not our equals. See how the people stare and point at us, Jethro. I should think they have never seen a race like ours with blue eyes and fair hair, though even among them there are varying shades of darkness. The nobles and upper classes are lighter in hue than the common people."

The surprise of the Egyptians was indeed great at the complexion of their captives, and the decoration of their walls has handed down in paintings which still remain, the blue eyes and fair hair of the Rebu. The rejoicings upon the return of the king went on for several days, at the end of that time the captives were distributed by the royal order. Some were given to the generals who had most distinguished themselves. Many were assigned to the priests, while the great bulk were sent to labour upon the public works.

The Rebu captives, whose singular complexion and fairness caused them to be regarded with special interest, were distributed among the special favourites of the king. Many of the girls were assigned to the queen and royal princesses, others to the wives of the priests and generals who formed the council of the king. The men were, for the most part, given to the priests for service about the temples.

To his great delight Amuba found that Jethro and himself were among the eight captives who were assigned to the service of the priests of one of the great temples. This was scarcely the effect of chance, for the captives were drawn up in line, and the number assigned to each temple were marched off together in order that there might be no picking and choosing of the captives, but that they might be divided impartially between the various temples, and as Jethro always placed himself by Amuba's side, it naturally happened that they fell to the same destination.

On reaching the temple the little band of captives were again drawn up, and the high-priest, Ameres, a grave and distinguished-looking man, walked along the line scrutinizing them. He beckoned to Amuba to step forward. "Henceforth," he said, "you are my servant. Behave well, and you will be well treated." He again walked down the line, and Amuba saw that he was going to choose another, and threw himself on his knees before him.

"Will my lord pardon my boldness," he said, "but may I implore you to choose yonder man who stood next beside me? He has been my friend from childhood, he covered me with his shield in battle, he has been a father to me since I have lost my own. Do not, I implore you, my lord, separate us now. You will find us both willing to labour at whatsoever you may give us to do."

The priest listened gravely.

"It shall be as you wish," he said, "it is the duty of every man to give pleasure to those around him if it lies in his power, and as your friend is a man of thews and sinews, and has a frank and honest face, he will assuredly suit me as well as another; do you therefore both follow me to my house."

The other captives saluted Amuba as he and Jethro turned to follow. The priest observed the action, and said to the lad:

"Were you a person of consequence among your people that they thus at parting salute you rather than your comrade, who is older than you?"

"I am the son of him who was their king," Amuba said. "He fell in action with your troops, and had not our city been taken, and the nation subdued by the Egyptians, I should have inherited the throne."

"Is it so?" the priest said. "Truly the changes and fortunes of life are strange. I wonder that, being the son of their king, you were not specially kept by Thotmes himself."

"I think that he knew it not," Amuba said. "We knew not your customs, and my fellow-captives thought that possibly I might be put to death were it known that I was a son of their king, and therefore abstained from all outward marks of respect, which, indeed, would to one who was a slave like themselves, have been ridiculous."

"Perhaps it is best so," the priest said thoughtfully. "You would not have been injured, for we do not slay our captives taken in war, still maybe your life will be easier to bear as the servant of a priest than in the household of the king. You had better, however, mention to no one the rank you have borne, for I might be reported to the king, and then you might be sent for to the palace; unless indeed you would rather be a spectator of the pomp and gaiety of the court than a servant in a quiet household."

"I would far rather remain with you, my lord," Amuba said eagerly. "You have already shown the kindness of your heart by granting my request, and choosing my comrade Jethro as my fellow slave, and I feel already that my lot will be a far happier one than I had ventured to hope."

"Judge not hastily by appearances," the priest said. "At the same time, here in Egypt, slaves are not treated as they are among the wild peoples of Nubia and the desert. There is a law for all, and he who kills a slave is punished as if he took the life of an Egyptian. However I think I can say that your life will not be a hard one; you have intelligence, as is shown by the fact that you have so rapidly acquired sufficient knowledge of our tongue to speak it intelligibly. Can you, too, speak our language?" he asked Jethro.

"I can speak a little," Jethro said; "but not nearly so well as Amuba. My lips are too old to fashion a strange tongue as rapidly as can this younger one."

"You speak sufficiently well to understand," the priest said, "and doubtless will in time acquire our tongue perfectly. This is my house."

The priest entered an imposing gateway, on each side of which stretched a long and lofty wall. At a distance of fifty yards from the gate stood a large dwelling, compared to which the royal abode which Amuba had been brought up in was but a miserable hut. Inclosed within the walls was a space of ground some three hundred yards square, which was laid out as a garden. Avenues of fruit trees ran all round it, a portion was laid out as a vineyard; while, separated from the rest by an avenue of palm-trees, was a vegetable garden.

In front of the house was a large piece of water, in which floated a gaily painted boat; aquatic plants of all kinds bordered its edges. Graceful palms grouped their foliage over it, the broad flat leaves of lilies floated on its surface, while the white flowers which Amuba had seen carried in all the religious processions, and by large numbers of people of the upper rank, and which he heard were called the lotus, rose above them. The two captives were struck with surprise and admiration at the beauty of the scene, and forgot for a moment that they were slaves, as they looked round at a vegetation more beautiful than they had ever beheld. A smile passed over the countenance of the priest.

"Perfect happiness is for no man," he said, "and yet methinks that you may in time learn at least contentment here."

Chapter 4

JUST as the priest finished speaking, a lad of about the same age as Amuba appeared at the portico of the house, and ran down to his father.

"Oh, father!" he exclaimed, "have you brought two of those strange captives home. We saw them in the procession, and marvelled greatly at the colour of their hair and their eyes. Mysa and I particularly noticed this lad, whose hair is almost the colour of gold."

"As usual, Chebron, your tongue outruns your discretion. This youth understands enough Egyptian to know what you are saying, and it is not courteous to speak of a person's characteristics to his face."

The lad flushed through his olive cheeks.

"Pardon me," he said courteously to Amuba. "I did not think for a moment that one who had but newly arrived among us understood our language."

"Do not apologize," Amuba replied with a smile. "Doubtless our appearance is strange to you, and indeed even among the peoples of Lydia and Persia, there are few whose hair and eyes are as fair as ours. Even had you said that you did not like our appearance I should not have felt hurt, for all people I think like that to which they are accustomed; in any case, it is good of you to say that you regret what you said; people do not generally think that captives have feelings."

"Chebron's apology was right," his father said. "Among us politeness is the rule, and every Egyptian is taught to be considerate to all people. It is just as easy to be polite as to be rude, and men are served better for love than for fear."

"And are they to stay here, father?" Chebron asked, "or have you only brought them for to-day?"

"They are to stay here, my son. I have chosen them from those set aside for our temple. I selected the younger because he was about your age, and it is good for a man to have one near him who has been brought up with him, and is attached to him; who, although circumstances may not have made them equal in condition, can yet be a comrade and a friend, and such, I hope, you will find in Amuba, for such he tells me is his name. I have said whom circumstances have placed in an inferior position, for after all circumstances are everything. This youth, in his own country, held a position even higher than you do here, for he was the son of the king; and since his father fell in battle, would now be the king of his people had they not been subjected to us. Therefore, Chebron, bear it always in mind that, although misfortune has placed him a captive among us, he is in birth your superior, and treat him as you yourself would wish to be treated did you fall a captive into the hands of a hostile nation."

"I will gladly treat you as my friend," the young Egyptian said frankly to Amuba. "Although you are so different from me in race, I can see in your face that you are true and loyal. Besides," he added, "I am sure that my father would not have bade me so trust you had he not read your character and been certain that you will be a fit friend for me."

"You and your father are both good," Amuba replied. "I know how hard is the lot of captives taken in war, for we Rebu had many slaves whom we took in various expeditions, and I was prepared to suffer. You can judge, then, how grateful I feel to our gods that they have placed me in hands so different from those I had looked for, and I swear to you, Chebron, that you shall find me faithful and devoted to you. So, too, will you find my friend, here, who in any difficulty would be far more able to render you service than I could. He was one of our bravest warriors. He drove my chariot in the great battle we fought with your people, and saved my life several times; and should you need the service of a strong and brave man, Jethro will be able to aid you."

"And have you been in battle?" Chebron asked in surprise.

"That was the first time I had ever fought with men," Amuba said; "but I had often hunted the lion, and he is almost as terrible an enemy as your soldiers. I was young to go to battle, but my father naturally wished me to take my place early among the fighting men of our nation."

"By the way, Chebron," Ameres said, "I would warn you, mention to no one the rank that Amuba held in his own country. Were it known he might be taken away from us to serve in the palace. His people who were taken captives with him said nothing as to his rank, fearing that ill might befall him were it known, and it was therefore supposed that he was of the same rank as the other captives, who were all men of noble birth among the Rebu. Therefore tell no one, not even your mother or your sister Mysa. If there is a secret to be kept, the fewer who know it the better."

While this conversation had been going on Amuba had been narrowly examining the lad who had promised to treat him as a friend.

Like his father he was fairer in complexion than the majority of the Egyptians, the lighter hue being, indeed, almost universal among the upper class. He was much shorter and slighter than the young Rebu, but he carried himself well, and had already in his manner something of the calm and dignity that distinguished Egyptians born to high rank. He was disfigured, as Amuba thought, by the custom, general throughout Egypt, of having his head smoothly shaven, except one lock which fell down over the left ear. This, as Amuba afterwards learned, was the distinguishing sign of youth, and would be shaved off when he attained man's estate, married, or entered upon a profession.

At present his head was bare, but when he went out he wore a close-fitting cap with an orifice through which the lock of hair passed out and fell down to his shoulder. He had not yet taken to the custom general among the upper and middle classes of wearing a wig. This general shaving of the head had, to Amuba, a most unpleasant effect until he became accustomed to it. It was adopted, doubtless, by the Egyptians for the purpose of coolness and cleanliness; but Amuba thought that he would rather spend any amount of pains in keeping his hair free from dust than go about in the fantastic and complicated wigs that the Egyptians wore.

The priest now led them within the house. On passing through the entrance they entered a large hall. Along its side ran a row of massive columns supporting a ceiling, which projected twelve feet from each wall; the walls were covered with marble and other coloured stones; the floor was paved with the same material; a fountain played in the middle, and threw its water to a considerable height, for the portion of the hall between the columns was open to the sky; seats of a great variety of shapes stood about the room; while in great pots were placed palms and other plants of graceful foliage. The ceiling was painted with an elaborate pattern in colours. A lady was seated upon a long couch. It had no back, but one end was raised as a support for the arm, and the ends were carved into the semblance of the heads of animals.

Two Nubian slave girls stood behind her fanning her, and a girl about twelve years old was seated on a low stool studying from a roll of papyrus. She threw it down and jumped to her feet as her father entered, and the lady rose with a languid air, as if the effort of even so slight a movement was a trouble to her.

"Oh, papa!—" the girl began, but the priest checked her with a motion of his hand.

"My dear," he said to his wife, "I have brought home two of the captives whom our great king has brought with him as trophies of his conquest. He has handed many over for our service and that of the temples, and these two have fallen to my share. They were of noble rank in their own country, and we will do our best to make them forget the sad change in their position."

"You are always so peculiar in your notions, Ameres," the lady said more pettishly than would have been expected from her languid movements. "They are captives; and I do not see that it makes any matter what they were before they were captives, so that they are captives now. By all means treat them as you like, so that you do not place them about me, for their strange coloured hair and eyes and their white faces make me shudder."

"Oh, mamma, I think it so pretty," Mysa exclaimed. "I do wish my hair was gold-coloured like that boy's instead of being black like everyone else's."

The priest shook his head at his daughter reprovingly; but she seemed in no way abashed, for she was her father's pet, and knew well enough that he was never seriously angry with her.

"I do not propose placing them near you, Amense," he said calmly in reply to his wife. "Indeed it seems to me that you have already more attendants about you than you can find any sort of employment for. The lad I have specially allotted to Chebron, as to the other I have not exactly settled as to what his duties will be."

"Won't you give him to me, papa?" Mysa said coaxingly. "Fatina is not at all amusing, and Dolma, the Nubian girl, can only look good-natured and show her white teeth, but as we can't understand each other at all I don't see that she is of any use to me."

"And what use do you think you could make of this tall Rebu?" the priest asked, smiling.

"I don't quite know, papa," Mysa said, as with her head a little on one side she examined Jethro critically, "but I like his looks, and I am sure he could do all sorts of things; for instance, he could walk with me when I want to go out, he could tow me round the lake in the boat, he could pick up my ball for me, and could feed my pets."

"When you are too lazy to feed them yourself," the priest put in. "Very well, Mysa, we will try the experiment. Jethro shall be your special attendant, and when you have nothing for him to do, which will be the best part of the day, he can look after the water-fowl. Zunbo never attends them properly. Do you understand that?" he asked Jethro.

Jethro replied by stepping forward, taking the girl's hand, and bending over it until his forehead touched it.

"There is an answer for you, Mysa."

"You indulge the children too much, Ameres," his wife said irritably. "I do not think in all Egypt there are any children as spoiled as ours. Other men's sons never speak unless addressed, and do not think of sitting down in the presence of their father. I am astonished indeed that you, who are looked up to as one of the wisest men in Egypt, should suffer your children to be so familiar with you."

"Perhaps, my dear," Ameres said with a placid smile, "it is because I am one of the wisest men in Egypt. My children honour me in their hearts as much as do those who are kept in slave-like subjection. How is a boy's mind to expand if he does not ask questions, and who should be so well able to answer his questions as his father? There, children, you can go now, take your new companions with you, and show them the garden and your pets."

"We are fortunate, indeed, Jethro," Amuba said as they followed Chebron and Mysa into the garden. "When we pictured to ourselves as we lay on the sand at night during our journey hither what our life would be, we never dreamt of anything like this; we thought of tilling the land, of aiding to raise the great dams and embankments, of quarrying stones for the public buildings, of a grinding and hopeless slavery, and the only thing that ever we ventured to hope for was that we might toil side by side, and now, see how good the gods have been to us. Not only are we together, but we have found friends in our masters, a home in this strange land."

"Truly it is wonderful, Amuba. This Priest Ameres is a most excellent person; one to be loved by all who come near him. We have indeed been most fortunate in having been chosen by him."

The brother and sister led the way through an avenue of fruit trees, at the end of which a gate led through a high paling of rushes into an inclosure some fifty feet square. It was surrounded by trees and shrubs, and in their shade stood a number of wooden structures. In the centre was a pool occupying the third of the area, and like the large pond before the house bordered with aquatic plants. At the edge stood two ibises, while many brilliantly plumaged water-fowl were swimming on its surface, or cleaning their feathers on the bank.

As soon as the gate closed there was a great commotion among the water-fowl; the ibises advanced gravely to meet their young mistress, the ducks set up a chorus of welcome, those on the water made for the shore, while those on land followed the ibises with loud quacking. But the first to reach them were two gazelles, which bounded from one of the wooden huts and were in an instant beside them, thrusting their soft muzzles into the hands of Chebron and Mysa, while from the other structures arose a medley of sounds— the barking of dogs and the sounds of welcome from a variety of creatures.

"This is not your feeding time, you know," Chebron said, looking at the gazelles, "and for once we have come empty-handed; but we will give you something from your stores. See, Jethro, this is their larder," and he led the way into a structure somewhat larger than the rest; along the walls were a number of boxes of various sizes, while some large bins stood below them. "Here, you see," he went on, opening one of the bins and taking from it a handful of freshly cut vetches, and going to the door and throwing it down before the gazelles, "this is their special food; it is brought in fresh every morning from our farm, which lies six miles away. The next bin contains the seed for the water-fowl. It is all mixed here you see. Wheat and peas and pulse and other seeds. Mysa, do give them a few handfuls, for I can hardly hear myself speak from their clamour.

"In this box above you see there is a pan of sopped bread for the cats. There is a little mixed with the water; but only a little, for it will not keep good. Those cakes are for them too. Those large, plain, hard-baked cakes in the next box are for the dogs; they have some meat and bones given them two or three times a week. These frogs and toads in this cage are for the little crocodile; he has a tank all to himself. All these other boxes are full of different food for the other animals you see. There's a picture of the right animal upon each, so there is no fear of making a mistake. We generally feed them ourselves three times a day when we are here, but when we are away it will be for you to feed them."

"And please," Mysa said, "above all things be very particular that they have all got fresh water; they do love fresh water so much, and sometimes it is so hot that the pans dry up in an hour after it has been poured out. You see, the gazelles can go to the pond and drink when they are thirsty, but the others are fastened up because they won't live peaceably together as they ought to do; but we let them out for a bit while we are here. The dogs chase the water-fowl and frighten them, and the cats will eat up the little ducklings, which is very wrong when they have plenty of proper food; and the ichneumon, even when we are here, would quarrel with the snakes if we let him into their house. They are very troublesome that way, though they are all so good with us. The houses all want making nice and clean of a morning."

The party went from house to house inspecting the various animals, all of which were most carefully attended. The dogs, which were, Chebron said, of a Nubian breed, were used for hunting; while on comfortable beds of fresh rushes three great cats lay blinking on large cushions, but got up and rubbed against Mysa and Chebron in token of welcome. A number of kittens that were playing about together rushed up with upraised tails and loud mewing. Amuba noticed that their two guides made a motion of respect as they entered the house where the cats were as well as towards the dogs, the ichneumon, and the crocodile, all of which were sacred animals in Thebes.

Many instructions were given by Mysa to Jethro as to the peculiar treatment that each of her pets demanded, and having completed their rounds the party then explored the garden, and Amuba and Jethro were greatly struck by the immense variety of plants, which had indeed been raised from seeds or roots brought from all the various countries where the Egyptian arms extended.

For a year the time passed tranquilly and pleasantly to Amuba in the household of the priest. His duties and those of Jethro were light. In his walks and excursions Amuba was Chebron's companion. He learned to row his boat when he went out fishing on the Nile. When thus out together the distinction of rank was altogether laid aside; but when in Thebes the line was necessarily more marked, as Chebron could not take Amuba with him to the houses of the many friends and relatives of his father among the priestly and military classes. When the priest and his family went out to a banquet or entertainment Jethro and Amuba were always with the party of servants who went with torches to escort them home. The service was a light one in their case; but not so in many others, for the Egyptians often drank deeply at these feasts, and many of the slaves always took with them light couches upon which to carry their masters home. Even among the ladies, who generally took their meals apart from the men upon these occasions, drunkenness was by no means uncommon.

When in the house Amuba was often present when Chebron studied, and as he himself was most anxious to acquire as much as he could of the wisdom of the Egyptians, Chebron taught him the hieroglyphic characters, and he was ere long able to read the inscriptions upon the temple and public buildings and to study from the papyrus scrolls, of which vast numbers were stowed away in pigeon holes ranged round one of the largest rooms in the house.

When Chebron's studies were over Jethro instructed him in the use of arms, and also practiced with Amuba. A teacher of the use of the bow came frequently—for Egyptians of all ranks were skilled in the use of the national weapon—and the Rebu captives, already skilled in the bow as used by their own people, learned from watching his teaching of Chebron to use the longer and much more powerful weapon of the Egyptians. Whenever Mysa went outside the house Jethro accompanied her; waiting outside the house she visited until she came out, or going back to fetch her if her stay was a prolonged one.

Greatly they enjoyed the occasional visits made by the family to their farm. Here they saw the cultivation of the fields carried on, watched the plucking of the grapes and their conversion into wine. To extract the juice the grapes were heaped in a large flat vat above which ropes were suspended. A dozen bare-footed slaves entered the vat and trod out the grapes, using the ropes to lift themselves in order that they might drop with greater force upon the fruit.

Amuba had learned from Chebron that, although he was going to enter the priesthood as an almost necessary preliminary for state employment, he was not intended to rise to the upper rank of the priesthood, but to become a state official.

"My elder brother will, no doubt, some day succeed my father as high-priest of Osiris," he told Amuba. "I know that my father does not think that he is clever, but it is not necessary to be very clever to serve in the temple. I thought that, of course, I too should come to high rank in the priesthood; for, as you know, almost all posts are hereditary, and though my brother as the elder would be high-priest, I should be one of the chief-priests also. But I have not much taste that way, and rejoiced much when one day saying so to my father, he replied at once that he should not urge me to devote my life to the priesthood, for that there were many other offices of state which would be open to me, and in which I could serve my country and be useful to the people. Almost all the posts in the service of the state are, indeed, held by the members of priestly families; they furnish governors to the provinces, and not infrequently generals to the army.

"'Some,' he said, 'are by disposition fitted to spend their lives in ministering in the temples, and it is doubtless a high honour and happiness to do so; but for others a more active life and a wider field of usefulness is more suitable. Engineers are wanted for the canal and irrigation works, judges are required to make the law respected and obeyed, diplomatists to deal with foreign nations, governors for the many people over whom we rule; therefore, my son, if you do not feel a longing to spend your life in the service of the temple, by all means turn your mind to study which will fit you to be an officer of the state. Be assured that I can obtain for you from the king a post in which you will be able to make your first essay, and so, if deserving, rise to high advancement.'"

There were few priests during the reign of Thotmes III who stood higher in the opinion of the Egyptian people than Ameres. His piety and learning rendered him distinguished among his fellows. He was high-priest in the temple of Osiris, and was one of the most trusted of the councillors of the king. He had by heart all the laws of the sacred books; he was an adept in the inmost mysteries of the religion. His wealth was large, and he used it nobly; he lived in a certain pomp and state which were necessary for his position, but he spent but a tithe of his revenues, and the rest he distributed among the needy.

If the Nile rose to a higher level than usual and spread ruin and destruction among the cultivators, Ameres was ready to assist the distressed. If the rise of the river was deficient, he always set the example of remitting the rents of the tenants of his broad lands, and was ready to lend money without interest to tenants of harder or more necessitous landlords.

Yet among the high priesthood Ameres was regarded with suspicion, and even dislike. It was whispered among them that, learned and pious as he was, the opinions of the high-priest were not in accordance with the general sentiments of the priesthood; that, although he performed punctiliously all the numerous duties of his office, and took his part in the sacrifices and processions of the god, he yet lacked reverence for him, and entertained notions widely at variance with those of his fellows.

Ameres was, in fact, one of those men who refused to be bound by the thoughts and opinions of others, and to whom it is a necessity to bring their own judgment to bear on every question presented to them. His father, who had been high-priest before him—for the great offices of Egypt were for the most part hereditary—while he had been delighted at the thirst for knowledge and the enthusiasm for study in his son, had been frequently shocked at the freedom with which he expressed his opinions, as step by step he was initiated into the sacred mysteries.

Already at his introduction to the priesthood, Ameres had mastered all there was to learn in geometry and astronomy. He was a skilful architect, and was deeply versed in the history of the nation. He had already been employed as supervisor in the construction of canals and irrigation works on the property belonging to the temple, and in all these respects his father had every reason to be proud of the success he had attained and the estimation in which he was held by his fellows. It was only the latitude which he allowed himself in consideration of religious questions which alarmed and distressed his father.

The Egyptians were the most conservative of peoples. For thousands of years no change whatever took place in their constitution, their manners, customs, and habits. It was the fixed belief of every Egyptian that in all respects their country was superior to any other, and that their laws and customs had approached perfection. All from the highest to the lowest were equally bound by these. The king himself was no more independent than the peasant; his hour of rising, the manner in which the day should be employed, the very quantity and quality of food he should eat, were all rigidly dictated by custom. He was surrounded from his youth by young men of his own age—sons of priests, chosen for their virtue and piety.

Thus he was freed from the influence of evil advisers, and even had he so wished it, had neither means nor power of oppressing his subjects, whose rights and privileges were as strictly defined as his own. In a country, then, where every man followed the profession of his father, and where from time immemorial everything had proceeded on precisely the same lines, the fact that Ameres, the son of the high-priest of Osiris, and himself destined to succeed to that dignity, should entertain opinions differing even in the slightest from those held by the leaders of the priesthood, was sufficient to cause him to be regarded with marked disfavour among them; it was indeed only because his piety and benevolence were as remarkable as his learning and knowledge of science that he was enabled at his father's death to succeed to his office without opposition.

Indeed, even at that time the priests of higher grade would have opposed his election; but Ameres was as popular with the lower classes of the priesthood as with the people at large, and their suffrages would have swamped those of his opponents. The multitude had, indeed, never heard so much as a whisper against the orthodoxy of the high-priest of Osiris. They saw him ever foremost in the sacrifices and processions; they knew that he was indefatigable in his service in the temple, and that all his spare time was devoted to works of benevolence and general utility; and as they bent devoutly as he passed through the streets they little dreamt that the high-priest of Osiris was regarded by his chief brethren as a dangerous innovator.

And yet it was on one subject only that he differed widely from his order. Versed as he was in the innermost mysteries, he had learned the true meaning of the religion of which he was one of the chief ministers. He was aware that Osiris and Isis, the six other great gods, and the innumerable divinities whom the Egyptians worshipped under the guise of deities with the heads of animals, were in themselves no gods at all, but mere attributes of the power, the wisdom, the goodness, the anger of the one great God—a God so mighty that His name was unknown, and that it was only when each of His attributes was given an individuality and worshipped as a god that it could be understood by the finite sense of man.

All this was known to Ameres and the few who, like him, had been admitted to the inmost mysteries of the Egyptian religion. The rest of the population in Egypt worshipped in truth and in faith the animal-headed gods and the animals sacred to them; and yet as to these animals there was no consensus of opinion. In one nome or division of the kingdom the crocodile was sacred; in another he was regarded with dislike, and the ichneumon, who was supposed to be his destroyer, was deified. In one the goat was worshipped, and in another eaten for food; and so it was throughout the whole of the list of sacred animals, which were regarded with reverence or indifference according to the gods who were looked upon as the special tutelary deities of the nome.

It was the opinion of Ameres that the knowledge, confined only to the initiated, should be more widely disseminated, and, without wishing to extend it at present to the ignorant masses of the peasantry and labourers, he thought that all the educated and intelligent classes of Egypt should be admitted to an understanding of the real nature of the gods they worshipped and the inner truths of their religion. He was willing to admit that the process must be gradual, and that it would be necessary to enlarge gradually the circle of the initiated. His proposals were nevertheless received with dismay and horror by his colleagues. They asserted that to allow others besides the higher priesthood to become aware of the deep mysteries of their religion would be attended with terrible consequences.

In the first place, it would shake entirely the respect and reverence in which the priesthood were held, and would annihilate their influence. The temples would be deserted, and, losing the faith which they now so steadfastly held in the gods, people would soon cease to have any religion at all. "There are no people," they urged, "on the face of the earth so moral, so contented, so happy, and so easily ruled as the Egyptians; but what would they be did you destroy all their beliefs, and launch them upon a sea of doubt and speculation! No longer would they look up to those who have so long been their guides and teachers, and whom they regard as possessing a knowledge and wisdom infinitely beyond theirs. They would accuse us of having deceived them, and in their blind fury destroy alike the gods and their ministers. The idea of such a thing is horrible."

Ameres was silenced, though not convinced. He felt, indeed, that there was much truth in the view they entertained of the matter, and that terrible consequences would almost certainly follow the discovery by the people that for thousands of years they had been led by the priests to worship as gods those who were no gods at all, and he saw that the evil which would arise from a general enlightenment of the people would outweigh any benefit that they could derive from the discovery. The system had, as his colleagues said, worked well; and the fact that the people worshipped as actual deities imaginary beings who were really but the representatives of the attributes of the infinite God, could not be said to have done them any actual harm. At any rate, he alone and unaided could do nothing. Only with the general consent of the higher priesthood could the circle of initiated be widened, and any movement on his part alone would simply bring upon himself disgrace and death. Therefore, after unburdening himself in a council composed only of the higher initiates, he held his peace and went on the quiet tenor of his way.

Enlightened as he was, he felt that he did no wrong to preside at the sacrifices and take part in the services of the gods. He was worshipping not the animal-headed idols, but the attributes which they personified. He felt pity for the ignorant multitude who laid their offerings upon the shrine; and yet he felt that it would shatter their happiness instead of adding to it were they to know that the deity they worshipped was a myth. He allowed his wife and daughter to join with the priestesses in the service at the temple, and in his heart acknowledged that there was much in the contention of those who argued that the spread of the knowledge of the inner mysteries would not conduce to the happiness of all who received it. Indeed he himself would have shrunk from disturbing the minds of his wife and daughter by informing them that all their pious ministrations in the temple were offered to non-existent gods; that the sacred animals they tended were in no way more sacred than others, save that in them were recognized some shadow of the attributes of the unknown God.

His eldest son was, he saw, not of the disposition to be troubled with the problems which gave him so much subject for thought and care. He would conduct the services consciously and well. He would bear a respectable part when, on his accession to the high-priesthood, he became one of the councillors of the monarch. He had common sense, but no imagination. The knowledge of the inmost mysteries would not disturb his mind in the slightest degree, and it was improbable that even a thought would ever cross his mind that the terrible deception practiced by the enlightened upon the whole people was anything but right and proper.

Ameres saw, however, that Chebron was altogether differently constituted. He was very intelligent, and was possessed of an ardent thirst for knowledge of all kinds; but he had also his father's habit of looking at matters from all points of view and of thinking for himself. The manner in which Ameres had himself superintended his studies and taught him to work with his understanding, and to convince himself that each rule and precept was true before proceeding to the next, had developed his thinking powers. Altogether, Ameres saw that the doubts which filled his own mind as to the honesty, or even expediency, of keeping the whole people in darkness and error would probably be felt with even greater force by Chebron.

He had determined, therefore, that the lad should not work up through all the grades of the priesthood to the upper rank, but should, after rising high enough to fit himself for official employment, turn his attention to one or other of the great departments of state.

Chapter 5

I AM going on a journey," Ameres said to his son a few days after the return from the farm. "I shall take you with me, Chebron, for I am going to view the progress of a fresh canal that is being made on our estate in Goshen. The officer who is superintending it has doubts whether, when the sluices are opened, it will altogether fulfill its purpose, and I fear that some mistake must have been made in the levels. I have already taught you the theory of the work, it is well that you should gain some practical experience in it; for there is no more useful or honourable profession than that of carrying out works by which the floods of the Nile are conveyed to the thirsty soil."

"Thank you, father. I should like it greatly," Chebron replied in a tone of delight, for he had never before been far south of Thebes. "And may Amuba go with us?"

"Yes; I was thinking of taking him," the high-priest said. "Jethro can also go, for I take a retinue with me. Did I consult my own pleasure I would far rather travel without this state and ceremony; but, as a functionary of state, I must conform to the customs. And, indeed, even in Goshen it is as well always to travel in some sort of state. The people there are of a different race to ourselves. Although they have dwelt a long time in the land and conform to its customs, still they are notoriously a stubborn and obstinate people, and there is more trouble in getting the public works executed there than in any other part of the country."

"I have heard of them, father. They belong to the same race as the shepherd kings who were such bitter tyrants to Egypt. How is it that they stayed behind when the shepherds were driven out?"

"They are of the same race, but they came not with them, and formed no part of their conquering armies. The shepherds, who, as you know, came from the land lying to the east of the Great Sea, had reigned here for a long time when this people came.

They were relations of the Joseph who, as you have read in your history, was chief minister of Egypt.

"He came here as a slave, and was certainly brought from the country whence our oppressors came. But they say that he was not of their race, but that his forefathers had come into the land from a country lying far to the east; but that I know not. Suffice it he gained the confidence of the king, became his minister, and ruled wisely as far as the king was concerned, though the people have little reason to bless his memory. In his days was a terrible famine, and they say he foretold its coming, and that his God gave him warning of it. So, vast granaries were constructed and filled to overflowing, and when the famine came and the people were starving the grain was served out, but in return the people had to give up their land. Thus the whole tenure of the land in the country was changed, and all became the property of the state, the people remaining as its tenants upon the land they formerly owned. Then it was that the state granted large tracts to the temples and others to the military order, so that at present all tillers of land pay rent either to the king, the temples, or the military order."

"Thus it is that the army can always be kept up in serviceable order, dwelling by its tens of thousands in the cities assigned to it. Thus it is that the royal treasury is always kept full, and the services of the temple maintained. The step has added to the power and dignity of the nation, and has benefited the cultivators themselves by enabling vast works of irrigation to be carried out—works that could never have been accomplished had the land been the property of innumerable small holders, each with his own petty interests."

"But you said, father, that it has not been for the good of the people."

"Nor has it in one respect, Chebron, for it has drawn a wide chasm between the aristocratic classes and the bulk of the people, who can never own land, and have no stimulus to exertion."

"But they are wholly ignorant, father. They are peasants, and nothing more."

"I think they might be something more, Chebron, under other circumstances. However, that is not the question we are discussing. This Joseph brought his family out of the land at the east of the Great Sea, and land was given to them in Goshen, and they settled there and throve and multiplied greatly. Partly because of the remembrance of the services Joseph had rendered to the state, partly because they were a kindred people, they were held in favour as long as the shepherd kings ruled over us. But when Egypt rose and shook off the yoke they had groaned under so long, and drove the shepherds and their followers out of the land, this people—for they had now so grown in numbers as to be in verity a people—remained behind, and they have been naturally viewed with suspicion by us. They are akin to our late oppressors, and lying as their land does to the east, they could open the door to any fresh army of invasion.

"Happily, now that our conquests have spread so far, and the power of the people eastward of the Great Sea has been completely broken, this reason for distrust has died out, but Joseph's people are still viewed unfavourably. Prejudices take long to die out among the masses, and the manner in which these people cling together, marrying only among themselves and keeping themselves apart from us, gives a certain foundation for the dislike which exists. Personally, I think the feeling is unfounded. They are industrious and hard working, though they are, I own, somewhat disposed to resist authority, and there is more difficulty in obtaining the quota of men from Goshen for the execution of public works than from any other of the provinces of Egypt."

"Do they differ from us in appearance, father?"

"Considerably, Chebron. They are somewhat fairer than we are, their noses are more aquiline, and they are physically stronger. They do not shave their heads as we do, and they generally let the hair on their faces grow. For a long time after their settlement I believe that they worshipped their own gods, or rather their own God, but they have long adopted our religion."

"Surely that must be wrong," Chebron said. "Each nation has its gods, and if a people forsake their own gods it is not likely that other gods would care for them as they do for their own people."

"It is a difficult question, Chebron, and one which it is best for you to leave alone at present. You will soon enter into the lower grade of the priesthood, and, although if you do not pass into the upper grades you will never know the greater mysteries, you will yet learn enough to enlighten you to some extent."

Chebron was too well trained in the respect due to a parent to ask further questions, but he renewed the subject with Amuba as they strolled in the garden together afterwards.

"I wonder how each nation found out who were the gods who specially cared for them, Amuba?"

"I have no idea," Amuba, who had never given the subject a thought, replied. "You are always asking puzzling questions, Chebron."

"Well, but it must have been somehow," Chebron insisted. "Do you suppose that anyone ever saw our gods? And if not, how do people know that one has the head of a dog and another of a cat, or what they are like? Are some gods stronger than others, because all people offer sacrifices to the gods and ask for their help before going to battle? Some are beaten and some are victorious; some win to-day and lose to-morrow. Is it that these gods are stronger one day than another? Or that they do not care to help their people sometimes? Why do they not prevent their temples from being burned and their images from being thrown down? It is all very strange."

"It is all very strange, Chebron. I was not long ago asking Jethro nearly the same question, but he could give me no answer. Why do you not ask your father—he is one of the wisest of the Egyptians."

"I have asked my father, but he will not answer me," Chebron said thoughtfully. "I think sometimes that it is because I have asked these questions that he does not wish me to become a high-priest. I did not mean anything disrespectful to the gods. But somehow when I want to know things, and he will not answer me, I think he looks sadly, as if he was sorry at heart that he could not tell me what I want to know."

"Have you asked your brother Neco?"

"Oh, Neco is different," Chebron said with an accent almost of disdain. "Neco gets into passions and threatens me with all sorts of things; but I can see he knows no more about it than I do, for he has a bewildered look in his face when I ask him these things, and once or twice he has put his hands to his ears and fairly run away, as if I was saying something altogether profane and impious against the gods."

On the following day the high-priest and his party started for Goshen. The first portion of the journey was performed by water. The craft was a large one, with a pavilion of carved wood on deck, and two masts, with great sails of many colours cunningly worked together. Persons of consequence travelling in this way were generally accompanied by at least two or three musicians playing on harps, trumpets, or pipes; for the Egyptians were passionately fond of music, and no feast was thought complete without a band to discourse soft music while it was going on. The instruments were of the most varied kinds; stringed instruments predominated, and these varied in size from tiny instruments resembling zithers to harps much larger than those used in modern times. In addition to these they had trumpets of many forms, reed instruments, cymbals, and drums, the last named long and narrow in shape.

Ameres, however, although not averse to music after the evening meal, was of too practical a character to care for it at other times. He considered that it was too often an excuse for doing nothing and thinking of nothing, and therefore dispensed with it except on state occasions. As they floated down the river he explained to his son the various objects which they passed; told him the manner in which the fisher-men in their high boats made of wooden planks bound together by rushes, or in smaller crafts shaped like punts formed entirely of papyrus bound together with bands of the same plant, caught the fish; pointed out the entrances to the various canals, and explained the working of the gates which admitted the water; gave him the history of the various temples, towns, and villages; named the many water-fowl basking on the surface of the river, and told him of their habits and how they were captured by the fowlers; he pointed out the great tombs to him, and told him by whom they were built.

"The largest, my son, are monuments of pride and folly. The greatest of the pyramids was built by a king who thought it would immortalize him; but so terrible was the labour that its construction inflicted upon the people that it caused him to be execrated, and he was never laid in the mausoleum he had built for himself. You see our custom of judging kings after their death is not without advantages. After a king is dead the people are gathered together and the question is put to them, 'Has the dead monarch ruled well?' If they reply with assenting shouts, he is buried in a fitting tomb which he has probably prepared for himself, or which his successor raises to him; but if the answer is that he has reigned ill, the sacred rites in his honour are omitted and the mausoleum he has raised stands empty forever.

"There are few, indeed, of the kings who have thus merited the execration of their people; for as a rule the careful manner in which they are brought up, surrounded by youths chosen for their piety and learning, and the fact that they, like the meanest of their subjects, are bound to respect the laws of the land, act as sufficient check upon them. But there is no doubt that the knowledge that after death they must be judged by the people exercises a wholesome restraint even upon the most reckless."

"I long to see the pyramids," Chebron said. "Are they built of brick or stone, for I have been told that their surface is so smooth and shiny that they look as if cut from a single piece?"

"They are built of vast blocks of stone, each of which employed the labour of many hundreds of men to transport from the quarries where they were cut."

"Were they the work of slaves or of the people at large?"

"Vast numbers of slaves captured in war laboured at them," the priest replied. "But numerous as these were they were wholly insufficient for the work, and well-nigh half the people of Egypt were forced to leave their homes to labour at them. So great was the burden and distress that even now the builders of these pyramids are never spoken of save with curses; and rightly so, for what might not have been done with the same labour usefully employed! Why, the number of the canals in the country might have been doubled and the fertility of the soil vastly increased. Vast tracts might have been reclaimed from the marshes and shallow lakes, and the produce of the land might have been doubled."

"And what splendid temples might have been raised!" Chebron said enthusiastically.

"Doubtless, my son," the priest said quietly after a slight pause. "But though it is right that the temples of the gods shall be worthy of them, still, as we hold that the gods love Egypt and rejoice in the prosperity of the people, I think that they might have preferred so vast an improvement as the works I speak of would have effected in the condition of the people, even to the raising of long avenues of sphinxes and gorgeous temples in their own honour."

"Yes, one would think so," Chebron said thoughtfully. "And yet, father, we are always taught that our highest duty is to pay honour to the gods, and that in no way can money be so well spent as in raising fresh temples and adding to the beauty of those that exist."

"Our highest duty is assuredly to pay honour to the gods, Chebron; but how that honour can be paid most acceptably is another and deeper question which you are a great deal too young to enter upon. It will be time enough for you to do that years hence. There, do you see that temple standing on the right bank of the river?—that is where we stop for the night. My messenger will have prepared them for our coming, and all will be in readiness for us."

As they approached the temple they saw a number of people gathered on the great stone steps reaching down to the water's-edge, and strains of music were heard. On landing Ameres was greeted with the greatest respect by the priests all bowing to the ground, while those of inferior order knelt with their faces to the earth, and did not raise them until he had passed on. As soon as he entered the temple a procession was formed. Priests bearing sacred vessels and the symbols of the gods walked before him to the altar; a band of unseen musicians struck up a processional air; priestesses and maidens, also carrying offerings and emblems, followed Ameres. He naturally took the principal part in the sacrifice at the altar, cutting the throat of the victim, and making the offering of the parts specially set aside for the gods.

After the ceremonies were concluded the procession moved in order as far as the house of the chief priest. Here all again saluted Ameres, who entered, followed by his son and attendants. A banquet was already in readiness. To this Ameres sat down with the principal priests, while Chebron was conducted to the apartment prepared for him, where food from the high table was served to him. Amuba and the rest of the suite of the high-priest were served in another apartment. As soon as Chebron had finished he joined Amuba.

"Let us slip away," he said. "The feasting will go on for hours, and then there will be music far on into the night. My father will be heartily tired of it all; for he loves plain food, and thinks that the priests should eat none other. Still, as it would not be polite for a guest to remark upon the viands set before him, I know that he will go through it all. I have heard him say that it is one of the greatest trials of his position that whenever he travels people seem to think that a feast must be prepared for him; whereas I know he would rather sit down to a dish of boiled lentils and water than have the richest dishes set before him."

"Is it going to be like this all the journey?" Amuba asked.

"Oh, no! I know that all the way down the river we shall rest at a temple, for did my father not do so the priests would regard it as a slight; but then we leave the boat and journey in chariots or bullock-carts. When we reach Goshen we shall live in a little house which my father has had constructed for him, and where we shall have no more fuss and ceremony than we do at our own farm. Then he will be occupied with the affairs of the estates and in the works of irrigation; and although we shall be with him when he journeys about, as I am to begin to learn the duties of a superintendent, I expect we shall have plenty of time for amusement and sport."

They strolled for an hour or two on the bank of the river, for the moon was shining brightly and many boats were passing up and down; the latter drifted with the stream, for the wind was so light that the sails were scarce filled; the former kept close to the bank, and were either propelled by long poles or towed by parties of men on the bank. When they returned to the house they listened for a time to the music, and then retired to their rooms. Amuba lay down upon the soft couch made of a layer of bulrushes, covered with a thick woolen cloth, and rested his head on a pillow of bulrushes which Jethro had bound up for him; for neither of the Rebu had learned to adopt the Egyptian fashion of using a stool for a pillow.

These stools were long, and somewhat curved in the middle to fit the neck. For the common people they were roughly made of wood, smoothed where the head came; but the head-stools of the wealthy were constructed of ebony, cedar and other scarce woods, beautifully inlaid with ivory. Amuba had made several trials to sleep with one of these head-stools, but had not once succeeded in going to sleep with one under his head, half an hour sufficing to cause such an aching of his neck that he was glad to take to the pillow of rushes to which he was accustomed. Indeed, to sleep upon the stool-pillows it was necessary to lie upon the side with an arm so placed as to raise the head to the exact level of the stool, and as Amuba had been accustomed to throw himself down and sleep on his back or any other position in which he first lay, for he was generally thoroughly tired either in hunting or by exercise of arms, he found the cramped and fixed position necessary for sleeping with the hard stool absolutely intolerable.

For a week the journey down the river continued, and then they arrived at Memphis, where they remained for some days. Ameres passed the time in ceremonial visits and by taking part in the sacrifices in the temple. Chebron and Amuba visited all the temples and public buildings, and one day went out to inspect the great pyramids attended by Jethro.

"This surpasses anything I have seen," Jethro said as they stood at the foot of the great pyramid of Cheops. "What a wonderful structure, but what a frightful waste of human labour!"

"It is marvellous indeed," Amuba said. "What wealth and power a monarch must have had to raise such a colossal pile! I thought you said, Chebron, that your kings were bound by laws as well as other people. If so, how could this king have exacted such terrible toil and labour from his subjects as this must have cost?"

"Kings should be bound by the laws," Chebron replied; "but there are some so powerful and haughty that they tyrannize over the people. Cheops was one of them. My father has been telling me that he ground down the people to build this wonderful tomb for himself. But he had his reward, for at his funeral he had to be judged by the public voice, and the public condemned him as a bad and tyrannous king. Therefore he was not allowed to be buried in the great tomb that he had built for himself. I know not where his remains rest, but this huge pyramid stands as an eternal monument of the failure of human ambition—the greatest and costliest tomb in the world, but without an occupant, save that Theliene, one of his queens, was buried here in a chamber near that destined for the king."

"The people did well," Jethro said heartily; "but they would have done better still had they risen against him and cut off his head directly they understood the labour he was setting them to do."

On leaving Memphis one more day's journey was made by water, and the next morning the party started by land. Ameres rode in a chariot, which was similar in form to those used for war, except that the sides were much higher, forming a sort of deep open box, against which those standing in it could rest their bodies. Amuba and Chebron travelled in a wagon drawn by two oxen; the rest of the party went on foot.

At the end of two days they arrived at their destination. The house was a small one compared to the great mansion near Thebes, but it was built on a similar plan. A high wall surrounded an inclosure of a quarter of an acre. In the centre stood the house with one large apartment for general purposes, and small bed-chambers opening from it on either side. The garden, although small, was kept with scrupulous care. Rows of fruit-trees afforded a pleasant shade. In front of the house there was a small pond bordered with lilies and rushes. A Nubian slave and his wife kept everything in readiness for the owner whenever he should appear. A larger retinue of servants was unnecessary, as a cook and barber were among those who travelled in the train of Ameres. The overseer of the estate was in readiness to receive the high-priest.

"I have brought my son with me," Ameres said when the ceremonial observances and salutations were concluded. "He is going to commence his studies in irrigation, but I shall not have time at present to instruct him. I wish him to become proficient in out-door exercises, and beg you to procure men skilled in fishing, fowling, and hunting, so that he can amuse his unoccupied hours with sport. At Thebes he has but rare opportunities for these matters; for, excepting in the preserves, game has become well-nigh extinct, while as for fowling, there is none of it to be had in Upper Egypt, while here in the marshes birds abound."

The superintendent promised that suitable men should be forthcoming, one of each caste; for in Egypt men always followed the occupation of their fathers, and each branch of trade was occupied by men forming distinct castes, who married only in their own caste, worked just as their fathers had done before them, and did not dream of change or elevation. Thus the fowler knew nothing about catching fish, or the fishermen of fowling. Both, however, knew something about hunting; for the slaying of the hyenas, that carried off the young lambs and kids from the villages, and the great river-horses, which came out and devastated the fields, was a part of the business of every villager.

The country where they now were was for the most part well cultivated and watered by the canals, which were filled when the Nile was high.

A day's journey to the north lay Lake Menzaleh—a great shallow lagoon, which stretched away to the Great Sea, from which it was separated only by a narrow bank of sand. The canals of the Nile reached nearly to the edge of this, and when the river rose above its usual height and threatened to inundate the country beyond the usual limits, and to injure instead of benefiting the cultivators, great gates at the end of these canals would be opened, and the water find its way into the lagoon. There were, too, connections between some of the lower arms of the Nile and the lake, so that the water, although salt, was less so than that of the sea. The lake was the abode of innumerable water-fowl of all kinds, and swarmed also with fish.

These lakes formed a fringe along the whole of the northern coast of Egypt, and it was from these and the swampy land near the mouths of the Nile that the greater portion of the fowl and fish that formed important items in the food of the Egyptians was drawn. To the south-east lay another chain of lakes, whose water was more salt than that of the sea. It was said that in olden time these had been connected by water both with the Great Sea to the north and the Southern Sea; and even now, when the south wind blew strong, and the waters of the Southern Sea were driven up the gulf with force, the salt water flowed into Lake Timsah, so called because it swarmed with crocodiles.

"I shall be busy for some days, to begin with," Ameres said to his son on the evening of their arrival, "and it will therefore be a good opportunity for you to see something of the various branches of sport that are to be enjoyed in this part of Egypt. The steward will place men at your disposal, and you can take with you Amuba and Jethro. He will see that there are slaves to carry provisions and tents, for it will be necessary for much of your sport that you rise early, and not improbably you may have to sleep close at hand."

In the morning Chebron had an interview with the steward, who told him that he had arranged the plan for an expedition.

"You will find little about here, my lord," he said, "beyond such game as you would obtain near Thebes. But a day's journey to the north you will be near the margin of the lake, and there you will get sport of all kinds, and can at your will fish in its waters, snare water-fowl, hunt the great river-horse in the swamps, or chase the hyena in the low bushes on the sand-hills. I have ordered all to be in readiness, and in an hour the slaves with the provisions will be ready to start. The hunters of this part of the country will be of little use to you, so I have ordered one of my chief men to accompany you.

"He will see that when you arrive you obtain men skilled in the sport, and acquainted with the locality and the habits of the wild creatures there. My lord your father said you would probably be away for a week, and that on your return you would from time to time have a day's hunting in these parts. He thought that as your time will be more occupied then, it were better that you should make this distant expedition to begin with."

An hour later some twenty slaves drew up before the house, carrying on their heads, provisions, tents, and other necessaries. A horse was provided for Chebron, but he decided that he would walk with Amuba. "There is no advantage in going on a horse," he said, "when you have to move at the pace of footmen, and possibly we may find something to shoot on the way."

The leader of the party, upon hearing Chebron's decision, told him that doubtless when they left the cultivated country, which extended but a few miles further north, game would be found. Six dogs accompanied them. Four of them were powerful animals, kept for the chase of the more formidable beast, the hyena or lion, for although there were no lions in the flat country, they abounded in the broken grounds at the foot of the hills to the south. The other two were much more lightly built, and were capable of running down a deer. Dogs were held in high honour in Egypt. In some parts of the country they were held to be sacred. In all they were kept as companions and friends in the house as well as for the purposes of the chase. The season was the cold one, and the heat was so much less than they were accustomed to at Thebes—where the hills which inclosed the plain on which the city was built cut off much of the air, and seemed to reflect the sun's rays down upon it—that the walk was a pleasant one.

Chebron and Amuba, carrying their bows, walked along, chatting gaily, at the head of the party. Jethro and Rabah the foreman came next. Then followed two slaves, leading the dogs in leashes, ready to be slipped at a moment's notice, while the carriers followed in the rear. Occasionally they passed through scattered villages, where the women came to their doors to look at the strangers, and where generally offerings of milk and fruit were made to them. The men were for the most part at work in the fields.

"They are a stout-looking race. Stronger and more bony than our own people," Chebron remarked to the leader of the party.

"They are stubborn to deal with," he replied. "They till their ground well and pay their portion of the produce without grumbling, but when any extra labour is asked of them there is sure to be trouble. It is easier to manage a thousand Egyptian peasants than a hundred of these Israelites, and if forced labour is required for the public service it is always necessary to bring down the troops before we can obtain it.

"But indeed they are hardly treated fairly, and have suffered much. They arrived in Egypt during the reign of Usertuen I., and had land allotted to them. During the reign of the king and other successors of his dynasty they were held in favour and multiplied greatly; but when the Theban dynasty succeeded that of Memphis, the kings, finding this foreign people settled here, and seeing that they were related by origin to the shepherd tribes who at various times have threatened our country from the east, and have even conquered portions of it and occupied it for long periods, regarded them with hostility, and have treated them rather as prisoners of war than as a portion of the people. Many burdens have been laid upon them. They have had to give far more than their fair share of labour towards the public works, the making of bricks, and the erection of royal tombs and pyramids."

"It is strange that they do not shave their heads as do our people," Chebron said.

"But I do not," Amuba laughed, "nor Jethro."

"It is different with you," Chebron replied. "You do not labour and get the dust of the soil in your hair. Besides, you do keep it cut quite short. Still, I think you would be more comfortable if you followed our fashion."

"It is all a matter of habit," Amuba replied. "To us, when we first came here, the sight of all the poorer people going about with their heads shaven was quite repulsive—and as for comfort, surely one's own hair must be more comfortable than the great wigs that all of the better class wear."

"They keep off the sun," Chebron said, "when one is out of doors, and are seldom worn in the house, and then when one comes in one can wash off the dust."

"I can wash the dust out of my hair," Amuba said. "Still I do think that these Israelites wear their hair inconveniently long; and yet the long plaits that their women wear down their back are certainly graceful, and the women themselves are fair and comely."

Chebron shook his head. "They may be fair, Amuba, but I should think they would make very troublesome wives. They lack altogether the subdued and submissive look of our women. They would, I should say, have opinions of their own, and not be submissive to their lords; is that not so, Rabah?"

"The women like the men have spirit and fire," the foreman answered, "and have much voice in all domestic matters; but I do not know that they have more than with us. They can certainly use their tongues; for, at times, when soldiers have been here to take away gangs of men for public works, they have had more trouble with them than with the men. The latter are sullen, but they know that they must submit; but the women gather at a little distance and scream curses and abuse at the troops, and sometimes even pelt them with stones, knowing that the soldiers will not draw weapon upon them, although not unfrequently it is necessary in order to put a stop to the tumult to haul two or three of their leaders off to prison."

"I thought they were viragoes," Chebron said with a laugh. "I would rather hunt a lion then have the women of one of these villages set upon me."

In a few miles cultivation became more rare; sandhills took the place of the level fields, and only here and there in the hollows were patches of cultivated ground. Rabah now ordered the slave leading the two fleet dogs to keep close up and be in readiness to slip them.

"We may see deer at any time now," he said. "They abound in these sandy deserts which form their shelter, and yet are within easy distance of fields where when such vegetation as is here fails them they can go for food."

A few minutes later a deer started from a clump of bushes. The dogs were instantly let slip and started in pursuit.

"Hurry on a hundred yards and take your position on that mound!" Rabah exclaimed to Chebron, while at the same time he signalled to the slaves behind to stop. "The dogs know their duty, and you will see they will presently drive the stag within shot."

Chebron called Amuba to follow him and ran forward. By the time they reached the mound the stag was far away, with the dogs labouring in pursuit. At present they seemed to have gained but little, if at all, upon him, and all were soon hidden from sight among the sandhills. In spite of the assurance of Rabah the lads had doubts whether the dogs would ever drive their quarry back to the spot where they were standing, and it was full a quarter of an hour before pursuers and pursued came in sight again. The pace had greatly fallen off, for one of the dogs was some twenty yards behind the stag; the other was out on its flank at about the same distance away, and was evidently aiding in turning it towards the spot where the boys were standing.

"We will shoot together," Chebron said. "It will come within fifty yards of us."

They waited until the stag was abreast of them. The dog on its flank had now fallen back to the side of his companion as if to leave the stag clear for the arrows of the hunters. The lads fired together just as the stag was abreast; but it was running faster than they had allowed for, and both arrows flew behind it. They uttered exclamations of disappointment, but before the deer had run twenty yards it gave a sudden leap into the air and fell over. Jethro had crept up and taken his post behind some bushes to the left of the clump in readiness to shoot should the others miss, and his arrow had brought the stag to the ground.

"Well done, Jethro!" Amuba shouted. "It is so long since I was out hunting that I seem to have lost my skill; but it matters not since we have brought him down."

The dogs stood quiet beside the deer that was struggling on the ground, being too well trained to interfere with it. Jethro ran out and cut its throat. The others were soon standing beside it. It was of a species smaller than those to which the deer of Europe belong, with two long straight horns.

"It will make a useful addition to our fare to-night," Rabah said, "although, perhaps, some of the other sorts are better eating."

"Do the dogs never pull them down by themselves?" Amuba asked.

"Very seldom. These two are particularly fleet, but I doubt whether they would have caught it. These deer can run for a long time, and although they will let dogs gain upon them they can leave them if they choose. Still I have known this couple run down a deer when they could not succeed in driving it within bowshot; but they know very well they ought not to do so, for, of course, deer are of no use for food unless the animals are properly killed and the blood allowed to escape."

Several other stags were started, but these all escaped, the dogs being too fatigued with their first run to be able to keep up with them. The other dogs were therefore unloosed and allowed to range about the country. They started several hyenas, some of which they themselves killed; others they brought to bay until the lads ran up and despatched them with their arrows, while others which took to flight in sufficient time got safely away, for the hyena, unless overtaken just at the start, can run long and swiftly and tire out heavy dogs such as those the party had with them.

After walking some fifteen miles the lads stopped suddenly on the brow of a sandhill. In front of them was a wide expanse of water bordered by a band of vegetation. Long rushes and aquatic plants formed a band by the water's edge, while here and there huts with patches of cultivated ground dotted the country.

"We are at the end of our journey," Rabah said. "These huts are chiefly inhabited by fowlers and fishermen. We will encamp at the foot of this mound. It is better for us not to go too near the margin of the water, for the air is not salubrious to those unaccustomed to it. The best hunting ground lies a few miles to our left, for there, when the river is high, floods come down through a valley which is at all times wet and marshy. There we may expect to find game of all kinds in abundance."

Chapter 6

THE tents, which were made of light cloth intended to keep off the night dews rather than to afford warmth, were soon pitched, fires were lighted with fuel that had been brought with them in order to save time in search for it, and Rabah went off to search for fish and fowl. He returned in half an hour with a peasant carrying four ducks and several fine fish.

"We shall do now," he said; "with these and the stag our larder is complete. Everything but meat we have brought with us."

Chebron, although he had kept on bravely, was fatigued with his walk and was glad to throw himself down on the sand and enjoy the prospect, which to him was a new one, for he had never before seen so wide an expanse of water.

When on the top of the hill he had made out a faint dark line in the distance, and this Rabah told him was the bank of sand that separated the lake from the Great Sea. Now from his present position this was invisible, and nothing but a wide expanse of water stretching away until it seemed to touch the sky met his view. Here and there it was dotted with dark patches which were, Rabah told him, clumps of water-fowl, and in the shallow water near the margin, which was but a quarter of a mile away, he could see vast numbers of wading birds, white cranes, and white and black ibises, while numbers of other water-fowl, looking like black specks, moved about briskly among them.

Sometimes with loud cries a number would rise on the wing, and either make off in a straight line across the water or circle round and settle again when they found that their alarm was groundless.

"It is lovely, is it not?" he exclaimed to Amuba, who was standing beside him leaning on his bow and looking over the water.

Amuba did not reply immediately, and Chebron looking up saw that there were tears on his cheeks.

"What is it, Amuba?" he asked anxiously.

"It is nothing, Chebron; but the sight of this wide water takes my thoughts homeward. Our city stood on a sea like this, not so large as they say is this Great Sea we are looking at, but far too large for the eye to see across, and it is just such a view as this that I looked upon daily from the walls of our palace, save that the shores were higher."

"Maybe you will see it again some day, Amuba," Chebron said gently.

Amuba shook his head.

"I fear the chances are small indeed, Chebron. Jethro and I have talked it over hundreds of times, and on our route hither we had determined that if we fell into the hands of harsh masters, we would at all hazards try some day to make our escape; but the journey is long and would lie through countries subject to Egypt. The people of the land to be passed over speak languages strange to us, and it would be well-nigh impossible to make the journey in safety. Still we would have tried it. As it is, we are well content with our lot, and should be mad indeed to forsake it on the slender chances of finding our way back to the land of the Rebu, where, indeed, even if we reached it, I might not be well received, for who knows what king may now be reigning there?"

"And if you could get away and were sure of arriving there safely, would you exchange all the comforts of a civilized country like Egypt for a life such as you have described to me among your own people?"

"There can be no doubt, Chebron, that your life here is far more luxurious and that you are far more civilized than the Rebu. By the side of your palaces our houses are but huts. We are ignorant even of reading and writing. A pile of rushes for our beds and a rough table and stools constitute our furniture; but, perhaps, after all one is not really happier for all the things you have. You may have more enjoyments, but you have greater cares. I suppose every man loves his own country best, but I do not think that we can love ours as much as you do. In the first place, we have been settled there but a few generations, large numbers of our people constantly moving west, either by themselves or joining with one of the peoples who push past us from the far East; besides, wherever we went we should take our country with us, build houses like those we left behind, live by the chase or fishing in one place as another, while the Egyptian could nowhere find a country like Egypt. I suppose it is the people more than the country, the familiar language, and the familiar faces and ways. I grant freely that the Egyptians are a far greater people than we, more powerful, more learned, the masters of many arts, the owners of many comforts and luxuries, and yet one longs sometimes for one's free life among the Rebu."

"One thing is, Amuba, you were a prince there and you are not here. Had you been but a common man, born to labour, to toil, or to fight at the bidding of your king, you might perhaps find that the life even of an Egyptian peasant is easier and more pleasant than yours was."

"That may be," Amuba said thoughtfully, "and yet I think that the very poorest among us was far freer and more independent than the richest of your Egyptian peasants. He did not grovel on the ground when the king passed along. It was open to him if he was braver than his fellows to rise in rank. He could fish, or hunt, or till the ground, or fashion arms as he chose; his life was not tied down by usage or custom. He was a man, a poor one, perhaps—a half savage one, if you will—but he was a man, while your Egyptian peasants, free as they may be in name, are the very slaves of law and custom. But I see that the meal is ready, and I have a grand appetite."

"So have I, Amuba. It is almost worth while walking a long way for the sake of the appetite one gets at the end."

The meal was an excellent one. One of the slaves who had been brought was an adept at cooking, and fish, birds, and venison were alike excellent, and for once the vegetables that formed so large a portion of the ordinary Egyptian repast were neglected.

"What are we going to do to-morrow, Rabah?" Chebron asked after the meal was concluded.

"I have arranged for to-morrow, if such is your pleasure, my lord, that you shall go fowling. A boat will take you along the lake to a point about three miles off where the best sport is to be had, then when the day is over it will carry you on another eight miles to the place I spoke to you of where good sport was to be obtained. I shall meet you on your landing there, and will have everything in readiness for you."

"That will do well," Chebron said. "Amuba and Jethro, you will, of course, come with me."

As soon as it was daylight Rabah led Chebron down to the lake, and the lad with Amuba and Jethro entered the boat, which was constructed of rushes covered with pitch, and drew only two or three inches of water. Two men with long poles were already in the boat; they were fowlers by profession, and skilled in all the various devices by which the water-fowl were captured. They had, during the night, been preparing the boat for the expedition by fastening rushes all round it; the lower ends of these dipped into the water, the upper ends were six feet above it, and the rushes were so thickly placed together as to form an impenetrable screen.

The boat was square at the stern, and here only was there an opening a few inches wide in the rushes to enable the boatman standing there to propel the boat with his pole. One of the men took his station here, the other at the bow, where he peered through a little opening between the rushes, and directed his comrade in the stern as to the course he should take. In the bottom of the boat lay two cats who, knowing that their part was presently to come, watched all that was being done with an air of intelligent interest. A basket well stored with provisions, and a jar of wine, were placed on board, and the boat then pushed noiselessly off. Parting the reeds with their fingers and peeping out, the boys saw that the boat was not making out into the deeper part of the lake, but was skirting the edge, keeping only a few yards out from the band of rushes at its margin.

"Do you keep this distance all the way?" Chebron asked the man with the pole.

The man nodded.

"As long as we are close to the rushes the water-fowl do not notice our approach, while were we to push out into the middle they might take the alarm; although we often do capture them in that way, but in that case we get to windward of the flock we want to reach, and then drift down slowly upon them, but we shall get more sport now by keeping close in. The birds are numerous, and you will soon be at work."

In five minutes the man at the bow motioned his passengers that they were approaching a flock of water-fowl. Each of them took up his bow and arrows and stood in readiness, while the man in the stern used his pole even more quickly and silently than before. Presently at a signal from his comrades he ceased poling. All round the boat there were slight sounds—low contended quacking, and fluttering of wings, as the birds raised themselves and shook the water from their backs. Parting the rushes in front of them, the two lads and Jethro peeped through them.

They were right in the middle of a flock of wild fowl who were feeding without a thought of danger from the clump of rushes in their midst. The arrows were already in their notches, the rushes were parted a little further, and the three shafts were loosed. The twangs of the bows startled the ducks, and stopping feeding they gazed at the rushes with heads on one side. Three more arrows glanced out, but this time one of the birds aimed at was wounded only, and uttering a cry of pain and terror it flapped along the surface of the water.

Instantly, with wild cries of alarm, the whole flock arose, but before they had fairly settled in their flight, two more fell pierced with arrows. The cats had been standing on the alert, and as the cry of alarm was given leaped overboard from the stern, and proceeded to pick up the dead ducks, among which were included that which had at first flown away, for it had dropped in the water about fifty yards from the boat. A dozen times the same scene was repeated until some three score ducks and geese lay in the bottom of the boat. By this time the party had had enough of the sport, and had indeed lost the greater part of their arrows, as all which failed to strike a bird aimed at went far down into the deep mud at the bottom and could not be recovered.

"Now let the men show us their skill with their throwing-sticks," Chebron said. "You will see they will do better with them than we with our arrows."

The men at once turned the boat's head towards a patch of rushes growing from the shallow water a hundred yards out in the lake. Many numbers of ducks and geese were feeding round it, and the whole rushes were in movement from those swimming and feeding among them, for the plants were just at the time in seed. The birds were too much occupied to mark the approach of this fresh clump of rushes. The men had removed the screen from the side of the boat furthest from the birds, and now stood in readiness, each holding half-a-dozen sticks about two feet long, made of curved and crooked wood.

When close to the birds the boat was swung round, and at once with deafening cries the birds rose; but as they did so the men with great rapidity hurled their sticks one after another among them, the last being directed at the birds which, feeding among the rushes, were not able to rise as rapidly as their companions. The lads were astonished at the effect produced by these simple missiles. So closely packed were the birds that each stick, after striking one, whirled and twisted among the others, one missile frequently bringing down three or four birds.

The cats were in an instant at work. The flapping and noise was prodigious, for although many of the birds were killed outright, others struck in the wing or leg were but slightly injured. Some made off along the surface of the water, others succeeded in getting up and flying away, but the greater part were either killed by the cats, or knocked on the head by the poles of the two fowlers. Altogether twenty-seven birds were added to the store in the boat.

"That puts our arrows to shame altogether, Amuba," Chebron said. "I have always heard that the fowlers on these lakes were very skilled with those throwing-sticks of theirs, but I could not have believed it possible that two men should in so short a space have effected such a slaughter; but then I had no idea of the enormous quantities of birds on these lakes."

Jethro was examining the sticks which, as well as the ducks, had been retrieved by the cats.

"They are curious things," he said to Amuba. "I was thinking before the men used them that straight sticks would be much better, and was wondering why they chose curved wood, but I have no doubt now the shape has something to do with it. You see, as the men threw they gave them a strong spinning motion. That seems the secret of their action. It was wonderful to see how they whirled about among the fowl, striking one on the head, another on the leg, another on the wing, until they happened to hit one plump on the body; that seemed to stop them. I am sure one of those sticks that I kept my eyes fixed on must have knocked down six birds. I will practice with these things, and if I ever get back home I will teach their use to our people. There are almost as many water-fowl on our sea as there are here. I have seen it almost black with them down at the southern end, where it is bordered by swamps and reed-covered marshes."

"How do they catch them there, Jethro?" Chebron asked.

"They net them in decoys, and sometimes wade out among them with their heads hidden among floating boughs, and so get near enough to seize them by the legs and pull them under water; in that way a man will catch a score of them before their comrades are any the wiser."

"We catch them the same way here," one of the fowlers who had been listening remarked. "We weave little bowers just large enough for our heads and shoulders to go into, and leave three or four of them floating about for some days near the spot where we mean to work. The wild fowl get accustomed to them, and after that we can easily go among them and capture numbers."

"I should think fowling must be a good trade," Chebron said.

"It is good enough at times," the man replied; "but the ducks are not here all the year. The long legged birds are always to be found here in numbers, but the ducks are uncertain and so are the geese. At certain times in the year they leave us altogether. Some say they go across the Great Sea to the north; others that they go far south into Nubia. Then even when they are here they are uncertain. Sometimes they are thick here, then again there is scarce one to be seen, and we hear they are swarming on the lakes further to the west. Of course the wading birds are of no use for food; so you see when the ducks and geese are scarce, we have a hard time of it. Then, again, even when we have got a boat-load we have a long way to take it to market, and when the weather is hot all may get spoiled before we can sell them; and the price is so low in these parts when the flocks are here, that it is hard to lay by enough money to keep us and our families during the slack time. If the great cities Thebes and Memphis lay near to us, it would be different. They could consume all we could catch, and we should get better prices, but unless under very favourable circumstances there is no hope of the fowl keeping good during the long passage up the river to Thebes. In fact, were it not for our decoys we should starve. In these, of course, we take them alive, and send them in baskets to Thebes, and in that way get a fair price for them."

"What sort of decoys do you use?" Jethro asked.

"Many kinds," the man replied. "Sometimes we arch over the rushes, tie them together at the top so as to form long passages over little channels among the rushes; then we strew corn over the water, and place near the entrance ducks which are trained to swim about outside until a flock comes near; then they enter the passage feeding, and the others follow. There is a sort of door which they can push aside easily as they pass up, but cannot open on their return."

"That is the sort of decoy they use in our country," Jethro said.

"Another way," the fowler went on, "is to choose a spot where the rushes form a thick screen twenty yards or so deep along the bank, then a light net two or three hundred feet long is pegged down on the shore behind them, and thrown over the tops of the rushes reaching to within a foot or two of the water. Here it is rolled up, so that when it is shaken out it will go down into the water. Then two men stand among the rushes at the ends of the net, while another goes out far onto the lake in a boat. When he sees a flock of ducks swimming near the shore he poles the boat towards them; not so rapidly as to frighten them into taking flight, but enough so to attract their attention and cause uneasiness. He goes backwards and forwards, gradually approaching the shore, and of course managing so as to drive them towards the point where the net is. When they are opposite this he closes in faster, and the ducks all swim in among the rushes. Directly they are in, the men at the ends of the net shake down the rolled up part, and then the whole flock are prisoners. After that the fowlers have only to enter the rushes, and take them as they try to fly upwards and are stopped by the net. With luck two or three catches can be made in one day, and a thousand ducks and sometimes double that number can be captured. Then they are put into flat baskets just high enough for them to stand in with their heads out through the openings at the top, and so put on board the boat and taken up the Nile."

"Yes, I have often seen the baskets taken out of the boats," Chebron said, "and thought how cruel it was to pack them so closely. But how do they feed them for they must often be a fortnight on the way?"

"The trader who buys them from us and other fowlers waits until he has enough together to freight a large craft—for it would not pay to work upon a small scale—accompanies them up the river, and feeds them regularly with little balls made of moistened flour, just in the same way they do at the establishments in Upper Egypt, where they raise fowl and stuff them for the markets. If the boat is a large one, he may take up forty or fifty thousand fowl, of course he takes two or three boys to help him, for it is no light matter to feed such a number, and each must have a little water as well as the meal. It seems strange to us here, where fowl are so abundant, that people should raise and feed them just as if they were bullocks. But I suppose it is true."

"It is quite true," Chebron replied. "Amuba and I went to one of the great breeding-farms two or three months ago. There are two sorts—one where they hatch, the other where they fat them. The one we went to embraced both branches, but this is unusual. From the hatching-places collectors go round to all the people who keep fowl for miles round and bring in eggs, and besides these they buy them from others at a greater distance. The eggs are placed on sand laid on the floor of a low chamber, and this is heated by means of flues from a fire underneath. It requites great care to keep the temperature exactly right; but of course men who pass their lives at this work can regulate it exactly, and know by the feel just what is the heat at which the eggs should be kept.

"There are eight or ten such chambers in the place we visited, so that every two or three days one or other of them hatches out and is ready for fresh eggs to be put down. The people who send the eggs come in at the proper time and receive each a number of chickens in proportion to the eggs they have sent, one chicken being given for each two eggs. Some hatchers give more, some less; what remain over are payment for their work; so you see they have to be very careful about the hatching. If they can hatch ninety chickens out of every hundred eggs, it pays them very well; but if, owing to the heat being too great or too little, only twenty or thirty out of every hundred are raised, they have to make good the loss. Of course they always put in a great many of the eggs they have themselves bought. They are thus able to give the right number to their customers even if the eggs have not turned out well.

"Those that remain after the proper number has been given to the farmers the breeders sell to them or to others, it bring no part of their business to bring up the chickens. The fattening business is quite different. At these places there are long rows of little boxes piled up on each other into a wall five feet high. The door of each of these boxes has a hole in it through which the fowl can put its head, with a little sort of shutter that closes down on it. A fowl is placed in each box. Then the attendants go round two together; one carries a basket filled with little balls of meal, the other lifts the shutter, as the fowl puts its head out, one catches it by the neck, makes it open its beak, and with his other hand pushes the ball of meal down its throat. They are so skilful that the operation takes only a moment; then they go on to the next, and so on down the long rows until they have fed the last of those under their charge. Then they begin again afresh."

"Why do they keep them in the dark?" the other fowler asked.

"They told us that they did it because in the dark they were not restless, and slept all the time between their meals. Then each time the flap is lifted they think it is daylight, and pop out their heads at once to see. In about ten days they get quite fat and plump, and are ready for market."

"It seems a wonderful deal of trouble," the fowler said. "But I suppose, as they have a fine market close at hand, and can get good prices, it pays them. It seems more reasonable to me than the hatching business. Why they should not let the fowls hatch their own eggs is more than I can imagine."

"Fowls will lay a vastly greater number of eggs than they will hatch," Chebron said. "A well-fed fowl should lay two hundred and fifty eggs in a year; and, left to herself, she will not hatch more than two broods of fifteen eggs in each. Thus, you see, as it pays the peasants much better to rear fowl than to sell eggs, it is to their profit to send their eggs to the hatching-places, and so to get a hundred and twenty-five chickens a year instead of thirty."

"I suppose it does," the fowler agreed. "But here we are, my lord, at the end of our journey. There is the point where we are to land, and your servant who hired us is standing there in readiness for you. I hope that you are satisfied with your day's sport."

Chebron said he was greatly pleased, in a few minutes the boat reached the landing-place, where Rabah was awaiting them. One of the fowlers, carrying a dozen of the finest fowls they had killed, accompanied them to the spot Rabah had chosen for the encampment. Like the last, it stood at the foot of the sand-hills, a few hundred yards from the lake."

"Is the place where we are going to hunt near here?" was Chebron's first question.

"No, my lord; it is two miles away. But, in accordance with your order last night, I have arranged for you to fish to-morrow. In the afternoon I will move the tents a mile nearer to the country where you will hunt, but it is best not to go too close, for near the edge of these great swamps the air is unhealthy to those who are not accustomed to it."

"I long to get at the hunting," Chebron said; "but it is better, as you say, to have the day's fishing first, for the work would seem tame after the excitement of hunting the river-horse. We shall be glad of our dinner as soon as we can get it, for although we have done justice to the food you put on board, we are quite ready again. Twelve hours of this fresh air from the sea gives one the appetite of a hyena."

"Everything is already in readiness, my lord. I thought it better not to wait for the game you brought home, which will do well to-morrow, and so purchased fish and fowl from the peasants. As we have seen your boat for the last two or three hours, we were able to calculate the time of your arrival, and everything is in readiness."

The dinner was similar to that on the previous day, except that a hare took the place of the venison—a change for the better, as the hare was a delicacy much appreciated by the Egyptians. The following day was spent in fishing. For this purpose a long net was used, and the method was precisely similar to that in use in modern times. One end of the net was fastened to the shore, the net itself being coiled up in the boat. This was rowed out into the lake, the fishermen paying out the net as it went. A circuit was then made back to the shore, where the men seized the two ends of the net and hauled it to land, capturing the fish inclosed within its sweep. After seeing two or three hauls made, the lads went with Jethro on board the boat. They were provided by the fishermen with long two-pronged spears.

The boat was then quietly rowed along the edge of the rushes, where the water was deeper than usual. It was, however, so clear that they could see to the bottom, and with their spears they struck at the fish swimming there. At first they were uniformly unsuccessful, as they were ignorant that allowance must be made for diffraction, and were puzzled at finding that their spears instead of going straight down at the fish they struck at seemed to bend off at an angle at the water's-edge. The fishermen, however, explained to them that an allowance must be made for this, the allowance being all the greater the greater the distance the fish was from the boat, and that it was only when it lay precisely under them that they could strike directly at it. But even after being instructed in the matter they succeeded but poorly, and presently laid down their spears and contented themselves with watching their boatmen, who rarely failed in striking and bringing up the prey they aimed at.

Presently their attention was attracted to four boats, each containing from six to eight men. Two had come from either direction, and when they neared each other volleys of abuse were exchanged between their occupants.

"What is all this about?" Chebron asked, as the two fishermen laid by their spears, and with faces full of excitement turned round to watch the boats.

"The boats come from two villages, my lord, between which at present there is a feud arising out of some fishing nets that were carried away. They sent a regular challenge to each other a few days since, as is the custom here, and their champions are going to fight it out. You see the number of men on one side are equal to those on the other, and the boats are about the same size."

Amuba and Jethro looked on with great interest, for they had seen painted on the walls representations of these fights between boatmen, which were of common occurrence, the Egyptians being a very combative race, and fierce feuds being often carried on for a long time between neighbouring villages. The men were armed with poles some ten feet in length, and about an inch and a half in diameter, their favourite weapons on occasions of this kind. The boats had now come in close contact, and a furious battle at once commenced, the clattering of the sticks, the heavy thuds of the blows, and the shouts of the combatants creating a clamour that caused all the water-fowl within a circle of half a mile to fly screaming away across the lake. The men all used their heavy weapons with considerable ability, the greater part of the blows being warded off. Many, however, took effect, some of the combatants being knocked into the water, others fell prostrate in their boats, while some dropped their long staves after a disabling blow on the arm.

"It is marvellous that they do not all kill each other," Jethro said. "Surely this shaving of the head, Amuba, which has always struck us as being very peculiar, has its uses, for it must tend to thicken the skull, for surely the heads of no other men could have borne such blows without being crushed like water-jars."

That there was certainly some ground for Jethro's supposition is proved by the fact that Herodotus, long afterwards writing of the desperate conflicts between the villagers of Egypt, asserted that their skulls were thicker than those of any other people.

Most of the men who fell into the water scrambled back into the boats and renewed the fight, but some sank immediately and were seen no more. At last, when fully half the men on each side had been put *hors de combat*, four or five having been killed or drowned, the boats separated, no advantage resting with either party; and still shouting defiance and jeers at each other, the men poled in the direction of their respective villages.

"Are such desperate fights as these common?" Chebron asked the fishermen.

"Yes; there are often quarrels," one of them replied, quietly resuming his fishing as if nothing out of the ordinary way had taken place. "If they are water-side villages their champions fight in boats, as you have seen; if not, equal parties meet at a spot halfway between the villages and decide it on foot. Sometimes they fight with short sticks, the hand being protected by a basket hilt, while on the left arm a piece of wood, extending from the elbow to the tips of the fingers, is fastened on by straps serving as a shield; but more usually they fight with the long pole, which we call the neboot."

"It is a fine weapon," Jethro said, "and they guard their heads with it admirably, sliding their hands far apart. If I were back again, Amuba, I should like to organize a regiment of men armed with those weapons. It would need that the part used as a guard should be covered with light iron to prevent a sword or ax from cutting through it; but with that addition they would make splendid weapons, and footmen armed with sword and a shield would find it hard indeed to repel an assault by them."

"The drawback would be," Amuba observed, "that each man would require so much room to wield his weapon that they must stand far apart, and each would be opposed to three or four swordsmen in the enemy's line."

"That is true, Amuba, and you have certainly hit upon the weak point in the use of such a weapon; but for single combat, or the fighting of broken ranks, they would be grand. When we get back to Thebes if I can find any peasant who can instruct me in the use of these neboots I will certainly learn it."

"You ought to make a fine player," one of the fishermen said, looking at Jethro's powerful figure. "I should not like a crack on the head from a neboot in your hands. But the sun is getting low, and we had best be moving to the point where you are to disembark."

"We have had another capital day, Rabah," Chebron said when they reached their new encampment. "I hope that the rest will turn out as successful."

"I think that I can promise you that they will, my lord. I have been making inquires among the villagers, and find that the swamp in the river-bed abounds with hippopotami."

"How do you hunt them?—on foot?"

"No, my lord. There is enough water in the river-bed for the flat boats made of bundles of rushes to pass up, while in many places are deep pools in which the animals lie during the heat of the day."

"Are they ferocious animals?" Amuba asked. "I have never yet seen one; for though they say that they are common in the Upper Nile, as well as found in swamps like this at its mouth, there are none anywhere in the neighbourhood of Thebes. I suppose that there is too much traffic for them, and that they are afraid of showing themselves in such water."

"There would be no food for them," Rabah said. "They are found only in swamps like this, or in places on the Upper Nile where the river is shallow and bordered with aquatic plants, on whose roots they principally live. They are timid creatures, and are found only in little frequented places. When struck they generally try to make their escape; for although occasionally they will rush with their enormous mouth open at a boat, tear it in pieces, and kill the hunter, this very seldom happens. As a rule they try only to fly."

"They must be cowardly beasts!" Jethro said scornfully. "I would rather hunt an animal, be it ever so small, that will make a fight for its life. However, we shall see."

Upon the following morning they started for the scene of action. An exclamation of surprise broke from them simultaneously when, on ascending a sand-hill, they saw before them a plain a mile wide extending at their feet. It was covered with rushes and other aquatic plants, and extended south as far as the eye could see.

"For one month in the year," Rabah said, "this is a river, for eleven it is a little more than a swamp, though the shallower boats can make their way up it many miles. But a little water always finds its way down, either from the Nile itself or from the canals. It is one of the few places of Northern Egypt where the river-horse is still found, and none are allowed to hunt them unless they are of sufficient rank to obtain the permission of the governor of the province. The steward wrote for and obtained this as soon as he knew by letter from your father that you were accompanying him, and would desire to have some sport."

"Are there crocodiles there?" Amuba asked.

"Many," Rabah replied, "although few are now found in the lakes. The people here are not like those of the Theban zone, who hold them in high respect—here they regard them as dangerous enemies, and kill them without mercy."

Chapter 7

GUIDED by Rabah the party now descended to the edge of the swamp. Here in the shallow water lay three boats, or rather rafts, constructed of bundles of bulrushes. They were turned up in front so as to form a sort of swan-necked bow, and in outline were exactly similar to the iron of modern skates. Upon each stood a native with a pole for pushing the rafts along, and three or four spears. These were of unusual shape, and the lads examined them with curiosity. They had broad short blades, and these were loosely attached to the shafts, so that when the animal was struck the shaft would drop out, leaving the head imbedded in its flesh. To the head was attached a cord which was wound up on a spindle passing through a handle.

"Those rafts do not look as if they would carry three," Chebron said.

"They will do so at a push," the man replied; "but they are better with two only."

"I will stop on shore, with your permission, Chebron," Jethro said. "I see there are a number of men here with ropes. I suppose they have something to do with the business, and I will accompany them."

"The ropes are for hauling the beasts ashore after we have struck them."

"Well, I will go and help pull them. I can do my share at that, and should be of no use on one of those little rafts; indeed, I think that my weight would bury it under the water."

"We have been out this morning, my lord," the boatman said, addressing Chebron, "and have found out that there is a river-horse lying in a pool a mile up the river. I think he is a large one and will give us good sport."

Chebron and Amuba now took their places on the two rafts; and the men, laying down the spears and taking the poles, pushed off from the shore. Noiselessly they made their way among the rushes. Sometimes the channels were so narrow that the reeds almost brushed the rafts on both sides; then they opened out into wide pools, and here the water deepened so much that the poles could scarce touch the bottom. Not a word was spoken, as the men had warned them that the slightest noise would scare the hippopotami and cause them to sink to the bottom of the pools, where they would be difficult to capture. After half an hour's poling they reached a pool larger than any that they had hitherto passed, and extending on one side almost to the bank of the river.

The man on his raft now signed to Chebron to take up one of the spears; but the lad shook his head and motioned to him to undertake the attack, for he felt that, ignorant as he was of the habits of the animal, it would be folly for him to engage in such an adventure. The man nodded, for he had indeed been doubting as to the course which the affair would take, for it needed a thrust with a very powerful arm to drive the spear through the thick hide of the hippopotamus. Amuba imitated Chebron's example, preferring to be a spectator instead of an actor in the unknown sport.

For three or four minutes the boats lay motionless, then a blowing sound was heard, and the boatmen pointed to what seemed to the boys two lumps of black mud projecting in inch or two above the water near the margin of the rushes. They could not have believed that these formed part of an animal, but that slight ripples widening out on the glassy water showed that there had been a movement at the spot indicated. With a noiseless push Chebron's hunter sent the boat in that direction, and then handed the end of the pole to Chebron, signing to him to push the boat back when he gave the signal.

When within ten yards of the two little black patches there was a sudden movement; they widened into an enormous head, the huge beast rose to his feet, startled at the discovery he had just made that men were close at hand. In an instant the hunter hurled his spear with all his force. Tough as was the animal's hide, the sharp head cut its way through. With a roar the beast plunged into the rushes, the shaft of the spear falling out of its socket as it did so, and the strong cord ran out rapidly from the reel held by the hunter. Presently the strain ceased. "He has laid down again in shelter," the hunter said; "we will now follow him and give him a second spear."

Pushing the rushes aside the boat was forced along until they again caught sight of the hippopotamus, who was standing up to his belly in water.

"Is he going to charge?" Chebron asked, grasping a spear.

"No, there is little chance of that. Should he do so and upset the boat, throw yourself among the rushes and lie there with only your face above water. I will divert his attention and come back and get you into the boat when he has made off."

Another spear was thrown with good effect. There was a roar and a great splash. Chebron thought that the animal was upon them; but he turned off and dashed back to the pool where he had been first lying.

"I thought that was what he would do," the hunter said. "They always seek shelter in the bottom of the deep pools; and here, you see, the water is not deep enough to cover him."

The boat again followed the hippopotamus. Amuba was still on his raft on the pool.

"What has become of him?" Chebron asked as they passed beyond the rushes.

"He has sunk to the bottom of the pool," Amuba replied. "He gave me a start, I can tell you. We heard him bursting through the rushes, and then he rushed out with his mouth open—a mouth like a cavern; and then just as I thought he was going to charge us, he turned off and sunk to the bottom of the pool."

"How long will he lie there?" Chebron asked the hunter.

"A long time if he is left to himself, but we are going to stir him up."

So saying he directed the boat towards the rushes nearest to the bank and pushed the boat through them.

"Oh, here you are, Jethro!" Chebron said, seeing the Rebu and the men he had accompanied standing on the bank.

"What has happened, Chebron?—have you killed one of them? We heard a sort of roar and a great splashing."

"We have not killed him, but there are two spear-heads sticking into him."

The hunter handed the cords to the men and told them to pull steadily, but not hard enough to break the cords. Then he took from them the end of the rope they carried and poled back into the pool.

"Those cords are not strong enough to pull the great beast to the shore, are they?" Chebron asked.

"Oh, no, they would not move him; but by pulling on them it causes the spear-heads to give him pain, he gets uneasy, and rises to the surface in anger. Then you see, I throw this noose over his head, and they can pull upon that."

In two or three minutes the animal's head appeared above the water. The instant it did so the hunter threw the noose. The aim was correct, and with a jerk he tightened it round the neck.

"Now, pull!" he shouted.

The peasants pulled, and gradually the hippopotamus was drawn towards the bank, although struggling to swim in the opposite direction.

As soon, however, as he reached the shallow water and his feet touched the ground he threw his whole weight upon the rope. The peasants were thrown to the ground and the rope dragged through their fingers as the hippopotamus again made his way to the bottom of the pool. The peasants regained their feet and again pulled on the cords and rope. Again the hippopotamus rose and was dragged to the shallow, only to break away again. For eight or ten times this happened.

"He is getting tired now," the hunter said. "Next time or the time after they will get him on shore. We will land then and attack him with spears and arrows."

The hippopotamus was indeed exhausted, and allowed itself to be dragged ashore at the next effort without opposition. As soon as it did so he was attacked with spears by the hunters, Jethro, and the boys. The latter found that they were unable to drive their weapons through the thick skin, and betook themselves to their bows and arrows. The hunters, however, knew the point at which the skin was the thinnest, and drove their spears deep into the animal just behind the fore leg, while the boys shot their arrows at its mouth. Another noose had been thrown over its head as it issued from the water, and the peasants pulling on the ropes prevented it from charging. Three or four more thrusts were given from the hunters; then one of the spears touched a vital part—the hippopotamus sank on its knees and rolled over dead.

The peasants sent up a shout of joy, for the flesh of the hippopotamus is by no means bad eating, and here was a store of food sufficient for the whole neighbourhood.

"Shall we search for another, my lord?" the hunter asked Chebron.

"No. I think I have had enough of this. There is no fun in killing an animal that has not spirit to defend itself. What do you think, Amuba?"

"I quite agree with you, Chebron. One might almost as well slaughter a cow. What is that?" he exclamed suddenly, as a loud scream was heard at a short distance away. "It is a woman's voice."

Chebron darted off in full speed in the direction of the sound, closely followed by Amuba and Jethro. They ran about a hundred yards along the bank, where they saw the cause of the outcry. An immense crocodile was making his way towards the river, dragging along with it the figure of a woman.

In spite of his reverence for the crocodile Chebron did not hesitate a moment, but rushing forward smote the crocodile on the nose with all his strength with the shaft of his spear. The crocodile dropped its victim and turned upon its assailant, but Jethro and Amuba were close behind, and these also attacked him. The crocodile seeing this accession of enemies now set out for the river, snapping is jaws together.

"Mind its tail!" one of the hunters exclaimed, running up.

But the warning was too late, for the next moment Amuba received a tremendous blow which sent him to the ground. The hunter at the same moment plunged his spear into the animal through the soft skin at the back of its leg. Jethro followed his example on the other side. The animal checked its flight, and turning round and round lashed with its tail in all directions.

"Keep clear of it!" the hunter shouted. "It is mortally wounded and will need no more blows."

In fact, the crocodile had received its death-wound. Its movements became more languid, it ceased to lash its tail, though it still snapped at those nearest to it, but gradually this action also ceased, its head sank, and it was dead. Jethro as soon as he had delivered his blow ran to Amuba.

"Are you hurt?" he asked anxiously.

"No, I don't think so," Amuba gasped. "The brute has knocked all the breath out of my body; but that's better than if he had hit me in the leg, for I think he would have broken it had he done so. How is the woman?—is she dead?"

"I have not had time to see," Jethro replied. "Let me help you to your feet, and let us see if any of your ribs are broken. I will see about her afterwards."

Amuba on getting up declared that he did not think he was seriously hurt, although unable for the time to stand upright.

"I expect I am only bruised, Jethro. It was certainly a tremendous whack he gave me, and I expect I shall not be able to take part in any sporting for the next few days. The crocodile was worth a dozen hippopotami. There was some courage about him."

They now walked across to Chebron, who was stooping over the figure of the crocodile's victim.

"Why, she is but a girl!" Amuba exclaimed. "She is no older than your sister, Chebron."

"Do you think she is dead?" Chebron asked in hushed tones.

"I think she has only fainted," Jethro replied. "Here," he shouted to one of the peasants who were gathered round the crocodile, "one of you run down to the water and bring up a gourd full."

"I don't think she is dead," Amuba said. "It seemed to me that the crocodile had seized her by the leg."

"We must carry her somewhere," Jethro said, "and get some woman to attend to her. I will see if there is a hut near." He sprang up to the top of some rising ground and looked round. "There is a cottage close at hand," he said as he returned. "I dare say she belongs there."

Bidding two of the peasants run to fetch some women, he lifted up the slight figure and carried her up the slope, the two lads following. On turning round the foot of a sand-hill they saw a cottage lying nestled behind it. It was neater and better kept than the majority of the huts of the peasants. The walls of baked clay had been whitewashed and were half covered with bright flowers. A patch of carefully cultivated ground lay around it. Jethro entered the cottage. On a settle at the further end a man was sitting. He was apparently of great age, his hair and long beard were snowy white.

"What is it?" he exclaimed as Jethro entered. "Has the God of our fathers again smitten me in my old age, and taken from me my pet lamb? I heard her cry, but my limbs have lost their powers, and I could not rise to come to her aid."

"I trust that the child is not severely injured," Jethro said. "We had just killed a hippopotamus when we heard her scream, and running up found a great crocodile dragging her to the river, but we soon made him drop her. I trust that she is not severely hurt. The beast seemed to us to have seized her by the leg. We have sent to fetch some women. Doubtless they will be here immediately. Ah! here's the water."

He laid the girl down upon a couch in the corner of the room, and taking the gourd from the peasant who brought it sprinkled some water on her face, while Amuba, by his direction, rubbed her hands. It was some minutes before she opened her eyes, and just as she did so two women entered the hut. Leaving the girl to their care, Jethro and the boys left the cottage.

"I trust that the little maid is not greatly hurt," Amuba said. "By her dress it seems to me that she is an Israelite, though I thought we had left their land behind us on the other side of the desert. Still her dress resembles those of the women we saw in the village as we passed, and it is well for her it does so, for they wear more and thicker garments than the Egyptian peasant women, and the brute's teeth may not have torn her severely."

In a few minutes one of the women came out and told them that the maid had now recovered and that she was almost unhurt. "The crocodile seems to have seized her by her garments rather than her flesh, and although the teeth have bruised her, the skin is unbroken. Her grandfather would fain thank you for the service you have rendered him."

They re-entered the cottage. The girl was sitting on the ground at her grandfather's feet holding one of his hands in hers, while with his other he was stroking her head. As they entered, the women, seeing that their services were no longer required, left the cottage.

"Who are those to whom I owe the life of my grandchild?" the old man asked.

"I am Chebron, the son of Ameres, high-priest of the temple of Osiris at Thebes. These are my friends, Amuba and Jethro, two of the Rebu nation who were brought to Egypt and now live in my father's household."

"We are his servants," Amuba said, "though he is good enough to call us his friends."

"'Tis strange," the old man said, "that the son of a priest of Osiris should thus come to gladden the last few hours of one who has always withstood the Egyptian gods. And yet had the crocodile carried off my Ruth, it might have been better for her, seeing that ere the sun has risen and set many times she will be alone in the world."

The girl uttered a little cry, and rising on her knees threw her arms around the old man's neck.

"It must be so, my Ruth. I have lived a hundred and ten years in the land of the heathen, and my course is run; and were it not for your sake I should be glad that it is so, for my life has been sorrow and bitterness. I call her my grandchild, but she is in truth the daughter of my grandchild, and all who stood between her and me have passed away before me and left us alone together. But she trusts in the God of Abraham, and He will raise up a protector for her."

Chebron, who had learned something of the traditions of the Israelites dwelling in Egypt, saw by the old man's words that Jethro's surmises were correct and that he belonged to that race.

"You are an Israelite," he said gently. "How is it that you are not dwelling among your people instead of alone among strangers?"

"I left them thirty years back when Ruth's mother was but a tottering child. They would not suffer me to dwell in peace among them, but drove me out because I testified against them."

"Because you testified against them?" Chebron repeated in surprise.

"Yes. My father was already an old man when I was born, and he was one of the few who still clung to the faith of our fathers. He taught me that there was but one God, the God of Abraham, of Isaac, and of Jacob, and that all other gods were but images of wood and stone. To that faith I clung, though, after awhile, I alone of all our people held to the belief. The others had forgotten their God and worshipped the gods of the Egyptians. When I would speak to them they treated my words as ravings and as casting dishonour on the gods they served.

"My sons went with the rest, but my daughter learned the true faith from my lips and clung to it. She taught her daughter after her, and ten years ago, when she too lay dying, she sent Ruth by a messenger to me, praying me to bring her up in the faith of our fathers, and saying that though she knew I was of a great age, she doubted not that when my time came God would raise up protectors for the child. So for ten years we have dwelt here together, tilling and watering our ground and living on its fruit and by the sale of baskets that we weave and exchange for fish with our neighbours. The child worships the God of our fathers, and has grown and thriven here for ten years; but my heart is heavy at the thought that my hours are numbered and that I see no way after me but that Ruth shall return to our people, who will assuredly in time wean her from her faith."

"Never, grandfather," the girl said firmly. "They may beat me, and persecute me, but I will never deny my God."

"They are hard people the Israelites," the old man said shaking his head, "and they are stubborn, and must needs prevail against one so tender. However all matters are in the hands of God, who will again reveal Himself in His due time to His people who have forgotten Him."

Amuba, looking at the girl, thought that she had more power of resistance than the old man gave her credit for. Her face was of the same style of beauty as that of some of the young women he had seen in the villages of the Israelites, but of a higher and finer type. Her face was almost oval, with soft black hair, and delicately marked eyebrows running almost in a straight line below her forehead. Her eyes were large and soft, with long lashes veiling them, but there was a firmness about the lips and chin that spoke of a determined will, and gave strength to her declaration "Never."

There was silence a moment, and then Chebron said almost timidly:

"My father, although high-priest of Osiris, is not a bigot in his religion. He is wise and learned, and views all things temperately, as my friends here can tell you. He knows of your religion; for I have heard him say that when they first came into this land the Israelites worshipped one God only. I have a sister who is of about the same age as Ruth, and is gentle and kind. I am sure that if I ask my father he will take your grandchild into his household to be a friend and companion to Mysa, and I am certain that he would never try to shake her religion, but would let her worship as she chooses."

The old man looked fixedly at Chebron.

"Your speech is pleasant and kind, young sir, and your voice has an honest ring. A few years back I would have said that I would rather the maiden were dead than a handmaid in the house of an Egyptian; but as death approaches we see things differently, and it may be that she would be better there than among those who once having known the true God have forgotten Him and taken to the worship of idols. I have always prayed and believed that God would raise up protectors for Ruth, and it seems to me now that the way you have been brought hither in these latter days of my life is the answer to my prayer. Ruth, my child, you have heard the offer, and it is for you to decide. Will you go with this young Egyptian lord and serve his sister as a handmaiden, or will you return to the villages of our people?"

Ruth had risen to her feet now, and was looking earnestly at Chebron, then her eyes turned to the faces of Amuba and Jethro, and then slowly went back again to Chebron.

"I believe that God has chosen for me," she said at last, "and has sent them here not only to save my life, but to be protectors to me; their faces are all honest and good. If the father of this youth will receive me, I will, when you leave me, go and be the handmaid of his daughter."

"It is well," the old man said. "Now I am ready to depart, for my prayers have been heard. May God deal with you and yours, Egyptian, even as you deal with my child."

"May it be so," Chebron replied reverently.

"I can tell you," Jethro said to the old man, "that in no household in Egypt could your daughter be happier than in that of Ameres. He is the lord and master of Amuba and myself, and yet, as you see, his son treats us not as servants, but as friends. Ameres is one of the kindest of men; and as to his daughter Mysa, whose special attendant I am, I would lay down my life to shield her from harm. Your grandchild could not be in better hands. As to her religion, although Ameres had often questioned Amuba and myself respecting the gods of our people, he has never once shown the slightest desire that we should abandon them for those of Egypt."

"And now," Chebron said, "we will leave you; for doubtless the excitement has wearied you, and Ruth needs rest and quiet after her fright. We are encamped a mile away near the lake, and will come and see you to-morrow."

Not a word was spoken for some time after they left the house, and then Chebron said:

"It really would almost seem as if what that old man said was true, and that his God had sent us there that a protector might be found for his daughter. It was certainly strange that we should happen to be within sound of her voice when she was seized by that crocodile, and be able to rescue her just in time. It needed, you see, first, that we should be there, then that the crocodile should seize her at that moment, and, lastly, that we should be just in time to save her being dragged into the river. A crocodile might have carried her away ten thousand times without any one being within reach to save her, and the chances were enormously against any one who did save her being in a position to offer her a suitable home at her father's death."

"It is certainly strange. You do not think that your father will have any objection to take her?" Amuba asked.

"Oh, no, he may say that he does not want any more servants in the house, but I am sure that when he sees her, he will be pleased to have such a companion for Mysa. If it was my mother I do not know. Most likely she would say no; but when she hears that it has all been settled, she will not trouble one way or the other about it. I will write my father a letter telling him all about it, and send off one of the slaves with it at once. He can get back to-morrow, and this will gladden the old man's heart to know that it is all arranged. I wish to tell my father, too, of my trouble."

"What trouble?" Amuba asked in surprise. "You have told me nothing about anything troubling you."

"Do you not understand, Amuba? I am in trouble because I struck the crocodile; it is an impious action, and yet what could I do?"

Amuba repressed an inclination to smile.

"You could do nothing else, Chebron, for there was no time to mince matters. He was going too fast for you to explain to him that he was doing wrong in carrying off a girl, and you therefore took the only means in your power of stopping him; besides, the blow you dealt him did him no injury whatever. It was Jethro and the hunter who killed him."

"But had I not delayed his flight, they could not have done so."

"That is true enough, Chebron; but in that case he would have reached the water with his burden and devoured her at his leisure. Unless you think that his life is of much more importance than hers, I cannot see that you have anything to reproach yourself with."

"You do not understand me, Amuba," Chebron said pettishly. "Of course I do not think that the life of an ordinary animal is of as much importance as that of a human being; but the crocodiles are sacred, and misfortune falls upon those who injure them."

"Then in that case, Chebron, misfortune must fall very heavily on the inhabitants of those districts where the crocodile is killed wherever he is found. I have not heard that pestilence and famine visit those parts of Egypt with more frequency than they do the districts where the crocodile is venerated."

Chebron made no answer. What Amuba said was doubtless true; but upon the other hand, he had always been taught that the crocodile was sacred, and if so he could not account for the impunity with which these creatures were destroyed in other parts of Egypt. It was another of the puzzles that he so constantly met with. After a long pause he replied:

"It may seem to be as you say; but you see, Amuba, there are some gods specially worshipped in one district, others in another. In the district that a god specially protects he would naturally be indignant were the animals sacred to him to be slain, while he might pay no heed to the doings in those parts in which, he is little concerned."

"In that case, Chebron, you can clearly set your mind at rest. Let us allow that it is wrong to kill a crocodile in the district in which he is sacred and where a god is concerned about his welfare, but that no evil consequences can follow the slaying of him in districts in which he is not sacred, and where his god, as you say, feels little interest in him."

"I hope that is so, Amuba; and that as the crocodile is not a sacred animal here no harm may come from my striking one, though

I would give much that I had not been obliged to do so. I hope that my father will regard the matter in the same light."

"I have no doubt that he will do so, Chebron, especially as we agreed that you did no real harm to the beast."

"Is it not strange, Jethro," Amuba said when Chebron had gone into the tent, "that wise and learned people like the Egyptians should be so silly regarding animals?"

"It is strange, Amuba, and it was hard to keep from laughing to hear you so gravely arguing the question with Chebron. If all the people held the same belief I should not be surprised; but as almost every animal worshipped in one of the districts is hated and slain in another, and that without any evil consequences arising, one would have thought that they could not but see for themselves the folly of their belief. What are we going to do to-morrow?"

"I do not think that it is settled, we have had one day at each of the sports. Rabah said that to-morrow we could either go out and see new modes of fishing, or accompany the fowlers and watch them catching birds in the clap-nets, or go out into the desert and hunt ibex. Chebron did not decide, but I suppose when he has finished his letter we shall hear what he intends to do."

After Chebron had finished his letter, which was a long one, he called Rabah and asked him to despatch it at once by the fleetest-footed of the slaves.

"He will get there," he said, "before my father retires to rest. If he does not reply at once, he will probably answer in the morning, and at any rate the man ought to be back before mid-day."

At dinner Amuba asked Chebron whether he had decided what they should do the next day.

"We might go and look at the men with the clap-nets," Chebron answered. "They have several sorts in use, and take numbers of pigeons and other birds. I think that will be enough for to-morrow. We have had four days' hard work, and a quiet day will be pleasant, and if we find the time goes slowly, we can take a boat across the lake and look at the Great Sea beyond the sand-hills that divide the lake from it; besides, I hope we shall get my father's answer, and I should like some further talk with that old Israelite. It is interesting to learn about the religion that his forefathers believed in, and in which it seems that he and his grandchild are now the last who have faith."

"It will suit me very well to have a quiet day, Chebron; for in any case I do not think I could have accompanied you. My ribs are sore from the whack the crocodile gave me with his tail, and I doubt whether I shall be able to walk to-morrow."

Indeed, the next morning Amuba was so stiff and sore that he was unable to rise from his couch.

Soon after breakfast the messenger returned, bringing a letter from Ameres. It was as follows:—

"It seems to me, Chebron, that Mysa has no occasion for further attendants; but as your story of this old Israelite and his daughter interests me, and the girl is of Mysa's age and might be a pleasant companion for her, I have no objection to her entering our household. I should have liked to talk with the old man himself, and to have heard from him more about the religion that Joseph and his people brought to Egypt. It is recorded in some of the scrolls that these people were monotheists; but although I have many times questioned Israelites, all have professed to be acquainted with no religion but that of Egypt. If you have further opportunity find out as much as you can from this old man upon the subject.

"Assure him from me that his daughter shall be kindly treated in my household, and that no attempt whatever will be made to turn her from the religion she professes. As to your adventure with the crocodile, I do not think that your conscience need trouble you. It would certainly be unfortunate to meet in Upper Egypt a crocodile carrying off a peasant, and I am not called upon to give an opinion as to what would be the proper course to pursue under the circumstances; but as you are at present in a district where the crocodile, instead of being respected, is held in detestation, and as the people with you would probably have overtaken and slain him even without your intervention, I do not think that you need trouble yourself about the knock that you gave him across his snout. Had I found myself in the position you did I should probably have taken the same course. With respect to the girl, you had best give them instructions that when the old man dies she shall travel by boat to Thebes; arrived there, she will find no difficulty in learning which is my house, and on presenting herself there she will be well received. I will write at once to Mysa, telling her that you have found a little Israelite handmaiden as her special attendant, and that, should the girl arrive before my return, she is at once to assume that position.

"It would not do for her to come here were her grandfather to die before we leave for home. In the first place, she would be in the way, and in the second, her features and dress would proclaim her to be an Israelite. The people in the village she passed through might detain her, and insist on her remaining with them; or, should she arrive here, the fact of her departing with us might be made a subject of complaint, and the Israelites would not improbably declare that I had carried off a young woman of their tribe as a slave. Therefore, in all respects it is better that she should proceed up the river to Thebes.

"As they are poor you had best leave a sum of money with them to pay for her passage by boat, and for her support during the voyage. I find that I shall have finished with the steward earlier than I had expected, and shall be starting in about three days to inspect the canals and lay out plans for some fresh ones; therefore, if by that time you have had enough sport to satisfy you, you had best journey back."

"My father has consented," Chebron said joyously as he finished the letter. "I felt that he would; still, I was anxious till I got the letter, for it would have been a great disappointment to the old man could it not have been managed. I will go off and tell him at once. I shall not want you this morning, Jethro; so you can either stay here with Amuba or do some fishing or fowling on the lake. The boat is all in readiness, you know."

Chebron went off to the cottage. Ruth was in the garden tending the vegetables, and he stopped to speak to her before entering.

"I have not heard yet," he said, "how it came about that you were seized by the crocodile."

"I hardly know how it was," she said. "I am in the habit of going down many times a day to fetch up water for the garden, and I always keep a look-out for these creatures before I fill my jar; but yesterday I had just gone round the corner of the sand-hill when I was struck down with a tremendous blow, and a moment afterwards the creature seized me. I gave a scream; but I thought I was lost, for there are no neighbours within sound of the voice, and my grandfather has not been able to walk for months. Then I prayed as well as I could for the pain, and God heard me and sent you to deliver me."

"It is not often that they go up so far from the river, is it?"

"Not often. But yesterday we had a portion of a kid from a neighbour and were cooking it, and perhaps the smell attracted the crocodile; for they say that they are quick at smell, and they have been known to go into cottages and carry off meat from before the fire."

"I see you walk very lame still."

"Yes. Grandfather would have me keep still for a day or two; but I think that as soon as the bruises die out and the pain ceases I shall be as well as ever. Besides, what would the garden do without water? My grandfather will be glad to see you, my lord; but he is rather more feeble than usual this morning. The excitement of yesterday has shaken him."

She led the way into the cottage.

"Your granddaughter has told me you are not very strong to-day," Chebron began.

"At my age," the old man said, "even a little thing upsets one, and the affair of yesterday was no little thing. I wonder much that the agitation did not kill me."

"I have satisfactory news to give you," Chebron said. "I yesterday despatched a message to my father, and have just received the answer." And taking out the scroll he read aloud the portion in which Ameres stated his readiness to receive Ruth in his household, and his promise that no pressure whatever should be put upon her to abandon her religion.

"The Lord be praised!" the old man exclaimed. "The very animals are the instruments of His will, and the crocodile that threatened death to the child was, in truth, the answer sent to my prayer. I thank you, my young lord; and as you and yours deal with my child, so may the God of my fathers deal with you. But she may stay on with me for the little time that remains, may she not?"

"Surely. We should not think of taking her now. My father sends instructions as to what she is to do, and money to pay for her journey up the Nile to Thebes. This is what he says." And he read the portion of the scroll relating to the journey. "And now," he said, "let me read to you what my father says about your religion. He is ever a searcher after truth, and would fain that I should hear from your lips and repeat to him all that you can tell me relating to this God whom you worship."

"That will I with gladness, my young lord. The story is easily told, for it is simple, and not like that of your religion with its many deities."

Chebron took a seat upon a pile of rushes and prepared to listen to the old man's story of the God of the Israelites.

Chapter 8

FOR two days longer the party lingered by the side of the lake fishing and fowling, and then returned across the desert to the head-quarters of Ameres. Two months were spent in examining canals and water-courses, seeing that the dykes were strengthened where needed, and that the gates and channels were in good repair. Levels were taken for the construction of several fresh branches, which would considerably extend the margin of cultivation. The natives were called upon to furnish a supply of labour for their formation; but the quota was not furnished without considerable grumbling on the part of the Israelites, although Ameres announced that payment would be given them for their work. At last, having seen that everything was in train, Ameres left one of his subordinates to carry out the work, and then started with his son for Thebes.

A fortnight after his return home he was informed that a young female, who said her name was Ruth, wished to see him. He bade the servant conduct her to him, and at the same time summon Chebron from his studies. The lad arrived first, and as Ruth entered presented her to his father.

"Welcome, child, to this house," the high-priest said. "I suppose by your coming that the old man, your great-grandfather, of whom my son has spoken to me, is no more?"

"He died a month since, my lord," Ruth replied; "but it was two weeks before I could find a passage in a boat coming hither."

"Chebron, tell Mysa to come here," Ameres said, and the lad at once fetched Mysa, who had already heard that an Israelite girl was coming to be her special attendant, and had been much interested in Chebron's account of her and her rescue from the crocodile.

"This is Ruth, Mysa," Ameres said when she entered, "who has come to be with you. She has lost her last friend, and I need not tell you, my child, to be kind and considerate with her. You know what you would suffer were you to be placed among strangers, and how lonely you would be at first. She will be a little strange to our ways, but you will soon make her at home, I hope."

"I will try and make her happy," Mysa replied, looking at her new companion.

Although the girls were about the same age, Ruth looked the elder of the two. Mysa was still little more than a child, full of fun and life. Ruth was broken down by the death of her grandfather and by the journey she had made; but in any case she would have looked older than Mysa, the difference being in manner rather than in face or figure. Ruth had long had many responsibilities on her shoulders. There was the care and nursing of the old man, the cultivation of the garden on which their livelihood depended, the exchange of its products for other articles, the preparation of the meals. Her grandfather had been in the habit of talking to her as a grown-up person, and there was an expression of thoughtfulness and gravity in her eyes. Mysa, on the contrary, was still but a happy child, who had never known the necessity for work or exertion; her life had been like a summer day, free from all care and anxiety. Naturally, then, she felt as she looked at Ruth that she was a graver and more serious personage than she had expected to see.

"I think I shall like you," she said when her examination was finished, "when we know each other a little better, and I hope you will like me; because, as my father says, we are to be together."

"I am sure we shall," Ruth replied, looking admiringly at Mysa's bright face. "I have never had anything to do with girls of my own age, and you will find me clumsy at first; but I will do my best to please you, for your father and brother have been very good to me."

"There, take her away, Mysa. I have told your mother about her coming, and want to go on with my reading," Ameres said. "Show her your garden and animals, and where she is to sleep; and give her in charge of old Male, who will see that she has all that she wants, and get suitable garments and all that is requisite."

Before many days were over Ruth became quite at home in her new abode. Her position was a pleasant one. She was at once companion and attendant to Mysa, accompanying her in her walks under the escort of Jethro, playing with her in the garden, helping her to feed the animals, and amusing her when she preferred to sit quiet by telling her about her life near the lake by the Great Sea, about the fowling and fishing there, and especially about the river course close to the cottage, with its hippopotami and crocodiles. Ruth brightened up greatly in her new surroundings, which to her were marvellous and beautiful; and she soon caught something of the cheerfulness of her mistress, and the laughter of the two girls was often heard rising from Mysa's inclosure at the further end of the quiet garden.

Shortly after the return from their visit to Lower Egypt an important event took place, Chebron being initiated into the lowest grade of the priesthood. His duties at first were slight; for aspirants to the higher order, who were with scarce an exception the sons of the superior priesthood, were not expected to perform any of the drudgery that belonged properly to the work of the lower class of the order. It was necessary to ascend step by step; but, until they arrived at the grade beyond which study and intelligence alone led to promotion, their progress was rapid, and they were expected only to take part in such services and ceremonies of the temple as required the attendance of all attached to it.

His duties, therefore, interfered but little with his studies or ordinary mode of life, and he was almost as much at home as before. He could now, however, enter the temples at all hours, and had access to the inner courts and chambers, the apartments where the sacred animals were kept, and other places where none but the priests were permitted to enter. He availed himself of this privilege chiefly of an evening. All the great courts were open to the sky, and Chebron loved to roam through them in the bright moonlight, when they were deserted by the crowd of worshippers and all was still and silent. At that time the massive columns, the majestic architecture, the strange figures of the gods, exercised an influence upon his imagination which was wanting in the daytime. Upon the altars before the chief gods fire ever burned, and in the light of the flickering flames the faces assumed life and expression.

Now and then a priest in his white linen robe moved through the deserted courts; but for the most part Chebron had undisturbed possession, and was free to meditate without interruption. He found that his mind was then attuned to a pitch of reverence and devotion to the gods that it failed to attain when the sun was blazing down upon the marble floor, and the courts were alive with worshippers. Then strive as he would he could not enter as he wanted into the spirit of the scene. When he walked in the solemn procession carrying a sacred vessel or one of the sacred emblems, doubts whether there could be anything in common between the graven image and the god it represented would occur to him.

He would wonder whether the god was really gratified by these processions, whether he felt any real pleasure in the carrying about of sacred vessels, emblems, and offerings of flowers. He was shocked at his own doubts, and did his best to banish them from his mind. At times it seemed to him that some heavy punishment must fall upon him for permitting himself to reason on matters so far beyond his comprehension, and he now rejoiced at what he before was inclined to regret, that his father had decided against his devoting his whole life to the service of the temple.

Sometimes he thought of speaking to his father and confessing to him that his mind was troubled with doubts, but the thought of the horror with which such a confession would be received deterred him from doing so. Even to Amuba he was silent on the subject, for Amuba he thought would not understand him. His friend believed firmly in the gods of his own country, but accepted the fact that the Egyptian deities were as powerful for good or evil to the Egyptians as were his own to the Rebu. And, indeed, the fact that the Egyptians were so great and powerful, and prevailed over other nations, was, he was inclined to think, due to the superior power of their gods.

The majesty of the temples, the splendour of the processions, and the devoutness with which the people worshipped their gods, alike impressed him; and although the strangeness of the images struck him as singular, he was ready to admit that the gods might take any shape they pleased. Thus, then, Chebron could look for no sympathy from him, and shrank from opening his mind to him. Nevertheless he sometimes took Amuba with him in his visits to the temple. The doors at all times stood open, and any could enter who chose, and had they in the inner courts met with any of the priests, Amuba would have passed unnoticed as being one of the attendants of the temple in company with Chebron.

But few words were exchanged between the lads during these rambles, for the awful grandeur of the silent temple and its weird aspect in the moonlight affected Amuba as strongly as it did Chebron. At times he wondered to himself whether if he ever returned home and were to introduce the worship of these terrible gods of Egypt, they would extend their protection to the Rebu.

Near the house of Ameres stood that of Ptylus, a priest who occupied a position in the temple of Osiris, next in dignity to that of the high-priest.

Between the two priests there was little cordiality, for they differed alike in disposition and manner of thought. Ptylus was narrow and bigoted in his religion, precise in every observance of ceremonial; austere and haughty in manner, professing to despise all learning beyond that relating to religion, but secretly devoured with jealousy at the esteem in which Ameres was held by the court, and his reputation as one of the first engineers, astronomers, and statesmen of Egypt. He had been one of the fiercest in the opposition raised to the innovations proposed by Ameres, and had at the time exerted himself to the utmost to excite such a feeling against him as would render it necessary for him to resign his position in the temple.

His disappointment had been intense, when—owing in no slight degree to the influence of the king himself, who regarded Ameres with too much trust and affection to allow himself to be shaken in his confidence even by what he held to be the erroneous views of the high-priest of Osiris—his intrigue came to nothing; but he had ever since kept an unceasing watch upon the conduct of his colleague, without, however, being able to find the slightest pretense for complaint against him. For Ameres was no visionary; and having failed in obtaining a favourable decision as to the views he entertained, he had not striven against the tide, knowing that by doing so he would only involve himself and his family in ruin and disgrace, without forwarding in the smallest degree the opinions he held.

He was thus as exact as ever in his ministration in the temple, differing only from the other performers of the sacred rites inasmuch as while they offered their sacrifices to Osiris himself, he in his heart dedicated his offerings to the great God of whom Osiris was but a feeble type or image.

A certain amount of intimacy was kept up between the two families. Although there was no more liking between the wives of the two priests than between their husbands, they were of similar dispositions—both were fond of show and gaiety, both were ambitious; and although in society both exhibited to perfection the somewhat gentle and indolent manner which was considered to mark high breeding among the women of Egypt, the slaves of both knew to their cost that in their own homes their bearing was very different.

In their entertainments and feasts there was constant rivalry between them, although the wife of the high-priest considered it nothing short of insolence that the wife of one inferior to her husband's rank should venture to compete with her; while upon the other hand, the little airs of calm superiority her rival assumed when visiting her excited the deepest indignation and bitterness in the heart of the wife of Ptylus. She, too, was aware of the enmity that her husband bore to Ameres, and did her best to second him by shaking her head and affecting an air of mystery whenever his name was mentioned, leaving her friends to suppose that did she choose she could tell terrible tales to his disadvantage.

Ameres on his part had never alluded at home either to his views concerning religion or to his difference of opinion with his colleagues. There was but little in common between him and his wife. He allowed her liberty to do as she chose, to give frequent entertainments to her female friends, and to spend money as she liked so long as his own mode of life was not interfered with. He kept in his own hands, too, the regulation of the studies of Chebron and Mysa.

One day when he was in his study his wife entered. He looked up with an expression of remonstrance, for it was an understood thing that when occupied with his books he was on no account to be disturbed except upon business of importance.

"You must not mind my disturbing you for once, Ameres; but an important thing has happened. Nicotis, the wife of Ptylus, has been here this afternoon, and what do you think she was the bearer of—a proposal from her husband and herself that their son Plexo should marry our Mysa."

Ameres uttered an exclamation of surprise and anger.

"She is a child at present; the thing is ridiculous!"

"Not so much of a child, Ameres, after all. She is nearer fifteen than fourteen, and betrothal often takes place a year earlier. I have been thinking for some time of talking the matter over with you, for it is fully time that we thought of her future."

Ameres was silent. What his wife said was perfectly true, and Mysa had reached the age at which the Egyptian maidens were generally betrothed. It came upon him, however, as an unpleasant surprise. He had regarded Mysa as still a child, and his affections were centred in her and Chebron; for his eldest son, who resembled his mother in spirit, he had but little affection or sympathy.

"Very well," he said at last in a tone of irritation very unusual to him, "if Mysa has reached the age when we must begin to think whom she is to marry, we will think of it, but there is no occasion whatever for haste. As to Plexo, I have marked him often when he has been here with Chebron, and I do not like his disposition. He is arrogant and overbearing, and, at the same time, shallow and foolish. Such is not the kind of youth to whom I shall give Mysa."

The answer did not quite satisfy his wife. She agreed with him in objecting to the proposed alliance, but on entirely different grounds. She had looked forward to Mysa making a brilliant match, which would add to her own consequence and standing. On ceremonial occasions, as the wife of the high-priest, and herself a priestess of Osiris, she was present at all the court banquets; but the abstemious tastes and habits of Ameres prevented her from taking the part she desired in other festivities, and she considered that were Mysa to marry some great general, or perhaps even one of the princes of the blood, she would then be able to take that position in society to which she aspired, and considered, indeed, that she ought to fill as the wife of Ameres, high-priest of Osiris, and one of the most trusted counsellors of the king.

Such result would certainly not flow from Mysa's marriage to the son of one of less rank in the temple than her husband, and far inferior in public estimation. Being content, however, that her husband objected to the match on other grounds, she abstained from pressing her own view of the subject, being perfectly aware that it was one with which Ameres would by no means sympathize. She therefore only said:

"I am glad that you object to the match, Ameres, and am quite in accord with you in your opinion of the son of Ptylus. But what reason shall I give Nicotis for declining the connection?"

"The true one, of course!" Ameres said in surprise. "What other reason could there be? In respect to position no objection could arise, nor upon that of wealth. He is an only son, and although

Ptylus may not have so large an income as myself (for I have had much state employment), he can certainly afford to place his son in at least as good a position as we can expect for Mysa. Were we to decline the proposal without giving a reason Ptylus would have good ground for offence.

"I do not suppose, Amense, he will be pleased at fault being found with his son, but that we cannot help. Parents cannot expect others to see their offspring with the same eyes that they do. I should certainly feel no offence were I to propose for a wife for Chebron to receive as an answer that he lacked some of the virtues the parents required in a husband for their daughter. I might consider that Chebron had those virtues, but if they thought otherwise why should I be offended?"

"It is not everyone who sees matters as you do, Ameres, and no one likes having his children slighted. Still, if it is your wish that I should tell Nicotis that you have a personal objection to her son, of course I will do so."

"Do not put it in that light, Amense. It is not that I have a personal objection to him. I certainly do not like him, but that fact has nothing to do with my decision. I might like him very much, and yet consider that he would not make Mysa a good husband; or, on the other hand, I might dislike him personally, and yet feel that I could safely intrust Mysa's happiness to him. You will say, then, to Nicotis that from what I have seen of Plexo, and from what I have learned of his character, it does not appear to me that a union between him and Mysa would be likely to conduce to her happiness; and that, therefore, I decline altogether to enter into negotiations for the bringing about of such a marriage."

Amense was well pleased, for she felt that this message, given in her husband's name, would be a great rebuff for her rival, and would far more than counterbalance the many triumphs she had gained over her by the recital of the number of banquets and entertainments in which she had taken part.

Had Amense been present when Nicotis informed Ptylus of the refusal of their proposal for the hand of Mysa, she might have felt that even the satisfaction of mortifying a rival may be dearly purchased.

"You know the woman, Ptylus, and can picture to yourself the air of insolence with which she declined our proposal. I wished at the moment we had been peasants' wives instead of ladies of quality. I would have given her cause to regret her insolence for a long time. As it was, it was as much as I could do to restrain myself, and to smile and say that perhaps, after all, the young people were not as well suited for each other as could be wished; and that we had only yielded to the wishes of Plexo, having in our mind another alliance which would in every respect be more advantageous. Of course she replied that she was glad to hear it, but she could not but know that I was lying, for the lotus flower I was holding in my hand trembled with the rage that devoured me."

"And it was, you say, against Plexo personally that the objection was made?" Ptylus said gloomily.

"So she seemed to say. Of course she would not tell me that she had set her mind on her daughter marrying one of the royal princes, though it is like enough that such is her thought, for the woman is pushing and ambitious enough for anything. She only said, in a formal sort of way, that while the alliance between the two families would naturally be most agreeable to them, her husband was of opinion that the dispositions of the young people were wholly dissimilar, and that he feared such a union would not be for the happiness of either; and that having perhaps peculiar ideas as to the necessity for husband and wife being of one mind in all matters, he thought it better that the idea should be abandoned. I had a mind to tell her that Ameres did not seem to have acted upon those ideas in his own case, for everyone knows that he and Amense have not a thought in common—that she goes her way and he goes his."

"Let them both beware!" Ptylus said. "They shall learn that we are not to be insulted with impunity. This Ameres, whom the people regard as so holy, is at heart a despiser of the gods. Had he not been a favourite of Thotmes he would ere now have been disgraced and degraded, and I should be high-priest in his place; for his son, Neco, is too young for such a dignity. But he is ascending in the scale, and every year that his father lives and holds office he will come more and more to be looked upon as his natural successor. A few more years and my chance will be extinguished."

"Then," Nicotis said decidedly, "Ameres must not hold office for many more years. We have talked the matter over and over again, and you have always promised me that some day I should be the wife of the high-priest, and that Plexo should stand first in the succession of the office. It is high time that you carried your promises into effect."

"It is time, Nicotis. This man has too long insulted the gods by ministering at their services, when in his heart he was false to them. It shall be so no longer; this last insult to us decides me! Had he agreed to our proposal I would have laid aside my own claims, and with my influence could have secured that Plexo, as his son-in-law, should succeed, rather than that shallow-brained fool, Neco. He has refused the offer, and he must bear the consequences. I have been too patient. I will be so no longer, but will act. I have a strong party among the upper priesthood who have long been of my opinion that Ameres is a disgrace to our caste and a danger to our religion. They will join me heart and soul, for they feel with me that his position as high-priest is an outrage to the gods. Ask me no questions, Nicotis, but be assured that my promises shall be kept. I will be high-priest; Plexo shall marry this child he fancies, for his doing so will not only strengthen my position, but render his own succession secure, by silencing those who might at my death seek to bring back the succession to Neco."

"That is well, Ptylus. I have long wondered that you were content to be lorded over by Ameres. If I can aid you in any way be sure that I will do so. By the way, Amense invited us to a banquet she is about to give next week. Shall we accept the invitation?"

"Certainly. We must not show that we are in any way offended at what has passed. As far as Ameres himself is concerned it matters not, for the man has so good an opinion of himself that nothing could persuade him that he has enemies; but it would not do, in view of what I have resolved upon, that any other should entertain the slightest suspicion that there exists any ill-feeling between us."

Great preparations were made by Amense for the banquet on the following week, for she had resolved that this should completely eclipse the entertainments of Nicotis. Ameres had, as usual, left everything in her hands, and she spared no expense. For a day or two previous large supplies of food arrived from the country farm and from the markets in the city; and early on the morning of the entertainment a host of professional cooks arrived to prepare the dinner. The head cooks superintended their labours. The meat consisted of beef and goose, ibex, gazelle, and oryx; for although large flocks of sheep were kept for their wool, the flesh was not eaten by the Egyptians. There were, besides, great numbers of ducks, quails, and other small fowl. The chief cooks superintended the cutting up of the meat and the selection of the different joints for boiling or roasting. One servant worked with his feet a bellows, raising the fire to the required heat; another skimmed the boiling caldrons with a spoon; and a third pounded salt, pepper, and other ingredients in a large mortar. Bakers and confectioners made light bread and pastry; the former being made in the form of rolls, sprinkled at the top with caraway and other seeds. The confectionery was made of fruit and other ingredients mixed with dough, and this was formed by a skilful workman into various artistic shapes, such as recumbent oxen, vases, temples, and other forms. Besides the meats there was an abundance of all the most delicate kinds of fish.

When the hour of noon approached Ameres and Amense took their seats on two chairs at the upper end of the chief apartment, and as the guests arrived each came up to them to receive their welcome. When all had arrived the women took their places on chairs at the one side of the hall, the men on the other. Then servants brought in tables, piled up with dishes containing the viands, and in some cases filled with fruits and decorated with flowers, and ranged them down the centre of the room.

Cups of wine were then handed round to the guests, lotus flowers presented to them to hold in their hands, and garlands of flowers placed round their necks. Stands, each containing a number of jars of wine, stoppered with heads of wheat and decked with garlands, were ranged about the room. Many small tables were now brought in, and round these the guests took their seats upon low stools and chairs—the women occupying those on one side of the room, the men those on the other. The servants now placed the dishes on the small tables, male attendants waiting on the men, while the women were served by females. Egyptians were unacquainted with the use of knives and forks, the joints being cut up by the attendants into small pieces, and the guests helping themselves from the dishes with the aid of pieces of bread held between the fingers. Vegetables formed a large part of the meal, the meats being mixed with them to serve as flavouring; for in so hot a climate a vegetable diet is far more healthy than one composed principally of meat. While the meal was proceeding a party of female musicians, seated on the ground in one corner of the room, played and sang.

The banquet lasted for a long time, the number of dishes served being very large. When it was half over the figure of a mummy, of about three feet in length, was brought round and presented to each guest in succession, as a reminder of the uncertainty of existence. But as all present were accustomed to this ceremony it had but little effect, and the sound of conversation and laughter, although checked for a moment, broke out again as soon as the figure was removed. Wine of many kinds was served during the dinner, the women as well as the men partaking of it.

When all was concluded servants brought round golden basins with perfumed water and napkins, and guests removed from their fingers the gravy that even with the daintiest care in feeding could not be altogether escaped. Then the small tables and stools were removed, and the guests took their places on the chairs along the sides of the room. Then parties of male and female dancers by turn came in and performed. Female acrobats and tumblers then entered, and went through a variety of performances, and jugglers showed feats of dexterity with balls, and other tricks; while the musicians of various nationalities played in turns upon the instruments in use in their own countries. All this time the attendants moved about among the guests, serving them with wine and keeping them supplied with fresh flowers. A bard recited an ode in honour of the glories of king Thotmes, and it was not until late in the evening that the entertainment came to an end.

"It has gone off splendidly," Amense said to Ameres when all was over, and the last guest had been helped away by his servants; for there were many who were unable to walk steadily unaided. "Nothing could have been better—it will be the talk of the whole town; and I could see Nicotis was devoured by envy and vexation. I do think great credit is due to me, Ameres, for you have really done nothing towards the preparations."

"I am perfectly willing that you should have all the credit, Amense," Ameres said wearily, "and I am glad that you are satisfied. To me the whole thing is tedious and tiresome to a degree. All this superabundance of food, this too lavish use of wine, and the postures and antics of the actors and dancers, is simply disgusting. However, if everyone else was pleased, of course I am content."

"You are the most unsatisfactory husband a woman ever had," Amense said angrily. "I do believe you would be perfectly happy shut up in your study with your rolls of manuscript all your life, without seeing another human being save a black slave to bring you in bread and fruit and water twice a day."

"I think I should, my dear," Ameres replied calmly. "At any rate, I should prefer it vastly to such a waste of time, and that in a form to me so disagreeable, as that I have had to endure to-day."

Chapter 9

IT was some days later that Chebron and Amuba again paid a visit to the temple by moonlight. It was well-nigh a month since they had been there; for, save when the moon was up, the darkness and gloom at the courts, lighted only by the lamps of the altars, was so great that the place offered no attractions. Amuba, free from the superstitions which influenced his companion, would have gone with him had he proposed it, although he too felt the influence of the darkness and the dim, weird figures of the gods, seen but faintly by the lights that burned at their feet. But to Chebron, more imaginative and easily affected, there was something absolutely terrible in the gloomy darkness, and nothing would have induced him to wander in the silent courts save when the moon threw her light upon them.

On entering one of the inner courts they found a massive door in the wall standing ajar.

"Where does this lead to?" Amuba asked.

"I do not know. I have never seen it open before. I think it must have been left unclosed by accident. We will see where it leads to."

Opening it they saw in front of them a flight of stairs in the thickness of the wall.

"It leads up to the roof," Chebron said in surprise. "I knew not there were any stairs to the roof, for when repairs are needed the workmen mount by ladders."

"Let us go up, Chebron; it will be curious to look down upon the courts."

"Yes, but we must be careful, Amuba; for, did any below catch sight of us, they might spread an alarm."

"We need only stay there a minute or two," Amuba urged. "There are so few about that we are not likely to be seen, for if we walk noiselessly none are likely to cast their eyes so far upwards."

So saying Amuba led the way up the stairs, and Chebron somewhat reluctantly followed him. They felt their way as they went, and after mounting for a considerable distance found that the stairs ended in a narrow passage, at the end of which was an opening scarce three feet high and just wide enough for a man to pass through. This evidently opened into the outer air, as sufficient light passed through to enable them to see where they were standing. Amuba crept out through the opening at the end. Beyond was a ledge a foot wide; beyond that rose a dome some six feet high and eight or ten feet along the ledge.

"Come on, Chebron; there is plenty of room for both of us," he said, looking backwards. Chebron at once joined him.

"Where can we be?" Amuba asked. "There is the sky overhead. We are twenty feet from the top of the wall, and where this ledge ends, just before it gets to the sides of this stone, it seems to go straight down."

Chebron looked round him.

"This must be the head of one of the statues," he said after a pause. "What a curious place! I wonder what it can have been made for. See, there is a hole here!"

Just in front of them was an opening of some six inches in diameter in the stone.

Amuba pushed his hand down.

"It seems to go a long way down," he said; "but it is narrowing," and removing his arm he looked down the hole.

"There is an opening at the other end," he said; "a small narrow slit. It must have been made to enable anyone standing here to see down, though I don't think, you could see much through so small a hole. I should think, Chebron, if this is really the top of the head of one of the great figures, that slit must be where his lips are. Don't you think so?"

Chebron agreed that is was probable.

"In that case," Amuba went on, "I should say that this hole must be made to allow the priests to give answers through the mouth of the image to supplications made to it. I have heard that the images sometimes gave answers to the worshippers. Perhaps this is the secret of it."

Chebron was silent. The idea was a painful one to him; for if this were so, it was evident that trickery was practiced.

"I think we had better go," he said at last. "We have done wrong in coming up here."

"Let me peep over the side first," Amuba said. "It seems to me that I can hear voices below."

But the projection of the head prevented his seeing anything beyond. Returning he put his foot in the hole and raised himself sufficiently to get on the top of the stone, which was here so much flattened that there was no risk of falling off. Leaning forward he looked over the edge. As Amuba had guessed would be the case, he found himself on the head of the principal idol in the temple. Gathered round the altar at its foot were seven or eight men, all of whom he knew by the whiteness of their garments to be priests. Listening intently he could distinctly hear their words. After waiting a minute he crawled back.

"Come up here, Chebron; there is something important going on."

Chebron joined him, and the two, lying close together, looked down at the court.

"I tell you we must do away with him," one of the group below said in tones louder than had been hitherto used. "You know as well as I do that his heart is not in the worship of the gods. He has already shown himself desirous of all sorts of innovations, and unless we take matters in our hands there is no saying to what lengths he may go. He might shatter the very worship of the gods. It is no use to try to overthrow him openly; for he has the support of the king, and the efforts that have been made have not in any way shaken his position. Therefore he must die. It will be easy to put him out of the way. There are plenty of small chambers and recesses which he might be induced to enter on some pretext or other, and then be slain without difficulty, and his body taken away by night and thrown into some disused catacombs.

"It would be a nine days' wonder when he was missed, but no one could ever learn the truth of his disappearance. I am ready to kill him with my own hands, and should regard the deed as one most pleasing to the gods. Therefore if you are ready to undertake the other arrangements, and two of you will join me in seeing that the deed is carried out without noise or outcry, I will take the matter in hand. I hate him, with his airs of holiness and his pretended love for the people. Besides, the good of our religion requires that he shall die."

There was a chorus of approbation from the others.

"Leave me to determine the time and place," the speaker went on, "and the excuse on which we will lead him to his doom. Those who will not be actually engaged with me in the business must be in the precincts of the place, and see that no one comes that way, and make some excuse or other should a cry by chance be heard, and must afterwards set on foot all sorts of rumours to account for his actions. We can settle nothing to-night; but there is no occasion for haste, and on the third night hence we will again gather here."

Chebron touched Amuba, and the two crept back to where they had been standing on the ledge.

"The villains are planning a murder in the very temple!" Chebron said. "I will give them a fright;" and applying his mouth to the orifice he cried:

"Beware, sacriligious wretches! Your plots shall fail and ruin fall upon you!"

"Come on, Chebron!" Amuba exclaimed, pulling his garment. "Some of the fellows may know the secret of this statue, and in that case they will kill us without mercy if they find us here."

Passing through the opening they groped their way to the top of the stairs, hurried down these as fast as they could in the darkness, and issued out from the door.

"I hear footsteps!" Amuba exclaimed as they did so. "Run for your life, Chebron!"

Just as they left the court they heard the noise of angry voices, and hurried footsteps close by. At full speed they ran through several courts and apartments.

"We had better hide, Amuba."

"It will be no use trying to do that. They will guard the entrance-gates, give the alarm, and set all the priests on duty in the temple in search. No, come along quickly. They cannot be sure that it is we who spoke to them, and will probably wait until one has ascended the stairs to see that no one is lurking there. I think we are safe for the moment; but there are no good hiding-places. I think you had better walk straight to the entrance, Chebron. Your presence here is natural enough, and those they post at the gates would let you pass out without suspicion. I will try to find myself a hiding-place."

"I certainly will not do that, Amuba. I am not going to run away and leave you in the scrape, especially as it was I who got us into it by my rashness."

"Is there any place where workmen are engaged on the walls?" Amuba asked suddenly.

"Yes, in the third court on the right after entering," Chebron replied. "They are repainting the figures on the upper part of the wall. I was watching them at work yesterday."

"Then in that case there must be some ladders. With them we might get away safely. Let us make for the court at once, but tread noiselessly, and if you hear a footstep approaching, hide in the shadow behind the statue. Listen! they are giving the alarm. They know that their number would be altogether insufficient to search this great temple thoroughly."

Shouts were indeed heard, and the lads pressed on towards the court Chebron had spoken of. The temple now was echoing with sounds, for the priests on duty, who had been asleep as usual when not engaged in attending to the lights, had now been roused by one of their number, who ran in and told them some sacrilegious persons had made their way into the temple.

"Here is the place," Chebron said, stopping at the foot of the wall.

Here two or three long light ladders were standing. Some of these reached part of the distance only up the walls, but the top of one could be seen against the skyline.

"Mount, Chebron! There is no time to lose. They may be here at any moment."

Chebron mounted, followed closely by his companion. Just as he gained the top of the wall several men carrying torches ran into the court and began to search along the side lying in shadow. Just as Amuba joined Chebron one of the searchers caught sight of them, and with a shout ran towards the ladder.

"Pull, Chebron!" Amuba exclaimed as he tried to haul up the ladder.

Chebron at once assisted him, and the foot of the ladder was already many feet above the ground before the men reached it.

The height of the wall was some fifty feet, and light as was the construction of the ladder, it was as much as the lads could do to pull it up to the top. The wall was fully twelve feet in thickness, and as soon as the ladder was up Amuba said:

"Keep away from the edge, Chebron, or it is possible that in this bright moonlight we may be recognized. We must be going on at once. They will tie the short ladders together and be after us directly."

"Which way shall we go?"

"Towards the outer wall, as far as possible from the gate. Bring the ladder along."

Taking it upon their shoulders they hurried along. Critical as the position was, Amuba could not help remarking on the singularity of the scene. The massive walls were all topped with white cement and stretched like broad ribbons, crossing and recrossing each other in regular parallelograms on a black ground.

Five minutes' running took them to the outer wall, and the ladder was again lowered and they descended, and then stood at its foot for a moment to listen. Everything was still and silent.

"It is lucky they did not think of sending men to watch outside the walls when they first caught sight of us, or we should have been captured. I expect they thought of nothing but getting down the other ladders and fastening them together. Let us make straight out and get well away from the temple, and then we will return to your house at our leisure. We had better get out of sight if we can before our pursuers find the top of the ladder, then as they will have no idea in which direction we have gone they will give up the chase."

After an hour's walking they reached home. On the way they had discussed whether or not Chebron should tell Ameres what had taken place, and had agreed that it would be best to be silent.

"Your father would not like to know that you have discovered the secret of the image, Chebron. If it was not for that I should say you had best have told him. But I do not see that it would do any good now. We do not know who the men were who were plotting or whom they were plotting against. But one thing is pretty certain, they will not try to carry out their plans now, for they cannot tell how much of their conversation was overheard, and their fear of discovery will put an end for the present to this scheme of theirs."

Chebron agreed with Amuba's views, and it was decided to say nothing about the affair unless circumstances occurred which might alter their intentions. They entered the house quietly and reached their apartment without disturbing any of the inmates.

On the following morning one of the priests of the temple arrived at an early hour and demanded to see Ameres.

"I have evil tidings to give you, my lord," he said. "Your son Neco has this morning been killed."

"Neco killed?" Ameres repeated.

"It is, alas, but too true, my lord! He left the house where he lives with two other priests but a short distance from the gate of the temple at his usual hour. It was his turn to offer the sacrifices at dawn, and it must have been still dark when he left the house. As he did not arrive at the proper time a messenger was sent to fetch him, and he found him lying dead but a few paces from his own door, stabbed to the heart."

Ameres waved his hand to signify that he would be alone, and sat down half-stunned by the sudden shock.

Between himself and his eldest son there was no great affection. Neco was of a cold and formal disposition, and although Ameres would in his own house have gladly relaxed in his case, as he had done in that of Chebron, the rigid respect and deference demanded by Egyptian custom on the part of sons towards their father, Neco had never responded to his advances and had been punctilious in all the observances practiced at the time. Except when absolutely commanded to do so, he had never taken a seat in his father's presence, had never addressed him unless spoken to, had made his appearance only at stated times to pay his respects to him, and when dismissed had gladly hurried away to the priest who acted as his tutor.

As he grew up the gap had widened instead of closing. Ameres saw with regret that his mind was narrow and his understanding shallow, that in matters of religion he was bigoted; while at the same time he perceived that his extreme zeal in the services of the temple, his absorption in ceremonial observances of all kind, were due in no slight degree to ambition, and that he was endeavouring to obtain reputation for distinguished piety with a view to succeeding some day to the office of high-priest. He guessed that the eagerness with which Neco embraced the first opportunity of withdrawing himself from his home and joining two other young priests in their establishment was due to a desire to disassociate himself from his father, and thus to make an unspoken protest against the latitude of opinion that had raised up a party hostile to Ameres.

Although living so close it was very seldom that he had, after once leaving the house, again entered; generally choosing a time when his father was absent and so paying his visits only to his mother. Still the news of his sudden death was a great shock, and Ameres sat without moving for some minutes until a sudden outburst of cries in the house betokened that the messenger had told his tidings to the servants, and that these had carried them to their mistress. Ameres at once went to his wife's apartment and endeavoured to console her, but wholly without success.

Amense was frantic with grief. Although herself much addicted to the pleasures of the world, she had the highest respect for religion, and the ardour of Neco in the discharge of his religious duties had been a source of pride and gratification to her. Not only was it pleasant to hear her son spoken of as one of the most rising of the young priesthood, but she saw that he would make his way rapidly and would ere long become the recognized successor to his father's office. Chebron and Mysa bore the news of their brother's death with much more resignation. For the last three years they had scarcely seen him, and even when living at home there had been nothing in common between him and them. They were indeed more awed by the suddenness of his death than grieved at his loss.

When he left them Ameres went at once to the house of Neco to make further inquiries into the matter. There he could learn nothing that could afford any clue. Neco had been late at the temple and had not returned until long after the rest of the household were in bed, and none had seen him before he left in the morning. No sound of a struggle or cry for help had been heard. His death had apparently been instantaneous. He had been stabbed in the back by some one who had probably been lurking close to the door awaiting his coming out.

The general opinion there and in the temple was that he must have fallen a victim to a feeling of revenge on the part of some attendant in the building who on his report had undergone disgrace and punishment for some fault of carelessness or inattention, in the services or in the care of the sacred animals. As a score of attendants had at one time or other been so reported by Neco, for he was constantly on the look-out for small irregularities, it was impossible to fix the crime on one more than another.

The magistrates, who arrived soon after Ameres to investigate the matter, called the whole of those who could be suspected of harbouring ill-will against Neco to be brought before them, and questioned as to their doings during the night. All stoutly asserted that they had been in bed at the time of the murder, and nothing occurred to throw a suspicion upon one more than another. As soon as the investigation was concluded Ameres ordered the corpse to be brought to his own house.

Covered by white cloths it was placed on a sort of sledge. This was drawn by six of the attendants of the temple; Ameres and Chebron followed behind, and after them came a procession of priests. When it arrived at the house, Amense and Mysa, with their hair unbound and falling around them received the body—uttering loud cries of lamentation, in which they were joined by all the women of the house. It was carried into an inner apartment, and there until evening a loud wailing was kept up, many female relatives and friends coming in and joining in the outcry. Late in the evening the body was taken out, placed upon another sledge, and followed by the male relatives and friends and by all the attendants and slaves of the house, was carried to the establishment of Chigron the embalmer. During the forty days occupied by the process the strictest mourning was observed in the house. No meat or wheaten bread was eaten, nor wine served at the table—even the luxury of the bath was abandoned. All the males shaved their eyebrows, and sounds of loud lamentation on the part of the women echoed through the house.

At the end of that time the mummy was brought back in great state, and placed in the room which was in all large Egyptian houses set apart for the reception of the dead. The mummy-case was placed upright against the wall. Here sacrifices similar to those offered at the temple were made. Ameres himself and a number of the priests of the rank of those decorated with leopard skins took part in the services. Incense and libation were offered. Amense and Mysa were present at the ceremony, and wailed with their hair in disorder over their shoulders and dust sprinkled on their heads. Oil was poured over the head of the mummy, and after the ceremony was over Amense and Mysa embraced the mummied body, bathing its feet with their tears and uttering expressions of grief and praises of the deceased.

In the evening a feast was held in honour of the dead. On this occasion the signs of grief were laid aside, and the joyful aspect of the departure of the dead to a happy existence prevailed. A large number of friends and relations were present. The guests were anointed and decked with flowers, as was usual at these parties, and after the meal the mummy was drawn through the room in token that his spirit was still present among them. Amense would fain have kept the mummy for some time in the house, as was often the practice, but Ameres preferred that the funeral should take place at once.

Three days later the procession assembled and started from the house. First came servants bearing tables laden with fruit, cakes, flowers, vases of ointment, wine, some young geese in a crate for sacrifice, chairs, wooden tables, napkins, and other things. Then came others carrying small closets containing the images of the gods; they also carried daggers, bows, sandals, and fans, and each bore a napkin upon his shoulder. Then came a table with offerings and a chariot drawn by a pair of horses, the charioteer driving them as he walked behind the chariot. Then came the bearers of a sacred boat and the mysterious eye of Horus, the god of stability. Others carried small images of blue pottery representing the deceased under the form of Osiris, and the bird emblematic of the soul. Then eight women of the class of paid mourners came along beating their breasts, throwing dust upon their heads, and uttering loud lamentations. Ameres, clad in a leopard skin, and having in his hands the censer and vase of libation, accompanied by his attendants bearing the various implements used in the services, and followed by a number of priests also clad in leopard skins, now came along. Immediately behind them followed the consecrated boat placed upon a sledge, and containing the mummy-case in a large exterior case covered with paintings. It was drawn by four oxen and seven men. In the boat Amense and Mysa were seated. The sledge was decked with flowers, and was followed by Chebron and other relatives and friends of the deceased, beating their breasts and lamenting loudly.

When they arrived at the sacred lake, which was a large piece of artificial water, the coffin was taken from the small boat in which it had been conveyed and placed in the baris, or consecrated boat of the dead. This was a gorgeously painted boat with a lofty cabin. Amense, Mysa, and Chebron took their places here. It was towed by a large boat with sails and oars. The members of the procession then took their places in other richly-decorated sailing boats, and all crossed the lake together. The procession was then reformed and went in the same order to the tomb. Here the mummy-case was placed on the slab prepared for it, and a sacrifice with libation and incense offered. The door of the tomb was then closed, but not fastened, as sacrificial services would be held there periodically for many years. The procession then returned on foot to the house.

During all this time no certain clue had been obtained as to the authors of the murder. Upon going up to the temple on the day of Neco's death Chebron found all sorts of rumours current. The affair of the previous night had been greatly magnified, and it was generally believed that a strong party of men had entered the temple with the intention of carrying off the sacred vessels, but that they had been disturbed just as they were going to break into the subterranean apartments where these were kept, and had then fled to the ladders and escaped over the wall before a sufficient force could be collected to detain them. It was generally supposed that this affair was in some way connected with the death of Neco. Upon Chebron's return with this news he and Amuba agreed that it was necessary to inform Ameres at once of their doings on the previous night. After the evening meal was over Ameres called Chebron into his study.

"Have you heard aught in the temple, Chebron, as to this strange affair that took place there last night? I cannot see how it can have any connection with your brother's death; still, it is strange. Have you heard who first discovered these thieves last night? Some say that it was Ptylus, though what he should be doing there at that hour I know not. Four or five others are named by priests as having aroused them; but curiously not one of these is in the temple to-day. I have received a letter from Ptylus saying that he has been suddenly called to visit some relations living on the sea-shore near the mouths of the Nile. The others sent similar excuses. I have sent to their houses, but all appear to have left at an early hour this morning. This is most strange, for none notified to me yesterday that they had occasion to be absent. What can be their motive in thus running away when naturally they would obtain praise and honour for having saved the vessels of the temple? Have you heard anything that would seem to throw any light upon the subject?"

"I have heard nothing, father; but I can tell you much. I should have spoken to you the first thing this morning had it not been for the news about Neco." Chebron then related to Ameres how he and Amuba had the night before visited the temple, ascended the stairs behind the image of the god, and overheard the plot to murder some unknown person.

"This is an extraordinary tale, Chebron," Ameres said when he had brought his story to a conclusion. "You certainly would have been slain had you been overtaken. How the door that led to the staircase came to be open I cannot imagine. The place is only used on very rare occasions, when it is deemed absolutely necessary that we should influence in one direction or another the course of events. I can only suppose that when last used, which is now some months since, the door must have been carelessly fastened, and that it only now opened of itself. Still, that is a minor matter, and it is fortunate that it is you who made the discovery. As to this conspiracy you say you overheard, it is much more serious. To my mind the sudden absence of Ptylus and the others would seem to show that they were conscious of guilt. Their presence in the temple so late was in itself singular; and, as you say, they cannot know how much of their conversation was overheard. Against whom their plot was directed I can form no idea; though doubtless, it was a personage of high importance."

"You do not think, father," Chebron said hesitatingly, "that the plot could have been to murder Neco? This is what Amuba and I thought when we talked it over this afternoon."

"I do not think so," Ameres said after a pause. "It is hardly likely that four or five persons would plot together to carry out the murder of one in his position; it must be some one of far greater importance. Neco may not have been liked, but he was certainly held in esteem by all the priests in the temple."

"You see, father," Chebron said, "that Ptylus is an ambitious man, and may have hoped at some time or other to become high-priest. Neco would have stood in his way, for, as the office is hereditary, if the eldest son is fitted to undertake it, Neco would almost certainly be selected."

"That is true, Chebron, but I have no reason to credit Ptylus with such wickedness; besides, he would hardly take other people into his confidence did he entertain such a scheme. Moreover, knowing that they were overheard last night, although they cannot tell how much may have been gathered by the listener, they would assuredly not have carried the plan into execution; besides which, as you say, no plan was arrived at, and after the whole temple was disturbed they would hardly have met afterwards and arranged this fresh scheme of murder. No. If Neco was killed by them, it must have been that they suspected that he was one of those who overheard them. His figure is not unlike yours. They may probably have obtained a glimpse of you on the walls, and have noticed your priest's attire. He was in the temple late, and probably left just before you were discovered. Believing, then, that they were overheard, and thinking that one of the listeners was Neco, they decided for their own safety to remove him. Of course it is mere assumption that Ptylus was one of those you overheard last night. His absence to-day is the only thing we have against him, and that alone is wholly insufficient to enable us to move in the matter. The whole affair is a terrible mystery; be assured I will do my best to unravel it. At present, in any case, we can do nothing. Ptylus and the four priests who are absent will doubtless return when they find that no accusation is laid against them. They will suppose that the other person who overheard them, whoever he was, is either afraid to come forward, or perhaps heard only a few words and is ignorant of the identity of the speakers. Indeed, he would be a bold man who would venture to prefer so terrible an accusation against five of the priests of the temple. I do not blame you in the matter, for you could not have foreseen the events that have happened. It was the will of the gods that you should have learned what you have learned; perhaps they intend some day that you shall be their instrument for bringing the guilty to justice. As to the conspiracy, no doubt, as you say, the plot, against whomsoever it was directed, will be abandoned, for they will never be sure as to how much is known of what passed between them, and whether those who overheard them may not be waiting for the commission of the crime to denounce them. In the meantime you will on no account renew your visit to the temple or enter it at any time, except when called upon to do so by your duties."

The very day after Neco's funeral Mysa and her mother were thrown into a flutter of excitement by a message which arrived from Bubastes. Some months before the sacred cat of the great temple there—a cat held in as high honour in Lower Egypt as the bull Apis in the Thebaid—had fallen sick, and, in spite of the care and attendance lavished upon it, had died. The task of finding its successor was an important and arduous one, and, like the bull of Apis, it was necessary not only that the cat should be distinguished for its size and beauty, but that it should bear certain markings. Without these particular markings no cat could be elevated to the sacred post, even if it remained vacant for years; therefore as soon as the cat was dead a party of priests set out from Bubastes to visit all the cities of Egypt in search of its successor.

The whole country was agitated with the question of the sacred cat, and at each town they visited lists were brought to the priests of all the cats which, from size, shape, and colour, could be considered as candidates for the office. As soon as one of the parties of the priests had reached Thebes Amense had sent to them a description of Mysa's great cat Paucis. Hitherto Amense had evinced no interest whatever in her daughter's pets, seldom going out into the garden, except to sit under the shade of the trees near the fountain for a short time in the afternoon when the sun had lost its power.

In Paucis, indeed, she had taken some slight interest; because, in the first place, it was only becoming that the mistress of the house should busy herself as to the welfare of animals deemed so sacred; and in the second, because all who saw Paucis agreed that it was remarkable alike in size and beauty, and the presence of such a creature in the house was in itself a source of pride and dignity. Thus, then, she lost no time in sending a message to the priests inviting them to call and visit her and inspect the cat. Although, as a rule, the competitors for the post of sacred cat of Bubastes were brought in baskets by their owners for inspection, the priests were willing enough to pay a visit in person to the wife of so important a man as the high-priest of Osiris.

Amense received them with much honour, presented Mysa to them as the owner of the cat, and herself accompanied the priests in their visit to the home of Mysa's pets. Their report was most favourable. They had, since they left Bubastes, seen no cat approaching Paucis in size and beauty, and although her markings were not precisely correct, they yet approximated very closely to the standard. They could say no more than this, because the decision could not be made until the return of all the parties of searchers to Bubastes. Their reports would then be compared, and unless any one animal appeared exactly to suit all requirements, a visit would be made by the high-priest of the temple himself to three or four of the cats most highly reported upon. If he found one of them worthy of the honour, it would be selected for the vacant position.

If none of them came up to the lofty standard the post would remain unfilled for a year or two, when it might be hoped that among the rising generation of cats a worthy successor to the departed one might be found. For themselves, they must continue their search in Thebes and its neighbourhood, as all claimants must be examined; but they assured Amense that they thought it most improbable that a cat equal to Paucis would be found.

Some months had passed, and it was not until a week after the funeral of Neco that a message arrived, saying that the report concerning Paucis by the priests who had visited Thebes was so much more favourable than that given by any of the other searchers of the animals they had seen, that it had been decided by the high-priest that it alone was worthy of the honour.

The messenger stated that in the course of a fortnight a deputation consisting of the high-priest and several lower functionaries of the temple, with a retinue of the lower clergy and attendants, would set out from Bubastes by water in order to receive the sacred cat, and to conduct her with all due ceremony to the shrine of Bubastes. Mysa was delighted at the honour which had befallen her cat. Privately she was less fond of Paucis than of some of the less stately cats; for Paucis, from the time it grew up, had none of the playfulness of the tribe, but deported itself with a placid dignity which would do honour to the new position, but which rendered it less amusing to Mysa than its humbler but more active companions.

Amense was vastly gratified at the news. It was considered the highest honour that could befall an Egyptian for one of his animals to be chosen to fill the chief post in one of the temples, and next in dignity to Apis himself was the sacred cat of the great goddess known as Baste, Bubastes, or Pasht.

As soon as the news was known, all the friends and acquaintances of the family flocked in to offer their congratulations; and so many visits were paid to Mysa's inclosure that even the tranquillity of Paucis was disturbed by the succession of admirers, and Amense, declaring that she felt herself responsible for the animal being in perfect health when the priests arrived for it, permitted only the callers whom she particularly desired to honour, to pay a visit of inspection to it.

Chapter 10

FOR several days, upon paying their morning visit to the birds and other pets in the inclosure in the garden, Chebron and Mysa had observed an unusual timidity among them. The wild fowl, instead of advancing to meet them with demonstrations of welcome, remained close among the reeds, and even the ibis did not respond at once to their call.

"They must have been alarmed at something," Chebron said the third morning. "Some bird of prey must have been swooping down upon them. See here, there are several feathers scattered about, and some of them are stained with blood. Look at that pretty drake that was brought to us by the merchants in trade with the far East. Its mate is missing. It may be a hawk or some creature of the weasel tribe. At any rate, we must try to put a stop to it. This is the third morning that we have noticed the change in the behaviour of the birds. Doubtless three of them have been carried off. Amuba and I will watch to-morrow with our bows and arrows and see if we cannot put an end to the marauder. If this goes on we shall lose all our pets."

Upon the following morning Chebron and Amuba went down to the inclosure soon after daybreak, and concealing themselves in some shrubs waited for the appearance of the intruder. The ducks were splashing about in the pond, evidently forgetful of their fright of the day before; and as soon as the sun was up the dogs came out of their house and threw themselves down on a spot where his rays could fall upon them, while the cats sat and cleaned themselves on a ledge behind a lattice, for they were only allowed to run about in the inclosure when some one was there to prevent their interference with birds.

For an hour there was no sign of an enemy. Then one of the birds gave a sudden cry of alarm, and there was a sudden flutter as all rushed to shelter among the reeds; but before the last could get within cover a dark object shot down from above. There was a frightened cry and a violent flapping as a large hawk suddenly seized one of the water-fowl and struck it to the ground. In an instant the watchers rose to their feet, and as the hawk rose with its prey in its talons they shot their arrows almost simultaneously. Amuba's arrow struck the hawk between the wings and the creature fell dead still clutching its prey. Chebron's arrow was equally well aimed, but it struck a twig which deflected its course and it flew wide of the mark.

Amuba gave a shout of triumph and leapt out from among the bushes. But he paused and turned as an exclamation of alarm broke from Chebron. To his astonishment, he saw a look of horror on his companion's face. His bow was still outstretched, and he stood as if petrified.

"What's the matter, Chebron?" Amuba exclaimed. "What has happened? Has a deadly snake bit you? What is it, Chebron?"

"Do you not see?" Chebron said in a low voice.

"I see nothing," Amuba replied, looking round, at the same time putting another arrow into his bow-string ready to repel the attack of some dangerous creature. "Where is it? I can see nothing."

"My arrow; it glanced off a twig and entered there; I saw one of the cats fall. I must have killed it."

Two years before Amuba would have laughed at the horror which Chebron's face expressed at the accident of shooting a cat, but he had been long enough in Egypt to know how serious were the consequences of such an act. Better by far that Chebron's arrow had lodged in the heart of a man. In that case an explanation of the manner in which the accident had occurred, a compensation to the relatives of the slain, and an expiatory offering at one of the temples would have been deemed sufficient to purge him from the offence; but to kill a cat, even by accident, was the most unpardonable offence an Egyptian could commit, and the offender would assuredly be torn to pieces by the mob. Knowing this, he realized at once the terrible import of Chebron's words.

For a moment he felt almost as much stunned as Chebron himself, but he quickly recovered his presence of mind.

"There is only one thing to be done, Chebron; we must dig a hole and bury it at once. I will run and fetch a hoe."

Throwing down his bow and arrows he ran to the little shed at the other end of the garden where the implements were kept, bidding a careless good-morning to the men who were already at work there. He soon rejoined Chebron, who had not moved from the spot from which he had shot the unlucky arrow.

"Do you think this is best, Amuba? Don't you think I had better go and tell my father?"

"I do not think so, Chebron. Upon any other matter it would be right at once to confer with him, but as high-priest it would be a fearful burden to place upon his shoulders. It would be his duty at once to denounce you; and did he keep it secret, and the matter be ever found out, it would involve him in our danger. Let us therefore bear the brunt of it by ourselves."

"I dare not go in," Chebron said in awestruck tones. "It is too terrible."

"Oh, I will manage that," Amuba said lightly. "You know to me a cat is a cat and nothing more, and I would just as soon bury one as that rascally hawk which has been the cause of all this mischief."

So saying he crossed the open space, and entering a thick bush beyond the cat-house, dug a deep hole; then he went into the house. Although having no belief whatever in the sacredness of one animal more than another, he had yet been long enough among the Egyptians to feel a sensation akin to awe as he entered and saw lying upon the ground the largest of the cats pierced through by Chebron's arrow.

Drawing out the shaft he lifted the animal, and putting it under his garment went out again, and entering the bushes buried it in the hole he had dug. He levelled the soil carefully over it, and scattered a few dead leaves on the top.

"There, no one would notice that," he said to himself when he had finished, "but it's awfully unlucky it's that cat of all others."

Then he went in, carefully erased the marks of blood upon the floor, and brought out the shaft, took it down to the pond and carefully washed the blood from it, and then returned to Chebron.

"Is it—" the latter asked as he approached. He did not say more, but Amuba understood him.

"I am sorry to say it is," he replied. "It is horribly unlucky, for one of the others might not have been missed. There is no hoping that now."

Chebron seemed paralyzed at the news.

"Come, Chebron," Amuba said, "it will not do to give way to fear; we must brave it out. I will leave the door of the cat-house open, and when it is missed it will be thought that it has escaped and wandered away. At any rate, there is no reason why suspicion should fall upon us if we do but put a bold face upon the matter; but we must not let our looks betray us. If the worst comes to the worst and we find that suspicions are entertained, we must get out of the way. But there will be plenty of time to think of that, all that you have got to do now is to try to look as if nothing has happened."

"But how can I?" Chebron said in broken tones. "To you, as you say, it is only a cat; to me it is a creature sacred above all others that I have slain. It is ten thousand times worse than if I had killed a man."

"A cat is a cat," Amuba repeated. "I can understand what you feel about it, though to my mind it is ridiculous. There are thousands of cats in Thebes, let them choose another one for the temple. But I grant the danger of what has happened, and I know that if it is found out there is no hope for us."

"You had nothing to do with it," Chebron said; "there is no reason why you should take all this risk with me."

"We were both in the matter, Chebron, and that twig might just as well have turned my arrow from its course as yours. We went to kill a hawk together and we have shot a cat, and it is a terrible business, there is no doubt; and it makes no difference whatever whether I think the cat was only a cat if the people of Thebes considered it as a god. If it is found out it is certain death, and we shall need all our wits to save our lives; but unless you pluck up courage and look a little more like yourself, we may as well go at once and say what has happened and take the consequences. Only if you don't value your life I do mine; so if you mean to let your looks betray us, say so, and stop here for a few hours till I get a good start."

"I will tell my father," Chebron said suddenly, "and abide by what he says. If he thinks it is his duty to denounce me, so be it; in that case you will run no risk."

"But I don't mind running the risk, Chebron; I am quite ready to share the peril with you."

"No; I will tell my father," Chebron repeated, "and abide by what he says. I am sure I can never face this out by myself, and that my looks will betray us. I have committed the most terrible crime an Egyptian can commit, and I dare not keep such a secret to myself."

"Very well, Chebron, I will not try to dissuade you, and I will go and see Jethro. Of course to him as to me the shooting of a cat is a matter not worth a second thought; but he will understand the consequences, and if we fly will accompany us. You do not mind my speaking to him? You could trust your life to him as to me."

Chebron nodded, and moved away towards the house.

"For pity sake, Chebron!" Amuba exclaimed, "do not walk like that. If the men at work get sight of you they cannot but see that something strange has happened, and it will be recalled against you when the creature is missed."

Chebron made an effort to walk with his usual gait, Amuba stood watching him for a minute, and then turned away with a gesture of impatience.

"Chebron is clever and learned in many things, and I do not think that he lacks courage; but these Egyptians seem to have no iron in their composition when a pinch comes. Chebron walks as if all his bones had turned to jelly. Of course he is in a horrible scrape; still, if he would but face it out with sense and pluck it would be easier for us all. However, I do think that it is more the idea that he has committed an act of horrible sacrilege than the fear of death that weighs him down. If it were not so serious a matter one could almost laugh at any one being crushed to the earth because he had accidentally killed a cat."

Upon entering the house Chebron made his way to the room where his father was engaged in study. Dropping the heavy curtains over the door behind him he advanced a few paces, then fell on his knees, and touched the ground with his forehead.

"Chebron!" Ameres exclaimed, laying down the roll of papyrus on which he was engaged and rising to his feet. "What is it, my son? Why do you thus kneel before me in an attitude of supplication? Rise and tell me what has happened."

Chebron raised his head, but still continued on his knees. Ameres was startled at the expression of his son's face. The look of health and life had gone from it, the colour beneath the bronze skin had faded away, drops of perspiration stood on his forehead, his lips were parched and drawn.

"What is it, my son?" Ameres repeated, now thoroughly alarmed.

"I have forfeited my life, father! Worse, I have offended the gods beyond forgiveness! This morning I went with Amuba with our bows and arrows to shoot a hawk which has for some time been slaying the water-fowl. It came down and we shot together. Amuba killed the hawk, but my arrow struck a tree and flew wide of the mark, and entering the cat's house killed Paucis, who was chosen only two days ago to take the place of the sacred cat in the temple of Bubastes."

An exclamation of horror broke from the high-priest, and he recoiled a pace from his son.

"Unhappily boy," he said, "your life is indeed forfeited. The king himself could not save his son from the fury of the populace had he perpetrated such a deed."

"It is not my life I am thinking of, father," Chebron said, "but first of the horrible sacrilege, and then that I alone cannot bear the consequences, but that some of these must fall upon you and my mother and sister; for even to be related to one who has committed such a crime is a terrible disgrace."

Ameres walked up and down the room several times before he spoke.

"As to our share of the consequences, Chebron, we must bear it as best we can," he said at last in a calmer tone than he had before used; "it is of you we must first think. It is a terrible affair; and yet, as you say, it was but an accident, and you are guiltless of any intentional sacrilege. But that plea will be as nothing. Death is the punishment for slaying a cat; and the one you have slain having been chosen to succeed the cat of Bubastes, is of all others the one most sacred. The question is, what is to be done? You must fly and that instantly, though I fear that flight will be vain; for as soon as the news is known it will spread from one end of Egypt to the other, and every man's hand will be against you, and even by this time the discovery may have been made."

"That will hardly be, father; for Amuba has buried the cat among the bushes, and has left the door of the house open so that it may be supposed for a time that it has wandered away. He proposed to me to fly with him at once; for he declares that he is determined to share my fate since we were both concerned in the attempt to kill the hawk. But in that of course he is wrong; for it is I, not he, who has done this thing."

"Amuba has done rightly," Ameres said. "We have at least time to reflect."

"But I do not want to fly, father. Of what good will life be to me with this awful sin upon my head? I wonder that you suffer me to remain a moment in your presence—that you do not cast me out as a wretch who has mortally offended the gods."

Ameres waved his hand impatiently.

"That is not troubling me now, Chebron. I do not view things in the same way as most men, and should it be that you have to fly for your life I will tell you more; suffice for you that I do not blame you, still less regard you with horror. The great thing for us to think of at present is as to the best steps to be taken. Were you to fly now you might get several days' start, and might even get out of the country before an alarm was spread; but upon the other hand, your disappearance would at once be connected with that of the cat as soon as it became known that she is missing, whereas if you stay here quietly it is possible that no one will connect you in any way with the fact that the cat is gone.

"That something has happened to it will speedily be guessed, for a cat does not stray away far from the place where it has been bred up; besides, a cat of such a size and appearance is remarkable, and were it anywhere in the neighbourhood it would speedily be noticed. But now go and join Amuba in your room, and remain there for the morning as usual. I will give orders that your instructor be told that you will not want him to-day, as you are not well. I will see you presently when I have thought the matter fully out and determined what had best be done. Keep up a brave heart, my boy; the danger may yet pass over."

Chebron retired overwhelmed with surprise at the kindness with which his father had spoken to him, when he had expected that he would be so filled with horror at the terrible act of sacrilege that he would not have suffered him to remain in the house for a moment after the tale was told. And yet he had seemed to think chiefly of the danger to his life, and to be but little affected by what to Chebron himself was by far the most terrible part of the affair—

the religious aspect of the deed. On entering the room where he pursued his studies he found Jethro as well as Amuba there.

"I am sorry for you, young master," Jethro said as he entered. "Of course to me the idea of any fuss being made over the accidental killing of a cat is ridiculous; but I know how you view it, and the danger in which it has placed you. I only came in here with Amuba to say that you can rely upon me, and that if you decide on flight I am ready at once to accompany you."

"Thanks, Jethro," Chebron replied. "Should I fly it will indeed be a comfort to have you with me as well as Amuba, who has already promised to go with me; but at present nothing is determined. I have seen my father and told him everything, and he will decide for me."

"Then he will not denounce you," Amuba said. "I thought that he would not."

"No; and he has spoken so kindly that I am amazed. It did not seem possible to me that an Egyptian would have heard of such a dreadful occurrence without feeling horror and detestation of the person who did it, even were he his own son. Still more would one expect it from a man who, like my father, is a high-priest to the gods."

"Your father is a wise as well as a learned man," Jethro said; "and he knows that the gods cannot be altogether offended at an affair for which fate and not the slayer is responsible. The real slayer of the cat is the twig which turned the arrow, and I do not see that you are any more to blame, or anything like so much to blame, as is the hawk at whom you shot."

This, however, was no consolation to Chebron, who threw himself down on a couch in a state of complete prostration. It seemed to him that even could this terrible thing be hidden he must denounce himself and bear the penalty. How could he exist with the knowledge that he was under the ban of the gods? His life would be a curse rather than a gift under such circumstances. Physically, Chebron was not a coward, but he had not the toughness of mental fibre which enables some men to bear almost unmoved misfortunes which would crush others to the ground. As to the comforting assurances of Amuba and Jethro, they failed to give him the slightest consolation. He loved Amuba as a brother, and in all other matters his opinion would have weighed greatly with him; but Amuba knew nothing of the gods of Egypt, and could not feel in the slightest the terrible nature of the act of sacrilege, and therefore on this point his opinion would have no weight.

"Jethro," Amuba said, "you told me you were going to escort Mysa one day or other to the very top of the hills, in order that she could thence look down upon the whole city. Put it into her head to go this morning, or at least persuade her to go into the city. If she goes into the garden she will at once notice that the cat is lost; whereas if you can keep her away for the day it will give us so much more time."

"But if Ameres decides that you had best fly, I might on my return find that you have both gone."

"Should he do so, Jethro, he will tell you the route we have taken, and arrange for some point at which you can join us. He would certainly wish you to go with us, for he would know that your experience and strong arm would be above all things needful."

"Then I will go at once," Jethro agreed. "There are two or three excursions she has been wanting to make, and I think I can promise that she shall go on one of them to-day. If she says anything about wanting to go to see her pets before starting, I can say that you have both been there this morning and seen after them."

"I do not mean to fly," Chebron said, starting up, "unless it be that my father commands me to do so. Rather a thousand worlds I stay here and meet my fate!"

Jethro would have spoken, but Amuba signed to him to go at once, and crossing the room took Chebron's hand. It was hot and feverish, and there was a patch of colour in his cheek.

"Do not let us talk about it, Chebron," he said. "You have put the matter in your father's hands, and you may be sure that he will decide wisely; therefore the burden is off your shoulders for the present. You could have no better counsellor in all Egypt, and the fact that he holds so high and sacred an office will add to the weight of his words. If he believes that your crime against the gods is so great that you have no hope of happiness in life, he will tell you so; if he considers that, as it seems to me, the gods cannot resent an accident as they might do a crime against them done willfully, and that you may hope by a life of piety to win their forgiveness, then he will bid you fly.

"He is learned in the deepest of the mysteries of your religion, and will view matters in a different light to that in which they are looked at by the ignorant rabble. At any rate, as the matter is in his hands, it is useless for you to excite yourself. As far as personal danger goes, I am willing to share it with you, to take half the fault of this unfortunate accident, and to avow that as we were engaged together in the act that led to it we are equally culpable of the crime.

"Unfortunately, I cannot share your greater trouble—your feeling of horror at what you regard as sacrilege; for we Rebu hold the life of one animal no more sacred than the life of another, and have no more hesitation in shooting a cat than a deer. Surely your gods cannot be so powerful in Egypt and impotent elsewhere; and yet if they are as powerful, how is it that their vengeance has not fallen upon other peoples who slay without hesitation the animals so dear to them?"

"That is what I have often wondered," Chebron said, falling readily into the snare, for he and Amuba had had many conversations on such subjects, and points were constantly presenting themselves which he was unable to solve.

An hour later, when a servant entered and told Chebron and Amuba that Ameres wished to speak to them, the former had recovered to some extent from the nervous excitement under which he had first suffered. The two lads bowed respectfully to the high-priest, and then standing submissively before him waited for him to address them.

"I have sent for you both," he said after a pause, "because it seems to me that, although Amuba was not himself concerned in this sad business, it is probable that as he was engaged with you at the time the popular fury might not nicely discriminate between you." He paused as if expecting a reply, and Amuba said quietly:

"That is what I have been saying to Chebron, my lord. I consider myself fully as guilty as he is. It was a mere accident that his arrow and not mine was turned aside from the mark we aimed at, and I am ready to share his lot, whether you decide that the truth shall be published at once, or whether we should attempt to fly."

Ameres bowed his head gravely, and then looked at his son.

"I, father, although I am ready to yield my wishes to your will, and to obey you in this as in all other matters, would beseech you to allow me to denounce myself and to bear my fate. I feel that I would infinitely rather die than live with this terrible weight and guilt upon my head."

"I expected as much of you, Chebron, and applaud your decision," Ameres said gravely.

Chebron's face brightened, while that of Amuba fell. Ameres, after a pause, went on:

"Did I think as you do, Chebron, that the accidental killing of a cat is a deadly offence against the gods, I should say denounce yourself at once, but I do not so consider it."

Chebron gazed at his father as if he could scarce credit his sense of hearing, while even Amuba looked surprised.

"You have frequently asked me questions, Chebron, which I have either turned aside or refused to answer. It was, indeed, from seeing that you had inherited from me the spirit of inquiry, that I deemed it best that you should not ascend to the highest order of the priesthood; for if so, the knowledge you would acquire would render you, as it has rendered me, dissatisfied with the state of things around you. Had it not been for this most unfortunate accident I should never have spoken to you further on the subject, but as it is I feel that it is my duty to tell you more.

"I have had a hard struggle with myself, and have, since you left me, thought over from every point of view what I ought to do. On the one hand, I should have to tell you things known only to an inner circle, things which were it known I had whispered to anyone my life would be forfeited. On the other hand, if I keep silent I should doom you to a life of misery. I have resolved to take the former alternative. I may first tell you what you do not know, that I have long been viewed with suspicion by those of the higher priesthood who know my views, which are the knowledge we possess should not be confined to ourselves, but should be disseminated, at least among that class of educated Egyptians capable of appreciating it.

"What I am about to tell you is not, as a whole, fully understood perhaps by any. It is the outcome of my own reflections, founded upon the light thrown upon things by the knowledge I have gained. You asked me one day, Chebron, how we knew about the gods—how they first revealed themselves, seeing that they are not things that belong to the world? I replied to you at the time that these things are mysteries—a convenient answer with which we close the mouths of questioners."

"Listen now and I will tell you how religion first began upon earth, not only in Egypt, but in all lands. Man felt his own powerlessness. Looking at the operations of nature—the course of the heavenly bodies, the issues of birth and life and death—he concluded, and rightly, that there was a God over all things, but this God was too mighty for his imagination to grasp.

"He was everywhere and nowhere, He animated all things, and yet was nowhere to be found; He gave fertility and He caused famine, He gave life and He gave death, He gave light and heat, He sent storms and tempests. He was too infinite and too various for the untutored mind of the early man to comprehend, and so they tried to approach Him piece-meal. They worshipped Him as the sun, the giver of heat and life and fertility; they worshipped Him as a destructive god, they invoked His aid as a beneficent being, they offered sacrifices to appease His wrath as a terrible one. And so in time they came to regard all these attributes of His—all His sides and lights under which they viewed Him—as being distinct and different, and instead of all being the qualities of one God as being each the quality or attribute of separate gods.

"So there came to be a god of life and a god of death, one who sends fertility and one who causes famine. All sorts of inanimate objects were defined as possessing some fancied attribute either for good or evil, and the one almighty God became hidden and lost in the crowd of minor deities. In some nations the fancies of men went one way, in another another. The lower the intelligence of the people the lower their gods. In some countries serpents are sacred, doubtless because originally they were considered to typify at once the subtleties and the destructive power of a god. In others trees are worshipped. There are peoples who make the sun their god. Others the moon. Our forefathers in Egypt being wiser people than the savages around them, worshipped the attributes of gods under many different names. First, eight great deities were chosen to typify the chief characteristics of the Mighty One. Chnoumis, or Neuf, typified the idea of the spirit of God—that spirit which pervades all creation. Ameura, the intellect of God. Osiris, the goodness of God. Ptah typified at once the working power and the truthfulness of God. Khem represents the productive power—the god who presides over the multiplication of all species; man, beast, fish, and vegetable—and so with the rest of the great gods and of the minor divinities, which are reckoned by the score.

"In time certain animals, birds, and other creatures whose qualities are considered to resemble one or other of the deities, are in the first place regarded as typical of them, then are held as sacred to them, then in some sort of way become mixed up with the gods and to be held almost as the gods themselves. This is, I think, the history of the religions of all countries. The highest intelligences, the men of education and learning, never quite lose sight of the original truths, and recognize the gods represent only the various attributes of the one Almighty God. The rest of the population lose sight of the truth, and really worship as gods these various creations, that are really but types and shadows.

"It is perhaps necessary that it should be so. It is easier for the grosser and more ignorant classes to worship things that they can see and understand, to strive to please those whose statues and temples they behold, to fear to draw upon themselves the vengeance of those represented to them as destructive powers, than to worship an inconceivable God, without form or shape, so mighty the imagination cannot picture Him, so beneficent, so all-providing, so equable and serene that the human mind cannot grasp even a notion of Him. Man is material, and must worship the material in a form in which he thinks he can comprehend it, and so he creates gods for himself with figures, likenesses, passions, and feelings like those of the many animals he sees around him.

"The Israelite maid whom we brought hither, and with whom I have frequently conversed, tells me that her people before coming to this land worshiped but one God like unto Him of whom I have told you, save that they belittled him by deeming that he was their own special God, caring for them above all peoples of the earth; but in all other respects He corresponded with the Almighty One whom we who have gained glimpses of the truth which existed ere the Pantheon of Egypt came into existence, worship in our hearts, and it seems to me as if this little handful of men who came to Egypt hundreds of years ago were the only people in the world who kept the worship of the one god clear and undefiled."

Chebron and Amuba listened in awe-struck silence to the words of the high-priest. Amuba's face lit up with pleasure and enthusiasm as he listened to words which seemed to clear away all the doubts and difficulties that had been in his mind. To Chebron the revelation, though a joyful one, came as a great shock. His mind, too, had long been unsatisfied. He had wondered and questioned, but the destruction at one blow of all the teachings of his youth, of all he had held sacred, came at first as a terrible shock. Neither spoke when the priest concluded, and after a pause he resumed.

"You will understand, Chebron, that what I have told you is not in its entirety held even by the most enlightened, and that the sketch I have given you of the formation of all religions is, in fact, the idea which I myself have formed as a result of all I have learned, both as one initiated in all the learning of the ancient Egyptians and from my own studies both of our oldest records and the traditions of all the peoples with whom Egypt has come in contact. But that all our gods merely represent attributes of the one deity, and have no personal existence as represented in our temples, is acknowledged more or less completely by all those most deeply initiated in the mysteries of our religion.

"When we offer sacrifices we offer them not to the images behind our altar, but to God the creator, God the preserver, God the fertilizer, to God the ruler, to God the omnipotent over good and evil. Thus, you see, there is no mockery in our services, although to us they bear an inner meaning not understood by others. They worship a personality endowed with principle; we the principle itself. They see in the mystic figure the representation of a deity; we see in it the type of an attribute of a higher deity.

"You may think that in telling you all this I have told you things which should be told only to those whose privilege it is to have learned the inner mysteries of their religion, that, maybe, I am untrue to my vows. These, lads, are matters for my own conscience. Personally, I have long been impressed with the conviction that it were better that the circles of initiates should be very widely extended, and that all capable by education and intellect of appreciating the mightiness of the truth should no longer be left in darkness. I have been over-ruled, and should never have spoken had not this accident taken place; but when I see that the whole happiness of your life is at stake, that should the secret ever be discovered you will either be put to death despairing and hopeless, or have to fly and live despairing and hopeless in some foreign country, I have considered that the balance of duty lay on the side of lightening your mind by a revelation of what was within my own. And it is not, as I have told you, so much the outcome of the teaching I have received as of my own studies and a conviction I have arrived at as to the nature of God. Thus, then my son, you can lay aside the horror which you have felt at the thought that by the accidental slaying of a cat you offended the gods beyond forgiveness. The cat is but typical of the qualities attributed to Baste. Baste herself is but typical of one of the qualities of One God."

"Oh, my father!" Chebron exclaimed, throwing himself on his knees beside Ameres and kissing his hand, "how good you are. What a weight have you lifted from my mind. What a wonderful future have you opened to me if I escape the danger that threatens me now. If I have to die I can do so like one who fears not the future after death. If I live I shall no longer be oppressed with the doubts and difficulties which have so long weighed upon me. Though till now you have given me no glimpse of the great truth, I have at times felt not only that the answers you gave me failed to satisfy me, but it seemed to me also that you yourself with all your learning and wisdom were yet unable to set me right in these matters as you did in all others upon which I questioned you. My father, you have given me life, and more than life—you have given me a power over fate. I am ready now to fly, should you think it best, or to remain here and risk whatever may happen."

"I do not think you should fly, Chebron. In the first place, flight would be an acknowledgment of guilt; in the second, I do not see where you could fly. To-morrow, at latest, the fact that the creature is missing will be discovered, and as soon as it was known that you had gone a hot pursuit would be set up. If you went straight down to the sea you would probably be overtaken long before you got there; and even did you reach a port before your pursuers you might have to wait days before a ship sailed.

"Then, again, did you hide in any secluded neighbourhood, you would surely be found sooner or later, for the news will go from end to end of Egypt, and it will be everyone's duty to search for and denounce you. Messengers will be sent to all countries under Egyptian government, and even if you passed our frontiers by land or sea your peril would be as great as it is here. Lastly, did you surmount all these difficulties and reach some land beyond the sway of Egypt, you would be an exile for life. Therefore I say that flight is your last resource, to be undertaken only if a discovery is made; but we may hope that no evil fortune will lead the searchers to the conclusion that the cat was killed here.

"When it is missed there will be a search high and low in which every one will join. When the conclusion is at last arrived at that it has irrecoverably disappeared all sorts of hypotheses will be started to account for it; some will think that it probably wandered to the hills and became the prey of hyenas or other wild beasts; some will assert that it has been killed and hidden away; others that it has made its way down to the Nile and has been carried off by a crocodile. Thus there is no reason why suspicion should fall upon you more than upon others, but you will have to play your part carefully."

Chapter 11

WHEN Chebron and Amuba returned to the room set apart for their use and study their conversation did not turn upon the slaying of the cat or the danger which threatened them, but upon the wonderful revelation that Ameres had made. Neither of them thought for a moment of doubting his words. Their feeling of reverence for his wisdom and learning would have been sufficient in itself for them to accept without a question any statement that he made to them. But there was in addition their own inward conviction of the truth of his theory. It appealed at once to their heads and hearts. It satisfied all their longing and annihilated their doubts and difficulties; cleared away at once the pantheon of strange and fantastic figures that had been a source of doubting amusement to Amuba, of bewilderment to Chebron.

"The Israelite maid Ruth was right, then," Amuba said. "You know that she told us that her forefathers who came down into Egypt believed that there was one God only, and that all the others were false gods. She said that He could not be seen or pictured; that He was God of all the heavens, and so infinite that the mind of man could form no idea of Him. Everything she said of Him seems to be true, except inasmuch as she said He cared more for her ancestors than for other men; but of course each nation and people would think that."

"It is wonderful," Chebron replied as he paced restlessly up and down the room. "Now that I know the truth it seems impossible I could have really believed that all the strange images of our temples really represented gods. It worried me to think of them. I could not see how they could be, and yet I never doubted their existence. It seems to me now that all the people of Egypt are living in a sort of nightmare. Why do those who know so much suffer them to remain in such darkness?"

"I understood your father to say, Chebron, that he himself is only in favour of the more enlightened and educated people obtaining a glimpse of the truth. I think I can understand that. Were all the lower class informed that the gods they worshipped were merely shadows of a great God and not real living deities, they would either fall upon and rend those who told them so as impious liars, or, if they could be made to believe it, they would no longer hold to any religion, and in their rage might tear down the temples, abolish the order of priesthood altogether, spread tumult and havoc throughout the land, rebel against all authority, destroy with one blow all the power and glory of Egypt."

"That is true," Chebron said thoughtfully. "No doubt the ignorant mass of the people require something material to worship. They need to believe in gods who will punish impiety and wrong and reward well-doing; and the religion of Egypt, as they believe it, is better suited to their daily wants than the worship of a Deity so mighty and great and good that their intellect would fail altogether to grasp Him."

Their conversation was suddenly interrupted by the entrance of Ruth.

"Paucis is missing. When we came back from our walk we went out to the animals, and the door of the house is open and the cat has gone. Mysa says will you come at once and help look for it? I was to send all the women who can be spared from the house to join in the search."

Work was instantly abandoned, for all knew that Paucis had been chosen to be the sacred cat at Bubastes; but even had it been one of the others, the news that it was missing would have caused a general excitement. So esteemed were even the most common animals of the cat tribe that, if a cat happened to die in a house, the inhabitants went into mourning and shaved their eyebrows in token of their grief; the embalmers were sent for, the dead cat made into a mummy, and conveyed with much solemnity to the great catacombs set aside for the burial of the sacred animals. Thus the news that Paucis was missing was so important that work was at once laid aside and the men and family slaves began to search the garden thoroughly, examining every bush and tree, and calling loudly to the missing animal. Chebron and Amuba joined in the search as actively as the rest.

"Where can it be?" Mysa exclaimed. "Why should it have wandered away? It never did so before, though the door of the cat-house is often left open all day. Where do you think it can have gone to? Do you think it could have got over the wall?"

"It could get over the wall easily enough," Chebron replied.

"It is a terrible misfortune!" continued Mysa with tears in her eyes. "Mamma fainted on hearing the news, and her women are burning feathers under her nose and slapping her hands and sprinkling water on her face. Whatever will be done if it does not come back before to-morrow, for I hear a solemn procession is coming from Bubastes to fetch it away? Poor dear Paucis! And it seemed so contented and happy, and it had everything it could want! What can have induced her to wander away?"

"Cats are often uncertain things," Amuba said. "They are not like dogs, who are always ready to follow their masters, and who will lie down for hours, ready to start out whenever called upon."

"Yes, but Paucis was not a common cat, Amuba. It did not want to catch mice and birds for a living. It had everything it could possibly want—cushions to lie on, fresh water and milk to drink, and plenty of everything to eat."

"But even all that will not satisfy cats when the instinct to wander comes upon them," Amuba said.

Ameres himself soon came out of the house, and, upon hearing that the cat was not to be found either in the garden or within, gave orders for the whole of the males of the household to sally out in the search, to inform all the neighbours what had happened, and to pray them to search their gardens. They were also to make inquiries of all they met whether they had seen a cat resembling Paucis.

"This is a very serious matter," Ameres said. "After the choice of the priest of Bubastes had fixed upon Paucis to be the sacred cat of the temple of Bubastes, the greatest care and caution should have been exercised respecting an animal towards whom all the eyes of Egypt were turned. For the last two or three weeks the question as to which cat was to succeed to the post of honour has been discussed in every household. Great has been the excitement among all the families possessing cats that had the smallest chance whatever of being selected; and what will be said if the cat is not forthcoming when the precession arrives to-morrow from Bubastes to conduct her there, I tremble to think of. The excitement and stir will be prodigious, and the matter will become of state importance. Well, do not stand here, but go at once and join in the search."

"I felt horribly guilty when talking to Mysa," Chebron said. "Of course she is very proud that Paucis was chosen for the temple, but I know that she has really been grieving over the approaching loss of her favourite. But of course that was nothing to what she will feel when she finds that no news whatever can be obtained of the creature; and it was hard to play the part and to pretend to know nothing about it, when all the time one knew it was lying dead and buried in the garden."

"Yes, I felt that myself," Amuba agreed, "but we cannot help it. Mysa will probably in the course of her life have very much more serious grief to bear than the loss of a cat."

All day the search was maintained, and when it was dark great numbers of men with torches searched every point far and near on that side of Thebes. The news had now spread far and wide, and numbers of the friends of the high-priest called to inquire into the particulars of the loss and to condole with him on the calamity which had befallen his house. Innumerable theories were broached as to the course the animal would have taken after once getting out of the garden, while the chances of its recovery were eagerly discussed. The general opinion was that it would speedily be found. A cat of such remarkable appearance must, it was argued, attract notice wherever it went; and even if it did not return of its own accord, as was generally expected, it was considered certain that it would be brought back before many hours.

But when upon the following morning it was found that it had not returned and that all search for it had been fruitless, there was a feeling akin to consternation. For the first time men ventured to hint that something must have befallen the sacred cat. Either in its rambles some evil dog must have fallen upon it and slain it, or it must have been carried off by a crocodile as it quenched its thirst at a pool. That it had fallen by the hand of man no one even suggested. No Egyptian would be capable of an act of such sacrilege. The idea was too monstrous to entertain for a moment.

Mysa had cried herself to sleep, and broke forth in fresh lamentation when upon waking in the morning she heard that her favourite was still absent; while her mother took the calamity so seriously to heart that she kept her bed. The slaves went about silently and spoke with bated breath, as if a death had taken place in the house. Ameres and Chebron were both anxious and disturbed, knowing that the excitement would grow every hour; while Amuba and Jethro, joining busily in the search and starting on horse-back the first thing in the morning to make inquiries in more distant localities, were secretly amused at the fuss and excitement which was being made over the loss of a cat.

It was well for the household of Ameres that he occupied so exalted a position in the priesthood. Had he been a private citizen, the excitement, which increased hour by hour when the vigilant search carried on far and wide for the missing cat proved fruitless, would speedily have led to an outbreak of popular fury. But the respect due to the high-priest of Osiris, his position, his well-known learning and benevolence rendered it impossible for the supposition to be entertained for a moment that the cat could have come to an untimely end within the limits of his house or garden, but it was now generally believed that, after wandering away, as even the best conducted of cats will do at times, it had fallen a victim to some savage beast or had been devoured by a crocodile.

So heavy was the penalty for the offence, so tremendous the sacrilege in killing a cat, that such an act was almost unknown in Egypt, and but few instances are recorded of its having taken place. As in the present case the enormity of the act would be vastly increased by the size and beauty of the cat, and the fact that it had been chosen for the temple of Bubastes, this seemed to put it altogether beyond the range of possibility that the creature had fallen by the hands of man. When a week passed without tidings it was generally accepted as a fact that the cat must be dead, and Ameres and his household, in accordance with the custom, shaved their eyebrows in token of mourning.

Although not suspected of having had anything to do with the loss of the cat, the event nevertheless threw a sort of cloud over the household of Ameres. It was considered to be such a terrible stroke of ill-luck that a cat, and above all such a cat, should have been lost upon the very eve of her being installed as the most sacred animal in the temple of Bubastes, that it seemed as if it must be a direct proof of the anger of the gods, and there was a general shrinking on the part of their friends and acquaintances from intercourse with people upon whom such a misfortune had fallen. Ameres cared little for public opinion, and continued on his way with placid calmness, ministering in the temple and passing the rest of his time in study.

The example of Ameres, however, was wholly lost upon his wife. The deference paid to her as the wife of the high-priest, and also to herself as the principal figure in the services in which women took part, was very dear to her, and she felt the change greatly. Her slaves had a very bad time of it, and she worried Ameres with constant complaints as to the changed demeanour of her acquaintances and his indifference to the fact that they were no longer asked to entertainments; nor was she in any way pacified by his quiet assurances that it was useless for them to irritate themselves over trifles, and that matters would mend themselves in time. But as the days went on, so far from mending things became worse, groups of people frequently assembled round the house, and shouts of anger and hatred were raised when any of the occupants entered or left. Even when Ameres was passing through the streets in procession with the sacred emblems hoots and cries were raised among the crowd. Chebron took this state of things greatly to heart, and more than once he implored his father to allow him to declare the truth openly and bear the consequences.

"I am not afraid of death, father. Have you not trained me to regard life as of no account? Do we not in our feasts always see the image of the dead man carried past to remind us that death is always among us? You have Mysa and my mother. I fear death far less than this constant anxiety that is hanging over us."

But Ameres would not hear of the sacrifice.

"I do not pretend that there is no danger, Chebron. I thought at first that the matter would soon pass over, but I own that I was wrong. The unfortunate fact that the creature was chosen as sacred cat for the temple at Bubastes has given its loss a prominence far beyond that which there would have been had it been an ordinary animal of its class, and the affair has made an extraordinary sensation in the city. Still I cannot but think that an enemy must be at work stirring up the people against me. I suspect, although I may be wrong, that Ptylus is concerned in the matter. Since he reappeared after his sudden absence following the night when you overheard that conversation, he has affected a feeling of warmth and friendship which I believe has been entirely feigned.

"Whether he was one of those you overheard I am unable to say, but his sudden disappearance certainly favours that idea. At any rate, he can have no real reason for any extra cordiality towards me at present, but would more naturally still feel aggrieved at my rejection of his son as a husband for Mysa. I thought at first when you told me what you had overheard that possibly it was a plot against my life. Now I feel sure of it.

"No doubt they believe, as no measures were taken, that their conversation was not overheard or that only a few words reached the listeners, and his manner to me is designed to allay any suspicion I might have conceived had as much of the conversation as was overheard been reported to me. It has had just the opposite effect. At any rate, an enemy is at work, and even were you to sacrifice yourself by admitting that you slew the missing animal, not only would your death be the result, but a general ruin would fall upon us.

"The mob would easily be taught to believe that I must to a great extent be responsible; the opinions I have expressed would be quoted against me, and even the favour of the king could not maintain me in my present position in defiance of popular clamour. No, my son, we must stand or fall altogether, Jethro offered yesterday if I liked to dig up the remains of the cat, carry it away and hide it under some rocks at a distance, but I think the danger would be greater than in allowing matters to remain as they are. It is certain that the house is watched. As you know, servants going in and out after nightfall have been rudely hustled and thrown down. Some have been beaten, and returned well-nigh stripped to the skin. I doubt not that these attacks were made in order to discover if they had anything concealed under their garments. Were Jethro to venture upon such an attempt he might either be attacked and the cat found upon him, or he might be followed and the place where he hid it marked down. Things must go on as they are."

Ameres did not tell Chebron the whole of the conversation he had had with Jethro. After declining his offer to endeavour to dispose of the body of the cat elsewhere he said:

"But, Jethro, although I cannot accept this perilous enterprise you have offered to undertake, I will entrust you with a charge that will show you how I confide in your devotion to my family. Should this storm burst, should the populace of this town once become thoroughly imbued with the idea that the sacred cat has been slain here, there will be an outburst of fanatical rage which will for the time carry all before it.

"For myself I care absolutely nothing. I am perfectly willing to die as soon as my time comes. I have done my work to the best of my power, and can meet the Mighty One with uplifted head. I have wronged no man, and have laboured all my life for the good of the people. I have never spared myself, and am ready for my rest; but I would fain save Chebron and Mysa from harm. Even in their wrath the populace will not injure the women, but Mysa without a protector might fall into evil hands. As to her, however, I can do nothing; but Chebron I would save. If he grows up he will, I think, do good in the world. He has not the strength and vigour of Amuba, but he is not behind other lads his age. He has been well educated. His mind is active and his heart good. I look to you, Jethro, to save him, it if be possible, with Amuba, for I fear that Amuba is in as much danger as he is.

"Should the slaves be seized and questioned, and perhaps flogged, till they say what they know, the fact would be sure to come out that the two lads were together among the animals on the morning before the cat was missed. It will be noticed, too, that they took with them their bows and arrows. It will therefore be assumed that the responsibility of the act lies upon both of them. Chebron, I know, would proclaim the truth if he had an opportunity for speech, but an angry crowd does not stop to listen, and the same fate will befall them both.

"You who are stranger to our manners can hardly conceive the frenzy of excitement and rage in which the population of Egypt are thrown by the killing of a cat. I doubt whether even the king's person would be held sacred were the guilt of such an offence brought home to him; and, of course, the fact that this unfortunate beast was to have gone to the temple of Bubastes makes the death a matter ten times graver than ordinary. Therefore should the storm burst, there is no hope for either of them but in flight. The question is, whither could they fly?

"Certainly they would be safe nowhere in Egypt. Nor, were it possible that they could journey north and reach the sea, could they do so before the news reached the ports. Naturally messengers would be sent to the frontier towns, and even the governors of the provinces lying east of the Great Sea would hear of it; and could they leave the country and cross the desert they might be seized and sent back on their arrival. For the same reason the routes from here to the ports on the Arabian Sea are closed to them. It seems to me that their only hope of safety lies in reaching the country far up the Nile and gaining Meroe, over whose people the authority of Egypt is but a shadow; thence possibly they might some day reach the Arabian Sea, cross that and pass up through the country east of the Great Sea, and travelling by the route by which you came hither reach your country. Long before they could leave the savage tribes and start upon their journey, this matter would have been forgotten, and whatever dangers might befall them, that of arrest for participation in this matter would not be among them.

"I know that your fidelity and friendship for the son of your late king would cause you to risk all dangers and hardships for his sake, and that if bravery and prudence could take him safely through such terrible dangers as would be encountered in such a journey as I speak of, you will conduct him through them. I ask you to let Chebron share your protection, and to render him such service as you will give to Amuba."

"I can promise that willingly, my lord," Jethro answered. "He has treated Amuba more as a brother than a servant since we came here, and I will treat him as if he were a brother to Amuba, now that danger threatens. The journey you speak of would, indeed, be a long and dangerous one; but I agree with you that only by accomplishing it is there even a chance of escape."

"Then I commit my son to your charge, Jethro, and I do so with full confidence that if it be possible for him to make this journey in safety he will do so. I have already placed in the hands of Chigron, the embalmer, a large sum of money. You can trust him absolutely. It is through my patronage that he has risen from being a small worker to be the master of one of the largest businesses in Egypt, and he has the embalming of all the sacred animals belonging to our temple and several others. He will hide the boys for a time until you are ready to start on your journey.

"When you are once a few days south of Thebes you will be fairly safe from pursuit, for they will never think of looking for you in that direction, but will make sure that you will attempt to leave the country either by sea, by the Eastern Desert, or that you may possibly try to reach some of the tribes in the west, and so to go down upon the Great Sea there. I thought at first that this might be the best direction; but the tribes are all subject to us and would naturally regard Egyptians going among them as fugitives from justice, and so hand them over to us."

"You can rely upon me, my lord, to carry out your directions and do all that is possible to serve the two lads. What the country through which we have to pass is like, or its inhabitants, I know not, but at least we will do our best to reach the Arabian Sea as you direct. Amuba is hardy and strong, and Chebron, though less powerful in frame, is courageous, and able to use his weapons. We should, of course, travel in disguise. But you spoke something about your daughter—in what way can I serve her? I have now accompanied her in her walks for months, and would lay down my life for her."

"I fear that you can do nothing," Ameres said after a pause. "We have many friends, one of whom will doubtless receive her. At first I would, if it were possible, that she should go to some relatives of mine who live at Amyla, fifty miles up the river. She was staying with them two years ago and will know the house; but I do not see how you could take her—the boys will be sufficient charge on your hands. She will have her mother with her, and though I fear that the latter has little real affection for her, having no time to think of aught but her own pleasure and amusement, she will be able to place her among the many friends she has.

"It is not her present so much I am thinking of as her future. I should like my little Mysa to marry happily. She is a little self-willed, and has been indulged; and although, of course, she would marry as I arrange for her, I would not give her to any one who was not altogether agreeable to her. I fear that should anything happen to me the same consideration might not be paid to her inclinations. However, Jethro, I see no manner in which you can be useful to Mysa. So far as she is concerned things must be left to take their own course."

"I trust," Jethro said, "that your foreboding will not be verified. I cannot believe that an absurd suspicion can draw away the hearts of the people from one whom they have so respected as yourself."

Ameres shook his head.

"The people are always fickle, Jethro, and easily led; and their love and respect for the gods renders it easy for anyone who works on that feeling to lash them into fury. All else is as nothing in their eyes in comparison with their religion. It is blind worship, if you will; but it is a sincere one. Of all the people in the world there are none to whom religion counts so much as to the Egyptians. It is interwoven with all their daily life. Their feasts and processions are all religious, they eat and drink and clothe themselves according to its decrees, and undertake no action, however trifling, without consulting the gods. Thus, therefore, while in all other respects obedience is paid to the law, they are maddened by any supposed insult to their religion, or any breach of its observances. I know that we are in danger. The ideas that I have held of the regeneration of the people by purifying their religious beliefs have been used as weapons against me. I know from what has come to my ears that it has been hinted among them that in spite of my high office I have no respect for the gods.

"The accusation is false, but none the less dangerous for that. Nothing is more difficult than to expose or annihilate a falsehood. It spreads like wild-fire, and the clearest demonstration of its falsity fails to reach a tithe of those who believe it. However, it is needless to speak of it now. You know what I wish you to do if danger comes—get the boys away, and conduct them to the place I have indicated. If they are from home seek them and take them there. Do not waste time in vain attempts to succour me. If you are attacked, and this may possibly be the case, make, I pray you, no resistance save such as may be needed to get away. Above all, do not try to interfere on my behalf. One man, though endowed with supernatural strength, cannot overcome a mob, and your trying to aid me would not benefit me, and might cost you your life, and so deprive Chebron and Amuba of their protector."

Jethro promised strictly to follow the instructions he had received, and to devote himself in case of need solely to insuring the safety of the boys.

Two days later, Ameres sent Chebron and Amuba away to the farm, and told them to remain there until he sent for them.

"You cannot go in and out here without unpleasantness," he said, "and had best be away. Your presence here can be of no use, and you are probably quite as much suspected as I am. As to your mother and sister, the present state of things is inconvenient to them, but that is all. There can be no danger for them; however violent a mob they would not molest females."

"Why should not you also, father, go away until the trouble is passed?"

"I cannot leave my duties, Chebron; nor would it benefit me if I did. I am convinced that this cry against us is a mere pretext which has been seized by enemies who dare not attack me openly. Were I to depart from Thebes my absence would be denounced as a proof of my guilt, and the people be inflamed more and more against me, and nowhere in Egypt should I be safe. My only course is to face the storm, trusting to the integrity of my life, to the absence of any deed which would offend the great God I believe in, and to the knowledge that my life is in His hands. When it is His will, and not before, it will return to Him who gave it me."

"Could you not apply to the king for guards?"

"The king spoke to me yesterday at the termination of the council," Ameres replied, "and told me that he had been informed of the murmurs of the populace against me. He said that as one of his most trusted counsellors, and as a high-priest of Osiris, he knew that the charges against me were baseless; but that in view of the proneness of the people of Thebes to excitement and tumult, he should be glad to order a company of soldiers to keep guard over my house. I refused. I said that I was conscious of no evil, that none could say that I was slack in my ministrations in the temple, or that I had ever spoken a word in disrespect of our religion. That as for the disappearance of the sacred cat, of which so much had been made, I had had no hand in it, and that whatever had happened to it had been, I was sure, the result of accident. Were I to have soldiers placed to guard me it would be a confession that I was conscious of ill-doing and knew that I had forfeited the protection of the gods. It would, too, help to keep up the talk and excitement, which I trust would die away ere long."

Chebron did not think of further questioning the orders of Ameres, and an hour later he and Amuba rode out to the farm. Before they started Ameres had a long talk with Chebron, and told him that he had placed him in charge of Jethro, in the event of any popular outbreak taking place.

"Remember, Chebron," he said, "that whatever comes of this affair you are not to blame yourself for the accident of killing the cat. All things are in the hands of the great God, and your arrow would not have struck the twig and flown straight to the heart of that creature had it not been His will. Moreover, you must always remember that the loss of this cat is but a pretext for the tumult.

"The populace believe that they are angry on account of the loss of the sacred cat, whereas, in fact, they are but instruments in the hands of my enemies. I have no doubt whatever now that the plot you overheard in the temple was directed against my life, and had not the loss of the cat happened opportunely and served them as a lever with which to work against me, the plot would have taken some other form. I trust sincerely that whatever fate may befall your sister she may never have to marry the son of the man who has plotted against my life. But it is no use thinking of that now. Should aught happen before we meet again, remember I have placed you in the hands of Jethro, and have delegated my authority to him. He is shrewd, strong, and courageous, and can be relied upon to do what is best. In Amuba you will find a friend who will be as a brother to you. So farewell, my son, and may the Great One who rules all things keep you!"

A stay at the farm had hitherto been regarded by Chebron as a delightful change from the city, but upon this occasion he proceeded there sad and depressed in spirit.

"Even here we are watched, you see, Chebron," Amuba said as they rode along. "Do you see those runners behind us? Doubtless they will follow us to the farm, and set a watch upon us there. However, there at least, they can search as much as they like, and find out nothing."

Chapter 12

THE days passed slowly at the farm. The lads went out listlessly to watch the cattle treading in the seed and the other operations on the lands, but they were too anxious as to what was going on in the city to feel the slightest interest in the work of the farm. The second and fourth days after their coming, Jethro had paid them a short visit to say that there was no change in the situation. The officer in command of some troops whom the king had sent down to within a short distance of the house had come down to the mob as they were shouting outside the gate, and threatened them with the severe displeasure of the king unless they desisted from their demonstrations, but had been answered with shouts, "The gods are above all kings, and not even kings can protect those who insult them." Amense, he said, on the occasion of his second visit, had left the house and taken up her abode with some relation in the city, declaring that the anxiety and disgrace were killing her. She had wished to take Mysa with her, but the girl had positively refused to leave her father; and as her mother seemed indifferent whether she went or stayed she had had her way. In a private talk with Amuba, Jethro said:

"It is a relief to us all that she has gone; she was bad enough before you went, but for the last three days she has been doing nothing but weep and bewail herself till the house has been well-nigh unbearable. Ameres goes backward and forward between his house and the temple, walking unmoved through those gathered near his door, who are for the most part quiet when he passes, being abashed by the presence of one who has so long been held in high esteem among them. As for Mysa, she seems to think only of her father. The Hebrew girl is a great comfort to her, for while the example of their mistress and the shouts of the populace have terribly scared the other maids, and they go about the house in fear and trembling, Ruth is quiet and self-contained as if she were again in her quiet cottage with her grandfather. She greatly comforts and sustains Mysa, and Ameres said to me only this morning that Mysa was fortunate indeed in that Chebron had furnished her with so brave and steadfast a companion at a time like this."

On the evening of the fifth day Jethro came suddenly in at the house. The boys started to their feet as he entered, for they saw at once that something terrible had happened. His face was stained with blood, his breath came short, for he had run for the six intervening miles between the farm and the city at the top of his speed.

"Quick, my lord!" he said, "there is not a moment to lose. The whole matter has been discovered, and ere long they will be here in pursuit of you."

"What of my father?" Chebron exclaimed.

"I will tell you all about it afterwards, Chebron. There is no time for talking now, his orders must be instantly carried out. Where are the fellows who are spying over you?"

"One of them is probably seated outside at the entrance to the farm. You must have passed him as you entered," Amuba replied. "I have not seen more than one at a time since they first came."

"Take up your arms and follow me," Jethro said, taking a heavy staff from the corner of the room, and, followed by the lads, he went outside the gate.

It was now getting dark, and as they passed out a man standing near approached as if to see who they were. Without a word Jethro sprang forward and brought down the staff with tremendous force upon his head, and the man fell without a cry upon the road.

"There is no fear of his giving the alarm," Jethro said grimly, and set off in a run in the direction of the city at a pace that taxed the powers of Chebron to keep up with. Once or twice as he ran the boy gasped out a question as to his father's safety, but Jethro did not appear to hear him, but kept on at a steady pace. Presently he stopped suddenly and listened. A vague, confused sound was heard in front of them, and Jethro quitted the road and took his course over the fields. Amuba heard the sound increase, and was presently conscious that a crowd of people were passing along the road.

"It is well I managed to get through," Jethro said. "They would have made short work of you both had they arrived at the farm and found you unprepared."

Jethro did not return to the road, but kept on in an oblique line towards the foot of the hills near the city.

"Where are you going, Jethro?" Amuba asked at last.

"I am going to Chigron, the embalmer. Ameres has arranged with him to hide you there for the present."

The boys knew the place, for they had more than once been there to watch the process of embalming the bodies and preparing them for burial. It was an extensive establishment, for Chigron was one of the most celebrated embalmers of the day; and not only did he embalm, but he kept with him men who performed the further processes required, namely, the wrapping up in the mummy cloths, and the construction of the great cases and the placing the bodies in them ready to be handed over to their friends. These were usually distinct and separate trades, the embalmers generally returning the bodies to the friends after they had completed the process of embalming. Another set of men then prepared the corpse for burial, while the mummy-cases or sarcophagi were prepared by men of another trade. Of the three trades, that of the embalmers was held in by far the highest respect, the work being considered as sacred and the embalmers ranking and associating with the priests.

In Chigron's establishment the men of the three trades worked apart and separate from each other; and although Chigron was in fact at the head of all, he personally superintended only the embalming, the men of the other trades being directed by their own masters, and it was as if the three establishments had been placed near each other simply for the purpose of convenience.

When they reached the house of Chigron Jethro went forward alone and knocked at the door. An attendant presented himself. "Give this ring to Chigron," Jethro said, "and say that the bearer of it would fain speak to him here."

In two or three minutes Chigron himself came out.

"I have brought the lads hither in obedience to the order of Ameres," Jethro said. "He told me that he had arranged the matter with you."

"And Ameres himself?" Chigron asked.

"He is no more," Jethro said. "The villains who sought his ruin have triumphed, and a furious mob this afternoon broke into his house and murdered him. Chebron does not know it yet, though he cannot but suspect that something terrible has happened, as I would not answer his questions, fearing that he might break down when his strength was most needed."

The Egyptian uttered an exclamation of sorrow. "Fools and madmen!" he exclaimed; "in all the land none were more worthy of honour than Ameres. He was just and generous, ever ready to befriend those who needed his aid, calm in judgment, and powerful in council. Surely the gods must be angry with Egypt when they suffered such a one to fall a victim to the passions of the mob. But where are the lads? I myself will conduct them to the place I have already prepared. The workers have all left, so there is no fear in passing through the house."

At Jethro's call the lads came up.

"Follow me, my lord," Chigron said to Chebron, "I have had everything in readiness for your reception for some days. Would that your visit had been made on some more cheerful occasion."

The embalmer led the way through the portion of the house occupied by himself, then he entered a large apartment whose floor was covered with saw-dust.

Here on slabs of stone lay a number of bodies of those in the first state of preparation, while in a still larger apartment behind were a number of stone baths each long enough to contain a body. These were occupied by the corpses which had undergone their first state of preparation, and which were now lying covered with a strong solution of salt and water. Beyond again were other chambers for the reception of bodies embalmed by other processes than that of salt.

Passing through a door at the rear the lads found themselves in the open air again. Above them the hill rose in a precipitous rock. Chigron led the way along the foot of this for some little distance, and then stopped at a portal hewn in the rock itself. All this time he had carried a lighted lamp, although the chambers in which the dead were lying were illuminated with lamps hanging from the ceiling. Upon entering the portal and closing the door behind him he produced from a niche in the wall several other lamps, lighted them, and gave one to each of his companions.

"This," he said, "was cut by a wealthy inhabitant of Thebes centuries ago as a tomb for himself and his family. What happened to him I know not, but the place was never used beyond this chamber, which has been utilized for mummies of sacred animals. Beyond in the main chamber everything is as it was left by those who formed it. There I have during the last ten days privately stored up such articles as would be necessary for you, and I trust that you will not find yourself uncomfortable."

Upon entering the apartment, which was some twenty feet square, they found that the embalmer had not exaggerated what he had done. A table with several settles stood in the middle; three couches piled with rushes were placed against the wall. Mats had been laid down to cover the floor and give warmth to the feet, and lamps ready for burning stood upon the table. In a corner stood two jars of wine, with drinking vessels.

"All is here except food," Chigron said. "That I could not prepare until I knew you were coming; but be assured that you shall be served regularly. There is no fear of intrusion from any employed in the establishment. They have no occasion to come out to the back of the house, and probably few know of the existence of the tomb. Should I have any ground for believing that there is danger, I will take other measures for your concealment. Should you need anything, do no hesitate to say so. I owe my position to the patronage of my lord Ameres, and there is nothing I would not do to ensure the safety of his son. And now, my lord, I will retire, and will presently send you by a trusty servant the food of which I have no doubt that you stand in need."

Chebron said a few words in thanks, but he was too anxious and full of grief to say more. Directly Chigron had left he turned to Jethro.

"Now, Jethro, tell me all; I am prepared for the worst. My dear father is no more. Is it not so?"

"It is true, Chebron," Jethro replied. "Your noble father has been killed by a base and cowardly mob urged on by some villains of the priesthood."

Chebron threw himself down on one of the couches and wept bitterly, while Amuba was almost as deeply affected, for Ameres had behaved to him with the kindness of a father. It was not until the following morning that Chebron was sufficiently recovered to ask Jethro to relate to him the details of his father's death.

"I was in the garden," Jethro began. "Mysa and Ruth were in a boat on the pond, and I was towing them when I heard a tumult at the gate. I pulled the boat ashore, and hurried them up to the house and told Mysa to retire to her apartment, and that she was not to leave it whatever noise she might hear, that being her father's command. Then I went out to the gate. Just as I got there it fell in, and a crowd of people rushed through. As there were only myself and two or three of the gardeners who had run up we could do nothing to stop them. Just as they reached the house your father came out into the portico and said, 'Good people, what will you have?'

"Those in front of him were silent a moment, abashed by his presence and the calm manner in which he spoke, but others behind set up a cry 'Where is the sacred cat? We will find it!' while others again shouted out 'Down with the impious priest!' Ameres replied, 'You can search the place if you will; though, indeed, it seems that you need not my permission, seeing that you have taken the matter into your own hands. Only I pray you enter not the house. There are the ladies of my family and other women there, and I swear to you that neither alive nor dead is the cat to be found there.'

"The cry was raised, 'Let us search the garden!' In all this it struck me that there were two parties among the mob, the one ignorant and bigoted, believing really that an offence had been committed against their gods; the other, men who kept in the background, but who were the moving spirits. I was not pleased when I saw the crowd so readily abandon the idea of searching the house and scatter themselves over the garden, for it seemed to me that from one of the gardeners or others they might have obtained some sort of clue that might put them on the road to discovery. I saw that several among the crowd had with them dogs trained for the chase, and this made me more uneasy. I told one of the men to run at once and summon the troops, and then followed the crowd.

"I was the more uneasy to see that without wasting time in searching elsewhere they made straight to the inclosure where the animals were kept. No sooner did they get there than they began to search, urging on the dogs to assist them. Suddenly I started, for there was a touch upon my shoulder, and looking round I saw

Ameres, 'Remember, my instructions, Jethro,' he said in a quiet voice; 'I commit Chebron to your charge.'

" 'Oh, my lord!' I exclaimed, 'why are you here? The troops are but a short distance away. Why do you not place yourself under their protection?'

" 'Because I have done no wrong, Jethro,' he replied calmly. 'I have not offended the gods, nor have I ever wronged one of my countrymen. Why should I fly?'

"At this moment there was a yell of rage among the crowd, and I knew that one of the accursed hounds must have smelled the dead cat and scratched the earth from over it. Then I heard a voice cry above the rest, 'See! even now the wounds are manifest; it has been pierced by an arrow, ever as I told you. The sacred cat has been slain!' Then the crowd turned. 'Fly, Jethro,' Ameres said. 'It is my last command.'

"But even then I could not obey him. There was death in the eyes of those who were rushing towards him shouting 'Down with the despiser of the gods! Down with the slayer of the sacred cat!' and seeing that, I rushed at them. After that all was confusion. I had caught up a staff from the portico as I passed, and with it I struck right and left. Many fell, I know, before they closed with me. Blows were showered upon me, and the staff then fell from my hands, but I fought with my naked fists. Several times I was beaten down, but each time I rose again. Then, as in a dream, I seemed to hear your father command, 'I commit Chebron to your care,' and I burst my way through them and threw myself upon a group standing further on, but I saw as I broke through them that I could do nothing there. Your father lay on the ground looking as calm and peaceful as when he had spoken to me but five minutes before; but his white garments were stained with blood, and the half of a dagger stood up just over his heart. There was no time to see more. His last command was to be obeyed, and shaking off those who tried to hold me, and evading the blows aimed at me with their knives, I fled. As I rushed out through the gate I saw the troops I had sent for coming towards the house. But they were too late now; besides, some of my pursuers were close behind me, and so without a pause I took the road to the farm. I think that is all I have to tell you."

Chebron was weeping bitterly, and Amuba, who was himself deeply affected, went over to him.

"Console yourself, Chebron. I know what you are feeling now, but do not blame yourself too greatly for the calamity. You know what your father said—that it was but an accident, and that it was doubtless the will of the great God that your arrow should fly as it did; and he himself declared that he believed that all this was but the result of conspiracy, and that, as we heard in the temple, there were men determined to take his life."

A few minutes later the embalmer entered bringing them food. He saw at once that Chebron had been informed of the fate that had befallen his father.

"Have you heard aught of what is passing in the city?" Amuba asked him.

"Yes," Chigron answered; "naught else is talked about. Many of those concerned in the deed escaped either by the entrance before the soldiers arrived there, or over the walls; but many were seized, and are now in prison for their sacrilegious deed in raising their hand against the person of the high-priest of Osiris. There were tumults in the city during the night, many maintaining that the deed was well done, others the contrary.

"Those who had been taken all declared that they had been informed by one who said he knew it for certain that the cat was buried in the inclosure, and that it had been slain by you and my young lord here, as you had been seen going with your bows and arrows to the inclosure and were there for some time, after which the cat was never seen again. The general opinion is that though the prisoners taken will be punished—some with flogging, some with death—your lives are also assuredly forfeited, and that even the friendship of the king for your father would not avail to protect you, for that he, like others, must obey the law, and that the law of Egypt is that whosoever shall take the life of a cat shall be slain."

"I am perfectly willing to die," Chebron said; "and my greatest regret now is that I did not follow my first impulse and denounce myself as the accidental killer of the cat. No blame could have then been attached to my father or to any but myself."

"The disgrace would have fallen upon your whole family," the embalmer said; "for those nearly related to one who performed an impious action must needs suffer with him. Not that I blame you, Chebron; for I know that your father did not do so. He told me when he arranged that I should, if needs be, furnish you with a hiding-place, that although you might need a refuge it would be for no fault of your own. I do not understand how he could have said so, seeing the terrible guilt of even accidentally taking the life of a cat, and specially of this cat, which was sacred above all others in the land. Still I know your father's wisdom equalled his goodness; and although I own that I cannot understand his saying, I am content to accept it, and will do all in my power to save you. Doubtless the search after you will be a hot one, but we must hope for the best."

"I will go out and see what is doing," Jethro said. "It may be that it will be more safe to move away at once than to remain here."

"In that case," the embalmer said, "you will need to be disguised before you start. It is known that Ameres had two fair-skinned slaves, and that one of them was concerned with my young lord here in the matter; also that the other, after fighting furiously in the garden, and, as I heard slaying several of his master's enemies, managed to make his escape. Fortunately I have the materials at hand. We use paints and stains in abundance for the sere clothes of the dead and the decorations of their coffins, and I can easily make you as dark as any of our people. That, with one of my wigs and Egyptian garments, will alter you so that, so long as you do not look any one fairly in the face, there will be no fear whatever of your discovery; but you must not look up, for even when I have blackened your lashes the lightness of your eyes would at once betray you."

In half an hour Jethro was transformed into a middle class-citizen of Thebes, and started on his mission of inquiry. During the day some officials came to the establishment and made many inquiries after the missing lads. Not contented with denials, they went through the whole buildings, examining all the chambers closely.

"It is known," they said to Chigron, "that they several times came here, and that Ameres was a patron of yours. It is our duty to search any house where shelter might have been given them, though we can hardly believe that any one would hold communication, far less receive into his house, persons guilty of such an act of sacrilege as they have been. However, there is no chance of their escaping us. Messages have been sent all over Egypt. Moreover, as they had no horses they cannot have gone far. Yours is the first house we have searched, for the servants all say the same—that the son of Ameres was frequently here."

"He was not here very frequently," Chigron replied, "though he certainly came sometimes, and was interested in watching the various processes."

Chebron had, in fact been several times to the embalmer's. Amuba had accompanied him, although he himself would have preferred staying away, for to him the whole scene was repulsive. Chebron's temperament differed, however, widely from that of his friend. The dead were sacred in Egypt, and all the rites and ceremonies connected with them bore a religious character. They had no fear of death, and deemed it but a sleep that would last three thousand years. It was for this reason the bodies of human beings and the sacred animals were so carefully embalmed and laid away either in massive tombs or rock-hewn caverns.

They believed, and as had been proved rightly, that the remains so carefully prepared would endure for that time, and thought that when the spirit returned to it it would resume its former shape in all particulars. Thus the dead of all ranks were embalmed; the process, however, in the case of the wealthy differing widely from that to which the bodies of the poorer classes were submitted. There were many kinds of embalming, varying according to the means of the family of the deceased. The process employed for the wealthy was a long and expensive one. First, an official called a scribe marked on the side of the corpse where an aperture should be made; this was cut by another person, who after doing so fled, pursued with execrations and pelted with stones, as although necessary the operation was considered a dishonourable one and as an injury to the sacred body. Through this aperture the embalmers removed the whole of the internal organs, which, after being cleansed and embalmed in spices, were deposited in four vases, which were subsequently placed in the tomb with the coffins. Each of these vases contained the parts sacred to a separate deity. The body was then filled with aromatic resin and spices, and rubbed for thirty days with a mixture of the same ingredients. In the case of the very wealthy the whole body was then gilt; in other cases only the face and portions of the body. The skin of the mummy so preserved is found to be of an olive colour, dry and flexible as if tanned; the features are preserved and appear as during life, and the teeth, hair of the head, and eyebrows are well preserved.

In some cases, instead of the aromatic resin, the bodies were filled with bitumen; in others saltpetre was used, the bodies being soaked in it for a long time and finally filled with resin and bitumen. In the second quality of mummies, those of persons of the middle class, the incision was not made, but resin or bitumen was used and the bodies soaked in salt for a long time. In the case of the poorer classes the bodies were simply dipped into liquid pitch. None of these, however, were treated in the establishment of Chigron, who operated only upon the bodies of the wealthy.

After the preparation was complete the body passed from the hands of the embalmers into those of another class, who enveloped it in its coverings. These were linen bandages, which in the case of the rich were sometimes a thousand yards in length. It was then inclosed in a sort of case fitting closely to the mummied body. This case was richly painted, covered in front with a network of beads and bugles arranged in a tasteful form, the face being overlaid with thick gold leaf and the eyes made of enamel. This again was placed in other cases, sometimes three or four in number, all similarly ornamented with painting and gilding, and the whole inclosed in a sarcophagus or coffin of wood or stone, profusely decorated with painting and sculpture. It was then handed over to the family of the deceased, and afterwards taken in solemn procession across the sacred lake, followed by the mourning relatives throwing dust upon their heads.

Every Egyptian city had a lake of this kind, either natural or artificial. Notice was given beforehand to the judges and public of the day on which the funeral would take place, and these assembled at the side of the lake, where the decorated boat in readiness for the passage was lying. Before the coffin could be placed upon the boat it was lawful for any person present to bring forward his accusation against the deceased. If it could be proved that he had led an evil life the judge declared that the body was deprived of the accustomed sepulture. If the accused failed to establish his charge he was subject to the heaviest penalties. If there was no accuser or if the accusation was not proved the judge declared the dead man innocent. The body was placed in the boat and carried across the lake, and then either taken to the family catacombs or to the room specially prepared for its reception in the house of the deceased.

The greatest grief and shame were felt by the family of those deprived of the right of sepulture, for they believed that thereby he was excluded from the mansions of the blessed, and that in the course of the transmigrations through which his spirit would pass before it again returned to a human form, it might be condemned to inhabit the body of an unclean animal.

As none from the lowest to the very highest rank could escape the ordeal of public accusation after death, there can be little doubt that this ceremony exercised a most wholesome effect upon the life of the Egyptians, and was most efficacious in repressing tyranny, cruelty, and vice of all kinds among them. Even the most powerful kings were restrained by the knowledge that should they give cause of complaint to their subjects they were liable after death to be accused and deprived of the right of lying in the mighty tombs they had so carefully prepared for their reception.

Chebron's brain therefore, while he was watching the process of embalming, was busy with thoughts and fancies as to the future of the spirit that had inhabited the body he looked at.

Had it already passed into the body of some animal? Was it still disconnected and searching for an abode? Through what changes would it pass and how long would be the time before it returned to this human tenement? For the three thousand years was believed to be the shortest period of transition through the various changes in the case of the man of the purest and most blameless life, while in other cases the period was vastly extended.

As Amuba was not gifted with a strong imagination, and saw in the whole matter merely the preservation of a body which in his opinion had much better have been either buried or placed on a funeral pile and destroyed by fire, these visits to the embalmers had constituted the most unpleasant part of his duties as Chebron's companion.

Jethro had anticipated when he left that his visit to the city would be of short duration, and that he should return in an hour at the latest; but as the day passed and night fell without his return the lads became exceedingly anxious, and feared that something serious had taken place to detain him. Either his disguise had been detected and he had been seized by the populace, or some other great misfortune must have befallen him.

It had been arranged indeed that they should that night have started upon their journey, and Jethro after his return was to have made out a list of such articles as he deemed necessary for their flight, and these Chigron had promised to purchase for him. Their plans, however, were completely upset by his non-appearance, and late in the afternoon Chigron himself went down into the city to ascertain, if he could, if Jethro had been discovered, for his name had been associated with that of the boys. It was not believed indeed that he had taken any actual part in the slaying of the cat, but it was deemed certain from his close connection with them, and his disappearance shortly before the time they had suddenly left the farm, that he was in league with them. Chigron returned with the news that so far as he could learn nothing had been heard of Jethro.

No other subject was talked of in the city but the event of the previous day, and the indignation of the people was equally divided between the murderers of Ameres and the slayers of the sacred cat. The boys were full of grief and perplexity. To Amuba Jethro had taken the place of an elder brother. He had cheered him in the darkest moment of his life and had been his friend and companion ever since, and the thought that ill might have befallen him filled him with sorrow. With this was mingled an intense anxiety as to the future. Without Jethro's strong arm and advice how was this terrible journey to be accomplished?

Chebron was in no state either to act or plan. A deep depression had seized upon him; he cared not whether he escaped or not, and would indeed have hailed detection and death as boons. Intense, therefore, was Amuba's relief when late in the evening a footstep was heard in the outer chamber, and Jethro entered. He sprang to his feet with a cry of gladness.

"Oh, Jethro! Thank the gods you have returned. I have suffered terribly on your account. What has happened to you, and so long delayed your return here?"

"There is fresh trouble," Jethro replied in a stern voice.

"Fresh trouble, Jethro? In what way?" And even Chebron, who had scarcely sat up languidly on his couch on Jethro's entrance, looked up with some interest for Jethro's answer.

"Mysa has been carried off," he replied grimly.

Chebron sprang to his feet. He was devoted to his sister, and for a moment this new calamity effaced the remembrance of those which had preceded it.

"Mysa carried off!" he exclaimed at the same moment as Amuba. "Who has done it?—when was it done?—how did you learn it?" were questions which broke quickly from the lads.

"On leaving here I went as arranged down into the city," Jethro replied. "There was no difficulty in learning what there was to learn, for all business seemed suspended and the streets were full of groups of people talking over the events of yesterday. The whole city is shaken by the fact that two such terrible acts of sacrilege as the slaying of the sacred cat of Bubastes and the murder of a high-priest of Osiris should have taken place within so short a time of each other. All prophesy that some terrible calamity will befall the land, and that the offended gods will in some way wreak their vengeance upon it. A royal order has been issued enjoining all men to search for and arrest every person concerned in the murder of Ameres, and doubtless the severest penalties will be dealt to them. The same decree orders your arrest wherever found, and enjoins upon all officials throughout the kingdom to keep a strict watch in the towns and villages, to examine any strangers who may present themselves, and to send hither bound in chains all young men who may fail to give a satisfactory account of themselves. Sacrifices will be offered up at all the temples throughout the land to appease the wrath of the gods. Messengers have been despatched in all directions in the provinces, and all seemed to consider it certain that in a few hours our hiding-place would be discovered. All made sure that we had made either for the sea-coast or the desert on one side or the other, and as the messengers would reach the coast long before we could do so, it was considered impossible for us to get through unnoticed.

"Then I went to the house, not intending to go in, but simply to see if those in the neighbourhood had heard any further news. The gates were open, and quite a crowd of people were passing in and out to gratify their curiosity by gazing on the scene. Relying upon my disguise I went in with the rest. None entered the house, for a guard of soldiers had been stationed there. I passed round at the back and presently Lyptis, the old female slave, came out to fetch water. I spoke to her in my assumed character, but she only shook her head and made no reply. Then believing that she, like all the others in the house, was attached to the family and could be trusted, I spoke to her in my natural voice, and she at once knew me. I made a sign to her to be silent and withdrew with her alone to some bushes. The tears were streaming down her face.

" 'Oh, Jethro!' she exclaimed, 'did the gods ever before hurl such calamities upon a household? My dear master is dead; my lord Chebron is hunted for as men hunt for a wild beast; my dear young mistress, Mysa, is missing!'

" 'Missing!' I exclaimed. 'What do you mean?'

" 'Have you not heard it?' she said.

" 'I have heard nothing!' I cried. 'Tell me all!'

" 'Just after the gates were beaten down and the crowd rushed along into the garden, four men burst into the house and ran from chamber to chamber until they entered that of my young mistress. We heard a scream, and a moment later they came out again bearing a figure enveloped in a wrapping. We strove to stop them, but there were naught but women in the house. They struck two of us to the ground, and rushed out. Some of us ran out into the garden crying for aid, but there we saw a terrible scene. A great struggle was going on, and presently you broke forth, covered with blood and wounds, and ran swiftly past. None heeded us or our cries.

" 'When the soldiers arrived we told the officer what had happened; but it was too late then, and nothing could be done. Had there been a guard over the house all these things would never have happened.'

"I asked her if she could describe to me the appearance of the men. She said that they were attired as respectable citizens, but that from their language and manner she believed that they were ruffians of the lowest class.

"For a time I was so overwhelmed with this news that I could think of nothing, but went out and roamed through the streets. At last I bethought me of the girl Ruth. She was with Mysa at the time, and might, if questioned, be able to tell me more than the old woman had done. I therefore returned, but had to wait for three hours before old Lyptis came out again.

" 'I want to speak to Ruth,' I said. 'Send her out to me.'

" 'Ruth has gone,' she said.

" 'Gone!' I repeated. 'When and whither?'

" 'That we know not. It was not until hours after Mysa was carried off that anyone thought of her. We were too overwhelmed with grief at the death of our dear lord and the loss of Mysa to give a thought to the young Israelite. Then one asked, where was she? No one had noticed her. We went to Mysa's chamber, thinking that the villains who carried our young mistress off might have slain her; but there were no signs of her there.'

" 'But she was with Mysa, was she not,' I asked, 'when the attack was made? Did she not pass in with her when she came in from the garden?'

" 'Yes,' she replied, 'they came in together and passed through us; for we gathered in the front chamber, being greatly frightened at the clamour at the gate. As they passed us our young mistress said, 'Keep silent, what is the use of screaming and crying?'

"I asked if she was sure Ruth was not carried off as well as Mysa.

" 'Quite sure,' she said. 'One bore a figure and the other three cleared the way.'

" 'And that was the last time,' I asked, 'that any of you saw the Israelite?'

" 'It was,' she answered. 'She must have passed out by the door at the end of the passage, which she might well have done without being observed by any of us.'

"This was a new mystery. Why Ruth should have fled I could not guess, because as soon as the soldiers appeared there was no more danger in remaining. Besides, I did not think Ruth was one to shrink from danger. However, there was no more to be learned, and I again went out into the streets."

Chapter 13

"PERHAPS Ruth had gone to tell my mother that Mysa was lost," Chebron suggested when Jethro had gone so far in his story.

"That could hardly have been," Jethro replied, "for I should have told you that your mother returned early this morning to the house with many relatives, and that all were weeping and mourning round the body of your father. Had Ruth gone to her, she would either have returned with her, or Lyptis would have heard where she was."

"Did you hear how my mother bore her misfortunes, Jethro?"

"She was overwhelmed with grief, Lyptis said, at your father's death—so overwhelmed that she seemed to have no thought for anything else. She had, of course, been told the night before that Mysa was missing; but it seemed to make no impression upon her. She only said that doubtless friends had carried her off to save her from the danger that Chebron's wickedness had brought upon us all. This morning she made some further inquiries, but did not seem in any serious alarm; but the magistrates, when they came last night to inquire into the whole matter, took note of Mysa having been carried off, and when on their coming again this morning they found that nothing had been heard of her, gave orders that a search should be made for her, and a proclamation was issued this afternoon denouncing punishment on those who carried her off, and enjoining all who could give any information on the subject to present themselves before them immediately.

"Since I came out from the house I have been wandering about trying to think what is best to be done, and hoping that something might occur to me which would put me upon the track of the villains who carried Mysa off."

"You do not think of carrying out our plans for to-morrow, Jethro?" Chebron asked anxiously. "We could never go away from here in ignorance of what had become of her."

"Certainly not, Chebron. I consider it my duty, as well as my inclination, to stay here until she is found. Your father spoke to me of her as well as of you, but as he did not see any way in which we could aid her he said that she must take her chance— meaning, take her chance under the guardianship of your mother to obtain some day a husband whom she could love. But the present misfortune entirely alters the case. She has need of our active help, and whatever are the risks we must postpone our start.

"Whether you will be able to stay here or not is doubtful. Each day that passes without news being received of your capture in the provinces north of us, will increase the belief that you are hiding somewhere in the neighbourhood of the city, and in that case the search will become more and more earnest. However, for a day of two we may be safe here. As to that, however, we must abide by Chigron's opinion. He is running no small risk in concealing us here, and if he considers the danger is becoming greater than he is willing to run, we must betake ourselves to the hills. There are lonely spots there where we could lie concealed for a long time, or at least, as long as such supplies of food and water as we could carry with us hold out. But, at any rate, we must set aside all thought of flight for the present, and devote all our energies to the discovery and rescue of Mysa."

"I do not think we have far to look for the contrivers of the outrage," Amuba said. "It seems to me that it is of a piece with the whole of the misfortunes that have befallen us. We know that Ameres refused the request of Ptylus for Mysa as a wife for his son. After that came the plot which we overheard in the temple for the murder of some one. The knowledge that they were overheard put a stop to that scheme. Then came the stirring up of the people, partly by the story of that unfortunate cat, partly by whispers that Ameres, although high-priest of Osiris, was yet a scorner of the gods. Then came the attack upon the house, in which, while the main body of the mob attacked Ameres, a chosen band carried off Mysa.

"This villain, Ptylus, had several motives to spur him on. In the first place, there was anger at the rejection of his son's suit; next, that he would at the death of Ameres, naturally succeed to the high-priesthood; thirdly, he may have thought that if he could obtain possession of Mysa and marry her to his son, she would bring with her no small portion of her father's lands as a dowry. With the influence which he, as high-priest would have with the king and council he could rely upon her obtaining a share of the estate, especially as the villain would calculate that Chebron as well as his father would be put out of the way.

"He has only to keep Mysa immured until his power as high-priest is consolidated, and then if he gain the consent of the king to the match Mysa could not refuse to accept the fate prepared for her."

"I think you have accurately reasoned out the case, Amuba, and that we have penetrated the whole conspiracy. The question is, what are we to do?"

"It must not be, Jethro!" Chebron cried excitedly, pacing up and down the chamber. "Mysa cannot bear Plexo. She spoke of him with something like horror when she heard of the proposal Ptylus made. I do not like him myself. He is thin lipped and crafty and cruel. Mysa had better be dead than married to him."

"I think I can promise you, Chebron," Jethro said grimly, "that that marriage shall never come about. We may not find Mysa, who may be hidden either in Ptylus's house, or in one of the many chambers of the temple, or in the caves near it; but, at any rate, I can find Plexo, and before we leave Egypt I will slay him as well as his father, whom I regard as the murderer of Ameres. I may not be able to do this and to get away, and in that case you must journey alone; but I am not going to quit Egypt and leave them to enjoy the gains of their crime." As he finished speaking Chigron entered.

"I was coming in to see if Jethro had returned."

He was told the reasons for his prolonged absence—the abduction of Mysa, and the determination to remain and search for her place of concealment. He shook his head.

"It is a rash resolution. Even were you free to come and go as you choose, your chance of finding out her hiding-place would be small indeed—hunted as you yourselves are, your quest seems to be an absolutely hopeless one. As to your remaining here long, I think it would be madness.

"It is not only for myself that I say this, but for you. In the first place, there are so many men employed here that your coming in and going out would be sure to be noticed by some one; in the second place, the cave would scarcely escape search a second time.

Were it not for my workmen I could conceal you in the house; and if I saw men in search of you approaching I could place you in one of the inner casings of the mummies, and put two or three more casings on. Then, lying as you would be among a number of corpses in a similar state of advancement towards burial, none would think of opening the cases.

"But with so many people about it would be well-nigh impossible to do this without observation—unless, indeed, the search was made at night or after the workmen had departed, which would hardly be likely to happen. Therefore I think it impossible for you to stay here more than another day or two; but there are many caves and burial-places higher up on the hill-side where you might be concealed. In many of these there are sarcophagi. If we choose one in which there are several coffins I can remove the mummies and their casings into another cave, so that, should a party of searchers approach the place, you can lie down in the sarcophagus and lower the lid down upon you."

"It would be sacrilege to move the dead," Chebron said with a shudder.

"It would be sacrilege for others," Chigron replied, "but not to us, whose business and duty it is to handle the dead. I can replace the mummies in their cases after you have left, and they will be none the worse for their temporary removal. It will be necessary, of course, that there should be no signs of habitation in the cave—nothing to excite their suspicions that it has been disturbed."

"I think that is a very good plan," Jethro said. "We can make sleeping-places in the open air near. We shall sleep in the open air on our journey, and it would be no hardship to begin at once. I should think it best to remove to one of these caves at once. There is never any saying when the searchers may be here again; therefore if you will, Chigron, I will at early daybreak go with you, choose a cave and make our arrangements."

"I think, indeed, that that will be the best plan," the embalmer agreed. "I will, of course, take care to bring you up every night a store of provisions. And now I will leave you to sleep."

It was long, however, before the occupants of the chamber threw themselves upon their piles of rushes. Sometimes they talked of Mysa, and discussed all possible plans for discovering where she was concealed. Then they wondered what had become of Ruth, who would be friendless in the great city, and might not have money sufficient to buy a meal with her.

"She had her ornaments," Jethro said; "a silver bracelet that Mysa gave her she always wore. She had two silver necklaces and ear-rings of her own. I should think they had been handed down to her from her mother; they seemed good and would fetch money. Ruth is a shrewd little maid; for though but fifteen years old she has long been accustomed to manage a house and look after her grandfather. Why she has run away I cannot think, except that perhaps from the noise and tumult she thought that all were going to be killed. But even in that case she would probably have found her way back by this morning, if not sooner."

"I cannot help thinking myself," Chebron said, "that she has followed Mysa. Although she has not been here for many months, I am sure that she was very fond of her."

"That she certainly was," Jethro said. "I often thought when I was walking behind them that it was pretty to see them together. Mysa knew so much more of everything; and yet it was the Hebrew maid who gave her opinion most decidedly, and Mysa listened to her as she talked in that grave way of hers as if she had been an elder sister. And you think she might have followed her? I hope that it may have been so. But in that case the women must have seen her."

"The women were scared out of their senses," Chebron said, "and, I have no doubt, were screaming and wringing their hands and attending to nothing else. If I could but be sure that Ruth is with Mysa I should feel less anxious, for I am certain she would be a comfort and support to her."

"She would indeed," Jethro agreed. "And moreover I should have greater hopes of finding where they are concealed; for if it be possible to get away and to spread the alarm I am sure that Ruth would seize the first opportunity promptly."

It was but a short time after they lay down that Chigron entered and said that morning was beginning to break. They at once rose and followed him. He led them along the foot of the hill for some distance, and then turning began to ascend at a spot where it sloped gradually. They passed many tombs, partly erected with masonry and partly cut out from the rock behind; and it was not until after walking fully half an hour that he stopped before the entrance of one of them.

"This is the one that I thought of as being suitable for the purpose," he said. "It is one of the most lonely, and there is little likelihood of any chance passer coming near it. In the second place, I know that the stone door which rolls across the entrance has not been cemented in its place. I know indeed to whom the tomb belongs. The last mummy was placed here but a short time back; and the son of the man then buried told me that he should not have it cemented because his wife was grievously sick, and he feared would shortly follow his father. Therefore there will be no difficulty in effecting an entry. In the second place, there is hard by a small tomb that was cut in the rock and then left—the owners changing their minds and having a larger tomb made lower down the hill. As nothing beyond the chamber and the narrow entrance were made, we can there hide the mummies from this chamber and heap stones and earth over the entrance, so that none would suspect its existence."

"Nothing could be better," Jethro said. "Let us set to work and prepare it at once."

The stone across the entrance to the tomb, which was but three feet high and of the same width, was pushed back without difficulty and they entered. Four wooden sarcophagi stood there. Jethro aided Chigron in opening three of these. The mummies in their cases were taken out, the outer cases opened and replaced in the coffins after the mummies with the inner cases had been removed from them. These were then carried to the unfinished tomb fifty yards away and there deposited. Stones were then piled together so as to conceal the entrance, and the men returned to the tomb.

"Here you will be perfectly safe," Chigron said. "You can keep the stone rolled back unless you see any one approaching; and you would be sure to make out any considerable number of searchers mounting the hillside long before they reach you. Should you see them, you will of course close the door, enter each of you one of the sarcophagi, lie down in the inner case, close the lid of the sarcophagus, and place the lid of the inner case over you. I think it unlikely in the extreme that any search will be made for you, or at any rate a search only of untenanted tombs. The fact of the stone here being left uncemented is a mere accident probably known only to myself and its owner. It is only as an extreme resource that you could need to take to these hiding-places. As far as passers-by are concerned you might remain outside altogether, but in that case you would run some risk of being noticed. You may be sure the hills will be closely scanned, and if figures were seen moving about here a party might set out to see whether these were the fugitives so eagerly sought for. Therefore I say, during the daytime keep yourselves concealed here. As soon as it is dark you can of course issue out and pass the night wherever you may think fit."

"We shall certainly follow your advice," Jethro said. "Undoubtedly the plan you propose is by far the safest. I cannot think that there is much chance of an earnest search being made among the tombs, though likely enough they may visit those which are open and empty; but as you say, they would never dream of examining the tombs in use, as they would naturally suppose that all were securely fastened. In case of the very worst, there are the coffins for us to betake ourselves to; and these assuredly, no one would think of examining."

"If you will come down," Chigron said, "as soon as it is dark, I will give you provisions for some days, together with the peasants' dresses I have prepared for you and the money Ameres committed to my charge. It is not likely that anything will occur to decide you to make a move suddenly, but it is best that you should have everything in readiness for so doing should the occasion possibly arise. I will come up myself to-morrow night, if all is well, an hour after sunset. I name the time exactly in order that if you sleep at any distance away you can be here at that hour to meet me; and now I leave you to the protection of the gods. This evening I shall dismantle the chamber you have used and remove all signs of its having been inhabited."

Chebron thanked the embalmer very earnestly for the kindness he had shown them, the trouble he had taken, and the risk he had run on their behalf.

"I would have done more if I could," Chigron said. "Your father's son has the highest claims upon me, and were it to half my fortune I would spend it to carry out the last wishes that Ameres expressed to me."

As soon as the embalmer left them the three friends sat down just within the entrance to the tomb, looking out over the quiet city laying in the plain below them.

"I wish we had our peasant dresses," Chebron said, "that we might go down with you and join in the search for Mysa."

"It would be too dangerous," Jethro said decidedly. "Too many have seen you taking part in the services and procession for you to have a chance of passing unnoticed. Amuba is less likely than you to be detected, and if his skin was stained, his eyebrows blackened, and his head shaved, he might manage to pass providing he walked with his eyes fixed on the ground; but in that way he would not have much chance of coming upon traces of Mysa.

"Any search you make must be at night. I shall today station myself near the house of Ptylus. I do not expect to gain any information from gazing at the high wall which surrounds it, but I will follow, as closely as I can without attracting observation, all the slaves or servants who may come out, especially if two issue forth together; I may then catch a few words of their talk, and possibly gather some clue to the mystery. Still I own that the chance is small, and you must not look forward in any way to my returning with news."

"I wish, Jethro," Chebron said, "that if possible you would again go to our house, see the old woman, and get her to bring out to you a suit of my priests' garments; with these I could at night enter the temple, and wander unquestioned through the chambers and courts. The nights are dark now, and unless I pass close to a lamp none could recognize me. We overheard one conversation of importance there, and it may be that I could overhear another."

"There would be danger in the attempt," Jethro said doubtfully.

"That matters not at all!" Chebron exclaimed impetuously. "All this trouble has come upon us through me, and even should there be some slight risk I would willingly face it; but in truth I think there is no chance whatever of my being recognized. See how often Amuba went there with me, and though the nights were always moonlit we never were once addressed, nor was it noticed that Amuba was not one of the regular attendants of the temple, who alone have a right to penetrate beyond the great courts.

"So be it, then," Jethro said. "Then you shall explore the temple, Amuba and I will search every cavern in the hills. There are many great tombs behind the temple, and just as we have selected such a hiding-place, Ptylus may have chosen one as a place of concealment for Mysa. There are many tombs there built by princes, nobles, and wealthy priests for their reception after death which could be turned into a comfortable dwelling. After we have spent some time in searching there, we must, if unsuccessful, try further away. Ptylus, no doubt, like Ameres, has country farms and residences, and she may be hidden in one of these."

"I believe myself," Amuba said, "that a better plan than yours will be for us to establish a watch over Plexo. Ptylus has his duties and is no doubt fully occupied in securing his election to the high-priesthood, but Plexo would most probably go sometimes to see Mysa in her place of imprisonment; he will naturally be anxious to conciliate or frighten her into giving her consent to marry him as soon as possible. Therefore, if we can but watch him sufficiently closely, he is sure to lead us at last to her."

"That will certainly be the best way, Amuba. I did not think of it before, but it is clearly the plan that promises the best chance of success. We might search the country for years without finding her; and although I wish to keep up your hopes, I really despaired in my own mind. But, as you say, if we follow Plexo, sooner or later he is sure to bring us to her. But to do so we shall want many disguises. I will think the matter over as I walk to-day, and when I see Chigron this evening will beg him to get the disguises that seem to him the best for us to use."

"As for me, Jethro," Chebron said, "I will visit the temple of an evening, as I said. But long before midnight all will be quiet there; so that will give me plenty of time for sleep, and in the daytime I will work with you. Get me a garb of a peasant woman. In such a dress and with a female head-covering I could surely get myself up so that even those who know me best would pass by without suspicion. Many women are taller than I am. The disguise would be out of the question for Amuba, who is well-nigh as tall as you are, besides being wide and strong-looking, but for me it would do well."

"Yes, I think you could pass as a woman," Jethro agreed; "and certainly the more of us there are to watch this rascal the better. But for myself I think that we are more likely to succeed by night than by day. Plexo, too, has his duties in the temple, and would be likely to pay his visits after dark. Then it would be a mere question of speed of foot, and Amuba and I used to be trained in running, and it will be a swift horse that will outpace us. And now I am going down to the city. I feel more hopeful than I did, lads, and for the first time begin to think that we have a chance of discovering where the villains have carried Mysa."

The day passed slowly to Chebron and Amuba. They would not show themselves outside the tomb, as Chigron had earnestly begged them not to do so; besides, there were frequently people about on the hillside, for many came daily to offer prayers at the tombs of their relatives. Still they had much to talk of—the chances of finding Mysa; the question with whom she should be placed if recovered; the prospects of the long and adventurous journey which lay before them. Amuba encouraged talk on all these points, and started the conversation afresh whenever it dropped, for he saw that the excitement concerning Mysa had done a great deal for Chebron. It had weaned his thoughts from the death of his father, and the consequences that had arisen from his unfortunate shot; it had given him fresh subject for thought, and had revived his spirits and interest in life. Both lads were glad when, late in the afternoon, they saw Jethro ascending the hill.

"I have no news," he said, as he came up to them. "I have been all day in the neighbourhood of the house of Ptylus, and have followed all who came out two together from it. I have overheard many scraps of conversation, and one and all talked upon the same subject, the death of Ameres and the sacred cat, and the want of success in the search for you. The fact of Mysa being carried off was spoken of once or twice; but I was convinced by the manner in which the slaves spoke to each other on the subject that they had not the slightest idea that their master was concerned in the matter, and they had assuredly no knowledge whatever of her being in the house.

"Of course it is possible that she might be there without its being generally known to all the slaves. Still you know how things leak out in a household, and how everything done by the master and mistress soon become public property; and had any one among them heard something unusual was going on, it would by this time have been known to all the servants. I hardly thought that Ptylus would have ventured to have her carried home, for he might suppose that her mother's suspicions might be directed towards him just as ours have been, and that if she made a complaint against him a search of his house might be ordered; besides, there are too many servants there for a secret to be kept. No, if a clue is to be obtained it will be in the temple or by our following Plexo."

As soon as it was dark they descended the hill together. Chebron had attired himself in the garments bearing the distinguishing marks of the priesthood that Jethro had brought up with him, having obtained them from old Lyptis. When near the house of the embalmer the lad stopped, and Jethro went on and returned in half an hour with the various disguises he had asked Chigron to obtain for him. All these with exception of the scant attire of two peasants, he hid for the present in some bushes near the path, then he rubbed Amuba's skin and his own with a fluid he had obtained from Chigron; and after putting on the peasants' clothes they took their way towards the house of Ptylus.

While Chebron went towards the temple, which was but a short distance from the house, Jethro and Amuba sat down by the wall close to the gate so that none would leave it without their knowledge. But beyond servants and visitors no one came out. At ten o'clock they heard the bolts of the gates fastened, but remained where they were until near midnight, when Chebron joined them. He had spent the time wandering from court to court of the temple, but beyond a solitary priest moving here and there replenishing the lamps of the altars he had seen no one, and had been himself entirely unnoticed. Amuba and Chebron were both inclined to be dispirited at the want of success of their watching, but Jethro chid them for their impatience.

"You do not suppose," he said, "that you are going to find out a secret so well hidden by a few hours' watching. It may be weeks before we succeed. To-morrow we will begin our watch two or three hours before sundown. I am better known to the servants at the house of Ptylus than you are, as I have often taken messages there; besides, in my disguise I could not so well loiter about without attracting attention as you could. I will, therefore, content myself with watching the northern road from the city upon the chance of his taking that way, while you dressed as peasants can watch the house itself. You, Chebron, might sit down by the wall fifty yards from the house on the north side, while you, Amuba, had best keep on the other side of the road and somewhat to the south of the gate. In this way you will be within sight of each other and yet not together; solitary figures are less likely to attract attention than two together, for it is for two boys that people will be looking. As I should scarcely know you myself now that your skins are darkened, there is, I trust, small fear of others detecting your disguise."

Accordingly the next day, three hours after noon, Amuba and Chebron, disguised as peasants, went down to the house of Ptylus and took their posts as arranged. Late in the afternoon Amuba noticed that one of the slaves from the house of Ptylus suddenly checked his walk as he passed Chebron and gazed fixedly at him. Amuba left the spot where he was standing and walked quickly in that direction. The slave spoke to Chebron, who rose to his feet. A moment later the slave seized him. As they were struggling Amuba ran up.

"Here is a find!" the slave exclaimed. "This is the slayer of the sacred cat. Aid me to drag him into the house of my master."

But to his surprise Amuba sprang upon him and struck him such a heavy blow in the face that he released his hold of Chebron and staggered backwards.

"Run for your life!" Amuba exclaimed to his friend. "I will take another route."

The slave, recovering from his blow, rushed at Amuba, shouting at the top of his voice:

"Death to the insulters of the gods! Death to the slayers of the sacred cat!"

But Amuba, who was now eighteen years of age, was at once stronger and more active than the slave, whose easy life in the household of the priest had unfitted him for such a struggle. Springing back to avoid the grasp of his assailant, Amuba struck him with all his strength in the face, and as he reeled backwards repeated the blow, and the man fell heavily to the ground. But several other people attracted by the conflict and the shouts of the slave, were running up, and Amuba took to his heels at the top of his speed. As he expected, the passers-by paused to assist the fallen man and to learn the cause of the fray before they took up the pursuit, and he was nearly two hundred yards away when he heard the cry again raised, "Death to the slayer of the sacred cat!"

By this time he was alongside of Chebron, who had paused to see the issue of the contest with the slave.

"Do you turn off, Chebron, and take a turning or two and conceal yourself, and then make your way up to the hill. I will keep straight on for awhile. I have more last than you have and can outrun these fellows, never fear. Do as I tell you," he said almost angrily as he saw that Chebron hesitated when they reached the next turning. "If we keep together they will overtake us both."

Chebron hesitated no longer, but took the turning indicated. Amuba slackened his speed now, judging correctly that his pursuers if they saw they gained upon him would not trouble themselves about his companion, of whose identity they were probably still ignorant. When, on looking back, he saw that all had passed the turning, he again quickened his speed. He was not afraid of being overtaken by those behind him, but that he might meet other people who, seeing the pursuit, would take him for a fugitive from justice, and endeavour to stop him. One or two did indeed make feeble attempts to do so, but did not care to grapple in earnest with a powerful young man, evidently desperate, and of whose crime they knew nothing.

As soon as he felt sure that Chebron was quite safe from pursuit, he turned off from the road he was following and struck across the country. A quarter of an hour's running took him fairly beyond the villas and detached houses scattered so thickly round Thebes. The ground here was closely cultivated. It was intersected everywhere by channels conveying the water needed for the irrigation of the crops. The holdings were small, and in the centre of each stood a little hut.

Some of these were inhabited, but for the most part the cultivators lived in the villages, using the huts only when it was necessary to scare away the birds and keep a close watch over their fruit. In some of these patches the fruit-trees were thick, and Amuba took advantage of the cover to turn off at right angles to the course he had been pursuing, and then shaping his course so as to keep in shelter of the trees, ran until he arrived at a hut whose door stood open. A glance within showed that it was not at present used by the owner. He entered and closed the door behind him, and then climbed up a ladder, and threw himself down on some boards that lay on the rafters for the storage of fruit, pulling the ladder up after him.

The last glimpse he had of his pursuers showed him that they were fully four hundred yards behind him when he turned off from the line he had been following, and he would have kept on and trusted to his speed and endurance to outrun them had he not been sure that many of the cultivators whom he had passed in his flight, and who had contented themselves with shouting threats at him for crossing their land, would, on learning from his pursuers the crime with which he was charged, join the pursuit. Thus fresh runners would be constantly taking up the chase, and he would eventually be run down; he therefore thought it best to attempt to conceal himself until night fell.

Scarcely had he thrown himself down when he heard loud shouts rise close at hand, and had no doubt that some labourer unobserved by him had noticed him enter the hut. He sprang down again from the loft, and seizing a stake which with several others was standing in a corner he again sallied out. As he did so he was suddenly grasped. Twisting himself free he saw a powerful Nubian armed with a hoe. Without a moment's hesitation Amuba spring at him with his stake. The Nubian parried the blow with his hoe, and in turn dealt a sweeping blow at the lad.

Amuba sprang back just in time, and before the negro could recover his guard, struck him a heavy blow on the wrist with his stake. The negro dropped his hoe, uttering a cry of pain and rage. Amuba followed up the blow on the wrist with one on the ankle, and as the man fell, bounded away again. But the negro's shouts had been heard, and the pursuers were now but fifty yards away. Amuba saw that their numbers had swollen considerably, and a doubt as to his ability to escape them for the first time entered his mind.

They were too close for any further attempts at concealment, and he had now only his speed to rely on. But he had already run nearly three miles, while many of those behind him were fresh, and he soon found that he could not again widen the space between them. For another two miles he still kept ahead, at first leaping the ditches lightly and without a pause, but at last often landing in the middle, and scrambling out with difficulty. He was becoming completely exhausted now. Those who had at first taken up the chase had long since abandoned it; but, as he had feared, fresh men constantly joined the ranks of his pursuers. They were but a few paces behind him when he found himself again on the highroad.

A few hundred yards away he saw a chariot approaching, and feeling that further flight was hopeless he turned stake in hand, to face his pursuers, who were but a few paces behind him. With cries of "Kill him!" "Death to the insulter of the gods!" they rushed at him. Panting and breathless he defended himself as best he could. But his guard was beaten down and blows were showered upon him.

He fell, but with a great effort struggled to his feet again; his senses were fast deserting him now, but he was conscious that the chariot drew up beside him, scattering his assailants right and left. He heard a voice raised in tones of indignant reproach, and a renewal of the cries of hatred. He felt strong arms round him; then he was lifted, and for a time became unconscious.

Chapter 14

WHEN Amuba recovered his senses he was lying in a heap at the bottom of the chariot. Two men were standing in the car beside him. The one he supposed to be the driver, the other the owner of the chariot.

In a few minutes the chariot turned off through a stately gateway. The driver leapt down and closed the gates, and then led the horses to the steps leading up to a splendid mansion. The man beside him called out, and two or three slaves ran down the steps. Then he was lifted out, carried into the house, and laid upon a couch. A cup of wine was placed to his lips, and after he had drunk a slave bathed his head with cold water, and bandaged up the numerous cuts from which blood was flowing.

This greatly refreshed him, and he raised himself on his arm. An order was given, and the slaves left the apartment, and Amuba looking up saw a tall and stately figure standing before him. He recognized him at once, for he had seen him following the king in one of the processions among the princes of Egypt.

"Who are you? And is it true what those men whom I found maltreating you averred, that you are the slayer of the cat of Bubastes?"

"My name is Amuba, my lord," the lad said, striving to stand upright, but his questioner signed to him to remain seated. "I am a Rebu taken prisoner of war, and handed as a slave to Ameres, high-priest of Osiris. I am not the slayer of the cat, but it is true that I was present at its death, and that it might just as well have been my arrow that accidentally pierced it as that of him who did so."

"Then it was an accident," the noble said.

"It was wholly an accident, my lord. We fired at a hawk that had been thinning the pet birds of my master's daughter. One of the arrows struck a tree, and glancing off entered the house in which the cat was kept and unfortunately caused its death. We regretted the accident bitterly, knowing how sacred was the animal in the sight of the Egyptians."

"And not in your sight, young man? You are not yet a follower of the gods of the Egyptians?"

"I am not, my lord," Amuba answered; "but at the same time I would not upon any account have willfully done aught to offend the religious opinions of others, although I myself have not been taught to consider the life of a cat as of more value than that of other animals."

"Then you worship the gods of your own people?"

Amuba was silent for a moment.

"I would answer frankly, my lord, and I hope that you will not be displeased. Since I have come to Egypt I have come to think that neither the gods of the Egyptians nor the gods my fathers worshipped are the true gods. I believe that there is one great God over all, and that the others are but as it were His attributes, which men worship under the name of gods."

The Egyptian uttered an exclamation of surprise.

"Whence did you obtain such a belief as this?" he asked.

Amuba was silent.

"It must have been from Ameres himself," the noble went on, seeing that the lad was reluctant to answer. "I knew him well, and also that he carried to an extreme the knowledge he had gained. But how came it that he should speak of such matters to you—a slave?"

"My master was good enough to make me a companion and friend to his son rather than a servant to him," Amuba replied, "partly because he thought that I should lead him to a more active life, which he needed, for he was over studious; partly because I had high rank in my own country, of which my father was the king. But he never spoke of this until after the accident of the cat. My friend Chebron was utterly cast down at the sin that he thought he had committed, and would at once have denounced himself, preferring death to living with such a burden upon his mind. Then his father, seeing that his whole life would be embittered, and that he would probably be forced to fly from Egypt and dwell in some other land, told him the belief which he himself held. I believed this all the more readily because I had heard much the same from an Israelite maiden who served my master's daughter."

Again Amuba's listener uttered an exclamation of surprise.

"I knew not," he said, after a pause, "that there was an Israelite who still adhered to the religion of their ancestors."

"The maiden told me that for the most part they had taken to the worship of the Egyptians, and indeed, so far as she knew, she was the last who clung to the old belief. She had been brought up by a great-grandfather who had been driven from his people and forced to dwell apart because he reproached them for having forsaken their God, and he instructed her in the faith he held, which was that there was but one God over all the earth."

"Do you know who I am?" the noble asked abruptly.

"I know that you are one of the princes of the land, my lord, for I have seen you in the procession following closely behind the king with his sons and other princes."

"I also am an Israelite. It seems strange to you, doubtless," he went on, as Amuba started in astonishment at hearing a prince of Egypt declare himself as belonging to the hated race. "Many years ago, at the time I was an infant, there was a great persecution of the Israelites, and as is supposed my father and mother, fearing for my life placed me in a little cradle and set me afloat on the water. It chanced—or was it chance or the will of God?—that the water took me to the spot where the Princess Thermuthis, the daughter of the then king, was bathing with her maidens. She had compassion upon me and adopted me, and as I grew up I had all the rights and privileges of her son, and rank, as you say, with the princes of Egypt. She called me Moses; for that was the name, as it seems, that was writ upon a piece of papyrus fastened to my cradle. I was instructed in all the learning of the Egyptians, and grew up as one of them. So I lived for many years, and had almost forgotten that I was not one of them; but now—" And here he stopped and began thoughtfully to pace up and down the apartment.

"What has become of the maiden of whom you spoke?" he asked suddenly stopping before Amuba.

"That I know not, my lord. Upon the day that Ameres was murdered by the mob his little daughter was carried off, and Ruth, for that is her name, has also been missing ever since. It is for that reason we have lingered here, otherwise we should have fled at once."

"You and the son of Ameres?"

"Yes, my lord, and another Rebu, one of my father's warriors, who was a fellow-captive with me, and also slave of Ameres. The high-priest had great confidence in him, and committed to him the mission of aiding Chebron to escape and of conducting us if possible back to my own land; but when we found that my young mistress was missing we decided to remain to search for her."

"What will you do when you find her?"

"If we can rescue her from those who have carried her away we shall hand her over to her mother, and then leave the land as we had intended. Unless, indeed you, my lord, in your goodness, could obtain for Chebron a pardon for an offence which was wholly accidental."

"That I can never do," Moses said. "This is wholly beyond my power; the king himself could not withstand the demand of the populace for his life. Until lately I might have in some way aided you, but I have no longer influence, and have myself fallen into disgrace at court."

After again pacing the apartment for some time, Moses went on:

"If you find this little Israelite maiden tell her that she is not the last of the Israelites who believes in the God of Abraham, our ancestor; tell her that Moses also holds to the faith. You again look surprised, young man, and you may well be so, seeing that I have from the days of my infancy been separated from my people.

"But our priests keep accurate records of all things connected with the countries and religion of the people with whom we come in contact. Thus, then, it was easy for me, who have access to all the stores of knowledge, to examine the rolls recording the first coming of my people, the rule of Joseph, the great governor, the coming of his relations here and their settlement in the country. Thus I learned that they worshipped one God, whom they believed to be the only God in the world. I have been interested deeply in the learning of the priesthood, and have long seen that behind all the forms and mysteries of the Egyptian religion this central idea seemed to be hidden. None with whom I have spoken acknowledged boldly that it was so; but I heard reports that Ameres was bold enough to entertain the idea that there was but one God, and that our far-back ancestors, who had first worshipped Him under the various attributes they ascribed to Him, came in course of time to lose the truth altogether and to regard shadows as substance. Therefore, I said to myself, I too will believe in the one God worshipped by my forefathers, hoping that in time it may be that I may learn more of Him.

"Until the last two or three years I have been content to live as one of the Egyptian princes; but of late my heart has turned much to my oppressed people, and I have determined upon doing what I can to relieve their burden. I have even raised my voice in the council in their favour, and this has created a coldness between the court and myself. They consider that I, having had the honour of adoption into the royal family, should myself forget, and allow others to forget, what they regard as my base origin. Sometimes I own, that I myself wonder that I should feel so drawn towards them, and even wish that I could forget my origin and give my whole mind to the duties and pleasures of my present rank; but I feel moved by a Spirit stronger than my own. But we must talk no longer; I see that you are now stronger. Do you think that you can walk?"

"Oh, yes," Amuba replied, getting up and walking across the apartment. "I have not lost much blood, and was only dizzy from their blows."

"Then it is better that you should leave at once. The people from whom I snatched you will have carried the news speedily to the city, and officials will doubtless soon arrive here to demand that you be given up to them. Take, therefore, another draught of wine and a piece of bread, I will then give you in charge of a trusty slave, who will lead you through the garden and through a small door at the back, and will guide you to any spot where you may wish to go. Even now, doubtless, a watch is being kept up in the front of the house. When the officials arrive I shall tell them the truth—that coming, as I drove, upon a lad who was being attacked and murdered by a number of brutal peasants, I carried him off in my chariot. As to the shouts I heard, that you were the slayer of the Cat of Bubastes, I regarded it as an invention designed to hinder me from interfering on your behalf; that I questioned you upon your arrival here, and finding that, as I had supposed, you were entirely innocent of the offence charged against you, I urged you to leave at once, letting you depart by the garden gate in order to escape the fury of your persecutors. As you are not an Israelite, no one can suppose that I could have any motive for shielding an offender from the punishment of his crimes. Do not thank me, for time presses, and you must be moving, so as to be well away before it is known that you have left. May the God we both worship, though as yet in ignorance, guide and preserve you and carry you and your friends through the dangers that beset you."

Moses drew back the curtains from before the entrance to the chamber and clapped his hands, and ordered the servant who answered the call to tell Mephres to come to him. An old slave speedily appeared, and Moses ordered him to take Amuba out by the private way, and to guide him by a quiet way back to the city. Then cutting short his guest's expressions of thanks for the great kindness he had rendered him, he hurried him away, for he knew that at any moment the officials might arrive from the city.

It was well that Amuba had been supplied with a guide, for upon issuing into the night air—for by this time darkness had fallen—he found that he could with difficulty direct his steps; his head throbbed as if it would split from the blows that had been dealt him, and every limb ached. The old slave, however, seeing that he stumbled as he walked, placed his staff in one of Amuba's hands, and taking him firmly by the arm led him steadily on. It seemed to the lad that he went on walking all night, and yet it was less than an hour after starting when his conductor found that he could go no further, and that he was wholly unable to answer his questions as to whither he wished to be guided. He determined to stop with him until he should be able to proceed again. He therefore led Amuba aside into an orchard, and there laid him down under the shelter of a tree, covering him with one of his own garments.

"It is well for the lad that my lord arrived just when he did," he said to himself as he sat down by the side of Amuba and listened to his heavy breathing—for all in the house had heard from the charioteer of the rescue of the lad from the hands of furious peasants.

"He must have been very near death when he was saved from their hands. Maxis said that his assailants shouted out that he was the slayer of the Cat of Bubastes about which such a turmoil has been made. Had it been so I do not think that my lord would have aided him thus to escape; though for my part I care not if he had killed all the cats in Egypt, seeing that in my native Libya we worship not the gods of the Egyptians."

Several times during the night the old man got up and plucked large handfuls of grass wet with dew and placed them on Amuba's head, and when he perceived the first faint gleam of morning in the sky he aroused him. Amuba sat up and looked round with an air of astonishment.

"Where am I?" he exclaimed.

"You are at present in an orchard, my young friend, though to whom it may belong I know not; but finding that you were unable to continue your journey I drew you aside here, and you have slept well all night, and I hope feel better for it, and able to proceed."

"I remember now," Amuba said; "it seemed to me that I walked for hours leaning on your arm."

"It was but an hour," the slave replied; "we are not yet two miles from my lord's house."

"And you have watched over me all night," Amuba said; "for it was, I know, but an hour after sunset when we started. Truly I am deeply indebted to you for your kindness."

"Speak not of it," the old man replied. "My lord gave you into my charge, and I cannot return until I can tell him that you are in safety. But if you are able to walk we must pass on, for there may be a search for you as soon as it is light."

"I am perfectly able to go on," Amuba said; "thanks to the wet grass I see you have been piling round my head, the heat seems to have passed away and the throbbing to have ceased."

Amuba was indeed now able to walk at a brisk pace.

"Which way do you want to go?" the slave asked him in a short time. "It is getting light enough now for me to see your face, and it will never do for you to meet anyone. Your head is still swollen, and there are marks and bruises and cuts all over the scalp. Your appearance will attract attention at once, and if any saw you who had heard of last evening's doings you would be at once suspected."

"I will make direct for the hills," Amuba said. "They are not far distant, and I can easily conceal myself among the rocks until sunset."

"Let us hurry on, then," the slave said; "it is but half an hour's walk. But as we may at any moment now meet peasants going to their work, I will go on ahead; do you follow a hundred yards behind me. If I see anyone coming I will lift my hand above my head, and do you at once step aside from the road into the vineyard or orchard, and lie there until they have passed."

Amuba followed these instructions, and it was more than an hour before he reached the foot of the hills, so often did he have to turn aside to avoid groups of peasants. At last he reached the foot of the rugged ascent. Here he took leave of his guide with many warm thanks for his kindness and services, and with a message of gratitude to his lord. Then Amuba ascended the hill for a short distance, and laid himself down among some great boulders.

Although greatly refreshed by his night's rest he was still weak and shaken, and felt altogether unequal to making his way along the hills for the four miles which intervened between himself and the hiding-place of his friends among the tombs above the city. He was soon asleep again, and the sun was already some distance down the sky when he awoke. He waited until it sank behind the brow of the hill above him, and then climbing some distance higher made his way along the hillside, having little fear that his figure would be noticed now that the hillside was in shadow. Darkness had just fallen when he arrived at the tomb they used as their shelter. A figure was standing there in deep shadow. As he turned the path and approached, it advanced to meet him. Then there was a cry of joy, and Jethro sprang forward and clasped him in his arms.

"My dear Amuba, I never thought to see you in life again!"

A moment later Chebron ran out, and in his turn embraced Amuba.

"I shall never forgive you, and I shall never forgive myself," he said reproachfully. "What right had you to take my danger upon yourself? It was wrong, Amuba; and I have suffered horribly. Even though we are as brothers, why should you sacrifice yourself for me, especially when it is my life and not yours that is forfeited? I told myself a thousand times last night that I was base and cowardly in allowing you and Jethro to risk your lives for me, when by giving myself up the rage of the people will be satisfied, and you could make your way out of this land without great danger. It was bad enough that you should share my risk, but when it comes to your taking it all upon your shoulders that I should escape free, I can accept such sacrifice no longer; and to-morrow I will go down and surrender myself."

Amuba was about to burst into remonstrance, when Jethro touched him as a sign to be silent. The Rebu knew how acutely Chebron had suffered and how he had spent the night in tears and self-reproaches, and felt that it was better to allow his present agitation to pass before arguing with him.

"Are you hungry, Amuba?" he asked.

"That I am, Jethro. I had nothing save a mouthful of bread since our meal here yesterday; and you will get no news out of me until I have eaten and drunk." A meal of cakes and cool fish and a draught of wine was soon taken; and Amuba said, "Now I will tell you all about it."

"We know the first part," Jethro said. "When I returned here yesterday evening I found Chebron almost beside himself with anxiety. He told me how he had been discovered by one of the slaves of Ptylus who knew him by sight; how you attacked the slave, rescued him from his hands, and then joined him in his flight; how you insisted that you should separate; and how the pursuers had all followed on your track, leaving him to return here unmolested. He had been here upwards of two hours when I arrived, and as the time had passed on without your return he had become more and more anxious. Of course I at once started out to gather news, and had the greatest difficulty in persuading him to remain here, for he scorned the idea of danger to himself from the search which would be sure to be again actively set on foot. However, as I pointed out it was necessary that if you returned you should find somebody here, he at last agreed to remain.

"When I got into the town I found the whole city in the streets. The news had come that the slayers of the cat had been discovered; that one had escaped, but that the other had been overtaken after a long chase; and that he had been set upon, and would have been slain, as he well deserved, had not one of the princes of the royal house arrived and carried him off in his chariot. The news excited the greatest surprise and indignation, and two officers of the city had gone out to the prince's mansion, which was six miles away from the city, to claim the fugitive and bring him to the town, when he would be at once delivered to the just anger of the populace.

"As soon as I learned this I started out along the road by which they would return, and hurried on past the people already gathered there. I had brought my sword with me, and my intention was that as the chariot returned with you I would leap upon it, surprise and slay the officials, and drive off with you; for I knew you would be able to take no part in making the escape, as I had heard that you were already insensible when carried off in the chariot. There were groups of people all along the road with torches, but I thought that a sudden surprise would probably be successful.

"At last I heard the chariot approaching. It was being driven more slowly than I had expected. As it came to a large group of people some distance ahead of me it stopped for a moment, and the official addressed the people. There was no shout or sound of exultation, and I felt convinced at once that either upon their arrival they had found that you were already dead, or that in some miraculous way you had escaped. I therefore hurried back to the next group. When the chariot came up there was a shout of, 'What is the news? Where is the malefactor?' The officials checked their horses and replied: 'A mistake has been made. The prince assures us that the lad was a poor slave, and wholly innocent of this affair. He has satisfied himself that in their jealousy for the honour of the gods the peasants who attacked the lad committed a grievous wrong, and fell upon a wholly innocent person. After assuring himself of this he had his wounds bound up and suffered him to depart. The prince intends to lay a complaint before the council against the persons who have cruelly maltreated and nearly murdered an innocent person, who, he stated, interfered in the matter because he saw a slave attacking a young lad, and who fled fearing trouble because of the punishment he had inflicted upon the aggressor.'

"The announcement was received in silence; but when the chariot had driven on again there was much murmuring. The account had certainly the appearance of truth; for it was already known by the narrative of the slave who recognized Chebron that the person who rescued him was a youth and a stranger to him, and that it was this youth who had been pursued while Chebron himself had escaped. Still there was murmuring the prince should in so important a matter have suffered the youth to depart without a more searching examination. Some said that even if the boy's story was true he deserved punishment for attacking the slave who had arrested Chebron, while others said that as he had certainly been beaten almost to death, he had been punished sufficiently. All agreed that no doubt the whole affair would be investigated.

"I hurried back again with the news, and all night we watched for you, and when morning came without your arrival we were almost as anxious as before, fearing that you had been too badly injured to rejoin us, and that to-day you would almost certainly be recaptured. As the search for Chebron would assuredly be actively carried out, I insisted on his remaining quiet here while I made frequent journeys down to the city for news; but beyond the certainty that you had not been recaptured, although a diligent search had been made for you as well as for Chebron, I learned nothing. Now, Amuba, I have relieved you of the necessity for much talk; you have only to fill in the gaps of the story and to tell us how it was that you persuaded the Egyptian prince of your innocence."

"It is rather a long story, Jethro; but now that I have had a meal I feel strong enough to talk all night, for I have had nearly twenty-four hours sleep. First, I will tell Chebron that when I took the pursuers off his track I had no idea of sacrificing myself, for I made sure that I should be able to outrun them, and I should have done so easily had it not been for fresh people constantly taking up the pursuit and at last running me down."

Amuba then related the whole story of his flight, his attack with the peasants and his rescue, and then recited the whole of his conversation with his rescuer, and his proceedings after leaving his house. "So you see," he concluded, "that strangely enough it was the teaching of your father, Chebron, and the tale that Ruth told us, and that her grandfather before told you, of the God of their forefathers, that saved my life. Had it not been that this prince of Israelitish birth also believed in one God, it could hardly be that he would have saved me from the vengeance of the people, for as he says he is in disfavour with the king, and his conduct in allowing me to go free merely on my own assertion of my innocence is likely to do him further harm. This he would assuredly never have risked had it not been for the tie between us of a common faith in one great God."

"It is a strange story," Jethro said when Amuba brought his narrative to a conclusion, "and you have had a marvellous escape. Had it not been for the arrival of this prince upon the spot at the very moment you must have been killed. Had he not have been of a compassionate nature, he would never, in the first place, have interfered on your behalf; and had it not been for your common faith, he would have held you until the officials arrived to claim you. Then, too, you were fortunate, indeed, in the kindness of your guide; for evidently had it not been for your long rest, and the steps he took to reduce the heat of your wounds, you must have fallen into the hands of the searchers this morning. Above all, I consider it extraordinary that you should at the critical moment have been rescued by perhaps the one man in Egypt who would have had the will and the courage to save you."

Upon the following morning Jethro and Amuba succeeded with some difficulty in dissuading Chebron from his determination to give himself up, the argument that had the most powerful effect being that by so doing he would be disobeying the last orders of his father. It was resolved that in future as a better disguise he should be attired as a woman, and that the watch upon the house of Ptylus should be recommenced; but that they should station themselves further away. It was thought, indeed, that the search in that neighbourhood was likely to be less rigorous than elsewhere, as it would not be thought probable that the fugitives would return to a spot where they had been recognized. Amuba's disguise was completely altered. He was still in the dress of a peasant, but, by means of pigments obtained from Chigron, Jethro so transformed him as to give him, to a casual observer, the appearance of advanced years.

They had had a long discussion as to the plan they would adopt, Amuba and Jethro wishing Chebron to leave the watching entirely to them. But this he would not hear of, saying that he was confident that, in his disguise as a woman, no one would know him.

"We must find out which way he goes, to begin with," he said. "After that none of us need go near the house. I will buy a basket and some flowers from one of the peasant women who bring them in, and will take my seat near the gate. By three o'clock Plexo will have finished his offices in the temple, and may set out half an hour later. I shall see at least which road he takes. Then, when you join me at dusk, one of you can walk a mile or two along the road; the other twice as far. We shall then see when he returns whether he has followed the road any considerable distance or has turned off by any cross-roads, and can post ourselves on the following day so as to find out more."

"The plan is a very good one, Chebron, and we will follow it. Once we get upon his trail I will guarantee that it will not be long before we trace him to his goal."

Accordingly that afternoon Chebron, dressed as a peasant woman, took his seat with a basket of flowers fifty yards from the entrance to the house of Ptylus. At about the time he expected Plexo and his father returned together from the temple. Half an hour later a light chariot with two horses issued from the gate. Plexo was driving and an attendant stood beside him. Chebron felt sure that if Plexo was going to visit Mysa he would take the road leading into the country, and the post he had taken up commanded a view of the point where the road divided into three— one running straight north along the middle of the valley, while the others bore right and left until one fell into the great road near the river, the other into that on the side of the valley near the hills. It was this last that Plexo took; and although he might be going to visit acquaintants living in the many villas scattered for miles and miles along the road-side, Chebron felt a strong hope that he was going to Mysa's hiding-place. As soon as it was dark he was joined by Jethro and Amuba.

"He started at three o'clock!" Chebron exclaimed as they came up to him, "and took the road leading to the foot of the hills."

"We will go on there at once," Jethro said. "He may return before long, and we must hurry. Do you walk quietly on, Chebron, and stop at the point where the road ahead runs into the main road. Amuba shall stop two miles further; I will go two miles further still. If he comes along the road past me we will begin at that point to-morrow."

Jethro had but just reached the spot at which he proposed to wait when he heard the sound of the wheels approaching, and a minute later the chariot drove along. The moon was not up, but the night was clear and bright; and, advancing as close he could to the passing chariot, he was able to recognize Plexo. The latter gave an angry exclamation as his horses shied at the figure which had suddenly presented itself, and gave a cut with his whip at Jethro. A minute later the chariot had disappeared and Jethro returned towards the city, picking up on his way Amuba and Chebron.

The next night Amuba took up his station a mile beyond the spot at which Jethro had seen the chariot, Jethro another mile ahead, while Chebron watched the cross-roads near the town; but this time it did not come along, although Chebron had seen him start the same hour as before.

"I hardly expected to see him to-night," Jethro said when he joined the others after fruitlessly waiting for three hours. "He will hardly be likely to visit her two days in succession. He will be more likely to leave her for a week to meditate on the hopelessness of refusing to purchase her liberty at the price of accepting him as her husband. Doubtless he has to-day merely paid a visit to some friends."

It was not, indeed, until the fourth night of waiting that Plexo came along. This time he did not pass Jethro at all, and it was therefore certain that he had turned off from the main road either to the right or left at some point between the post of Jethro and that of Amuba. When this was determined they agreed, after a consultation, not to return to their hiding-places near Thebes that night, but to lie down under some trees by the road-side until morning broke, and then to examine the road carefully. It was not likely that another chariot would pass before morning, and they might be able to follow the tracks along the dusty road.

In this way they discovered the road where he had turned off; but beyond this the tracks did not show, as the road was hard and almost free from dust. It lay, as they expected, towards the hills; but there were so many country mansions of the wealthy classes dotted about, and so many cross-roads leading to these and to the farm-houses of the cultivators, that they felt they were still far from attaining the object of their search.

After some discussion it was agreed that they should ascend the hills and remain there during the day, and that Jethro should return to the town as soon as it became dark to obtain a store of provisions sufficient to last them for a week. This was done, and the next day they separated at dawn and took up their places on the hills at a distance of about a mile apart, choosing spots where they commanded a view over the valley, and arranging to meet at a central point when night came on.

Chapter 15

SIX days passed without their watch being rewarded; then Chebron, whose post was just opposite the road where they had traced the wheels, saw a chariot turn from the main road into it. As many others had taken that course every day he did not at first feel very hopeful, although the time precisely tallied with that at which Plexo should have arrived had he started at the same hour as before. As it came near, however, he became convinced that it was the vehicle he was looking for. The horses tallied in colour with those of Plexo, and the colour of his dress could even at that distance be distinguished. This time, however, he was not accompanied by a servant, but by a figure the whiteness of whose garment showed him also to be a priest. "That must be Ptylus," he said to himself, "my father's murderer. Would I were down by the edge of the road, with my bow and arrows; high-priest as he has now become, I would send an arrow through his heart!"

The chariot turned off by the road parallel to that which had been followed from Thebes, and so close to the foot of the hills that from Chebron's post he could no longer see it. As soon as it was out of sight he leapt to his feet and hurried along the hills to join Amuba, whose post was next to his own. He found his friend had already gone on, and he hurried breathlessly on until he reached Jethro, who had been joined by Amuba a few minutes before.

"Have you seen them?" he exclaimed.

"I have seen them and marked them down," Jethro replied. "You see that roof among those trees at the foot of the hill half a mile further along? They turned off the road and entered those trees. Our search is over at last."

"What had we better do, Jethro? Wait until they have left again, and then go down?"

"No," Jethro said sternly. "There are two things to be done— the one is to rescue Mysa; the other to punish the murderer of Ameres. But even did we determine to delay our vengeance I should say we must still press on. You saw that arch-villain Ptylus with his son. He has assuredly come for some purpose; probably he may intend to terrify the girl until he drives her into taking some solemn oath that she will accept Plexo as her husband. What can a girl of that age do in the hands of unscrupulous villains like these? It may be that this fox Plexo has been trying flattery; and, finding that fail, has called in Ptylus, who can threaten her with the anger of these gods of hers, to say nothing of perpetual imprisonment and harsh treatment. We will therefore push on at once. Amuba and I carry our stout peasant staves, while you, Chebron, have your dagger concealed under that female dress. We shall have all the advantage of surprise in our favour. It is not likely that there are more than one or two men there, with perhaps a female servant. Ptylus would not wish the secret to be known to more than was absolutely necessary. Of course it is possible that the four men who carried her off may all be on guard there, but if so, it makes but six; and that with the surprise, and what with their not knowing how numerous we are, that number should not be more than sufficient for us to dispose of without difficulty. At any rate, were there twenty I would not hesitate; honest men need never fear an encounter with rogues."

"Especially," Amuba said, "when the honest men possess such sinews as yours, Jethro, and a good heavy cudgel in their hands."

Jethro smiled, but was in too earnest a mood to answer, and at once led the way along the hillside until immediately behind the house among the trees; then they descended, climbing with some difficulty over the wall surrounding the wood, and entered the inclosure. Treading as lightly as possible Jethro and his companions passed through the wood and made their way up to the house. It was small but handsomely built, and was surrounded with a colonnade supported by carved pillars. The garden immediately around it was evidently carefully tended, and the house, from its secluded position, was well fitted as a place of sojourn for a wealthy priest or noble desirous of a few days' rest and retirement from the bustle of the great city. As all were barefooted they passed across the garden to the colonnade without the slightest sound. As they reached it Jethro held up his hand for them to stop, for the sound of voices came through the wide doorway of an apartment opening out to the colonnade.

Both Chebron and Amuba at once recognized the voice of Ptylus.

"I will put up with no more of this folly, Mysa. You should think yourself fortunate in the extreme, in the position in which you are, belonging to a disgraced family, to receive such an offer as my son makes to you. I will have an answer at once. You will either swear before the gods that you accept Plexo as your future husband, that you will reply to all who question you that you have been staying here by your own free will, and that you remained in concealment simply because you were overwhelmed with horror at the terrible act of the sacrilege committed by your brother, or you will this night be confined in a tomb, where you will remain alone and without the light of day until you agree to my conditions. You don't think, you little fool, that I, Ptylus, high-priest of Osiris, am to be thwarted in my plans by the opposition of a child like you."

Here a voice, which the three listeners recognized to their surprise as that of Ruth, broke out:

"Do not listen to him, Mysa. Whatever comes of it, never consent to lie before God, as this wicked man would have you. You call yourself a high-priest, sir. What must be the worth of the gods you pretend to worship if they suffer one like you to minister to them? Were they gods, and not mere images of stone, they would strike you dead at the altar."

A furious exclamation broke from Ptylus, and he stepped forward and seized the Hebrew girl roughly by the shoulder, only to start back with another exclamation as Ruth struck him with her open hand, with all her force, on the cheek.

"Drag her hence, Plexo!" he exclaimed. But at this moment the entrance was darkened, and the three listeners sprang into the room.

Ptylus had the courage that distinguished his race, and although for a moment startled at the sudden entry he did not recoil, but drawing his sword from his girdle he said haughtily:

"Who are you, and what means this intrusion?"

"We are those whom you have been hunting to death, Ptylus; and we come here as avengers of blood. As you brought about the murder of Ameres, so you must die—to say naught of your offence in carrying off the daughter of the man you slew."

Without a word Ptylus rushed upon Jethro with his sword, thinking to make short work of this insolent peasant; but as he did so, Jethro whirled his massive club round his head, and catching the blow upon it, shivered the sword in pieces.

Ptylus stopped his arm, and, gazing steadily at his opponent, said:

"Wretch, do you dare to murder the high-priest of Osiris?"

"No," Jethro said, "but I dare to execute him," and he brought his heavy club down with all his strength upon the head of the priest.

At this moment Plexo, who had stolen unobserved from the room the instant the others entered, returned, followed by three armed men. Chebron and Amuba were so intent upon the combat between Jethro and the priest, that they did not notice the entrance of Plexo, who, with uplifted knife, sprang upon Chebron.

There was a scream of warning, and quick as thought Ruth sprang forward and pushed Plexo as he sprang through the air. The sudden shock threw both to the ground. Ruth sprang to her feet again, but Plexo lay there motionless. The three armed men stood for a moment stupefied at the fall of their two employers, and then, seeing two men and a woman, rushed forward to attack them. One sweeping blow with Jethro's staff felled the first of his assailants to the ground; the other paused irresolute.

"Drop your weapons, or you are dead men!" Jethro exclaimed. "You are outnumbered; and if you move, you die!"

As Chebron had now thrown back his female robe and drawn his dagger, and taken his place at the door, while Jethro and Amuba were advancing against them, the two men dropped their weapons.

"Hold out your hands," Jethro said. "My son, stand over them with your club, and break the skull of either who may move."

The men did as they were ordered. Jethro tore strips of cloth off their garments, twisted them into ropes, and bound their wrists firmly together. The meaning tone in which Jethro had called Amuba his son had not escaped either Amuba or Chebron, who saw that Jethro was desirous of concealing their names. Mysa, who had raised a cry of joy when Jethro first spoke, had sunk terrified upon a couch, and had hidden her face in her hands during the short encounter; while Ruth had stood silent and vigilant beside her, moving only when Plexo rushed at Chebron, and retiring to

Mysa's side again as soon as she had regained her feet. She, too, understood Jethro's motives in calling Amuba his son, and stooping over Mysa she said:

"It is all over now, Mysa, but remain quiet at present. Do not speak until you see what is going to be done."

As soon as the men were tied Jethro secured in the same manner the man who was lying stunned from his blow. Then he turned to Plexo, who had not moved since he had fallen. He half turned him round, and uttered a low exclamation of surprise.

"Gastrion," he said to Chebron, "go with the young lady into the garden, and remain there until we join you."

Chebron passed out on to the colonnade, following Mysa and Ruth. The moment they were unobserved Mysa threw her arms round him, and burst into tears with joy.

"Oh, Chebron!" she exclaimed, "you have arrived just in time. I thought we were never going to get away from that dreadful man; and I don't know what I should have done if it hadn't been for Ruth. And, oh ! they have been telling me such terrible things— but they can't be true—that our dear father had been killed; and that it was you, Chebron, who killed dear Paucis; but of course I did not believe them—I knew it was all their wickedness."

"Never mind about that, dear," Chebron said; "we will talk about all this afterwards. The first thing is to get you away from this place. Jethro and Amuba will soon decide what is best to be done. Are there any others in the house?"

"There is one other man," Ruth replied, "and an old woman; I think the other man is at the door with the chariot."

"I had better tell Jethro," Chebron said, and he again went into the room and told Jethro what he had heard.

"We will seize the woman first," Jethro said, "and then go out round the house and come down from the other way upon the chariot. The man will have heard the outcry; and if we came suddenly out of the door, might leap into the chariot and drive off before we could overtake him. But if we come upon it from behind we shall secure him."

"But you have forgotten to bind Plexo," Chebron said.

"Plexo is dead," Jethro replied. "As he fell his arm was beneath him, and the knife with which he had been intending to strike you pierced his heart. I am very glad that you observed the way I spoke to Amuba. It was of the greatest importance that the name should not be mentioned. This affair will cause a tremendous excitement. There is nothing to connect us with Ptylus, and it may be supposed that it is the work of some malefactors, who came down from the hills in search of plunder. The fact that Mysa was here and was carried away is not in itself any proof that we had a hand in it, for Libyan robbers might well have carried her and Ruth away to make slaves of. Plexo caught but a glimpse of us, and doubtless only rushed out and called to the men to come to his father's assistance. At any rate, let there be no names mentioned. Now let us finish our work here."

The female servant was soon found and bound; then the four prisoners were placed in different rooms, and fastened securely to the wall or pillars.

"Never put two prisoners together," Jethro said; "always remember that. Tie one man up and you may keep him; tie up two and they are sure to escape. They can bite through each other's cords, or untie the knot with their teeth, or possibly even with their fingers."

"Now, what is the next thing to do?" Amuba asked.

"The next thing is to have a consultation. Do you, Chebron, go out into the garden to the girls. Amuba and I will deal with the other man."

As soon as Jethro and Amuba had left him Chebron rejoined the girls.

"You saved my life, Ruth. I shall never forget it."

"You saved me from the crocodile, my lord. It was but a push and he fell. I scarce know how it was done."

"Your quickness saved my life all the same, Ruth. I had not noticed him till you cried out, and then it would have been too late. We have been anxious for you also, Ruth. We hoped that you might be with Mysa, but none saw you go out with her."

"My place was with my mistress," Ruth said quietly. "And she was more than a mistress—she was as a friend to me."

"But how came you here, Chebron," Mysa again asked, "and why are you dressed up like a peasant woman? It is not seemly in any man, much less in you, a priest. And Amuba and Jethro, too; they are dressed as peasants, and their faces seem changed, I do not know how. They look darker, and I should not have known them had I not recognized Jethro's voice."

"It is a long story, dear, and I will tell you all presently, and we want to hear your story too. Ah! here come the others. It is to them, Mysa, far more than to me that you owe your rescue. I may know more of the learning of our people, but I have none of the readiness and coolness of Amuba, while Jethro is as prudent as he is brave. It would have fared hardly with me as well as with you, Mysa, had it not been for these good friends."

Mysa went up to them as they approached.

"Oh, Jethro! I feel how much I owe to you; and to you Amuba. My courage had all but given way, although Ruth strove so hard to give me hope, and I fear I could not have long withstood the threats of that bad man. You cannot tell what joy I felt when I recognized your voice."

"Our joy was as great in finding you as yours in seeing us," Jethro replied. "Amuba and I would gladly have laid down our lives for you. And now let us have a consultation; there is much to decide upon and arrange. Let us go round to the garden at the other side of the house. There we can sit and talk, and at the same time keep watch that no one else enters. It is not likely that any one will do so, for the place is secluded, and none would know that these men were here; still a peasant might enter to sell fowls or fruit, therefore it were best to keep an eye upon the entrance."

They went round to some seats placed beneath trees on the other side of the house. A fountain worked by the water of a little rill on the hillside played in front of them, and a few tame water-fowl swam in the shallow basin around it. Everything was still and peaceful, and to Chebron it seemed as if the events of the last three weeks had been a hideous dream, and that they were again sitting in the garden of their house at Thebes.

"Now, first of all," Mysa said, "I must have my questions answered. How are my father and mother and everyone?"

Jethro took Amuba's arm and turned away. "We will leave you, Chebron, to tell Mysa what has taken place. It will be better for you to do so alone."

Ruth rose from her seat to leave also, but Mysa put her hand on her arm.

"I am frightened, Ruth; stay with me."

"You told me, Mysa," Chebron began, "that they had told you tales that our father was dead, and that it was I who killed Paucis."

"Yes; but I did not believe them, Chebron. Of course I did not for a moment—at least not for a moment about you. But when I thought of those bad men at the gate, and the crash we heard, and the noise of the people rushing in shouting, I thought—I was afraid—that perhaps it might be true about our father. But, oh, Chebron, surely it is not so?"

"Alas, Mysa, it is true! They cruelly slew our father. I wish I had been there to have fallen by his side; but you know Amuba and I were away. Jethro fought desperately to the last, and would have died with him had not our father himself commanded that in case anything happened to him he was to take charge of me, and to carry me out of the land."

Mysa was crying bitterly now. Presently she looked up.

"But why should you want to leave the land, Chebron? Surely—surely it is not true that you——"

The thing seemed too terrible for her to put into words.

"That I killed poor Paucis? That is true also, Mysa."

Mysa gave a little cry of horror.

"Oh, Ruth!" she cried, "this is too dreadful!"

Ruth put her arms round the sobbing girl. "You may be sure, Mysa, that your brother did not do it intentionally."

"But it is all the same," Mysa cried. "It was the sacred cat, you know—the Cat of Bubastes."

"It was, Mysa; and I thought at first, as you did, that although it was the result of an accident the anger of the gods would be poured out against me, that I was as one accursed, whose life was forfeited in this world, and whose spirit was destined to dwell in unclean beasts after death. But when I told my father all, he reassured me, and told me not to fear in any way the wrath of the gods."

He then related to his sister the manner in which the cat had been killed, the steps he and Amuba had taken to conceal the body, and his avowal to his father of his fault.

"I see it was not your fault, Chebron. But you know the laws of Egypt, and the punishment for killing even a common cat. How could our father say that the gods would not be angry?"

"I cannot tell you all he said, Mysa; though some day had I remained with you I might have done so. But he did say so, and you know how wise and good he was. Therefore I want you to remember what he said, so that when I am gone you will not all your life think of me as one accursed."

"Oh! I should never do that!" Mysa exclaimed, starting up and throwing her arms round her brother's neck. "How could you think so? But why are you talking about going, and where are you going?"

"I am going, Mysa, because the people of Egypt do not view this matter in the same light as my father, but are hunting all the land to find and slay me and Amuba; for, not knowing the exact truth, they put us down as equally guilty. So we must fly. Our father gave full directions to Jethro, and we should by this time have been a long distance away had it not been that we stayed to find and rescue you."

"Then if the other things they told me are true, Chebron, it may be true too that the letter they showed me ordering me to consent to marry Plexo was from my mother. How could she tell me that when she knew that I hated him, and she has over and over again spoken scornfully of his family before me?"

"What did she say?" Chebron asked.

"She said that now disgrace had fallen on the family I might think myself very fortunate in obtaining such an offer."

Chebron was silent. He knew that his mother had never shown any earnest love either for Mysa or himself, that her thoughts were entirely devoted to dress and entertainments, and that any love she had to give had been bestowed upon his brother.

"I fear it is true, Mysa."

"But I will never marry Plexo!" Mysa exclaimed passionately. "My father always said I should never marry a man I disliked."

"You will never marry Plexo, Mysa—he is dead."

Ruth uttered an exclamation.

"He died by his own hand, Ruth—that is, by an accident. As he fell his dagger pierced his own heart, and when Jethro went to look at him he was dead."

"The Lord requited him for his evil," Ruth said firmly. "All things are in His hands. As I did not mean to slay him, I lament not over his death. Besides, he strove to take your life, and had I had a dagger in my hand I should assuredly have used it."

"Then what is to become of me?" Mysa asked.

"You must go back to your mother, Mysa. There is naught else for you to do."

"I will not!" Mysa exclaimed. "She never loved me. She would have married me against my will to Plexo, although she knew he was bad, and that I hated him. She would make me marry some one else who was rich, regardless of my wishes. No, Chebron, nothing shall make me go back to her."

Chebron looked perplexed.

"Here come Jethro and Amuba, dear. You had best talk it over with them. I see nothing else for you to do."

As Jethro came up Mysa walked to meet him.

"I will not go back to my mother, Jethro!" she exclaimed impetuously. "She wanted me to marry Plexo. She would give me to some one else, and my father always said I should only marry some one I liked. You can never be so cruel as to give me up to her?"

"I know that your father's wishes were strong upon that point," Jethro said; "for he spoke to me of you when he gave me his commands respecting Chebron. He said that he wished that I could watch over you as over him, and it was because of what he had said that I disregarded his orders as to our instant flight, and lingered here in hopes of freeing you. Still I see not anything else to be done. Your mother doubtless wrote while still overpowered by grief at your father's loss, and thought that she was acting for your welfare in securing you so advantageous a marriage in spite of the cloud under which your family was resting."

"I will not go to her!" Mysa repeated. "She thought of herself, as she always did, and not of me in any way. You know it was so, Chebron—you cannot deny it!"

Chebron was silent. His whole affection had been given to his father, for his mother he had comparatively little. As a child he had seldom been allowed to come into the room where she was. She declared that his noise was too much for her, that his talk made her head ache, and that his fidgeting about was too much to be borne. Nor since that time had he been much more with her. It was his father who had seen to his welfare and that of Mysa, who would put aside his grave studies to walk and talk with them, who was always indulgent, always anxious to give them pleasure. He therefore thoroughly entered into Mysa's feelings, but saw no possible alternative for her.

"But where could you go, Mysa?" Jethro asked. "Where could you be placed? Wherever you were your mother in time would be sure to hear of it and would re-claim you."

"I shall go with Chebron, and you, and Amuba," Mysa said positively.

"Impossible!" Jethro replied. "We are going upon a tremendous journey, full of danger and fatigue. We are going among unknown and savage peoples; the chances are a hundred to one against our ever arriving at the end of our journey. If this is so to myself and to young men like Chebron and Amuba—for they are now past eighteen, and will speedily be men—what chance would there be of success with you with us?"

"I can walk as well as Chebron," Mysa said. "You know that, Chebron. And I suppose I could suffer hardship just as well. At any rate, I would rather suffer anything and be with him and all of you than stop here. The people have murdered my father. My mother would sell me to the highest bidder. If the chances are so great that you will never get through your journey in safety, my being with you cannot make them so much greater. I have only Chebron in the world, and I will go where he goes, and die where he dies. The gods can protect me just as well on a journey as here. Have they not protected you now, and Chebron too, by what he says? You will take me with you, dear Jethro, won't you?" she urged pleadingly. "You say my father wished you to watch over me; do not forsake me now. Ruth will come with us too—will you not, Ruth?—I am sure she will not be more afraid of the journey than I am."

"I will assuredly go if you go, Mysa. The God of Israel can take us safely through all dangers if it be His will."

Jethro was silent. Such an addition to his charge would assuredly add immensely to the difficulties of the journey; but on the other hand he remembered the anxiety of Ameres about Mysa, and he asked himself what his late master would have wished had he known how matters stood. He glanced at Amuba and Chebron and saw at once that their wishes agreed with those of Mysa. He turned away abruptly, and for some minutes paced up and down the garden. Then he returned to the group, among whom not a word had been exchanged since he left them.

"Mysa," he said gravely, "this is a great thing that you ask; there is no disguising that your presence will add greatly to our difficulties, will add also to our perils, and may render it impossible for me to carry out your father's wishes and to conduct Chebron to a land where he will be beyond the persecution of Egypt. Such an enterprise must be undertaken in no light spirit. If you go you must be prepared to face death in all forms—by hunger and thirst and the weapons of the wild natives. It may even be that your lot may be that of slavery among them. It is a terrible journey for men, more terrible still for women; still, if you are resolved, resolved with the strength and mind of a woman and not of a child, that after having once turned your back upon Egypt you will never repent the step you have taken or wish to return, but will be steadfast under all the trials that may befall us, then I say that you shall share our lot."

Mysa uttered an exclamation of joy.

"I promise, Jethro; and whatever may happen—hardship, danger, or death—you shall never hear a word of complaint from me. Are you not glad, Ruth?"

"I think it well," Ruth said gravely. "It is a great undertaking; but I think that God's hand is in it. I, too, would fain leave this land of idols; and except those here I have none in the world to care for."

"And now, Jethro," Amuba said, "what had we best do? It is already almost dark, therefore we could set out at once. Could we make use of the chariot?"

Jethro considered for a short time.

"Except for carrying any things we may want for our first start, I do not see that we can do so," he said; "for where we leave the chariot to-morrow morning it would be found, and when it is known that Ptylus' chariot was missing it would soon be recognized as his, and thus a clue be afforded to the fact that we had fled south. As to travelling in it beyond to-night, it would be out of the question. Besides, it will only hold three at the most. No, if we use it at all it must be to drive north, and so throw them off the scent. I think it will be worth doing that."

"I will undertake that part of the business," Amuba said. "There will be much for you to do to-morrow, Jethro, which only you can arrange. There's the boat to be hired, stores laid in, and all got in readiness. I think the best plan will be for you both to start at once with the girls for Thebes. You and Chebron can occupy your hiding-place on the hill, and Chigron will be glad to take the girls into his house. There is no danger of an immediate search being made for them.

"To-night when the priest and his son do not return their servants will suppose that they have slept here. It will not be until late to-morrow afternoon that there will be any alarm or any likelihood of a messenger being sent over here, then the consternation and confusion that will be caused will be so great that probably no one will think of carrying the news to the officials until the next morning. Besides, until the story of Mysa's having been here and of her being missing is generally known, there is no reason that what has taken place should be attributed to us; therefore, for the next eight-and-forty hours I think that they would be perfectly safe at the embalmer's. I will drive the chariot thirty or forty miles north, then turn the horses loose where they are sure to be noticed ere long, and will return on foot and join you in your hiding-place to-morrow night."

"I think your plan is a very good one, Amuba. Before we start I will make a search through the house. There will be nothing we want to take with us, nor would we touch any of the treasure of the villains were the house full or it; but if I toss some of the things about it will look as if robbery had been the motive of what has taken place. The men in bonds can know nothing of the real state of things. Plexo, when he rushed out for their aid, could have had no time to do more that to tell them to take up their arms and follow him; indeed, it is doubtful whether he himself had any idea that we were aught but what we seemed. Therefore, the first impression assuredly will be that we were malefactors of the worst kind, escaped slaves, men with no respect for the gods; for assuredly no Egyptians, even the worst of criminals, would, in cold blood, have laid hands on the high-priest of Osiris."

"They laid hands on my father," Chebron said bitterly.

"Yes, but not in cold blood. Reports had first been spread among them that he was untrue to the gods, and then they were maddened by fanaticism and horror at the death of that sacred cat. But in cold blood, as I said, no Egyptian, however vile and criminal, would lift his hand against a priest. You may as well come with me, Amuba; it would be strange if one of us only took part in the search."

In ten minutes Jethro and Amuba had turned the place into confusion in forcing open chests and cabinets and littering the floor with garments; then taking a few of the most valuable vases and jewels they threw them into the pond round the fountain, where they would be concealed from view by the water-lilies which floated on its surface.

They examined afresh the fastenings of the captives, and felt assured that by no possibility could they free themselves.

"They will be sure to be freed by to-morrow night," Amuba said, "otherwise I should not like to leave them here to die of hunger and thirst."

"I should be only too glad," Jethro said, "if I thought there was a chance of their being here forty hours instead of twenty. Doubtless this is not the first evil business they have carried out for their villain master, and they may think themselves lucky indeed that we do not take what would be in every way the safest and best course, namely, to run a sword through their bodies and silence them forever. If I thought they could tell anything I would do so now; but I really do not think that anything they can tell will add to our danger. Of course the priest's wife knows that Mysa is hidden here, and will proclaim the fact that she has been here and is now missing, as she would consider it might afford a clue for the apprehension of those who attacked the house and slew her husband and son; therefore I do not see that there would be much to be gained by silencing these people; but if you think differently I will finish them at once."

Amuba shook his head, for although human life in those days was thought little of, save by the Egyptians themselves, he shrank from the thought of slaying captives in cold blood.

"No, they can tell nothing, Jethro. You had best be moving; there is nothing more to talk over. I think all our plans were arranged long ago; except, of course, that you must get rather a larger boat than you had intended, together with garments for the girls. I think it would be best that Chebron should still be disguised as a woman; but we can settle that to-morrow night. There is a good store of dresses for us to choose from at Chigron's."

Amuba led the horses to a stone water-trough and allowed them to quench their thirst. Then he mounted the chariot and drove off, while the rest of the party set out on foot for Thebes. It was so late before they reached Chigron's house that they thought it better not to arouse the inmates, as comment would be excited by the arrival of women at so late an hour and unexpected by the master; the girls, therefore, passed the night in the rock chamber behind the building, while Jethro and Chebron lay down outside.

As soon as dawn broke they moved some distance away. Jethro went to the house as soon as there was a sign that there was any one astir, and told Chigron that they had discovered and rescued Mysa. Chigron was much disturbed when he heard of the death of the high-priest and his son.

"I don't say these men were not villains, Jethro; but that two high-priests should be slaughtered in the course of a month is enough to bring the anger of all the gods upon Egypt. However, the poor girls are not responsible for it in any way, and I will willingly shelter them, especially as it is but for one night; but I own that I shall be vastly relieved when I know that you are all fairly on your journey."

"That I can well understand," Jethro said; "and believe me, the gratitude of those you have sheltered, which you will have as long as they live, may well outweigh any doubts that may present themselves as to whether you have acted wisely in aiding those who are victims to the superstitions of your countrymen."

Chigron called his servants and told them that he had just heard of the arrival from the country of some friends, and ordered a room to be prepared for them. He then went out and returned an hour later with the two girls. He led them quietly into the house and direct to the apartment prepared for them, so that they were unseen by any of the servants.

Then he called an old servant on whose fidelity he could rely, and charged her to wait upon them during the day, and to suffer none other to enter the apartment. He bade her convey the impression to the other servants that the visitors were aged women, and to mention that they intended to make a stay of a few hours only, until some friends with whom they were going to stay should send in a cart to carry them to their farm in the country. The old woman at once prepared baths for the girls and then supplied them with a meal, after which they lay down on couches and were soon fast asleep; for the excitement of the preceding evening and the strangeness of their position in the comfortless stone chamber had prevented their closing an eye during the night, and they had spent the hours in talking over the terrible loss Mysa had sustained, and the journey that lay before them.

Half an hour later Chigron went out again and was soon joined by Jethro, who had now resumed his attire as a citizen of middle class. It was necessary that Chigron should accompany him and take the chief part in making the arrangements; for although Jethro had learned, in his two years' captivity, to speak Egyptian fluently, he could not well pass as a native. Chigron therefore did most of the bargaining, Jethro keeping somewhat in the background.

They first took their course down to the river bank. Here innumerable craft lay moored; for the Nile was the highway of Egypt, and except for short journeys all traffic was carried on on its waters. As soon as it was known that they were looking for a boat they were surrounded by the owners of the various craft, each praising the speed, safety, and comfort of his boat. Chigron, however, was some time before he made his choice; then he fixed upon a boat that seemed well suited for the purpose. She carried a mast and large sail to take advantage of favourable winds. She was light and of very small draught, and, being constructed entirely for passenger traffic, she had a large cabin—divided into two parts for the accommodation of ladies—the crew, consisting of the captain and four men, sleeping on the deck.

"I think your boat will do very well," he said to the captain, "provided we can come to terms. My friend is going up with his family as far as Syene at any rate, and possibly on to Ibsciak; his business may take him even further. What will buy your terms a week?"

"I suppose my lord will provide food for the crew as well as for his own family?"

"That will be the best way," Jethro said.

"Then will he pay for extra hands where the current runs so strong that the crew cannot tow the boat unaided against it?"

Jethro assented.

"And will he return with it, or remain for awhile at the end of the journey?"

"It is probable that his business may detain him there for a considerable time," Chigron replied. "He has relations there with whom he will wish to make a stay. But this should make no difference; you will have no difficulty in obtaining passengers or freight for your journey down."

It was a long time before a bargain was struck, for Chigron knew that the boatman would consider it strange indeed were the terms he first asked to be accepted. But at last an arrangement satisfactory to both parties was concluded. It was arranged that the start should take place early on the following morning, and Chigron then proceeded with Jethro to make the purchases requisite for the voyage—mats, cushions, and curtains for furnishing the boat, cooking utensils and provisions for the crew and passengers. Of these, however, it was not necessary to take a very large quantity, as the boat would lie up to the bank every night near one of the frequent villages, and here there would be no difficulty in purchasing provisions of all kinds.

Some jars of good wine were, however, among the stores purchased, and in addition to these were several bales of costly merchandise and a large stock of such articles as would be useful for trade with the natives of the wilder parts of the country. A supply of arms—bows, arrows, and lances—was also placed on board. It was late in the afternoon before all these things were got on board the boat and everything arranged in order. Having seen all complete, Chigron returned with Jethro to his house. Jethro, after seeing the girls, who had just woke up and partaken of a meal, went up to the hiding-place on the hill and found that Amuba had just joined Chigron there.

"Is all going on well?" the lads asked as he entered.

"Everything is in readiness. The boat is hired and furnished. I have a good store of merchandise for trading in Meroe, besides trinkets of many kinds for the peoples lying between Meroe and the Red Sea. So far everything promises well. The boatmen belong to the Upper Nile, and their dialect differs too widely from that spoken here for them to be able to distinguish that I do not talk pure Egyptian. I wondered why it was that Chigron was such a long time in making his choice between the boats, when, as far as I could see, there were scores that would have equally suited our purpose. But I found afterwards that it was the boatmen rather than the boat which he was selecting, and that he chose those coming from far up the river, partly because their speech differed so widely from that of Thebes that they would not detect the roughness of my tongue; and secondly, because they would be more likely to continue the voyage further to the south than would the boatmen of this part, who would regard it as a serious undertaking to proceed beyond Ibsciak. Therefore we need fear no suspicion on the part of our boatmen. I suppose you disposed of the chariot as we arranged, Amuba?"

"Yes, I drove north for five hours and then turned aside into a wood. Here I loosed the horses so that they could feed as they chose. They would doubtless by morning stray into the fields, and so attract attention. Then there would be a search to see to whom they belonged, and the chariot would be found. By the time that the news spreads that Ptylus is dead, and also that his chariot and horses are missing, and have doubtless been taken off by those who had attacked him, the tidings that the chariot is found will have been taken to the nearest town, and it will shortly be reported all over the country that we are making north, and the search for us will be made in that direction only."

"Are you going back to the house, Jethro?"

"Yes, Chigron has given out to his servants that the visitors are relatives of mine, and as I have been frequently seen going in and out in this garb they are now accustomed to me; and it will be natural for me to sleep there to-night and to start with them in the morning. We shall start exactly at sunrise. You had better wait at a distance from the house and follow us, coming up and joining us just as we reach the river-side. The boat will be taken above the city to the highest steps; and we shall be able to proceed to that point without entering the town itself. Be careful with your disguises. The news of the death of Ptylus will not, I hope, be generally known in the city until we are fairly afloat. Were it otherwise it would be dangerous for you to run the risk of being seen abroad."

Chapter 16

LATE at night Jethro again went up to the hiding-place on the hill. Chigron had just returned from another visit to the city. He said:

"The whole of the town is in an uproar. The news that Ptylus and his son have been found slain has been received, and the excitement is tremendous. The death by violence of two high-priests of Osiris within so short a time is regarded as a presage of some terrible national misfortune. That one should have been slain was an almost unprecedented act—an insult of a terrible kind to the gods; but this second act of sacrilege has almost maddened the people. Some regard it as a judgment of Osiris, and deem that it is a proof that, as a few ventured to whisper before, the death of Ameres was brought about by an intrigue among a party of the priests, headed by Ptylus. Others see in it a fresh proof of the anger of the god against Egypt.

"The king himself will, it is said, take part in services of propitiation in the temple of Osiris to-morrow; sacrifices are to be offered, they say, in all the temples. A solemn fast will be proclaimed to-morrow, and all the people, high and low, are to shave their eyebrows and to display the usual signs of mourning. So far I have heard nothing as to the fact that two girls who were in the house are discovered to be missing, but to-morrow, when those who were in the house are questioned by the magistrates, this fact will doubtless come out, and the men will own that by the orders of Ptylus they carried Mysa away at the time the attack on the house was made.

"At present, however, there is no question of women in the case; and I can go down to the boat with the girls in company with Chigron without any fear whatever. But it is better that you should not be with us when we embark; for when the matter comes to be talked over, someone who sees us embark might notice that our number tallies with that of the three persons present when Ptylus was killed, and the two missing girls. Therefore Chigron's opinion is that it will be safer for you to start at once and walk to Mita, a village twenty miles up the river. There the boat will lie up to-morrow night, and as soon as it is dark you can come on board. I shall tell the boatmen that I expect you to join us there, as you have gone on ahead to transact some business for me in the neighbourhood."

"That is certainly the best plan," Amuba agreed. "There are too many who know Chebron by sight for it to be safe for him to go down to the boat here and embark in broad daylight. I will take two hours' sleep before I start; for as I did not sleep last night, and have walked forty miles since I left the chariot, I feel in need of a little repose before I start again. I was foolish not to have slept this afternoon, for I have since midday been hiding near; but there was so much to think about that I had no inclination to do so, especially as I believed that we should have a night's rest here."

"I will wake you," Chebron said. "I have been asleep the better part of the day, having had nothing to do since we arrived here yesterday evening."

Chebron sat watching the stars until he saw that they had made two hours' journey through the sky. Then he roused Amuba. Both now laid aside their garments as peasants and put on the attire prepared for them as the sons of a small trader. Amuba had submitted, although with much disgust, to have his head shaved on the night following the death of Ameres, and it was a satisfaction to him to put on a wig; for accustomed as he was to see the bare heads of the peasants, it was strange and uncomfortable to him to be going about in the same fashion.

As soon as they were dressed they started, made their way down to the bank of the river above the town, and walked along the broad causeway by the stream until within a mile or two of their destination. Then they turned off towards a clump of trees which were visible by the first gleam of dawn a quarter of a mile away. Here they slept for some hours, and late in the afternoon returned to the side of the river and strolled quietly along, watching the boats. Those in the middle of the stream were making their way down with the current lightly and easily, the crews often singing merrily, rejoicing over the approaching meeting with their friends after an absence of many weeks. The boats going up the stream were all close to the bank, the crews walking along the causeway and labouring at the tow-ropes, for there was not enough wind to render the sails of any utility in breasting the stream. The craft were of various kinds, some shapeless and rudely fashioned, used in conveying corn from the country higher up down to Thebes, and now returning empty. Others were the fancifully-painted boats of the wealthy, with comfortable cabins and sails of many colours richly decorated and embroidered. These were carrying their owners up or down the river, between their country mansions and the city.

It was half an hour after sunset when the two friends arrived at Mita. Darkness falls quickly in Egypt after the sun has gone down, and their features could scarcely have been recognized had they been met by anyone acquainted with them in the streets. The scene in the streets of the little village was a busy one. Its distance from Thebes rendered it a general halting-place for the night of the boats which had left the capital early, and a great number of these were already moored off the bank, while others were arriving in quick succession. The boatmen and passengers were busy making their purchases at the shops; fishermen, with well-filled baskets, were shouting the praises of their fish; fowlers, with strings of ducks and geese hanging from poles from their shoulders, were equally clamorous in offering them for sale.

The shops of the fruiterers and bakers and those of the vendors of the vegetables that formed so large a portion of the diet of the Egyptians, were all crowded, and the wine-shops were doing a brisk business.

Chebron and Amuba made their way through the busy scene, keeping a sharp look-out for Jethro, for they considered it certain, that owing to the early start the boat was to make that it would have arrived there some hours before, and that he would be on the look-out for them. In a few minutes they saw him looking into one of the shops. He started as they went up to him and touched him, for he had not perceived them before.

"All well?" Amuba asked.

"Everything has gone off admirably. We got off without the slightest trouble. But come on board at once; the girls are anxious about you, although I assured them that there was not the slightest risk of your being discovered on your way here."

So saying, Jethro led the way to the boat, which was moored by the bank a hundred yards above the village, "in order," Jethro said, "that they could make an early start in the morning, and be off before the rest of the boats were under way."

"Here are your brothers," Jethro said in a loud voice as he stepped on board. "I found them dawdling and gossiping in the street, forgetting altogether that you were waiting for your evening meal until they came on board."

Both entered the cabin, which was about eight feet wide and twelve feet long, but not high enough for them to stand upright. The floor was spread with a thick carpet; cushions and pillows were arranged along each side, and thick matting hung from the top. In the daytime this was rolled up and fastened, so that the air could play through the cabin, and those within could look out at the river; but at present it closed the openings and kept out both the night air and the glances of passers-by. At the other end was a door opening into the smaller cabin allotted to the girls. A lamp swung from the beams overhead. Mysa gave a cry of pleasure as they entered and was about to spring to her feet, when Jethro exclaimed:

"Mind your head, child! You are not accustomed to these low quarters yet."

"Thank the gods we are together again!" Mysa said, as Chebron, after embracing her, sat down on the cushion beside her. "I feel almost happy now, in spite of the dreadful times that have passed."

"It does feel homelike here," Chebron said, looking round, "especially after sleeping in the open air on the hard ground, as we have been doing for the last month."

"I should hardly have known you, Amuba," Mysa said. "You do look so different in your wig, and with your skin darkened."

"I must look horrible," Amuba replied rather ruefully.

"You don't look so nice," Mysa replied frankly. "I used at first to think that short, wavy, golden hair of yours was strange, and that you would look better in a wig like other people; but now I am sorry it is gone."

"Here is our meal," Jethro said, as the hangings that served as a door were drawn aside, and one of the men entered bearing a dish of fried fish and another of stewed ducks, which he placed on the floor.

Jethro produced some cups and a jar of wine from a locker in the cabin, and then the men, by his orders, brought in a jar of water for the use of the girls. Then sitting round the dishes they began their meal, Jethro cutting up the food with his dagger, and all helping themselves with the aid of their fingers and pieces of bread, that served them for the purpose of forks. Mysa had been accustomed always to the use of a table; but these were only used in the abodes of the rich, and the people in general sat on the ground to their meals.

"We have not begun our hardships yet," Mysa said, smiling. "I should not mind how long this went on. I call this much better than living in a house; don't you, Ruth?"

"It is more natural to me than that great house of yours," Ruth replied; "and of course to me it is far more homelike and comfortable. For I do not think I was a favourite among the other servants; they were jealous of the kindness you showed me."

"There is one thing I wanted to say," Jethro said. "It is better that we should not call each other by our names. I am sure that the boatmen have no suspicion here that we are other than what we seem to be; but they can hardly help hearing our names, for all Egypt has rung with them for the last month, and it would be well if we change them for the present. You must of necessity call me father, since that is the relation I am supposed to bear to you. Amuba can become Amnis and Chebron Chefu."

"And I will be Mytis," Mysa said. "What name will you take, Ruth? There is no Egyptian name quite like yours."

"It matters not what you call me," Ruth said.

"We will call you Nite," Mysa said. "I had a great friend of that name, but she died."

"And there is one thing, Nite," Chebron said, "that I wish you to understand. Just now you spoke to me as my lord Chebron. That sort of thing must not be any longer. We are all fugitives together, and Mysa and I have no longer any rank. Jethro and Amuba are of high rank in their own country, and if we ever get safely to their own people they will be nobles in the land, while we shall be but strangers, as he was when he and Jethro came into Egypt. Therefore any talk of rank among us is but folly. We are fugitives, and my life is forfeited if I am discovered in my own land. Jethro is our leader and guardian, alike by the will of our father and because he is older and wiser than any of us. Amuba is as my elder brother, being stronger and braver and more accustomed to danger than I; while you and Mysa are sisters, inasmuch as you are both exiled from your own land, and are friendless, save for each other and us."

"I am glad to hear you say that, brother," Mysa said. "I spoke to her last night about it, for she would insist on treating me as if she were still my servant; which is absurd, and not nice of her, when she is going out with us to share our dangers only because she loves me. It is I rather who should look up to her, for I am very helpless, and know nothing of work or real life, while she can do all sorts of things; besides, when we were captives it was she who was always brave and hopeful, and kept up my spirits when, I do think, if it had not been for her I should have died of grief and terror."

"By the way," Jethro said, "we have not heard yet how it was that you were together. We heard of your being carried off, but old Lyptis told me that no one had seen aught of you."

"They were all scared out of their senses," Ruth said scornfully. "The men suddenly ran into the room and seized Mysa, and twisted a shawl round her head before she had time to call out. I screamed, and one of them struck me a blow which knocked me down. Then they carried her off. I think I was stunned for a moment. When I recovered I found they were gone. I jumped up and ran along the passage and through the hall, where the women were screaming and crying, and then out of the house through the garden, and out of the gate. Then I saw four men at a short distance off carrying Mysa to a cart standing a hundred yards away. I ran up just as they laid her in it. One of them turned upon me with a dagger. I said:

"Let me go with her, and I will be quiet. If not, I will scream; and if you kill me, it will only set the people on your traces.

"The men hesitated, and I ran past them and climbed into the cart, and threw myself down by Mysa, and then they drove off."

"It was brave and good of you, Ruth," Jethro said, laying his hand on the girl's shoulder; "but why did you not scream when you first came out of the gate? It might have brought aid, and prevented Mysa from being carried off."

"I thought of that," Ruth said, "but there were numbers of rough men still coming in at the gate; and knowing how the people had been stirred up to anger against us, I did not know what might happen if I gave the alarm. Besides, I was not sure at first that these men, although they seemed so rough and violent, were not really friends, who were taking away Mysa to save her from the popular fury."

"Yes, that might have been the case," Jethro agreed. "At any rate, child, you acted bravely and well. We were hoping all along that you were with Mysa, for we know what a comfort you would be to her. Only, as the women all declared you did not pass out after her, we did not see how that could be. And now, Mytis and Nite, you had better retire to your own cabin to rest; for though you have both kept up wonderfully, all this has been a great strain for you, and you are both looking fagged and heavy-eyed. To-night you can sleep in comfort; for, for the present, I think that there is no occasion whatever for the slightest anxiety."

It was some time before Jethro and his companions lay down to sleep. They talked long and earnestly of the journey that lay before them; and when they had exhausted this topic, Chebron said:

"Till now, Jethro, I have not asked you about my father's funeral. When is it to be? I have thought of it often, but as you did not speak I thought it better not to question you."

"I was glad you did not," Jethro replied. "It will be in about ten days' time. As I believed you guessed, Chigron is embalming him; the process will not be complete for another four days, and, as you know, the relatives do not see the corpse after it is in the hands of the embalmer until it is swathed and in the coffin. Chigron has done so much that must have been against his conscience that I did not like him to be asked to allow you to break through that custom, which to him is a sort of religion; besides, dear lad, I thought it better for yourself not to renew your griefs by gazing on a lifeless face.

"During the last month you have fortunately had so much to distract your thought that you have not had time to dwell upon your loss. Moreover, you have needed all your strength and your energy for your search for your sister, and right sure am I that your father, who was as sensible as he was wise—and the two things do not always go together—would be far better pleased to see you energetic and active in your search for your sister, and in preparation for this new life on which we are entering, than in vain regrets for him; therefore, lad, for every reason I thought it better to keep silent upon the subject. It may be a satisfaction, however, for you to know that everything will be done to do honour to the dead.

"The king and all the great men of Egypt will be present, and Thebes will turn out its thousands to express its grief for the deed done by a section of its population. Had it not been for the express commands of your father I should have thought that it might have been worth while for you to present yourself on that occasion, and it may be that for once even the fanatics would have been satisfied to have pardoned the offence of the son because of the wrong done to the father. However, this affair of Ptylus puts that out of the question, for when it is generally known that Mysa was carried off when Ptylus was slain, public opinion will arrive at the truth and say that the fugitives of whom they were in search, the slayers of the sacred cat, were the rescuers of the daughter of Ameres and the slayers of the high-priest."

"You are right, Jethro, it will be better for me not to have seen my father; I can always think of him now as I saw him last, which is a thousand times better than if he dwelt in my memory as he lies in the cere-clothes in the embalming room of Chigron. As to what you say about my appearing at the funeral, I would in no case have done it; I would a thousand times rather live an exile or meet my death at the hands of savages than crave mercy at the hands of the mob of Thebes, and live to be pointed at all my life as the man who had committed the abhorred offence of killing the sacred cat."

The conversation in the cabin had all been carried on in an undertone; for although through an opening in the curtains they could see the crew—who had been eating their meal by the light of a torch of resinous wood, and were now wrapped up in thick garments to keep off the night dew—chatting merrily together and occasionally breaking into snatches of song, it was prudent to speak so that not even a chance word should be overheard. The boatmen, indeed, were in high spirits. Their home lay far up near the borders of Upper Egypt, and it was seldom indeed that they obtained a job which gave them the chance of visiting their friends. Thus the engagement was most satisfactory to them, for although their leader had haggled over the terms, he and they would gladly have accepted half the rate of pay rather than let such an opportunity slip. As Chebron finished speaking they were preparing for the night by laying down a few mats on the boards of the fore-deck. Then they huddled closely together, pulled another mat or two over them, extinguished the torch, and composed themselves to sleep.

"We will follow their example; but a little more comfortably, I hope," Jethro said.

The cushions and pillows were arranged, the lamp turned low, and in a short time all on board the boat were sound asleep. No ray of light had entered the cabin when Amuba was awakened by a movement of the boat, caused by a stir among the crew. He felt his way to the door and threw back the hangings and looked out; there was a faint greenish yellow light in the east, but the stars were still shining brightly.

"Good-morning, young master!" the captain said. "I hope you have slept well."

"So well that I could hardly believe it was morning," Amuba replied. "How long will it be before you are off?"

"We shall be moving in ten minutes; at present there is not light enough to see the shore."

"Chefu, are you awake?"

"Yes," Chebron answered sleepily, "I am awake; thanks to your talking. If you had lain quiet we might have slept for another hour yet."

"You have had plenty of sleep the last twenty-four hours," Amuba retorted. "Take a cloth and let us land and run along the banks for a mile, and have a bathe before the boat comes along."

"It is very cold for it," Chebron said.

"Nonsense! The water will refresh you."

"Come along, Chefu," Jethro said, "your brother is right; a dip will refresh us for the day."

The Egyptians were most particular about bathing and washing. The heat and dust of the climate rendered cleanliness an absolute necessity, and all classes took their daily bathe—the wealthy in baths attached to their houses, the poor in the water of the lakes or canals. Jethro and the two lads leapt ashore and ran briskly along the bank for about a mile, stripped and took a plunge into the river, and were dressed again just as the boat came along with the four men towing her, and the captain steering with an oar at the stern. It was light enough now for him to distinguish the faces of his passengers, and he brought the boat straight alongside the bank. In a few minutes the girls came out from their cabin, looking fresh and rosy.

"So you have been bathing?" Mysa said. "We heard what you were saying, and we have had our bath too."

"How did you manage that?" Chebron asked.

"We went out by the door at the other side of our cabin in our woollen robes, on to that little platform on which the man is standing to steer, and poured jars of water over each other."

"And you both slept well?"

"Yes, indeed, and without waking once till we heard Amnis call you to get up."

"You disturbed everyone, you see, Amnis," Chebron said.

"And a very good thing too," Amuba laughed. "If we had not had our bath when we did, we should not have got an opportunity all day. Now we all feel fresh."

"And ready for something to eat," Mysa put in.

"What would you like, Mytis?" Ruth asked. "I am a capital cook, you know, and I don't suppose the men will be preparing their breakfast for a long time yet."

"I think that will be a very good plan, Mytis," Jethro said; "but we will divide the labour between us. The two boys shall stir up the brands smoldering on the flat stone hearth forward, I will clean and get ready some fish, Nite shall cook them, while Mytis shall, under her directions, make us some cakes and put them into the hot ashes to bake. We shall have to shift for ourselves later on. There is nothing like getting accustomed to it. Of course the men will cook the principal meals, but we can prepare little meals between times. It is astonishing how many times you can eat during the day when you are in the open air."

In half an hour the meal, consisting of the fish, light dough-cakes, which Mysa had with much amusement prepared under Ruth's direction, and fruit, was ready. The latter consisted of grapes and melons. The meal was greatly enjoyed, and by the time it was finished the sun was already some distance up the sky. For an hour the party sat on the deck forward watching the boats coming down the stream and villages on the opposite shore; but as the sun gained power they were glad to enter the cabin. The mats were rolled up now to allow a free passage of air, and as they sat on the cushions they could look out on both sides.

Day after day passed quietly and smoothly. The men generally towed the boat from sunrise until eleven o'clock in the day, then they moored her to the bank, prepared a meal, and after eating it went ashore if there were trees that afforded a shade there, or if not, spread out some mats on the poles over the boat and slept in their shade till three o'clock. Then they towed until sunset, moored her for the night, cooked their second meal, talked and sang for an hour or two, and then lay down for the night. Sometimes the wind blew with sufficient strength to enable the boat to stem the stream close inshore by means of the sail alone; then the boatmen were perfectly happy, and spent their day in alternate eating and sleeping. Generally the passengers landed and walked alongside of the boat for an hour or two after they had had their early breakfast, and again when the heat of the day was over; it made a change, and at the same time kept their muscles in a state of health and activity.

"We may have to make long journeys on foot," Jethro said, "and the more we can accustom ourselves to walking the better."

The time passed so quietly and pleasantly that both Mysa and Chebron at times blamed themselves for feeling as light-hearted as they did; but when the latter once said so to Jethro he replied:

"Do not be uneasy on that score. Remember that in the first place it is a comfort to us all that you and your sister are cheerful companions. It makes the journey lighter for us. In the next place, good spirits and good health go together; and although, at present, our life is an easy one, there will be need for health and strength presently. This flight and exile are at present blessings rather than misfortunes to you. Just as Amuba's captivity following so closely upon the death of his father and mother was to him."

"I can hardly believe," Mysa said, "that we are really going upon a dangerous expedition. Everything is so pleasant and tranquil. The days pass without any care or trouble. I find it difficult to believe that the time is not very far off when we shall have to cross deserts, and perhaps to meet savage beasts and wild people, and be in danger of our lives."

"It will be a long time first, Mytis. It will be months before we arrive at Meroe, the capital of the next kingdom, which lies at the junction of the two great arms of this river. Up to that point I do not think there will be dangers, though there may be some little difficulty, for they say there are tremendous rapids to be passed. It is only lately that the king overran Meroe, defeated its armies, and forced it to pay tribute, but as there is a considerable trade carried on with that country I do not think there is any danger of molestation. It is on leaving Meroe that our difficulties will commence; for, as I hear, the road thence to the east through the city of Axoum, which is the capital of the country named Abyssinia, passes through a wild land abounding with savage animals; and again, beyond Axoum the country is broken and difficult down to the sea.

"Chigron told me, however, that he had heard from a native of Meroe who had worked for him that there is a far shorter road to the sea from a point at which the river takes a great bend many hundreds of miles below the capital. When we get higher up we can of course make inquiries as to this. I hope that it may prove to be true, for if so, it will save us months of travel."

Several large towns were passed as they journeyed upwards. Hermonthis, standing on the western bank, by which they were travelling, was the first passed. Then came Esneh, with grand temples dedicated to Kneph and Neith, and standing where the Nile Valley opens to a width of five miles. Then they passed Eilithya, standing on the eastern bank, with many temples rising above it, and with the sandstone rock behind it dotted with the entrances to sepulchres.

A few miles higher up they passed Edfu. Above this the valley gradually narrowed, the hills closing in until they rose almost perpendicularly from the edge of the stream. Here were temples erected especially for the worship of the Nile and of his emblem the crocodile. It appeared to the Egyptians the most appropriate place for the worship of the river, which seemed here to occupy the whole width of Egypt. Here, too, were vast quarries, from which the stone was extricated for the building of most of the temples of Upper Egypt.

Sixteen miles higher Ombi was passed, with its great temple in honour of the crocodile-headed god Sebak. Along this part of the river the country was comparatively barren, and the villages small and far apart. In the narrow places the river at times ran so rapidly that it was necessary to hire a number of peasants to assist the boatmen to drag the boat against the stream, and the progress made each day was very slight.

Four days after leaving Ombi they arrived at Syene[1], by far the largest town they had come to since leaving Thebes. This brought the first stage of their journey to an end. Hitherto they had been travelling along a tranquil river, running strongly at times, but smooth and even. Before them they had a succession of cataracts and rapids to pass, and a country to traverse which, although often subjugated, was continually rising against the power of Egypt.

At Syene they remained for three days. They would gladly have pushed on without delay, for although the Egyptian authority extended further up the river, Syene was the last town where the governor would concern himself with the affairs of Egypt, or where fugitives from justice were likely to be arrested. However, as it was customary to give boatmen a few days of repose after their labour, and before undertaking the still more severe work which lay before them, Jethro thought it better to avoid any appearance of haste.

There was much to be seen that was new to them at Syene. A great trade was carried on with Meroe. Most of the merchants engaged in it dwelt here, buying on the one hand the products of Upper and Lower Egypt and sending or taking them up the river, and on the other hand buying the products of Meroe and despatching them to Thebes. The streets were filled with a mingled population. Egyptians with their spotless garments and tranquil mien; merchants absorbed in business; officers and soldiers in large numbers, for Syene was an important military station; officials belonging to the great quarries near, and gangs of slaves of many nationalities working under their orders.

Wild-looking figures moved among the crowd, their garments, thrown loosely round them, affording a striking contrast to the cleanness of those of the Egyptians, while their unkempt hair was in equally strong contrast to the precise wigs of the middle-class Egyptians and the bare heads of the lower class. Their skins, too, were much darker in colour, though there was considerable variation in this respect. Among them were a sprinkling of men of entirely different type, almost black in hue, with thicker lips and flatter features. These were Ethiopians, whose land lay beyond that of Meroe and who had also felt the weight and power of the arms of Egypt.

"These people of Meroe," Amuba said, "are very similar in feature to the Egyptians, Chebron. And their tongue is also not unlike yours; I can understand their speech."

"Our oldest books," Chebron said, "say that we are kindred people, and are Asiatic rather than African in our origin. The people of Meroe say that their far-back ancestors came from Arabia, and first spreading along the western shore of the Red Sea, ascended to the high lands and drove out the black people who inhabited them.

"As to our own origin, it is vague; but my father has told me that the opinion among those most skilled in the ancient learning is that we too came from Arabia. We were not all one people, that is certain; and it is comparatively of recent years, though a vast time as far as human lives go, that the people of the Thebaid—that is, of Upper Egypt—extended their dominion over Lower Egypt, and made the whole country one nation. Even now, you know, the king wears two crowns—the one of Upper Egypt, the other of the lower country. Along the shores of the Great Sea to the west are Libyans and other people similar in race to ourselves. My father considered that the tribes which first came from Asia pressed on to the west, driving back and exterminating the black people. Each fresh wave that came from the east pushed the others further and further, until at last the ancestors of the people of Lower Egypt arrived and settled there.

"In Meroe the temples and religion are similar to our own. Whether they brought that religion from Arabia, or whether we planted it there during our various conquests of the country, I cannot tell you; but certain it is that there is at present but little more difference between Upper Egypt and Meroe than there is between Upper Egypt and the Delta."

"And beyond Meroe the people are all black like those we see here?"

"So I believe, Amuba. Our merchants penetrate vast distances to the south exchanging our products for gold and ivory, and everywhere they find the country inhabited by black people living in wretched villages, without, as it seems, any government, or law, or order, waging war with each other and making slaves, whom they also sell to our merchants. They differ so wholly from us that it is certain that we cannot come from the same stock. But they are strong and active and make excellent slaves. Lying between Meroe and the sea, the country called Abyssinia is also inhabited by a race of Arab blood, but differing more from us than those of Meroe.

"They have great towns, but I do not think that their religion is the same as ours; our traders say that their language can be understood by them, although more rough and unpolished. I have heard my father say that he considered that all the country lying east of the Nile, and of its eastern branch that rises in Abyssinia and is called the Tacazze, belongs to Asia rather than to Africa."

The party found that the death by violence of two successive high-priests of Osiris was one of the principal topics of conversation in Syene, but none appeared to think that there was the remotest probability of any concerned in the occurrences making for the south. However, Jethro thought it prudent that the whole party should not land together, and therefore Amuba and Chebron usually went one way, and he with the girls another. They paid visits to the sacred island of Ebo opposite the town, and to the quarries of Phile, four miles away. Here they saw the gangs of slaves cutting out colossal statues, obelisks, and shrines from the solid rock.

First the outline was traced on the rock, then the surrounding stone was removed with chisels and wedges, and at last the statue or obelisk was itself severed from the rock. Then it was hewn and sculptured by the masons, placed on rollers and dragged by hundreds of men down to the landing-place below the rapids, and these placed on rafts to be floated down the river to its destination. They saw many of the masses of stone in all stages of manufacture. The number of slaves employed was enormous, and these inhabited great buildings erected near the quarries, where also were barracks for the troops who kept guard over them.

Watching the slaves at their painful labour, Jethro and Amuba were both filled with gratitude at the good fortune that had placed them with Ameres instead of sending them to pass their lives in such unceasing and monotonous toil. Among the slaves were several whom, by their complexion and appearance, they judged to be Rebu. As at first all those brought to Egypt had been distributed among the priests and great officers, they supposed that either from obstinacy, misconduct, or from attempts to escape, they had incurred the displeasure of their masters, and had been handed over by them for the service of the state.

Had the slaves been in the hands of private masters, Jethro and Amuba, who were filled with pity at seeing their countrymen in such a state, would have endeavoured to purchase them and take them with them upon their journey. This was out of the question now, nor was it possible to hold any communication with them, or to present them with a small sum of money to alleviate their misery, without exciting suspicion. The whole party were heartily glad when on the morning of the fourth day after their arrival the boat was pushed off from the shore and the work of ascending the rapids began.

Chapter 17

THE river had begun to rise before they left Thebes, and although it had not yet reached its highest point, a great volume of water was pouring down; and the boatmen assured Jethro that they would be able to ascend the cataract without difficulty, whereas when the Nile was low there was often great danger in passing, and at times indeed no boats could make the passage. Ten men were engaged in addition to the crew to take the boats up beyond the rapids.

But although assured that there was no danger, the girls declared that they would rather walk along the bank, for the hurry and rush of the mighty flood, rising sometimes in short angry waves, were certainly trying to the nerves. Jethro and the lads of course accompanied them, and sometimes seized the rope and added their weight when the force of the stream brought the men towing to a stand-still and seemed as if it would, in spite of their efforts, tear the boat from their grasp. At last the top of the rapids was gained, and they were glad to take their places again in the boat as she floated on the quiet water. So a month passed—sometimes taken along by favourable winds, at others being towed along quiet waters close to the shore, at others battling with the furious rapids. They found that the cataract they had first passed was as nothing to those higher up. Here the whole cargo had to be unloaded and carried up to the top of the rapids, and it needed some forty men to drag the empty boat through the turmoil of waters, while often the slightest error on the part of the helmsman would have caused the boat to be dashed to pieces on the great rocks rising in the midst of the channel. But before arriving at the second cataract they had tarried for several days at Ibsciak, the city to which their crew belonged.

They had passed many temples and towns during the hundred and eighty miles of journey between Syene and this place, but this was the largest of them. Here two great grotto temples were in course of construction, the one dedicated to the gods Amun and Phre, and built at the expense of Rameses himself, the other dedicated to Athor by Lofreai, the queen. On these temples were engraved the records of the victories of Rameses over various nations of Africa and Asia.

Jethro offered, if the boatmen wished to make a longer stay here, that he would charter another boat to take them further; but they declared their willingness to proceed at the end of a week after their arrival, being well satisfied with their engagement and treatment. After passing the second cataract they arrived at another large town named Behni.[1] This was a very large city, and abounded with temples and public buildings. The largest temple was dedicated to Thoth. All along the river a belt of cultivated land extended for some miles back from the bank; this was dotted with numerous villages, and there was no difficulty whatever in obtaining food of all kinds.

At last they reached Semneh, the point to which the boatmen had agreed to take them. This was the furthest boundary to which at that time the Egyptian power extended. The river here took a great bend to the east, then flowing south and afterwards again west, forming a great loop. This could be avoided by cutting across the desert to Merawe, a flourishing town which marked the northern limit of the power of Meroe, the desert forming a convenient neutral ground between the two kingdoms. Sometimes Egypt under a powerful king carried her arms much further to the south, at other times a warlike monarch of Meroe would push back the Egyptian frontier almost to Syene; but as a rule the Nile as far south as Semneh was regarded as belonging to Egypt.

The traders arriving at Semneh generally waited until a sufficient number were gathered together to form a strong caravan for mutual protection against the natives inhabiting the desert, who held themselves independent alike of Egypt and of Meroe, and attacked and plundered parties crossing the desert, unless these were so strong and well-armed as to be able to set them at defiance. Erecting two tents, and landing their goods and merchandise, Jethro and his party encamped near the river-bank. They had not yet settled whether they would cross the desert or continue their journey by water.

The choice between the two routes was open to them; for although the traders usually crossed the desert, taking with them their lighter and more valuable merchandise, the heavier goods made the long detour in boats, going up in large flotillas, both for protection against the natives and for mutual aid in ascending the rapids which had to be encountered. There was no difficulty in hiring another boat, for it was the universal rule to make a transhipment here, as the Egyptian boatmen were unwilling to enter Meroe. The transport beyond this point, therefore, was in the hands of the people of this country.

In consultation with the traders gathered at Semneh Jethro learned that it was by no means necessary to proceed up the river to the city of Meroe[2] and thence eastward through Axoum, the capital of Abyssinia, to the sea, but that a far shorter road existed from the eastern most point of the bend of the river direct to the sea. There were, indeed, several large Egyptian towns upon the Red Sea, and from these a flourishing trade was carried on with Meroe and Abyssinia; and the first merchant to whom Jethro spoke was much surprised to find that he was in ignorance of the existence of the route he had described.

The journey, although toilsome, was said to be no more so than that from Meroe through Axoum, while the distance to be traversed was small in comparison. After much consultation it was therefore agreed that the best plan was to dispose of the merchandise that they had brought with them to one of the traders about to proceed south, retaining only sufficient for the payment of the men whom it would be necessary to take with them for protection on their journey. Jethro had no difficulty in doing this, alleging as his reason for parting with his goods that he found that the expenses to Meroe would greatly exceed the sum he had calculated upon, and that therefore he had determined to proceed no further. As they thought it best to allow six months from the date of their departure from Thebes to elapse before they entered any large Egyptian town, they remained for nearly two months at Semneh, and then finding that a flotilla of boats was ready to ascend the river they made an arrangement with some boatmen for the hire of their craft to the point where they were to leave the river and again set out on their journey.

The difficulties of the journey were very great. After travelling for some sixty miles they came to rapids more dangerous than any they had passed, and it took the flotilla more than a fortnight passing up them, only four or five boats being taken up each day by the united labours of the whole of the crews. There was great satisfaction when the last boat had been taken up the rapids, and there was a general feast that evening among the boatmen. During the whole time they had been engaged in the passage a number of armed scouts had been placed upon the rocky eminences near the bank; for the place had an evil reputation, and attacks were frequently made by the desert tribesmen upon those passing up or down upon the river.

So far no signs of the presence of hostile natives had been perceived. The usual precautions, however, had been taken; the cargoes had all been carried up by hand and deposited so as to form a breastwork, and as night closed in several sentries were placed to guard against surprise. It had been arranged that the men belonging to the boats each day brought up should that night take sentinel duty; and this evening Jethro, his companions, and boatmen were among those on guard. Many of the boats had left Semneh before them, and they had been among the last to arrive at the foot of the cataracts, and consequently came up in the last batch.

As owners they had been exempt from the labours of dragging up the boats, and had spent much of their time during the enforced delay in hunting. They had obtained dogs and guides from the village at the foot of the cataracts and had had good sport among the ibex which abounded in the rocky hills. The girls had seldom left their cabin after leaving Semneh. There was nothing remarkable in the presence of women in a boat going so far up the river, as many of the traders took their wives on their journeys with them. When, however, they journeyed beyond Semneh they left them there until their return, the danger and hardships of the desert journey being too great for them to encounter, and it was therefore thought advisable that the girls should remain in seclusion.

Jethro, Amuba, and Chebron were standing together at one of the angles of the encampment when the former suddenly exclaimed:

"There are men or animals moving on that steep hill opposite! I thought several times I heard the sound of stones being displaced.

I certainly heard them then." Then turning round he raised his voice: "I can hear sounds on the hill. It were best that all stood to their arms and prepare to resist an attack."

In an instant the sound of song and laughter ceased amid the groups assembled round the fires and each man seized his arms. There was a sharp ringing sound close to Jethro, and stooping he picked up an arrow which had fallen close to him.

"It is an enemy!" he shouted. "Draw up close to the breastwork and prepare to receive them. Scatter the fires at once and extinguish the blazing brands. They can see us, while themselves invisible."

As he spoke a loud and terrible yell rose from the hill-side and a shower of arrows was poured into the encampment. Several men fell, but Jethro's orders were carried out and the fires promptly extinguished.

"Stoop down behind the breastwork," Jethro shouted, "until they are near enough for you to take aim. Have your spears ready to check their onslaught when they charge."

Although Jethro held no position entitling him to command, his orders were as promptly obeyed as if he had been in authority. The men recognized at once, by the calmness of his tones, that he was accustomed to warfare, and readily yielded to him obedience. In a minute or two a crowd of figures could be seen approaching, and the Egyptians, leaping to their feet, poured in a volley of arrows. The yells and screams which broke forth testified to the execution wrought in the ranks of the enemy, but without a check they still rushed forward. The Egyptians discharged their arrows as fast as they could during the few moments left them, and then, as the natives rushed at the breastwork, they threw down their bows, and grasping the spears, maces, swords, axes, or staves with which they were armed, boldly met the foe.

For a few minutes the contest was doubtful, but encouraged by the shouts of Jethro, whose voice could be heard above the yells of the natives, the Egyptians defended their position with vigour and courage. As fast as the natives climbed over the low breastwork of merchandise they were either speared or cut down, and after ten minutes' fierce fighting their attack ceased as suddenly as it had begun, and as if by magic a dead silence succeeded the din of battle.

"You have done well, comrades," Jethro said, "and defeated our assailants; but we had best stand to arms for awhile, for they may return. I do not think they will, for they have found us stronger and better prepared for them than they had expected. Still, as we do not know their ways, it were best to remain on our guard."

An hour later, as nothing had been heard of the enemy, the fires were relighted and the wounded attended to. Sixteen men had been shot dead by the arrows of the assailants and some fifty were more or less severely wounded by the same missiles, while eighteen had fallen in the hand-to-hand contest at the breastwork. Thirty-seven natives were found dead inside the breastwork. How many had fallen before the arrows of the defenders the latter never knew, for it was found in the morning that the natives had carried off their killed and wounded who fell outside the inclosure. As soon as the fighting was over Chebron ran down to the boat to allay the fears of the girls and assure them that none of their party had received a serious wound, Jethro alone having been hurt by a spear thrust, which, however, glanced off his ribs, inflicting only a flesh wound, which he treated as of no consequence whatever.

"Why did not Amuba come down with you?" Mysa asked. "Are you sure that he escaped without injury?"

"I can assure you that he has not been touched, Mysa; but we are still on guard, for it is possible that the enemy may return again, although we hope that the lesson has been sufficient for them."

"Were you frightened, Chebron?"

"I felt a little nervous as they were coming on, but when it came to hand-to-hand fighting I was too excited to think anything about the danger. Besides, I was standing between Jethro and Amuba, and they have fought in great battles, and seemed so quiet and cool that I could scarcely feel otherwise. Jethro took the command of everyone, and the rest obeyed him without question, but now I must go back to my post. Jethro told me to slip away to tell you that we were all safe, but I should not like not to be in my place if they attack again."

"I have often wondered, Ruth," Mysa said when Chebron had left them, "what we should have done if it had not been for Jethro and Amuba. If it had not been for them I should have been obliged to marry Plexo, and Chebron would have been caught and killed at Thebes. They arrange everything, and do not seem afraid in the slightest."

"I think your brother is brave, too," Ruth said; "and they always consult with him about their plans."

"Yes; but it is all their doing," Mysa replied. "Chebron, before they came, thought of nothing but reading, and was gentle and quiet. I heard one of the slaves say to another that he was more like a girl than a boy; but being with Amuba has quite altered him. Of course, he is not as strong as Amuba, but he can walk and run and shoot an arrow and shoot a javelin at a mark almost as well as Amuba can; still he has not so much spirit. I think Amuba always speaks decidedly, while Chebron hesitates to give an opinion."

"But your brother has a great deal more learning than Amuba, and so his opinion ought to be worth more, Mysa."

"Oh, yes, if it were about history or science; for anything of that sort of course it would, Ruth, but not about other things. Of course, it is natural that they should be different, because Amuba is the son of a king."

"The son of a king?" Ruth repeated in surprise.

"Yes, I heard it when he first came; only father said it was not to be mentioned, because if it were known he would be taken away from us and kept as a royal slave at the palace. But he is really the son of a king, and as his father is dead he will be king himself when he gets back to his own country."

"And Jethro is one of the same people, is he not?" Ruth asked.

"Oh, yes! they are both Rebu. I think Jethro was one of the king's warriors."

"That accounts," Ruth said, "for what has often puzzled me. Jethro is much the oldest of our party, and altogether the leader, and yet I have observed that he always speaks to Amuba as if the latter were the chief."

"I have not noticed that," Mysa said, shaking her head; "but I do know, now you mention it, that he always asked Amuba's opinion before giving his own."

"I have constantly noticed it, Mysa, and I wondered that since he and Amuba were your father's slaves he should always consult Amuba instead of your brother; but I understand now. That accounts, too, for Amuba giving his opinion so decidedly. Of course, in his own country, Amuba was accustomed to have his own way. I am glad of that, for I like Amuba very much, and it vexed me sometimes to see him settling things when Jethro is so much older. And you think if he ever gets back to his own country he will be king?"

"I am not sure," Mysa said doubtfully. "Of course, he ought to be. I suppose there is some other king now, and he might not like to give up to Amuba."

"I don't suppose we shall ever get there," Ruth said. "Amuba said the other day that this country lay a great distance further than the land my people came from a long time ago."

"But that is not so very far, Ruth. You said that the caravans went in six or seven days from that part of Egypt where you dwelt to the east of the Great Sea where your father came from."

"But we are a long way from there, Mysa."

"But if it is only six or seven days' journey why did not your people go back again, Ruth?"

"They always hoped to go back some day, Mysa; but I don't think your people would have let them go. You see, they made them useful for building and cutting canals and other work. Besides, other people dwell now in the land they came from, and these would not turn out unless they were beaten in battle. My people are not accustomed to fight; besides, they have stopped so long that they have become as the Egyptians. For the most part they talk your language, although some have also preserved the knowledge of their own tongue. They worship your gods, and if they were not forced to labour against their will I think now that most of them would prefer to live in ease and plenty in Egypt rather than journey into a strange country, of which they know nothing except that their forefathers hundreds of years ago came thence. But here are the others," she broke off as the boat heeled suddenly over as some one sprang on board. "Now we shall hear more about the fighting."

The next day the journey was continued, and without further adventure the flotilla arrived at last at the town where the party would leave the river and strike for the coast. Having unloaded their goods and discharged the boat, Jethro hired a small house until arrangements were made for their journey to the sea-coast. El Makrif[3] was a place of no great importance. A certain amount of trade was carried on with the coast, but most of the merchants trading with Meroe preferred the longer but safer route through Axoum. Still parties of travellers passed up and down and took boat there for Meroe; but there was an absence of the temples and great buildings which had distinguished every town they had passed between Thebes and Semneh.

Jethro upon inquiry found that there were wells at the camping-places along the whole route. The people were wild and savage, the Egyptian power extending only from the sea-shore to the foot of the hills, some fifteen miles away. Occasionally expeditions were got up to punish the tribesmen for their raids upon the cultivated land of the coast, but it was seldom that the troops could come upon them, for, knowing every foot of the mountain, these eluded all search by their heavy-armed adversaries. Jethro found that the custom was for merchants travelling across this country to pay a fixed sum in goods for the right of passage. There were two chiefs claiming jurisdiction over the road, and a messenger was at once despatched to the nearest of these with the offer of the usual payment and a request for an escort.

A week later four wild-looking figures presented themselves at the house and stated that they were ready to conduct the travellers through their chief's territory. Jethro had already made arrangements with the head man of the place to furnish him with twelve men to carry provisions necessary for the journey, and upon the following morning the party started, and Mysa and Ruth assumed the garb of boys, Jethro finding that although traders might bring up the ladies of their family to Semneh, or even take them higher up the river in boats, they would never think of exposing them to the fatigue of a journey across the mountains, and that the arrival of two girls at the Egyptian town on the sea would therefore assuredly attract remark, and possibly inquiry, on the part of the authorities.

For the first few hours the girls enjoyed the change of travelling after the long confinement on the boat, but long before nightfall they longed for the snug cushions and easy life they had left behind. The bearers, heavy laden as they were, proceeded at a steady pace that taxed the strength of the girls to keep up with after the first few miles were passed. The heat of the sun was intense. The country after a short distance had been passed became barren and desolate. They did not suffer from thirst, for an ample supply of fruit was carried by one of the bearers, but their limbs ached, and their feet, unused to walking, became tender and painful.

"Can we not stop for awhile, Jethro?" Mysa asked beseechingly.

Jethro shook his head.

"We must keep on to the wells. They are two hours further yet. They told us at starting that the first day's journey was six hours' steady walking."

Mysa was about to say that she could walk no further, when Ruth whispered in her ear:

"We must not give way, Mysa. You know we promised that if they would take us with them, we would go through all difficulties and dangers without complaining."

The admonition had its effect. Mysa felt ashamed that she had been on the point of giving way on the very first day of their starting on their real journey, and struggled bravely on; but both girls were utterly exhausted by the time they arrived at the wells. They felt rewarded, however, for their sufferings by the hearty commendation Jethro bestowed upon them.

"You have held on most bravely," he said; "for I could see you were terribly fatigued. I am afraid you will find it very hard work just at first, but after that it will be more easy to you. Tomorrow's journey is a shorter one."

It was well that it was so, for the girls were limping even at the start, and needed the assistance of Jethro and the boys to reach the next halting-place; and as soon as the tent, which was separated into two parts by hangings, was erected, they dropped upon their cushions, feeling that they could never get through another day's suffering like that they had just passed.

Jethro saw that this was so, and told their escort that he must halt next day, for that his young sons had been so long in the boat that the fatigue had quite overcome them; he accompanied the intimation with a present to each of the four men.

They offered no objections, while the porters, who were paid by the day, were well contented with the halt. The day's rest greatly benefited the girls, but it was not long enough to be of any utility to their feet; these, however, they wrapped in bandages, and started in good spirits when the porters took up the loads. They were now following the course of what in wet weather was a stream in the mountains. Sometimes the hills on either side receded a little, at others they rose almost perpendicularly on either side of the stream, and they had to pick their way among great boulders, and rocks. This sort of walking, however, tired the girls less than progressing along a level. Their feet were painful, but the soft bandages in which they were enveloped hurt them far less than the sandals in which they had at first walked, and they arrived at the halting-place in much better condition than on the previous occasions.

"The worst is over now," Jethro said to them encouragingly. "You will find each day's work come easier to you. You have stood it far better than I expected; and I feel more hopeful now that we shall reach the end of our journey in safety than I have done since the evening when I first agreed to take you with us."

While passing through some of the ravines the party had been greatly amused by the antics of troops of apes. Sometimes these sat tranquilly on the hillside, the elder gravely surveying the little caravan, the younger frisking about perfectly unconcerned. Sometimes they would accompany them for a considerable distance, making their way along the rough stones of the hillside at a deliberate pace, but yet keeping up with the footmen below.

As the ape was a sacred animal in Egypt, Mysa was gladdened by their sight, and considered it a good omen for the success of their journey. The men who escorted them told them that if undisturbed the apes never attack travellers, but if molested they would at once attack in a body with such fury that even four or five travellers together would have but little chance of escape with their lives. During the first week's journey they saw no other animals; although at night they heard the cries of hyenas, who often came close up to the encampment, and once or twice a deep roar which their guide told them was that of a lion.

On the seventh day, however, soon after they had started upon their march, the sound of breaking branches was heard among some trees a short distance up the hillside, and immediately afterwards the heads of four or five great beasts could be seen above the mimosa-bushes which extended from the wood to the bottom of the hill. The bearers gave a cry of terror, and throwing down their loads took to their heels. The four men of the escort stood irresolute. Although none of Jethro's party had before seen an elephant, they knew from pictures and carvings, and from the great statues in the Island of Elephanta, what these great creatures were.

"Will they attack us?" Jethro asked the men.

"They do not often do so," one of them replied; "although at times they come down and waste the fields round villages, and will sometimes slay any they come across. But it is best to get out of their way."

Jethro pointed out a few of the more valuable packages, and taking these up they entered the bushes on the other slope of the hill, and made their way among them as far as they could. This was, however, but a short distance, for they were full of sharp thorns, and offered terrible obstacles to passage. All of the party received severe scratches, and their garments suffered much, in making their way but twenty yards into the bush.

"That will do," Jethro said. "We shall be torn to pieces if we go further; and we are as much concealed from sight here as we should be another hundred yards further. I will see what they are doing."

Standing up and looking cautiously through the screen of feathery leaves, Jethro saw that the elephants were standing immovable. Their great ears were erected, and their trunks outstretched as if scenting the air. After two or three minutes' hesitation they continued to descend the hill.

"Are they afraid of men?" Jethro asked one of the escort.

"Sometimes they are seized with a panic, and fly at the approach of a human being; but if attacked they will charge any number without hesitation."

"Do you ever hunt them?"

"Sometimes; but always with a great number of men. It is useless to shoot arrows at them; the only way is to crawl out behind and cut the back sinews of their legs. It needs a strong man and a sharp sword, but it can be done. Then they are helpless, but even then it is a long work to despatch them. Generally we drive them from our villages by lighting great fires and making noise. Solitary elephants are more dangerous than a herd. I have known one of them to kill a dozen men, seizing some in his trunk and throwing them in the air as high as the top of a lofty tree, dashing others to the ground and kneeling upon them until every bone is crushed to pieces."

The elephants had now reached the bottom of the valley, and the chief of the escort held up his hand for perfect silence. All were prepared to fight if the elephants pursued them into the bushes, for further retreat was impossible. Amuba and Chebron had fitted their arrows into the bowstrings, and loosened their swords in the scabbards. The four natives had drawn the short heavy swords they carried, while Jethro grasped the ax that was his favourite weapon. "Remember," he had whispered to the boys, "the back sinews of the legs are the only useful point to aim at; if they advance, separate, and if they make towards the girls try to get behind them and hamstring them."

There was a long pause of expectation. The elephants could be heard making a low snorting noise with their trunks; and Jethro at last raised himself sufficiently to look through the bushes at what was going on. The elephants were examining the bundles that had been thrown down.

"I believe that they are eating up our food," he whispered as he sat down again.

Half an hour elapsed, and then there was a sound of breaking the bushes. Jethro again looked out.

"Thank the gods!" he exclaimed, "they are going off again."

Trampling down the mimosa thicket as if it had been grass, the elephants ascended the opposite hill and at last re-entered the wood from which they had first emerged. The fugitives waited for a quarter of an hour and then made their way out again from the thicket, Jethro cutting a path with his ax through the thorns. An exclamation of surprise broke from them as they gained the open ground. The whole of their stores were tossed about in the wildest confusion. Every one of the packages had been opened. Tents, garments, and carpets hung upon the bushes as if the animals had tossed them contemptuously there as being unfit to eat. Everything eatable had disappeared. The fruit, grain, and vegetables had been completely cleared up. The skins of wine were burst; but the contents had been apparently appreciated, for none remained in the hollows of the rocks.

"What greedy creatures!" Mysa exclaimed indignantly; "they have not left us a single thing."

"They do not often get a chance of such dainty feeding," Amuba said. "I don't think we ought to blame them, especially as they do not seem to have done very much damage to our other goods."

"Look how they have trampled down the bushes as they went through. I wish their skins were as thin as mine," Mysa said as she wiped away the blood from a deep scratch on her cheek; "they would keep up in their own woods then and not come down to rob travellers."

"At any rate, Mysa, we ought to feel indebted to them," Chebron said, "for not having pushed their investigations further. We should have had no chance either of escape of resistance in these bushes. Jethro told us to move round and attack them from behind; but moving round in these thorns is all very well to talk about, but quite impossible to do. Two minutes of active exercise and there would not be a morsel of flesh left on one's bones."

It was two or three hours before the bearers came back one by one. They were assailed with fierce reproaches by Jethro for the cowardice which had been the means of losing all the provisions. Four of their number were at once paid off and sent back, as there was no longer anything for them to carry. The others would have left also had it not been for the escort, who threatened death if they did not at once take up their burdens and proceed. For Jethro had been liberal with his stores, and they were as indignant as he was himself at the sudden stoppage of their rations.

Three days later they arrived at a small village, which marked the commencement of the territory of the second chief through whose country the road ran. Here the escort and carriers left them, their place being supplied by natives of the village. There was no difficulty in obtaining a supply of grain and goat's-milk cheese; but these were a poor substitute for the stores that the elephants had devoured. They were too glad, however, at having accomplished half the toilsome journey to murmur at trifles, and after a day's halt proceeded on their way. Another fortnight's travel and they stood on the lower slopes of the hills, and saw across a wide belt of flat country the expanse of the sea glistening in the sun.

Two more days' journey and they reached the Egyptian trading station. This was situated on a little peninsula connected with the mainland by a narrow neck of land, across which a massive wall had been built to repulse the attacks of the wild tribesmen, who frequently swept down and devastated the cultivated fields up to the very wall. As soon as they entered the town Jethro was ordered by an official to accompany him to the house of the governor. Taking Chebron with him, he left it to Amuba to arrange for the use of a small house during their stay.

The governor's inquiries were limited to the state of the country, the behaviour of the tribesmen along the road, the state of the wells, and the amount of provisions obtainable along the line of route.

"There are a party of Arab traders from the other side who wish to pass up to carry their goods either to Semneh or Meroe, but I have detained them until news should reach me from above, for if any wrong should happen to them their countrymen might probably enough hold us responsible for their deaths, and this might lead to quarrels and loss of trade; but since you have passed through with so small a party there can be no fear, and they can arrange with the people who brought you down as the amount to be paid to the chiefs for free passage."

He inquired Jethro's reason for making the journey over the mountains instead of proceeding by the Nile. He replied that he had received an advantageous offer for all his merchandise and had disposed of it to a trader going up to Meroe, and that as the Nile had now fallen and the danger in passing down the cataracts was considerable, he thought it better to make a short land journey, and to travel by sea to Lower Egypt; especially as he was told that the natives were now friendly, and that no difficulty would be met with on the way. Another reason for his choosing that route was that he might determine whether on his next venture it would not be more advantageous to bring down his merchandise by ship, and start from the sea-shore for Meroe.

"Undoubtedly it would be better," the governor said; "but it were wiser to sail another two days' journey down the coast and then to journey by way of Axoum."

A week's rest completely recruited the strength of the girls, and Jethro then engaged a passage in a trading ship which was going to touch at various small ports on its way north.

Chapter 18

THE journey was a long one. The winds were often so light that the vessels scarcely moved, and the heat was greater than anything they had felt during their journey. They stopped at many small ports on the Arabian side; the captain trading with the natives—selling to them articles of Egyptian manufacture, and buying the products of the country for sale in Egypt. The party had, before starting, arranged that they would land at Ælana, a town lying at the head of the gulf of the same name, forming the eastern arm of the Red Sea.[1] By so doing they would avoid the passage through Lower Egypt. The question had not been decided without long debate. By crossing from Arisinoe[2] to Pelusium they would at the latter port be able to obtain a passage in a Phoenician trader to a port in the north of Syria, and there strike across Asia Minor for the Caspian. Jethro was in favour of the route, because it would save the girls a long and arduous journey up through Syria. They, however, made light of this, and declared their readiness to undergo any hardships rather than to run the risk of the whole party being discovered either upon landing at Arsinoe or on their journey north, when they would pass through the very country that Amuba and Chebron had visited and that was inhabited by Ruth's people.

All allowed that the time had long since passed when the authorities would be keeping up a special watch for them; but as upon entering port a scribe would come on board and make a list of the passengers with their place of birth and vocation, for registration in the official records, it would be difficult in the extreme to give such answers as would avoid exciting suspicion.

When the vessel reached the mouth of the long and narrow gulf the party were struck by the grandeur of the mountains that rose from the water's-edge on their left.

The captain told them that the chief of these was known as Mount Sinai, and that barren and desolate as the land looked, it contained valleys where sheep were pastured, and where wandering tribes found a subsistence. No hint had been given to the captain that they had any intention of cutting short their voyage before arriving at Arsinoe, for it would have seemed an extraordinary proceeding for a trader journeying with his family to leave the ship at any of the Arabian ports. While sailing up the gulf Mysa complained of illness, and indeed so overpowered was she by the heat that there was but little fiction in the complaint. Upon arriving at Ælana Jethro had her carried on shore, and, hiring a house there, stayed on shore while the ship was in port.

There was a small Egyptian garrison in the town, which carried on a considerable trade with Moab and the country to the east. No attention, however, was paid to the landing of the traders, for, as the country beyond the walls of the town lay beyond the limit of Egyptian rule, the landing and departure of persons at the port was a matter of no interest to the authorities. Two days later Jethro went on board again and said that his young son was so ill that there was no chance of him being able to proceed on the journey, and that therefore he must forfeit the passage money paid to Arsinoe.

He said that as it might be many weeks before another vessel would come along, he should endeavour to pay his way by trading with the natives, and he therefore wished to purchase from him a portion of his remaining goods suitable for the purpose. As the captain saw that he would save the provisions for five persons for a month or six weeks that the voyage would yet last, and at the same time get rid of some of his surplus cargo, he assented without question to Jethro's proposal. Several bales of goods were made up, consisting principally of cloths of various texture and colour of Egyptian manufacture, trinkets, and a selection of arms.

These were landed, and two days later the vessel set sail. Jethro called upon the Egyptian commandant, and by making him a handsome present at once enlisted his aid in his enterprise. He said that as he had been detained by the illness of his son, and it might be a long time before any vessel came, he thought of getting rid of the rest of the merchandise he had brought with him by trading with the people of Moab.

"That you can do if you reach Moab," the Egyptian said, "for traders are everywhere well received; but the journey from here is not without dangers. It is a country without a master; the people have no fixed abodes, moving here and there according as they can find food for their animals, sometimes among the valleys of Sinai, sometimes in the desert to the east. These people plunder any whom they may come across, and not content with plunder might slay or carry you away as slaves. Once you have passed through as far as Moab you are safe; as you would also be if you journeyed to the west of the Salt Lake, into which runs the river Jordan. There are many tribes there, all living in cities, warlike and valorous people, among whom also you would be safe. We have had many wars with them, and not always to our advantage. But between us is a sort of truce—they do not molest our armies marching along by the sea-coast, nor do we go up among their hills to meddle with them. These are the people who at one time conquered a portion of Lower Egypt, and reigned over it for many generations until, happily, we rose and drove them out."

"Is the journey between this and the Salt Lake you speak of an arduous one?"

"It is by no means difficult, except that it were best to carry water upon the journey, for the wells are few and often dry; but the country is flat for the whole distance, indeed, there is a tradition that this gulf at one time extended as far north as the Salt Lake. The road, therefore, though stony and rough, offers no difficulties whatever; but I should advise you, if you determine upon the journey, to leave your son behind."

"It is better for him to travel than to remain here without me," Jethro said; "and if we go up through the people you speak of to the west of the lake and river, it would be but a short journey for us after disposing of our goods to make our way down to a port on the Great Sea, whence we may take ship and return quickly to Pelusium and thus arrive home before we should find a ship to take us hence."

"That is so," the Egyptian said. "The winds are so uncertain on these seas that, as far as time goes, you might journey by the route you propose and reach Egypt more speedily than you would do if you went on board a ship at once. The danger lies almost entirely in the first portion of your journey. The caravans that go hence once or twice a year through Moab to Palmyra are numerous and well armed, and capable of resisting an attack by these robber tribesmen. But one left a few weeks ago, and it may be some months before another starts."

"What animals would you recommend me to take with me?"

"Beyond all doubt camels are the best. They are used but little in this country, but come down sometimes with the caravans from Palmyra; and I believe that there is at present in the town an Arab who possesses six or seven of them. He came down with the last caravan, but was taken ill and unable to return with it. Doubtless you could make a bargain with him. I will send a soldier with you to the house he occupies."

Jethro found that the man was anxious to return to his own country, which lay on the borders of Media, and therefore directly in the direction which Jethro wished to travel. He was, however, unwilling to undertake the journey except with a caravan, having intended to wait for the next however long the time might be; but the sum that Jethro offered him for the hire of his animals as far as Palmyra at last induced him to consent to make the journey at once, bargaining, however, that a party of ten armed men should be hired as an escort as far as the borders of Moab. Highly pleased with the result of his inquiries, Jethro returned home and told his companions the arrangements he had made.

"I have only arranged for our journey as far as Palmyra," he said, "as it would have raised suspicion had I engaged him for the whole journey to Media; but of course he will gladly continue the arrangement for the whole journey. He has bargained for an escort of ten men, but we will take twenty. There is ample store of your father's gold still unexhausted; and, indeed, we have spent but little yet, for the sale of our goods when we left the boat paid all our expenses of the journey up the Nile. Therefore, as this seems to be the most hazardous part of our journey, we will not stint money in performing it in safety. I have told him that we shall start in a week's time. It would not do to leave earlier. You must not recover too rapidly from your illness. In the meantime I will make it my business to pick out a score of good fighting men as our escort."

In this the Egyptian captain was of use, recommending men whose families resided in Ælana, and would therefore be hostages for their fidelity. This was necessary, for no small portion of the men to be met with in the little town were native tribesmen who had encamped at a short distance from its walls, and had come in to trade in horses or the wool of their flocks for the cloths of Egypt. Such men as these would have been a source of danger rather than a protection.

By the end of the week he had collected a party of twenty men, all of whom were to provide their own horses. The sum agreed upon for their escort was to be paid into the hands of the Egyptian officer, who was to hand it to them on their return, with a document signed by Jethro to the effect that they had faithfully carried out the terms of their agreement.

Jethro found that the expense of the escort was less than he had anticipated, for when the men found that the party would be a strong one, therefore capable of protecting itself both on the journey out and on its return, they demanded but a moderate sum for their services. When the owner of the camels learned that they had decided positively to pass to the east of the Salt Lake, he advised them strongly, instead of following the valley of Ælana to the Salt Lake, where it would be difficult to obtain water, to take the road to the east of the range of hills skirting the valleys, and so to proceed through Petra and Shobek and Karik to Hesbon in Moab. This was the route followed by all the caravans. Villages would be found at very short distances, and there was no difficulty whatever about water.

"My camels," he said, "can go long distances without water, and could take the valley route, but the horses would suffer greatly."

Jethro was glad to hear that the journey was likely to be less toilsome than he had anticipated; and all the arrangements having been concluded, the party started soon after dawn on the day at first fixed upon.

The girls were still in male attire, and rode in large baskets, slung one on each side of a camel. The camel-driver walked at the head of the animal, leading it by a cord. Its fellows followed in a long line, each fastened to the one before it. Jethro, Amuba, and Chebron, all armed with bows and arrows, as well as swords, rode beside the girls' camel. Half the escort went on ahead, the other half formed the rear-guard.

"Which is the most dangerous part of the journey?" Jethro asked the camel-driver.

"That on which we are now entering," he replied. "Once we arrive at Petra we are comparatively safe; but this portion of the journey passes over a rough and uninhabited country, and it is across this line that the wandering tribesmen pass in their journeys to or from the pastures round Mount Sinai. The steep hills on our left form at once a hiding-place and a look-out. There they can watch for travellers passing along this road, and swoop down upon them."

"How long shall we be reaching Petra?"

"It is three days fair travelling; but as the beasts are fresh, by journeying well on to sundown we could accomplish it in two days. After that we can travel at our ease, the villages lie but a few miles apart."

"Let us push on, then, by all means," said Jethro. "We can stay a day at Petra to rest the beasts, but let us get through this desolate and dangerous country as soon as we can."

The girls had been greatly amused at first at the appearance of the strange animal that was carrying them; but they soon found that the swinging action was extremely fatiguing, and they would have gladly got down and walked.

Jethro, however, said that this could not be, for the pace of the animal, deliberate though it seemed, was yet too great for them to keep up with on foot, and it was needful for the first two days to push on at full speed.

The sun blazed with tremendous force, and was reflected from the black rock of the hills and the white sand lying between the stones that everywhere strewed the plain along which they were travelling, and the heat was terrible. After travelling for three hours they halted for an hour, and Jethro managed, with the poles that had been brought to form the framework of tents, and some cloths, to fasten an awning over the baskets in which the girls were riding. The camels had lain down as soon as they halted, and the girls stepped into the baskets before they arose. They gave a simultaneous cry as the animal rose. They had prepared for him to rise on his fore legs, and when his hind quarter suddenly rose in the air they were almost thrown from their baskets.

"I don't like this creature a bit," Mysa said as they moved on. "Who would suppose that he was going to get up the wrong way first? Besides, why does he keep on grumbling? I am sure that Ruth and I cannot be such a very heavy load for such a great beast. I believe he would have bit us as we got in if the driver had not jerked the rope at its head. It must be much nicer to sit on a horse. I am sure that looks easy enough."

"It is not so easy as it looks, Mysa," Chebron replied; "besides, you know women never do ride horses."

"They do in our country," Amuba said. "When we get there, Mysa, I will teach you how to sit on them."

"Ah! it is a long way off, Amuba," Mysa replied; "and I believe this creature has made up his mind to shake us to pieces as soon as he can."

"You should not try to sit stiff," Jethro said. "Sit quite easily, and sway backwards and forwards with the motion of the basket. You will soon get accustomed to it, and will find that ere long you will be able to sleep as if in a cradle."

They travelled on until the sun was just sinking, and then prepared to camp for the night. They had brought with them several skins of water, and from these a scanty drink was given to each of the horses. A few handfuls of grain were also served out to each. The drivers stuck their spears firmly into the ground, and to these fastened them. The camels were made to kneel down so as to form a square. In the centre of this the tent was pitched for the girls, the horses being arranged in a circle outside.

The men had all brought with them flat cakes, and with these and a handful of dates they made their meal; and there was no occasion for lighting a fire, for Jethro's party had brought an ample store of cooked provisions for their own use. In a short time quiet reigned in the camp. The journey had been a hot and fatiguing one, and the men wrapping themselves in their cloaks lay down, each by his spear, and were soon asleep, with the exception of four who took their posts as sentries. Jethro had agreed with Amuba and Chebron that they also would divide the night between them, taking it by turns to keep watch.

The men of the escort were, however, of opinion that there was very little probability of any attack before morning, even had they been watched by a party among the hills.

"They could hardly hope to take us by surprise, for they would be sure that we should set a watch in the darkness. They could not make their way down the hills without some noise; besides, they believe the power of evil are potent at night, and seldom stir out of their camps after dark. If we are attacked at all, it is likely to be just before sunrise."

Jethro had therefore arranged that Chebron should keep the first watch, Amuba the second, and that he himself would take charge four hours before daylight.

The night passed without any cause for alarm. As soon as daylight broke the camp was astir. Another ration of water and grain was served out to the horses, a hasty meal was made by the men, and just as the sun rose the cavalcade moved on. They had journeyed but half a mile, when from behind a spur of hills running out in the plain a large party was seen to issue forth. There must have been fully a hundred of them, of whom some twenty were mounted and the rest on foot. The travellers halted and had a short consultation. Jethro with one of the escort then rode out to meet the advancing party, waving a white cloth in token of amity. Two of the Arabs rode forward to meet them. It was some time before Jethro returned to the party, who were anxiously awaiting the termination of the colloquy.

"What do they say, Jethro?" Amuba asked as he rode up.

"He says, to begin with, that we ought to have purchased from him the right of travelling across the country. I said that I would gladly have paid a moderate sum had I been aware that such was required, but that as he was not in Ælana I could not tell that he claimed such a right. At the same time I was ready to make an offer of four rolls of Egyptian cloth. He rejected the offer with scorn, and after a long conversation let me know pretty plainly that he intended to take all our goods and animals, and that we might think ourselves fortunate in being allowed to pursue our way on foot. I said that I would consult my friends; that if they agreed to his terms we would keep the white flag flying, if we refused them, we would lower it."

"Then you may as well lower it at once, Jethro," Amuba said. "We might as well be killed at once as be plundered of all we possess by the Arab rascals. Besides, as there are three and twenty of us, and all well armed we ought to be able to cut our way through them. At the worst the girls could mount behind us, and we could make a circuit so as to avoid the footmen, and if the horsemen ventured to attack us we could soon give a good account of them."

"Yes. But we should lose our seven camel-loads of goods, and we shall want them for trade as we go along," Jethro said. "I propose that we should form the camels into a square, as we did last night, that you two and six of the men armed with bows and arrows shall occupy it and take care of the girls, while the rest of us charge the Arabs. If we can defeat the horsemen it is probable that the men on foot will draw off. But while we are doing so some of those on foot may rush forward and attack you. We will take care not to pursue, and you can rely upon our coming to your assistance as soon as you are attacked."

"I think that is the best plan, Jethro. We can keep them off for some time with our bows and arrows, for certainly Chebron and I can bring down a man with each shot at a hundred yards."

Jethro chose six of the men who professed themselves to be good archers. Their horses' legs were tied and the animals thrown down just outside the square formed by the kneeling camels. Strict instructions were given to the girls to lie down, and the saddles and bales were arranged outside the camels to shield them from missiles. Then when all was prepared the white flag was lowered, and Jethro with his fourteen men rode at full gallop against the Arabs.

Trusting to their somewhat superior numbers the Arab horsemen advanced to meet them; but Jethro's party, obeying his orders to keep in a close line together with their spears levelled in front of them, rode right over the Arabs, who came up singly and without order. Men and horses rolled over together, several of the former transfixed by the spears of the horsemen. Jethro called upon his men to halt, and turned upon the Arabs.

Some of the latter fled towards the footmen, who were running up to their assistance, but were pursued and cut down. Others fought to the last silently and desperately; but these, too, were slain. As soon as the footmen approached they opened fire with slings and stones. Jethro rallied his men and formed them in line again, and at their head charged the Arabs. The latter fought steadily. Giving way for a moment, they closed in round the little party of horsemen, throwing their javelins, and hacking at them with their swords. Jethro spurred his horse into their midst, dealing blows right and left with his heavy ax. His followers pressed after him, and after hard fighting cut their way through their opponents.

Again and again the maneuvre was repeated, the resistance of the Arabs weakening, as most of their best men had fallen, while the large shields carried by the horsemen repelled the greater part of the missiles they hurled at them. Another minute or two and the Arabs broke and fled from the hills, leaving over twenty of their number on the ground, in addition to the whole of their mounted men. Jethro had now time to look round, and saw for the first time that he had not, as he supposed been engaged with the whole of the enemy's party. While some fifty of them had attacked him, the rest had made direct for the camels, and were now gathered in a mass around them.

With a shout to his men to follow him Jethro galloped at full speed towards the Arabs, and with a shout flung himself upon them clearing his way through them with his ax. He was but just in time. A desperate conflict was raging across the camels. At one point several of the Arabs had broken into the square, and these were opposed by Amuba, Chebron, and one of the men, while the others still held back the Arabs on the other side. The arrival of Jethro, followed closely by the rest of his men, instantly put a stop to the conflict.

The Arabs no longer thought of attacking, but with cries of dismay started for the hills, hotly pursued by the horsemen, who followed them until they reached the foot of the rocks. As soon as the Arabs gained their fastnesses they again betook themselves to their slings, and the horsemen fell back to the camels. Jethro had not joined in the pursuit, but as soon as the Arabs fled had leapt from his horse.

"You were almost too late, Jethro," Amuba said.

"I was, indeed," Jethro replied. "I thought that I was engaged with the whole of the footmen, and in the heat of the fight did not notice that a party had moved off to attack you. You are terribly hurt, I fear, both you and Chebron. Are both the girls unharmed?"

Mysa and Ruth had both risen to their feet as soon as the attack ceased.

"We are both safe," Mysa replied. "But oh, how terribly you are hurt, both of you; and Jethro, too, is wounded!"

"My wound is nothing," Jethro said; "let us look to those of Chebron first," for Chebron had sat down against one of the camels.

"Do not be alarmed," Chebron said faintly. "I think it is only loss of blood; my shield covered my body."

"Now, girls," Jethro said, "do you get beyond the camels, open one of the bales of cloth, and set to work tearing it up in strips for bandages. I will look after these two."

After an examination of their wounds Jethro was able to say that he did not think that any of them would have very serious consequences. Both had been wounded in the leg with javelins, the side of Chebron's face was laid open by a sword cut, and a spear had cut through the flesh and grazed the ribs on the right side.

Amuba's most serious wound had been inflicted by a javelin thrown at him sideways. This had passed completely through his back under both shoulder-blades and had broken off there. Jethro cut off the ragged end, and taking hold of the point protruding behind the left arm, drew the shaft through. Then taking some of the bandages from the girls, he bound up all the wounds, and then proceeded to examine those of the men who were already occupied in stanching the flow of blood from their comrades' wounds. It was found that one of the defenders of the square was dead and three others severely wounded.

Of Jethro's party two had fallen and all had received wounds more or less severe. Had it not been for the shields that covered their bodies, few would have emerged alive from the conflict; but these gave them an immense advantage over the Arabs, who carried no such means of protection. The owner of the camels had escaped unhurt, having remained during the fight hidden under some bales. As soon as the wounds were all bandaged, and a drink of wine and water had been served out to each, the camels were unbound and permitted to rise.

Three of the men most seriously wounded, being unable to sit on their horses, were placed on the bales carried by camels, and the party again set out. It was well that they were obliged to proceed at the pace of the camels, for several men could scarcely sit their horses, and could not have done so at a pace exceeding a walk.

"Now, Amuba, let us hear about your fight," Jethro said. "I have not had time to ask a question yet."

"There is naught to tell," Amuba said. "We saw you charge down upon their horsemen and destroy them, and then ride into the middle of their foot. At once a party of about thirty strong detached themselves and made straight for us. As soon as they came within range of our arrows, we began. I shot four before they reached us, and I think Chebron did the same; but the men with us shot but poorly, and I do not think that they can have killed more than seven or eight between them. However, altogether, that accounted for about half their number, and there were only about fifteen who got up to a hand-to-hand fight with us. For a bit, aided by our breastwork, we kept them out. But at last they managed to spring over, and although we were doing our best and several of them had fallen, we had been wounded, and it would have gone very hard with us in another minute or two if you had not come up to the rescue. Now let us hear what you were doing."

Jethro then described the encounter he and his party had with the footmen.

"They fight well, these Arabs," he said, "and it was well for us that we all carried shields; for had we not done so they would have riddled us with their javelins. As you see, I had a narrow escape; for had that dart that went through my ear been an inch or two to the right it would have pierced my eye. I have two or three nasty gashes with their swords on the legs, and I think that most of the other men came out worse than I did. It was lucky that they did not strike at the horses; but I suppose they wanted them, and so avoided inflicting injury on them. However, it has been a tough fight, and we are well out of it. I hope I shall not be called on to use my battle-ax again until I am fighting in the ranks of the Rebu."

Chapter 19

WHEN they neared Petra a horn was heard to blow, and people were seen running about among the houses.

"They take us for a party of Arabs," one of the horsemen said. "As I have often been through the town and am known to several persons here, I will, if you like, hurry on and tell them that we are peaceful travellers."

The party halted for a few minutes and then moved slowly forward again. By the time they reached the town the news that the party were traders had spread, and the people were issuing from their houses. These were small, and solidly built of stone. They were but one story high. The roof was flat, with a low wall running round it, and the houses had but one door, opening externally. This was very low and narrow, so that those inside could offer a determined resistance against entry. As the town stood on the slope of a hill, and the roofs of the lower houses were commanded by those from above, the place was capable of offering a determined resistance against marauding tribes. The head man of the place met the travellers and conducted them to an empty house, which he placed at their disposal, and offered a present of fowls, dates, and wine. The news that a heavy defeat had been inflicted upon one of the wandering bands excited satisfaction, for the interference of these plunderers greatly affected the prosperity of the place, as the inhabitants were unable to trade with Ælana unless going down in very strong parties. Every attention was paid to the party by the inhabitants. Their wounds were bathed and oil poured into them, and in the more serious cases boiled herbs of medicinal virtue were applied as poultices to the wounds.

Petra at that time was but a large village, but it afterwards rose into a place of importance. The travellers remained here for a week, at the end of which time all save two were in a fit state to continue their journey.

Without further adventure the journey was continued to Moab. On their arrival here the escort was dismissed, each man receiving a present in addition to the stipulated rate of pay that they were to draw upon their return to Ælana.

Moab was a settled country. It contained no large towns; but the population, which was considerable, was gathered in small villages of low stone-built houses, similar to those in Petra. The inhabitants were ready to trade. Their language was strange to Jethro and Amuba; but it was closely related to that spoken by Ruth, and she generally acted as interpreter between Jethro and the natives. After travelling through Moab, they took the caravan road across the desert to the north-east, passed through the oasis of Palmyra, a large and flourishing city, and then journeyed on to the Euphrates. They were now in the country of the Assyrians, and not wishing to attract attention or questions, they avoided Nineveh and the other great cities, and kept on their way north until they reached the mountainous country lying between Assyria and the Caspian.

They met with many delays upon the way, and it was six months after leaving Ælana before, after passing through a portion of Persia, they reached the country inhabited by the scattered tribes known by the general name of Medes, and to whom the Rebu were related. Through this country Thotmes had carried his arms and most of the tribes acknowledged the dominion of Egypt, and paid a tribute to that country, Egyptian garrisons being scattered here and there among them.

Jethro and Amuba now felt at home, but as they determined that when they reached their own country they would, until they found how matters were going on there, disguise their identity, they now travelled as Persian traders. Long before reaching Persia they had disposed of the stock of goods with which they started, and now supplied themselves with articles of Persian manufacture. They thus passed on unquestioned from village to village, as the trade in those regions was entirely carried on by Persian merchants, that country having already attained a comparatively high amount of civilization; while the Median tribes, although settled down into fixed communities, had as yet but little knowledge of the arts of peace. The party journeyed in company with some Persian traders, and gradually worked their way north until they arrived at the first Rebu village.

They had many times debated the question of the part they should here play, and had agreed that it would be better to continue to maintain their character as Persian traders until they had learned the exact position of affairs. In order to be able to keep up their disguise they had laid in a fresh stock of Persian goods at the last large town through which they passed. Had Jethro been alone he could at once have declared himself, and would have been received with joy as one who had made his way back from captivity in Egypt; but for Amuba there would have been danger in his being recognized until the disposition of the occupant of the throne was discovered. There would, indeed, have been small chance of his being recognized had he been alone. Nearly four years had elapsed since he had been carried away captive, and he had grown from a boy into a powerful young man; but had Jethro been recognized his companion's identity might have been suspected, as he was known to have been the special mentor and companion of the young prince.

As to Amuba, he had no desire whatever to occupy the throne of the Rebu, and desired only to reside quietly in his native country. The large sum that Ameres had handed over to the care of Jethro had been much diminished by the expenses of their long journey, but there was still ample to insure for them all a good position in a country where money was not abundant.

In their journey through Persia they had picked up many of the words of that language differing from those of the Rebu, and using these in their conversation they were able to pass well as traders who in their previous journeys in the land had acquired a fair knowledge of the dialect of the people. They soon learned that an Egyptian garrison still occupied the capital, that the people groaned under the exaction necessary to pay the annual tribute, and that General Amusis, who had, as Amuba's father expected he would do, seized the throne of the Rebu after the departure of the main Egyptian army, was in close intimacy with the Egyptian officials, and was in consequence extremely unpopular among the people. He had, on his accession to power, put to death all the relatives of the late king, and there could be little doubt that did he suspect that Amuba had returned from Egypt he would not hesitate to remove him from his path.

Amuba had several long consultations with Jethro as to his course. He repeated to him the conversation that he had had with his father on the day previous to the battle in which the latter was slain, how he had warned him, against the ambition of Amusis, and advised him, rather than risk the chances of civil war in endeavouring to assert his rights, to collect a body of adherents, and to seek a new home in the far west. Jethro, however, was strongly of opinion that the advice, although excellent at the time, was no longer appropriate.

"To begin with, Amuba, you were then but a boy of sixteen, and engaged as we were in war with Egypt, the people would naturally have preferred having a well-known and skilful general at their head to a boy whom they could not hope would lead them successfully in war. You are now a man. You have had a wide experience. You have an acquaintance with the manners and ways of our conquerors, and were you on the throne could do much for the people, and could promote their welfare by encouraging new methods of agriculture and teaching them something of the civilization in Egypt.

"In the second place, in the four years that have elapsed Amusis has had time to make himself unpopular. The necessity for heavy taxation to raise the annual tribute has naturally told against him, to say nothing of the fact that he is said to be on friendly terms with our foreign oppressors. Therefore the chances would be all in your favour."

"But I have no desire to be king," Amuba replied. "I want to live in quiet contentment."

"You are born to be king, Prince Amuba," Jethro said; "it is not a matter of your choice. Besides, it is evident that for the good of the people it is necessary that the present usurper should be overthrown and the lawful dynasty restored. Besides this, it is clear that you cannot live in peace and contentment as you say; you might at any moment be recognized and your life forfeited. As to the original plan, I am sure that your father would not have advocated it under the changed circumstances; besides, I think you have had your fair share of wandering and dangers.

"Moreover, I suppose you would hardly wish to drag Mysa with you on your journey to an unknown country, where all sorts of trials and struggles must unquestionably be encountered before you succeed in founding a new settlement. I suppose," he said with a smile, "you would not propose leaving her here to whatever fate might befall her. I fancy from what I have seen during the last six months that you have altogether other intentions concerning her."

Amuba was silent for some time.

"But if Amusis is supported by the Egyptians," he said at last, "and is viewed by them as their ally, I should not be able to overthrow him without becoming involved in hostilities with them also. It is not," he went on, seeing that Jethro was about to speak, "of the garrison here that I am thinking, but of the power of Egypt behind it. Did I overthrow Amusis and defeat the Egyptians, his friends, I should bring upon my country a fresh war with Egypt."

"Egypt is, as we have found, a very long way off, Amuba. Occasionally a warlike monarch arises under whom her arms are carried vast distances, and many nations are brought under her sway, but such efforts are made but rarely, and we lie at the extremest limit of her power. Thotmes himself has gained sufficient glory. He was absent for years from his country, and at the end of long journeyings returned home to enjoy the fruits of his victories. It is not likely that he would again start on so long an expedition merely to bring so distant a corner of the land subject to Egypt again under her sway. The land is stripped of its wealth; there is nothing to reward such vast toil and the outlay that would be required to carry out such an expedition, and it may be generations before another monarch may arise thirsting like Thotmes for glory, and willing to leave the luxuries of Egypt for a course of distant conquest.

"Besides, Egypt has already learned to her cost that the Rebu are not to be overcome bloodlessly, and that defeat is just as likely as victory to attend her arms against us. Therefore I do not think that the thought of the vengeance of Egypt need deter you. In other respects the present occupation by them is in your favour rather than otherwise, for you will appear before the people not only as their rightful king but as their liberator from the hated Egyptian yoke."

"You are right, Jethro," Amuba said after a long silence; "it is my duty to assert my rights and to restore the land to freedom. My mind is made up now. What is your advice in the matter?"

"I should journey through the land until we reach a port by the sea frequented by Persian traders, and should there leave the two girls in charge of the family of some trader in that country; there they can remain in tranquillity until matters are settled. Chebron will, I am sure, insist upon sharing our fortunes. Our long wanderings have made a man of him, too. They have not only strengthened his frame and hardened his constitution, but they have given stability to his character. He is thoughtful and prudent, and his advice will always be valuable, while of his courage I have no more doubt than I have of yours. When you have once gained your kingdom you will find in Chebron a wise counsellor, one on whom you can lean in all times of difficulty.

"When we have left the girls behind we will continue our journey through the land, and gradually put ourselves into communication with such governors of towns and other persons of influence as we may learn to be discontented with the present state of things, so that when we strike our blow the whole country will declare for you at once. As we travel we will gradually collect a body of determined men for the surprise of the capital. There must be numbers of my old friends and comrades still surviving, and there should be no difficulty in collecting a force capable of capturing the city by a surprise."

Jethro's plans were carried out, and the girls placed under the care of the wife of a Persian trader in a seaport close to the frontier of Persia, the others then started upon their journey, still travelling as Persians. Jethro had little difficulty in discovering the sentiments of the principal men in the towns through which they passed. Introducing himself first to them as a Persian trader desirous of their protection in travelling through the country, he soon disclosed to them his own individuality.

To many of them he was known either personally or by repute. He informed them that he had escaped from Egypt with Amuba, but he led them to believe that his companion was waiting in Persian territory until he learnt from him that the country was ripe for his appearance; for he thought it best in no case to disclose the fact that Amuba was with him, lest some of those with whom he communicated would endeavour to gain rewards from the king by betraying him. His tidings were everywhere received with joy, and in many cases Jethro was urged to send at once for Amuba and to show him to the people, for that all the land would instantly rise on his behalf.

Jethro, however, declared that Amuba would bide his time, for that a premature disclosure would enable the king to call together a portion of the army which had formerly fought under his order, and that with the assistance of the Egyptians he might be able to form a successful resistance to a popular rising.

"I intend," he said, "if possible, to collect a small force to seize the person of the usurper by surprise, and so paralyse resistance; in which case there would only be the Egyptians to deal with, and these would be starved out of their fortress long before assistance could reach them."

After visiting most of the towns Jethro and his companions journeyed through the villages remote from the capital. Here the king's authority was lightly felt save when troops arrived once a year to gather in the taxes. Less caution was therefore necessary, and Jethro soon made himself known, and began to enlist men to the service. This he had no difficulty in doing. The news that an attempt was at once to be made to overthrow the usurper and to free the land of the Egyptians, and that at the proper time the rightful king would present himself and take the command, was received with enthusiasm.

In each valley through which they passed the whole of the young men enrolled themselves, receiving orders to remain perfectly quiet and to busy themselves in fabricating arms, of which the land had been stripped by the Egyptians, until a messenger arrived summoning them to meet at the rendezvous on an appointed day.

In six weeks the numbers of the enrolled had reached the point that was considered necessary for the enterprise, and the day was fixed on which they were to assemble among the hills a few miles distant from the town. Upon the appointed day the bands began to arrive. Jethro had purchased cattle and provisions, and receiving each band as it arrived formed them into companies and appointed their leaders. Great fires were lighted, and the cattle slaughtered. Chebron aided in the arrangements; but Amuba, by Jethro's advice, passed the day in a small tent that had been pitched in the centre of the camp.

By the evening the whole of the contingents had arrived, and Jethro saw with satisfaction the spirit that animated them all, and the useful if somewhat rough weapons that they had fashioned. When all had assembled he drew them up in a body; and after a speech that excited their patriotic feeling to the utmost, he went to the tent, and leading Amuba forth presented him to them as their king.

He had in his journeys through the towns procured from some of the principal men arms and armour fitted for persons of high rank, which had been lying concealed since the conquest by the Egyptians. Amuba was accoutered in these, and as he appeared at the door of his tent a wild shout of greeting burst from the troops, and breaking their ranks they rushed forward, and throwing themselves on their faces round him, hailed him as their king and promised to follow him to the death.

It was a long time before the enthusiasm and excitement abated, then Amuba addressed his followers, promising them deliverance from the Egyptian yoke, and from taxation under which they so long groaned.

A week was spent in establishing order and discipline in the gathering, sentries being placed at a distance round the camp to prevent any stranger entering, or any one leaving to carry the news to the city. In the meantime trusted men were sent to the town to ascertain the exact position of affairs there, and to learn whether the garrison had been placed on their guard by any rumours that might have reached the town of disaffection in the country districts. They returned with the intelligence that although reports had been received that the late king's son had escaped captivity in Egypt, and would shortly appear to claim his rights, the news had been received with absolute incredulity, the king and his Egyptian allies scoffing at the idea of a captive making his escape from Egypt and traversing the long intervening distance. So completely had been the quiet throughout the country since the Egyptian occupation that the garrison had ceased to take any precautions whatever. No watch was set, and the gates of the city were seldom closed even at night.

The plans were now finally arranged. Jethro, with a band of two hundred men, was to enter the town in the daytime; some going down to the next port and arriving by sea, others entering singly through the gates. At midnight they were to assemble in the square round the palace, which was to be suddenly attacked.

Amuba, with the main body, was to approach the city late in the evening, and to station themselves near one of the gates.

Jethro was before the hour named for the attack to see whether this gate was open and unguarded, and if he found that it was closed and under charge of an Egyptian guard, he was to tell off fifty men of his command to attack and overpower the Egyptians, and throw open the gate the instant they heard the trumpet, which was to be the signal for the attack of the palace. Jethro's party were, therefore, the first to start, going off in little groups, some to the neighbouring ports, others direct to the city. Jethro himself was the last to set out, having himself given instructions to each group as they started as to their behaviour and entry into the city, and the rendezvous at which they were to assemble. He also arranged that if at any time they should hear his call upon the horn, which was to be repeated by three or four of his followers, who were provided with similar instruments, they were to hurry to the spot at the top of their speed.

"One can never tell," he said, when he told Amuba the orders he had given, "what may happen. I believe that every man here is devoted to you, but there may always be one traitor in a crowd; but even without that, some careless speech on the part of one of them, a quarrel with one of the king's men or with an Egyptian, and the number of armed men in the city might be discovered, for others would run up to help their comrade, and the broil would grow until all were involved. Other reasons might render it advisable to strike at an earlier hour than I arranged."

"I cannot think so," Amuba replied. "I should say if anything were to precipitate affairs it would be most prejudicial. You, with your small force, would be certain to be overwhelmed by the large body of followers whom, as we have learned, the king keeps in his palace, to say nothing of the Egyptians. In that case not only would you lose your lives, but you would put them so thoroughly upon their guard that our enterprise at night would have little chance of success."

"That is true," Jethro said; "and I certainly do not mean to make the slightest variation from the plan we agreed upon unless I am driven to it. Still it is as well to be prepared for everything."

"Of course I know that you will do nothing that is rash, Jethro. After being all these years my guide and counsellor, I know that you would do nothing to endanger our success now that it seems almost assured."

Jethro had in fact a reason for wishing to be able to collect his men suddenly which he had not mentioned to Amuba. He thought it possible that, as he had said, at the last moment the plot might by some means or other be discovered. And his idea was that if that were the case he would instantly gather his followers and attack the palace, trusting to surprise and to his knowledge of the building in the endeavour to fight his way to the king's abode and slay him there, even if he himself and his men were afterwards surrounded and cut to pieces. The usurper once removed, Jethro had no doubt that the whole nation would gladly acknowledge Amuba, who would then have only the Egyptian garrison to deal with.

No such accident, however, happened. The men entered the town unnoticed. Those who had come by boat, and who were for the most part natives of villages along the shore, remained in the lower town near the landing-place. Such of them as had friends went to their houses. Those who entered the gates sauntered about the town singly or in pairs, and as their weapons were hidden they attracted no notice, having the appearance of men who had come in from the country round to dispose of their produce or the spoils of the chase, or to exchange them for such articles as were required at home. Jethro went at once to the house of an old friend with whom he had already communicated by messenger.

The house was situated on the open space facing the palace. Here from time to time he received messages from his sub-leaders, and learned that all was going on well. He heard that the continual rumours from the country of the approaching return of the son of the late king had at last caused some anxiety to the usurper, who had that morning seized and thrown into prison several leading men who were known to be personally attached to the late king. Not, indeed, that he believed that Amuba could have returned; but he thought it possible that some impostor might be trading on his name.

Several bodies of men had been despatched from the town to the places whence these rumours had been received, to ascertain what truth there was in them, and to suppress at once any signs of revolt against the king's authority. This was highly satisfactory news to Jethro, as in the first place it showed that the king did not dream of danger in his capital; and, in the second place, it reduced the number of fighting men in the palace to a number but slightly exceeding the force at his own disposal.

Jethro did not stir abroad until nightfall, his face being so well-known in the town that he might at any moment be recognized. But as soon as it was dark he went out, and, accompanied by his friend, went round the town. He found that some changes had taken place since he had last been there. The Egyptians had entirely cleared away the huts towards the end of the rock furthest from the sea, and had there erected large buildings for the use of the governor, officers, and troops; and had run a wall across from the walls on either side, entirely separating their quarter from the rest of the town. Jethro's friend informed him that the erection of these buildings had greatly added to the hatred with which the Egyptians were regarded, as they had been erected with forced labour, the people being driven in by the thousands, and compelled to work for many months at the buildings.

Jethro learned that as soon as the inner wall was completed the Egyptians had ceased altogether to keep watch at the gates of the city walls, but that they had for a long time kept a vigilant guard at the gate leading to their quarters through the new wall. For the last year, however, owing to the absence of any spirit of revolt among the Rebu, and to their confidence in the friendship of the king, they had greatly relaxed their vigilance.

By nine o'clock all was quiet in the town. Jethro sent out a messenger by the road by which Amuba's force would approach, to tell him that the city walls were all unguarded, and that he had better enter by the gate half an hour before midnight, instead of waiting until he heard the signal for attack. He could then move his men up close to the Egyptian wall so as to attack that gate when the signal was given, otherwise the Egyptians would be put on their guard by the sound of fighting at the palace before he could arrive at their gate.

At the time he had named Jethro went to the gate by which Amuba was to enter, and soon heard a faint confused noise, and a minute or two later a dark mass of men were at the path at the gate. They were headed by Amuba. Jethro at once explained to him the exact position; and his companion placed himself by the side of Amuba to act as his guide to the Egyptian wall.

Jethro then returned to the rendezvous, where his men were already drawn up in order. Midnight was now close at hand. Quietly the band crossed the square to the gate of the palace; then Jethro gave a loud blast of his horn, and in an instant a party of men armed with heavy axes rushed forward and began to hew down the gate. As the thundering noise rose on the night air cries of terror, and the shouts of officers were heard within the royal inclosure. Then men came hurrying along the wall, and arrows began to fall among the assailants; but by this time the work of the axmen was nearly done, and in five minutes after the first blow was struck the massive gates fell splintered and Jethro rushed in at the head of his band.

The garrison, headed by the usurper himself, endeavoured to stem their inrush; but, taken by surprise, half-armed, and ignorant of the numbers of their assailants, they could not long withstand the determined onslaught of Jethro's men. Jethro himself made his way through the crowd of fighting men and engaged in a hand-to-hand fight with the usurper, who, furious with rage and despair at the sudden capture of the palace, fought but wildly, and Jethro's heavy ax soon terminated the conflict by hewing clean through helmet and head.

The fall of the usurper was for the moment unnoticed in the darkness and confusion, but Jethro shouted to his men to hold their hands and fall back. Then he called upon the garrison to surrender, telling them that Amusis had fallen, and that Amuba, the son of Phrases, had arrived, and was now king of the Rebu.

"We do not war against our own people. The Egyptians are our only enemies. Some of you may know me. I am Jethro, and I call upon you to join us and make common cause against the Egyptians, who are even now being attacked by our young king."

The garrison were but too glad to accept the terms. Fear rather than love had attached them to Amusis; and they were delighted to escape the prospect of death, which had the moment before stared them in the face, and to swear allegiance to their rightful king. As Jethro ceased, therefore, shouts of "Long live Amuba, king of the Rebu!" rose from them.

"Form up in order instantly under your captains," Jethro commanded, "and follow us."

The fray had been so short that it was but ten minutes from the moment when Jethro's horn had given the signal for attack to that when he led his force, now increased to twice its former dimensions, to the assistance of Amuba. When he reached the wall that separated the Egyptian barracks from the rest of the town he found that Amuba had entered without resistance and had captured two or three buildings nearest to the gate, surprising and slaying their occupants; but beyond that he had made no progress. The Egyptians were veterans in warfare, and after the first moment of surprise had recovered their coolness, and with their flights of arrows so swept the open spaces between the buildings that the Rebu could make no progress.

Jethro ordered the troops who had just joined him, all of whom carried bows and arrows, to ascend the walls and open fire upon the buildings occupied by the Egyptians. Then he with his own band joined Amuba.

"All has gone well," he said. "The palace is captured and Amusis slain. I would do nothing further to-night. The Egyptians are four thousand strong, while we have but half that number. It would be madness to risk a repulse now. I will send off messengers at once to the governors of all the towns and to our friends there, informing them that the usurper is slain, that you are proclaimed king and are now besieging the Egyptians in their quarters, and ordering them to march thither at once with every man capable of bearing arms.

"In three days we shall have twenty thousand men here, and the Egyptians, finding their position hopeless, will surrender; whereas if you attack now we may be repulsed and you may be slain, and in that case the country, left without a leader, will fall again into slavery."

Amuba, whose armour had already been pierced by several arrows and who was bleeding freely, was with some difficulty persuaded by Jethro to adopt his counsel. He saw at last that it was clearly the wisest plan to adopt, and orders were at once issued to the men to desist from further assaults, but to content themselves with repelling any attacks the Egyptians might make.

These, however, were too ignorant as to the strength of their assailants to think of taking the offensive, and until morning both sides contented themselves with keeping up an incessant fire of arrows against the openings in the buildings occupied by their foes. In the morning Amuba ordered some green branches to be elevated on the flat terrace of the house he occupied. The signal was observed, and the fire of the Egyptians ceased. As soon as it did so Jethro presented himself on the terrace, and a minute or two later the Egyptian governor appeared on the terrace of the opposite building. Not a little surprised was he to hear himself addressed in his own language.

"In the name of King Amuba, son of King Phrases and lawful ruler of the Rebu, I, Jethro his general, summon you to surrender. The usurper Amusis is dead and the whole land has risen against you. Our force is overpowering—resistance can only result in the death of every Egyptian under your orders. Did we choose we could starve you out, for we know that you have no more than a week's provisions in your magazines.

"There is no possibility that assistance can reach you. No messenger could pass the watchers in the plain; and could they do so your nearest force is hundreds of miles away, and is of no strength to fight its way hither. In the name of the king I offer to allow you to depart, carrying with you your arms and standards. The king has been in your country. He knows how great and powerful is your nation, and fain would be on terms of friendship with it; therefore he would inflict no indignity upon you. The tribute which your king laid upon the land is far more than it can pay, but the king will be willing to send every year, to the nearest garrison to his frontiers, a tribute of gold and precious stones of one fifth the value of that which has been until now wrung from the land. This he will do as a proof of the honour in which he holds your great nation, and as a recognition of its power. The king ordered me to say that he will give you until to-morrow morning to reflect over his offer. If it is refused the whole garrison will be put to the sword."

So saying Jethro descended from the terrace, leaving the Egyptians to consider the terms he proposed.

Chapter 20

THE offer that Amuba had made through Jethro was a politic one, and he was influenced by two motives in granting a delay of twenty-four hours before receiving the answer. In the first place, he felt sure that his own force would, before the conclusion of the time, be trebled in strength, and that should the Egyptians refuse he would be able to repel any efforts they might make to cut their way out until he would be at the head of such a force that he could at will either storm their position or, as he intended, beleaguer them until starvation forced them to surrender.

In the second place, he thought that the Egyptian answer, if given at once, would probably be a refusal; but the time for reflection would enable them to look their position in the face and to recognize its hopelessness. On the one side would be certain defeat and death, on the other their general would lead out his command intact and without dishonour. Although he had threatened to put the garrison to the sword in case they refused, Amuba had no intention to carry out his threat, but on the contrary had determined that even were the Egyptians forced to surrender by famine he would freely grant them the same terms he now offered.

He knew the proud and haughty nature of the Egyptians, and that the news of the massacre of a great garrison and the successful rising of a tributary province would excite such deep feeling that sooner or later an army would be despatched to avenge the disaster. If, however, the garrison left the country with their arms and standards no disgrace would be inflicted upon the national arms, and as a tribute, however much reduced, would still be paid, they could still regard the Rebu as under their domination. The reduction of the tribute indeed, would be an almost imperceptible item in the revenue of Egypt.

Leaving Jethro in command of the beleaguering force, Amuba, accompanied by Chebron, who had been by his side during the fighting, and a small body-guard, went back into the town.

The news of his coming had already spread, and the inhabitants, who had remained in their houses in terror during the, to them, unaccountable tumult of the night, had now poured out into the streets, the great space in front of the palace being densely packed with people. As Amuba approached a deafening shout of welcome was raised; the gates of the prisons had been thrown open, and those arrested the previous day, and many others of the principal captains of his father's army, thronged round him and greeted him as their king.

With difficulty a way was cleared to the gate of the royal inclosure. Amuba, after entering, mounted the wall and addressed a few words to the people. He told them that in defiance of all probability he had escaped from his captivity in Egypt and had made his way back to his native land, intent not so much on claiming his rightful position there as of freeing them from the power of their oppressors. He promised them that he would always respect their rights and usages, and should endeavour to follow in the footsteps of his father. Then he retired to the palace, where he held a council with the captains and leading men in the city. Orders were at once issued for every man capable of bearing arms to provide himself with some kind of weapon, and to assemble at noon in the great square.

Lists were drawn up of all the officers of the late army still living in the town, and when the gathering took place at noon these were appointed to form the men into companies, to appoint sub-officers, to see to the state of the arms, and as far as possible, to supply deficiencies. A larger proportion than was expected of the three thousand men that assembled were found to be provided with weapons. Although nominally all arms had been surrendered to the Egyptians, great numbers of spear and arrow-heads, swords, and axes had been buried. Shafts had been hastily made for the spears, and bows used for the purposes of the chase were now brought out to do service as fighting weapons.

Many hundreds of spears and swords had been found in the stores at the palace, and when these were served out most of the men had a weapon of some sort. They were at once marched up to the Egyptian inclosure. Those with bows and arrows were placed upon the walls, the rest were massed near the gate in readiness to advance to the assistance of the band within should the Egyptians make an attempt to cut their way out. In point of numbers Amuba's force were now superior to those of the Egyptians, but he was well aware that the superior arms and discipline of the latter would enable them to make a successful sortie should they determine to do so.

The women of the town were ordered to set to work to grind the grain served out from the magazine in the palace, and to bake bread both for the fighting men present and for those expected to arrive. By noon the latter began to flock in, the contingents from the towns arriving in regular order, while the shepherds and villagers straggled in irregularly as the news reached them of the events of the previous night. By evening fully ten thousand men had arrived, and as the Egyptians had remained quiet all day Amuba had every hope that they had decided to accept the terms he offered, and that there would be no occasion for further fighting. The troops, however, remained under arms all night, ready to repel an attack, and in the morning Amuba and Jethro mounted together on to the terrace of the building from which the parley had taken place on the previous day.

A few minutes later the Egyptian governor and a group of his officers appeared on the opposite house.

"This is King Amuba," Jethro said in a loud voice. "He is here to confirm the terms offered yesterday, and to receive your answer."

"We are ready," the Egyptian governor said, "to retire beyond your frontier, carrying with us our arms, standards, and valuables, it being understood that we make no surrender whatever, but that we march out on equal terms, holding, as we do, that we could, if we chose, cut our way out in spite of any resistance."

"You may hold that belief," Amuba said (and the Egyptian was astonished at finding that the king, as well as his general, was capable of conversing in the Egyptian tongue); "and, indeed, knowing and honouring the valour of the Egyptian troops, I admit it is possible that, although with great loss, you might make your way out, but more than that you could not do. You could not hold the country, for you have a nation against you. It is doubtful whether you could reach the frontier. Surely it is better, then, that you should leave with honour and without loss."

"As to the tribute that you offer," the Egyptian commander said, "I have no power to agree to any diminution of the terms imposed by the king, and if it be his will that an army invades your country to enforce the former terms, I, with the troops here, must march as ordered, without imputation of having behaved treacherously."

"That is quite understood," Amuba said; "but I trust, my lord, that you having seen for yourself how poor is our country, how utterly unable to continue to pay the tribute formerly demanded from us, which has already impoverished us to the last degree, will represent the same in your despatches to the king, and will use your good offices in obtaining his favourable consideration of our case. I can promise you that the tribute shall be paid regularly. I regard Egypt as the greatest power in the world, and I am most desirous to continue in friendly relations with it, and I swear to you that it will be no fault of mine if any complaint reach you of trouble on our part."

Amuba's speech was well calculated to soothe the pride of the Egyptian. The latter was perfectly conscious, although he spoke confidently, that it would be no easy matter for his troops to cut their way through the narrow gateway held by the masses of the Rebu, still less to make their way, harassed as he was, to their frontier. If he returned with his troops intact and in good condition he could so represent circumstances that no blame or discredit would fall upon him; and personally he was exceedingly pleased at the prospect of the termination of his soldiering at a post so far removed from Egypt and civilization. He therefore agreed to the terms Amuba proposed, and after a short parley the conditions of the evacuation of the town by the Egyptians were arranged.

Amuba agreed to withdraw his men from the buildings that they occupied, and also from the gate, and to place them all upon the walls, thus saving the Egyptians the humiliation of passing through lines of armed men, and avoiding the risk of a broil arising between the soldiers. He at once issued the necessary orders, and the Rebu retired to the walls, where they could defend themselves in case of any treachery on the part of the Egyptians, and the inhabitants of the city were all ordered back from the road leading from the entrance to the Egyptian inclosure to the gate in the city walls. An hour later the Egyptians drew up in order in their inclosure.

Each man carried with him food sufficient for a week's subsistence, and Amuba had arranged that a certain number of bullocks should be sent forward at once to each halting-place on the way to the frontier, and that there a herd sufficient for their subsistence during their march to the nearest Egyptian garrison should be awaiting them. In firm and steady order the Egyptians marched out. The images and symbols of the gods were carried aloft, and the bearing of the soldiers was proud and defiant, for they, too, were doubtful whether the Rebu might not intend to make an attack upon them, the terms granted them seeming to be almost too good to be trusted. No sooner had the rear of the column passed out through the city gate than the Rebu with shouts of joy flocked down from the walls, and the city gave itself up to rejoicing.

Jethro had at once sent out messengers to see that the oxen were collected at the points agreed upon, and to issue orders that the population along the line of march should all retire before the arrival of the Egyptians, who might otherwise have been tempted to seize them and carry them off as slaves with them in their retreat.

For the next few days Amuba's time was wholly occupied in receiving deputations from the various towns and districts, in appointing fresh officials, and in taking measures for the re-arming of the people and their enrollment in companies, so that the country should be in a position to offer a desperate resistance should the Egyptians determine to recapture it. It was certain that many months must elapse before any force capable of undertaking their invasion could march from Egypt; but Amuba was determined that no time should be lost in making preparations, and he decided that something of the tactics and discipline of the Egyptians should be introduced into the Rebu army.

He had on the very night of the surprise of the town sent on a message to inform the girls of his success, and that neither Chebron nor himself was hurt. Having by unremitting work got through his most pressing business, he left Jethro, who was now formally appointed general-in-chief, to carry on the work, and started with Chebron to fetch the girls to his capital. But he was now obliged to travel with a certain amount of state, and he was accompanied by twenty of the leading men of the Rebu in chariots, and by an escort of light-armed horsemen. At each town through which he passed he was received with rapturous greetings and hailed as king and deliverer of the nation.

Two days after starting he arrived at the little seaport, and after receiving the usual greeting from the inhabitants and holding an audience at which he received the principal inhabitants who came to tender their allegiance, he made his way to the house of the Persian merchant where he had placed the girls. As his chariot stopped at the door the merchant appeared on the threshold and made a profound prostration. He had until the arrival of Amuba at the town been in entire ignorance that those who had placed the girls under his charge were other than they seemed. He knew indeed from their ignorance of his language that the girls were not Persians, but supposed that they were female slaves who had been brought from a distance, with a view, perhaps, of being presented as an offering to the king.

After a word or two with him, Amuba and Chebron entered the house and ascended to the apartment which had been set aside for the girls. They were standing timidly at one end of the room, and both bent profoundly as he entered. Amuba for a moment paused in astonishment, and then burst into a fit of laughter.

"Is this your sister, Chebron, who thus greets her old friend in such respectful fashion? Am I myself or some one else?"

"You are King Amuba," Mysa said, half-smiling, but with tears in her eyes.

"That is true enough, Mysa; but I was always prince, you know. So there is nothing very surprising in that."

"There is a great difference," Mysa said; "and it is only right where there is such a difference of rank——"

"The difference of rank need not exist long, Mysa," Amuba said, stepping forward and taking her hand. "Chebron, who is your brother, and like a brother to me, has given me his consent, and it rests only with you whether you will be queen of the Rebu and Amuba's wife. You know that if I had not succeeded in winning a throne I should have asked you to share my lot as an exile, and I think you would have said yes. Surely you are not going to spoil my triumph now by saying no. If you do I shall use my royal power in earnest and take you whether you will or not."

But Mysa did not say no, and six weeks later there was a royal wedding in the capital. Amuba had at once allotted one of the largest houses in the royal inclosure to Chebron, and to this he took Mysa while Amuba was making the tour of his country, receiving the homage of the people, hearing complaints, and seeing that the work of preparation for the defence of the country was being carried on, after which he returned to the capital. The wedding was celebrated in great state, though it was observed that the religious ceremonies were somewhat cut short, and that Amuba abstained from himself offering sacrifice on the altars of the gods. The ceremony was a double one, for at the same time Chebron was united to Ruth.

For the next year the preparations for war went on vigourously and the Rebu army was got into a state of great efficiency. Amuba and Jethro felt confident that it could successfully withstand any invading force from Egypt, but, as they had hoped, Egypt made no effort to regain her distant conquest, but was content to rank the land of the Rebu among the list of her tributary nations, and to accept the diminished tribute.

Once prepared for war Amuba turned his attention to the internal affairs of the country. Many of the methods of government of Egypt were introduced. Irrigation was carried out on a large scale, and the people were taught no longer to depend solely upon their flocks and herds. Stone took the place of mud in the buildings of the towns, rigorous justice was enforced throughout the land, wagons and carts similar to those of Egypt took the place of pack animals, which had hitherto been used for transport; improved methods of agriculture were taught, and contentment and plenty reigned in the land.

Chebron remained Amuba's chief minister, adviser, and friend, and under their joint efforts the Rebu rose from the condition of a mere settled tribe to that of a small but flourishing nation.

Another change was made, but more slowly. Soon after his ascension Amuba assembled many of the leading men and chief-priests in the country, and explained to them the convictions held by himself and Chebron and their wives, that there was but one God who ruled over the world, and that this knowledge was the highest wisdom of the Egyptians. He explained to the priests that he did not wish to overthrow the temples or disturb the worship of the former gods, but that he desired that the people not remain in ignorance, but should be taught that the gods as they worshipped them were but symbols or images of the one great God. He said he had no thought of enforcing his convictions upon others, but that all would be free to worship as they pleased, and that at all times he and Chebron would be ready to confer with those who wished to inquire into these matters.

In this matter alone Amuba met with much opposition in carrying out his plans, and had he been less popular than he was with the people his efforts might have cost him his throne and his life; but the Rebu were devoted to him, and as the priests came gradually to see that the change would not diminish their power, their opposition died away, especially as many of the younger men were soon convinced by the arguments of the king and his minister, and preached the new religion with enthusiasm among the people. But it was not until many years after that Amuba had the satisfaction of knowing that the one God was worshipped among his people. He was well aware that the success of the work was to no small extent due to the earnestness with which Mysa and Ruth had laboured among the wives and daughters of the nobles.

"How strangely things turn out," Chebron said one day ten years after their arrival in the land, when the little party who had travelled so long together were gathered in a room in the palace. "At one time it seemed that that unlucky shot of mine would not only bring ruin on all connected with me, but be a source of unhappiness to me to the end of my life. Now I see, that except for the death of my father, it was the most fortunate event of my life. But for that, I should all my life have gone on believing in the gods of Egypt; but for that although you, Amuba and Jethro, might some day have made your escape, Mysa and I would assuredly never have left Egypt, never have known anything of the life of happiness and usefulness that we now enjoy. All this I consider I owe to the fortunate shot that killed the Cat of Bubastes."